M000239694

HMH SOCIAL STUDIES

HMH

SOCIOLOGY

Printed in the U.S.A.
ISBN 978-0-544-85936-4

1 2 3 4 5 6 7 8 9 10 0918 25 24 23 22 21 20 19 18 17

4500652471 A B C D E F G

Content Reviewer

Dr. Tracey Steele
Wright State University
Criminology, Gender and Sexuality

Educational Reviewers

Anna Bryant
Mills E. Godwin High School
Richmond, VA

Jennifer Matasovsky
Hamilton Southeastern High School
Fishers, IN

Mary-Elizabeth Maynard
Leominster High School
Leominster, MA

Glenn Mechem
Union High School
Union, MO

Greg Talberg
Howell High School
Howell, MI

Contents

2

1

3

CHAPTER 5

CHAPTER 6

CHAPTER 7

CHAPTER 8

We Can Do It!
WAR PRODUCTION CO-ORDINATING COMMITTEE

UNIT 4 Social Institutions

The Family

CHAPTER 12

The Economy and Politics

CHAPTER 13

CHAPTER 14

UNIT 5 The Changing Social World

Reference Section

Features

Quick Lab

Apply your knowledge with a range of quick in-class activities.

Applying What You've Learned

Explore topics in sociology in depth with labs, experiments, and simulations.

Labs

Simulations

Experiments

Online Resources

Explore a whole new world of online learning. Go online to find all the components and resources for this book, including labs, quizzes, and more.

ONLINE QUIZZES
Take a practice quiz for each section in each chapter.

KEEP IT CURRENT
Link to the Current Events site for regularly updated stories on sociology as well as other social studies topics.

CASE STUDY

Examine major topics in sociology through Case Studies.

TECHNOLOGY FOCUS

Explore how technological advances affect culture and society.

CURRENT RESEARCH IN SOCIOLOGY

Explore the latest research in the field of sociology.

SOCIOLOGY IN TODAY'S WORLD

Apply sociological concepts to understand important issues in the world today.

CULTURAL DIVERSITY AND SOCIOLOGY

Learn about diversity and the different cultures of the world in sociology.

CULTURAL DIVERSITY AND SOCIOLOGY

Expand your knowledge of sociology to a global level.

CAREERS IN SOCIOLOGY

Explore career possibilities in different fields of sociology.

Statistically Speaking...

Analyze the data that supports sociological concepts.

U.S. HEALTH-CARE SPENDING DOLLAR

Note: Due to rounding, percentages may not add up to 100.

Source: Centers for Medicare and Medicaid Services, Office of the Actuary, National Health Statistics Group, 2014

CHARTS, GRAPHS, MAPS, AND TIME LINES

Analyze information presented visually to learn more about sociology.

Charts

Graphs

Maps

Time Lines

Review key concepts with these summaries of important facts.

Perspectives on

Compare different views on aspects of society.

How to Use Your Textbook

HMH Social Studies: Sociology was created to make your study of sociology an enjoyable, meaningful experience. Take a few minutes to become familiar with the book's easy-to-use organization and special features.

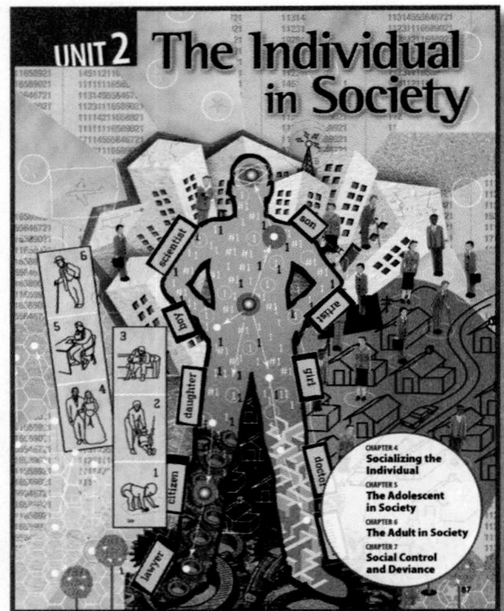

Unit

Unit Openers list the chapter titles within each unit to preview the material you are about to explore.

Careers in Sociology features appear at the end of each unit. Each one profiles a career area within sociology and includes a short activity on how to write using ASA style the way sociologists do.

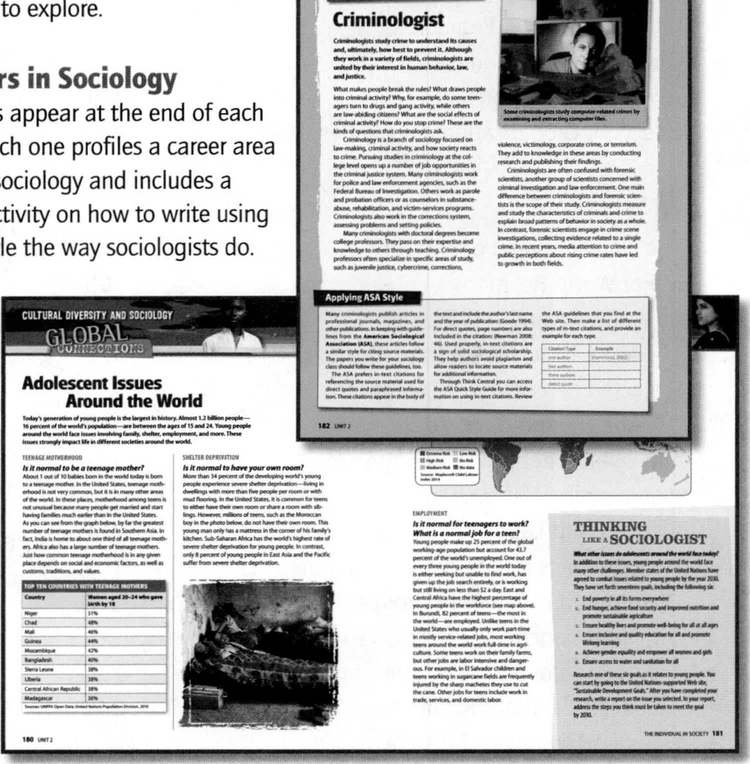

Cultural Diversity and Sociology: Global Connections features at the end of each unit connect sociology content to places around the world and provide an opportunity to think like a sociologist.

Chapter

Chapter Openers include a Case Study that deals with a real-world application or example of chapter content. Chapter openers also feature Chapter at a Glance, which summarizes the key points from each section.

Chapter Reviews provide a full array of assessments and direct you to online features.

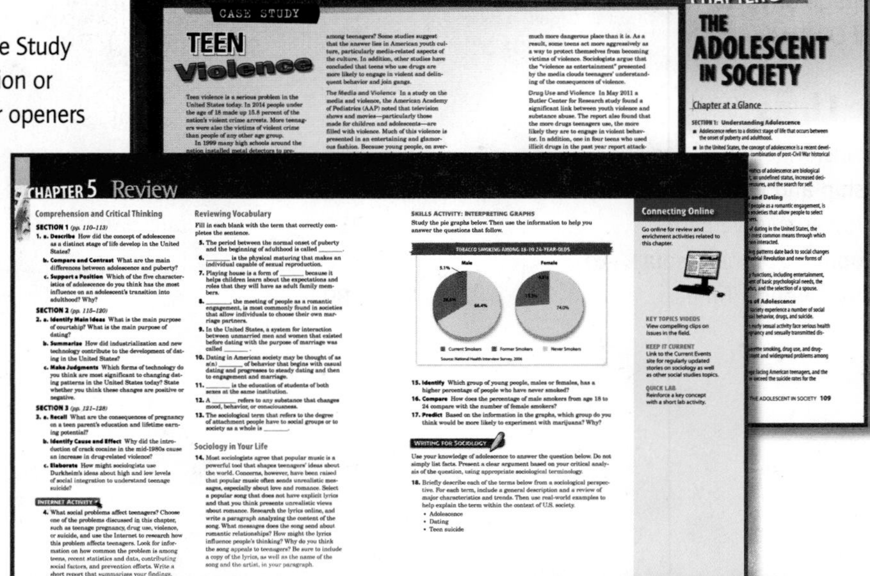

Section

Each section begins with a Main Idea statement, Reading Focus questions, and Vocabulary terms. In addition, each section includes the following special features:

Taking Notes graphic organizers help you record key ideas as you read.

Sociology Close Up features begin each section with an engaging story, example, or anecdote.

Reading Check questions throughout each section provide frequent opportunities to review and assess your understanding of what you read.

Section Assessments help you demonstrate your understanding of main ideas and key content. There is also assessment practice online.

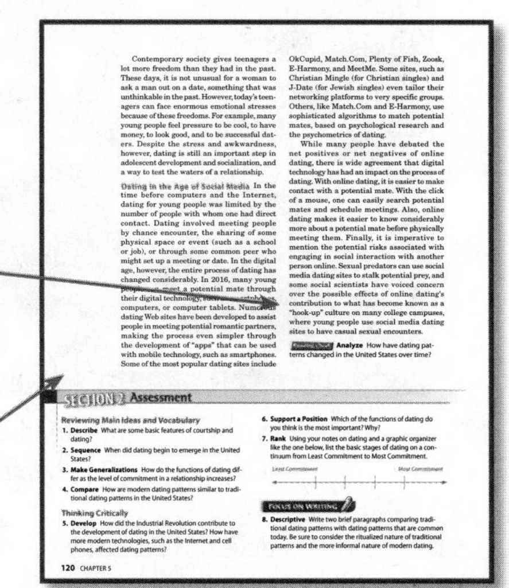

Hands-On Activities

HMH Social Studies: Sociology provides many opportunities for you to learn sociology content by completing individual and group activities.

Applying What You've Learned features at the end of each chapter provide opportunities to complete individual and group labs, simulations, and experiments.

Quick Labs in each chapter help you learn and apply chapter content by completing a short activity.

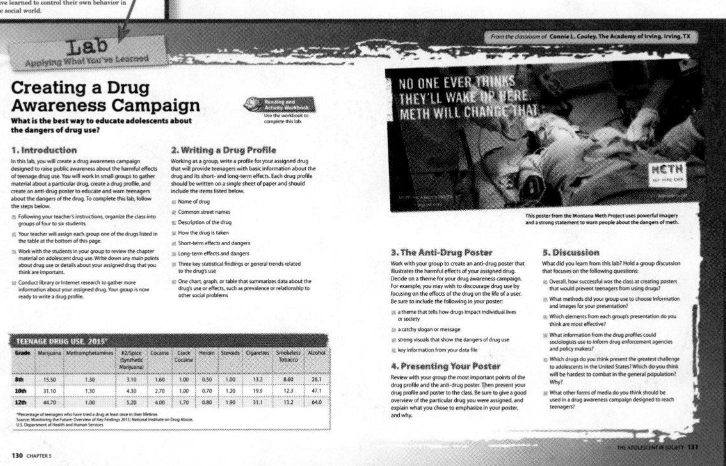

Time Line of Sociology

▲ **1837** Harriet Martineau publishes *Society in America.*

▲ **1848** Karl Marx and Friedrich Engels publish the *"Communist Manifesto."*

▲ **1897** Émile Durkheim publishes his study *Suicide.*

1892 The University of Chicago establishes the first department of sociology in the United States.

1798 Eli Whitney develops interchangeable parts for manufacturing, helping to spur the growth of the Industrial Revolution.

1800 **1850** **1900**

▼ **1819** The British Cotton Mills and Factories Act places some limits on child labor.

▼ **1889** Jane Addams opens Hull House settlement.

▲ **1851** Herbert Spencer publishes his study *Social Statics.*

1838 Auguste Comte gives the social science of sociology its name.

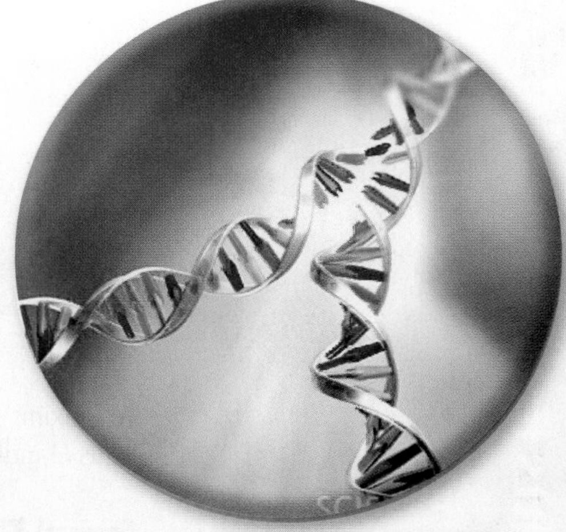

▲ **1920** American women gain the right to vote with the passage of the Nineteenth Amendment.

▲ **2003** Scientists with the Human Genome Project announce they have mapped the human genetic code.

1931 Jane Addams receives the Nobel Peace Prize.

1993 Apartheid ends in South Africa.

1945 World War II ends.

1950

2000

▲ **1908** The Ford Motor Company produces the first Model T automobile.

1980 CNN, the world's first 24-hour cable news network is established.

▼ **1963** Martin Luther King Jr. delivers his "I Have a Dream" speech in Washington, D.C.

▼ **1989** The Berlin Wall falls, marking the end of the Cold War.

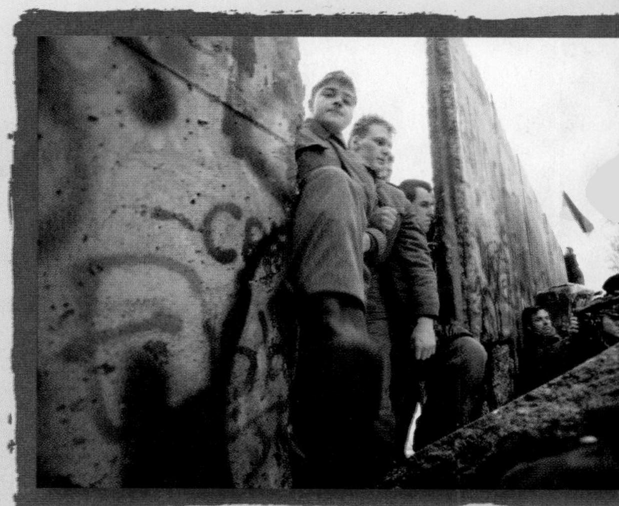

SKILLS HANDBOOK

To maximize your study and understanding of sociology, use the Skills Handbook to review and practice a variety of key skills.

Identifying Main Ideas and Details

Define the Skill

The **main idea** is the central thought in a passage. It is a general statement that conveys the key concept the author wants the reader to know. The main idea can come at the beginning, middle, or end of a passage, although it is most often found at the beginning. The main idea can be one or two sentences and can be implied or directly stated.

Details are statements that support or explain the main idea. Details are specific and provide additional information to the reader, such as the *who, what, when, where, why,* and *how* of the main idea. Details include statements, statistics, examples, explanations, and descriptions.

Learn the Skill

Read the passage below and note how the details support the main idea.

> The family provides many, if not most, of the socialization experiences of early childhood. Infants and very young children are particularly likely to spend almost all of their time in a family setting. As children grow older, forces outside of the family increasingly influence them. In particular, children begin to relate more and more to their peer groups.

Main Idea
The family provides many, if not most, of the socialization experiences of early childhood.

Details		
Detail 1	**Detail 2**	**Detail 3**
Infants and very young children are particularly likely to spend almost all of their time in a family setting.	*As children grow older, forces outside of the family increasingly influence them.*	*In particular, children begin to relate more and more to their peer groups.*

Apply the Skill

Turn to Section 2 of the chapter titled "Gender, Age, and Health" and locate the subhead titled "Americans with Disabilities." Use a graphic organizer like the one above to identify the main idea and details of the passage.

1. Identify the main idea in the passage. Restate it in your own words.
2. What details support the main idea?
3. Explain how the details add to the main idea.

SKILLS HANDBOOK

Identifying Cause and Effect

Define the Skill

Identifying cause and effect can help you to become a critical thinker and to better understand what you read. A **cause** is something that brings about an action or condition. Often, a cause will be directly stated in the text, but sometimes it will be implied, or stated indirectly. An **effect** is an event that happens as the result of a cause. A cause may have more than one effect. Similarly, an effect may have several causes. By identifying causes and effects, you will be able to determine why certain events occurred, whether certain events are related, and what the relationship is between events.

Learn the Skill

Use the following strategies to identify cause and effect.

> In 1995, residents of the South Pacific island nation of Fiji got television for the first time. They received only one channel, which broadcast programming from the United States, Great Britain, and Australia. Three years later Harvard researcher Dr. Anne E. Becker found a significant increase in symptoms of eating disorders among teenage girls.
>
> In traditional Fijian society, a robust body is the norm, and commenting that someone had gained weight is a compliment. After exposure to Western mass media, Fijian teens wanted to look like the actresses they saw on television. According to Becker's study, girls who said they watched television three or more nights a week were 50 percent more likely to see themselves as too fat and 30 percent more likely to diet than girls who watched less often.

1 Identify the causes of events. Look for reasons that prompted a given event to occur. Words such as *since, because, so, therefore,* and *found* can signal a causal relationship among events.

2 Identify the effects of events. Look for phrases and clue words that indicate consequences, such as *thus, brought about, according to, consequently,* and *as a result.*

3 Connect causes and effects. Consider why certain causes led to an event and why the event turned out as it did. Remember that an event can be both a cause and an effect.

Apply the Skill

1. What was the cause of the events described in the passage?
2. List the various effects described in the passage.
3. What is the ultimate outcome described in the passage? Why might that outcome have resulted from the cause you identified?

Identifying Problems and Solutions

Define the Skill

People have always faced problems and sought solutions to those problems. As a result, sociologists describing social issues often structure their writing by identifying a problem and then describing its actual or possible solutions. By **identifying problems and solutions,** you can better understand the challenges that people face and the means by which they resolve such difficulties.

Learn the Skill

Look for problems that are identified in the reading and then determine what solutions may be appropriate. Some problems have more than one solution.

The Internet has made personal information more accessible to thieves. One important piece of personal information thieves often seek is Social Security numbers because they can be used to find other personal and financial information. It is difficult to protect these numbers because they are used for so many purposes.

How can you protect yourself from identity theft? Shred documents with personal information, such as credit card applications. Protect your wallet, and keep your Social Security card in a secure location. Watch out for online scams. Also, monitoring your bank statements and checking your credit report regularly will help you detect identity theft early, which may limit damage.

Problem
With the Internet, personal information is now more accessible.

Solution 1
Shred documents with personal information.

Solution 2
Keep your Social Security card in a secure location.

Solution 3
Monitor your bank statements and check your credit report regularly.

Apply the Skill

Use a graphic organizer like the one above to identify the problems and solutions in the following passage.

Almost 46.7 million Americans still live in poverty. In addition, the poverty rate is about the same as it was in the early 1970s. Nevertheless, the situation has improved in some ways. In 1966, for example, poverty among elderly Americans was almost three times as high as among the general population. Today the poverty rate for people 65 and older is lower than the rate for the country as a whole. This improvement is due mainly to increased Social Security benefits and the introduction of Medicare, the government-sponsored health-insurance program for people 65 and older.

1. What is the problem presented in this passage?
2. Identify one solution to the problem.

Drawing Conclusions

Define the Skill

Writing in the social sciences provides you with facts and information. But often you have to determine the meaning of events and information on your own. You need to combine the facts and information, along with your prior knowledge, to draw conclusions about the reading. In **drawing conclusions,** you analyze the reading and form opinions about its meaning.

Learn the Skill

To draw conclusions, combine the information you find in the reading with what you already know. Look for a common link or theme. Then put it all together.

Drawing on the work of Faraday and Swan, Thomas Edison developed the first usable and practical lightbulb in 1879. The new invention caused a sensation. Having created a demand for lightbulbs, Edison then needed to supply the electricity that powered them. So he built the world's first central electric power plant in New York City. The plant illuminated several city blocks. As a result of Edison's work, life during the Industrial Age became easier and more convenient.

Information gathered from the passage you are reading	+	What you already know about the topic	=	What all the information adds up to—your conclusion
Thomas Edison invented the lightbulb in 1879 and built the world's first central electric plant.		Electricity is a huge part of people's lives today and is used in many capacities in everyday life.		The invention of the lightbulb was one of the first steps towards the modernized world we know today.

Apply the Skill

Read the following sentences. Think about what you know about parental and peer influences today. Use the process above to draw conclusions about the passage.

Parents often worry that their adolescent children's needs for peer approval will influence them to engage in risky or unacceptable behavior. However, the assumption that parents and peers often pull an adolescent in different directions does not seem to be borne out by reality.

In fact, parental and peer influences often coincide to some degree. For example, research suggests that peers are more likely to urge adolescents to work for good grades and complete high school than they are to try to involve them in drug abuse, sexual activity, or delinquency.

1. How do parents sometimes misjudge adolescent peer influence?
2. What can you conclude about how adolescents evaluate the influence of peers and parents?

Interpreting Line and Bar Graphs

Define the Skill

Graphs are diagrams that present statistical or numeric data. They can display amounts, trends, ratios, or changes over time. A **line graph** is a visual representation of data organized so that you can see a pattern of change over time. In most cases, the *vertical axis* of a line graph shows quantities while the *horizontal axis* shows time. A **bar graph** compares quantities. A single bar graph compares one set of data, while a double bar graph compares two sets of data. Knowing how to interpret line graphs and bar graphs can help you recognize trends and patterns.

Learn the Skill

Use the following strategies to interpret the line graph.

1 Read the title of the graph. The title tells you the subject or purpose of the graph.

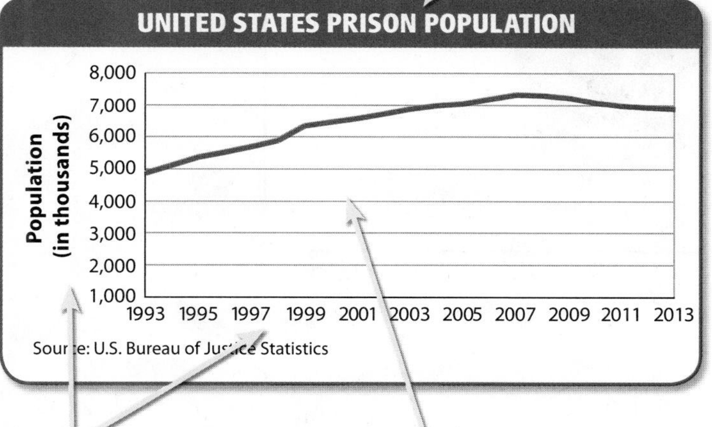

2 Read the horizontal and vertical axis labels. The labels explain what the graph measures and gives the units of measurement.

3 Analyze the information on the graph. Look at the slant of the line. The closer the line is to being parallel to the horizontal axis, the slower the change. The closer the line is to being perpendicular to the horizontal axis, the quicker the change.

Use the following strategies to interpret the bar graph.

1 Read the title of the graph. Read the title and the legend to determine the subject of the graph.

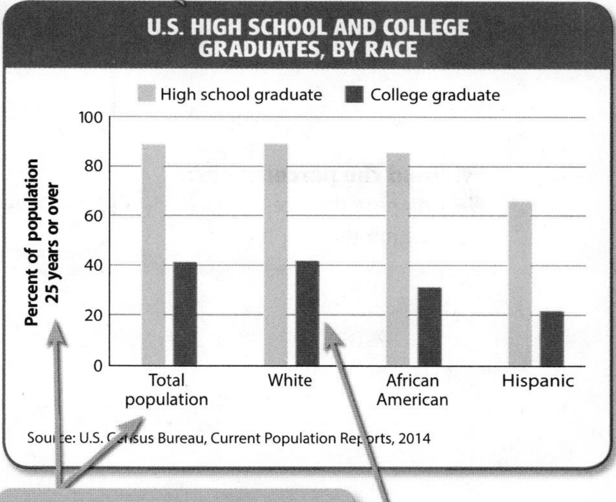

2 Read the horizontal and vertical axis labels. The labels tell what the bar graph measures and gives the units of measurement.

3 Analyze the information on the graph. Compare the amounts shown on the bar graph.

Apply the Skill

1. What information does the line graph compare?
2. What information does the bar graph compare?
3. What conclusion can you draw from the data in the bar graph?

Interpreting Pie Graphs

SKILLS HANDBOOK

Define the Skill

A **pie graph** is a circular chart that shows how individual parts relate to the whole. The circle of the pie symbolizes the whole amount. The slices of the pie represent the individual parts of the whole. Knowing how to interpret pie graphs will allow you to better understand and evaluate data.

Learn the Skill

Use the following strategies to interpret the pie graph.

1 Read the title of the graph. The title tells you the subject or purpose of the graph.

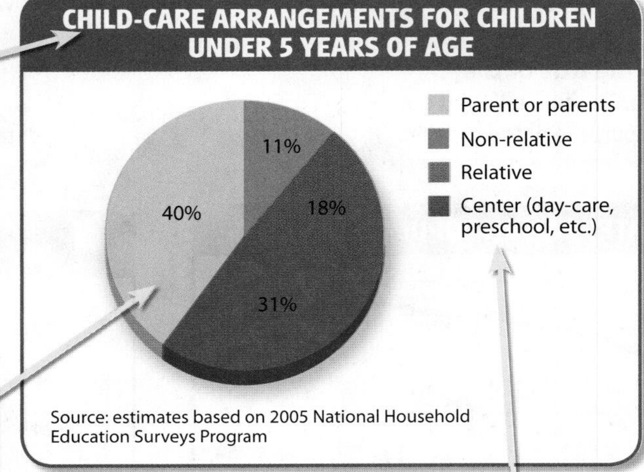

2 Read the percentages. Compare the sizes of each piece within the graph.

3 Analyze the information on the graph. Determine what the percentages tell about the subject of the pie graph.

Apply the Skill

1. What information does the pie graph compare?
2. What percentage of children are cared for by relatives?
3. According to this graph, who do parents rely on the most to care for their children?

Interpreting Charts

Define the Skill

Charts are visual representations of information. Sociologists use charts to organize, condense, simplify, and summarize information in a convenient format. *Simple charts* combine or compare information. *Tables* classify information by groups. Numbers, percentages, dates, and other data can be classified in the columns and rows of a table for reference and comparison. *Diagrams* illustrate the steps involved in a process so that the information is easier to understand. Knowing how to read and use charts allows you to interpret, compare, analyze, and evaluate information.

Learn the Skill

Use the following strategies to interpret the chart.

1 Read the title of the chart. The title tells you the subject of the chart.

2 Look at the way the information is organized. Charts can be organized alphabetically, chronologically, or by topic.

3 Analyze the information found in the chart. Interpret, compare, and contrast the information in the chart to draw conclusions and make inferences or predictions.

THE RESEARCH PROCESS

QUICK FACTS

Sociologists generally follow a seven-step process when conducting empirical research.

Step 1 Define the Problem
The researcher selects a topic for study and develops operational definitions of key concepts.

Step 2 Review the Literature
The researcher reviews existing literature on the topic.

Step 3 Form a Hypothesis
The researcher develops a testable hypothesis on the research topic.

Step 4 Choose a Research Design
The researcher develops a plan for collecting, analyzing, and evaluating data.

Step 5 Collect the Data
The researcher gathers and carefully records data.

Step 6 Analyze the Data
The researcher objectively analyzes the data to determine whether the data support the research hypotheses.

Step 7 Present Conclusions
The researcher presents the research findings to other sociologists.

Apply the Skill

1. How is the information in the chart organized?
2. How could this information be useful to a sociologist?
3. According to the chart, what does a researcher do in Step 6?

Interpreting Thematic Maps

Define the Skill

Thematic maps provide information in spatial terms. You can use thematic maps to compare how various social issues are reflected in different places. Thematic maps can show information such as population density, economic activity, political and military alliances, and movement of people and goods.

Learn the Skill

Use the following strategies to interpret thematic maps.

1 Read the title and legend. The title will help you identify the subject and the purpose of the map. The legend explains the meaning of the colors on the map.

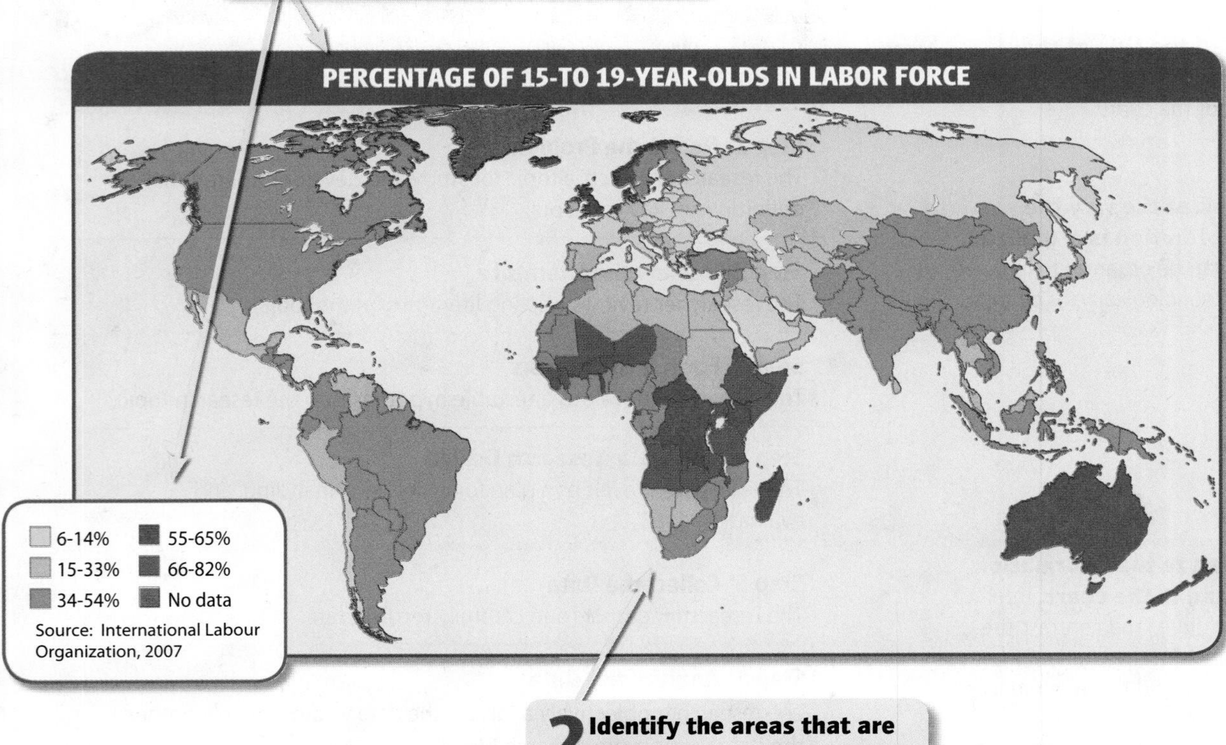

2 Identify the areas that are different. Note which parts of the map have different percentage ranges.

Apply the Skill

1. What is the purpose of this thematic map?
2. What percentage of 15- to 19-year-olds in the United States are in the labor force?

Analyzing Primary Sources

SKILLS HANDBOOK

Define the Skill

A **primary source** is a document or other artifact created by people who are present at events either as witnesses or participants. Usually, you can identify a primary source by reading for first-person clues, such as *I*, *we*, and *our*. Primary sources are valuable tools because they give firsthand information about an event or time period.

Learn the Skill

Use the following strategies to analyze primary sources.

In 1903 W.E.B. Du Bois published a classic work titled The Souls of Black Folk. *The book is partly autobiographical, and in the following excerpt, Du Bois reveals how he felt when he first learned, as a schoolboy, that he was "different from the others" and "shut out from their world." The incident may seem trivial, but it had a profound effect on him for the rest of his life.*

"It is in the early days of rollicking boyhood that the revelation first bursts upon one, all in a day, as it were. I remember well when the shadow swept across me. I was a little thing, away up in the hills of New England . . . In a wee wooden schoolhouse, something put it into the boys' and girls' heads to buy gorgeous visiting-cards—ten cents a package—and exchange. The exchange was merry, till one girl, a tall newcomer, refused my card . . . Then it dawned upon me with a certain suddenness that I was different from the others; or like, mayhap, in heart and life and longing, but shut out from their world by a vast veil. I had thereafter no desire to tear down that veil, to creep through; I held all beyond it in common contempt, and lived above it in a region of blue sky and great wandering shadows. That sky was bluest when I could beat my mates at examination-time, or beat them at a foot-race . . ."

1 Identify the author or creator of the primary source and when the source was created. The author and the date the primary source was created give you a context in which to place the document.

2 Compare details in the primary source to what you know about the event, situation, or time period. The time frame of the primary source allows you to make connections between your previous knowledge and the information the document provides.

3 Determine why the author created the primary source. Each document has a particular purpose and can be used by its author to inform, persuade, direct, or influence the audience.

Apply the Skill

1. Recall what you have learned in other social studies classes. What era or situation is Du Bois describing in this excerpt?
2. How does Du Bois's memoir affect your knowledge of that era or situation?

Analyzing Secondary Sources

SKILLS HANDBOOK

Define the Skill

A **secondary source** is an account created by someone who was not present at the actual event about which he or she is writing. Writers of secondary sources rely on primary sources in order to write their secondary source accounts. Secondary sources often contain summaries and analyses of events. Your textbook, for example, can be considered a secondary source. Before determining whether a document is a primary or secondary source, you must pay attention to how the document is presented.

Learn the Skill

Use the following strategies to analyze secondary sources.

1 Identify the source. Examine any source information to learn the origins of the document and its author.

Christopher Browning's book, *Ordinary Men: Reserve Police Battalion 101 and the Final Solution in Poland* describes the events and motives that caused 500 middle-class, middle-aged German men to terrorize Jews in Poland in July of 1942. It was easier for most of these policemen to join in the killing than to break ranks and refuse to participate. By November of 1943, these ordinary civilians had murdered at least 85,000 Jewish people.

Before the killing began the commanding officer, Major Trapp, explicitly offered to excuse any man who did not want to participate in the impending mass murder. Trapp's offer thrust responsibility onto each man individually. Still, between 80 to 90 percent of the men participated in the killing, finding it too difficult not to conform. Unlike soldiers, these policemen had the burden of choice. They were not "just following orders." Rather, the pressure to conform to their peers' expectations was paramount.

In his book, Browning notes that no member of Reserve Police Battalion 101 who refused to participate was physically harmed or punished. Instead, outright refusal to participate brought more subtle consequences, such as the threat of isolation from the group.

2 Analyze the summary of historical events provided by the source. The author of a secondary source usually offers a summary of events or of a time period.

3 Identify the author's purpose. Look for clues that indicate the intention of the author.

Apply the Skill

1. How do you know that this passage is not a primary source?
2. Why might this passage actually be called a tertiary source?
3. What is this writer's point of view? What can you conclude is Christopher Browning's point of view?

Interpreting Cartoons

Define the Skill

Although most **cartoons** are just meant to be funny, many of them can also shed light on social science concepts. Some cartoons, including political or editorial cartoons, express specific points of view. Cartoons that appear in popular magazines or newspapers may also present a certain viewpoint. Cartoons of this type often poke fun at the foibles of modern life. Artists may use exaggeration, either in the text or the drawing, to help make their point. Although some cartoons are not at all realistic, for the reader to understand them and the humor there must be some elements in the cartoon to which the reader can relate.

Learn the Skill

Use the acronym **BASIC** to analyze cartoons.

"I'm sorry, but I WILL NOT have any member of my electorate flirting with a THIRD PARTY such as him!"

Background Knowledge Place the cartoon in its context. Use your prior knowledge of what is being depicted to analyze the cartoon's message about the particular issue, person, or event.

Argument Determine what message the artist is trying to convey. Analyze the message that the artist is sending to the audience.

Symbolism Analyze any symbols in the cartoon. Symbols can be used to represent large groups that cannot be depicted easily or to stand for a person or an event. Symbols can also be used to simplify the cartoon or make its message clearer to the audience.

Irony Examine any irony that is present in the cartoon. Irony is the use of words or images to express something other than, and often the opposite of, their literal meaning.

Caricature Caricature, or exaggeration, is often used in cartoons. Exaggerated facial features or figures are used to make a point. Analyze any caricature present in the cartoon and consider what the meaning of such exaggerations might be.

Apply the Skill

1. On what issue is the artist commenting?
2. What elements are exaggerated in the cartoon?
3. How does the artist convey a message to the audience?

Determining Relevance

Define the Skill

When conducting research, you will likely be faced with a great variety of different sources. Identifying which sources will help you is an important task. One step in identifying your sources is to determine their relevance. **Determining relevance** means deciding if a piece of information is related to your topic. It also involves identifying *how* something is related to your topic.

Learn the Skill

Use the following strategies to determine the relevance of information.

1 Identify the specific topic. Determine what types of sources address your research topic. Define your specific task to narrow down what types of information you need. Write down any questions for which you need answers.

2 Locate a variety of sources. Use several resources to track down sources. Textbooks, encyclopedias, periodicals, and electronic databases are just a few types of resources you can use.

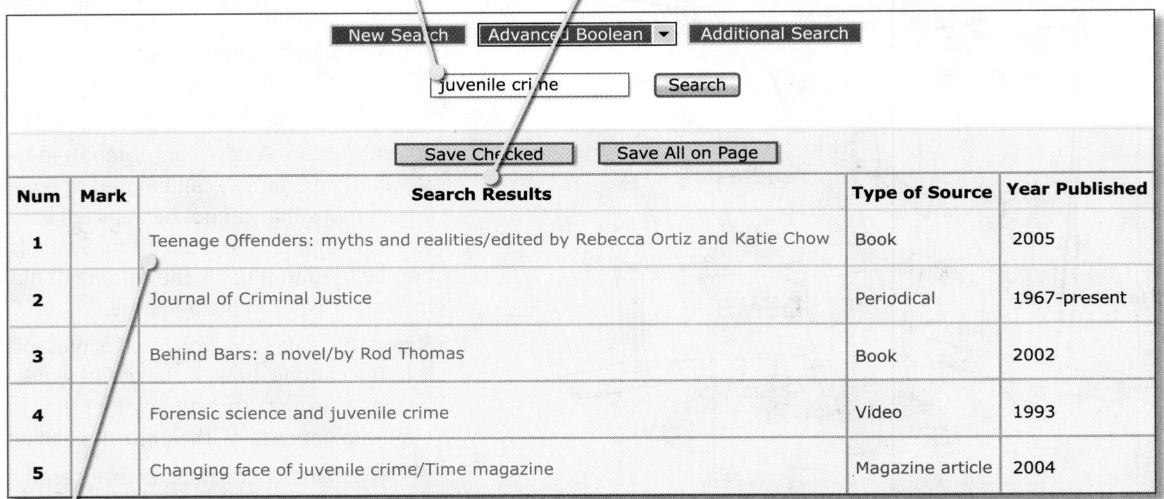

Num	Mark	Search Results	Type of Source	Year Published
1		Teenage Offenders: myths and realities/edited by Rebecca Ortiz and Katie Chow	Book	2005
2		Journal of Criminal Justice	Periodical	1967-present
3		Behind Bars: a novel/by Rod Thomas	Book	2002
4		Forensic science and juvenile crime	Video	1993
5		Changing face of juvenile crime/Time magazine	Magazine article	2004

3 Examine the sources carefully. Identify the purpose of the source and the information it provides.

4 Determine what information is useful for your topic. Decide if the information in the sources can help you answer the list of questions you created.

Apply the Skill

1. List several resources you might use to find information on the topic of juvenile crime.
2. How might you evaluate each of the sources listed above?
3. What sources from the list above would be relevant to your research? Explain.

Developing and Testing Hypotheses

Define the Skill

A **hypothesis** is a testable statement about the relationship between two or more factors. Hypotheses are possible explanations based on facts. Because they can be tested, hypotheses can be proved or disproved.

Learn the Skill

Use the following strategies to learn to develop and test hypotheses.

1 Identify the question. Examine the issue at hand to find the trend, relationship, or event that you want to explain.

Question: What has caused the drop in Monroeville's crime rate?

2 Examine the facts. Identify all the facts surrounding the question. The facts may support several different conclusions.

FACTS:
- Crime rates in the city of Monroeville have declined for five consecutive years.
- Monroeville's crime rate used to be the highest in the county.
- This year unemployment rates dropped to an all-time low.
- The population of Monroeville has increased by 26 percent since the new factory opened six years ago.
- Monroeville has hired three new police officers in the last three years.

3 Consider what you already know about the issue. Use your own prior knowledge to help you formulate a hypothesis.

4 Develop a hypothesis that addresses the question. Analyze the facts and your own knowledge to form a conclusion, explanation, or prediction.

Hypothesis: The availability of jobs in Monroeville has led to the drop in the town's crime rate.

FACTS THAT SUPPORT HYPOTHESIS:	FACTS THAT REFUTE HYPOTHESIS:
Monroeville's population has increased 25 percent in six years.	Monroeville has three new police officers.

5 Test your hypothesis. Conduct research to test your hypothesis. Identify facts that support or refute your conclusion. Depending on your findings, you may need to modify your hypothesis.

SKILLS HANDBOOK

Apply the Skill

1. Develop a list of facts and a hypothesis that might explain why voter turnout rates among young voters has increased in recent years.
2. Use a graphic organizer like the one above to test your hypothesis.

Evaluating Information on the Internet

Define the Skill

The **Internet** is an international computer network that connects schools, businesses, government agencies, and individuals. Every Web site on the Internet has its own address called a *URL*. Each URL has a domain. The *domain* tells you the type of Web site you are visiting. Common domains in the United States are .com, .net, .org, .edu, and .gov. A Web site with the domain .edu means that it is sponsored by an educational institution. A Web site with the domain .gov means that it is sponsored by a government institution. The collection of Web sites throughout the world is called the *World Wide Web*.

The Internet can be a valuable research tool. Evaluating the content found on the Internet will help you determine its accuracy and reliability.

Learn the Skill

Use the following strategies to evaluate information on the Internet.

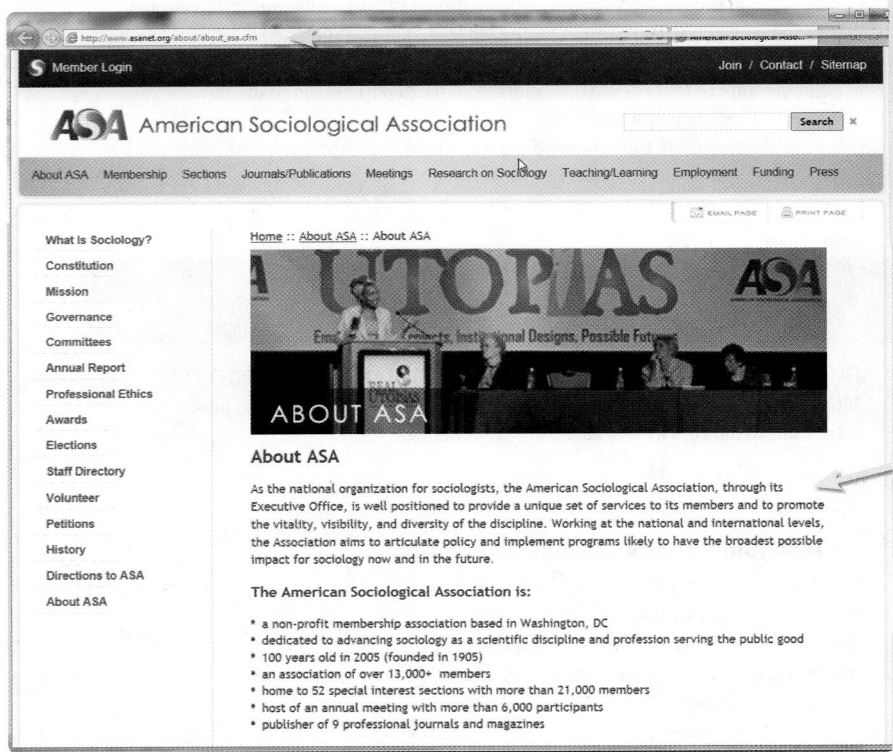

1 Identify the Web site's domain. Determine who sponsors the Web site. Web sites sponsored by reputable organizations, educational institutions, and government agencies usually provide accurate and reliable information.

2 Understand the purpose of the site. Find out whether the purpose of the site is to inform, to persuade, or to entertain.

3 Identify the author and check for bias. Not all sites provide you with an author. If the site does, try to determine the author's credentials. If the site does not, decide whether the Web site presents balanced information or is overly biased toward a certain point of view.

Apply the Skill

1. What is the domain of the Web site? Do you think the information on the Web site will be reliable? Why or why not?
2. What is the purpose of this Web site?
3. Do you think this Web site presents a balanced point of view or a biased point of view? Explain your response.

Synthesizing Information from Multiple Sources

Define the Skill

An important critical thinking skill is synthesizing information. **Synthesizing information** means combining information from different sources. Each source you use might provide different information on a particular topic or issue. Synthesizing the information from all of your sources will help you to produce a new idea, point of view, or interpretation.

Learn the Skill

Use the following strategies to practice synthesizing information from multiple sources.

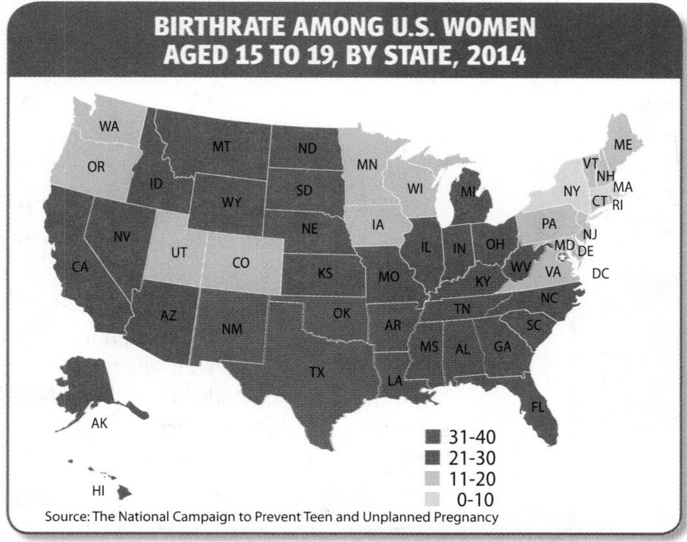

Source: The National Campaign to Prevent Teen and Unplanned Pregnancy

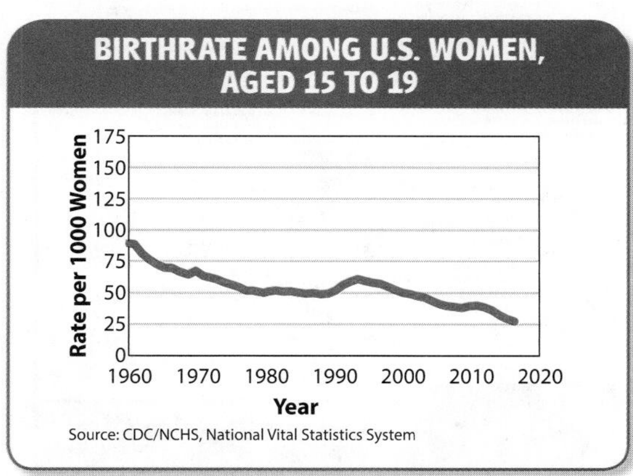

Source: CDC/NCHS, National Vital Statistics System

1 Evaluate each source. Analyze each source to determine if the source is valid and reliable. Determine if the various sources are comparable.

2 Examine the information from each source. Identify the key facts presented in each source separately. Make a list of the information that each source provides.

3 Compare the information from your various sources. Identify similarities and differences between the sources and analyze relationships between the sources.

4 Synthesize the information from the sources. Draw conclusions based on the information from each of your sources. Use your conclusions to create your own interpretation, point of view, or idea on the topic.

Apply the Skill

1. Are the sources above valid and reliable? How can you tell?
2. What similarities and differences exist between the two sources?
3. What conclusions can you draw based on the information in these two sources?

Building Your Vocabulary

HMH Social Studies: Sociology helps you build your vocabulary by focusing on two types of vocabulary words. Terms that are essential to your mastery of the course content are listed at the beginning of every section and are highlighted in yellow. You will encounter the definitions of these words as you read each section. The definitions are also in the Glossary. Academic Vocabulary words are words you need to know for other classes, too. They are underlined in the text and defined in the margins. On the following page is a list of these Academic Vocabulary words, along with their definitions.

Vocabulary Throughout each section you will find vocabulary words highlighted in yellow that you will need to know. Be on the lookout for these words as you read.

school invo...
influential agen...
media, involves no
The **mass media** are
...ication that reach
personal contact
information a...

Academic Vocabulary Words that are important in all classes, not just sociology, are defined in the margin under the heading Academic Vocabulary. You will run into these academic words in other social studies courses.

ACADEMIC VOCABULARY
coeducational the education of students of both sexes at the same institution

Academic Vocabulary/Definition

administrative type of job that organizes and assists, such as a secretary

apprentice a person acquiring a trade or skills under supervision

arbitrary determined by personal preference, notion, or whim

assimilate to integrate or fit into

charismatic having a special charm or appeal that arouses loyalty or enthusiasm

civil disobedience the nonviolent refusal to obey the law as a way to advocate change

coeducational the education of students of both sexes at the same institution

conformity behavior in accordance with accepted rules or conventions

continuum a coherent whole characterized as a collection, sequence, or progression

dementia progressive deterioration of the cognitive and intellectual functions of the brain, such as memory loss

diagnoses more than one diagnosis

differentiate to identify or create difference between

disillusion to free someone from a naive or idealized belief

disproportionate in greater or lesser numbers than an equal share

domestic produced in a particular country; opposite of foreign

eligibility quality of being qualified or worthy of being chosen

empirical based on experiment or observation

enable make possible or supply an opportunity

epidemic an outbreak of disease affecting large numbers of people

ethics rules and standards of behavior governing the conduct of a person or group

feral wild or untamed

folklore traditional customs, tales, sayings, dances, or art forms preserved among a people

ghettos sections of a city where minority groups live, often because of economic or social pressure

ideology a belief system

informal economy unofficial economic activities that take place without government approval, and outside of mainstream business and industry

interval space or time between two points

linear relating to or resembling a straight line

means of production the materials and methods used to produce goods and services

model a representation or simulation of an object or theory

oligarchy situation in which a few people rule the many

personality disorder a long-term and deeply ingrained pattern of socially unacceptable behavior that is harmful to the person who displays it and to others

perspective point of view

policy plan or guiding principle

propaganda organized and deliberate attempt to shape public opinion

proponent one who argues in support of something

rebuke sharp criticism or expression of disapproval

sanction penalty, punishment

scope range or room in which to function

social advancement the process of moving up through the ranks of a class system

social environment contact with other people

synthesize to blend

vice legal term for offenses involving immorality, such as prostitution and gambling

voting bloc a group whose shared concerns motivate how they vote in elections

Using Statistics

Analyzing Observations

Conducting a research study is actually only a small part of the research process. Imagine that you decide to conduct a survey about the amount of television teenagers watch daily. After you have conducted interviews and received dozens of completed questionnaires you would probably feel overwhelmed by the amount of data you had collected. What is the next step?

When faced with this situation, sociologists use mathematical procedures, involving statistics to organize, analyze, and interpret the data. Sociologists then use the statistical analyses to construct charts and graphs. In short, statistics help sociologists make sense of their research findings.

Understanding Frequency

One of the most common forms of statistical analysis researchers use to organize their data is the frequency distribution. A frequency distribution is a way of arranging data to determine how often a certain piece of data—such as a score, salary, or age—occurs. In setting up a frequency distribution, researchers arrange the data from highest to lowest, and enter a mark when a piece of data occurs. The sum of each group's marks determines the frequency.

If there are too many different pieces of data to list individually, as is sometimes true for class scores, a researcher may substitute specific numerical spans, called class intervals, for individual scores. Again, the data are arranged from highest to lowest. A frequency distribution would allow a teacher to see at a glance how well a group of students did on a test, for instance, but it does not provide any information about individual performance.

Understanding Bell Curves

A useful statistical concept for sociologists is the bell curve, or normal curve. The bell curve is an ideal, a hypothetical standard against which actual categories of people or things (such as scores) can be measured and compared. Usually, bell curves are used to categorize characteristics of people in large groups. The closer the group comes to the center of the curve, where the most "normal" traits congregate, the more validity the study appears to have.

For example, the bell curve, "Distribution of IQ Scores," shown on the following page, illustrates a hypothetical standard against which actual IQ scores can be compared. This bell curve is a model of an ideal. It shows what would happen if the largest number of scores fell exactly in the middle of a range of scores. A comparison of the actual scores against this bell curve tells a researcher how representative the IQ test really is.

Correlations represent the relationship between two variables. When two variables show a positive correlation, one rises as the other rises. If the two variables are negatively correlated, one of the variables rises as the other falls. A bell curve is a normal frequency distribution. This means that after counting the frequency of specific data, researchers can create an arrangement, or distribution, that is concentrated on or near the curve's center, which represents the norm. The fewest entries of data should appear at the far ends of the distribution—away from the highly concentrated norm.

It follows then that when the graphed results of an experiment come close to matching a bell curve, the results are assumed to be highly representative of that experiment. If most scores or data cluster towards the ends of the curve, however, the experiment or test is assumed to be unrepresentative of the group.

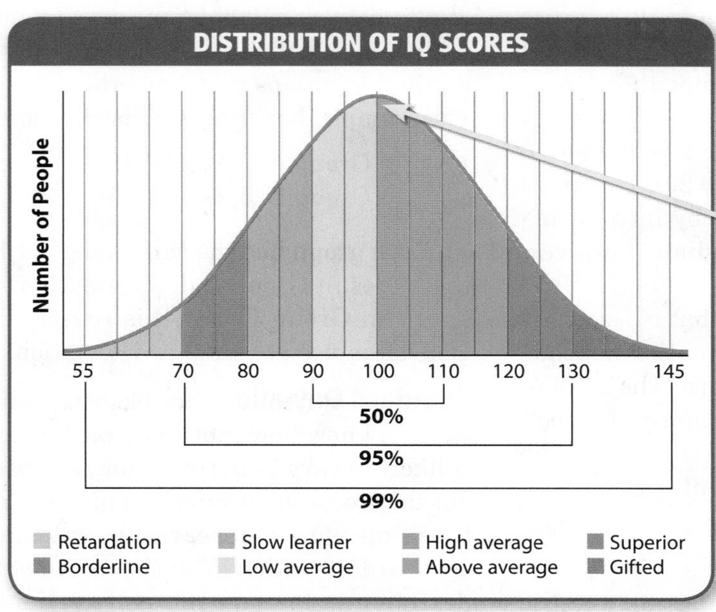

This bell curve is a model of an ideal. It shows what would happen if the largest number of scores fell exactly in the middle of a range of scores. A comparison of the actual scores against this bell curve tells a researcher how representative the IQ test really is.

Bell curves and frequency distributions seem very complicated. However, they are simply ways to condense information and put it in a visual form. Within moments of glancing at a real plotted curve and the bell curve beside it, researchers can judge approximately how far from the norm their experimental group was, and how closely their results conform to what is "perfectly" normal.

Mode, Mean, and Median: Measures of Central Tendency

Three other measures are used to compare data that fall within the central points of a distribution: the mode, the mean, and the median.

Mode Simply, the mode is the piece of data that occurs most often in a given set of numbers. To find the mode, examine any frequency distribution and choose the number that appears most often. The mode is of limited use to researchers because "occurring most often" in a distribution may mean, for example, that this number occurred only twice among fifty different test scores.

Mean The mean is an average. The mean is found by adding all the scores or data together and then dividing that sum by the number of scores. The formula for finding the mean is:

$$\text{mean} = \frac{\text{sum of the scores}}{\text{number of scores}}$$

A significant disadvantage of using the mean is that any extreme score, whether high or low, distorts a researcher's results. For instance, if five waiters earn $300, $350, $325, $390, and $600 per week respectively, the mean—or average—weekly salary for this group would be $393. Yet four of the five waiters earn less than the average amount. In this circumstance, using the mean would not necessarily be representative of the waiters' wages.

Median The median is the score or piece of data that falls precisely in the middle of all the scores when they are arranged in descending order. Exactly half of the students score above the median, and exactly half score below it. In the previous example of waiters' salaries, the median would be $350, because two waiters earned more and two earned less.

The median, unlike the mean, is usually an actual number or score. To find the median of an even number of scores, you would find the median of the two numbers that fall in the middle, and then take the mean of those two central numbers in the distribution.

One major advantage of the median is that extreme scores, high or low, will not affect it. For example, examine the following two distributions:

Group X: 4, 10, 16, 18, 22
Group Y: 4, 10, 16, 18, 97

The median for each group is 16, because that number falls precisely in the middle of all the scores. However, the mean for Group X is 14 (4 + 10 + 16 + 18 + 22 = 70; 70 ÷ 5 = 14), while the mean for Group Y is 29 (4 + 10 + 16 + 18 + 97 = 145; 145 ÷ 5 = 29). The mean changes dramatically simply by introducing one extreme score. The median, however, remains the same.

The kind of central point that researchers choose to use in any given situation depends on what they are trying to learn. The median is not the best choice in all instances. In a bell curve—the idealized norm—the mode, the mean, and the median are identical.

Variability

Knowing what the mode, the mean, and the median are tells a researcher a great deal but not everything about the data. Researchers also need to know how much variability there is among the scores in a group of numbers. That is, researchers must discover how far apart the numbers or scores are in relation to the mean. For this purpose, sociologists use two measures: the range and the standard deviation.

Range The range is the mathematical difference between the highest and lowest scores in a frequency distribution. If the highest grade in a class is 100 and the lowest is 60, the range is 40 (100 – 60 = 40). Two groups of numbers may have the same mean but different ranges. For example, consider the batting averages of two baseball teams:

Team A: 210 250 285 300 340
Team B: 270 270 275 285 285

The mean for each team is 277. However, the range for Team A is 130 points, whereas the range for Team B is 15 points. This would tell a researcher that Team B is more alike in its batting abilities than is Team A.

The range tells a sociologist how similar the subjects in each group are to one another in terms of what is being measured. This information could not be obtained from the mode, mean, or median alone, since each is just one number and not a comparison.

The disadvantage of the range, though, is that it takes only the lowest and highest scores of a frequency distribution into account. The middle numbers may be substantially different in two groups that have the same range. For example, here are two distributions:

Group A: 5, 8, 12, 14, 15
Group B: 5, 6, 7, 8, 15

Each group has the same range of 10. But the scores in Group A differ greatly from the scores in Group B. For this reason, sociologists often use the standard deviation.

Standard Deviation Sociologists sometimes want to know how much any particular score is likely to vary from the mean, or how spread out the scores are around the mean. To derive these measures, researchers calculate the standard deviation. The closer the standard deviation is to zero, the more reliable that data tends to be.

Let's say that the standard deviation of Team A's batting average is about 44.2, and the standard deviation of Team B's batting average is 6.8. From this information we know that the typical score of Team A will fall within 44.2 points of the mean, and the typical score of Team B will be within 6.8 points of the mean. This tells us that the quality of batting is more consistent on Team B than on Team A.

Two bell curves can have the same mode, mean, and median, but different standard deviations. If you were plotting two bell curves on a line graph, and one curve had a much larger standard deviation than the other, the curve with the larger standard deviation would show a more pronounced bell shape on the graph.

Correlation Correlation is a measure of the relationship between two variables. A variable is any behavior or condition that can change in quantity or quality. Examples of variables that people frequently encounter are age, hair color, weight, and height. Correlation and causation are two types of relationships between variables that have great importance for sociologists.

When two variables are related, they are said to have a correlation. Changes in variables often occur together. Sometimes, an increase or decrease in one is accompanied by a corresponding increase or decrease in the other. For example, a decrease in someone's caloric intake is accompanied by a decrease in that person's weight. Such variables are said to be positively correlated. Sometimes, when one variable increases, the other decreases, or vice-versa. These variables are said to be negatively correlated.

Correlation Coefficient The correlation coefficient describes the degree of relationship between variables. The concept of correlation allows researchers to predict the value of one variable if they know the value of the other and the way that the variables are correlated. A perfect positive correlation would have a coefficient of +1.00; a perfect negative correlation has a coefficient of –1.00. A correlation coefficient of zero indicates that there is no correlation between two variables.

Perfect positive correlations (+1.00 coefficient), when graphed, form a straight line that leans to the right; a perfect negative correlation (–1.00 coefficient), shown on a line graph, would form a straight line that leans to the left. In reality, few correlations are perfect. While one variable may increase or decrease in relation to the other, both variables probably will not change to the same degree.

Here is an example of a strong negative correlation with predictive potential: the more hours a person spends commuting to work, the less he or she enjoys driving. We can predict that if the person shortens the commute, his or her enjoyment of driving will increase.

Causation Although correlation is an important concept in statistics, it does not explain everything about relationships between variables. For one thing, correlation does not speak to the concept of causation. No correlation, of any degree, in itself proves that one variable causes another.

It is difficult to determine whether one variable actually causes another. Researchers determine causal relationships scientifically rather than relying on the intuitive sense of causality that may be implied in a correlation. They compare the differences between an experimental group—the group that displays the condition that is being studied— and a control group, in which this condition is not present. The independent variable is the variable being manipulated by the researcher.

If Group A is exposed to a virus and gets sick, and Group B is exposed to the same virus but has been vaccinated and does not become ill, there appears to be a causal relationship at work. It seems that the vaccine protected Group B from the virus, and therefore from illness. But researchers probably would want to examine how the vaccine actually worked—if it did. It may have been coincidental that Group B remained well.

POSITIVE AND NEGATIVE CORRELATIONS

Positive Correlation

Generally speaking, people who have a higher need for achievement achieve higher salaries.

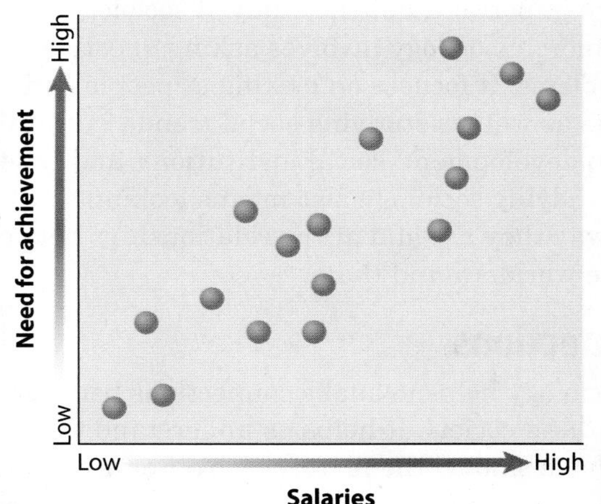

Negative Correlation

Generally speaking, the immune systems of people who are under high amounts of stress tend to function more poorly than the immune systems of people who are under less stress.

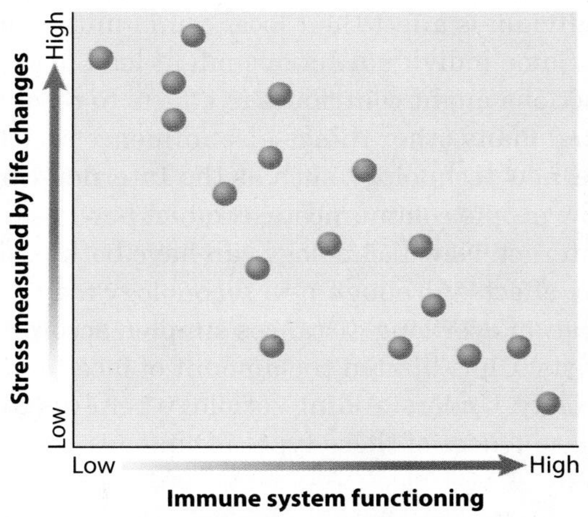

Why Sociology Matters

Sociology is the study of society. In order to understand society we must be able to see the world through the eyes of others. By using this sociological imagination you can understand the world around you.

Sociology and Your World

When you think of sociology, what comes to mind? Maybe you think of people conducting surveys or interviewing people in a neighborhood to learn more about their lives. Perhaps you simply picture people analyzing census data. These things are important, but the study of sociology includes much more. Sociology involves asking questions and solving problems. It focuses on looking at people and their ways of life as well as studying social trends, cultural changes, human development, social institutions, and collective behavior. Studying sociology also means looking at why things are the way they are and at the relationships between humans and the world around them.

Making Connections

The study of sociology helps us make connections between human behavior and society. It helps us understand the processes that have shaped the features we observe around us today, as well as the ways those features may be different tomorrow. In short, sociology helps us understand the processes that have created a world that is home to more than 6.5 billion people.

Sociology and You

Anyone can influence the society of our world. For example, the actions of individuals affect their local community and social networks. Some individual actions might lead to social conflict. Other actions might contribute to efforts to resolve social conflict. And many other things also influence sociology. For example, new technology, such as the Internet, can greatly affect how people communicate, conduct business, and generally interact. New technology can have both positive and negative effects. Although new technology may make communication over long distances simpler, according to some sociologists it has limited the amount of face-to-face interaction in society. Understanding sociology helps us to evaluate the consequences of these types of changes.

UNIT 1 Culture and Social Structure

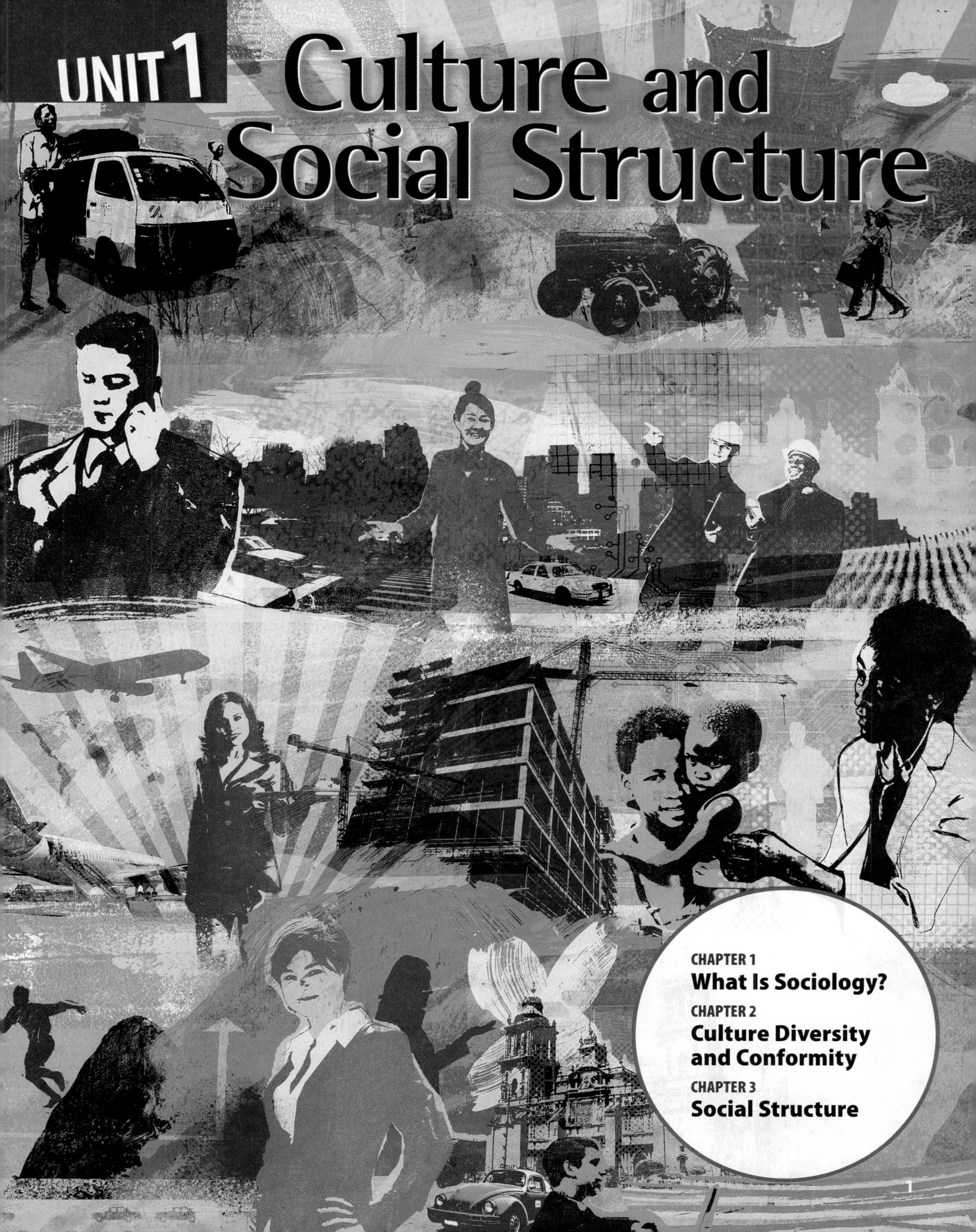

CASE STUDY

STREET SCIENCE

Sudhir Venkatesh, now a professor of sociology, stands in the Chicago neighborhood he studied as a student.

Sudhir Venkatesh's first visit to the Robert Taylor Homes, a sprawling public housing project on Chicago's South Side, did not go too well. Venkatesh, a graduate student at the time, planned to interview residents for a research paper on poverty. However, members of a local street gang grabbed him and held him hostage for 24 hours. When they released him, the gang leader, J.T., gave Venkatesh some advice—get to know people before you ask them questions.

Venkatesh took the suggestion to heart. He returned to the projects several times in the next few months and got to know J.T. quite well. Venkatesh found the gang leader fascinating. J.T. was college educated and had once held a management-level job. He returned to the neighborhood and became a gang leader to find the prestige and money that had escaped him in the business world.

A friendship with J.T. gave Venkatesh access to practically every aspect of life in the neighborhood. For close to seven years, Venkatesh spent a good part of his time there, watching and listening, gathering information for his research. He discovered that the neighborhood, in sociological terms, was a "shady world." Pretty much the whole community lived "off the books." Mainstream economic activities were few and far between. Many people made a living through illegal means. Most got by through practical barter arrangements. For example, a doctor treated patients in return for hot meals. A business owner allowed homeless people to sleep in his store at night in return for their acting as security guards. Also, neighborhood residents sought their own solutions to problems rather than calling on the police or others in official positions. Venkatesh got involved in this process. Several people asked him to mediate disputes over economic transactions. They felt that since Venkatesh was familiar with the neighborhood but not really part of it, he would make decisions that treated all parties fairly.

Venkatesh's fascination with J.T. led him to spend more and more time with the gang leader. At one point, he even took over for

The Robert Taylor Homes, once the largest housing project in the United States, were demolished in the early 2000s.

J.T. In response to Venkatesh's challenge that the job looked easy, J.T. suggested that Venkatesh try being gang leader for a day. Soon, however, this involvement with the illegal side of neighborhood life began to worry Venkatesh. When he readily took part in the beating of a neighborhood thug, he knew he had crossed the line from observer to accessory.

Venkatesh's professors, fearing for his safety, suggested that he step back from his research. One urged him to refocus his studies and take a more traditional approach to the issue of poverty. Even Venkatesh began to doubt that what he was doing had any academic value.

After considerable thought, Venkatesh continued on and completed the research as planned. His book based on that research, *Off the Books: The Underground Economy of the Urban Poor,* discussed the violence of day-to-day life and the illegal activities of J.T. and his drug-dealing gang. However, it also described a community of people who looked out for each other and community leaders who got things done despite having few resources. Further, it showed that the families in the projects were little different from other families—mothers and fathers did their utmost to make a decent life for themselves and their children. Venkatesh noted that the sociological studies he had read in preparation for his research had defined poverty in terms of what was missing. In *Off the Books,* he hoped to present the issue of poverty in terms of what was actually there.

What do you think?

1. What did Sudhir Venkatesh learn from the community he studied?
2. Do you think that to really understand a situation, you need to be part of it? Why or why not?

CHAPTER 1

WHAT IS SOCIOLOGY?

Chapter at a Glance

SECTION 1: Examining Social Life

- The social sciences are disciplines that study human social behavior or institutions and functions of human society in a scientific manner. Sociology is the social science that studies human society and social behavior.
- The sociological perspective is a way of looking at the world that enables sociologists to see beyond commonly held beliefs to the hidden meanings behind human actions.

SECTION 2: The Development of Sociology

- Social upheaval in Europe during the late 1700s and 1800s encouraged scholars to closely study society.
- European scholars such as Auguste Comte, Harriet Martineau, Herbert Spencer, Karl Marx, Émile Durkheim, and Max Weber made important contributions to the development of the academic discipline of sociology.
- The Chicago School of sociologists introduced new ways to analyze society.

SECTION 3: Modern Perspectives

- Sociology employs three major theoretical perspectives—functionalism, conflict, and interactionism.
- The functionalist perspective focuses on order and stability, the conflict perspective focuses on power relations, and the interactionist perspective focuses on how individuals interact with one another in everyday life.
- Sociologists employ two levels of analysis: macrosociology, which focuses on large-scale systems or society as a whole, and microsociology, which focuses on small-group settings.

SECTION 4: Conducting Sociological Research

- Sociologists employ a seven-step process when they conduct research.
- Research approaches available to sociologists include survey, analysis of existing documents, observation, and experiment.

SECTION 1

Examining Social Life

Before You Read

Main Idea

Sociology is a social science that looks at human society. Viewing the world from a sociological perspective enables sociologists to see beyond commonly held beliefs to the hidden meanings behind human actions.

Reading Focus

1. What is sociology, and how does it compare to other social sciences?
2. How do sociologists view and think about society?

Vocabulary

social sciences
sociology
social interaction
social phenomena
anthropology
psychology
social psychology
economics
political science
history
sociological perspective
sociological imagination

TAKING NOTES Use a graphic organizer like this one to compare the focus of sociology with the focus of the other social sciences.

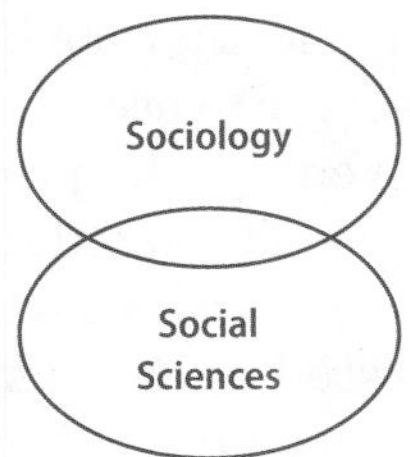

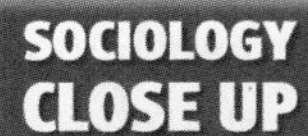

Why are so many Americans getting tattoos? For many young people, a tattoo is a form of rebellion—a challenge to the accepted standards of appearance. For others, it's a symbol of belonging. Sports teammates, fraternity and sorority members, or groups of friends get tattoos to show that they have had some shared experience. Women, who make up almost half of tattooed Americans, also have a number of reasons for marking their bodies. For some, a tattoo is a declaration of independence from traditional feminine roles. Other women, however, see the tattoo as an enhancement of feminine beauty. For many heavily tattooed Americans, the reasons are almost tribal. Their tattoos are a form of reconnection to a long-lost past when body marking symbolized status, achievement, courage, and strength.

Regardless of their reasons, quite a few Americans are getting tattooed. A recent survey showed that 21 percent of adults in the United States have at least one tattoo. This number rises to 72 percent among adults under the age of 40. Further, 30 percent of those with tattoos stated that having a tattoo made them feel more sexy. ■

While many Americans still look upon tattoos negatively, the norm against body marking is losing its authority, especially among the young.

Sociology and Other Social Sciences

Looking for an individual's motivation behind actions such as body marking, as well as the meaning and effects of such actions, is the realm of social science. The **social sciences** are disciplines that study human social behavior or institutions and the functions of human society in a scientific manner. These sciences include sociology, anthropology, psychology, economics, and political science. In addition, history is also often categorized as a social science.

Sociology The social science that studies human society and social behavior is called **sociology.** Sociologists, for the most part, are interested in **social interaction**—how people relate to one another and influence each other's behavior. Consequently, sociologists tend to focus on the group rather than on the individual. Sociologists do this by examining **social phenomena**—observable facts or events that involve human society.

Anthropology Similar to sociology in its subject matter, **anthropology** is the comparative study of past and present cultures. Anthropologists often concentrate on examining past cultures and present simple—or less advanced—societies. Sociology, on the other hand, is most interested in group behavior in complex, or more advanced, societies. Recently, however, many anthropologists have turned their attention to complex societies. For example, urban anthropologists examine such things as the cultural characteristics of neighborhoods in large modern cities.

Psychology The social science that studies behavior and mental processes is **psychology.** It differs from sociology primarily in that it focuses on individual behavior rather than on group behavior. In addition, it draws more heavily on the tools of the natural sciences to gather and analyze information. Areas of interest to psychologists include personality, perception, motivation, and learning. Despite differences in emphasis and methods of analysis, sociology and psychology are related. This is particularly true in the area of **social psychology,** the study of how the social environment affects an individual's behavior and personality.

THE SOCIAL SCIENCES

The social sciences are a group of related disciplines that study society and human relationships. These disciplines overlap, but each one has a distinct point of view.

Sociology
The study of human social behavior from a group perspective.

Anthropology
The comparative study of past and present cultures. In terms of subject matter, anthropology is the social science most similar to sociology.

Psychology
The study of behavior and mental processes. Social psychology, the study of how the social environment affects individual personality and behavior, uses approaches similar to those of sociology.

Economics
The study of the production, distribution, and consumption of goods and services. Sociology is interested in the impact of the distribution of goods and services on inequality.

Political Science
The study of the organization and operation of governments. Government, particularly its impact on people's lives, is also of interest to sociologists.

History
The study of past events in human societies. Sociology sometimes looks to past events for explanations of present-day social phenomena.

Economics Analyzing the choices people make in an effort to satisfy their needs and wants is the focus of **economics.** Economists study the processes by which goods and services are produced, distributed, and consumed. In addition, they examine the effects of government policies on economic growth and stability. Sociologists share many areas of interest with economists. For example, the effect of economic factors on various groups in society has attracted the attention of sociologists since the earliest days of the discipline.

Political Science The examination of the principles, organization, and operation of government is the focus of **political science.** The interests of sociology and political science often overlap. Areas of mutual interest include voting patterns, the concentration of political power, and the formation of politically based groups.

The Sociological Imagination

The sociological imagination enables the sociologist to see the broad social issues behind individual problems while appreciating that those broad social issues affect the lives of individuals. For example, the sociological imagination moves the sociologist beyond the private concerns of the unemployed individual to the see the social phenomenon of unemployment. At the same time, however, it allows the sociologist to understand unemployment in terms of the lives of the unemployed.

C. Wright Mills suggested that the sociological imagination involves seeing the world in terms of biography and history. What do you think he meant by this?

Private Troubles–Being Unemployed

Public Issue–Unemployment

History The social science that studies the people and events of the past is **history.** Occasionally, sociologists focus on the past in their work. For example, some sociologists study past events in an effort to explain current social behaviors and attitudes.

Over time, the divisions between the social sciences have become less distinct. Many sociologists now borrow freely from other social sciences in an effort to better understand the social forces that shape our world.

Reading Check **Summarize** What are the social sciences?

Thinking Like a Sociologist

Did you know that you are surrounded by the subject of sociology? Think about how your life is influenced by the values, beliefs, lifestyles, and experiences of those around you. Historic events, too, help to shape who you are. Even new technologies may affect your view of the world. Skimming some newspaper articles illustrates this. Consider these two stories:

Impact of the Internet Several studies suggest that the Internet has helped to create a new form of isolation. A growing number of people, these studies note, are spending more time online and less time with family and friends. Other studies suggest that Internet use may have a positive impact. Many people who connect on the Internet tend to spend just as much time connecting through more traditional modes of communication such as the telephone and face-to-face meetings. Internet use also may be broadening horizons. Easy access to many of the world's newspapers has resulted in more people being interested in international affairs.

Crime Trends According to figures from the Bureau of Justice Statistics (BJS), the violent crime rate was 20.1 victimizations per 1,000 U.S. residents age 12 and older in 2014. Violent crime here includes rape or sexual assault, robbery, aggravated assault and simple assault. These numbers did not change significantly from 2013 to 2014.

The Sociological Perspective You've probably seen stories on these or other topics of sociological interest in the newspapers or on television. But if such stories appear in the media, then why study sociology? Most importantly, because sociology can help you gain a new perspective on yourself and the world around you. This new view involves looking at social life in a scientific, systematic way, rather than depending on common-sense explanations usually found in the media. By adopting a **sociological perspective,** you can look beyond commonly held beliefs to the hidden meanings behind human actions.

Looking at these two news stories from the sociological perspective, sociologists would try to find patterns. Do factors such as friends, family, gender, race, or education affect Internet use or crime? Would looking at the influence of television or music provide any clues? Finding the answers to such questions helps sociologists to develop a better understanding of these issues.

The sociological perspective helps you see that all people are social beings. It tells you that your behavior is influenced by social factors and that you have learned your behavior from others. The sociological perspective can also help you broaden your view of the social world. It tells you that there are many different perceptions of social reality. Using the sociological perspective allows you to see beyond your own day-to-day life by viewing the world through others' eyes.

Further, the sociological perspective can help you find an acceptable balance between your personal desires and the demands of your social environment. If you always do what you want to do, you are likely to conflict with others a great deal of the time. On the other hand, if you always do what others want, you will not grow as an individual. Applying the sociological perspective can help you find an acceptable point between these two extremes.

ACADEMIC VOCABULARY
perspective point of view

The Sociological Imagination Perhaps most importantly, the sociological perspective can help you view your own life within a larger social and historical context. It can give you insights into how your social environment shapes you and how you, in turn, can shape your social environment. This ability to see the connection between the larger world and your personal life is what sociologist C. Wright Mills called the **sociological imagination.** Mills described the sociological imagination as "the capacity to range from the most impersonal and remote [topics] to the most intimate features of the human self—and to see the relations between the two." All good sociologists and students of society, Mills added, must possess this ability.

Reading Check **Find the Main Idea** What is the sociological perspective?

SECTION 1 Assessment

Reviewing Main Ideas and Vocabulary

1. **Define** What is sociology?
2. **Explain** Why do sociologists focus on group behavior rather than individual behavior?
3. **Recall** What do sociologists examine in their study of human behavior?

Thinking Critically

4. **Analyze** How does applying the sociological perspective enable sociologists to develop a greater understanding of social issues?
5. **Draw Conclusions** Why did C. Wright Mills think that employing the sociological imagination was important to the study of sociology?
6. **Compare and Contrast** Using your notes and a graphic organizer like the one below, note how sociology is similar to or different from the other social sciences.

	Similarities with Sociology	Differences from Sociology
Anthropology		
Psychology		
Economics		

FOCUS ON WRITING

7. **Expository** Write two or three paragraphs explaining how a sociological imagination can enhance your everyday life. Consider the importance of viewing your own life within a larger social and historical context.

SECTION 2

The Development of Sociology

Before You Read

Main Idea
Social upheaval in Europe during the late 1700s and 1800s encouraged scholars to closely study society. Their work led to the development of the academic discipline of sociology.

Reading Focus
1. What factors led to the development of sociology?
2. How did early European scholars lay the foundations of sociology?
3. What contributions did later European scholars make to the development of sociology?
4. How did American scholars contribute to the field of sociology?

Vocabulary
social Darwinism
function
Verstehen
ideal type

TAKING NOTES Use a graphic organizer like this one to gather information about the development of sociology.

Early Sociologists	Areas of Interest
Comte	
Martineau	
Spencer	
Marx	
Durkheim	

Survival of the FITTEST

The life of London's poor is vividly illustrated by this sketch of a family huddled in a dank city alleyway.

SOCIOLOGY CLOSE UP ***How did one early sociologist view the problem of poverty?*** In the late 1800s the city of London was plagued with poverty. Estimates suggested that as much as one third of the population of Britain's capital were destitute. The living conditions of the city's poor were nothing short of horrendous. A visitor to London in the 1870s recalled that he saw "stifling alleys thick with . . . troops of pale children crouching on filthy staircases; the street benches at London Bridge where all night whole families huddle close, heads hanging, shaking with cold."

Even though the British government assisted the worst off, the vast majority of London's poor fell through the cracks in the welfare system. Calls for action to help the poverty-stricken grew. Many religious leaders charged that it was a moral outrage that so many people lived in squalor in one of the world's greatest cities.

But not everyone viewed the situation so sympathetically. Social philosopher Herbert Spencer believed that society was moving toward perfection. To provide assistance to the poor, he stated, would impede this process. Spencer believed that for society to reach its perfect state, all that was weak and not of use had to be discarded or allowed to fall away—a theory Spencer called "survival of the fittest." ■

The Development of Sociology

The nature of social life and human interaction has been of interest to scholars such as Herbert Spencer throughout history. However, a separate academic discipline dedicated to the analysis of society—sociology—did not develop until the 1800s.

Several factors led to the development of sociology as a distinct field of study. The rapid social and political changes that took place in Europe as a result of the Industrial Revolution were of primary importance. The rural economy, with its farms and cottage industries, gave way to an economy based on large-scale production. The factory replaced the home as the main site for manufacturing. With the growth of factories came the growth of cities, as people left their homes in the countryside in search of work.

The rapid growth of urban populations produced a multitude of social problems. The number of people seeking work outpaced available jobs. Housing shortages developed, crime increased, and pollution became a major problem. In addition, many people found it difficult to adapt to the impersonal nature of urban life. Over time, it became more difficult to ignore the effect of society on the individual. Individual liberty and individual rights became the focus of a wide variety of political movements and gave rise to the American and French Revolutions.

These sweeping political, social, and economic changes caused some scholars to question the traditional explanations of life. A similar situation had developed in the physical sciences in the 1700s. Many scientists rejected traditional religious explanations of the physical world. Rather, they speculated that the physical world operated according to systematic properties and laws. They attempted to prove their beliefs through observation, experiments, and careful collection and analysis of information. In the 1800s some scholars believed that the social world was based on a set of basic principles that could be studied and analyzed through the use of scientific research methods.

Reading Check **Draw Conclusions** Why do you think social upheaval encouraged scholars to analyze society?

Early European Scholars

Sociology took root in the 1800s, primarily in France, Germany, and Britain. These countries had most strongly felt the effects of the Industrial Revolution. Auguste Comte, Harriet Martineau, Herbert Spencer, and Karl Marx were perhaps the most influential of the early sociologists.

Auguste Comte Many people consider French philosopher Auguste Comte (1798–1857) the founder of sociology as a distinct subject. He was one of the first scholars to apply the methods of the physical sciences to the study of social life. He also coined the term *sociology* to describe the study of society.

Like most French scholars of his day, Comte was intrigued by the causes and consequences of the French Revolution. As a result, Comte began to focus on two basic areas of study—social order and social change. He suggested that certain processes, which he called *social statics,* hold society together. Similarly, Comte argued that society changes through definite processes, which he called *social dynamics.* The basic principles of these two social forces, Comte believed, could be uncovered through the methods of scientific research. He hoped this knowledge could be used to reform society.

Throughout his life, Comte suffered from depression and other emotional problems. At one point he began to practice what he called "cerebral hygiene," which involved ignoring the publications of other scholars in order to keep his mind pure. Even so, Comte's work had an enormous influence on early sociology. Today, most of his ideas regarding society have been refuted. However, more than 150 years after Comte's death, sociologists are still concerned with his basic issues of order and change.

Harriet Martineau Harriet Martineau (1802–1876) was born to a middle class English family. Her parents valued learning, and they made sure she received a good education. After her father died, Martineau was forced to support herself. She was determined to make a living as a writer. Even though she received little help or encouragement from publishers, she succeeded. By the 1830s, she was a respected author in Britain.

In 1837—a year or so before Auguste Comte coined the term *sociology*—Martineau published *Society in America*. Based on observations she made while traveling in the United States, the book was a review of how well the United States lived up to its promise of democracy. The topics on which Martineau reported in her book—including marriage, the family, race relations, education, and religion—established the focus of sociological study. Her detached style of reporting also set the standard for objectivity in sociological research. Despite the pioneering nature of Martineau's study, it was largely ignored by early sociologists.

Martineau's next major sociological work, however, did make an impression on the world of sociology. In 1853 she published a translation of Comte's *Positive Philosophy*. This book introduced Comte's ideas concerning the study of society to English speakers and had an enormous influence on scholars in Britain and the United States.

Martineau's views on the role of the scholar also had an impact. She believed that scholars should advocate change to solve the problems that they studied. As a result, she spoke out in favor of women's rights, religious tolerance, and the end of slavery.

Herbert Spencer Although trained as a civil engineer, Herbert Spencer (1820–1903) spent most of his time on the study of the natural and social sciences. Combining these areas, Spencer adopted a biological model of society. In a living organism, he suggested, the biological systems work together to maintain the organism's health. Spencer attributed a similar process to society. Like a living organism, society is a set of interdependent parts that work together to maintain the system over time.

Spencer was strongly influenced by the views of Charles Darwin, a pioneering English naturalist. As a result, Spencer used Darwin's theory of the evolution of biological organisms to describe the nature of society. Spencer considered social change and unrest to be natural occurrences during a society's evolution toward stability and perfection. Because he believed that the best aspects of society would survive over time, Spencer thought that no steps should be taken to correct social ills.

Spencer also believed that only the fittest societies would survive over time, leading to a general upgrading of the world as a whole. Although the phrase "survival of the fittest" is often credited to Charles Darwin, it was coined by Spencer to describe this process. Because of its similarities to Darwin's ideas, Spencer's view of society became known as **social Darwinism.**

Spencer's ideas gained a wide following, particularly in Britain and France. However, like Comte, Spencer refused to read the writings of scholars whose ideas differed from his own. As a result, he disregarded the rules of careful scholarship and made scientifically unfounded claims about society. Over time, Spencer's social Darwinism fell out of favor among the world's sociologists.

Auguste Comte

Contribution Among the first scholars to apply the methods of the physical sciences to the study of society; coined the word *sociology* and is considered the founder of the subject.

Major Works *Plan of the Scientific Operations Necessary for Reorganizing Society* (1822), *Positive Philosophy* (1830–1842), *System of Positive Polity* (1851–1854)

Harriet Martineau

Contribution Conducted early sociological studies in Britain and the United States; advocate of the idea that scholars should try to improve society, not just study it; best known for translating Comte's works into English.

Major Works *Society in America* (1837), *How to Observe Morals and Manners* (1838)

Karl Marx Karl Marx (1818–1883) was born to middle-class parents in a part of Prussia that is now Germany. He attended several universities and received a doctorate degree in 1841. Marx was unable to get a teaching position because of his political views. Instead, he worked as a writer and editor for a radical newspaper. In time the government closed the newspaper because of its revolutionary point of view. Marx moved to the more liberal atmosphere of Paris. However, the French soon expelled him at the request of the Prussian government. Marx moved on to Brussels, returned for a short time to Paris and Prussia, and finally settled in London. There, he earned a scant living from his writings. Marx died in poverty and obscurity. Nevertheless, his writings have influenced generations of scholars and social critics around the world.

Marx believed that the structure of a society is influenced by how its economy is organized. According to Marx, society is divided into two classes—the *bourgeoisie* (boozh-wah-ZEE), or capitalists, and the *proletariat,* or workers. The bourgeoisie own the means of production—the materials and methods used to produce goods and services. The proletariat, on the other hand, own only the labor needed to produce goods and provide services.

Marx held that this imbalance in power would inevitably lead to conflict between the capitalists and the workers. This class conflict would end only when the proletariat united to overthrow those in power. After this rebellion, Marx said, the victorious workers would build a classless society in which each citizen would contribute "according to his ability" and would be rewarded "according to his needs."

Marx did not really consider himself a sociologist. Nevertheless, his belief that a society's economic system strongly influences its social structure has had a lasting influence on sociology. His emphasis on conflict as the primary cause of social change led to the development of one of the major sociological perspectives—conflict theory.

Reading Check **Contrast** How did Herbert Spencer's approach to social problems differ from the approaches of other early sociologists?

Later European Scholars

In the late 1800s, Émile Durkheim and Max Weber (VAY-buhr) made major contributions that built on the foundations laid by earlier sociologists. Their work helped to get sociology recognized as an academic subject.

Émile Durkheim While a French Jew by birth, Émile Durkheim (1858–1917) was educated in both France and Germany. In his late twenties he accepted a teaching position at the University of Bordeaux in France. There, Durkheim developed the country's first university sociology course. Durkheim was also the first to systematically apply the methods of science to the study of society.

Like Comte, Durkheim was concerned with social order. Like Spencer, Durkheim saw society as a set of interdependent parts that maintain the system throughout time. However, he viewed the role of these interdependent parts in terms of their functions.

Herbert Spencer

Contribution Applied the principles of biology to society; popularized the evolutionary theory of social change and coined the phrase "survival of the fittest."

Major Works *Social Statics* (1851), *First Principles* (1862), *The Study of Sociology* (1872), *The Principles of Sociology* (1876–1896)

Karl Marx

Contribution Emphasized the primary role that conflict plays in social change and advocated revolution to speed up the process of change; his ideas led to the development of the conflict perspective in sociology.

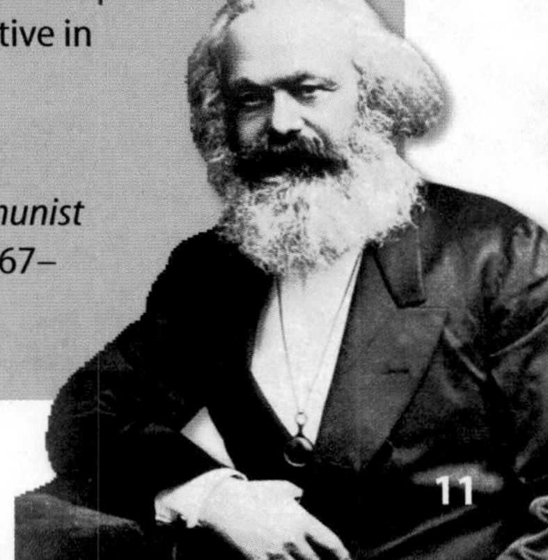

Major Works *The Poverty of Philosophy* (1847), *The Communist Manifesto* (1848), *Capital* (1867–1894)

A **function** is the consequence that an element of society produces for the maintenance of its social system. Durkheim was particularly interested in the function of religion in maintaining social order, because he believed that shared beliefs and values were the glue that held society together. Durkheim's functionalist view of society has been very influential in modern American sociology.

The basis of Durkheim's scientific analysis of society was his belief that sociologists should only study features of society that are directly observable. Ideas about observable phenomena, Durkheim noted, can be tested by applying the scientific tool of statistical analysis. Durkheim used this approach in his 1897 study, *Suicide,* which examined suicide rates in several European countries. The first true sociological study, *Suicide* is still consulted by sociology professors and students today.

Max Weber Born in Prussia to wealthy parents, Max Weber (1864–1920) received his doctoral degree from the University of Berlin in 1889. Later he attained a teaching position at that same university. A few years after, he took a position as professor of economics at the University of Heidelberg. There, he produced some of his most important writings.

Unlike earlier sociologists, Weber was interested in separate groups within society rather than in society as a whole. This emphasis on groups led Weber to focus more on the effect of society on the individual. Weber also thought that sociologists should go beyond studying what can be directly observed and attempt to uncover people's feelings and thoughts. Weber proposed doing this by using the principle of ***Verstehen*** (fer-SHTAY-en). *Verstehen* involves an attempt to understand the meanings individuals attach to their actions. In essence, with *Verstehen* one puts oneself in the place of others and tries to see situations through their eyes.

In addition to *Verstehen,* Weber employed the concept of ideal type in much of his work. An **ideal type** is a description comprised of the essential characteristics of a feature of society. Sociologists construct an ideal type first by examining many different examples of the feature and then by deducing its essential characteristics. Yet any particular example of the feature might not contain all of the characteristics described in the ideal type. For example, the ideal type for a school might not be a perfect representation of your school. However, you would recognize it as a general description of an educational institution.

Reading Check **Contrast** How did Weber's sociological focus differ from that of Durkheim?

American Scholars

The study of society gained an academic foothold in the United States in the late 1800s with the establishment of a sociology department at the University of Chicago. Members of the department adopted a very distinctive style of thinking about society, which became known as the "Chicago School." Like Weber, Chicago School sociologists were interested in

Émile Durkheim

Contribution Described society as a set of interdependent parts, with each part serving a specific function; believed that sociologists should focus on observable social phenomena; influential in the development of the functionalist perspective in sociology.

Major Works *The Division of Labor in Society* (1893), *The Rules of Sociological Method* (1895), *Suicide: A Study in Sociology* (1897), *Elementary Forms of the Religious Life* (1912)

Max Weber

Contribution Developed the concept of the ideal type, a model against which social reality can be measured; believed that sociology should attempt to understand the meanings that individuals attach to their actions; his work influenced the development of the interactionist perspective in sociology.

Major Works *The Protestant Ethic and the Spirit of Capitalism* (1905), *Economy and Society* (1922)

Statistically Speaking...

Hull House Studies Perhaps Jane Addams' best demonstration of her commitment to both social reform and sociological analysis was *Hull House Maps and Papers*. Published in 1895, this study's most striking aspect was the color-coded maps that showed race, ethnicity, and income levels on Chicago's West Side. During her study Addams discovered the following:

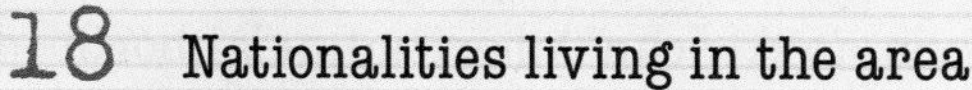

18 Nationalities living in the area

$9.44 Average weekly wage for garment workers

12 Hours per day worked by garment workers

$1.25 Average daily wage for laborers

17–32 Weeks per year laborers were unemployed

$8.47 Average monthly rent

Thinking Critically **Draw Conclusions** Why were the Hull House studies important for the development of sociology?

Jane Addams (above) thought that analyzing social problems was the first step to solving them. She presented some of her findings in color-coded maps like this one below, which shows differences in family income.

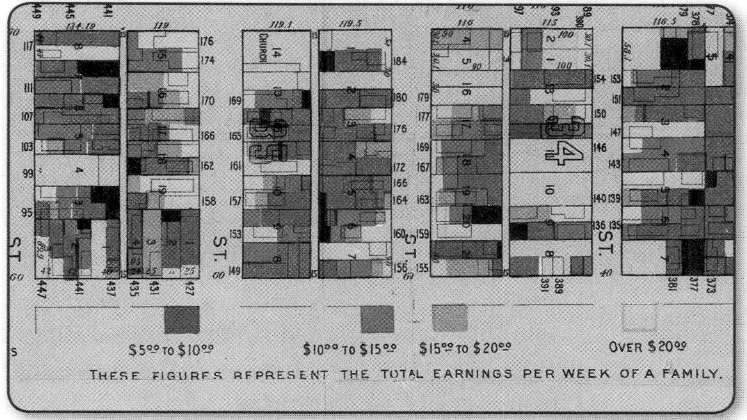

group interactions and the impact of society on individual development. Work in this area by Chicago School members Charles Horton Cooley and George Herbert Mead led to the development of the interactionist perspective of sociology.

Chicago School sociologists also believed that the study of society should be accompanied by an effort to find practical solutions to social problems. Jane Addams, a part-time professor at the University of Chicago, was a leading proponent of this practical approach to the study of social issues.

Jane Addams Jane Addams (1860–1935) was born into a wealthy Illinois family in 1860. Her family, like Harriet Martineau's, valued learning. Addams attended Rockford College and earned a bachelor's degree. She then went on to medical school in Philadelphia, but had to quit soon after because of poor health.

In the 1880s Addams visited London, where she saw Toynbee Hall, a settlement house that provided assistance for the poor. Addams became determined to open a similar center in the United States. In 1889 she set up Hull House on the West Side of Chicago. There, she offered welfare, educational, and recreational services for poor residents of the neighborhood.

Addams soon realized that if she wanted to solve the problems of the poor, she needed to know the exact nature of those problems.

W.E.B. Du Bois

Contribution Used community studies to underscore the significance of race in American society; believed that sociologists should be involved in social reform as well as academic study.

Major Works *The Philadelphia Negro: A Social Study* (1899), *The Souls of Black Folk* (1903)

ACADEMIC VOCABULARY

empirical based on experiment or observation

She undertook a series of surveys of poor people and the conditions in which they lived. She published her results in 1895. Entitled *Hull House Maps and Papers,* the study covered such subjects as wage levels, sweatshops, child labor, the immigrant experience, and living conditions in poverty-stricken neighborhoods. This groundbreaking work provided the first serious discussion of the effects of two major social forces—industrialization and urbanization.

Addams was an early member of the American Sociological Society. She spoke at national conferences and was a frequent contributor to the *American Journal of Sociology.* However, most sociologists did not give her work serious consideration. They considered her a social worker rather than a sociologist.

W.E.B. Du Bois Although he was not a member of the Chicago School, W.E.B. Du Bois (1868–1963) took a similar approach to studying society, mixing social analysis with social reform. A gifted scholar, Du Bois was the first African American to earn a doctorate at Harvard. After studying at the University of Berlin in Germany, where he came under the influence of Max Weber, Du Bois returned to the United States to teach.

In 1899, he published his first major work, *The Philadelphia Negro.* This examination of life in an African American neighborhood in Philadelphia was among the first empirical community studies undertaken in the United States. Its findings underscored Du Bois's strongly-held belief that race was an issue that needed to be addressed. Du Bois published many more studies of race in the United States. He also took action to improve the lives of African Americans, helping to found the National Association for the Advancement of Colored People (NAACP) in 1909.

Du Bois's work was of the utmost importance to an understanding of American society. However, his findings—and remedies—ran counter to the accepted views on race. As a result, his contribution to the development of sociology went unrecognized.

Reading Check **Summarize** What was the Chicago School's approach to studying society?

SECTION 2 Assessment

Reviewing Main Ideas and Vocabulary

1. **Recall** Why was Herbert Spencer's view of society referred to as social Darwinism?
2. **Identify** What in sociological terms is a function?
3. **Explain** What did Max Weber mean by the term *Verstehen*?

Thinking Critically

4. **Evaluate** Why do you think the concept of the ideal type is a useful sociological tool?
5. **Draw Conclusions** How did sociologists of the Chicago School continue a sociological tradition established by most of the founders of sociology?
6. **Summarize** Using your notes and a graphic organizer like the one below, briefly describe the development of sociology as a distinct academic subject.

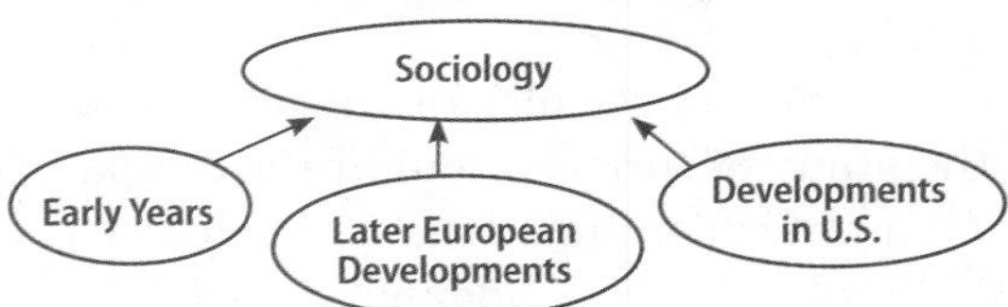

FOCUS ON WRITING

7. **Expository** Write two paragraphs explaining why you think Jane Addams's and W.E.B. Du Bois's work was ignored by their contemporaries. Consider the issues Addams and Du Bois addressed and the generally accepted sociological views of those issues.

SECTION 3

Modern Perspectives

Before You Read

Main Idea

Sociology employs three major theoretical perspectives—functionalism, which focuses on order and stability; conflict, which focuses on power relations; and interactionism, which focuses on how individuals interact with one another in everyday life.

Reading Focus

1. In what ways do the three major theoretical perspectives in sociology differ in their focus?
2. How do the three theoretical perspectives differ in terms of their levels of analysis?

Vocabulary

theory
theoretical perspective
functionalist perspective
dysfunction
manifest function
latent function
conflict perspective
feminist perspective
interactionist perspective
symbol
symbolic interaction
macrosociology
microsociology
globalization

TAKING NOTES Use a graphic organizer like this one to take notes on the three theoretical perspectives used in sociology.

Functionalist	
Conflict	
Interactionist	

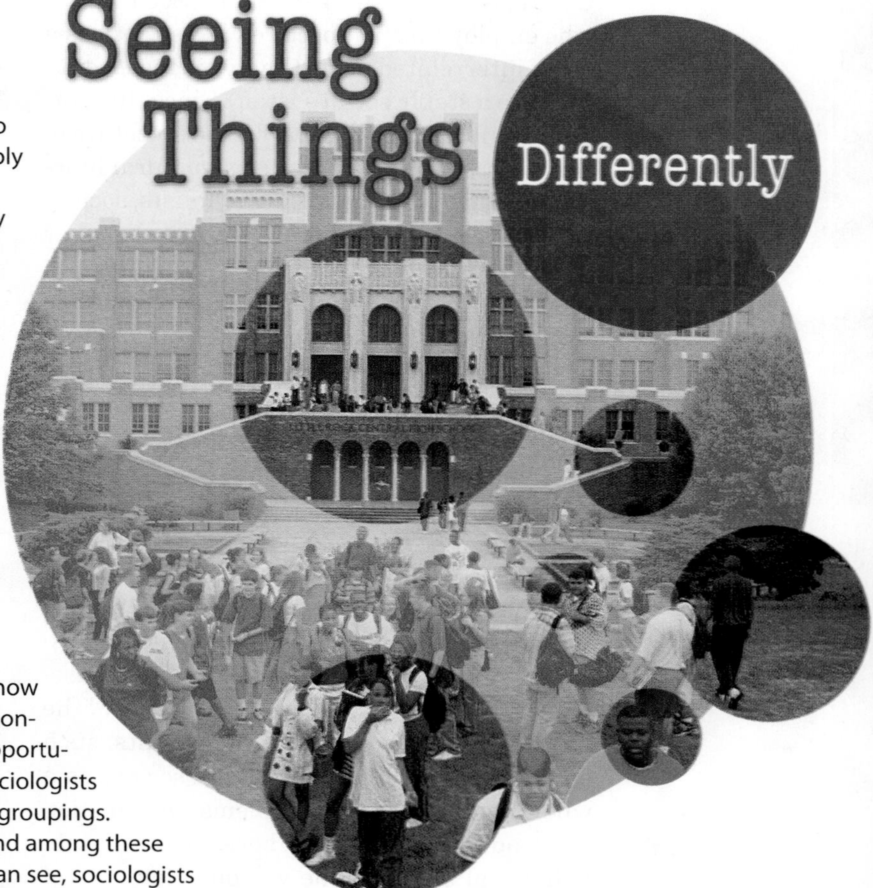

SOCIOLOGY CLOSE UP ***How do sociologists view what goes on in your school?*** What do you see in this photograph? Probably a group of students gathering outside a school. If you asked sociologists that question, you would get a very different answer. Actually, you would almost certainly get several answers. Asking sociologists to analyze a social setting could result in something like the movie *Rashomon,* which tells the story of an event from the viewpoint of the participants and eyewitnesses—and each version is very different from the others.

Looking at this scene, some sociologists would see an orderly world. The young people are performing an appropriate role—that of student. The school is performing its proper task, preparing students to be productive citizens in American society. Other sociologists would see a setting where there is competition for resources. They would want to know about the power relationships within the school and how the distribution of resources is affected by those relationships. They would also want to know what kinds of opportunities are available for minority students. Still other sociologists would see a setting made up of many relatively small groupings. They would want to know how relationships within and among these groupings affect what goes on in the school. As you can see, sociologists view social settings through several different lenses. ■

Major Theoretical Perspectives

In their effort to explain the social world, sociologists develop **theories,** or explanations of the relationships among particular phenomena. Theories provide guidance for sociologists in their work and help them to interpret their findings. Sociologists not only develop theories to explain specific phenomena, they also adopt broad theoretical perspectives to provide a foundation for their inquiries. A **theoretical perspective,** or a school of thought, is a general set of assumptions about the nature of things. In the case of sociology, a theoretical perspective outlines specific ideas about the nature of social life.

Three broad theoretical perspectives form the basis of modern sociology. These are the functionalist perspective, the conflict perspective, and the interactionist perspective. Essentially, each one is a lens that presents a slightly different image of society or focuses on different aspects of social life.

Functionalist Perspective The **functionalist perspective** is broadly based on the ideas of Comte, Spencer, and Durkheim. Sociologists who employ this perspective view society as a set of interrelated parts that work together to produce a stable social system. Since this perspective focuses so heavily on the structure of society, it is sometimes called structural functionalism. According to functionalists, society is held together through consensus. In other words, most people agree on what is best for society and work together to ensure that the social system runs smoothly. Topics of interest to functionalist sociologists include the functions that family, religion, education, and the economy serve in society.

Like Durkheim, functionalists view the various elements in society in terms of their functions, or their positive consequences for society as a whole. Recognizing that not everything in society operates smoothly, functionalists also label certain elements as dysfunctional. A **dysfunction** is the negative consequence an element has for the stability of the social system. Dysfunctional elements, such as crime, disrupt the working of society as a whole and create social problems. Dysfunction can lead to social change, because to reestablish social stability the various elements of society must adapt and adjust.

In addition to being either positive or negative, functions can be either manifest or latent. A **manifest function** is the intended and recognized consequence of some element of society. For example, a manifest function of the automobile is to provide speedy transportation from one location to another. A **latent function,** on the other hand, is the unintended and unrecognized consequence of an element of society. A latent function of the automobile is to gain social standing through the display of wealth.

Conflict Perspective People who employ the **conflict perspective** focus on the forces in society that promote competition and change. Following in the tradition of Karl Marx, conflict theorists are interested in how those who possess more power in society exercise control over those with less power in society. Conflict theorists do not limit their attention to acts of violent conflict. They are also interested in nonviolent competition between various groups in society—men and women, people of different ages, or people of different racial or national backgrounds. Some of the topics that conflict sociologists research include decision-making in the family, relationships among racial groups, and disputes between workers and employers.

According to conflict theorists, competition over scarce resources is at the basis of social conflict. Because resources such as power and wealth are in limited supply, people must compete with one another for them. Once particular groups gain control of society's resources, they tend to establish rules and procedures that protect their interests at the expense of other groups. This behavior leads to social conflict as those with less power attempt to gain access to desired resources. Conflict, in turn, leads to social change. Thus, conflict theorists see social change as an inevitable feature of our society.

Feminist theory is often seen as an extension of the conflict perspective because it focuses on an area of inequality—gender. The **feminist perspective,** sociologists Claire M. Renzetti and Daniel J. Curran state, involves viewing society as "a sex/gender system in which men dominate women, and that which is considered masculine is more highly valued than that which is considered feminine."

This system of gender inequality, feminist theorists charge, is created by society and is not the result of biology. Further, this system is reinforced by social institutions such as the family, religion, and education.

Feminist theorists argue that the study of sociology has played a role in perpetuating this system of gender inequality. Traditional approaches to the subject have misrepresented or completely ignored the lives of women. However, feminist theorists state, the experience of women should be central to the study of social life. Further, the knowledge gained from this study should be used to bring about social change to end gender inequality.

Interactionist Perspective As you have learned, functionalists and conflict theorists tend to focus on society in general or on large groups within society. However, some sociologists adopt an **interactionist perspective,** which focuses on how individuals interact with one another in society. These sociologists are interested in the ways in which individuals respond to one another in everyday situations. They are also interested in the meanings that individuals attach to their own actions and to the actions of others. Interactionist theorists are indebted to the work of Max Weber, particularly the principle of *Verstehen.* The interactionist perspective is used to study topics such as child development, relationships within small groups, and mate selection.

Interactionists are particularly interested in the role that symbols play in our daily lives. A **symbol** is anything that represents something else. Such things as physical objects, gestures, words, and events can serve as symbols. In order for something to serve as a symbol, however, members of society must agree on the meaning that is attached to it. The American flag, the bald eagle, Fourth of July celebrations, and Uncle Sam are examples of symbols that people readily accept as representations of the United States. In the case of gestures, a salute is accepted as a sign of respect for authority, while a raised, shaking fist is understood to signify a threat of physical harm.

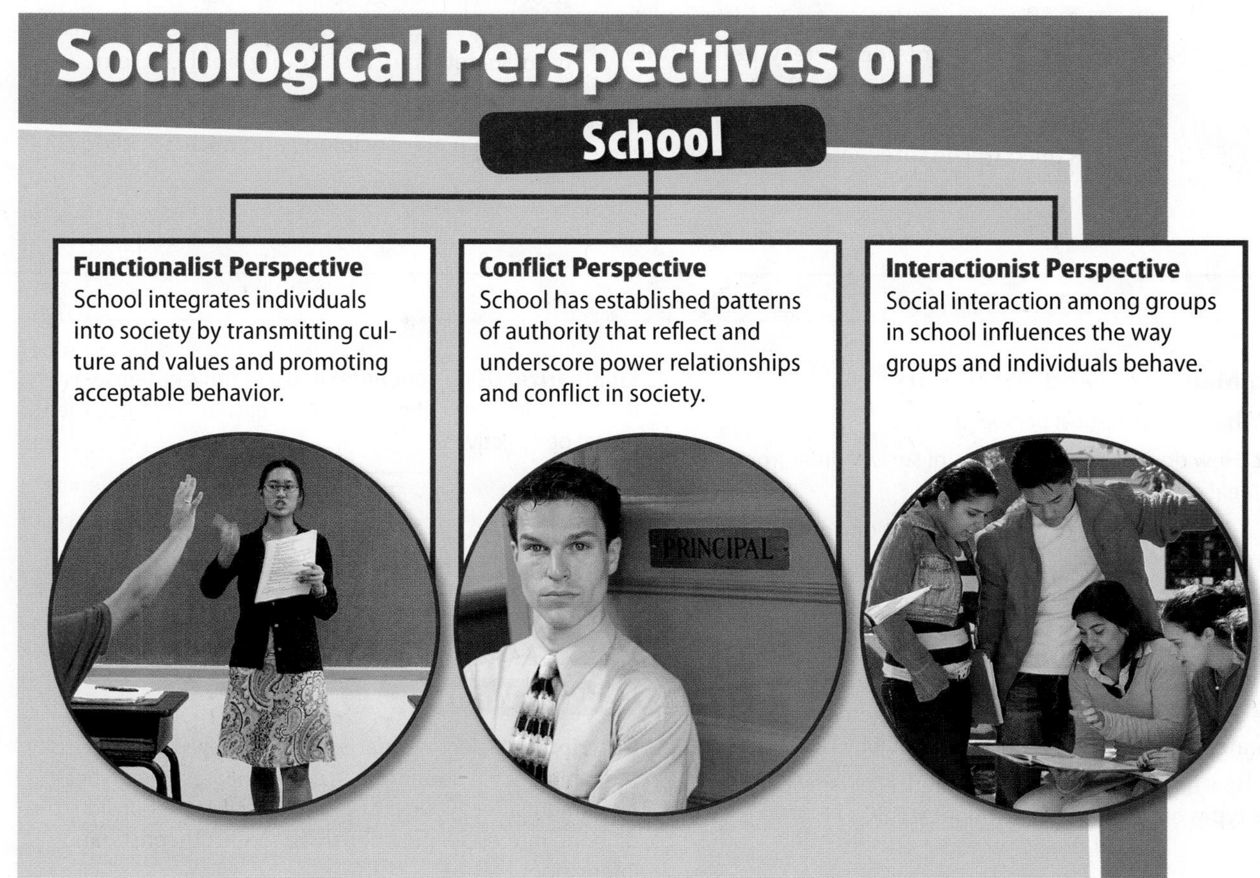

Sociological Perspectives on
School
Functionalist Perspective
School integrates individuals into society by transmitting culture and values and promoting acceptable behavior.
Conflict Perspective
School has established patterns of authority that reflect and underscore power relationships and conflict in society.
Interactionist Perspective
Social interaction among groups in school influences the way groups and individuals behave.
PRINCIPAL

Interactionists focus on how people use symbols when interacting. This process, called **symbolic interaction,** has three essential elements—meaning, language, and thought. The individual responds to people and things based on the meanings he or she gives to those people or things. These meanings arise out of the social interaction, through the vehicle of language, that the individual has with others. Finally, the individual adjusts and modifies these meanings through thought—a kind of internal conversation. This involves imagining how others see things. Interactionists, then, see social interaction as more than individuals reacting to each other's actions. Rather, it involves individuals constantly defining and interpreting each other's actions.

Reading Check **Summarize** What are the three sociological perspectives and on what does each perspective focus?

Levels of Analysis

One major difference among the major sociological perspectives is the level of analysis that each one employs. The level used by the functionalist and conflict perspectives is called **macrosociology.** This involves the study of large-scale systems or society as a whole. It also includes the analysis of long-term processes, such as industrialization. The level of analysis used in the interactionist perspective is referred to as **microsociology.** This involves looking at small-group settings and the everyday face-to-face interactions among group members. This level of analysis would be used to measure the impact of teacher expectations on student academic performance.

Which level of analysis provides the best explanation of the social world? Obviously, the "big-picture" provided by the macrosociological approach is of the utmost value. However, society consists of individuals interacting with each other. So, microsociology offers important insights. For example, let's look again at your school. Macrosociological analysis explains how your school fits into the workings of the education system or society itself. Microsociology, with its focus on everyday interaction, provides details of the inner workings of the school. Each level of analysis, then, can assist you in your study of society.

Regardless of the level of analysis or theoretical approach they adopt, more and more sociologists are beginning to look at society from a global perspective. **Globalization** is the development of economic, political, and social relationships that stretch worldwide. This process, sociologists recognize, requires them to look at social life not only in terms of their own society but also in a global context.

Reading Check **Contrast** What is the difference between macrosociology and microsociology?

SECTION 3 Assessment

Reviewing Main Ideas and Vocabulary

1. **Define** What is a theoretical perspective?
2. **Contrast** How do functional elements of society differ from dysfunctional elements?
3. **Identify** Give an example of a manifest function and a latent function.
4. **Recall** Which theoretical perspectives employ macrosociological analysis?

Thinking Critically

5. **Evaluate** Do you think that feminist theory should be seen as a separate theoretical perspective? Why or why not?
6. **Discuss** How might a sociologist's theoretical perspective affect the types of issues he or she might study?
7. **Summarize** Using your notes and a graphic organizer like the one below, describe the focus of each of the three theoretical perspectives.

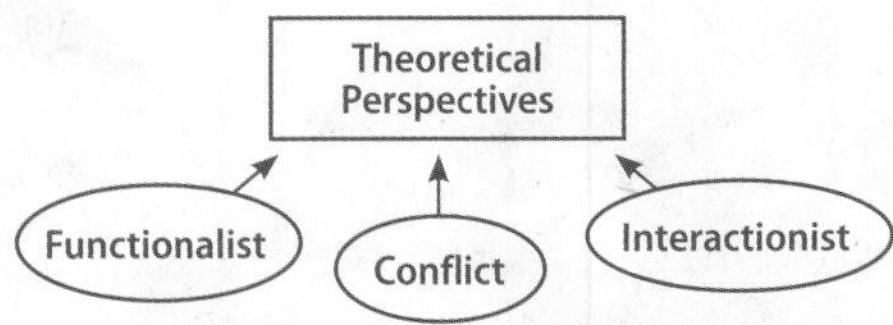

FOCUS ON WRITING

8. **Descriptive** Select a social issue in the news. Write an essay describing how adopting each of the theoretical perspectives might affect your view of that social issue. Consider the differing interests of functionalists, conflict theorists, and interactionists.

CURRENT RESEARCH IN SOCIOLOGY

The Spread of Hip-Hop

Globalization, the worldwide spread of political, economic, and social institutions through trade and the exchange of ideas, has influenced the way sociologists look at social phenomena. In the past, many sociologists limited their academic focus to their own societies. Today, however, sociologists often try to put the issues they study in a global context. A look at hip-hop provides an illustration of this change.

Chinese youth, like this teenager in Shanghai, began to adopt hip-hop fashions and attitudes in the late 1990s and early 2000s.

The first major studies on hip-hop looked at it through an American lens, focusing on its impact on African American youth (Rose, 1994). More recent studies, however, have taken a global perspective, looking at hip-hop's spread to other areas of the world and characterizing it as a global youth movement (Mitchell, 2001, Condry, 2006).

Hip-hop's spread was greatly assisted by the multinational media companies (Watkins, 2007). Beginning in the 1990s, they aggressively marketed hip-hop related music and movies on the world market. Assisted by the fashion business and major American sports franchises, the media giants brought the hip-hop way of life—music, dance, clothes, and attitudes—to a global audience. In a short time, young people from London to Moscow to Mumbai had adopted hip-hop culture.

Even though their introduction to hip-hop came through big business, young people worldwide quickly recognized and seized upon hip-hop's questioning of mainstream values. The vocal dissent of some young urban African Americans struck a chord. In short time, young people who saw themselves as outside society's mainstream adopted hip-hop as their vehicle of protest (Watkins).

THE GLOBAL SPREAD OF HIP-HOP

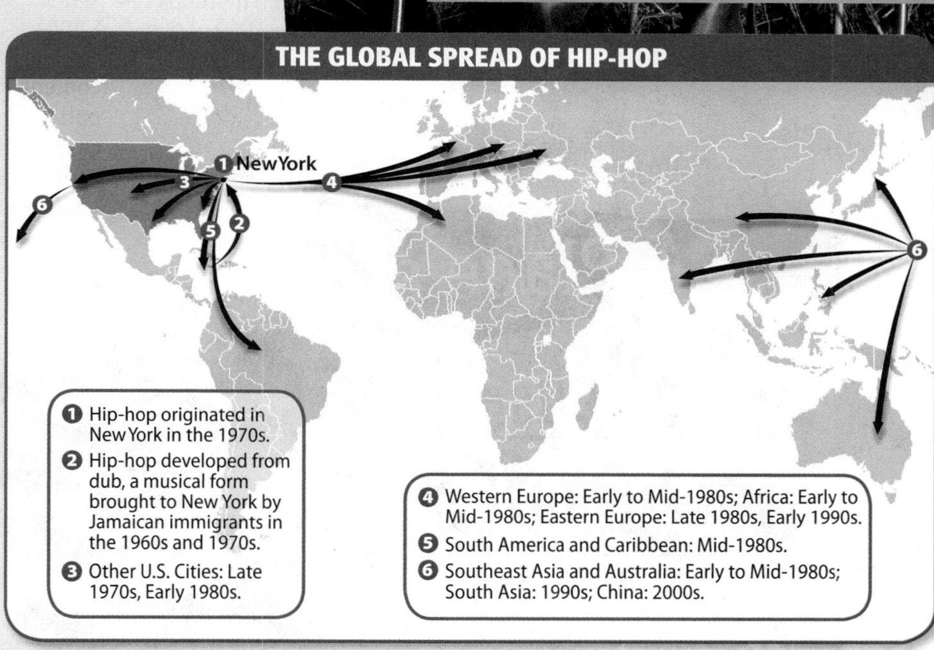
1 New York
2
3
4
5
6
1 Hip-hop originated in New York in the 1970s.
2 Hip-hop developed from dub, a musical form brought to New York by Jamaican immigrants in the 1960s and 1970s.
3 Other U.S. Cities: Late 1970s, Early 1980s.
4 Western Europe: Early to Mid-1980s; Africa: Early to Mid-1980s; Eastern Europe: Late 1980s, Early 1990s.
5 South America and Caribbean: Mid-1980s.
6 Southeast Asia and Australia: Early to Mid-1980s; South Asia: 1990s; China: 2000s.

Not content to mimic American performers, these young people localized hip-hop, adapting "the template to fit their own language and political concerns" (Mitchell). In France and Britain, for example, young Muslims have used hip-hop to combat prejudice against their faith. In Spain, hip-hop has become a voice for the Basque separatist movement. In New Zealand, Maori performers combine American styles with traditional music to tell their story. Many Eastern Europeans, however, favor American styles as a way to declare a break with the Communist past.

From the global perspective, hip-hop, which started on the streets of New York, has become the voice of the world's streets. As the title of one study on hip-hop noted, it is the "global noise" (Mitchell).

Thinking Critically

1. **Draw Conclusions** Why do some sociologists consider hip-hop a global youth movement?
2. **Discuss** Many studies of cultural spread suggest that American culture often overpowers local culture. Why does the spread of hip-hop not fit this description?

SECTION 4

Conducting Sociological Research

Before You Read

Main Idea
Sociologists use several approaches to conducting research. Regardless of the approaches they use, all sociologists follow a seven-step research process.

Reading Focus
1. What are the seven steps in the research process?
2. How do sociologists uncover causation and correlation?
3. What basic research methods do sociologists employ?
4. How do ethical issues affect sociological research?

Vocabulary
scientific method
hypothesis
variable
correlation
survey
sample
historical method
content analysis
participant observation
case study
experiment
statistical analysis

TAKING NOTES Use a graphic organizer like this one to take notes on the various research methods that sociologists use.

Surveys	Analysis of Existing Sources
Observation	Experiments

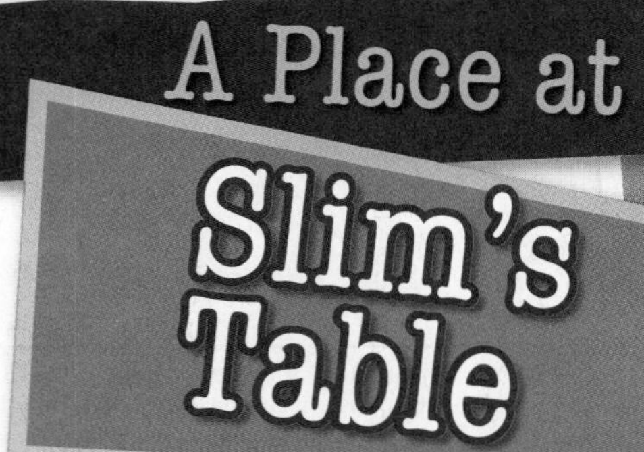

Mitchell Duneier (standing) talks to Slim (to the left of Duneier) and his friends.

SOCIOLOGY CLOSE UP ***How do sociologists conduct research?*** The Valois restaurant is located in Chicago's Hyde Park community. The Valois serves hearty food cafeteria style to African American and white residents of the neighborhood and students from the nearby University of Chicago.

Mitchell Duneier, then a graduate student in the university's sociology department, ate at the Valois often during the late 1980s. While eating his food, Duneier often watched the other diners. One group of older African American men particularly caught his attention. Over breakfast or after-dinner coffee, these working men animatedly discussed the experiences of the day or the latest stories in the news. At first, they seemed like a group of equals. After a while, however, Duneier noticed that the others showed special deference to Slim. This "unimposing but . . . dignified" man commanded respect from other regulars, too—so much so that they referred to the group as "Slim's Table."

Over the next four years, Duneier observed the interactions among Slim's group, noting the values and beliefs that drove their lives. The result was *Slim's Table,* a study that showed the African American working class living lives of pride and principle—a story very different from that in the mainstream media. Sometimes, doing something as simple as taking a seat at a restaurant table can provide sociologists with new insights into social life. ■

The Research Process

As you recall, sociology is the science that studies human society and social behavior. Because sociology is a science, it seeks answers to questions through empirical research. This type of research relies on the use of experience, observation, and experimentation to collect facts, or data. If something can be seen, smelled, tasted, touched, or heard, it is considered to be empirical.

Sociologists, like most scientists, collect empirical data by using the scientific method. The **scientific method** is an objective, logical, and systematic way of collecting empirical data and arriving at reasoned conclusions. Researchers who employ the scientific method (1) try to prevent their own notions, values, and biases from interfering in the research process; (2) use careful and correct reasoning in drawing conclusions from their data; and (3) carry out research in a thoughtful, organized, and methodical manner.

Sociologists generally follow a series of seven steps when conducting their research. These steps include defining the problem, reviewing the literature, forming a hypothesis, choosing a research design, collecting the data, analyzing the data, and presenting conclusions. Émile Durkheim's classic 1897 study of the social causes of suicide provides the earliest example of the application of these steps to a sociological problem.

THE RESEARCH PROCESS

Sociologists follow a seven-step process when conducting empirical research.

Step 1 Define the Problem
The researcher selects a topic for study and develops operational definitions of key concepts.

Step 2 Review the Literature
The researcher reviews existing literature on the topic.

Step 3 Form a Hypothesis
The researcher develops a testable hypothesis on the research topic.

Step 4 Choose a Research Design
The researcher develops a plan for collecting, analyzing, and evaluating data.

Step 5 Collect the Data
The researcher gathers and carefully records data.

Step 6 Analyze the Data
The researcher objectively analyzes the data to determine whether it supports the research hypotheses.

Step 7 Present Conclusions
The researcher presents the research findings to other sociologists.

Defining the Problem The first step in the research process involves selecting a topic for study and developing operational definitions of key concepts. An operational definition is a definition that is stated in terms of measurable characteristics. For example, Durkheim wished to study the effect of social integration on suicide rates among various groups of individuals. In order to do this, he had to define suicide and social integration in terms that would enable him to measure both concepts.

Reviewing the Literature Good sociological research is conducted within the context of an existing body of knowledge. To determine how others have approached a research problem and what conclusions they have reached, sociologists review the published reports of studies that have a bearing on their research interests. This review not only provides researchers with valuable insights that help guide their work, it also prevents the unnecessary duplication of research efforts.

Thus when Durkheim began his study of suicide, he examined the existing literature to determine how other researchers explained the phenomenon. Durkheim also reviewed the available statistics on suicide. What he found led him to dismiss the psychological explanations that were popular in the literature and to concentrate his attention on social factors.

Forming a Hypothesis Once the existing literature has been reviewed, sociologists develop testable hypotheses. A **hypothesis** is a statement that predicts the relationship between two or more variables. Durkheim, for example, hypothesized that suicide rates within groups vary inversely with the degree to which group members are integrated into society. In other words, Durkheim predicted that the more family, religious, and community bonds group members have, the less likely they are to commit suicide.

Choosing a Research Design The next step in the research process involves selecting a research design. A research design is a plan for collecting, analyzing, and evaluating data. Not all research problems lend themselves to every data collection technique. Selecting the correct research design, therefore, is extremely important. Most of the data collection methods used by sociologists fall into four categories: surveys, experiments, observational studies, and the analysis of existing sources.

Once the data are collected, many sociologists employ some form of statistical analysis to evaluate their findings. For example, Durkheim statistically analyzed existing sources—official suicide records from various European nations—to test his hypotheses.

Collecting the Data Once they have developed a research design, sociologists must follow the design in collecting their data. Different research designs require taking different factors into consideration. However, regardless of the method being used, information must be carefully recorded. Careless data collection can affect the accuracy of the research findings.

Analyzing the Data The analysis of data is a very important step. Even if the proper research design has been used and data have been carefully collected, the accuracy of findings can be affected by how the data are analyzed. Researchers must be careful to maintain their objectivity and not read more into the data than is there. Research findings are only as good as the methods used to collect and analyze the data.

The purpose of data analysis is to determine whether the data support the research hypotheses. When Durkheim analyzed his data on suicide, he found that rates varied among different groups within society. For example, he found that Catholics had lower rates of suicide than did Protestants and that married people, particularly those with children, were less likely than single people to commit suicide. He attributed these findings to the weakness of social bonds among Protestants and single individuals. Durkheim reasoned that the importance of individual actions in the religious values and practices of Protestantism would lead Protestants to rely on themselves rather than on others in times of crisis. Similarly, he reasoned that unmarried individuals generally have fewer people on whom to rely for support. These findings led Durkheim to confirm his hypothesis that suicide rates vary inversely with the degree of social integration.

Presenting Conclusions The last step in the research process involves drawing conclusions from the data and presenting the research findings to others. Sociologists generally report their findings in professional journals, in scholarly books, and at professional meetings. By reporting their research findings, sociologists add to the body of sociological knowledge. They also make it possible for other sociologists to evaluate the data and the research process. One method of evaluation sociologists sometimes use is to replicate, or repeat, the research. When sociologists do not supply enough information to allow their research to be repeated by others, the findings are often viewed as suspicious.

Reading Check **Sequence** What are the seven steps in the research process?

Causation and Correlation

Like all scientists, sociologists want to uncover the causal connections between events. Things do not just happen. There is a cause behind each occurrence. Whether the subject under discussion is biological growth, riots, atomic fission, or wars—all events have causes.

Sociologists study cause and effect by examining the relationships among variables. A **variable** is a characteristic that can differ from one individual, group, or situation to another in a measurable way. Anything that can vary in amount or quality from case to case can be considered a variable. Age, race, income, level of education, and marital status are just a few of the things that can serve as sociological variables. A causal relationship exists when a change in one variable causes a change in another variable.

When examining cause and effect, sociologists distinguish between two types of variables: independent variables and dependent variables. An independent variable is a variable that causes a change in another variable. A dependent variable, on the other hand, is the variable that is changed by the independent variable. In a study of teenage drug use, for instance, the level of drug use might be the dependent variable, while the independent variables might include school grades or teenage attitudes toward drug use. In this instance, sociologists might be interested in determining if the level of drug use is influenced by grades in school or attitudes toward drug use. For example, is drug use lower among students who are on the honor roll at school?

The first step in determining cause and effect is to establish whether a correlation exists between two variables. A **correlation** exists when a change in one variable is regularly associated with a change in another variable. Correlations may or may not be causal. In addition, correlations may be either positive or negative. In the case of a positive correlation, both variables change in the same direction. Cigarette smoking, for example, is positively correlated with diseases such as lung cancer. The higher the rate of cigarette use, the higher the rate of lung cancer. In the case of a negative correlation, the variables change in opposite directions. For example, as individuals age they need fewer hours of sleep to feel well rested.

In some cases, variables appear to be correlated, but the relationship actually is spurious. A spurious correlation exists when variables appear to be related but actually are being affected by the existence of a third variable. For example, hospitalization and death appear to be highly correlated. However, this does not mean that hospitalization causes death. It is more likely that a third variable—serious illness—is responsible for the high correlation. Thus, hospitalization and death are spuriously correlated.

Sociologists determine whether variables are causally related, correlated, or spuriously correlated through the use of controls. In sociological terms, controls are ways of excluding the possibility that outside variables are affecting the relationship between the two variables under investigation. For example, suppose that a group of sociologists finds that the level of government spending on social programs and the level of voter participation are positively correlated in most nations of the world. To determine whether increased government spending causes higher rates of voter participation, the sociologists might control for the level of economic development in each nation. If the sociologists find that both the level of government spending and the level of voter participation are related to the level of economic development in a nation, they will conclude that the correlation between government spending and voter participation is spurious.

Spurious Correlation

"A spurious correlation exists where variables appear to be related but actually are being affected by a third variable."

Suppose that studies show that students who get good grades are also members of the school band. Does this mean that involvement in the school band causes students to get good grades? Not necessarily. There might be a third variable—such as a general desire to do well in school—that encourages both good grades and involvement in extracurricular activities such as the band. ***Why is spurious correlation an important concept for researchers?***

Reading Check **Contrast** How do positive correlations and negative correlations differ?

Basic Research Methods

There are four broad categories of research methods that sociologists employ to collect data on society and human behavior. These categories are surveys, the analysis of existing sources using techniques such as the historical method and content analysis, observational studies, and experiments. Sociologists also employ various techniques to analyze their data once the collection process is completed. The most common of these techniques involve some form of statistical analysis.

Surveys The **survey** allows sociologists to collect data on attitudes and opinions from large numbers of people. Two techniques are commonly used to gather survey data—questionnaires and interviews.

A questionnaire is a list of questions or statements to which people are asked to respond in writing. Questionnaires can be administered in person or on the Internet or sent through the mail. This technique has the advantage of making it possible to collect information from a large number of people in a relatively short period of time. However, questionnaires also have several disadvantages. For example, they do not enable sociologists to know if the respondents have interpreted the questions correctly. Furthermore, researchers must rely solely on survey answers in drawing conclusions.

An interview is like a questionnaire, but respondents answer questions orally. Interviews can be administered in person or over the telephone. This makes it easier for researchers to determine if respondents understand the questions. It also makes it possible for researchers to ask for clarifications and to note context clues, such as facial expressions, hesitations, or side comments. One disadvantage of interviews is that they are more time consuming and expensive to administer than are questionnaires.

Whether sociologists use questionnaires or interviews, they must first select the people they wish to question. Unless a population is very small, it is impractical to survey everyone in the population. Therefore, sociologists generally survey a **sample,** or a small number of people, drawn from the larger population. For a sample to be useful to the researcher, it must be representative of the population from which it is drawn. To help ensure representativeness, sociologists generally rely on random

Conducting Interviews

Your school probably uses some form of Internet filtering system to block student access to various Web sites. What do your classmates think of this school policy? Find out by interviewing them.

PROCEDURE

1. Conduct background reading to discover why schools and other institutions such as public libraries use Internet filters.
2. Based on your reading, develop a hypothesis on students' attitudes to the use of Internet filters.
3. Write three to five questions for your interview. Remember that you are looking for attitudes and opinions, so do not write questions that can be answered with "Yes" or "No."
4. Select four or five classmates to interview. Try to get a cross-section of the class population in your interview sample.
5. Conduct your interviews, spending one or two minutes for each question. Note respondents' answers.

ANALYSIS

1. Review the results of the interviews. Did any respondents express strong opinions for or against Internet filtering? What reasons did they give for those opinions?
2. How well do the results support your hypothesis? Do you need to adjust your hypothesis? If so, how?

samples. A random sample is chosen in such a way that every member of the population has an equal chance of being included.

A famous example of the consequences of not using a random sample is provided by the presidential election poll conducted by the *Literary Digest* in 1936. The magazine selected its respondents from telephone directories and automobile registration lists. The results of this survey of over 2 million Americans indicated that Republican Alfred E. Landon would beat Democrat Franklin D. Roosevelt by a margin of 15 percentage points. The magazine was quite embarrassed when Roosevelt won by a landslide.

Why was the magazine's survey so far off the mark? During the Great Depression, only members of the middle and upper classes could afford telephones and automobiles. Members of the middle and upper classes were mostly Republican in the 1930s. Thus, Republicans were vastly overrepresented in the sample. Members of the much larger working class, on the other hand, were not included in the survey. It was the working class, most of whom were Democrats, that was primarily responsible for Roosevelt's large margin of victory.

Analysis of Existing Sources One of the techniques used to analyze existing sources is the **historical method.** It involves examining any materials from the past that contain information of sociological interest. These materials can include such things as toys, clothes, pictures, tools, or furniture. However, more often they consist of written documents, such as diaries, newspapers, magazines, government records, laws, and letters.

The historical method enables researchers to make comparisons between events of today and events that happened in the recent past or long ago. It also provides a way to study trends. In the case of personal material, such as letters and diaries, the historical method allows researchers to view the private, unguarded feelings of individuals who lived in an earlier time.

Content analysis is another technique used to analyze existing sources. The process involves counting the number of times a particular word, phrase, idea, event, symbol, or other element appears in a given context. Content analysis can be used to analyze any form of recorded communication. Common sources of information include television, radio, sound recordings, movies, photographs, art work, newspapers, magazines, books, and personal or government documents.

Content analysis is a popular research technique among sociologists because it is easy to use and is inexpensive. Researchers merely have to count the number of times the characteristics of interest appear in the source. In recent years, computer programs have made the evaluation of data collected through content analysis even simpler.

Observational Studies In observational studies, researchers observe the behavior of individuals and groups in actual social settings. Data can be collected in two ways, through detached observation or through participant observation.

In detached observation, researchers observe the situation under study from a distance. Since researchers do not participate in the situation being studied, individuals often do not realize that they are being observed. This method has the advantage of making it less likely that behavior will be affected by the known presence of a researcher. However, by remaining detached, social researchers sometimes miss important details.

A more accurate picture of a situation often can be achieved through participant observation. In **participant observation,** researchers become directly involved in the situation under investigation. Sometimes researchers make their identities known to the people being studied. At other times, researchers remain anonymous. The latter technique has the advantage of increasing the chances that the subjects of the study will act naturally.

CASE STUDY CONNECTION

Street Science Sudhir Venkatesh acted as a participant observer to gather information for his study on poverty.

A **case study** is an intensive analysis of a person, group, event, or problem. Case studies tend to rely on observational techniques. However, researchers often use survey methods and the analysis of existing source materials in their investigations. It is not so much the technique that distinguishes case studies, but rather the focus of the investigation.

Case studies are particularly useful in analyzing infrequent or temporary events such as riots or natural disasters. Like observational studies, case studies have the advantage of providing a picture of a real-life situation.

TECHNOLOGY FOCUS

Mapping Social Networks

The social network, the web of relationships formed by the sum total of a person's interactions with others, is a topic of great interest in sociology. To explain social networks to others, sociologists often use graphics. These map-like images use points to show social actors and lines to show interaction among those actors.

Initially, network maps were hand-drawn and very simple. Over time, innovations added sophistication. The introduction of computing in the 1950s allowed researchers to use various forms of mathematical analyses on their data. This made mapping far more accurate. By the 1970s, computer programs had been developed that not only analyzed the data, but also produced printable images of the dots and lines. A further programming development in the 1980s enabled researchers to produce images on screen.

Perhaps the greatest revolution in network imaging came with the advent of the Web, because this added the viewer of the images to the mix. After accessing images on the Internet, the viewer can manipulate them—enlarging, shrinking, or rotating them, isolating particular aspects of the network, and so on. These capabilities make the analysis of the complicated concept of social interaction much easier.

This social network map shows friendship ties among a group of teenagers in Dublin, Ireland.

Thinking Critically

Draw Conclusions Why are graphics so important to the analysis and understanding of social networks?

Experiments In an **experiment,** data is gathered under controlled conditions set by the researcher. In this way, the researcher is able to focus on the effects produced by an independent variable. Most sociological experiments use two groups. The experimental group is exposed to the independent variable, while the control group is not. Every effort is made to ensure that all other conditions are the same for both groups. This makes it possible for the researcher to conclude that the experiment's results are caused by the independent variable, not by something else.

The experimental method has some limitations. Most experiments are conducted in a laboratory, so the conditions created may not accurately reflect conditions in real life. Further, the laboratory atmosphere may cause research subjects to behave differently than they would in a normal social setting.

Statistical Analysis Statistical analysis involves the use of mathematical data. Provided the data can be translated into numbers, statistical analysis can be used with any of the research methods previously discussed. **Statistical analysis** entails analyzing data that have already been collected to determine the strength of the relationship that may exist between two or more variables.

Sociologists use a wide range of statistical methods, many of them very complicated. Students of sociology, however, can analyze and interpret a great deal of sociological information if they have a basic understanding of a few statistical concepts. The most important of these concepts are the three measures of central tendency or statistical average: the mode, the mean, and the median.

In statistical analysis, the same data will produce different averages depending on which of the three measures of central tendency is used. Firstly, the mode is the number that occurs most often in the data. Secondly, the mean is the measure obtained by adding up all of the numbers in the data and dividing that number by the total number of cases. This mean is the measure that people most often think of when they think of averages. Finally, the median is the number that divides the range of data into two equal parts.

The above methods are only some of those used by sociologists to collect, analyze, and evaluate data. It is important to note that sociologists will often use more than one method in the research process.

Reading Check **Summarize** What research approaches might a case study employ?

Ethical Issues in Research

When conducting research, sociologists are guided by ethics. They follow ethical standards to foster professional integrity and to ensure the welfare of the people with whom they work. The American Sociological Association (ASA), the professional organization of sociologists, has established specific ethical guidelines. By and large, these guidelines focus on the issues of confidentiality, deception, and informed consent.

Sociologists have an obligation to ensure that confidential information provided by research participants is protected. This ensures the value and integrity of the research because participants are more likely to disclose true information, feelings, and observations when they know what they say will remain confidential.

Sometimes, however, the issue of confidentiality is not straightforward. Researchers whose studies touch on criminal behavior may have to deal with legal questions. For example, some of Sudhir Venkatesh's subjects were involved in illegal activities. Suppose the police had wanted to see Venkatesh's research notes. Should he violate confidentiality and hand over the notes? Or should he continue to protect his research subjects? In making such decisions, sociologists have to balance confidentiality with accepted standards of conduct and the needs of the law.

Another question that sociologists may confront when conducting research concerns the use of deception. For example, some sociologists may conceal the fact that they are conducting research. Others may mislead subjects as to the real nature of the research being undertaken. For the most part, sociologists accept the use of deception when the potential benefits of the research outweigh the potential harm.

To protect research subjects from deceptive practices and to ensure that they fully understand the nature and risks of the research, sociologists usually obtain informed consent. This means that subjects agree to participate only after they have been given an explanation of the research. Informed consent gives participants a degree of control over their part in the research. It also provides some legal protection for the researchers.

Reading Check **Find the Main Idea** What ethical issues do sociological researchers face?

CASE STUDY CONNECTION

Street Science In discussing his work, Sudhir Venkatesh noted that his friendship with gang members created ethical issues.

ACADEMIC VOCABULARY

ethics rules and standards of behavior governing the conduct of a person or group

SECTION 4 Assessment

Reviewing Main Ideas and Vocabulary

1. **Define** What is the scientific method?
2. **Analyze** What is the importance of correlation in sociological research?
3. **Describe** How do sociologists conduct participant observation?
4. **Recall** For what purpose do sociologists use statistical analysis?

Thinking Critically

5. **Explain** Why is it important that sociologists provide enough information about their research so that others are able to repeat it?
6. **Support a Position** Do you think it is ever ethical to use deception in sociological research? Why or why not?
7. **Compare and Contrast** Using your notes and a graphic organizer like the one below, describe the major research methods and discuss their usefulness for sociological research.

Method	Definition	Advantages	Disadvantages
Survey			
Analysis of Existing Documents			
Observation			
Experiment			

FOCUS ON WRITING

8. **Expository** Suppose you wanted to conduct research into the connection between Internet use and social isolation. Write a brief essay explaining which research method you would use and why.

Lab
Applying What You've Learned

Who's at Your Table?

Use the workbook to complete this lab.

How different does your life appear when you view it through the eyes of a sociologist?

1. Introduction

Thinking like a sociologist involves looking at things from a different perspective. In this lab you will step back and observe an activity in your life from an outsider's viewpoint. In order to complete this lab you will observe the dynamics of your table in the school cafeteria in much the same way that Mitchell Duneier observed "Slim's Table." Duneier revealed to his subjects who he was and what he was doing, so Slim and his friends were aware that they were being observed. However, you will be "undercover"—your status as an observer will not be known.

Your task in this lab is to analyze the social interaction of the people at your table in the school cafeteria. It will be necessary for you to detach yourself from the setting and think about and analyze the situation objectively as a sociologist would. After making your observations, you will compile notes of your experience and write a paper describing your observations and conclusions. Then you will pair up with another student and compare and contrast the observations that you made of your respective tables.

2. Conducting Your Observation

In this lab you will be working independently. Follow these steps to complete your observation.

- Observe the people at your table in the school cafeteria.
- Be sure that the subjects of your observation are unaware of your purpose and your status as an observer.
- Study the dynamics of the situation and form opinions to answer the following questions:
  - Who are the leaders at the table? What traits do they possess that result in their having this role?
  - Who are the followers? What traits do they possess that result in their having this role?
  - Who instigates the conversations?
  - Does anyone control the conversation? How do they manage this control?
  - What subjects are discussed? Why are these subjects chosen and not others?
  - What interests and qualities do the members of the table have that draw them together?
  - Is everyone welcome at the table or is seating limited to a select group? If seating is limited, how are boundaries set to establish the table as a closed group?
  - How diverse is the group at your table? If it is not diverse, what do you think the reason is for this? If it is, what factors encourage this diversity?
- Write a brief essay describing the social interaction you observed. Use the answers to the questions above and any other observations you made to write your essay. Be sure to support your opinions directly with your observations.
- Bring your completed essay to the next class. Following your teacher's instructions, pair up with another student. Compare and contrast the notes both of you have for your tables.

3. Discussion and Evaluation

What did you learn from this lab? Hold a group discussion that focuses on the following questions:

- How difficult was it to remove yourself from your usual position as group member and take on the role of a detached observer?
- Was it difficult to observe and not participate? Do you think your observations would have been useful if you had participated? Why or why not?
- Did anyone notice a difference in your behavior?
- Would you have been able to gather the same information if you had been actively taking notes during the observation? Why or why not?
- What did you observe that surprised you the most? What would it have taken for you to make this observation without this assignment?
- Had you ever thought of the people you identified as "leaders" and "followers" in those terms? Which category would you put yourself in?
- How would continuing this activity over a longer period of time affect your observations? Would your observations be more or less accurate?
- Would it be harder or easier to observe a lunch table with which you had no personal connection? What obstacles might this type of observation present?
- Were there any major differences between your observations and the observations of other students in the classroom?
- How would things differ if you were observing students in a classroom setting instead of the school cafeteria? How would they be similar?
- What other social settings do you think would be interesting to observe from a sociological perspective? Explain why you would choose these settings and how you would observe them.

Alecia & Patti—have an opinion on everything, but only when they're asked.

Derek—the leader, when he speaks, everyone listens.

CHAPTER 1 Review

Comprehension and Critical Thinking

SECTION 1 *(pp. 4–7)*

1. a. **Identify Main Ideas** What is the main focus of sociology?

   b. **Analyze** What ideas and approaches has sociology borrowed from the other social sciences?

   c. **Elaborate** What does it mean to have a sociological imagination? Illustrate your answer with examples.

SECTION 2 *(pp. 8–14)*

2. a. **Identify** Which early sociologists laid the foundations for the discipline of sociology?

   b. **Identify Cause and Effect** What social and political factors led to the development of sociology as a distinct academic discipline?

SECTION 3 *(pp. 15–18)*

3. a. **Recall** What are the three main theoretical perspectives in sociology, and which of the founders of sociology are connected to each?

   b. **Draw Conclusions** How might a sociologist's theoretical perspective influence the choice of social issues he or she studies?

   c. **Support a Position** Which of the three theoretical perspectives do you think provides the fullest explanation of human behavior? Explain your answer.

SECTION 4 *(pp. 20–27)*

4. a. **Identify Supporting Details** What are the advantages and disadvantages of the survey method of research?

   b. **Evaluate** Are there any circumstances under which a sociologist might violate a research subject's confidentiality? Why or why not?

INTERNET ACTIVITY

5. Use the Internet to research the development of sociology. Find information about the founders of the subject and the contributions they made to its development. Also note the events that influenced their thinking on society. Use your findings to write an illustrated essay on the development of the field of sociology.

Reviewing Vocabulary

Fill in each blank with the term that correctly completes the sentence.

6. The ________ are the disciplines that study human social behavior or the institutions and functions of human society in a scientific manner.
7. By adopting a ________ , sociologists are able to look beyond commonly held beliefs to the hidden meanings behind human actions.
8. According to Émile Durkheim, a ________ is the consequence that an element of society produces for the maintenance of its social system.
9. Max Weber urged sociologists to use ________ , which involves the attempt to understand the meanings individuals attach to their actions.
10. An ________ is a description of a social phenomenon comprised of that phenomenon's essential characteristics.
11. A ________ , or a school of thought, is a general set of assumptions about the nature of things.
12. Anything that people accept as representing something else is called a ________ .
13. ________ is the level of analysis that involves looking at small-group settings and the everyday face-to-face interactions among group members.
14. The objective, logical, and systematic way of collecting empirical data and arriving at conclusions is called the ________ .
15. ________ involves counting the number of times a particular word, phrase, idea, event, symbol, or other element appears in a given context.
16. The standards for proper and responsible behavior are called ________ .

Sociology in Your Life

17. Attend a school-related activity, such as a school board meeting, a PTA meeting, a sports event, or a performance by the school band or theater group. Carefully observe the behavior of all the people involved in the activity—both participants and spectators—and take notes on what you see. Based on your notes, write a one-paragraph analysis of the event you attended from the functionalist, conflict, or interactionist perspective.

Skills Activity: Interpreting Cartoons

Study the cartoon below. Then use the information to help you answer the questions that follow.

"Mr. Bigmeister says you may come in, but *only* if you promise to respect the present hierarchy of dominance."

18. Identify Main Ideas What issue is being addressed in the cartoon?

19. Draw Conclusions What is the cartoonist's point of view on this issue? Explain your answer.

20. Elaborate How might a feminist theorist analyze the situation shown in the cartoon?

Writing for Sociology

Use your knowledge of the social sciences to answer the question below. Do not simply list facts. Present a clear argument based on your critical analysis of the question, using appropriate sociological terminology.

21. Imagine that you are a sociologist serving as a member of a panel studying homelessness. What aspects of this issue would interest you as a sociologist? Write a brief report comparing your views on homelessness with those of the other members of the panel, who represent the disciplines listed below.

- Anthropology
- Economics
- Psychology

Connecting Online

Go online for review and enrichment activities related to this chapter.

KEY TOPICS VIDEOS
View compelling clips on issues in the field.

KEEP IT CURRENT
Link to the Current Events site for regularly updated stories on sociology as well as other social studies topics.

QUICK LAB
Reinforce a key concept with a short lab activity.

CASE STUDY

BODY RITUAL AMONG THE NACIREMA

Ceremonies and rituals—formal patterns of behavior that symbolically express shared beliefs—are an integral part of any culture. They provide sociologists with insight into a culture's system of values and beliefs. In the 1950s anthropologist Horace Miner examined some of the rituals of the Nacirema culture. The following is an excerpt from the article he wrote on his findings, "Body Ritual Among the Nacirema."

> *[The Nacirema] are a North American group living in the territory between the Canadian Cree, the Yaqui and Tarahumare of Mexico, and the Carib and Arawak of the Antilles. Little is known of their origin, although tradition states that they came from the east. . .*
>
> *Nacirema culture is characterized by a highly developed market economy which has evolved in a rich natural habitat. While much of the people's time is devoted to economic pursuits, a large part of the fruits of these labors and a considerable portion of the day are spent in ritual activity. The focus of this activity is the human body, the appearance and health of which loom as a dominant concern in the ethos of the people. While such a concern is certainly not unusual, its ceremonial aspects and associated philosophy are unique.*
>
> *The fundamental belief underlying the whole system appears to be that the human body is ugly and that its natural tendency is to debility and disease. Incarcerated in such a body, man's only hope is to avert these characteristics through the use of ritual and ceremony. Every household has one or more shrines devoted to this purpose. . .*
>
> *The focal point of the shrine is a box or chest which is built into the wall. In this chest are kept the many charms and magical potions without which no native believes he could live. These preparations are secured from a variety of specialized practitioners. The most powerful of these are the medicine men, whose assistance must be rewarded with substantial gifts. However, the medicine men do not provide the curative potions for their clients, but decide what the ingredients should be and then write them down in an ancient and secret language. This writing is understood only by the medicine men and by the herbalists who, for another gift, provide the required charm. . .*
>
> *Beneath the charm-box is a small font. Each day every member of the family, in succession, enters the shrine room, bows his head before the charm-box, mingles different sorts of holy water in the font, and proceeds with a brief rite of ablution [bathing]. The holy waters are secured from the Water Temple of the community,*

where the priests conduct elaborate ceremonies to make the liquid ritually pure. . .

The daily body ritual performed by everyone includes a mouth-rite. Despite the fact that these people are so punctilious [careful] about care of the mouth, this rite involves a practice which strikes the uninitiated stranger as revolting. . . The ritual consists of inserting a small bundle of hog hairs into the mouth, along with certain magical powders, and then moving the bundle in a highly formalized series of gestures. . .

A distinctive part of the daily body ritual . . . is performed only by men. This part of the rite includes scraping and lacerating the surface of the face with a sharp instrument. Special women's rites are performed only four times during each lunar month, but what they lack in frequency is made up in barbarity. As part of this ceremony, women bake their heads in small ovens for about an hour.

Can you identify the culture Miner studied? If not, read the word Nacirema backwards. Miner's study attempts to show that the values and culture of one society may seem strange, even ridiculous, to others.

What do you think?

1. What are the various items and rituals described by Miner?
2. What other aspects of American culture lend themselves to being analyzed in this way? Choose one and write a piece using the same point of view as Miner.

CHAPTER 2

CULTURAL DIVERSITY AND CONFORMITY

Chapter at a Glance

SECTION 1: The Meaning of Culture

- Culture is made up of the material and nonmaterial products of human groups.
- A society is a group of interdependent people who share a common culture and feeling of unity. Society differs from culture, in that societies are made up of people and cultures are made up of products.
- All cultures share certain elements: technology, symbols, language, values, and norms.

SECTION 2: Cultural Variation

- Cultures can be very different from one another in many ways. There are, however, certain features that all cultures share. These are known as cultural universals.
- Variations exist between societies, but they also exist within societies. Subcultures and countercultures are examples of variations with societies.
- Sociologists must take care to view cultural variations without bias, allowing each culture to be judged by its own standards and not those of another culture.

SECTION 3: The American Value System

- Over the years, sociologists have identified what they believe are the core values of American society.
- Among these values are work, individualism, morality and humanitarianism, personal achievement, and others.
- American values have not stayed the same over time, however. New values, such as respect for the environment, regularly develop and become part of American culture.

SECTION 1

The Meaning of Culture

Before You Read

Main Idea
Culture is made up of all the shared products, both physical and abstract, of human groups. While specific products differ between cultures, all cultures are made up of the same five basic components.

Reading Focus
1. What is the meaning of the term *culture,* and how do material culture and nonmaterial culture differ?
2. What are the basic components of culture?

Vocabulary
culture
material culture
nonmaterial culture
society
values
norms
folkways
mores
laws

TAKING NOTES As you read, use a graphic organizer like this one to take notes on the components of culture.

Component	Explanation

Car Culture U.S.A.

The Wigwam Village Motel, in Holbrook, Arizona, gave drivers a fun place to rest while traveling on Route 66—the "Main Street of America."

SOCIOLOGY CLOSE UP ***How did the car influence American culture?*** Americans have always been in love with their cars. The attitude of "just get in your car and go!" has lured millions to seek the freedom of the open road since the mid-1930s. After World War II a specific "car culture" blossomed along Route 66, a highway that stretched 2,448 miles between Chicago and Los Angeles.

What made driving this route a unique culture? Partly, it was the mythology that surrounded the journey. To many, a road trip vacation on Route 66 was like taking the old pioneer trail. Native American imagery was common along the road in the Southwest, from tepee motels to pueblo "trading posts." Cowboy and Spanish motifs were also common. This combination of ideas and material things is what defines a culture, as you'll see throughout this section. ■

What Is Culture?

Most sociologists believe that, unlike other animals, humans are not controlled by natural instincts. Because humans are not locked into a set of predetermined behaviors, they are able to adapt to and change their environment. The methods by which collections of people—be they small groups or entire societies—deal with their environment form the foundation of their culture.

Culture consists of all the shared products of human groups. These products include not only physical objects, but also the beliefs, values, and behaviors shared by a group. The physical objects that people create and use form a group's **material culture.** Examples of material culture include automobiles, books, buildings, clothing, computers, and cooking utensils. Abstract human creations form a group's **nonmaterial culture.** Examples of nonmaterial culture include beliefs, family patterns, ideas, language, political and economic systems, rules, skills, and work practices.

In everyday speech, people tend to use the terms *society* and *culture* interchangeably. However, sociologists distinguish between the two terms. A **society** is a group of interdependent people who have organized in such a way as to share a common culture and feeling of unity. Society consists of people, and culture consists of the material and nonmaterial products that people create.

Reading Check **Contrast** What is the difference between a society and a culture?

The Components of Culture

Culture is both learned and shared. This idea does not mean that everyone in the United States dresses the same way, belongs to the same church, or likes the same type of music. However, it does mean that most people in the United States choose from among the same broad set of material and nonmaterial elements of culture in dealing with and making sense of their environment.

Specific examples of the material and nonmaterial elements of culture vary from society to society, but all cultures have certain basic components such as technology, symbols, language, values, and norms.

Technology A society's culture consists of not only physical objects but also the rules for using those objects. Sociologists sometimes refer to this combination of objects and rules as technology. Using items of material culture, particularly tools, requires various skills, which are part of the nonmaterial culture. For example, knowledge of computer languages and the ability to access and surf the Internet are skills related to the computer. Sociologists are not only interested in skills but also in the rules of acceptable behavior when using material culture. For example, the practice of "hacking"—accessing Web sites or computer systems illegally—is considered unacceptable behavior.

Symbols The use of symbols is the very basis of human culture. It is through symbols that we create our culture and communicate it. As you learned in the previous chapter, a symbol is anything that represents something else. In other words, a symbol has a shared meaning attached to it. Any word, gesture, image, sound, physical object, event, or element of the natural world can serve as a symbol as long as people recognize that it carries a particular meaning. A church service, a class ring, the word *hello,* the Lincoln Memorial, and a handshake are examples of common symbols in the United States. Although specific examples vary from culture to culture, all cultures communicate symbolically.

Language One of the most obvious aspects of any culture is its language. Language is the organization of written or spoken symbols into a standardized system. When organized according to accepted rules of grammar, words can be used to express any idea. In the United States most people learn to speak an American form of English and use this language as their primary means of communication. English is the principal language used in schools, in books and magazines, on radio and television, and in business dealings, even though there are members of American society who do not speak English. Have you ever visited a foreign country and been unable to speak the language? If so, you realize how important the use of language is in daily life.

Values Language and other symbols are important partly because they allow us to communicate our values to one another and to future generations. **Values** are shared beliefs about what is good or bad, right or wrong, desirable or undesirable. The types of values held by a group help to determine the character of its people and the kind of culture they create. A society that values war and displays of physical strength above all else will be very different from one that places emphasis on cooperation and sharing. The Yanomamö of South America and the San of southern Africa provide examples of how different value systems produce different cultures.

The Elements of Culture

A culture is made up of all the shared products of a human group—everything from physical objects to beliefs, values, and behaviors. While cultures may differ from society to society, they all consist of the same key elements: technology, symbols, language, values, and norms. ***Which element of culture do you feel is most important? Why?***

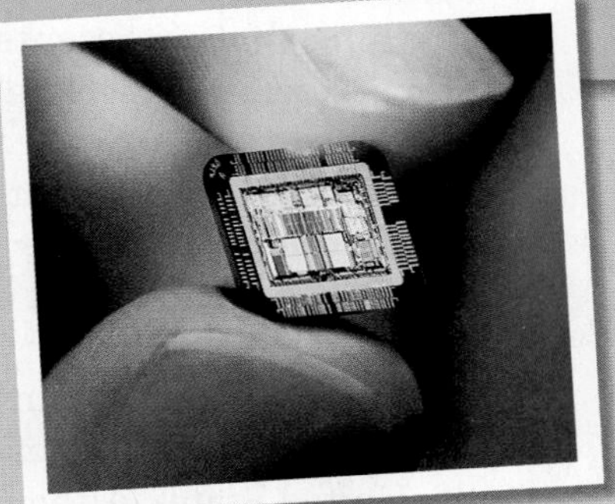

Technology For sociologists, technology refers not only to physical objects but also to the rules established for using those objects. So, technology involves an understanding of how a silicon chip works as well as the chip itself.

Symbols A symbol is any commonly understood gesture, word, object, sound, or design that has come to stand for something else. For example, the yin-yang symbol originated in China, but it has long been recognized as a symbol of harmony in many cultures.

The Yanomamö are farmers who live in villages along the border between Brazil and Venezuela. Warfare and feats of male strength play such an important role in the Yanomamö way of life that anthropologist Napoleon Chagnon called them the Fierce People. Although farming villages normally support between 500 and 1,000 people, Yanomamö villages rarely have as many as 200 people. Conflicts within the village usually cause groups to split off and form new settlements. Hostilities do not end with the splitting up of the village. Most instances of warfare occur between villages that were originally part of the same settlement.

In contrast, the way of life of the San people of southern Africa is based on cooperation. San groups have their own territories, and they take great care not to trespass on the lands of others. Within groups, all members who are able take part in the search for food. The group shares the food with all members. If food is in short supply, the group breaks into smaller units. When food is plentiful, these small units come back together.

Norms All groups create **norms** to enforce their cultural values. Norms are shared rules of conduct that tell people how to act in specific situations. For example, in the United States the value of a democratic government is reinforced through norms governing political participation, respect for the American flag, and the treatment of elected officials. It is important to keep in mind that norms are expectations for behavior, not actual behavior. The fact that a group has norms governing certain behaviors does not necessarily mean that the actions of all individuals will be in line with those norms. In the United States, there are norms concerning financial responsibility, but some people do not pay their bills.

A tremendous number of norms exists in our society ranging from the unimportant, such as covering your mouth when you yawn, to the very important, such as not committing murder. While some norms apply to everyone in society, others are applied selectively. For example, no one in American society is legally allowed to marry more than one person at a time. But only selected groups of people, such as children and the clergy of some religions, are forbidden from marrying at all.

Even important norms are sometimes applied selectively. The norm against taking life, for example, is applied differently to soldiers and police officers acting in the line of duty than it is to most members of society. Norms also vary in the strictness of enforcement. In recognition of all these variations, sociologists distinguish between two types of norms: folkways and mores (MAWR–ayz).

Folkways are norms that describe socially acceptable behavior but do not have great moral significance attached to them. In essence, they outline the common customs of

Language Perhaps the most important element of culture is language, the organization of written or spoken symbols into a standardized system. In countries such as Canada, several languages are part of the culture. Above, a sign uses both English and Cree, a Native American language.

Values In sociological terms, values are shared beliefs about what is good, desirable, and proper. Respect for one's elders is an important value in many cultures. In Thailand, the new year festival, Songkran, is a time to honor one's elders.

Norms Cultural values are enforced by norms—shared rules of conduct people follow in their relations with one another. Some norms, such as obeying traffic signals, are formalized as written laws.

everyday life. All of the following are folkways: do not put food in your mouth with a knife; when lowering the American flag, do not allow it to touch the ground; shake hands when you are introduced to someone; do not jostle and push people when waiting in line; get to class on time; do your homework. Failure to abide by such rules usually results in a reprimand or a minor punishment. Some degree of nonconformity to folkways is permitted because it does not endanger the stability of society.

Mores, on the other hand, have great moral significance attached to them. This relation exists because the violation of such rules endangers society's well-being and stability. For example, dishonesty, fraud, and murder all greatly threaten society. These are deviances from cultural mores.

Societies have established punishments for violating mores in order to protect the social well-being. These serious mores are formalized as **laws**—written rules of conduct enacted and enforced by the government. Most laws enforce mores essential to social stability, such as those against arson, murder, rape, and theft. However, laws may also enforce less severe folkways, such as not parking in spaces reserved for drivers with disabilities.

Reading Check **Identify** What are the key components of culture?

SECTION 1 Assessment

Reviewing Main Ideas and Vocabulary

1. **Describe** What is the difference between material and nonmaterial culture?
2. **Recall** Is technology part of material culture or nonmaterial culture or both? Explain.
3. **Explain** Use the Yanomamö and San cultures to explain how different value systems produce different cultures.

Thinking Critically

4. **Support a Position** Give and defend your opinion about the way the norm against taking life is applied to soldiers.
5. **Analyze** In your own words, explain how folkways and mores are different.
6. **Draw Conclusions** Using your notes and a graphic organizer like this one, give two examples of how each of the components of culture is important to your life.

Component	How It's Important

FOCUS ON WRITING

7. **Descriptive** Write two paragraphs describing a culture within the United States to which you belong. For example, you might write about a club or a team of which you are a part.

SECTION 2

Cultural Variation

Before You Read

Main Idea

There are many elements that all cultures share. Many cultural variations exist, however, and cultures change over time.

Reading Focus

1. What do most cultures have in common with each other?
2. What factors account for cultural variations within cultures?
3. How have some social scientists responded to cultural variation?
4. How does cultural change occur?

Vocabulary

cultural universals
subculture
counterculture
ethnocentrism
cultural relativism
cultural diffusion
cultural lag
cultural leveling

TAKING NOTES Use a graphic organizer like this one to take notes on cultural variation.

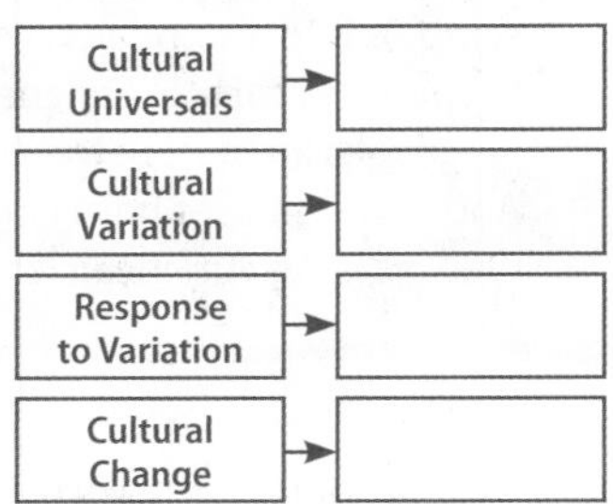

Time for Dinner

SOCIOLOGY CLOSE UP ***How do everyday activities such as eating dinner differ from culture to culture?*** You are visiting Tokyo, and Japanese friends have invited you to dinner. They tell you they will be dining in traditional Japanese style. Do you know what to expect? Here are some guidelines.

Bring a small gift to your friends to show your appreciation for their hospitality. On entering the house, take off your shoes and put on the slippers they offer you. They will probably suggest that you take the place of honor at the table. Decline a couple of times before accepting. The table will be very low to the floor, because the Japanese do not use chairs. You will have to kneel or sit on the floor. If you sit, do not stretch your legs out under the table. It is considered bad manners to point the soles of your feet at someone. During the meal, lift your bowl to your chest, then grip a bite-sized piece of food with your chopsticks and move it from the bowl to your mouth. Slurping while eating soup or noodles is acceptable. Never pour a drink for yourself. Pour drinks for others; someone else at the table will fill your glass. After the meal, do not leave a mess. Place chopsticks on your plate and fold your napkin neatly. This is probably a little different from a dinner at your house, right? ■

What Do We All Have in Common?

Everyday activities, such as having dinner with friends, show that cultures can differ widely. To get an idea of how diverse world cultures are, you might consider language. Estimates suggest that up to 7,000 languages are spoken in the world, 90 percent of these are used by less than 100,000 people, and 46 languages have only a single speaker! In addition, because there may be dialects of the same basic language, even people who speak the same language may have difficulty understanding one another. In the Spanish language, for example, speakers living in Latin America speak different dialects from speakers living in Spain.

You may be wondering how cultures can be so different when all humans have the same basic needs. The answer is that we have the ability to meet our needs in a vast number of ways. Only biological makeup and the physical environment limit this ability. Nevertheless, some needs are so basic that all societies must develop certain features to ensure their fulfillment. These features, common to all cultures, are called **cultural universals.**

In the 1940s anthropologist George Murdock examined hundreds of different cultures in an attempt to determine what general traits are common to all cultures. Murdock used his research to compile a list of more than 65 cultural universals. Among these universals are body adornment, cooking, dancing, family, feasting, forms of greeting, funeral ceremonies, gift giving, housing, language, medicine, music, folklore and myths, religion, sports, and toolmaking.

Murdock also found that although survival may dictate the need for cultural universals, the specific nature of these traits can vary widely. One factor that gives rise to families is the need to care for young children. He argued that in all cultures, the purpose of the family is the same. The family ensures that new members will be added to society and cared for until old enough to fend for themselves. In addition, the family introduces children to the components of their culture.

The makeup of a family, however, varies from culture to culture. In most of the Western world, a family consists of one or both parents and their children. In some cases, grandparents may also be included in the definition.

CULTURAL UNIVERSALS

Anthropologist George Murdock identified more than 65 cultural universals—features that are common to all cultures. How these universals are expressed, however, differs from culture to culture.

Arts and Leisure
athletic sports, dancing, decorative art, games, music

Basic Needs
clothing, cooking, housing

Beliefs
body adornment, dream interpretation, folklore, funeral rites, religious ritual, weather control

Communication and Education
education, greetings, language

Family
courtship, family feasting, kin groups, marriage

Government and Economy
calendar, division of labor, government, law, property rights, status differentiation, trade

Technology
medicine, toolmaking

In some parts of the world, a family might look completely different and include a man, his several wives, and their children. While the structure of family may be different, Murdock argued that the existence and purpose of families compose a cultural universal.

Reading Check **Find the Main Idea** What are cultural universals?

ACADEMIC VOCABULARY
folklore
traditional customs, tales, sayings, dances, or art forms preserved among a people

Cultural Variations

Cultural variations exist not only among societies but also within societies. Among the major sources of cultural variation within a society are the unique cultural practices of various subgroups.

As an American, you share a common culture with all other Americans. American culture is a collection of traits, complexes, and patterns that, by and large, are distinct from those of other societies. In addition to these broad cultural features, some groups in society share values, norms, and behaviors that are not shared by the entire population.

Statistically Speaking...

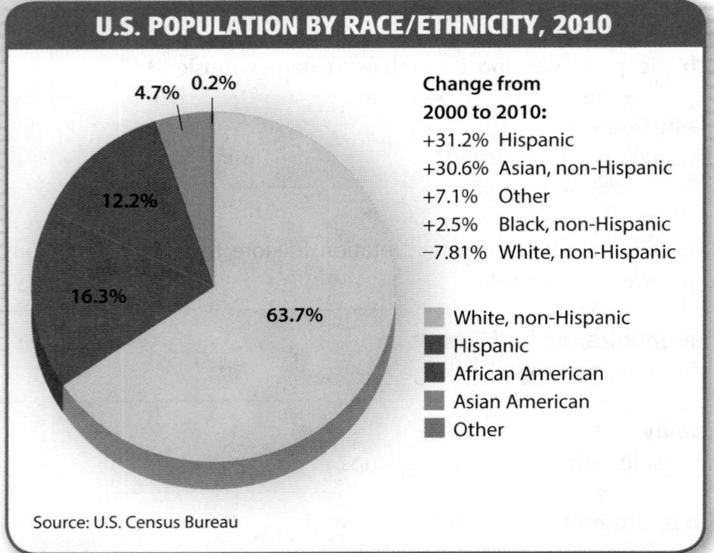

The Diverse U.S. Population Ethnic and racial diversity in the United States has greatly influenced American culture, and the makeup of the population is constantly changing.

96% Growth in the Asian American population by 2050

86% Growth in the Hispanic population by 2050

32% Growth in the African American population by 2050

Skills Focus INTERPRETING GRAPHS Will the African American population catch up to the Hispanic population by 2050? Explain.

Source: US Census Bureau

The unique cultural characteristics of these groups form a **subculture.** Criminologist Edwin Sutherland developed the idea of subcultures in the 1920s through his work on crime and juvenile delinquency. In addition to deviant subcultures, sociologists today recognize age, gender, ethnic, religious, political, geographic, social-class, and occupational subcultures.

Most subcultures do not reject all of the values and practices of the larger society. For example, residents of San Francisco's Chinatown have many broad American cultural traits, such as going to public schools, playing with toys, and working at similar jobs. The culture of the Chinatown residents also includes the Chinese language and specific foods and celebrations that are not shared by most Americans. Likewise, the residents of Little Havana in Miami and the Navajo of the Southwest have their own languages and other cultural traits that are not shared by the larger American society.

Subcultures have also developed around age groups. Youth subcultures have existed in the United States since the early 1900s. Characteristics of these youth cultures have included owning fast cars, listening to rock or hip-hop music, and wearing certain clothes. Some teenagers today consider themselves part of "emo" culture, which has its own distinct style of music, dress, and hairstyles.

Most subcultures do not present a threat to society. Modern society is dependent on various subcultures—such as the military, the police, lawyers, physicians, teachers, and religious leaders—to provide important functions. Furthermore, subcultures, particularly those based on race and ethnicity, add diversity and may make society more open to change.

In some instances, however, subcultural practices are consciously intended to challenge the values of the larger society. Sometimes a group rejects the major values, norms, and practices of the larger society and replaces them with a new set of cultural patterns. Sociologists call the resulting subculture a **counterculture.** The cyberpunk movement, anarchists, organized crime families, and the hippie movement of the 1960s are examples of countercultures in the United States.

The Mafia provides an extreme example of a counterculture. It rejects accepted societal norms, such as obeying the law, and creates its own cultural practices. To begin with, its day-to-day operations—the drug trade, illegal gambling, money laundering, and so on—are all against the law. Further, entrance to and promotion within the Mafia often requires violent acts such as beatings and murder. In fact, practically every aspect of life in the Mafia is a challenge to accepted norms.

Reading Check Contrast What is the difference between a subculture and a counterculture?

Response to Variation

The study of variations in cultures presents challenges for social scientists. Cultural variations are what make societies interesting to study. However, social scientists must be careful to remain critical of biases in their observations and conclusions.

Ethnocentrism Turn back to the beginning of this section and reread the description of Japanese customs. Do some of them seem odd? It is not unusual for people to have a negative response to cultural traits that differ drastically from their own. This tendency to view one's own culture and group as superior is called **ethnocentrism.** People in all societies are, at times, ethnocentric. From the functionalist viewpoint, this belief that the characteristics of one's group or society are right and good helps to build group unity. In contrast, the conflict perspective argues that belief in the superiority of a group or society often results in one group or society seeing others as inferior. This tends to encourage discrimination against those seen as inferior. Further, when ethnocentrism becomes extreme, culture can stagnate. By limiting the pool of acceptable members, groups and societies run the risk of excluding new influences that might prove beneficial.

Even anthropologists and sociologists struggle with ethnocentrism. Napoleon Chagnon's first impression of the Yanomamö of South America was filtered through the standards of his own culture. Everything about the Yanomamö culture contradicted his expectations of how people should look and act. Chagnon admits that when he began to study the Yanomamö, their appearance and behavior horrified him. He even questioned the switch he had made from a career in civil engineering to anthropology! Over time, however, Chagnon was able to see the Yanomamö from a less ethnocentric point of view.

Cultural Relativism Like Chagnon, sociologists attempt to keep an open mind toward cultural variations. To do so, they adopt an attitude of **cultural relativism,** which is the belief that cultures should be judged by their own standards rather than by applying the standards of another culture. In other words, researchers who practice cultural relativism attempt to understand cultural practices from the points of view of the members of the society being studied.

Cultural relativism helps sociologists and anthropologists understand practices that seem strange or different from those of their own culture. In *Cannibals and Kings,* anthropologist Marvin Harris explored the religious prohibition in India against killing cows even when food shortages exist. He suggested that the prohibition was related to the development of Indian agriculture. Cows played a vital role in feeding the Indian people, even though cows themselves were not eaten. Cattle provided the power for plowing, which prepared the land for planting. Therefore, a large number of cows were needed to ensure good harvests. In addition, cows provided milk, a traditionally important part of the Indian diet. When viewed from this perspective, it is possible to see that the prohibition against killing cows has practical benefits.

CASE STUDY CONNECTION

Nacirema Body Ritual Before you knew who the "Nacirema" were, did their rituals seem weird to you? Ethnocentrism is a common, negative reaction to unfamiliar customs.

Reading Check **Identify Cause and Effect** How might ethnocentrism cause discrimination?

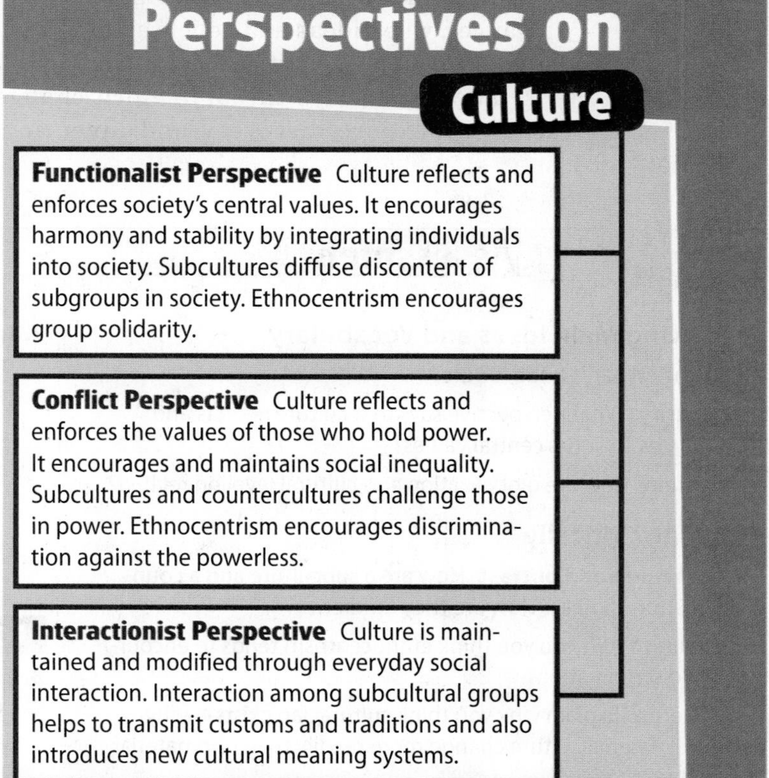

Perspectives on
Culture
Functionalist Perspective Culture reflects and enforces society's central values. It encourages harmony and stability by integrating individuals into society. Subcultures diffuse discontent of subgroups in society. Ethnocentrism encourages group solidarity.
Conflict Perspective Culture reflects and enforces the values of those who hold power. It encourages and maintains social inequality. Subcultures and countercultures challenge those in power. Ethnocentrism encourages discrimination against the powerless.
Interactionist Perspective Culture is maintained and modified through everyday social interaction. Interaction among subcultural groups helps to transmit customs and traditions and also introduces new cultural meaning systems.

Cultural Change

All cultures around the world are constantly changing. Sometimes this change comes very slowly. At other times, change happens suddenly. Change can occur in both material and nonmaterial culture, and a change in one area of life normally means that other areas will change, too.

The Process of Change Perhaps the most common way that change takes place is through a process called **cultural diffusion.** This involves the spreading of culture traits—ideas and beliefs as well as material objects—from one society to another. The more contact a society has with other societies, the more culture traits it will borrow. Today, with mass transportation and instant communication through the media, the telephone, and the Internet, cultural diffusion sometimes takes place almost instantly.

Sociologist William Ogburn noted that not all cultural traits change at the same rate. Some traits change rapidly, Ogburn observed, while the transformation of others may take considerable time. Material culture tends to change more readily than nonmaterial culture. Ogburn referred to the time between changes, when ideas and beliefs are adapting to new material conditions, as **cultural lag.**

Two other ways through which change takes place are discovery and invention. Discovery occurs when people recognize new uses for existing elements in the world or begin to understand them in new ways. Invention occurs when people use existing knowledge to create something that did not previously exist. Discovery often leads to invention. For example, scientists discovered nuclear fission in 1934. By 1951 a nuclear reactor that generated electricity had been invented.

Cultural Leveling Globalization—the development of economic and social relationships that stretch across the world—and the quickening rate of diffusion have brought about a situation that sociologist James Henslin calls **cultural leveling.** This is a process in which cultures become more and more alike.

Examples of cultural leveling abound. McDonald's has nearly 33,000 restaurants in over 100 countries, while Starbucks has more than 24,000 coffee houses in some 70 countries. Other American enterprises, such as Pizza Hut and Burger King, also have a world presence. Further, from the street corners of every major world city to the foothills of Tibet, a New York Yankees cap seems to be a must-have fashion item for many young people. Some sociologists suggest that cultural leveling is the first step toward the development of one global culture.

Reading Check **Summarize** What are the major processes of cultural change?

SECTION 2 Assessment

Reviewing Main Ideas and Vocabulary

1. **Recall** What is a subculture?
2. **Identify** What perspective says that culture reflects and enforces society's central values?
3. **Explain** How are globalization and cultural leveling related?

Thinking Critically

4. **Compare and Contrast** How are a subculture and a counterculture similar? How are they different?
5. **Evaluate** Why do you think ethnocentrism tends to encourage discrimination?
6. **Develop** Explain why you think cultural lag exists—why does material culture change more readily than nonmaterial culture?
7. **Interpret** Using your notes and a graphic organizer like this one, explain how each perspective on culture relates to cultural variation.

Functionalist Perspective	Conflict Perspective	Interactionist Perspective

FOCUS ON WRITING

8. **Expository** Write a few paragraphs on your opinion of cultural leveling. Is it a good or bad thing for people and cultures to become more alike? Why? For whom is it good or bad? Give a few other examples of cultural leveling that you have noticed in the world today.

The Adaptive American Culture

A long history of immigration to the United States has greatly influenced American culture. Immigrants incorporate their culture into American culture. As a result, these new cultural traditions influence many aspects of daily life, including business practices, advertising, and what Americans choose to eat.

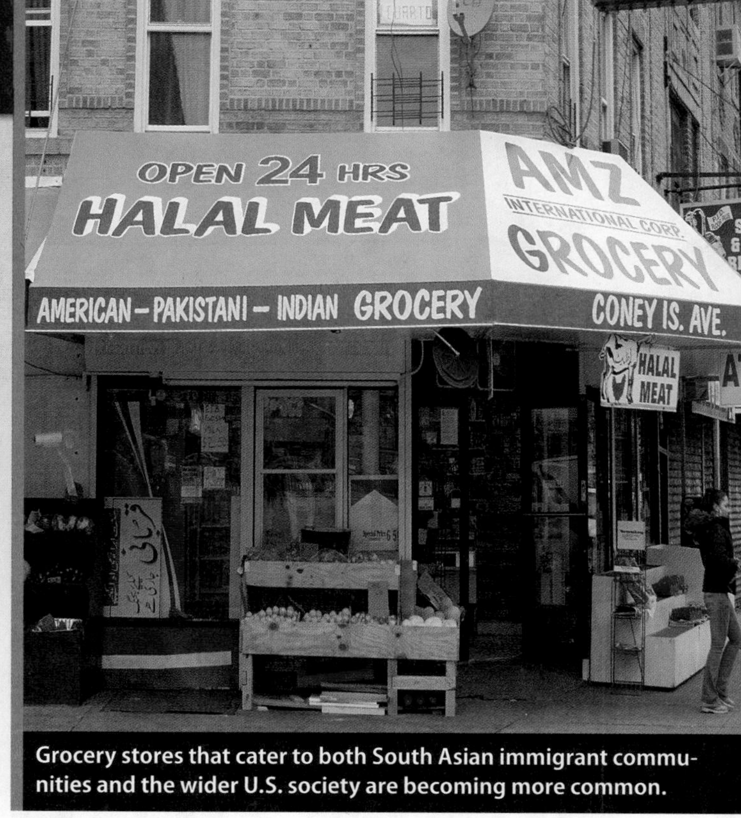

Grocery stores that cater to both South Asian immigrant communities and the wider U.S. society are becoming more common.

In the past few decades, large numbers of immigrants from Mexico and other Latin American countries have greatly influenced American culture. The following 2004 article "Hispanic Nation" from *Business Week* describes how this trend began.

Latinos, as many prefer to be called, officially passed African Americans last year to become the nation's largest minority. Their numbers are so great that, like the postwar baby boomers before them, the Latino Generation is becoming a driving force in the economy, politics, and culture. . .

Hispanics' soaring buying power increasingly influences the food Americans eat, the clothes they buy, and the cars they drive. Companies are scrambling to revamp products and marketing to reach the fastest-growing consumer group. . .

For more than 200 years, the nation has succeeded in weaving the foreign-born into the fabric of U.S. society, incorporating strands of new cultures along the way. With their huge numbers, Hispanics are adding all kinds of new influences. Cinco de Mayo has joined St. Patrick's Day as a public celebration in some neighborhoods, and burritos are everyday fare. More and more, Americans hablan Español.

The cultural influence of Hispanic immigrants is visible in many areas. For example, Mexican foods such as tortillas and salsa have become common across the United States. Americans now buy billions of dollars' worth of tortillas each year, and salsa is more popular than ketchup.

The growth in popularity of Spanish-language television, such as Telemundo and Univision, has also changed the way large corporations advertise, as Telemundo viewers alone have grown to more than 1.1 million viewers in the United States in 2014.

They're not just viewers, however. They're also consumers, and the amount of money they have to spend has become quite substantial. One estimate from 2012 suggested that Hispanic buying power in the United States would rise to $1.5 trillion in 2015.

Immigration from some South Asian nations, such as India and Pakistan, has become significant as well. According to U.S. government statistics, between 2004 and 2013, 851,806 Indians and 160,991 Pakistanis obtained legal permanent resident status in the United States. The U.S. government states that a further 51,293 Indian immigrants were designated unauthorized between 2005 and 2013.

In the not too distant past, Pakistani or Indian cuisine was considered extremely exotic. Today, especially in cities with large South Asian populations, this is no longer so. "Bollywood" movies from India are also gaining popularity in the United States. In 2005 they earned an estimated $100 million here.

Thinking Critically

1. **Evaluate** How have immigrant groups influenced American culture in your community?
2. **Discuss** What are some examples of how food, business practices, and advertising have changed because of immigration?

SECTION 3

The American Value System

Before You Read

Main Idea
Even though American society is quite diverse, there are certain core values that the vast majority of Americans share.

Reading Focus
1. What are traditional American values?
2. How have our values changed since the 1970s?

Vocabulary
self-fulfillment
narcissism

TAKING NOTES As you read, use a graphic organizer like this one to take notes on the values of American society.

Traditional American Values	Changing American Values

"Work Is Its Own Reward"

"Can Jennifer come out and work?"

SOCIOLOGY CLOSE UP ***How important is work in the American value system?*** Hard work has always been a cornerstone value of American culture. The United States has a long tradition of people going to work very young, working their way "up the ladder," and succeeding in a variety of ways.

The story of Andrew Carnegie illustrates what many see as "the American Dream." Carnegie's family emigrated from Scotland to Pennsylvania in 1848 when he was 12. He immediately went to work in a textile mill. Fifty years later—after success in the railroad business, as an investor, and in the steel industry—Carnegie was worth over $250 million. By the time he died in 1919, he had given about $350 million to various charities.

But you don't have to be a multimillionaire to gain respect for your hard work. U.S. Attorney Patrick Fitzgerald's father worked as a doorman in New York City. Fitzgerald went to work young as well, as a school janitor to make money for college. During summer breaks from college, he worked as a doorman, like his father, to save for the next term. Throughout his career as an attorney, one word has always been applied to him: *workaholic.* As U.S. Attorney for the Northern District of Illinois, Patrick Fitzgerald has garnered nearly universal respect for his dedication, fairness, and achievement.

Showing initiative as a young person and working through adversity continue to be truly valued in the United States. As you will read, hard work is but one of a number of traditional American values. ■

Traditional American Values

Ethnic, racial, religious, social-status, and geographical variations in American society make for a diverse culture. Nevertheless, the vast majority of Americans share certain values. Sociologists refer to these values when they speak of traditional American culture.

In his highly-regarded study *American Society: A Sociological Interpretation,* sociologist Robin M. Williams identified 15 traditional values he believes are central to the American way of life. Among these values are personal achievement, progress and material comfort, work, individualism, efficiency and practicality, morality and humanitarianism, equality and democracy, and freedom.

Personal Achievement Most Americans value personal achievement. This value is not a surprise considering that the United States was built primarily by people who believed in individualism and competition. This belief in the importance of personal achievement is most evident in the area of employment, where achievement often is measured in terms of power and wealth.

Progress and Material Comfort Americans have always looked to the future with optimism. They believe that through hard work and determination, living standards will continue to improve. This belief in progress is paired with a belief in the ability of science and technology to make the world a better and more comfortable place. Both views are important because most Americans also place a high value on material comfort.

Work Most Americans value work, regardless of the rewards. Americans view discipline, dedication, and hard work as signs of virtue. But this can be taken to the extreme. Often, people work long hours at the expense of their family lives but are still praised. On the other hand, Americans tend to view those who choose not to work as lazy or even immoral.

Individualism For most Americans, individual effort is the key to personal achievement. They believe that success comes through hard work and initiative. This emphasis on individualism has a negative side, however. Most Americans feel that if a person does not succeed, that person is to blame.

AMERICAN VALUES

American society is made up of many diverse groups, but there is a core set of values that the majority of these groups share.

Personal Achievement
Doing well at school and at work is important. Gaining wealth and prestige is a sign of success.

Progress and Material Comfort
History is marked by ongoing progress, and this progress improves people's lives.

Work
Discipline, dedication, and hard work are signs of virtue.

Individualism
Hard work, initiative, and individual effort are the keys to personal achievement.

Efficiency and Practicality
Every problem can be solved through efficiency and practicality. Getting things done well in the shortest time is very important.

Morality and Humanitarianism
Judgments should be based on a sense of right and wrong. This sense of morality also involves helping the less fortunate.

Equality and Democracy
Everyone should have an equal chance at success and the right to participate freely in government.

Freedom
Personal freedoms, such as freedom of religion, speech, and the press, are central to the American way of life.

Efficiency and Practicality Americans tend to be practical and inventive people. They believe that every problem has a solution. Problem solving involves discovering the most efficient way of dealing with a situation or determining the most practical response to the issue at hand. As a result, Americans tend to judge objects on their usefulness and judge people on their ability to get things done.

Morality and Humanitarianism The United States was founded on strong religious faith, on a belief in justice and equality, and on charity toward the less fortunate. Most Americans place a high value on morality and tend to view the world in terms of right and wrong. At the same time, they are quick to help those who are less fortunate than themselves.

Quick Lab

American Values: What's Your Opinion?

Do young Americans still uphold traditional American values? Or are the core values of American culture changing? Poll your fellow students to discover what they think.

PROCEDURE

1. Review the traditional American values listed in this section.
2. Working in a group with two or three classmates, develop a questionnaire addressing these values. Each question should take the form of a statement on one of the values with several possible responses—strongly agree, somewhat agree, somewhat disagree, and strongly disagree, for example.
3. Make copies of your questionnaire and distribute them to the rest of the class.

ANALYSIS

1. Collate all the responses to the questionnaires and present your findings to the class.
2. Lead a class discussion of your findings, using questions such as: Which core values do young people still hold? Which core values seem to be falling out of favor? Are there other values that should be considered core American values?

Equality and Democracy The United States was founded on the principle of human equality. The Declaration of Independence proclaims, "We hold these truths to be self-evident, that all men are created equal." Many Americans believe that to have equality, there must be an equality of opportunity and an equal chance at success. Although Americans value equal opportunity, they do not necessarily believe that everyone will be equally successful. The values of hard work and personal achievement lead most Americans to view success as a reward that must be earned.

The belief in equality extends to the form of government that Americans value: democracy. Americans believe that every citizen has the right to express his or her opinions and to participate freely in choosing representatives in government.

Freedom Freedom is an important value for most Americans. Americans particularly value personal freedoms of choice such as the freedoms of religion, speech, and the press, which are guaranteed in the U.S. Constitution. Americans steadfastly protect these freedoms from direct government interference in their daily lives and in business dealings.

Other Core Values These values are not the only values that help define American culture. Williams also included nationalism and patriotism, science and rationality, and racial and group superiority in his list of core values. Another sociologist, James Henslin, suggested that additional values such as education might be included. Many Americans think that everyone should achieve the highest level of education that his or her abilities will allow. Americans tend to unfavorably view those who deliberately choose not to fulfill their educational potential. Henslin also pointed out that religious values are important in American culture. While Americans do not expect people to belong to a church, temple, or mosque, they do expect them to live according to basic religious principles. Finally, Henslin suggested romantic love was another core American value. Americans strongly believe that people should marry primarily because they fall in love with each other.

Even though values are vital to the stability of society, they may sometimes produce conflict. Not everyone agrees on what are acceptable American values. Even when people agree, they may not uphold all values to the same degree. Strongly upholding the value of personal achievement, for example, may weaken an individual's commitment to such values as morality and equality.

Reading Check **Summarize** List and describe four traditional American values.

Our Changing Values

The problem of conflicting values is complicated by the fact that values, like all aspects of society, are dynamic. Over time, some values change and new ones emerge. In recent years sociologists have traced the development of several related new values in the United States. These values, which include leisure, physical fitness, and youthfulness, might be grouped under the term self-fulfillment.

Self-fulfillment is a commitment to the full development of one's personality, talents, and potential. The emergence of this value can be seen in the large and growing self-help industry. Seminars, television programs, and books offer people ideas on how to improve their personal and professional lives. At the same time, health clubs and diet centers promise to transform people's health and looks.

This growing emphasis on personal fulfillment created debate among social scientists. In his book *The Culture of Narcissism,* social historian Christopher Lasch went so far as to consider this emphasis on personal fulfillment a personality disorder. He termed this disorder **narcissism,** which means extreme self-centeredness. Sociologist Daniel Bell also saw dangers in the focus on the self. He felt that it weakened the established values of hard work and moderation and threatened the stability of the capitalist system. Psychologist and survey researcher Daniel Yankelovich took a different view. He admitted that this new value probably indicated that Americans believed less in hard work than did earlier generations. However, he viewed this shift toward self-fulfillment as a beneficial change. It marked a movement away from satisfaction based on material gain, he suggested.

Studies during the 1990s noted the emergence of other new American values, such as concern for the environment. Public opinion polls during that time reflected a growing support among Americans for environmental protection. Throughout much of the 1990s, for example, more than 60 percent of Americans said that they favored protecting the environment, even if it limited economic growth. However, during the 2000s, this number fell to about 50 percent.

The emergence of environmentalism illustrates how values often change. For long periods in American history, the desire for progress led people to alter the natural world. Americans cleared forests, diverted rivers, and built factories and roads in an effort to improve life in the United States. After a time, however, it became clear that some of these actions had damaged the environment. This damage had an adverse effect on quality of life. Americans then began to realize that they value the environment as well as progress.

ACADEMIC VOCABULARY

personality disorder a long-term and deeply ingrained pattern of socially unacceptable behavior that is harmful to the person who displays it and to others

Reading Check **Analyze** In what ways have American values changed?

SECTION 3 Assessment

Reviewing Main Ideas and Vocabulary

1. **Describe** Name and describe 5 of the 15 American values identified by the sociologist Robin M. Williams.
2. **Recall** What does the emergence of environmentalism in the 1990s illustrate about values?

Thinking Critically

3. **Draw Conclusions** In your own words, explain how the American values of equality and democracy are linked.
4. **Explain** In what ways might one of Williams's other core values that help to define American culture, "racial and group superiority," conflict with some of his 15 traditional American values?
5. **Categorize** Using your notes on the values of American society and a graphic organizer like this one, decide whether each value reflects practical concerns, idealistic goals, or a little of both.

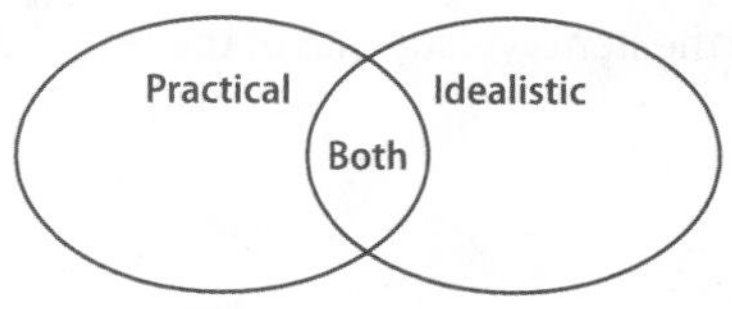

FOCUS ON WRITING

6. **Descriptive** Choose two American values that you feel strongly about (positively or negatively). Write one paragraph on each one, describing your feelings and explaining why you feel the way you do.

Lab

Applying What You've Learned

Analyzing Material Culture

Reading and Activity Workbook

Use the workbook to complete this lab.

How can material culture be used to tell about cultural values and differences?

1. Introduction

Values are a key component of society. They enable us to share and pass on what is important to us and form the basis for our expectations for behavior. While every culture has a broad set of shared values, some cultures have subcultures that hold different values. Even within subcultures values can vary from person to person. Such is the case with American teenagers.

In this lab you will compare your values against the values of others who are also in the American Teen subculture. This lab will give you the opportunity to compare your values with the values of your peers and see how they are similar or different. To complete this lab follow the steps below.

- Review the chapter material on the concept and components of culture. Pay special attention to the terms material culture, values, ethnocentrism, cultural relativism, and subculture. Write down a few main points on these concepts and any others that you think might be important to identifying and understanding cultural differences.
- Select two personal items to share with the class. One should be something you highly value, and one should be something you value little.
- Write a paragraph explaining why you selected each item and how you value it.
- Participate as a class in a presentation where everyone's items will be given a positive or negative value.
- Explain why you selected your items and talk about your valuation of the items versus that of the rest of the class.

2. Selecting Your Items

Following your teacher's instructions about appropriateness, select two personal items to share with the class. Use the following as a guide for making your selections.

- Go home and evaluate the items in your room. As you do so, think about why you have what you have in your room. What value do you give to the items in your room? Why do you have the various items? Is it for sentimental reasons? Are the items kept for their usefulness?
- Choose two items to take to the next class. The items you choose should be on opposite ends of the spectrum. In other words, one item should be most valued and the other least valued. You can think in whatever terms of value you want to: valuable/worthless, pretty/ugly, good/bad, etc.
- Each item can be anything that has a positive or negative value for you. Remember that can mean different things for different people. For example: A concert ticket might be highly valued if it was a from a happy couple's first date. On the other hand, it might have no value if it was the occasion of a couple's break up.
- Place your items in a bag or box so that they are not clearly visible.
- Upon arriving to class, give the box or bag to your teacher or place it in a designated spot.

Sample Items

Guitar
Stuffed animal
Eyeglasses
Workshirts or ID
Favorite shirt
Seashells
Paperweight
Football or sports equipment
Jewelry — rings, necklaces, etc.
Driver's License

3. Analyzing Your Selection

After selecting your two items, write a detailed analysis of your choices. The analysis should explain your thought process during the selection process. This part of the activity will help you with your part of the presentation. Consider the following questions as you write your analysis paper.

- How difficult was it to select only two items from your room?
- What process did you use to eliminate items and settle on the two you chose?
- What were some of the items you considered, but did not choose? Why?
- Which item did you assign a negative value to? Why have you kept it? What value or purpose does it hold for you?

4. Presenting and Judging the Items

Once everyone is ready for the presentation, your teacher will begin unveiling the items. As each item is revealed it will be presented to the class. The teacher will lead a discussion about what value they give to the item. Then the class should decide on which side of the spectrum it should be placed. Should it be placed on the good/valuable/pretty side or the bad/worthless/ugly side? The items should be clearly placed on one side of a table or the room to designate what value the class has given them. This procedure is repeated with each item until all items have been given a value.

After all the items have been given a value by the class it is time for each student to come forward and claim their items. Each student should give a complete explanation of their items, explaining why they chose them and what value they give them. They should also compare how they valued their item with how the class valued the item.

5. Discussion

Once all items have been claimed by their owners, the teacher will lead the class in a discussion about the lab. Consider some of the discussion questions listed below.

- Were you surprised by the values assigned to items by your classmates compared to how you valued them? Why?
- Why is there such variation in results among a group that is similar in age?
- Did your opinion of an object change upon hearing the owner's explanation of their item? Why or why not?
- How do you think a person's age might change the values assigned to each object? Would a 5-year-old think differently about the items? A 50-year-old?
- Would a person from another part of the country think differently about the items? What about a person from another part of the world?

CHAPTER 2 Review

Comprehension and Critical Thinking

SECTION 1 *(pp. 34–37)*

1. **a. Identify** What is the central characteristic that makes something a successful symbol?

   b. Contrast How are folkways different from laws?

   c. Support a Position Do you think folkways are necessary for our culture to exist? Why or why not?

SECTION 2 *(pp. 38–42)*

2. **a. Recall** What is the most common way that cultural change takes place?

   b. Contrast What is ethnocentrism? How does it differ from cultural relativism?

   c. Make Judgments Is the existence of countercultures valuable or harmful to society? Why?

SECTION 3 *(pp. 44–47)*

3. **a. Recall** What new American values have emerged in recent years?

   b. Analyze How might a strong commitment to such values as personal achievement and individualism affect an individual's economic decisions?

   c. Evaluate Briefly describe the differing opinions of the emergence of the value of self-fulfillment. In your opinion, which one is correct? Why?

INTERNET ACTIVITY

4. How have important counterculture movements challenged the values of the larger society? Choose one of the following counterculture movements: the cyberpunk movement, anarchists, or hippies. Use the Internet to research the group of your choosing. Write a report that gives a historical overview of the movement. When, where, and why did it begin? When did the movement reach its height? Is it ongoing, or has its influence worn out?

Reviewing Vocabulary

Match the terms below with their correct definitions.

5. cultural diffusion
6. nonmaterial culture
7. personality disorder
8. mores
9. subculture
10. narcissism
11. norms
12. material culture
13. cultural lag

A. extreme self-centeredness

B. norms that have great moral significance attached to them

C. situation in which some aspects of a culture change less rapidly than others

D. a group with its own unique values, norms, and behaviors that exists within a larger culture

E. abstract human creations, such as ideas, language, rules, political systems, and so on

F. shared rules of conduct that tell people how to act in specific situations

G. the spreading of cultural traits from one society to another

H. a long-term and deeply ingrained pattern of socially unacceptable behavior that is harmful to the person who displays it and to others

I. physical objects created by human groups

Sociology in Your Life

14. Simply by living in the United States, you are immersed in the broader American culture. But are you a member of a subculture? Since sociologists recognize age, gender, ethnic, religious, political, geographic, social-class, and occupational subcultures, you almost can't avoid it. Within your school there is an overarching culture, but there are certainly numerous subcultures operating as well. Think about a subculture that you belong to and that is meaningful to you. It can be any of the ones mentioned here or another that you recognize and feel strongly about. Write a paragraph that describes your chosen subculture. How is this subculture's values different from those of the wider, dominant culture? What accepted values (if any) does your subculture reject? Does your subculture seriously challenge the values of the larger society? Is it a counterculture?

Skills Activity: Interpreting Graphs

The bar graph below shows how the opinions of Americans about whether the environment or the economy should be given priority have changed between the years 2000 and 2008. Study the graph and answer the questions that follow.

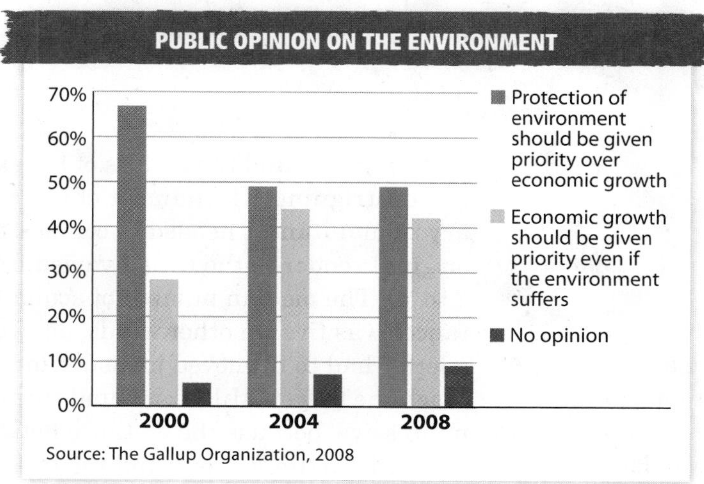

Source: The Gallup Organization, 2008

15. Analyze Which category between which two years saw the greatest change in support?

16. Compare In which year does the total number of people who want to give priority to the economy or have no opinion fall well short of the number of people who want to give priority to the environment?

17. Develop Judging strictly by numerical change, does this graph suggest that over time, fewer people support protecting the environment or more people support emphasizing the economy? Explain.

Writing for Sociology

Use your knowledge of the components of culture to answer the question below. Do not simply list facts. Present a clear argument based on your critical analysis of the question, using the appropriate sociological terminology.

18. Briefly describe each of the components of culture below. For each, say whether it is part of material culture, nonmaterial culture, or both. Then give an example of each and explain how it is relevant to your everyday life.

- Symbols
- Values
- Norms

Connecting Online

Go online for review and enrichment activities related to this chapter.

KEY TOPICS VIDEOS
View compelling clips on issues in the field.

KEEP IT CURRENT
Link to the Current Events site for regularly updated stories on sociology as well as other social studies topics.

QUICK LAB
Reinforce a key concept with a short lab activity.

CASE STUDY

Six Degrees of Separation

Imagine that you are on vacation in France. At a café, you share a table with another American whom you have never met before. Much to your surprise, you discover that even though you live more than 1,000 miles apart, you have a mutual friend. "Small world!" you both remark.

Events like these captivated social psychologist Stanley Milgram. He wondered if it would be possible to randomly select two people and connect them through their social networks. Milgram created a rather inventive experiment to test his hypothesis. He asked people in Kansas and Nebraska to get letters to a "target"—a named person in Massachusetts.

The Experiment The letter senders had to follow certain rules. First, unless they knew the target personally, they could not directly contact him or her. Instead, they had to send the letter to a personal acquaintance—someone they knew on a first-name basis—who might know the target. The sender included information about the target to help the acquaintance locate him or her. If the acquaintance did not know the target personally he or she sent the letter to another acquaintance. Senders could dispatch the letter to only one person—not to several at the same time. This process continued until the letter reached its destination.

Milgram found the results of his experiment intriguing. The number of intermediary acquaintances needed to connect the original sender to the target varied from 2 to 10. The median number of acquaintances was five. In other words, on average a letter had to be moved just six times to reach the target. Milgram found this quite impressive, because the distance between the initial letter senders and the target stretched more than 1,300 miles. However, he also realized that the median number gave a misleading picture of closeness between sender and target. They were not five people apart. Rather, they were five groups of acquaintances—or social networks—apart.

Six Degrees of Separation Milgram's experiment entered popular culture shortly after playwright John Guare published *Six Degrees of Separation.* In 1993, three students took the premise of the play—that anyone in the world is separated by at most six connections from anyone else—and turned it into a trivia game. Called *Six Degrees of Kevin Bacon,* the game challenged players to link actor Kevin Bacon to other actors through co-starring roles. Today there are versions of the game focusing on practically every major Hollywood actor.

According to small-world experiments, on average it would take five intermediaries to connect you with a perfect stranger.

The Experiment Revisited Psychology professor Judith Kleinfeld was fascinated by the "six degrees of separation" phenomenon. She decided to ask her students to replicate Milgram's experiment. When she studied the original documentation, however, she made some surprising finds. Several similar studies that contradicted Milgram's findings had been ignored. Also, Milgram's results were suspect, too. Many of the letters never got to the target, but that was not factored into the equation that produced "six degrees of separation." Perhaps it's not such a small world after all, Kleinfeld concluded.

At the same time that Kleinfeld was looking into Milgram's original work, sociologist Duncan Watts attempted to replicate the experiment using e-mail. Called the Small World Research Project, it lasted two years and involved some 60,000 participants. The results showed that the initial e-mailers and the targets were separated by an average of six degrees!

The idea that two strangers are connected through a chain of just six links has become embedded in popular culture. However, the concept on which it is based—the small-world problem—is of great importance to sociology. For example, it may help to explain how and why rumors, fads and fashions, and even disease spread through social networks.

What do you think?

1. What do Milgram's and Watts's work appear to establish about the interconnectedness of people?
2. In Watts's experiment, e-mailers who forwarded to an acquaintance rather than a close friend tended to be more successful in reaching the target. Why do you think this is so?

CHAPTER 3
SOCIAL STRUCTURE

Chapter at a Glance

SECTION 1: Building Blocks of Social Structure

- Social structure is the network of interrelated statuses and roles that guides human interaction.
- A status is a socially defined position in society, while a role is the behavior, or the rights and obligations, attached to a status.
- A social institution is a system of statuses and roles organized to satisfy one or more of society's basic needs.

SECTION 2: Types of Social Interaction

- There are five common forms of social interaction—exchange, competition, conflict, cooperation, and accommodation.
- Exchange, cooperation, and accommodation tend to stabilize the social structure, while competition and conflict tend to encourage social change.

SECTION 3: Types of Societies

- Sociologists classify societies according to subsistence strategies, or the ways societies use technology to meet the needs of their members.
- Sociologists recognize three broad categories of society—preindustrial, industrial, and postindustrial.

SECTION 4: Groups Within Society

- Groups are the foundation of social life. They differ in terms of size, life, organization, and purpose.
- Groups perform important functions, such as setting membership boundaries, choosing leaders, fulfilling goals, and controlling members' behavior.

SECTION 5: The Structure of Formal Organizations

- Formal organizations are complex secondary groups created to achieve specific goals. Most are structured as bureaucracies.
- Max Weber noted that all bureaucracies, regardless of their goals or purposes, have common characteristics.
- Formal and informal structures can affect the efficiency of bureaucracies.

SECTION 1

Building Blocks of Social Structure

Before You Read

Main Idea
Social structure is the network of interrelated statuses and roles that guides human interaction. A status is a socially defined position in society, while a role is the behavior attached to a status.

Reading Focus
1. What do sociologists mean by the term *status?*
2. How are status and roles related?
3. What are social institutions?

Vocabulary
social structure
status
role
ascribed status
achieved status
master status
role set
role conflict
role strain
role exit
social institution

TAKING NOTES Use a graphic organizer like this one to take notes on two major components of social structure—status and role.

Social Structure	
Status	Role

Juggling Roles

SOCIOLOGY CLOSE UP

Where do you fit in society? Meet Alan—he's a little confused as to where he fits in. He seems to perform so many different roles in society. At home, for example, he's a son, a grandson, an older brother, and a younger brother. When his sister and her family drop by for dinner, he takes on two more roles: brother-in-law and uncle. In the neighborhood, everybody knows him as a skateboarder and music fanatic.

At school, the situation is no better. There he's a senior, a football player, a basketball player, the captain of the chess team, and an honors student. New roles seem to pop up regularly. Soon he'll be the class valedictorian and a graduate. Then he'll move on to the role of college freshman. There's no escape from the confusion in his working life. On weekends he's a lifeguard. During the week, he works part-time as a delivery driver at the grocery store.

So, who is the real Alan? Actually, he's everything from son to delivery driver. Each role is just a small piece in the jigsaw puzzle that society knows as Alan.

Status

Sociologists have viewed society as a system of interrelated parts—as a structure—since the time of Auguste Comte. However, social structure as a concept has often been very loosely defined. Throughout this textbook, the term **social structure** will mean the network of interrelated statuses and roles that guide human interaction. A **status** is a socially defined position in a group or in a society. Each status has attached to it one or more roles. A **role** is the behavior—the rights and obligations—expected of someone occupying a particular status.

Ascribed and Achieved Statuses Each individual in society occupies several statuses. For example, an individual can be a student, a daughter, a sister, an African American, and a member of a sports team all at the same time. Statuses are ways of defining where individuals fit in society and how they relate to others in society.

While some statuses are assigned, others are gained through effort. An **ascribed status** is assigned according to qualities beyond a person's control. Ascribed statuses are not based on an individual's abilities, efforts, or accomplishments. Rather, they are based on a person's inherited traits or are assigned automatically when a person reaches a certain age. You hold the status of teenager or young adult, for example, because of your age. You did nothing to earn this status, and you cannot change it. Other examples of ascribed statuses include your gender, family heritage, and race.

Individuals acquire an **achieved status** through their own direct efforts. These efforts include special skills, knowledge, or abilities. For example, a person achieves the status of basketball player because of his or her physical skills and knowledge of the game. Similarly, someone achieves the status of actor because of his or her acting abilities.

Unlike their ascribed statuses, people have some control over their achieved statuses. In a complex society such as the United States, the list of achieved statuses is almost endless. For example, occupations are achieved statuses. Other achieved statuses include husband or wife, parent, high school or college graduate, and athlete.

Social Statuses

Status describes an individual's position in a group or society. Since individuals belong to more than one group, they have many different statuses. Statuses can be ascribed—given to an individual regardless of his or her abilities—or achieved—gained through the individual's talent, effort, or accomplishments.

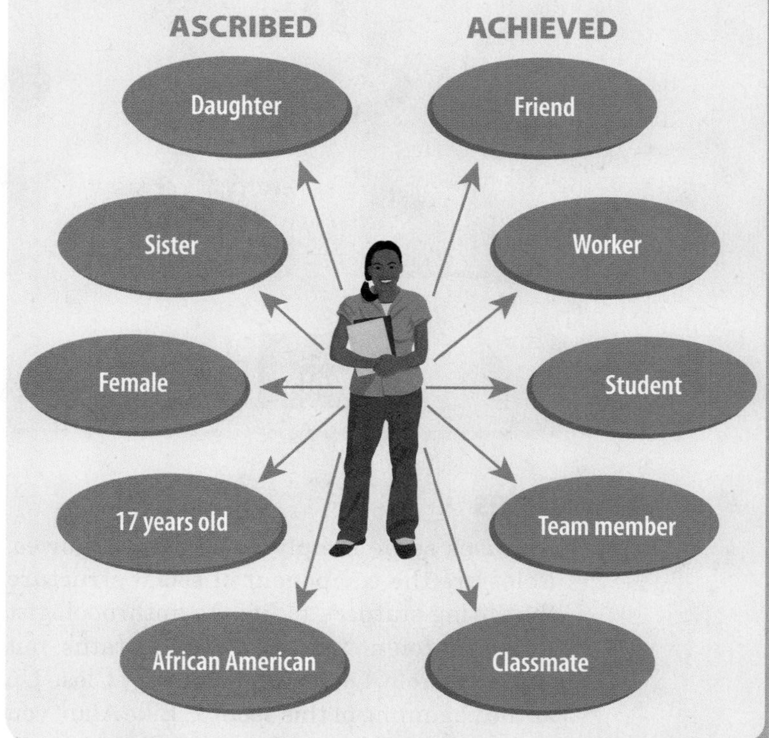

Master Status All individuals hold many statuses. Not all of these statuses are of equal importance. For most people, one status tends to take rank above all others. This **master status** plays the greatest role in shaping a person's life and determining his or her social identity. A master status can be either achieved or ascribed. In the United States, an adult's master status is usually achieved. For example, occupation, wealth, marital status, or parenthood can serve as a master status.

A person's master status changes over time. During the teenage years, being a student often serves as a master status. During much of adulthood, master status is often based on one's occupation. Finally, in late adulthood, generally after a person retires, volunteer work, grandparenthood, or past accomplishments serve as a master status.

Reading Check **Contrast** What is the difference between ascribed status and achieved status?

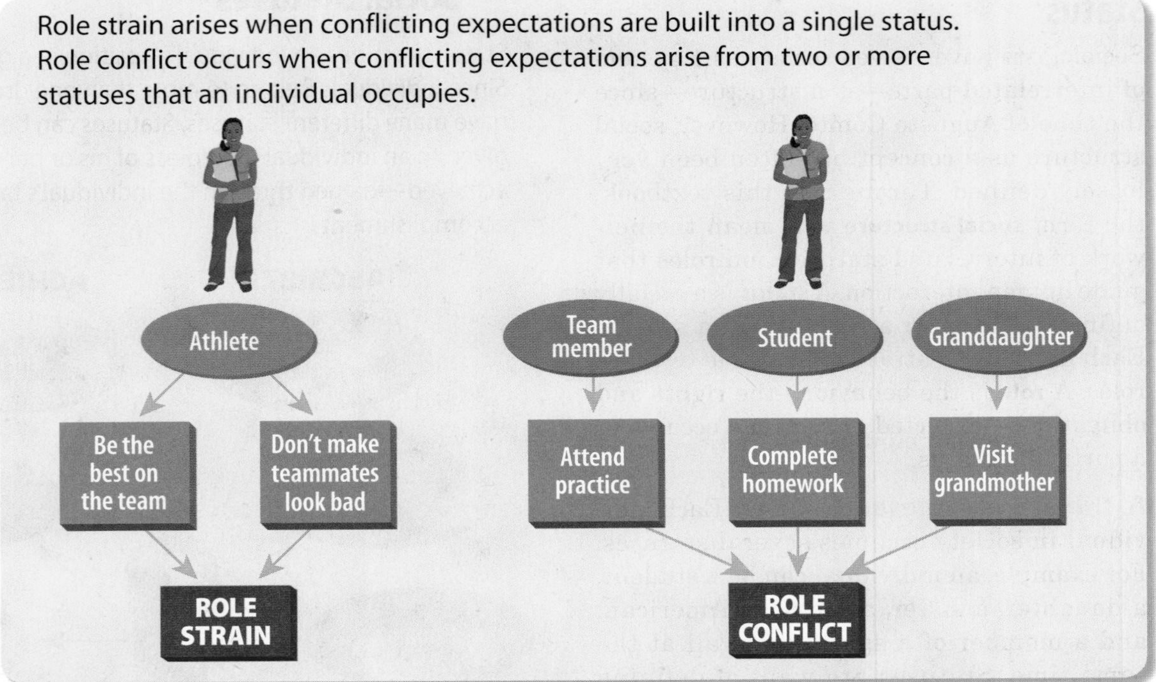

Roles

Statuses serve simply as social categories. Roles are the component of social structure that bring statuses to life. As anthropologist Ralph Linton noted, you *occupy* a status, but you *play* a role. Look at the Sociology Close Up at the beginning of this section. Like Alan, you play many different roles every day. At home you probably play the role associated with the status of son or daughter. At school you play the role associated with the status of student. You may also play the roles that go along with the status of reporter on the school newspaper or of sports team member.

Most of the roles that you perform have reciprocal roles. These are corresponding roles that define the patterns of interaction between related statuses. For example, one cannot fulfill the role associated with the status of husband without having someone else perform the role that goes along with the status of wife. Some other statuses that require reciprocal roles are doctor-patient, teacher-student, coach-athlete, employer-employee, and sales clerk-customer.

Role Expectations and Role Performance

Ideally, when people interact with one another their behavior corresponds to the particular roles they are playing. The socially determined behaviors expected of a person performing a role are called role expectations. For example, doctors are expected to treat their patients with skill and care. Parents are expected to provide emotional and physical security for their children. Police officers are expected to uphold the law.

In reality, people's role performance—their actual role behavior—does not always match the behavior expected by society. Some doctors do not give their patients the best possible care. Some parents mistreat their children. Some police officers break the law. Occasionally, this problem arises because role behaviors considered appropriate by a certain segment of society are seen as inappropriate by society as a whole. Even when someone tries to fulfill a role in the manner expected by society, actual performance may fall short of expectations. This problem occurs, in part, because each of us is asked to perform many roles, some of which are contradictory.

Role Conflict, Role Strain, and Role Exit

Even within a single status, there are interrelated roles to perform. Sociologists call the different roles attached to a single status a **role set.** Each of us, because we hold more than one status, must deal with many role sets in our daily lives. The often contradictory expectations within and between our role sets can lead to role conflict and role strain.

Role conflict occurs when fulfilling the role expectations of one status makes it difficult to fulfill the role expectations of another status. For example, to be a good employee an individual needs to go to work. However, to be a good parent, that individual needs to stay home and take care of a sick child. **Role strain,** on the other hand, occurs when a person has difficulty meeting the role expectations of a single status. The boss who must maintain the morale of workers while getting them to work long periods of overtime is likely to experience role strain.

Another situation where role performance does not match expectations is **role exit.** This is the process people go through to detach from a role that has been central to their self-identity. Ex-convicts, divorced people, mothers who have lost custody of their children, former nuns and priests, and retirees all experience this process. Sociologist Helen Rose Ebaugh suggests that people go through certain common stages on their way to creating a new identity as an "ex." First they begin to experience disillusionment with the old role. Then they start to search for alternative roles. Finally they reach a turning point and make the decision to depart the old role. Conflict occurs because throughout this process, society expects the "ex" to behave according to his or her old identity.

Reading Check **Identify Cause and Effect** Why do role conflict and role strain occur?

Social Institutions

Statuses and their related roles determine the structure of the various groups in society. When these statuses and roles are organized to satisfy one or more of the basic needs of society, the group is called a **social institution.** The basic needs of a society include providing physical and emotional support for its members, transmitting knowledge, producing goods and services, and maintaining social control. Sociologists have recognized several significant social institutions. The most important are listed below.

- **The family,** the most universal social institution, takes responsibility for raising the young and teaching them accepted norms and values.
- **The economic institution** organizes the production, distribution, and consumption of goods and services.
- **The political institution** is the system of norms that governs the exercise and distribution of power in society.
- **Education** ensures the transmission of values, patterns of behavior, and certain skills and knowledge.
- **Religion** provides a shared, collective explanation of the meaning of life.

Reading Check **Find the Main Idea** What purpose do social institutions serve?

SECTION 1 Assessment

Reviewing Main Ideas and Vocabulary

1. **Identify** Give an example of an ascribed status and an example of an achieved status.
2. **Define** What is master status?
3. **Explain** How are status and role related?
4. **Identify Main Ideas** What is the situation called in which contradictory expectations arise from a single status held by an individual?

Thinking Critically

5. **Categorize** Use a web diagram to create your own social status set. Which one is your master status?
6. **Elaborate** How might a conflict theorist argue that certain ascribed statuses can be an individual's master status?
7. **Explain** Using your notes and a graphic organizer like the one below, briefly discuss how status and role affect human interaction.

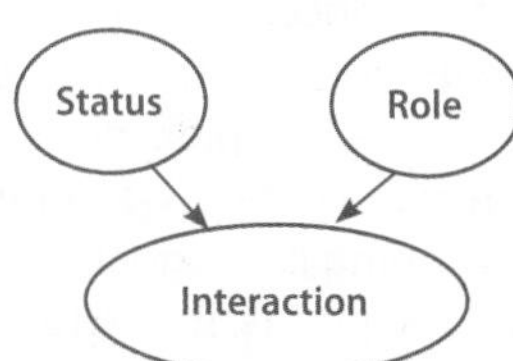

FOCUS ON WRITING

8. **Expository** Study the example of role conflict in the diagram in this section. Write one or two paragraphs suggesting how this conflict might be resolved. In writing your paragraphs, consider the reasons for the conflict and possible individual or group resolutions to the conflict.

SECTION 2

Types of Social Interaction

Before You Read

Main Idea
Sociologists identify five common forms of social interaction: exchange, competition, conflict, cooperation, and accommodation.

Reading Focus
1. What is the basis of exchange?
2. What are the similarities and differences between competition and conflict?
3. Why is cooperation important for society?
4. How do individuals and groups use accommodation to settle disputes?

Vocabulary
exchange
reciprocity
exchange theory
competition
conflict
cooperation
accommodation

TAKING NOTES Use a graphic organizer like this one to take notes on the five types of social interaction.

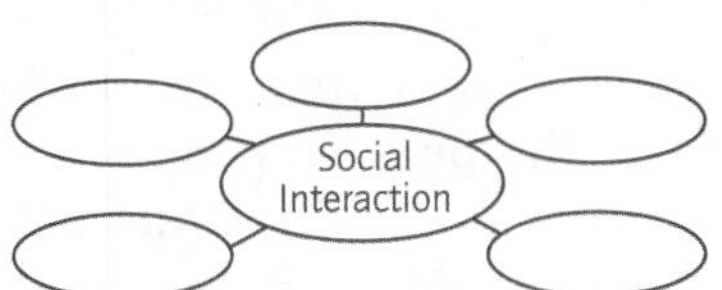

WAR of WORDS

SOCIOLOGY CLOSE UP ***How do you interact with other people?*** Does one form of interaction dominate American society? Linguistics professor Deborah Tannen thinks most Americans interact with each other through competition or conflict. In her book *The Argument Culture,* Tannen suggests that, through their culture, Americans learn to approach human interaction as a duel of wills in which all issues have only two sides. This approach is based on the assumption that contention is the best way to get things done. In addition, it presupposes that there will be winners and losers. Even everyday phrases, such as "the war on drugs," "the fight against cancer," and "to join the fray" frame life in terms of a contest in which winning or losing is the major concern.

Tannen challenges the argument culture, pointing out that most issues are a complex mix of many views. Focusing on just the extremes of these views rarely gets to the truth. Further, when winning is the goal, the parties in an argument are looking to score points, not to further understanding. However, Tannen accepts that argument does have its place in interaction. To stand up for right against wrong, she says, is acceptable and necessary. ■

In the argument culture, Deborah Tannen suggests, interaction can become a little like "a shoot-out between two gunslingers."

Exchange

When you play a role, most of the time you have to interact with others. This interaction can take many forms. Some kinds of interaction help stabilize the social structure. Others promote change. The most common form of social interaction is exchange. Whenever people interact in an effort to receive a reward or a return for their actions, an **exchange** has taken place. Almost all daily interaction involves exchange. In fact, sociologist Peter Blau suggested that exchange is the most basic and common form of interaction. Dating, family life, friendship, and politics all involve exchanges. **Reciprocity**—the idea that if you do something for someone, that person owes you something in return—is the basis of exchange. The reward might be nonmaterial—a simple "thank you" from your parents for washing the dishes, for example. The reward could also be material, such as the wage you receive for working at a supermarket.

Efforts to explain this type of social interaction led to the emergence of **exchange theory.** Exchange theorists believe that people are motivated by self-interest in their interactions with other people. In other words, people do things primarily for rewards. Behavior that is rewarded tends to be repeated. However, when the costs of an interaction outweigh the rewards, individuals are likely to end the relationship. According to exchange theorists, most of social life can be explained as the attempt to maximize rewards while minimizing costs. This careful review of the costs and benefits of alternative actions in sociological terms mirrors the economic concept of rational choice theory.

Some sociologists have suggested that exchange theory has weaknesses. For example, it fails to explain why people join certain organizations. Why would a worker join a trade union if all workers get union-negotiated wage increases whether they are members or not? Also, exchange theory appears to run counter to some social norms. Altruism, or the unselfish concern for the welfare of others, and other similar norms seem to be a matter of morality rather than rational choice.

Reading Check **Analyze** How do exchange theorists view social interaction?

Competition and Conflict

Imagine that you have applied for an after-school job at a local store. When you arrive for your interview, you find that you are competing with several other applicants for the job. **Competition** occurs when two or more people or groups oppose each other to achieve a goal that only one can attain.

Competition is a common feature of Western societies. Some social scientists consider it to be the cornerstone of the capitalist economic system and the democratic form of government. Advancement in business and success in school are achieved through competition. As long as competition follows accepted rules of conduct, most sociologists view it as a positive means of motivating people to perform the roles society asks of them. On the negative side, competition can lead to psychological stress, a lack of cooperation in social relationships, inequality, and even conflict.

The main emphasis in competition is on achieving the goal. With conflict, however, the emphasis is on defeating the opponent. **Conflict** is the deliberate attempt to control a person by force, to oppose someone, or to harm another person. Unlike competition, conflict has few rules of accepted conduct, and even these often are ignored. Conflict may range from the deliberate snubbing of a classmate to the killing of an enemy.

Sociologist Georg Simmel identified four sources of conflict: wars, disagreements within groups, legal disputes, and clashes over ideology, such as religion or politics. Sometimes conflicts begin as competition. Rival businesses may first engage in intense competition for customers. Over time, however, the emphasis may shift from attracting customers to undermining the other business.

Although we tend to think of conflict as negative, some sociologists suggest that conflict serves some useful purposes. For example, conflict reinforces group boundaries and strengthens group loyalty by focusing attention on an outside threat. In addition, conflict can also lead to social change by bringing problems to the forefront and forcing opposing sides to seek solutions.

Reading Check **Contrast** How do competition and conflict differ?

Social Interaction

Social interaction is the way people relate to one another and influence each other's behavior. The nature of social interaction changes according to the social setting in which it takes place. Sociologists have recognized five forms of social interaction: exchange, competition, conflict, cooperation, and accommodation. ***How might cooperation work alongside another form of interaction such as competition?***

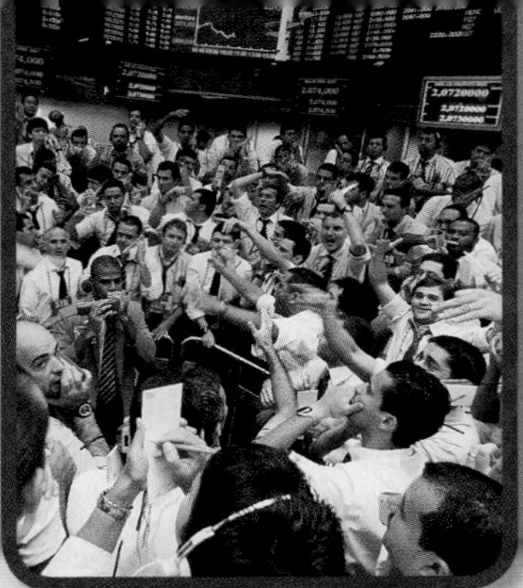

Exchange The most common form of interaction, exchange, takes place when people interact in the hope of receiving some reward. The rules of exchange tend to be informal. Wait staff provide good service to customers in the hope of receiving a "thank you" and a good tip.

Competition When two or more people or groups oppose each other to achieve a goal that only one can attain, competition is taking place. This type of interaction is governed by mutually acceptable formal rules. Traders on the stock exchange floor compete to buy and sell shares at the most advantageous prices.

Cooperation

The members of a football team work together to win a game. The pep club, school band, and student body also contribute to this effort by encouraging the team. If, in the end, the team takes a trophy, it will be through the shared efforts of the entire school. Similarly, the employees of a corporation work together to increase sales for the organization. If their efforts are successful, everyone in the corporation benefits. In both of these examples, the people involved are cooperating to achieve a desired goal. **Cooperation** occurs when two or more people or groups work together to achieve a goal that will benefit more than one person.

Cooperation is a social process that gets things done. No group can complete its tasks or achieve its goals without cooperation from its members. Cooperation is often used along with other forms of interaction. Competition may be used along with cooperation to motivate members to work harder for the group. For example, individuals who go out for a team sport often compete with one another to make the varsity team.

Reading Check **Draw Conclusions** How does cooperation benefit society?

Accommodation

In many of your interactions, you neither cooperate nor engage in competition or conflict. You simply come to an accommodation with the other party in the interaction. In other words, you give a little, and you take a little. **Accommodation** is a state of balance between cooperation and conflict.

One way to remember this concept is by thinking about staying at a motel. The owner of the motel is accommodating you by letting you stay for the night in exchange for a payment of $60. If the owner were cooperating with you, he would let you stay for free. On the other hand, if the owner refused to let you stay under any condition, you would be in a conflict situation.

Accommodation helps to ensure social stability. It can take a number of different forms, the most common being compromise, truce, mediation, and arbitration.

- **Compromise** A compromise occurs when the two parties at odds each give up something to come to a mutual agreement. For example, you and a friend want to see different movies. To compromise, you might choose a third movie that you both would like to see.

Conflict The aim of conflict is to oppose, control, or harm a person or group through the use of force. With conflict, rules do not exist or are ignored. Using military might to control dissent is an example of conflict over ideology.

Cooperation With cooperation, individuals join together to achieve a common goal—usually one that benefits the whole community. Rules, both formal and informal, may play a part in cooperative efforts. People coming together to build houses for the homeless is an example of cooperation.

Accommodation With accommodation, conflict and cooperation are balanced. The various forms of accommodation, such as compromise, truce, mediation, and arbitration, tend to be guided by formal rules. The United Nations uses accommodation to find solutions to international conflicts.

- **Truce** Another form of accommodation is the truce, which temporarily brings a halt to the competition or conflict until a compromise can be reached. In wartime, the adversaries sometimes call a truce and stop fighting while a compromise, in the form of a peace treaty, is worked out.
- **Mediation** Sometimes, when two parties cannot reach a compromise through their own efforts, they will use mediation. This form of accommodation involves calling in a third party who acts as adviser and counselor to guide the two parties toward an agreement. The United Nations, for example, often acts as a mediator to resolve conflicts between member countries.
- **Arbitration** If mediation fails, the parties may use arbitration. In arbitration, a third party makes a decision that is binding on both parties. Employers and labor unions sometimes use arbitration in wage disputes. When negotiation and mediation fail, they bring in an outside arbitrator to impose a settlement.

Reading Check **Summarize** What are the four types of accommodation?

SECTION 2 Assessment

Reviewing Main Ideas and Vocabulary

1. **Describe** What role does reciprocity play in exchange?
2. **Recall** How might conflict have a positive impact on society?
3. **Identify** What type of interaction is being used when people work together to rebuild their damaged homes after a tornado?
4. **Define** What is meant by the term *accommodation?*

Thinking Critically

5. **Compare and Contrast** What are the similarities and differences between exchange and cooperation?
6. **Explain** Which types of interaction can lead to a disruption of social stability? Support your answer with examples.
7. **Sequence** Using your notes and a graphic organizer like the one below, sequence the four forms of accommodation in terms of their ease of achievement. Explain your placements with annotations.

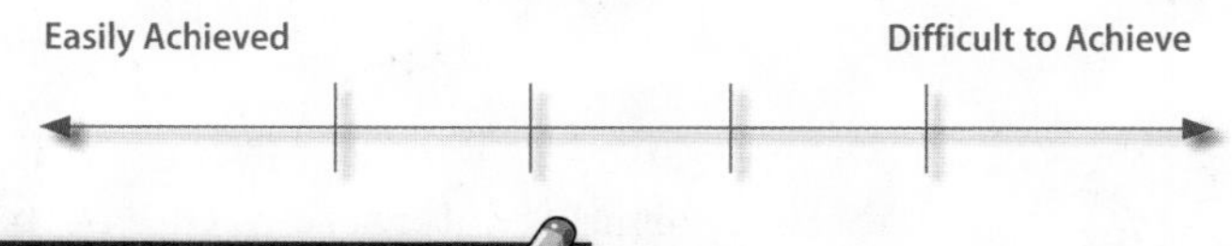

FOCUS ON WRITING

8. **Descriptive** Write a brief essay showing how you might employ several forms of interaction involving another person or group. As you write, consider examples of how you have used each form of interaction with family members or friends.

SECTION 3

Types of Societies

Before You Read

Main Idea
Sociologists classify societies according to how each uses technology to meet the needs of its members. Sociologists recognize three broad categories of society—preindustrial, industrial, and postindustrial.

Reading Focus
1. What are the types of preindustrial societies?
2. What is the main economic activity in industrial societies?
3. How do postindustrial societies and industrial societies differ?
4. What concepts have sociologists used to contrast societies?

Vocabulary
group
subsistence strategies
preindustrial society
division of labor
barter
industrial society
postindustrial society
mechanical solidarity
organic solidarity
Gemeinschaft
Gesellschaft

TAKING NOTES Use a graphic organizer like this one to take notes on the different types of societies.

Types of Society	Characteristics
Preindustrial	
Industrial	
Postindustrial	

People on the Move

SOCIOLOGY CLOSE UP ***What is life like in a preindustrial society today?*** Some Mongolians still follow a traditional pastoral lifestyle. Living in small groups, they drive their "five treasures"—herds of cattle, sheep, goats, horses, and camels—from pasture to pasture as the seasons change. Since they are constantly on the move, everything they own has to be portable. Even their tentlike homes, or yurts, can be folded and stowed on the backs of pack animals. Yurts are made of felt stretched over a wooden frame and can be erected or dismantled in minutes.

Mongolian herders follow a way of life that has been practiced for centuries. The modern world, however, has begun to intrude on their traditional culture. Cell phones are popular, and jeeps and motorcycles have gained favor as a means of transportation. Some yurts have been redesigned to support solar panels that power electric lights, televisions, and radios. It may be only a matter of time before the herders abandon their nomadic ways in favor of these modern conveniences. ■

By dismantling a yurt, these Mongolian herders prepare to move their home to a new location.

Preindustrial Societies

Role behavior often takes place in groups. In sociological terms, a **group** is a set of people who interact on the basis of shared expectations and who possess some degree of common identity. The largest and most complex groups that sociologists study are societies. Sociologists tend to classify societies according to **subsistence strategies,** or the ways societies use technology to provide for the needs of their members. There are three broad subsistence categories: preindustrial, industrial, and postindustrial.

In a **preindustrial society,** food production, which is carried out through the use of human and animal labor, is the main economic activity. Preindustrial societies can be subdivided according to their level of technology and their method of producing food. These subdivisions are hunter-gatherer, pastoral, horticultural, and agricultural.

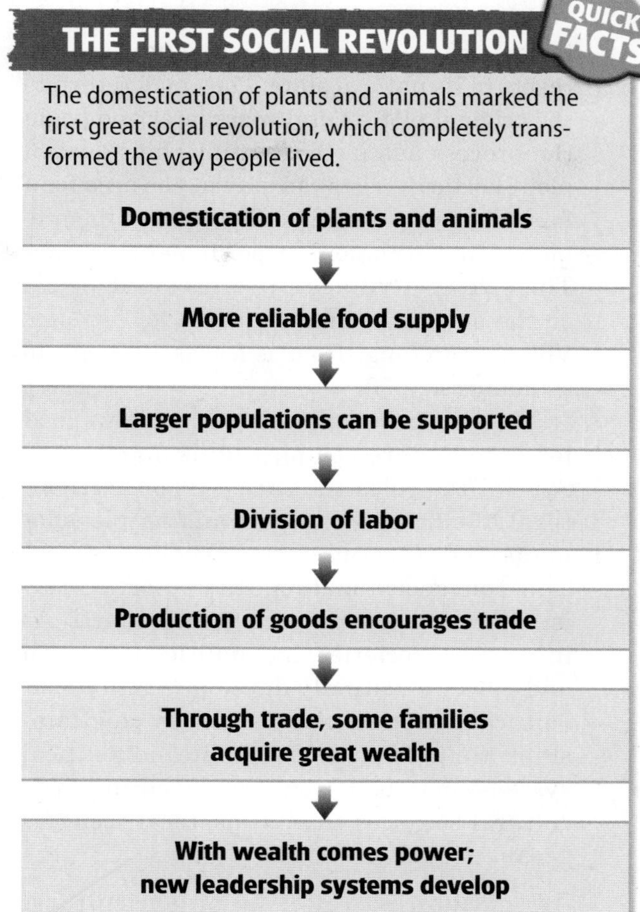

QUICK FACTS
THE FIRST SOCIAL REVOLUTION
The domestication of plants and animals marked the first great social revolution, which completely transformed the way people lived.
Domestication of plants and animals
More reliable food supply
Larger populations can be supported
Division of labor
Production of goods encourages trade
Through trade, some families acquire great wealth
With wealth comes power; new leadership systems develop

Hunter-Gatherer Societies The method of producing food used in hunter-gatherer societies is the daily collection of wild plants and the hunting of wild animals. Hunter-gatherers move around constantly in search of food. As a result, they do not build permanent villages or create a wide variety of artifacts. The need for mobility also limits the size of hunter-gatherer societies. Such societies rarely exceed 100 people. Statuses within the group are relatively equal, and decisions are reached through general agreement. The family forms the main social unit, with most societal members being related by birth or by marriage. The family also carries out most social functions.

Pastoral Societies Pastoralism is a slightly more efficient form of subsistence. Rather than searching for food on a daily basis, members of a pastoral society rely on domesticated herd animals to meet their food needs. Pastoralists live a nomadic life, moving their herds from pasture to pasture. Because their food supply is far more reliable, pastoral societies can support larger populations. Since there are food surpluses, fewer people are needed to produce food. So the **division of labor**—the specialization by individuals or groups in the performance of specific economic activities—becomes more complex. For example, some people become craftworkers, producing tools, weapons, and jewelry.

The production of goods encourages trade. This trade, in turn, helps to create inequality, as some families acquire more goods than others do. These families often acquire power through their increased wealth. The passing on of property from generation to generation helps to centralize wealth and power. In time, hereditary chieftainships—the typical form of government in pastoral societies—emerge.

Horticultural Societies Fruits and vegetables grown in garden plots that have been cleared from the jungle or forest provide the main source of food in a horticultural society. Horticultural societies have a level of technology and complexity similar to pastoral societies. Some horticultural groups use the-slash-and-burn method to raise crops. The wild vegetation is cut and burned, and the ashes are used as fertilizer. Horticulturists use human labor and simple tools to cultivate the land for one or more seasons.

When the land becomes barren, horticulturists clear a new plot and leave the old plot to revert to its natural state. They may return to the original plot several years later and begin the process again. By rotating their garden plots, horticulturists can stay in one area for a fairly long period of time. This allows them to build semipermanent or permanent villages. The size of a village's population depends on the amount of land available for farming. Villages can range from as few as 30 people to as many as 2,000.

As with pastoral societies, surplus food leads to a more complex division of labor. Specialized roles that are part of horticultural life include those of craftspeople, shamans—or religious leaders—and traders. This role specialization allows horticulturists to create a wide variety of artifacts. As in pastoral societies, inequalities in wealth and power eventually develop within horticultural societies, and hereditary chieftainships are prevalent. Economic and political systems may be better developed in horticultural societies than in pastoral societies because of the more settled life.

Agricultural Societies In an agricultural society, animals are used to pull plows to till the fields. This technological innovation allows agriculturists to plant more crops than is possible when only human labor is used. Irrigation further increases crop yields, as does terracing, the practice of cutting fields into the sides of hills.

Higher crop yields allow agricultural societies to support large populations. Most people still work in food production, but many are able to engage in specialized roles. In turn, specialization leads to the development of cities, as individuals engaged in specialized roles come together in central areas. As the number of cities within a society increase, power often becomes concentrated in the hands of a single individual. This power is transferred from generation to generation, usually in the form of a hereditary monarchy.

Leaders of agricultural societies build powerful armies to provide protection from outside attack. The leaders also construct roads. Efficient transportation systems help increase trade, and this, in turn, leads to a number of significant cultural advances. For example, many agricultural societies abandon **barter**—the exchange of goods or services—to facilitate trade. In its place, they use money as the medium of exchange. Many agricultural societies also develop a system of writing to assist in keeping records.

Sharp status differences arise in agricultural societies. Most people belong to one of two groups: landowners or peasants. The small group of landowners controls the wealth and power in society. The large peasant group provides the labor on which the landowners' wealth and power depend.

Reading Check **Identify Supporting Details** What two developments changed life in preindustrial societies?

The Transformation of Society

Society was transformed by four revolutions—the domestication of plants and animals, the development of agriculture, industrialization, and the information age. ***Why do you think the rate of societal change is increasing?***

The Domestication Revolution The earliest humans were nomadic hunter-gatherers who constantly moved in search of food. About 10,000 years ago, some hunter-gatherers learned how to domesticate plants and animals. This led to a more settled life.

The Agrarian Revolution The invention of the plow about 6,000 years ago ushered in the second great social revolution—the development of agriculture. Permanent settlements and larger food surpluses contributed to the growth of cities. In turn, cities brought new forms of leadership.

Industrial Societies

In an **industrial society** the emphasis shifts from the production of food to the production of manufactured goods. This shift is made possible by changes in production methods. In preindustrial societies, production is based on human and animal labor. Production is slow, and the amount that can be produced is limited. In industrial societies the bulk of production is carried out with machines. Thus, production can be increased by adding more machines or by developing new technologies.

Industrialization affects population size by increasing food production. The more food produced, the more people the society can support. Industrialization also changes the nature of the economy by reducing the demand for agricultural laborers. These workers are free to transfer their labor to the production of goods. The size of the industrial workforce also increases as new technologies make it possible to manufacture a wider variety of goods.

With industrialization, the location of work changes. In preindustrial societies most economic activities are carried out within the home setting. With the development of machines, production moves from the home to factories. As factories are built in cities, many people move to these areas. This trend leads to urbanization—the concentration of the population in cities.

The nature of work changes, too. In preindustrial societies, craftspeople are responsible for manufacturing an entire product. With the use of machines, the production process is divided into a series of specific tasks, with each task being assigned to a different person. This process greatly increases productivity. However, it serves to reduce the level of skill required of most workers and tends to create boredom on the job.

Industrialization also changes the role of various institutions in society. In preindustrial societies the family is the primary social institution. However, in industrial societies social processes such as education take place outside the bounds of the family. The need for mass literacy leads industrial societies to establish programs of compulsory education.

One positive effect of industrialization is that it brings more freedom to compete for social position. In preindustrial societies most social statuses are ascribed. In industrial societies, however, most statuses are achieved. As a result, individuals have more control over their position in the social structure.

Reading Check **Identify Cause and Effect** How does industrialization lead to urbanization?

Postindustrial Societies

The United States, like many Western countries, is no longer an industrial society. Rather, it is a **postindustrial society,** where the economic emphasis is on the provision of information and services rather than on manufacturing. Some 39.6 million workers in the United States are involved in information and

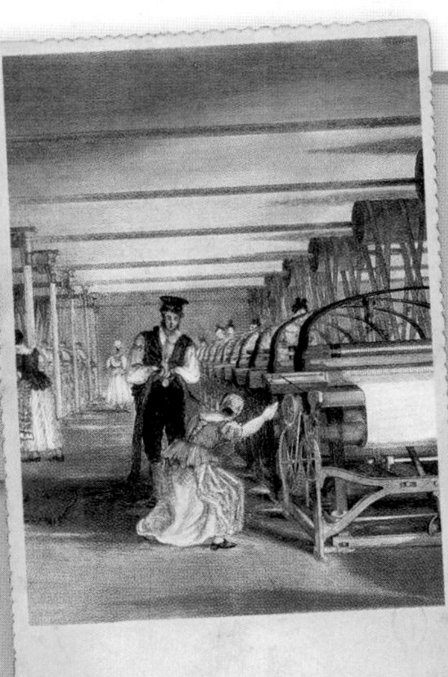

The Industrial Revolution With the Industrial Revolution in the late 1700s, the emphasis of society shifted from food production to the production of manufactured goods. Industrialization changed the location and nature of work. It also changed the social structure, since in industrial societies most statuses are achieved.

The Information Revolution The development of the computer in the second half of the 1900s brought about postindustrial society. In this type of society, information is the chief commodity. Most people do not produce any concrete goods; rather, they use or apply information to provide services.

services. Less than 1.3 million work in agriculture and about 12 million in manufacturing.

Many significant social changes result from the transition to a postindustrial society. For example, the standard of living improves as wages increase for much of the population. In general, postindustrial societies place strong emphasis on roles of science and education in society. Technological advances are viewed as the key to future prosperity. The rights of individuals and the search for personal fulfillment also take on added importance. Belief in these rights leads to a strong emphasis on social equality and democracy.

Reading Check **Find the Main Idea** On what economic activity are postindustrial societies based?

Contrasting Societies

Sociologists have long been interested in how the social structures of preindustrial and industrial societies differ. Émile Durkheim used the concepts of mechanical and organic solidarity to contrast societies. According to Durkheim, preindustrial societies are held together by **mechanical solidarity.** By this Durkheim meant that when people share the same values and perform the same tasks, they become united in a common whole. As the division of labor within societies becomes more complex, mechanical solidarity gives way to **organic solidarity.** This refers to the impersonal social relationships that arise with increased job specialization. Individuals can no longer provide for all of their own needs, and they become dependent on others for their survival. Thus, many societal relationships are based on need rather than on values.

The German sociologist Ferdinand Tönnies (TUHRN-yuhs) distinguished two ideal types of societies based on the structure of social relationships and the degree of shared values among societal members. He called these two types of societies ***Gemeinschaft*** (guh-MYN-shahft), the German word meaning "community," and ***Gesellschaft*** (guh-ZEL-shahft), the German word meaning "society."

In a *Gemeinschaft,* most people know one another. Relationships are close, and activities center on family and community. In a *Gemeinschaft,* people share a strong sense of group solidarity. A preindustrial society or a rural village in a more complex society are examples of a *Gemeinschaft.* In a *Gesellschaft* most social relationships are based on need rather than on emotion. Thus, relationships are impersonal and often temporary. Traditional values are generally weak, and individual goals are more important than group goals. A modern urban society such as the United States is an example of a *Gesellschaft.*

Reading Check **Contrast** How are social relationships in a *Gemeinschaft* different from those in a *Gesellschaft?*

SECTION 3 Assessment

Reviewing Main Ideas and Vocabulary

1. **Identify** What feature do sociologists tend to use to classify societies?
2. **Identify Cause and Effect** What developments led to a more settled life in horticultural and pastoral societies?
3. **Recall** What system of exchange was replaced by the use of money in many agricultural societies?
4. **Define** What does the term *barter* mean?

Thinking Critically

5. **Make Generalizations** How do the statuses held by people tend to change as societies become more complex?
6. **Infer** Why do you think some sociologists refer to postindustrial societies as information societies?
7. **Sequence** Using your notes and a graphic organizer like the one here, arrange the six types of society in order of complexity. For each entry, add a brief description of the society's level of complexity.

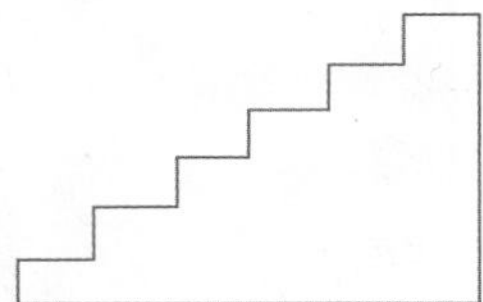

FOCUS ON WRITING

8. **Expository** Write a brief essay contrasting the social structures of simple and complex societies. In writing your essay, consider Émile Durkheim's concepts of mechanical and organic solidarity and Ferdinand Tönnies's concepts of *Gemeinschaft* and *Gesellschaft.*

The New Barter

One of the major cultural developments of agricultural societies was the creation of a money system. In some postindustrial societies, the method of trade that the money system replaced—barter—has made something of a comeback in recent years. It has certainly found favor with American businesses. Estimates suggest that in the early 21st century nearly half a million North American companies were involved in the commercial barter industry. The value of the retail trade transactions these companies make averaged well over $10 billion a year globally as of 2008.

How the New Barter Works

The commercial barter of the 21st century differs greatly from barter of the past. Companies rarely trade directly with one another, swapping one product or service for another. Rather, they work through a clearinghouse known as a barter exchange. There were about 500 of these exchanges in North America by the early 2000s, with a total membership of well over 450,000 businesses. A member company sells its products or services to the exchange for "barter dollars" or "trade credits." These "dollars" or "credits" are entered into the company's account with the exchange. The company then draws on the account to pay for goods or services that it wants to buy. In essence, a barter exchange acts as a marketplace for its members to buy and sell products and services among themselves.

Barter exchanges handle almost every type of trade. Most member companies are looking to sell products and buy advertising. For example, one fruit-juice company partially financed an advertising campaign by bartering 2 million pounds of guava jelly!

Of course, barter exchanges do not offer their services for free. Companies pay a membership fee, usually between $100 and $700, to join an exchange group. The exchange also charges a commission of 10 to 15 percent on every barter transaction and has other monthly fees.

Reasons for Growth

The commercial barter industry has grown rapidly over the past two decades. For example, the value of barter transactions increased by as much as 8 percent per year between the mid-1990s and early 2000s. Retail trade experts predict that this annual growth will rise to 10 percent. One reason for this rapid growth is the development of new computer technology. Computers make the recording and tracking of trades—many of which involve several companies—much easier. The Internet also allows exchanges to locate potential trade partners in distant markets.

There are many advantages to barter trade. To begin with, it provides a way to dispose of outdated inventory or excess capacity. For example, a hotel can reduce the number of empty rooms during the off-season by trading hotel stays for barter credits. Another company might use its credits to buy the hotel stays, which it could use for sales meetings or promotional giveaways. Barter also allows companies to conserve cash for absolutely essential services. In addition, barter provides a way for companies to buy services that, under normal circumstances, might be beyond their means.

The rapid growth of commercial barter has begun to change the face of business in the United States. Further, barter exchanges now include foreign companies, which has affected trade worldwide. As a result, the way we view and use money is changing. Obviously, such a change is having a major effect on social interaction—an effect that sociologists are seeking to analyze and explain.

The new barter enables some interesting exchanges—a fruit-juice company paying for an advertising campaign with cases of guava jelly, for example.

Thinking Critically

1. **Analyze** Why has the new barter grown, and how does it differ from barter in the past?
2. **Discuss** What effect do you think the expansion of commercial barter will have on society in the United States? Explain your answer.

Groups Within Society

Before You Read

Main Idea
Groups are the foundation of social life and they differ in terms of size, organization, and purpose. Groups also perform many important functions in society.

Reading Focus
1. How do sociologists define the term *group?*
2. What types of groups do sociologists recognize?
3. What are the main functions of groups?

Vocabulary
dyad
triad
formal group
informal group
primary group
secondary group
reference group
in-group
out-group
electronic community
social network
leaders

TAKING NOTES Use a graphic organizer like this one to take notes on the different types of groups.

Group Type	Characteristics

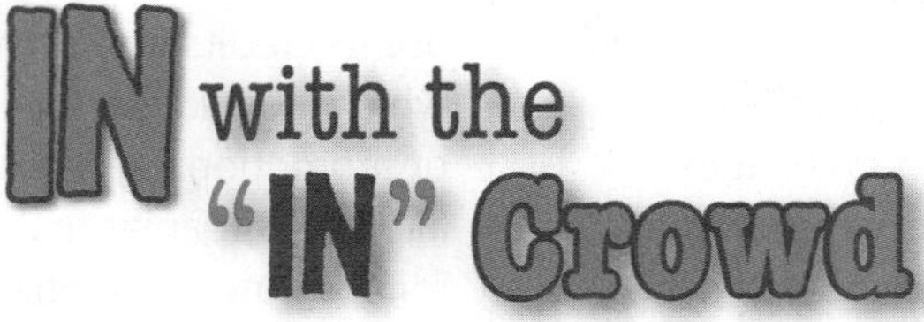

SOCIOLOGY CLOSE UP ***In which group do you belong?*** Alex is a Drama Guy, a member of the high school Theater Club. It's a pretty exclusive group—just 25 students out of a school population of about 1,500. The label "drama guy" was given to Alex by one of his classmates. It was intended as a put-down, but Alex and the other Theater Club members—even the girls—seized on it. They now wear it with pride, emblazoned on the back of the bright red T-shirts that they've adopted as their "uniform." The Drama Guys have other ways to let the world know who they are. When they meet, for example, they loudly greet each other with the words, "Well met, friend."

Alex spends most of his time with the Drama Guys. When not in class, they usually gather at the "Backlot Upstairs," a rehearsal room on the top floor of the main school building. Outside of school, they meet at Danny's Deli. There, they occupy the booths in the back room, making it clear by their behavior that outsiders are not welcome. Of course, the Drama Guys—just like the girls in this cartoon—think they are cool and that just about everyone else in school is not. However, they hold the greatest disdain for athletes. "I mean," Alex says, "some of those jocks think Shakespeare is a warm-up exercise for javelin throwers." ■

It's simple—you can't have an in-crowd unless you leave somebody out of it—without uncool, there is no cool. So basically, you're nothing without me. HA!
Streeter
Suzie would later win a Nobel Prize for her Theory of Special Social Relativity.

Sociologists would agree with this cartoon—you cannot have an in-group without setting boundaries to show who does not belong.

Defining Groups

Just like Alex, every individual in society participates in groups. In fact, sociologists such as David Orenstein consider "groups and group activities . . . the very foundation upon which social life is structured." A group can be very small—two people on a date, for example. Or it can be very large—500 soldiers at boot camp. A group can be very intimate, as in the case of the family. It can also be very formal, as in the case of sociologists attending an American Sociological Association conference.

In sociological terms, a group has four major features. First, it must consist of two or more people. Second, there must be interaction among members. If you exchange greetings with a friend in the hall at school, for example, interaction has taken place. As you recall, interaction occurs whenever the actions of one person cause another person or persons to act. Third, group members must have shared expectations. Fourth, the members of the group must possess some sense of common identity.

The last three features—interaction, shared expectations, and a common identity—distinguish a group from an aggregate or a social category. When people gather in the same place at the same time but lack organization or lasting patterns of interaction, they form an aggregate. Passengers on an airplane, the crowd at a baseball game, or people standing in a ticket line at the movies are examples of aggregates. In the case of social categories, it is not necessary for people to interact in any way. A social category is simply a means of classifying people according to a shared trait or a common status. Students, women, teenagers, and left-handed people are examples of social categories.

Size All groups are not the same. Obviously, they can differ in size. While some groups are very small, other groups are enormous. The smallest group possible, a group with two members, is called a **dyad.** In a dyad each member of the group has direct control over the group's existence. If one member leaves the group, the group ends. Consequently, decision making in a dyad can be difficult. If the two members fail to agree, one member must convince the other to change his or her position or the group may cease to exist.

QUICK FACTS

GROUP SIZE AND RELATIONSHIPS

Group size has a huge impact on social interaction among group members. Adding one or two members can dramatically alter group dynamics.

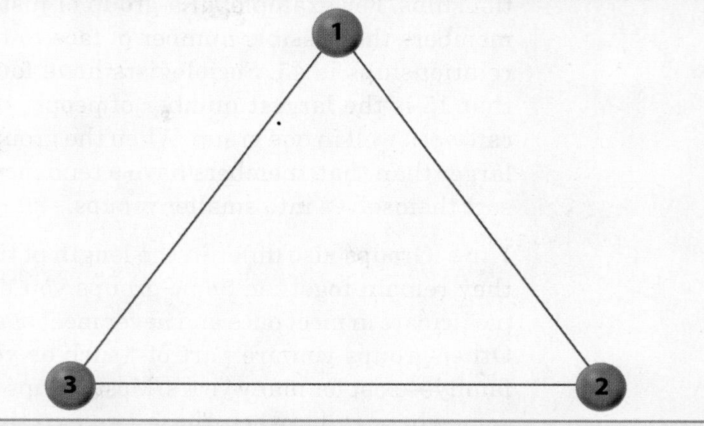

Group of 3
There are just three possible face-to-face relationships in a group with three members. Interaction tends to be personal and intimate.

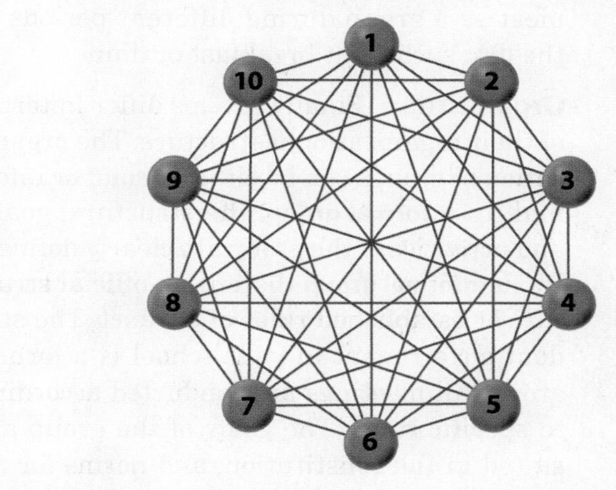

Group of 10
With a 10-member group, there are 45 possible face-to-face relationships. As a result, interaction is often less intense and intimate.

According to sociologist Georg Simmel, a major change occurs when group size increases from two to three members. With a three-person group, or **triad,** the group takes on a life of its own, independent of any individual member. No one person can disband the group. In addition, decision making in a triad is often easier than in a dyad, since two-against-one alliances can form in cases of disagreement.

How large can a small group be? Sociologists consider a small group one with few enough members that everyone is able to interact on a face-to-face basis. The more members, the greater the number of face-to-face relationships. For example, in a group of just 10 members the possible number of face-to-face relationships is 45. Sociologists have found that 15 is the largest number of people that can work well in one group. When the group is larger than that, members have a tendency to sort themselves into smaller groups.

Time Groups also differ in the length of time they remain together. Some groups you may participate in meet once and never meet again. Other groups you are part of—such as your family—exist for many years. Most groups fall somewhere in between these two extremes. However, regardless of the life of the group, interaction is not continuous. Few people spend 24 hours a day in a group setting, even with their families. Instead, family members meet as a group during different periods of the day, such as at breakfast or dinner.

Organization Finally, groups differ in terms of their organizational structure. The organization of groups can be either formal or informal. In a **formal group,** the structure, goals, and activities of the group are clearly defined. In an **informal group** there is no official structure or established rules of conduct. The student government in your school is a formal group. All meetings are conducted according to specific rules. The goals of the group are stated in the constitution, and norms for all occasions are listed in the bylaws. Your circle of friends would be an example of an informal group, because you do not have rules or structure for meetings.

Reading Check **Identify Supporting Details** In what ways do groups differ?

Types of Groups

We all are members of different types of groups. The most common types of groups recognized by sociologists include primary groups, secondary groups, reference groups, in-groups, and out-groups. Since the development of the Internet, sociologists have noted the emergence of a new kind of group, electronic communities.

Primary and Secondary Groups One of the easiest ways to classify groups is according to the degree of intimacy that occurs among group members. Charles Horton Cooley used the term *primary group* to describe those involving the most intimate relationships. "By primary groups," Cooley said, "I mean those characterized by intimate face-to-face association and cooperation. They are primary in several senses, but chiefly in that they are fundamental in forming the social nature and ideals of the individual."

A **primary group** is a small group of people who interact over a relatively long period of time on a direct and personal basis. In primary-group relationships the entire self of the individual is taken into account. The relationships are intimate and often face-to-face. Communication is deep and intense, and the structure is informal. Family relationships are probably the most common primary relationships.

Against this, Cooley contrasted secondary groups. A **secondary group** is a group in which interaction is impersonal and temporary in nature. Examples of secondary groups include a classroom, a factory, and a political party.

Secondary-group relationships involve a reaction to only a part of the individual's self. Secondary-group relationships also tend to be casual and limited in personal involvement. The person's importance to the group lies in the function that he or she performs in the group. An individual can be replaced easily by anyone who can carry out the specific tasks needed to achieve the group's goals. This characteristic is particularly important because secondary groups are generally organized around specific goals.

Suppose, for example, you work at a cement factory. Your job involves loading cement into sacks. The factory management has little interest in your personality. Whether you attend religious services regularly and what you do with your leisure time is of little concern to them. They are interested only in your ability to load cement into the sacks. If you cannot handle the responsibilities of the job adequately, you will likely be replaced by someone else who can.

It is also possible for primary and secondary relationships to exist in the same group. Within most secondary groups to which you

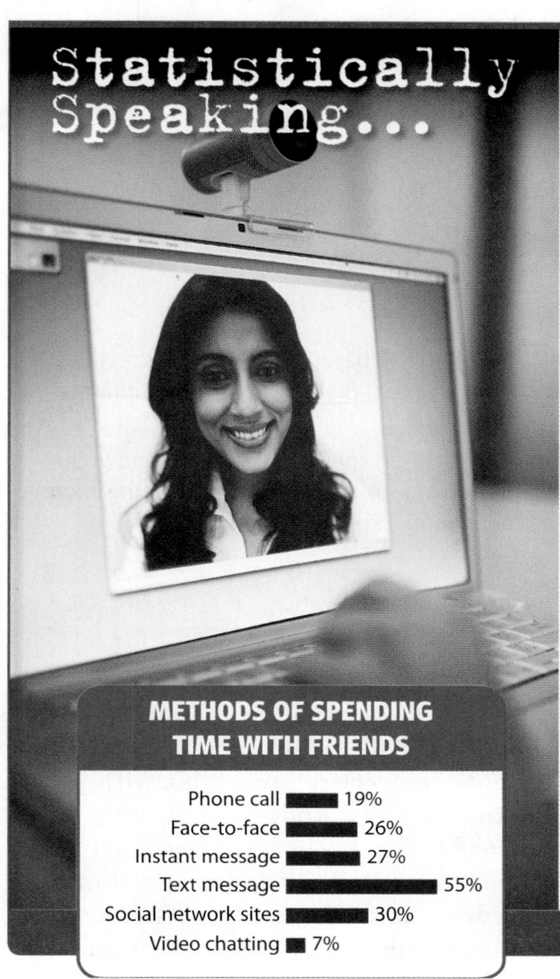

METHODS OF SPENDING TIME WITH FRIENDS

Phone call	19%
Face-to-face	26%
Instant message	27%
Text message	55%
Social network sites	30%
Video chatting	7%

Social Networking Web sites such as Facebook provide a virtual community where people can "gather." Members create their own online profile and "meet" using a host of communication methods, including voice, chat, instant message, and video. This mode of group interaction is growing in popularity among young Americans.

Social Media Sites Used Most Often by Teens:

41% Facebook

20% Instagram

11% Snapchat

6% Twitter

5% Google+

3% Tumblr

1% Vine

Skills Focus **INTERPRETING GRAPHS** What in the graph suggests that virtual communication encourages rather than discourages traditional forms of communication?

Sources: Pew Internet & American Life Project

belong, you occasionally develop primary relationships. These relationships provide you with the regular interaction and friendship lacking in the secondary group.

Reference Groups People usually perform their social roles and judge their own behaviors according to standards set by a particular group. They do not have to belong to this group. When people identify with the group's standards and attitudes, the group influences their behavior. Any group with whom individuals identify and whose attitudes and values they adopt is called a **reference group.**

Groups of friends or school clubs serve as reference groups for many students. Members of a particular occupation often serve as reference groups for adults. As children grow up or as adults adjust to changing social conditions, they often change their reference groups. The choice of reference groups is particularly important because groups can have both positive and negative effects on behavior.

In-Groups and Out-Groups All groups have boundaries—methods of distinguishing between members and nonmembers. When these boundaries are clearly marked, group members tend to think in terms of in-groups and out-groups. The group that a person belongs to and identifies with is an **in-group.** Any group that the person does not belong to or identify with is an **out-group.** Both primary and secondary groups can serve as in-groups and out-groups.

Most in-groups exhibit three basic characteristics. First, group members tend to separate themselves from other groups through the use of symbols. For example, groups often use badges, clothing, names, or slogans as forms of identification. Second, members view themselves positively and often view out-groups in negative terms. Finally, these feelings of superiority often lead in-groups to compete with out-groups. Usually, such competition is relatively peaceful. However, it can turn into conflict and violence.

Quick Lab

Tracking Groups

To which primary and secondary groups, in-groups and out-groups, and electronic communities do you belong? Find out by keeping track of your group activity.

Group	Group Type	Formal/Informal

PROCEDURE

1. Review the content on primary and secondary groups, in-groups and out-groups, and electronic communities.
2. Discuss the information with classmates and identify examples of the various group types at your school.
3. Track your group activity through the day, both at home and at school. Record your observations on a chart like the one to the right.

ANALYSIS

1. Review your results. Then based on their various features, place the groups on a continuum from formal to informal.
2. Compare your continuum with those of your classmates. Which groups most often appear at the formal end of the continuum? Which groups appear most often at the informal end of the continuum? Explain why this is so.

Electronic Communities Some sociologists have suggested that computer technology—most notably the Internet—has given rise to a new type of group. In an **electronic community,** people interact with one another regularly on the Internet. The earliest of these communities were based on Usenet, a system of Internet discussion groups called newsgroups. By the early 2000s, more sophisticated software enabled the creation of online communities such as Facebook, where members create personal profiles, share content, and interact with one another. Facebook, the most popular form of social media community, has been joined by many newer media-sharing applications, such as Instagram, Snapchat, Twitter, Tumblr, and Vine. Some members of these electronic communities exhibit behaviors similar to those of primary-group members in the "real world." They argue, engage in intellectual discussions, share intimate details of their lives, gossip, play games, and even flirt. The only difference is that they do it online rather than face-to-face.

CASE STUDY CONNECTION

Six Degrees of Separation "Small-world" studies look at connections among social networks, not among individuals.

Social Networks We all belong to more than one group and interact with more than one set of people, whether on the Internet or in the "real world." The web of relationships formed by the sum total of a person's interactions with other people is termed a **social network.** Social networks include both direct and indirect relationships. We have direct relationships with those whom we interact with in our primary and secondary group relationships. We have indirect relationships with people we know or who know us but with whom we have little or no interaction, such as the friends of a friend. This idea of distant connectedness is the basis of the "small-world" studies conducted by Stanley Milgram and Duncan Watts.

Unlike groups, social networks do not have clear boundaries and do not give rise to a common sense of identity. Yet they do provide us with a feeling of community and with opportunities for social interaction and career advancement. In some instances, knowing the "right" person can mean the difference between getting or not getting a job. Social networks also provide a support system that can help us through stressful periods.

Reading Check **Find the Main Idea** How do primary groups and secondary groups differ?

Group Functions

In order to exist, all groups must fulfill several basic functions. Groups must define their boundaries so that members can tell who belongs and who does not. To do this, groups use an array of methods, including symbols, such as uniforms or other styles of dress; gestures, such as hand signals or handshakes; and language.

Groups must also select **leaders**—people who influence the attitudes and opinions of others. In some cases leadership roles are assigned. For example, the board of directors of a corporation selects the company's chief executive officer. With other groups, individuals achieve leadership because of some ability, such as soccer skills or expertise at chess. Still other groups use elections to choose leaders. Members of many professional associations cast ballots to select their presidents.

Studies suggest that regardless of how they are selected, leaders fall into two categories. *Instrumental leaders* are task-oriented. They find specific means that will help the group reach its goals. *Expressive leaders,* on the other hand, are emotion-oriented. They find ways to keep the group together and to maintain morale. Groups need both kinds of leadership to be successful. An instrumental leader might develop a game plan for the football team to win a championship. At the same time, an expressive leader might use fight songs and chants to keep team spirits high in the days before the big game.

Groups also need to perform the related functions of setting goals, assigning tasks, and making decisions. If groups have no purpose, then there is no reason for them to exist. Therefore, groups set goals. The nature and scope of these goals varies from group to group. The goals for an informal group may be as simple as maintaining the group. Formal groups may have very large goals. For example, the American Sociological Association has a very broad goal—advancing sociology as a science and profession. In contrast, the goal of a National Football League team is fairly narrow in scope—to win the Super Bowl.

To achieve their goals, groups need to assign tasks to their members. Knowing what is being done, and who is doing it, helps strengthen members' support for the group. Setting goals and assigning tasks involves making decisions. Whatever a group's decisions, the methods of making them must be acceptable to members.

Finally, groups need to control their members' behavior. If members constantly violate group norms, the group cannot long survive. The group, therefore, needs to employ effective sanctions to ensure conformity to norms. Primary groups generally allow a greater level of nonconformity than do secondary groups. Interestingly, people tend to show a greater commitment to primary-group norms. This is because they place a high value on primary-group membership. In turn, members tend to belong to primary groups longer than secondary groups. Conformity is linked to the importance that people attach to a particular group.

ACADEMIC VOCABULARY

conformity behavior in accordance with accepted rules or conventions

Reading Check **Summarize** What types of leadership do groups need to be successful?

SECTION 4 Assessment

Reviewing Main Ideas and Vocabulary

1. **Identify** Give an example of a group, an aggregate, and a social category.
2. **Describe** What changes take place in a group when it moves from a dyad to a triad?
3. **Contrast** How do groups and social networks differ?
4. **Explain** What functions does a leader perform for a group?

Thinking Critically

5. **Make Generalizations** What roles do members play in primary groups and secondary groups?
6. **Elaborate** Why are reference groups important for an individual's social development? Illustrate your answer with examples.
7. **Summarize** Using your notes and a graphic organizer like the one below, describe the types of groups that sociologists recognize.

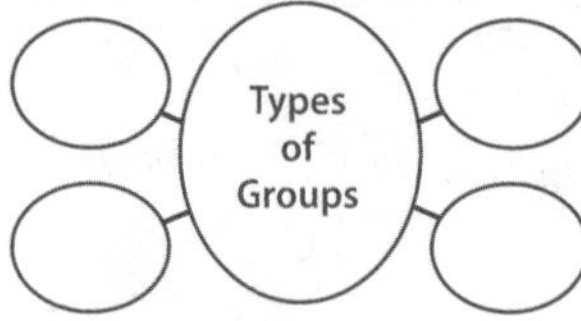

FOCUS ON WRITING

8. **Descriptive** Select a formal and an informal group to which you belong. Write two paragraphs comparing the ways leaders might help you fulfill each group's goals. In writing your paragraphs, consider the methods instrumental leaders and expressive leaders might use.

SECTION 5

The Structure of Formal Organizations

Before You Read

Main Idea
Formal organizations are complex secondary groups created to achieve specific goals. Most are structured as bureaucracies. Formal and informal structures can affect the efficiency of bureaucracies.

Reading Focus

1. How do sociologists view formal organizations?
2. What are the main characteristics of Max Weber's model of bureaucracies?
3. What types of relationships are found in formal organizations?
4. What problems do bureaucracies face?

Vocabulary
formal organization
bureaucracy
rationality
voluntary association
alienation
iron law of oligarchy

TAKING NOTES Use a graphic organizer like this one to take notes on the major characteristics of bureaucracy.

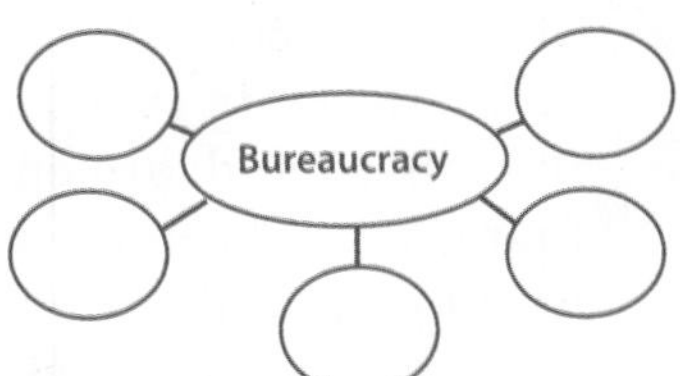

Passing the TEST

To get a job with the Chinese government, applicants had to take a state exam. Many exam questions focused on the ideas of the philosopher Confucius.

SOCIOLOGY CLOSE UP ***How did people get jobs in the Chinese bureaucracy?*** The Han dynasty, which ruled China from about 200 B.C. to A.D. 200, oversaw a massive empire that covered more than 1.5 million square miles. Han emperors established a bureaucracy some 130,000 strong to govern this empire. Most Han emperors filled the ranks of the bureaucracy with their loyal followers. Emperor Wudi, who ruled from 141 to 87 B.C., came up with another way to fill these government positions. Applicants would take a state exam that tested their knowledge of the teachings of Confucius, a philosopher who had lived in the fifth century B.C.

Wudi surrounded himself with Confucian scholars and listened carefully to their advice. They told him Confucius had taught that gentlemen should practice "reverence, generosity, truthfulness, diligence, and kindness." Wudi thought that all his government officials should have these qualities. So he set up schools where applicants could study Confucius's works and other important subjects. They then took state exams in history, law, poetry, and Confucianism. The exams were tough and very stressful. Some lasted all day and required memorizing whole books. The few who passed—about 2 percent of applicants—went on to a career in government. This idea that there are specific qualifications for jobs and positions are awarded based on education and testing is still followed by bureaucracies today. ■

Formal Organizations

Sociologists use the term **formal organization** to describe a large, complex secondary group that has been established to achieve specific goals. Formal organizations include a variety of groups such as schools, businesses, government agencies, religious organizations, youth organizations, political organizations, volunteer associations, labor unions, and professional associations.

Most formal organizations are structured in a form that is known as a bureaucracy. A **bureaucracy** is a ranked authority structure that operates according to specific rules and procedures. Bureaucracies existed in ancient times in Mesopotamia, Egypt, China, and Rome. However, they rose to prominence during the Industrial Revolution.

Industrialization is part of the process that sociologists refer to as the rationalization of society. **Rationality** involves subjecting every feature of human behavior to calculation, measurement, and control. Bureaucracies were created to rationally organize groups to complete a set of goals. Today we use the word *bureaucracy* to refer to any organization that has many departments, or bureaus. If you have ever applied for a driver's license, registered to vote, or been admitted to a large hospital, you have dealt with a bureaucracy.

Reading Check **Find the Main Idea** What is the relationship between a formal organization and a bureaucracy?

Weber's Model of Bureaucracies

The German sociologist Max Weber developed a theoretical model of bureaucracies that is still widely used by sociologists today. According to Weber's model, bureaucracies, whether they are designed to run a school, a hospital, or a business, have the following five characteristics:

- **Division of labor** Work is divided among specialists in various positions. Each specialist is expected to perform specific duties.
- **Ranking of authority** There are clear-cut lines of responsibility, and each individual is responsible to a supervisor at a higher level.
- **Employment based on formal qualifications** Specific qualifications are required for each job, and individuals are hired on the basis of tests, education, or previous experience. Also, in a bureaucracy, the job—not the jobholder—is important. Therefore, everyone from an entry-level worker to the chief executive is replaceable.
- **Written rules and regulations** There are objective rules, regulations, and routine procedures that identify the exact responsibilities and authority of each person on the staff. Established rules, regulations, and procedures also protect workers from arbitrary dismissal.
- **Specific lines of promotion and advancement** It is assumed that employees expect a career with the organization. Thus, there are clear-cut lines of promotion and advancement. Among the rewards for remaining with the organization are job security and seniority.

The chart on the next page shows the bureaucratic organization of a large school system. Notice how the job titles represent specific duties. Also, notice that lines of authority and responsibility are clearly indicated. All members of the organization, then, know what they should be doing and to whom they should report.

Remember that Weber's model of bureaucracy is an ideal type. In other words, it describes the essential characteristics of bureaucracies. The structures of formal organizations conform to the model to varying degrees. Many governmental agencies and large business corporations fit these characteristics very rigidly. Some other organizations—voluntary associations, for example—may be much less bureaucratic. Typically, a **voluntary association** is a nonprofit organization formed to pursue some common interest. As the name suggests, membership is voluntary. Many officeholders and workers are unpaid volunteers. Examples of voluntary associations include amateur sports teams, professional associations, service clubs, charities, and political interest groups.

Reading Check **Summarize** What are the five characteristics of bureaucracies?

Relationships in Formal Organizations

According to Weber's model, bureaucracies are formal, impersonal structures. However, informal structures based on strong primary relationships may exist within the most rigid bureaucracies, creating what sociologist Charles Page called "bureaucracy's other face." Sometimes, informal structures displace the formal. For example, the director of sales in a large corporation may play golf every weekend with the director of purchasing. Or, they may have gone to the same college and now attend the same religious services. The rules and regulations of the purchasing department are quite inflexible. However, because of their friendship, the director of purchasing waives the rules for the director of sales.

The importance of primary-group relationships within formal organizations was first noted in a research project at the Hawthorne, Illinois, plant of the Western Electric Company. The intended purpose of the study, conducted between 1927 and 1932, was to determine how various factors affected worker productivity.

As part of the research, sociologists Fritz Roethlisberger and W.J. Dickson studied

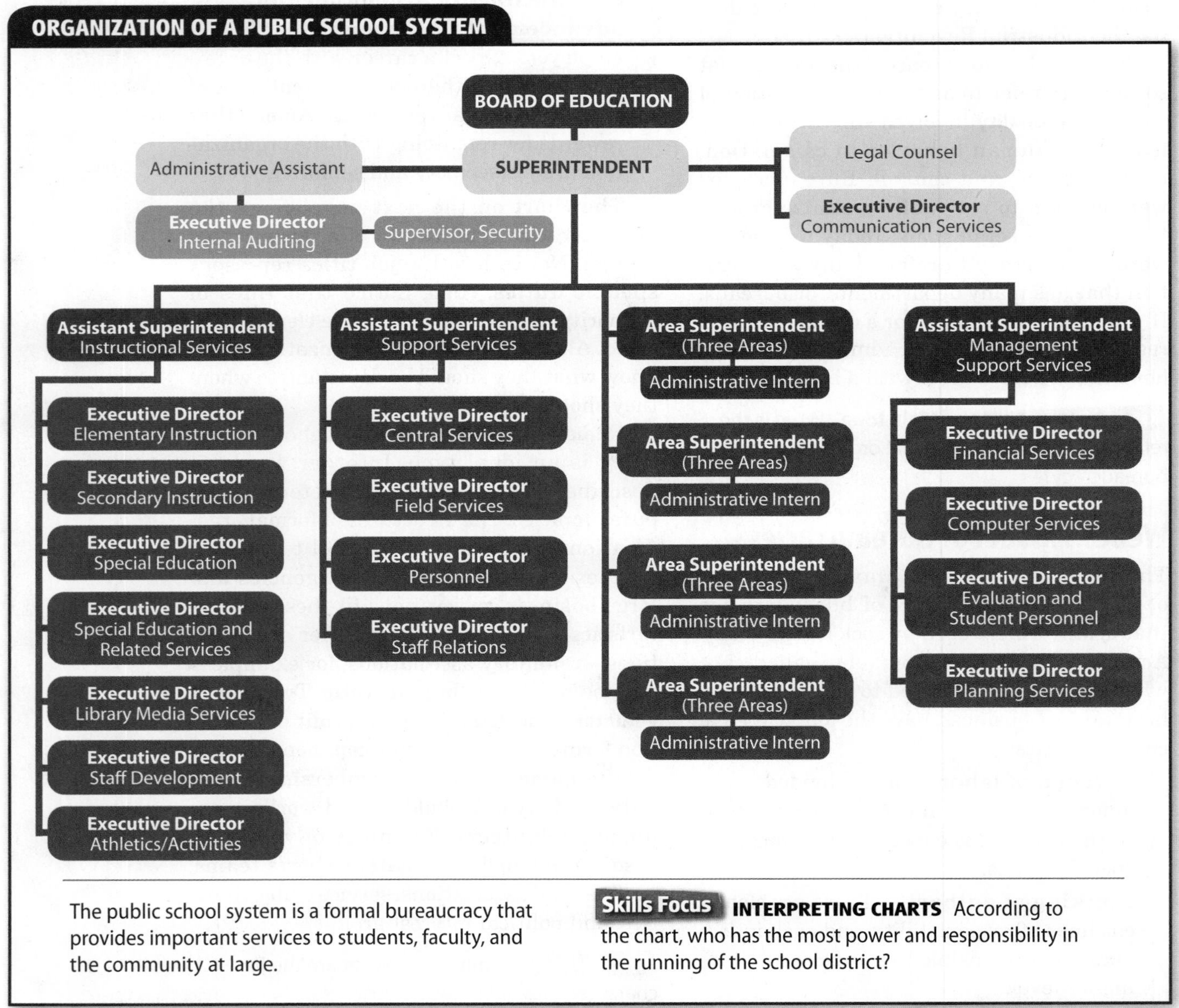

The public school system is a formal bureaucracy that provides important services to students, faculty, and the community at large.

Skills Focus **INTERPRETING CHARTS** According to the chart, who has the most power and responsibility in the running of the school district?

the interaction among a group of employees assigned the task of wiring telephone circuits. This task involved three worker roles: wirer, solderer, and inspector. The wirers connected the proper wires together. The solderers then sealed these connections with molten metal. Finally, the inspectors examined the completed circuits to make sure they met specifications. The company paid workers according to the number of circuits, or units, they completed.

Management assumed that each worker would try to complete as many units as possible in order to make more money. However, this was not the case. An informal structure developed among the workers. Together, they decided what the norms would be for a day's production. Workers who produced more were called rate-busters. Those who produced less were called chiselers. Workers who gave any information to a supervisor were called squealers. Conformity to the norms was enforced through a system of negative sanctions, such as ridicule, exclusion, and—occasionally—physical force. This informal structure operated independently of the formal structure of the organization and was far more important to the individual workers.

Reading Check **Analyze** What is "bureaucracy's other face?"

Problems of Bureaucracies

Some scholars have suggested that Weber's theoretical model views bureaucracies in a positive light, as the best method of coordinating large numbers of people to achieve large-scale goals. Weber also suggested that bureaucracies create order by clearly defining job tasks and rewards. Further, they also provide stability, since individuals come and go but the organization continues. However, this view is a rather broad overstatement of the effectiveness of bureaucracies. In reality, bureaucracies have several significant weaknesses as well.

One reason why actual bureaucracies are less effective is that they no longer fulfill their original goals. Sometimes, bureaucracies undergo a process called goal displacement, in which they abandon their original purpose in favor of another. Often, this new goal simply is self-continuation. For example, certain government agencies emphasize their need to exist, regardless of whether or not they continue to provide useful services. A study of the Environmental Protection Agency provides a striking illustration of this. Researchers found that officials' actions often favored survival of the agency over enforcement of environmental standards.

TECHNOLOGY FOCUS

The Impact of Telecommuting

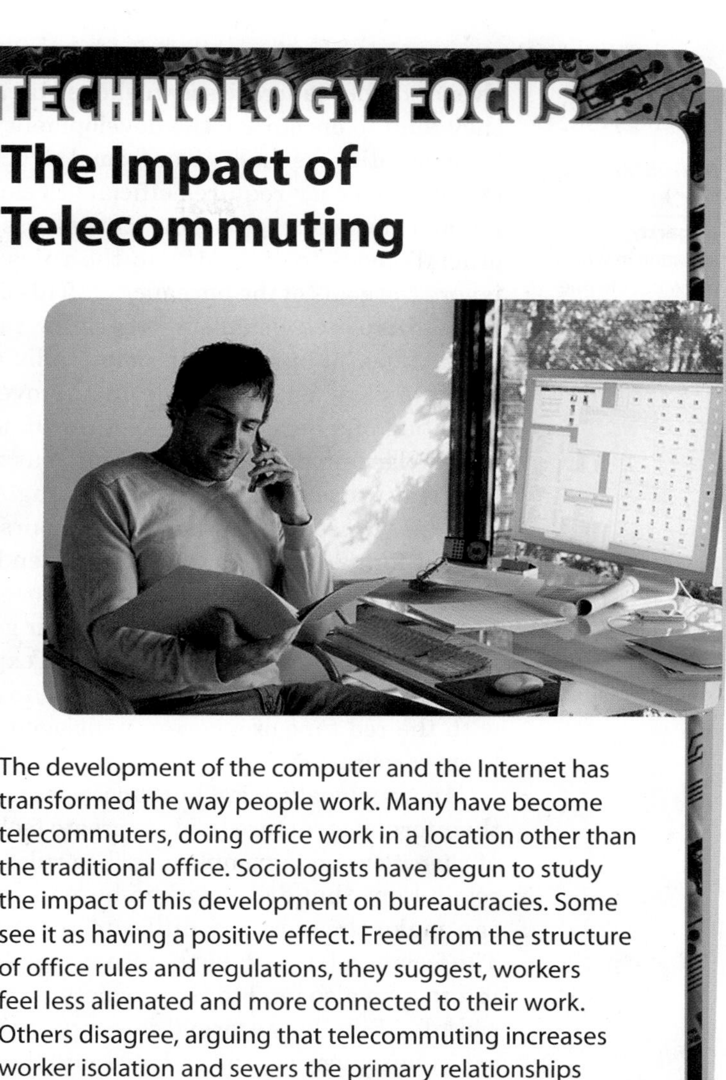

The development of the computer and the Internet has transformed the way people work. Many have become telecommuters, doing office work in a location other than the traditional office. Sociologists have begun to study the impact of this development on bureaucracies. Some see it as having a positive effect. Freed from the structure of office rules and regulations, they suggest, workers feel less alienated and more connected to their work. Others disagree, arguing that telecommuting increases worker isolation and severs the primary relationships that make office life bearable. Further, they charge, many telecommuters fear that their absence from the office will adversely affect their chances for promotion.

Thinking Critically

Support a Position Is telecommuting a positive development or a negative development for bureaucracies? Why?

ACADEMIC VOCABULARY

oligarchy situation in which a few people rule the many

Sociologists have suggested that the effectiveness of bureaucracies is weakened because they tend to encourage the development of a bureaucratic personality. The formal structure of a bureaucracy requires officials to closely follow rules and regulations. However, some officials focus too intently on the rules and ignore the goals of the bureaucracy. This often leads to a related weakness—the proliferation of "red tape," or bureaucratic delay. Individual officials play a limited role in the overall operation of a bureaucracy. As a result, their knowledge and power is often limited as well. This may cause people to become entangled in red tape. Consequently, they spend hours filling out forms, standing in seemingly endless lines, or being shuffled from one department to another before they accomplish their goals. You probably know stories or have had experiences about how frustrating it can be to deal with the red tape of a government agency or large corporation.

Another weakness of bureaucracies is that their formal structure tends to create feelings of **alienation** among employees. The rules and regulations that drive work in bureaucracies can make the workday dull and repetitive. The formal relationships that frame employee interaction also tend to strip variety from the workday. Finally, the formal career paths typical in bureaucracies often leave middle- and lower-level employees with little chance of advancement. As a result, employees feel disconnected from their work and the workplace, which they see as cold and uncaring.

A final weakness of bureaucracies concerns their tendency to result in oligarchies. In bureaucracies, power tends to concentrate in the hands of a few people at the top. These people then use their position to promote their own interests over the interests of the organization. Sociologist Robert Michels called this tendency of organizations to become increasingly dominated by small groups of people the **iron law of oligarchy.**

Some critiques of bureaucratic effectiveness have made their point through humor. In his book *The Peter Principle,* Laurence J. Peter suggested that employees in a bureaucracy often are promoted to positions for which they have little ability. Bureaucracies are able to function, he added, only because not all officials have been promoted to their "level of incompetence." Parkinson's Law is another humorous criticism of bureaucracies. C. Northcote Parkinson argued that "work expands to fill the time available for its completion." Bureaucrats with "full" work days hire subordinates to assist them. In time, these subordinates find that their work days are full and request that subordinates be hired to assist them!

Reading Check **Draw Conclusions** How does goal displacement affect bureaucracies?

SECTION 5 Assessment

Reviewing Main Ideas and Vocabulary

1. **Summarize** What is the relationship between a formal organization and a bureaucracy?
2. **Identify** Define and give an example of a voluntary organization.
3. **Explain** How does the formal structure of bureaucracies create feelings of alienation?
4. **Define** What is the iron law of oligarchy?

Thinking Critically

5. **Evaluate** Is Max Weber's model of bureaucracies an effective analytic tool? Why or why not?
6. **Elaborate** How effective are bureaucracies?
7. **Summarize** Using your notes and a graphic organizer like the one below, apply Weber's bureaucracy model to an organization you are familiar with. Note how well your chosen organization corresponds to Weber's five characteristics.

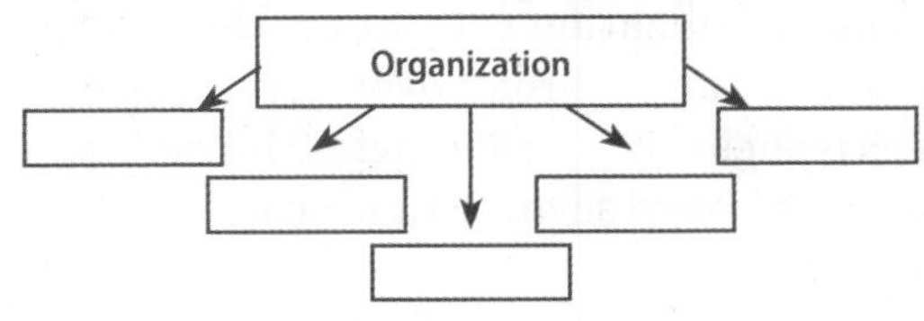

FOCUS ON WRITING

8. **Expository** Write a short essay on whether formal structure or informal structure has a greater effect on bureaucratic operations. In writing your essay, consider the primary group relationships that may develop in bureaucracies and the weaknesses created by the formal structure of bureaucracies.

CURRENT RESEARCH IN SOCIOLOGY

The McDonaldization of Society

In his discussion of bureaucracies, Max Weber suggested that as society progressed it would become more and more rational. In other words, social life would be increasingly guided by rules, regulations, and formal structures. The sociologist George Ritzer (1993, 2014) recognizes Weber's prediction of increasing rationality in a process he calls *McDonaldization*. Today's rational systems, Ritzer suggests, essentially follow the characteristics of the fast-food restaurant, McDonald's.

The fast-food model, Ritzer states, has permeated practically every aspect of social life—so much so that the United States is rapidly becoming "McAmerica." Ritzer sees four prongs to the McDonaldization process: efficiency, calculability, predictability, and control.

Efficiency McDonald's operations, Ritzer says, are efficient. The company has made rational calculations to find "the optimum method for getting from one point to another." McDonaldization requires that every step in the production process is carefully planned to ensure speed with the minimum cost and effort.

Calculability In the McDonald's system, measurement of outcomes is based on quantity rather than quality. The size and cost of the product and the speed of delivery are emphasized. Similarly, workers are judged not on how well they do their jobs, but how quickly. With McDonaldization, Ritzer concludes, quantity becomes the equivalent of quality.

Predictability With predictability, customers are guaranteed a uniform product, regardless of where or when they buy. The setting where purchases are made is predictable, too, right down to the greeting customers receive when they enter. With McDonaldization there are no surprises.

Control McDonaldization requires that the behavior of both workers and customers is tightly controlled. Workers are trained to do their tasks in a precise way, and supervisors monitor them closely to ensure that they are following correct procedures. Customers' behavior is influenced by their interaction with workers and the surroundings. With the fast-food restaurant, Ritzer says, that behavior is "eat quickly and leave."

Obviously, there are some benefits to McDonaldization. Transactions, whether they involve buying burgers or health care, are convenient and familiar. However, there are drawbacks, too. Predictability removes the human aspect from the equation, so there is no room for innovation. Also, efficiency and control often call for machines to replace human labor, which greatly reduces face-to-face interaction.

Social life, George Ritzer suggests, has begun to resemble drive-through food service—predictable and efficient but impersonal.

Thinking Critically

1. **Explain** What are the costs and benefits of McDonaldization?
2. **Discuss** How is a large suburban shopping mall an example of McDonaldization?

Are You In or Are You Out?

What makes a group an in-group or an out-group?

Reading and Activity Workbook
Use the workbook to complete this simulation.

1. Introduction

In this simulation, you will work in small groups to explore the symbiotic relationship between in-groups and out-groups. You will identify in-groups and out-groups to simulate, define the groups' boundaries, and perform a simulation with a companion group. After simulations have been completed, groups will describe and explain the boundaries they established. Finally, groups will come together as a class to discuss and evaluate the activity. To complete this activity, follow the steps below.

- As a class, hold a brainstorming session to identify and list on the board the various in-groups and out-groups in your high school.
- Following your teacher's instructions, organize the class into an even number of groups. At the start of the activity, groups will pair off and select from the list on the board an in-group and an opposing out-group to simulate. Once this decision has been made, each group will go back to working alone.

2. Setting Group Boundaries

Each group will come up with its own boundaries—the characteristics that identify members and set the boundary for those outside the group. These might include:

- form of greeting (spoken and nonspoken)
- style of clothing and hairstyle
- other symbols, such as badges
- language/slang
- location—a place that your group considers its own
- personal space boundaries/eye contact
- form of closure/good-bye (spoken and nonspoken)

Groups should brainstorm ideas for each boundary, noting them in a chart like that on the next page. Groups should refer to the chart when making their final decisions on boundaries.

- Group members must decide unanimously on how they are going to carry out these boundaries in the simulation and how they will be presented to the class. The boundaries will be written down and illustrated for presentation to the class later. At this stage you should create any props you need to act out and demonstrate your boundaries.
- Each group should select someone to perform the following tasks:
  - a moderator to keep everyone on task
  - a secretary to record information and put the group's boundaries into writing
  - an artist to illustrate the boundaries on the poster and give directions on making props for the simulation/presentation
  - a director to guide the acting out of the boundaries
  - a presenter to present the group's boundaries to the class

Once all groups have assigned roles and completed their boundaries, the simulations can begin. Groups should pair off as they did at the beginning of the activity.

3. Simulation and Presentation

Pairs of groups should perform their simulations. Then each group should present and explain their boundaries to the class.

- During the simulation, proceed through all your group's boundaries. While the in-group/out-group relationship is one of opposition, antagonism, and competition, silence should be the sole means of simulating this. Exceptions would be if your language/slang, greeting, or good-bye requires a spoken word. No disrespectful or antagonistic behavior should be simulated.
- During the presentation, each group will present their boundaries and explain the importance and meanings behind them. Other groups will have the opportunity to comment on how they might have misinterpreted the boundaries of the presenting group.

4. Discussion and Evaluation

What did you learn from this simulation? Hold a group discussion that focuses on the following questions.

- If you could describe this role-play simulation in one word, what word would you use?
- Did not being able to speak with the opposing group lead to more or less competition and/or conflict? How do you think being able to speak with the opposing group would affect the relationship between the two groups?
- Which of the boundaries was the hardest to convey without speaking? How did not being able to speak affect what you experienced?
- Which boundaries did you feel were most important to get across to your opposing group?
- Is it inevitable that in-groups and out-groups will form? Why or why not?
- What advantage is there to having in-groups and out-groups?
- How easily are the boundaries set by these groups overcome? Is it easier to cross the boundaries of an in-group or an out-group?
- How do your experiences from the simulation illustrate issues from our past? How do your experiences from the simulation illustrate current issues?
- Consider the effect of global communication and computer technology on in-groups and out-groups. Do you think technological advances will strengthen or weaken the boundaries set by in-groups and out-groups? Can you think of examples you have personally experienced to illustrate and support your answer?

SETTING GROUP BOUNDARIES

Greetings/Good-byes	Clothing/Hairstyles	Other Symbols	Language	Personal Space	Location

CHAPTER 3 Review

Comprehension and Critical Thinking

SECTION 1 *(pp. 54–57)*

1. a. **Identify Main Ideas** How do a person's statuses differ from his or her roles?
   b. **Explain** Identify three sets of reciprocal roles not mentioned in the chapter. Explain how the roles in each set are reciprocal.
   c. **Elaborate** Identify an example of role conflict not mentioned in the chapter. How might an individual resolve such a conflict?

SECTION 2 *(pp. 58–61)*

2. a. **Identify Main Ideas** What are the five most common forms of interaction recognized by sociologists?
   b. **Elaborate** List several examples of interaction you have had with other people. How might an exchange theorist interpret these interactions?

SECTION 3 *(pp. 62–66)*

3. a. **Describe** Identify and describe the three broad categories of societies used by sociologists.
   b. **Contrast** How do the six types of societies discussed in the chapter differ in terms of social structure?

SECTION 4 *(pp. 68–73)*

4. a. **Recall** What, according to sociologist David Orenstein, is the importance of groups?
   b. **Contrast** How does interaction among group members differ between primary and secondary groups?
   c. **Elaborate** How have your group memberships changed from your time in elementary school to today? Why do you think these changes have taken place?

SECTION 5 *(pp. 74–78)*

5. a. **Identify** What, according to Max Weber's theoretical model, are the major characteristics of bureaucracies?
   b. **Support a Position** Which of the criticisms of bureaucracies outlined in the chapter do you think has the greatest impact on bureaucratic effectiveness? Give reasons for your answer.

Reviewing Vocabulary

Identify the term from the chapter that best fits each of the following descriptions.

6. the network of interrelated statuses and roles that guide human interaction
7. plays the greatest role in shaping a person's life and determining his or her social identity
8. situation where people interact in an effort to receive a reward or a return for their actions
9. the state of balance between cooperation and conflict
10. a society that relies on domesticated herd animals to meet its food needs
11. a society in which much of the economy is involved in providing information and services
12. a group whose members interact over a relatively long period of time on a direct and personal basis
13. a group in which interaction is impersonal and temporary in nature
14. a large, complex group that has been established to achieve specific goals
15. a situation in which a few people rule the many

INTERNET ACTIVITY

16. Select a group with strong self-identity, such as a branch of the military or a religious order. Use the Internet to research the methods members of your selected group use to separate themselves from members of out-groups. Present your findings in a brief essay.

Sociology in Your Life

17. In a group with two or three classmates, brainstorm instances when you have used the forms of accommodation in settling a conflict with a family member or a friend. Select one of these instances and create a skit to show the original conflict and how accommodation was reached. Perform the skit for the rest of the class.

Skills Activity: Interpreting Primary Sources

In the following excerpt, Terrence E. Deal and Allan A. Kennedy describe the cultural network of a typical corporation. Study the excerpt and answer the questions that follow.

> "Everyone in a strong culture has a job—but he also has another job. This 'other job' won't get stamped on a business card, but that doesn't matter. In many ways this work is far more important than budgets, memos, policies, and five-year plans. Spies, storytellers, priests, whisperers, cabals—these people form the *hidden hierarchy* which looks considerably different from the organization chart. In the hidden hierarchy, a lowly junior employee doubles as a highly influential spy. Or an 'unproductive' senior manager gets the best office in the building, precisely because he does little but tells good stories—an ability that makes him tremendously valuable in a corporation as an interpreter of events. As consultants, we've found that these 'other jobs' are critical to the effective management of any successful organization. They make up what we call the cultural network.
>
> This network is actually the primary means of communication within the organization; it ties together all parts of the company without respect to positions or titles. The network is important because it not only transmits information but also interprets the significance of the information for employees . . . The real business goes on in the cultural network."
>
> —Deal, Terrence E., and Allan A. Kennedy, *Corporate Cultures: The Rites and Rituals of Corporate Life.* (Da Capo Press, 2000).

18. Identify What is the hidden hierarchy of an organization?

19. Analyze What function does a cultural network serve?

20. Make Judgments Do the authors think formal structure or informal structure is more important to the functioning of an organization? Support your answer with the information from the excerpt.

Writing for Sociology

Use your knowledge of formal organizations to answer the question below. Do not simply list facts. Present a clear argument based on your critical analysis of the question, using appropriate sociological terminology.

21. Write journal entries on daily life in the three broad categories of society below. Include information on subsistence strategies and social structure.

- Preindustrial societies
- Industrial societies
- Postindustrial societies

Connecting Online

Go online for review and enrichment activities related to this chapter.

KEY TOPICS VIDEOS
View compelling clips on issues in the field.

KEEP IT CURRENT
Link to the Current Events site for regularly updated stories on sociology as well as other social studies topics.

QUICK LAB
Reinforce a key concept with a short lab activity.

World Cultures

Sociologists have a rich source of material for their studies—the great diversity of world cultures. Our world is home to an incredible variety of cultures, social systems, and ways of life. Language and religion, two of the most basic building blocks of culture, are both extremely varied and complex, both between and within societies. Other components of culture, such as technology, symbols, norms, and values, add to the diversity of world cultures.

WAYS OF LIFE

How do ways of life vary around the world?

Think about your lifestyle for a minute. Your lifestyle includes just about everything you do—what you eat, what you wear, how you talk, where you travel, and what you like to do for fun. So your lifestyle says a lot about who you are and the society and culture that you are a part of. Now think about the lifestyle of the person in the photograph below. How do you think his way of life is different from yours? How might it be the same? What might his lifestyle indicate about his culture and society? The world is filled with an incredible richness of cultures and ways of life, and while societies around the world have much in common, each is also unique.

LANGUAGES

What languages do most people speak?

Language is the vehicle for our expression of thoughts, ideas, and beliefs. As such, it is one of the most fundamental human and cultural characteristics. And the diversity of the world's languages is reflected in the diversity of its cultures. The language in the world with the most native speakers is Chinese (Mandarin), with more than 950 million. Spanish and English are next, with 405 million and 360 million native speakers, respectively. In addition to these major world languages, thousands of other languages are spoken around the world. However, that number is rapidly declining as the world's smaller languages disappear.

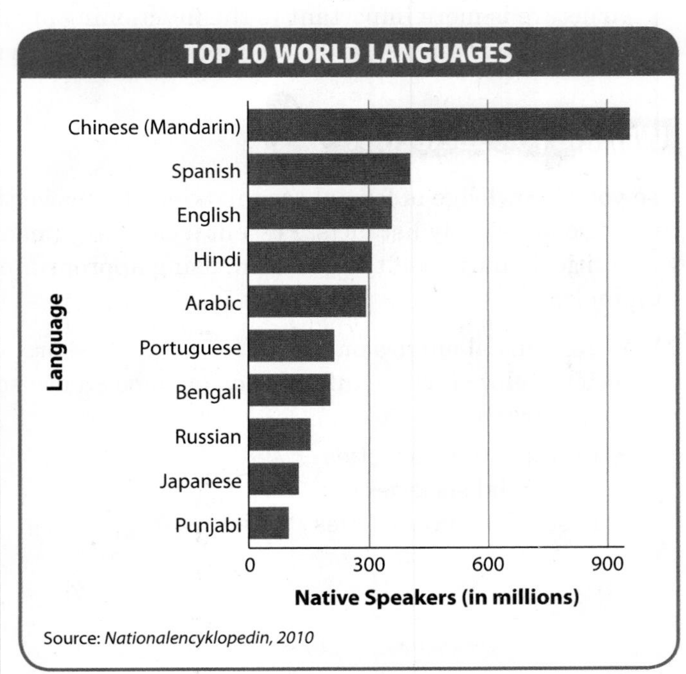

Source: *Nationalencyklopedin, 2010*

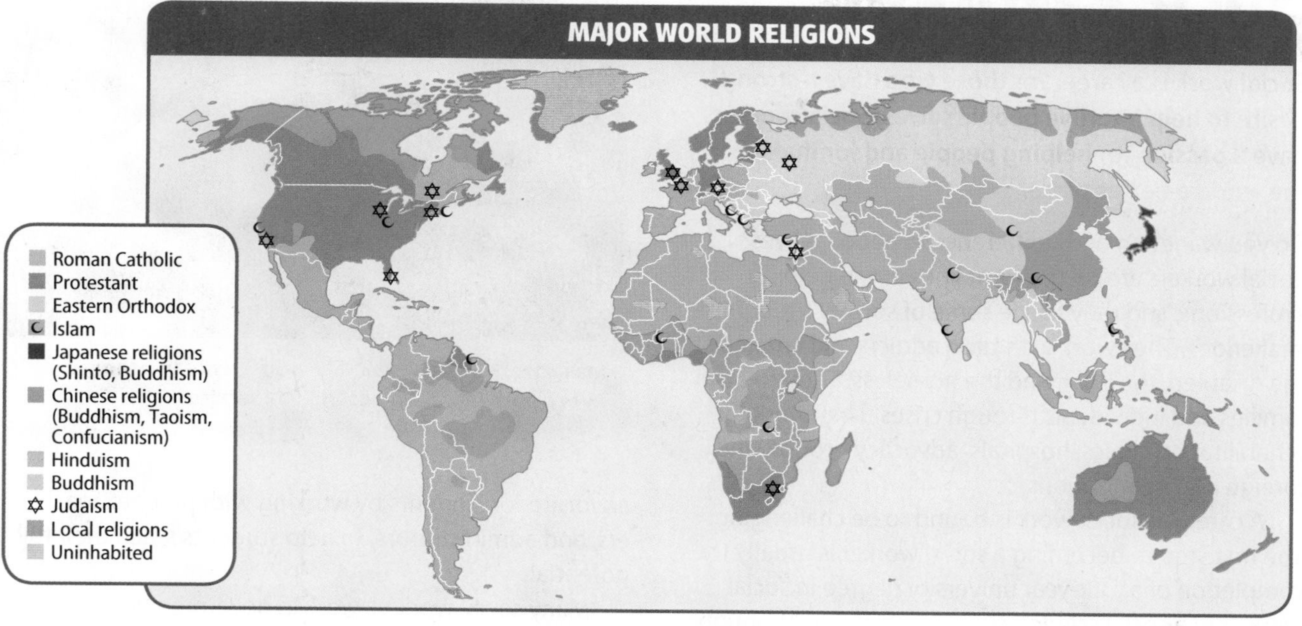

RELIGIONS

What are some of the world's major religions?

Like languages, the religions of the world are extremely varied and complex. The major religions, both in numbers of followers and in area, are Christianity and Islam. As you can see on the map, Christianity (including Roman Catholic, Protestant, and Eastern Orthodox) is the main religion in most of the Americas, Europe, and Russia, while Islam is the main religion in most of North Africa, the Middle East, and Central Asia. Other major world religions include Hinduism, Buddhism, and Judaism. It is important to keep in mind, however, that the map above represents a huge generalization—it shows only the major or dominant religion in an area, but there is often great religious diversity within any one place. For example, consider the United States. As the map shows, most people in the United States are Protestants, but there are hundreds of different Christian denominations in the country. In addition, there are followers of many other religions in the United States; they just are not in the majority. As you can see, the religious makeup of the world's cultures is extremely complex, both across and within societies.

THINKING LIKE A SOCIOLOGIST

How do other aspects of culture vary around the world?

In addition to ways of life, languages, and religions, many other components of culture vary from place to place. Select two different countries and one of the components of culture listed below.

1. Music
2. Dance
3. Literature
4. Architecture
5. Art

Research how your chosen component of culture is both similar and different in the two countries you have chosen. Be sure to find out what the component's major characteristics are, how it is used and valued in each society, and and how it reflects each society's culture and way of life. When you are done, write a short report that summarizes your findings.

CAREERS IN SOCIOLOGY

Social Worker

Social workers strive to make a difference in people's lives by providing counseling and services.

Social work is a career for those who have a strong desire to help improve people's lives. Social workers have a passion for helping people and for making the world a better place.

Do you want to make a difference in people's lives? Social workers are on the front lines of the helping professions, and they tackle some of society's toughest challenges. They work with drug addicts and criminals, the disabled, the poor, and the homeless. They counsel families and individuals through crises. They work for rehabilitation clinics, hospitals, advocacy groups, and foreign aid organizations.

A career in social work is bound to be challenging. The first step to becoming a social worker is usually the completion of a four-year university degree in social work or in a social science, such as sociology. Although a bachelor's degree is sufficient for entry into the field, a master's degree in social work (MSW) has become standard for most positions.

Many social workers specialize in serving the needs of a particular segment of the population or in working in a particular setting. For example, child, family, and school social workers provide services to improve the psychological health and social functioning of children and adults. Services they may provide include assisting single parents, arranging adoptions, helping parents find jobs, or locating foster homes for neglected or abused children. Others specialize in supporting the needs of senior citizens. School social workers often provide a bridge between home and school. They advocate for students by working with parents, teachers, and administrators, to help students reach their full potential.

Many social workers work in governmental agencies, treatment centers, and hospitals to improve people's psychological and physical health. Medical and public health social workers often help people and their loved ones cope with the effects of chronic, acute, or terminal illnesses, such as cancer and AIDS. Those who specialize in mental health and substance abuse assess and treat people who experience mental illness or problems with drug and alcohol addiction.

Social workers also work as administrators, planners, and policymakers to develop social programs aimed at combating child abuse, homelessness, drug addiction, poverty, or violence. Still others choose to obtain doctorates in social work to teach and research at the college or university level.

Applying ASA Style

Many social workers publish articles in professional journals. In keeping with the guidelines from the **American Sociological Association (ASA)**, these articles follow a similar style for citing electronic resources (e-resources). The papers you write for your sociology class should follow these guidelines, too.

The ASA provides direction for citing the most common types of e-resources used by sociologists. The first type includes journal articles, periodicals, reports, and books published on the Internet. The second type includes other Internet sources, such as Web sites and blogs. Lastly, the ASA provides guidelines for other forms of media, such as DVDs and CD-ROMs.

Through Think Central you can access the ASA Quick Style Guide for more information on using e-resources. Review the ASA guidelines that you find at the Web site. Then practice writing a citation for each type of e-resource listed below.

E-Resource	Example
Article	
Book	
Web Site	
DVD	

UNIT 2 The Individual in Society

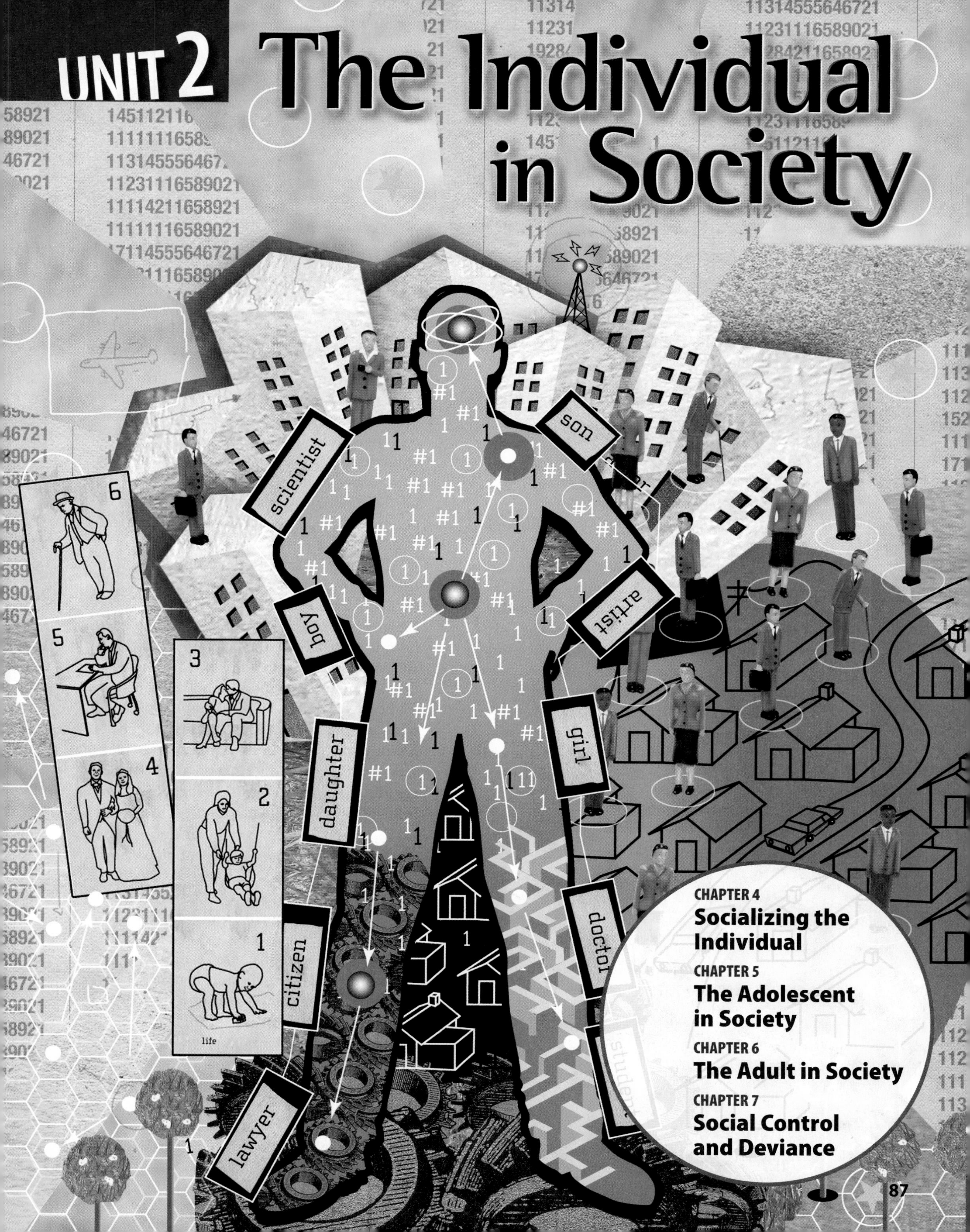

CASE STUDY

Identical Strangers

These photos show Paula Bernstein, left, and Elyse Schein, not long after they were adopted.

Identical twins Paula Bernstein and Elyse Schein met for the first time at age 35. Adopted as infants and raised in separate homes, neither knew about her twin sister. Then one day Schein, who had been searching for information about her birth mother, received a letter from the adoption agency informing her that she was the "younger" of twin girls born in October 1968.

Unbeknownst to them, the women had been part of a psychological study in the 1960s and 1970s that separated identical twins. In an effort to determine the influence of nature versus nurture, or heredity versus environment, researchers tracked the development of the study's participants. Although the adoptive parents were aware that the children were participating in some kind of scientific study, they were not informed of the study's true purpose. Shockingly, they were not told that the children had been separated from their twins.

At the time that Schein and Bernstein were born, the state of New York did not require adoption agencies to keep siblings together. Indeed, Viola Bernard, the psychiatric consultant for the adoption agency that placed Schein and Bernstein, supported a policy of separating twins. She believed that doing so allowed the children to establish their own personalities.

For psychiatrist Peter Neubauer, the adoption agency's policy presented an opportunity for a unique twin study. Scientists have used twin studies for decades in their efforts to determine the roles of heredity and environment in the development of personality, intelligence, and certain diseases. The studies continue to be a valuable research tool. However, a study like Neubauer's would be considered unethical today. Modern guidelines regulate behavior studies and require the informed consent of the participants.

Surprisingly, Neubauer never published his study. He instead donated his findings to Yale University, which will keep the papers sealed until 2066. Schein's and Bernstein's repeated efforts to gain access to the data have been unsuccessful. However, the two women have made their own observations about nature and nurture.

In their adoptive families, the sisters had different experiences. Schein's adoptive mother passed away when she was 6, and her father remarried soon after. Her older brother, also adopted, was diagnosed with schizophrenia. Schein attended a state university in

Bernstein, left, and Schein after their reunion

New York and then studied film in Prague. When she discovered her twin Paula, she was living alone in Paris.

Paula Bernstein had a happy childhood in suburban New York with her parents and older brother, who was also adopted. She attended the prestigious Wellesley College and earned a master's degree in cinema studies at NYU. When the adoption agency contacted her about her twin Elyse, she was living in Brooklyn with her husband and daughter.

When they met, Schein and Bernstein were amazed at the similarities between them. Schein was a filmmaker and Bernstein had worked as a film critic. As she talked to Elyse, Paula was shocked to see how many facial expressions and mannerisms they shared. They both had the same liberal political views. Both had faced bouts with depression.

Amidst all the similarities, there were also differences. Both women had cultivated their own styles and attitudes toward life. They looked alike, but neither would have been mistaken for the other.

The sisters believe that heredity is important. In an interview, Bernstein acknowledged that genetics play a huge role. She commented that she could see her personality in Schein. Schein even wondered, if they had been raised by each other's families, would Schein have turned out like Bernstein and Bernstein like Schein? After some time together, both twins think not. As far as these twins are concerned, both nature and nurture have played an active role in shaping who they are today.

What do you think?

1. Why would Neubauer's study be considered unethical today?
2. Which do you think is more important, nature or nurture?

CHAPTER 4

SOCIALIZING THE INDIVIDUAL

Chapter at a Glance

SECTION 1: Personality Development

- People develop their personalities over the course of their lives.
- While scientists have debated for years whether nature or nurture plays a bigger role in personality development, most social scientists today believe that environmental factors have the biggest influence.
- According to social scientists, the principal factors that influence personality and behavior are heredity, birth order, parental characteristics, and cultural environment.
- Studies of isolated children suggest the importance of environment in personality development.

SECTION 2: The Social Self

- Through socialization, people learn the basic values and behavior patterns of a culture and develop a sense of self.
- John Locke believed that humans were blank slates that could be socialized to have any type of character.
- According to Charles Horton Cooley, we develop our sense of self through an interactive process based on how we think we appear to others.
- George Herbert Mead proposed that we are socialized through a three-step process called role-taking, in which we learn to internalize the expectations of society.
- Sociologist Erving Goffman developed the theory of impression management, in which the self that we present to the world changes based on circumstance.

SECTION 3: Agents of Socialization

- The primary agents of socialization in the United States are the family, the peer group, the school, and the mass media.
- As the principal socializer of young children, the family is the most important agent of socialization in most societies.
- As children grow older, forces outside the family—such as friends, school, and mass media—increasingly influence them.
- Resocialization, or the process of learning new values and norms, can be voluntary or involuntary.

SECTION 1

Personality Development

Before You Read

Main Idea
Although the nature versus nurture debate has raged for decades, most social scientists believe a blend of the two influences personality.

Reading Focus
1. What is the history behind the nature versus nurture debate?
2. What are the main factors that affect personality development?
3. How does social environment influence personality?

Vocabulary
personality
heredity
instinct
sociobiology
aptitude

TAKING NOTES Use a graphic organizer like this one to take notes on the factors that affect personality development.

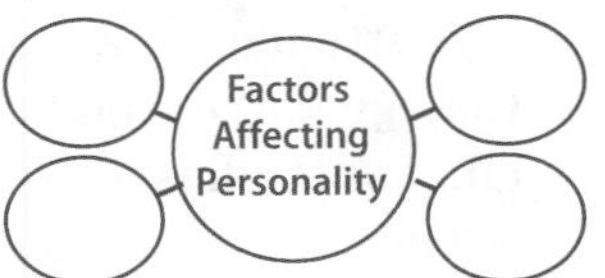

Pieces of the Personality Puzzle

What makes you the person that you are? Maybe you're good at basketball, like your dad, and you're the star center forward on the varsity team. Or perhaps you inherited your mother's ear for music and you spend your afternoons rehearsing with your band. Are you the oldest child in your family, responsible for taking care of your younger siblings? Or are you the baby, clowning around and making people laugh? Do you go to church every Sunday with your dad? Do you want to be a lawyer like your mom? The answers to these questions, and to hundreds of others like them, explain who you are. Even the fact that you live in the United States plays a role in shaping you. These factors—heredity, birth order, parental characteristics, and cultural environment—all influence your personality and make up the pieces of the unique puzzle that is you. ■

Nature Versus Nurture

To social scientists, **personality** is the sum total of behaviors, attitudes, beliefs, and values that are characteristic of an individual. Our personality determines how we adjust to our environment and how we react in specific situations. No two individuals have exactly the same personality. People's personalities continue to develop throughout their lifetimes. However, the rate of personality development varies from individual to individual.

For years, social scientists have debated what determines personality and social behavior. Some argue that it is **heredity**—the transmission of genetic characteristics from parents to children. Others suggest that the social environment determines personality. This debate is usually seen in terms of nature versus nurture, or inherited genetic traits versus environment and social learning.

The nature viewpoint that held sway in the 1800s states that much of human behavior is instinctual. An **instinct** is an unchanging, biologically inherited behavior pattern. Instinct is most often applied to animal behavior. For example, birds possess the instinct to migrate at particular times of the year. Supporters of the nature argument extended this notion of the biological basis of behavior to humans. They claimed that instinctual drives were responsible for practically everything, such as laughing, motherhood, warfare, and even the creation of society itself. In the early 1900s, social scientists claimed to have identified more than 10,000 human instincts.

From the nurture point of view, a person's behavior is the result of social environment and learning. Russian scientist Ivan Pavlov's work helped this viewpoint gain acceptance. Pavlov found that supposedly instinctual behavior could be taught. Pavlov knew that dogs would salivate when they were fed because saliva aids digestion. Pavlov rang a bell when he fed the dogs. Eventually, he rang the bell but did not feed them. The dogs still salivated. They had learned to salivate at the sound of the bell. American psychologist John B. Watson suggested that what applied to dogs also applied to humans. He claimed that he could take healthy infants and train them to be anything—doctors, artists, or thieves.

The emergence of sociobiology in the 1970s reemphasized the nature viewpoint. **Sociobiology** is the systematic study of the biological basis of all social behavior. Sociobiologists argue that such varied traits as religion, cooperation, competition, and envy are rooted in humans' genetic code. In general, sociobiologists argue that biological factors determine most of human social life.

Reading Check **Summarize** What arguments have been made to support each side in the nature versus nurture debate?

Factors in Personality Development

Most social scientists assume that personality and social behavior result from a blend of genetics and environment. They believe that environmental factors have the greatest influence. Heredity, birth order, parents, and the cultural environment are among the principal factors influencing personality and behavior.

ACADEMIC VOCABULARY

social environment contact with other people

Heredity Everyone has characteristics that are present at birth, such as body build, hair type, eye color, and skin pigmentation. Hereditary characteristics also include certain aptitudes. An **aptitude** is a capacity to learn a particular skill or acquire a specific body of knowledge. For example, a natural talent for music or art would be considered an aptitude. Elyse Schein and Paula Bernstein both pursued careers related to film, suggesting a shared aptitude for the subject.

CASE STUDY CONNECTION

Identical Strangers Despite being raised in separate households, identical twins Schein and Bernstein both showed an aptitude for film.

Most social scientists believe that some aptitudes can be learned as well as inherited. Some social scientists believe that inherited aptitudes develop due to environmental factors. Specifically, parents' responses can encourage or discourage the development of aptitudes. For example, if a child shows verbal aptitude, parents often respond with praise. They may read to the child. These actions encourage the development of the child's innate talent. Parental reinforcement may also affect how such personality traits as shyness, sociability, and aggression develop.

Humans also inherit certain basic needs. Like all animals, humans have biological drives. The hunger drive makes you want to eat. However, drives do not determine your specific behavior. The hunger drive does not tell you when, what, or how to eat. You learn such things through interaction with others. Heredity provides you with biological needs, but culture determines how you meet them.

Heredity also plays a role in shaping personalities by setting limits on individuals. If heredity endowed you with a five-foot-tall frame, you are not likely to play professional basketball. However, you may not do so even if you are seven feet tall. Inherited characteristics limit what is possible, not determine what a person will do. No one factor alone decides what kind of personality someone will have.

Birth Order Our personalities are also influenced by whether we have brothers, sisters, both, or neither. Children with siblings have a different view of the world than do children who have no brothers or sisters. The order in which we are born into our families also influences our personalities. That being said, the relationship between birth order and personality or IQ has been found to be moderated by family size.

It is commonly thought that firstborn children are more likely to be achievement-oriented and responsible than are later-born children. However, while some research showed that a majority of astronauts were firstborn, this research did not account for family size. It is possible that families who raised astronauts had fewer children, thus increasing the resources the parents had to devote to each child. More recent research has found that even when controlling for family size, some birth order effects seem to be real. One study in 2007 found a relationship between birth order and intelligence, and a 2009 study found birth order influences whom we choose as friends and spouses.

Parental Characteristics Personality development in children is also influenced by the characteristics of their parents. For example, the age of parents can have a bearing on their children's development. Parents who are in their early twenties when their children are born are likely to relate differently to their offspring than parents who are in their mid- to late thirties. Other differences between sets of parents are also likely to affect their children's personality development. Some parental characteristics that can influence a child's personality are level of education, religious orientation, economic status, cultural heritage, and occupational background.

The Cultural Environment Culture has a strong influence on personality development. Generally, the cultural environment determines the basic types of personalities that will be found in a society. Each culture gives rise to a series of personality traits—model personalities—that are typical of members of that society. For example, in the United States competitiveness, assertiveness, and individualism are common personality traits.

A powerful example of the effects of cultural environment on personality development is the Ik (eek) of northern Uganda. Prior to World War II, the Ik were hunters and gatherers who lived in a mountainous region of northern Uganda. Ik villagers were like one large family. Children viewed every adult in the village as a parent and all other children as brothers and sisters. However, after World War II the Ugandan government turned much of the Ik's land into a national park. The government then resettled the Ik on barren land. Faced with insufficient food sources, the Ik's social structure soon collapsed. In frustration, the Ik turned on each other.

Today Ik children are generally thrown out of their homes at the age of three. They survive by forming age bands—groups of children of the same general age. These bands, which serve as protection against older children, are short-lived. By the time a child reaches the age of 12 or 13, he or she has formed and broken several protective alliances and has decided that in most instances acting alone is better. Parents do not help their children, and adult children do not assist their aged parents. To survive the Ik culture, one must be strong and clever. In this way, the culture of the Ik influences the personality of Ik children.

How we experience our culture also influences our personalities. For example, our

Birth Order

Famous Examples of Only/ Firstborn Children	Famous Examples of Middle Children	Famous Examples of Last-Born Children
• Franklin D. Roosevelt	• John F. Kennedy	• Ronald Reagan
• Bill Clinton	• Bill Gates	• Jim Carrey
• J. K. Rowling	• Donald Trump	• Cameron Diaz
• Tiger Woods	• Princess Diana	• Stephen Colbert
• Kate Middleton	• Kim Kardashian	• Jennifer Lawrence

Quick Lab

Are You a Product of Your Cultural Environment?

This simple experiment should shed some light on how much your cultural environment influences you.

PROCEDURE

1. Answer the questions below on a blank sheet of paper. This is a test, so do not look up any of the answers.
   - **a. Is yak butter an important part of people's diets in India, Russia, or Tibet?**
   - **b. Do you think the word *Chomolungma,* which means "Goddess Mother of the World" in English, describes a spiritual leader, an Eastern religion, or a mountain?**
   - **c. If someone gave you Lapsang Souchong, would you eat it, drink it, or wear it?**
2. Ask your teacher for the answers, to see how you did.

ANALYSIS

1. How many questions did you answer correctly? Chances are that you did not know most of the answers. The test focused on aspects of Tibetan culture. If you had grown up in Tibet, the answers would have seemed obvious.
2. Relate the test to American culture. For example, what if, in the first question, "peanut butter" replaced "yak butter" and "United States" replaced "Tibet"? Or suppose the second question asked you to identify an American icon instead. You might take it for granted that everyone would know the answers then.
3. As a class, discuss the influence of your cultural environment.

experiences may differ depending on whether we are born male or female. Boys and girls are treated differently almost from the moment of birth. As they grow, male and female children are often nudged in different directions. Areas of difference include fields of interest, clothing, types of activities, speech habits, and ideas. All of these cultural differences in attitudes, expectations, and behavior affect the personalities of male and female adults.

Regardless of gender, subcultural differences also affect how our personalities develop. Someone from an Italian American family has a different experience from that of someone raised in a Polish American family. Both of these experiences differ from growing up in an American family with no clear ethnic pattern. Similarly, the region of the country or the type of neighborhood in which an individual is raised also affects personality.

Reading Check **Find the Main Idea** How do heredity, birth order, parental characteristics, and cultural environment influence personality?

Influence of Social Environment

Remarkably, several recorded instances exist in which children have been raised without the influence of a social environment. These feral children had few human characteristics other than appearance. They had acquired no reasoning ability, no manners, and no ability to control their bodily functions or move about like other human beings. Sociological studies of feral children point strongly to the conclusion that our personality comes from our social environment.

Anna and Isabelle Kingsley Davis's studies of Anna and Isabelle provide evidence of the devastating effect of isolation during childhood. Anna was born to an unmarried woman, a fact that enraged the woman's father. Because of the grandfather's hostility, Anna was confined to an attic room where she was given only a minimum of care. She was undernourished and emaciated and received almost no human contact. She was not spoken to, held, bathed, or loved.

Anna was discovered by a social worker in 1938. At six years of age, Anna could not walk, talk, or feed herself. Over time, though, Anna learned to walk, feed herself, and brush her teeth. She could also talk in phrases and follow simple directions. However, Anna died at age 10, probably due to her earlier isolation.

The story of Isabelle has a somewhat happier ending. Isabelle was found at about the same time as Anna. The child's grandfather kept her and her deaf mother confined to a dark room. Isabelle had the advantage of her mother's company. But because she and her

ACADEMIC VOCABULARY
feral wild or untamed

mother communicated only through gestures, Isabelle did not learn to speak. When she was found at age six, she behaved in many ways like an infant.

Isabelle was at first thought to be mentally disabled and incapable of speech. However, after months of intensive training she began to speak. After two years, Isabelle had reached a level of social and mental development consistent with her age group. Davis concluded that Isabelle's constant contact with her mother and skillful training by specialists allowed her to overcome her early social deprivation.

Genie Sometimes it is impossible to reverse the effects of prolonged isolation. This situation proved true in the case of Genie, who was discovered in 1970 when she was 13 years old. Genie's father had confined her from the age of 20 months to a small bedroom. Her world was almost totally silent, and she was beaten if she made noise. Whenever Genie's father interacted with her, he behaved like an angry dog, barking, growling, and baring his teeth. Consequently, Genie did not learn to talk.

When Genie was found, she could not stand straight and had the social and psychological skills of a one-year-old. Even after eight years of training, Genie had not progressed past the level of a third-grade student. Although she had learned to speak and to conform to basic social norms, Genie was unable to function as an adult. At age 21, she was placed in a facility for people with developmental disabilities.

Institutionalization Sociologists have also studied the human development of children living in institutions such as orphanages and hospitals. These children may show some of the characteristics of isolated children. In 1945 psychologist Rene Spitz studied a group of infants living in an orphanage. The children were given food and medical care but had little human contact. The nurses, although well-trained and efficient, had little time to hold or talk to the children. Within two years, about a third of the children in the study had died. They seemed to have wasted away from a lack of attention. Of those who survived, fewer than 25 percent could walk by themselves, dress themselves, or use a spoon. Only one child could speak in complete sentences.

The cases of Anna, Isabelle, Genie, and the institutionalized infants illustrate how important human interaction is for social and psychological development. Recent research continues to support these findings. Although foster care and orphanages are not seen as harmful today, studies of Romanian orphanages show that most young residents have learning delays and problems forming attachments to others. Children who lack a caring environment develop their mental, physical, and emotional skills at a much slower pace.

Reading Check **Identify Cause and Effect** How did isolation affect Anna, Isabelle, and Genie?

SECTION 1 Assessment

Reviewing Main Ideas and Vocabulary

1. **Explain** What do most modern social scientists think about the roles of nature and nurture in shaping personality?
2. **Recall** What are some of the parental characteristics that can influence a child's personality?

Thinking Critically

3. **Support a Position** What do you think is the most important influence on personality and social behavior? Explain your answer.
4. **Identify Cause and Effect** According to research by Rene Spitz, what effect does lack of close human contact have on institutionalized children?
5. **Categorize** Using your notes and a graphic organizer like the one below, explain how aspects of the factors affecting personality fit in the nature versus nurture debate.

Nature	Nurture

FOCUS ON WRITING

6. **Expository** Write two paragraphs explaining what factors might have led to the different levels of success in the efforts to teach Anna, Isabelle, and Genie to function normally.

SECTION 2

The Social Self

Before You Read

Main Idea
The theories of Locke, Cooley, and Mead explain how people are socialized and develop a sense of self. Once a sense of self exists, people change how they present it to others.

Reading Focus
1. What are three theories to explain the development of self?
2. How does our environment affect the presentation of self?

Vocabulary
socialization
self
looking-glass self
role-taking
significant others
generalized other
I
me
dramaturgy
impression management

TAKING NOTES Use a graphic organizer like this one to take notes on the development and presentation of self.

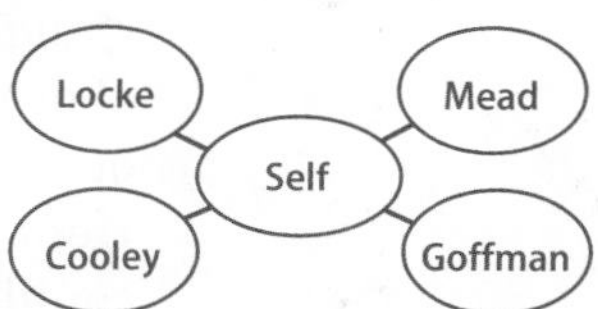

Mirror, Mirror On the Wall

SOCIOLOGY CLOSE UP ***Do you ever think about how other people see you?*** You probably do without even realizing it. According to one sociologist, as you interact with people, you pick up cues about their opinions of you. In response, you form your sense of self.

Each different group of people that you spend time with plays a role in defining your sense of self. Your parents probably do not see you in the same way that your friends do. You also act differently depending on the group you are with. As a result, your sense of self is never permanently fixed. It is always developing through interactions with others. ■

The Development of Self

At birth, human beings cannot talk, walk, feed themselves, or protect themselves. They know nothing about the norms of society or how to follow them. However, through interaction with their social and cultural environments, people are transformed into participating members of society. The interactive process through which people learn the basic skills, values, beliefs, and behavior patterns of a society is called **socialization.**

A number of theories exist to explain how people become socialized and develop a sense of self. Your **self** is your conscious awareness of possessing a distinct identity that separates you and your environment from other members of society. This section examines three of these theories of socialization—those of John Locke, Charles Horton Cooley, and George Herbert Mead.

Locke: The Tabula Rasa John Locke, an English philosopher from the 1600s, insisted that each newly born human being is a tabula rasa, or clean slate, on which just about anything can be written. Locke claimed that each of us is born without a personality. We acquire our personalities as a result of our social experiences. Locke believed that human beings could be molded into any type of character. He further believed that, if given a newborn infant, he could shape that child's personality, giving it whatever characteristics he chose. As you recall, more than 200 years later, psychologist John B. Watson made a similar claim.

Today few people would take such an extreme view. Nevertheless, many of our basic assumptions about socialization are related to Locke's views. Most sociologists think of socialization as a process by which individuals absorb the aspects of their culture with which they come into contact. Through the socialization process, they develop the sense of being distinct members of society.

Cooley: The Looking-Glass Self Social psychologist Charles Horton Cooley was one of the founders of the interactionist perspective in sociology. He is most noted for developing the idea of the primary group and for his theory explaining how individuals develop a sense of self. The concept of the looking-glass self is central to Cooley's theory. The **looking-glass self** refers to the interactive process by which we develop an image of ourselves based on how we imagine we appear to others. Other people act as a mirror, reflecting back the image we project through their reactions to our behavior.

According to Cooley, the development of the looking-glass self is a three-step process. First, we imagine how we appear to others. Second, based on their reactions to us, we attempt to determine whether others view us as we view ourselves. Finally, we use our perceptions of how others judge us to develop feelings about ourselves.

The process of identity development begins very early in childhood. According to Cooley, a newborn baby has no sense of person or place. The entire world appears as one mass. Then various members of the child's primary group—parents, brothers, sisters, other family members, and friends—interact with the growing infant. They pick up the child. They talk to him or her. They reward or punish the child's behavior. They provide the child with a mirror that reflects his or her image. From this interactive process, the child develops a sense of self.

This theory puts a great deal of responsibility on parents and other primary-group members who have contact with children. Parents who think little of a child's ability, or children who perceive this attitude from their parents, will likely give rise to feelings of inferiority in the child. On the other hand, parents who treat their children as capable and competent are likely to produce children who are capable and competent.

Cooley was quick to note that although this process starts early in childhood, it continues throughout life. Individuals adjust their self-images continually as they reinterpret the way they think others view them.

Mead: Role-Taking American philosopher George Herbert Mead, another founder of the interactionist perspective, developed ideas related to Cooley's theories. According to Mead, seeing ourselves as others see us is only the beginning. Eventually we not only see ourselves as others see us but actually take on, or pretend to take on, the roles of others. This act of **role-taking** forms the basis of the socialization process by allowing us to anticipate what others expect of us. We learn to see ourselves through the eyes of others and then act accordingly.

Mead proposed that we first internalize the expectations of the people closest to us. These people include parents, siblings, relatives, and others who directly influence our socialization. Although Mead may not have used the term, sociologists now refer to such people as **significant others.** As an individual ages, significant others become less important in shaping his or her sense of self.

Instead, the expectations and attitudes of society take on added importance in guiding our behavior and reinforcing our sense of self. Mead called the internalized attitudes, expectations, and viewpoints of society the **generalized other.** We internalize the generalized other through the process of role-taking.

Children are not automatically capable of role-taking. They must develop the necessary skills through social interaction. As the chart on this page illustrates, Mead visualized role-taking as a three-step process.

Under about three years of age, children lack a sense of self. Consequently, they can only imitate the actions of others, usually those of family members and others in their immediate environment. Such mimicking is not role-taking, but rather preparation for learning expectations associated with roles.

At about the age of three, children begin to play and act out the roles of specific people. They may dress up in their parents' clothes, play house, or pretend to be doctors, policemen, superheroes, or princesses. For the first time, they are trying to see the world through someone else's eyes.

By the time children reach school age, they begin to take part in organized games. Organized games require children not only to take on roles of their own but also to anticipate the actions and expectations of others. Because it requires internalizing the generalized other, the game stage of role-taking most closely resembles real life.

Through role-taking, individuals develop a sense of self. According to Mead, the self consists of two related parts—the "I" and the "me." The **I** is the unsocialized, spontaneous, self-interested component of personality and self-identity. The **me,** on the other hand, is the part that is aware of the expectations and attitudes of society—the socialized self.

In childhood, the I component of personality is stronger than the me component. Through the process of socialization, however, the me gains power by acting together with the I and bringing actions in line with the expectations of society. The me never totally dominates the I. To become a well-rounded member of society, a person needs both aspects of the self.

Reading Check **Contrast** How do the three theories of socialization differ?

Mead's Development of Self

According to Mead, children become capable of role-taking through a three-step process. As individuals progress through the steps and the self develops, they are able to internalize the expectations of more and more people. Finally, their ability to interact with others grows until they are able to take on the role of the generalized other, or society as a whole.

Step 1: Imitation

Under age 3 When they are very young, children do not see themselves as separate from other people. They do not yet have a sense of self and can only imitate other people's gestures and speech. This mimicking is not role-taking, but rather preparation for it.

Step 2: Play

Ages 3 to 6 At this age, children begin to see themselves in relation to others. They are able to recognize specific roles and begin to act out those roles by dressing up. These roles can range from the everyday, such as pretending to be a doctor, to the more fantastic, such as playing princess.

Step 3: Organized Games

Over age 6 or 7 About the time children reach school age, they begin to take part in organized games and team sports. These activities require children to take on their own roles as well as to anticipate the actions of others.

The Presentation of Self

ACADEMIC VOCABULARY

proponent one who argues in support of something

Sociologist Erving Goffman followed in Mead's footsteps as a proponent of interactionism. In 1959, after extensive observations, Goffman proposed the idea of dramaturgy. According to **dramaturgy,** social interaction is like a drama being performed on a stage. People are like an audience, judging each others' performances and trying to determine each individual's true character. As a result, most people make an effort to play their roles well and manage the impressions that the audience receives. Goffman called this presentation of self **impression management.**

Goffman suggested that we spend much of our time with others managing their impressions. In doing so, we are changing the self that we display. In a study of how college students react to exam grades, sociologists Daniel Albas and Cheryl Albas observed a classic example of such behavior. Those students who received good grades reacted differently depending on whether the interaction was with someone who also did well or someone who did poorly. In interactions between two students with high marks, both individuals felt comfortable sharing their success. However, in interactions with students who received poor grades, those with higher marks tended to downplay their success, even chalking it up to luck in some cases. In the same interactions, the students with lower marks tried to appear gracious and congratulate their fellow students on their scores.

Goffman's work is a logical progression from Cooley and Mead. Cooley and Mead focused on how we create and develop a self. Goffman examined how we change that self depending on our audience.

Reading Check **Analyze** According to Goffman, why does our presentation of self change?

SOCIALIZATION AND THE SELF

There are several theories about how the self emerges and develops.

John Locke: The Tabula Rasa
Each person is born as a blank slate. Humans, who aquire their personalities through interaction, can be molded into any type of character.

Charles Horton Cooley: The Looking-Glass Self
Humans form images of themselves based on how they seem to others. We imagine how we appear to others, judge whether they see us as we see ourselves, and use our judgments to form our sense of self.

George Herbert Mead: Role-Taking
Beyond seeing ourselves as others do, we begin to anticipate what others expect. After a three-step process, we take on the roles of others.

Erving Goffman: Impression Management
Social interaction is like performing for an audience. We change our personalities based on what impression we want to convey.

SECTION 2 Assessment

Reviewing Main Ideas and Vocabulary

1. **Identify** Who bears most of the responsibility for socialization in Cooley's theory?
2. **Define** What is the generalized other?
3. **Sequence** What are the three steps children go through when developing the skills needed for role-taking, and why is each step significant?

Thinking Critically

4. **Predict** If a parent understood and agreed with Cooley's looking-glass self theory, how do you think it would affect his or her behavior?
5. **Explain** According to Mead, what are the two components of self, and how are they related?
6. **Sequence** Using your notes and a graphic organizer like the one below, explain the steps in the process of impression management.

□ → □ → □

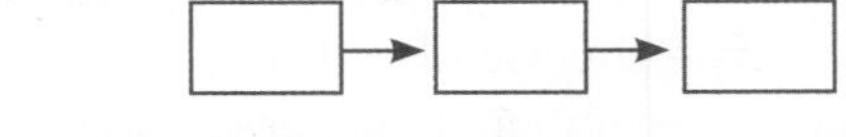

7. **Expository** Using all three theories of socialization (Locke, Cooley, and Mead) discussed in this section, write a short essay explaining the role of others in a person's sense of self.

SECTION 3

Agents of Socialization

Before You Read

Main Idea

There are four primary agents of socialization in the United States: family, peer group, school, and the mass media. In some cases, people may undergo voluntary or involuntary resocialization.

Reading Focus

1. What are the primary agents of socialization in the United States?
2. What are the two kinds of resocialization?

Vocabulary

agents of socialization
peer group
mass media
resocialization
total institution

TAKING NOTES Use a graphic organizer like this one to take notes on the primary agents of socialization in American society.

Family	Peer Group	School	Mass Media

This illustration contrasts a beautiful princess with an ugly villainess to highlight the distinction between good and evil.

SOCIOLOGY CLOSE UP ***How do fairy tales help to socialize children?*** According to child psychologist Bruno Bettelheim, fairy tales are important because they help children master the problems of growing up. They also serve as an introduction to the real world. The message of the tales is that good and bad, virtue and evil exist in everything. Fairy tales also teach children that difficulties in life are unavoidable and must be met head on. Children see the fairy-tale hero confront evil and, through cleverness or bravery, find a way to triumph. By identifying with the hero, children learn socially acceptable behaviors before they are old enough to grasp adult moral issues.

The structure of the fairy tale is ideally suited to the way young children think. Children cannot understand the complexities of the adult world, so situations and people are either right or wrong, good or bad. Fairy tales mimic this simplified view of the world. For example, the witch is bad and ugly. The princess is kind and beautiful. The prince is strong and brave. Good always triumphs over evil.

The subject matter of fairy tales also plays an important role in socialization. Love, fear, death, isolation, and abandonment are all prominent themes. Addressing such subjects allows young children to confront fears they might not be able to express. More than just beloved stories, fairy tales help mold social behavior by providing a way for children to grasp the contradictions of human nature and explore their fears. ■

Primary Agents

The views of Locke, Cooley, and Mead provide theoretical explanations of the socialization process. This section examines some specific forces and situations that shape socialization. Sociologists use the term **agents of socialization** to describe the specific individuals, groups, and institutions that enable socialization to take place. In the United States, the primary agents of socialization include the family, the peer group, the school, and the mass media.

The Family The family is the most important agent of socialization in most societies. It is the principal socializer of young children. Children first interact with others and first learn the values, norms, and beliefs of society through their families.

Socialization in a family setting can be both deliberate and unintended. A father may teach his children about the importance of telling the truth or being considerate of others. A mother may instruct her children on how to spend and save money. These are deliberate, or intended, socialization activities.

There also are unintended socialization activities. Many times these activities have a greater effect on children than do deliberate attempts at socialization. For example, suppose a father explains to his child the importance of being polite. However, the child sees several situations in which the father is impolite. Is the child likely to follow what the father says or what he actually does? Unintended socialization is very common. Parents may take deliberate action to try to influence a child in one direction. However, on numerous occasions they send out unintended messages that push the child in another direction.

Whether deliberate or unconscious, the socialization process differs from family to family, for all families are not the same. The number of children and the number of parents vary from family to family. In addition, one-parent families may be headed by a father or a mother. Also, relationships with other family members—grandparents, uncles, and aunts—may vary. Further, families differ according to the combination of subgroups to which they belong. These subgroups include racial or ethnic group, social class, religious group, and geographic region. For example, one family may be African American, middle class, Baptist, and live in the South. Another may be Italian American, working class, Catholic, and live in the Midwest. All these differences affect the way a family socializes its children. Thus, socialization produces a society of individuals who share in the patterns of the larger culture but who retain certain unique personality and behavior characteristics.

The Peer Group The family provides many, if not most, of the socialization experiences of early childhood. Infants and very young children are particularly likely to spend almost all of their time in a family setting. As children grow older, forces outside of the family increasingly influence them. In particular, children begin to relate more and more to their peer groups. A **peer group** is a primary group composed of individuals of roughly equal age and similar social characteristics.

Peer groups are particularly influential during the pre-teenage and early teenage years. Indeed, winning peer acceptance is a powerful force in the lives of young people of this age group. Without peer acceptance, they could be labeled as misfits, outsiders, or a similar disparaging term. To win this acceptance, young people willingly adopt the values and standards of the peer group. In essence, they shape themselves into the kind of person they think the group wants them to be.

Peer-group socialization is different from socialization within the family. The norms and values imparted by the family usually focus on the larger culture. However, in peer groups the focus is the subculture of the group. Peer-group goals are sometimes at odds with the goals of the larger society. Parents in particular become alarmed if they come to believe that the norms and values of the peer group are more important to their children than those of society as a whole.

The School For most young people, school occupies large amounts of time and attention. Between the ages of 5 and 18, young people spend some 30 weeks a year in school. Therefore, the school plays a major role in socializing individuals. Class activities are planned for the deliberate purpose of teaching basic reading, writing, arithmetic, and other skills. Extracurricular activities, such as school clubs, dances, and athletic events, are intended to also prepare the student for life in society.

Schools also attempt to transmit cultural values, such as patriotism, responsibility, and good citizenship.

A large amount of unintentional socialization also occurs within the school. Teachers may become models for students in such areas as manners of speech or styles of dress. In addition, schools contain many peer groups that influence the habits of their members.

The Mass Media Socialization in the family, the peer group, and the school involves personal contact. Another influential agent of socialization, the mass media, involves no face-to-face interaction. The **mass media** are instruments of communication that reach large audiences with no personal contact between those sending the information and those receiving it. The major forms of mass media are books, films, the Internet, magazines, newspapers, radio, and television.

Of these various forms of mass media, television probably has the most influence on the socialization of children. Some 99 percent of the homes in the United States have television sets, with an average of more than two sets per home. More importantly, research shows that most children watch an average of 24.7 hours each week. Further, watching television is their primary after-school activity. American children spend about 900 hours per year in school. In that same time, they watch about 1,200 hours of television.

The effect of television on children is a topic of ongoing debate. On the negative side, research indicates that by age 18, most children will have witnessed 150,000 fictional acts of violence, and 16,000 thirty-second TV commercials. Several studies have found a connection between television violence and aggressive youth behavior. These studies suggest that television violence encourages viewers to act in aggressive ways and to see aggression as a valid way to solve problems. The studies also show that because television violence often appears painless or not harmful, it invites viewers to be less sensitive to the suffering of others. The studies conclude that television violence appears to make viewers fearful of the world around them.

Another long-standing criticism of television is that it presents an image of a society limited to white middle-class values. The life experiences of many racial, religious, and economic groups are often either ignored or portrayed in a negative light.

On the positive side, television expands the viewers' world. It can be a powerful educational tool. Television brings far-off places into viewers' homes, makes world events immediate, and introduces viewers to subjects they otherwise might never encounter.

Reading Check **Find the Main Idea** Which agent of socialization is the most important?

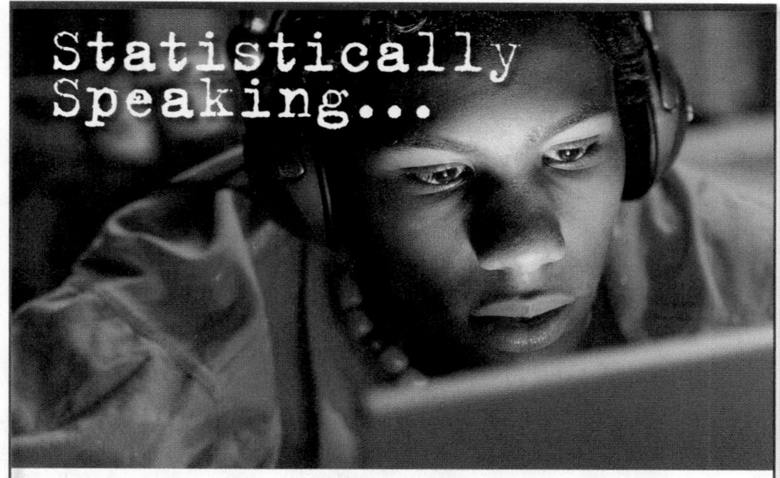

The Internet Since the 1990s, the Internet has come to play an increasingly large role in people's lives, including children. As a result, its significance as an agent of socialization has expanded.

81% Percentage of American households with school-aged children that have Internet access

2005 Year by which nearly all U.S. public schools had Internet connectivity

34.8% Percentage of children ages 3 to 5 using the Internet, compared to 50.3% of 6- to 9-year-olds, 71.9% percent of 10- to 14-year-olds, and 81.2% of 15- to 17-year-olds

92% Percentage of teens who report going online daily — including 24% who say they go online "almost constantly"

71% Percentage of teens who use Facebook

Skills Focus **INTERPRETING CHARTS** What is the relationship between age and Internet use among children and teens?

Sources: Child Trends DataBank (2015). *Home computer access and internet use*; Pew Research Center Teens Relationships Survey, Sept 25-Oct 9, 2014.

Resocialization

The development of self is a lifelong process. At certain points during the life course, individuals may experience resocialization. **Resocialization** involves a break with past experiences and the learning of new values and norms. There are two kinds of resocialization—voluntary and involuntary.

Total Institutions

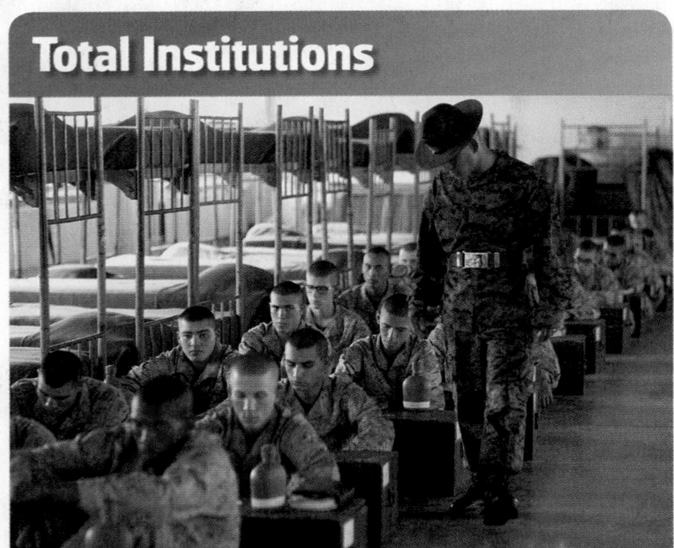

Total institutions such as military boot camps attempt to resocialize individuals by removing all semblance of a personal identity. ***What examples of this technique are shown in this image?***

Voluntary Resocialization Individuals who choose to assume a new status are undergoing voluntary resocialization. For example, a teenager who goes to college learns a whole new set of rules and behaviors. Every time we learn norms that differ from our previous experiences, we are being resocialized.

Involuntary Resocialization In some cases, resocialization occurs against a person's wishes. This kind of involuntary resocialization of an individual often takes place in a total institution, a rather unique agent of socialization. A **total institution** is a setting in which people are isolated from the rest of society for a specific period of time and are subject to tight control. Prisons, military boot camps, monasteries, and psychiatric hospitals are all examples of total institutions.

The goal of resocialization in most total institutions is to change an individual's personality and social behavior. To do so, these institutions strip away all semblance of individual identity and replace it with an institutional identity—uniforms, standard haircuts, and so on. The individual is denied the freedoms of the outside world. These actions weaken the person's sense of self, making it easier for those in power to convince that person to conform to new patterns of behavior.

Reading Check **Contrast** In what ways do voluntary and involuntary resocialization differ?

SECTION 3 Assessment

Reviewing Main Ideas and Vocabulary

1. **Define** What is an agent of socialization?
2. **Contrast** How is peer group socialization different from socialization within the family?
3. **Summarize** What are some possible positive and negative effects of television viewing on young people?

Thinking Critically

4. **Make Generalizations** Why are institutions such as family and school important?
5. **Evaluate** Do you think intended or unintended socialization is more common in schools? Explain.
6. **Make Judgments** What is your opinion about the techniques used by total institutions to resocialize their members?
7. **Compare and Contrast** Using your notes and a graphic organizer like the one below, compare and contrast total institutions with other agents of socialization.

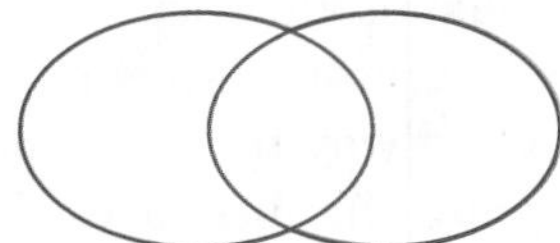

FOCUS ON WRITING

8. **Expository** Choose a mass medium, such as the Internet or newspapers, and write a paragraph evaluating how effective the medium is as an agent of socialization. Consider people's access and the medium's positive and negative effects.

CULTURAL DIVERSITY AND SOCIOLOGY

Socialization Around the World

The primary agents of socialization—family, peer group, education, and mass media—tend to be the same in most cultures. However, the importance placed on each agent can vary from society to society. In rare cases, an agent can be ignored completely. Each agent's importance can also change with time, as a society shifts and adapts to outside influences.

Amish The Amish are members of a conservative Christian group who first came to North America in the 1700s. The Amish have traditions that are distinct from the majority American culture. They make an effort to maintain this separation and to preserve their cultural heritage.

Children attend parochial schools within the Amish community, up to the eighth grade, when their education stops. By controlling education in this manner, the Amish are preserving their culture. Amish children learn values without being exposed to outside ideas. They also tend to be separated from non-Amish peers.

As part of their religion, the Amish avoid modern conveniences. They don't use electricity from public utility lines and avoid televisions and computers. As a result, they are isolated from much of the mass media that socializes other American youth.

East Asia Many East Asian cultures emphasize the importance of education. One reason for this emphasis is the belief that to get the best jobs, students must attend the best schools. Competition for these slots begins as early as age 4 or 5. By the time these students are in high school and are facing entrance exams to the top universities, the pressure is intense.

To improve their odds of acceptance into the best schools, many East Asian students use private tutoring. In 2012, for example, South Koreans spent over $17.7 billion on learning aids such as tutors, practice exam services, and special academies called "cram schools." These cram schools offer classes after school and on the weekends and are also popular in Japan and China. Some students attend cram schools every day in the hopes of gaining entry to the best schools.

South Korean students study at a cram school, or *hagwon.*

Most Amish communities avoid modern technology. These Amish use traditional methods to build a barn.

Fiji In 1995, residents of the South Pacific island nation of Fiji got television for the first time. They received only one channel, which broadcast programming from the United States, Great Britain, and Australia. Three years later Harvard University researcher Anne E. Becker found a significant increase in symptoms of eating disorders among teenage girls.

In traditional Fijian society, a robust body is the norm, and commenting that someone has gained weight is a compliment. After exposure to Western mass media, however, Fijian teens wanted to look like the actresses they saw on television. According to Becker's study, girls who said they watched television three or more nights a week were 50 percent more likely to see themselves as too fat and 30 percent more likely to diet than girls who watched less often.

Thinking Critically

1. **Compare and Contrast** How are the Amish and East Asian approaches to education similar to each other? How are they different?
2. **Discuss** Are some agents of socialization more important than others in your culture? Explain.

Simulation
Applying What You've Learned

A Personality for Every Occasion

What is your personality and how is it displayed in different social settings?

Use the workbook to complete this simulation.

1. Introduction

This simulation will help you review how an individual's personality develops and how it is shaped by social interaction. In this activity you will explore two concepts regarding your personality. The traits that you inherit from your family and the behaviors that you develop from interacting with your environment are both key factors in determining your personality. Once set, your personality remains stable. However, how you present yourself changes depending on the social setting and the people you are interacting with.

First, you will analyze your life and the factors that you believe shaped your personality. You will begin by creating a time line of the major events of your life. You will then analyze the time line to determine how these events might have affected the development of your personality. You will also consider how your personality is similar to or different from the other members of your family. After analyzing all of these factors, you will write an essay discussing your observations and conclusions.

Using the contents of your essay, you will work in pairs to role-play your personality in different social settings. You and your partner will take on the roles of different people as you act out these situations. Finally, you will come together as a class to discuss what you have learned from this simulation.

2. Personality Analysis

Working by yourself, create a time line that documents your life. Start with your birth and continue to the present.

1. Include the following types of events: divorce; moving; changing schools; a death in the family; the birth of a sibling; relationship with a boyfriend or girlfriend; academic problems or achievements; accomplishments; or pursuing a talent, such as music, art, or sports.
2. Now add major events that were happening in the world to your time line, such as September 11, 2001, or the 2008 and 2012 presidential elections. Include significant local events, as well as national or global events.
3. Think about how each event made you feel and how it might have affected you. Note those feelings on your time line. For example, did it make you feel shy or outgoing? Worried about the future or challenged to work harder? More or less family oriented? More or less confident in yourself?
4. Finally, consider whether any of these events, or your reaction to them, might have been influenced by heredity. For instance, did you inherit your father's musical ability and decide to join the choir?

Use your time line to analyze your personality. How has each event in your life shaped you? Compare your personality to the other members of your immediate family. Write an essay explaining your conclusions about your personality. Attach your time line to your essay and turn it in.

Sample Time Line

2000
Born in Dallas, TX: my grandparents came to visit

1. **2001**
September 11 terrorist attacks: I was too young to remember

2003
Little brother Tim born: I no longer got all the attention; had to look after him

2005
Started kindergarten: met my best friend Justin

2. **2007**
Tested for gifted and talented program at school: made me feel more confident

3. Role-play Social Situations

Now that you have analyzed your personality, you will role-play a series of scenarios to determine how you display your personality differently in different social situations. Follow these steps:

- Following your teacher's instructions, form a pair with another student.
- Take a few minutes to briefly discuss what each of you learned from your personality analyses.
- Your task is to role-play a conversation in which one of you will act as yourself while the other takes on a series of roles to simulate different situations. Then, you will switch places. While you play the role of yourself, your partner will take on each of the following roles:
    - your best friend
    - your older sibling or cousin
    - your parent or guardian
    - your teacher
- During each conversational role-play, you should answer the following questions:
    - What did you do on Friday night?
    - How was school today?
    - How are you doing on your homework?
- Remember that not only your answers, but also your behavior and demeanor might change in each situation. Behave as you actually would in each situation, not as you think you should or as you would like to act.

4. Discussion

What did you learn from this simulation? Hold a group discussion that focuses on the following questions:

- How difficult was it to analyze your personality once you completed your time line?
- What events made it easy to see the development of your personality? What events were difficult to analyze? Why?
- Comparing the effect of your family on you to the effect of the events in your life, which do you think has had the greater impact? Explain.
- Do you think it will ever be possible to resolve the nature versus nurture debate? Why or why not?
- During the role-play, how did your reaction to the question differ depending on who was asking it? Why do you think it differed?
- What is the purpose of personas, or the differing sides of our personalities that we show people?
- How can personas be positive? How can personas be negative?
- What would the world be like without personas? What if everyone said and did exactly what they felt like all of the time? Would you enjoy interacting with people who acted like this? Why or why not?

2008
Obama elected president: my parents were excited

3 **Mom and Dad got divorced:** hard on me and my brother
2012

4 **2014**
Started playing guitar: Dad gave me one of his old acoustic guitars

2016
Started dating Jess: made me more outgoing

CHAPTER 4 Review

Comprehension and Critical Thinking

SECTION 1 *(pp. 90–94)*

1. a. **Identify** What do social scientists believe are the principal factors that influence personality development?
   b. **Draw Conclusions** Why do you think sociologists study people who were isolated during childhood?
   c. **Predict** Do you think future research into genetics will sway social scientists toward the nature side of the nature versus nurture debate? Explain your answer.

SECTION 2 *(pp. 95–98)*

2. a. **Recall** According to Cooley, when does the process of development of self end?
   b. **Infer** What is the role of self in the socialization process?
   c. **Elaborate** What are some possible ways that an individual might change how he or she presents himself or herself to different audiences?

SECTION 3 *(pp. 99–102)*

3. a. **Describe** How do total institutions resocialize their members?
   b. **Make Generalizations** In what ways might the mass media, particularly television, reinforce and counteract the effects of the other agents of socialization?
   c. **Predict** How do you think agents of socialization in another country may be similar to or different than ours? What do you think explains these similarities and differences?

INTERNET ACTIVITY

4. How do social scientists develop theories? Choose one of the theories about the development or presentation of the self discussed in this chapter and use the Internet to research the social scientist who proposed the theory. Look for the individual's research or observations that might have led to the theory, information on possible influences on their thinking, and other prominent theories the individual might have also proposed. Write a short profile on your chosen social scientist that summarizes your findings.

Reviewing Vocabulary

Match the terms below with their correct definitions.

5. personality	**10.** self
6. heredity	**11.** generalized other
7. social environment	**12.** agents of socialization
8. sociobiology	**13.** resocialization
9. socialization	**14.** total institution

A. the systematic study of the biological basis of all social behavior

B. your conscious awareness of possessing a distinct identity that separates you and your environment from other members of society

C. a setting in which people are isolated from society for a set period of time and are subject to tight control

D. behaviors, attitudes, beliefs, and values that are characteristic of an individual

E. contact with other people

F. the specific individuals, groups, and institutions that enable socialization to take place

G. the interactive process through which people learn the basic skills, values, beliefs, and behavior patterns of a society

H. a break with past experiences and the learning of new values and norms

I. the internalized attitudes, expectations, and viewpoints of society

J. the transmission of genetic characteristics from parents to children

Sociology in Your Life

15. The culture of someone's community has a strong influence on his or her personality. However, the culture of a community can change over time. What effect does your community's culture have on you? Has the culture of your community changed over the past ten years? How might future changes in your community and other communities in the United States affect your personality traits and those of other Americans? Write a report in which you analyze these questions about the impact of culture on personality.

SKILLS ACTIVITY: INTERPRETING GRAPHS

According to a recent study of 14-year-olds, those who watch three or more hours of television a day are more likely to skip homework, get poor grades, and hate school than peers who watch an hour or less per day. Study the bar graph below and answer the questions that follow.

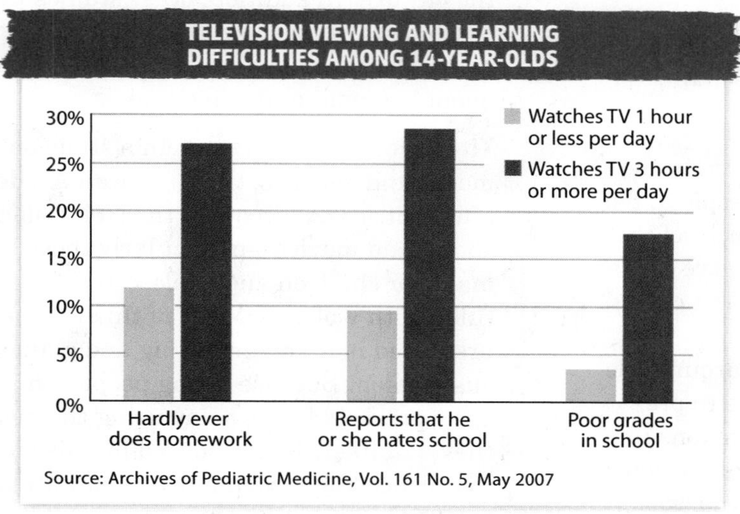

16. Identify Which category shows the greatest difference between the two groups of respondents?

17. Compare How many more teens who watch three hours or more of television a day get poor grades than those who watch an hour or less?

18. Predict Based on the data in the graph, which group do you think would be more likely to report having trouble paying attention in school?

WRITING FOR SOCIOLOGY

Use your knowledge of socialization to answer the question below. Do not simply list facts. Present a clear argument based on your critical analysis of the question, using appropriate sociological terminology.

19. Briefly describe each of the agents of socialization listed below. For each agent, include a general description and a discussion of its significance in the socialization process.

- Family
- Peer group
- School
- Mass media

Connecting Online

Go online for review and enrichment activities related to this chapter.

KEY TOPICS VIDEOS
View compelling clips on issues in the field.

KEEP IT CURRENT
Link to the Current Events site for regularly updated stories on sociology as well as other social studies topics.

QUICK LAB
Reinforce a key concept with a short lab activity.

CASE STUDY

TEEN Violence

Teen violence is a serious problem in the United States today. In 2014 people under the age of 18 made up 15.8 percent of the nation's violent crime arrests. More teenagers were also the victims of violent crime than people of any other age group.

In 1999 many high schools around the nation installed metal detectors to prevent students from carrying weapons into school. This safety measure was influenced by the Columbine High School massacre in Colorado that same year, when 12 students and a teacher were murdered by two of the school's students. Since Columbine, more than 50 school shootings have occurred on high school campuses across the nation. In 2005 seven people were murdered by a student at Red Lake High School in Minnesota in the nation's second deadliest high school shooting.

With the growing incidence of school violence, sociologists have been searching for clues to the causes of teen violence. What accounts for the prevalence of violence among teenagers? Some studies suggest that the answer lies in American youth culture, particularly media-related aspects of the culture. In addition, other studies have concluded that teens who use drugs are more likely to engage in violent and delinquent behavior and join gangs.

The Media and Violence In a study on the media and violence, the American Academy of Pediatrics (AAP) noted that television shows and movies—particularly those made for children and adolescents—are filled with violence. Much of this violence is presented in an entertaining and glamorous fashion. Because young people, on average, spend six hours a day using the media, they will likely be influenced by this view of violence. Some young people imitate the behavior they have seen others exhibit. The AAP suggests that if young people see their heroes resorting to violence to solve problems, they will do the same. In time, some young people accept violence as a legitimate form of behavior.

Citing several studies, the AAP argues that exposure to media violence is connected to several teen-related problems. Media violence may encourage aggressive behavior. For example, after playing video games, some teenagers show more aggression and exhibit violent behavior. In addition, the AAP asserts that the media's heavy emphasis on violence makes the world look like a

In Red Lake, Minnesota, victims of a deadly school shooting are memorialized with crosses. Seven people were murdered at the local high school, including 15-year-old Thurlene Stillday (shown at left).

much more dangerous place than it is. As a result, some teens act more aggressively as a way to protect themselves from becoming victims of violence. Sociologists argue that the "violence as entertainment" presented by the media clouds teenagers' understanding of the consequences of violence.

Drug Use and Violence In May 2011 a Butler Center for Research study found a significant link between youth violence and substance abuse. The report also found that the more drugs teenagers use, the more likely they are to engage in violent behavior. In addition, one in four teens who used illicit drugs in the past year report attacking others with the intent to harm.

According to a recent national poll conducted by the Partnership for a Drug-Free America, many teens think adults should be doing more to solve the drug problem. The poll also found that teens strongly associate violence with drug use. Almost 80 percent of the teens polled said that they believed teens who use drugs are more likely to be exposed to violence.

Teen Violence and Society According to sociological studies on teen violence, violent teens do not transition well into adulthood. Many are filled with anger during adolescence and are prone to lashing out and blaming others for their problems. They might also be seeking revenge against bullies or groups of teens who have rejected them. Sociologist Katherine Newman tries to explain the mind of the violent teen by stating, "this is someone who is a failed joiner, who is trying to gain access to peer groups that reject him."

What do you think?

1. What are some of the causes of teen violence?
2. What else do you think can be done to prevent teen violence? Discuss.

CHAPTER 5

THE ADOLESCENT IN SOCIETY

Chapter at a Glance

SECTION 1: Understanding Adolescence

- Adolescence refers to a distinct stage of life that occurs between the onset of puberty and adulthood.
- In the United States, the concept of adolescence is a recent development, resulting from a combination of post-Civil War historical events.
- The five leading characteristics of adolescence are biological growth and development, an undefined status, increased decision making, increased pressures, and the search for self.

SECTION 2: Teenagers and Dating

- Dating, or the meeting of people as a romantic engagement, is most commonly found in societies that allow people to select their own marriage partners.
- Before the development of dating in the United States, the courtship system was the most common means through which unmarried men and women interacted.
- Traditional American dating patterns date back to social changes brought about by the Industrial Revolution and new forms of technology.
- Dating today serves many functions, including entertainment, socialization, the fulfillment of basic psychological needs, the achievement of social status, and the selection of a spouse.

SECTION 3: Challenges of Adolescence

- Adolescents in American society experience a number of social challenges related to sexual behavior, drugs, and suicide.
- Teenagers who engage in early sexual activity face serious health challenges, including pregnancy and sexually transmitted diseases.
- Alcohol consumption, cigarette smoking, drug use, and drug-related violence are persistent and widespread problems among teenagers.
- Suicide is a major challenge facing American teenagers, and the suicide rates for teens now exceed the suicide rates for the general population.

SECTION 1

Understanding Adolescence

Before You Read

Main Idea
Adolescence is a time of great change and an important transition to adulthood.

Reading Focus
1. How has the concept of adolescence developed as a distinct stage of the life cycle in the United States?
2. What are the five general characteristics of adolescence?

Vocabulary
adolescence
puberty
anticipatory socialization

TAKING NOTES As you read, use a graphic organizer like this one to take notes on the characteristics of adolescence.

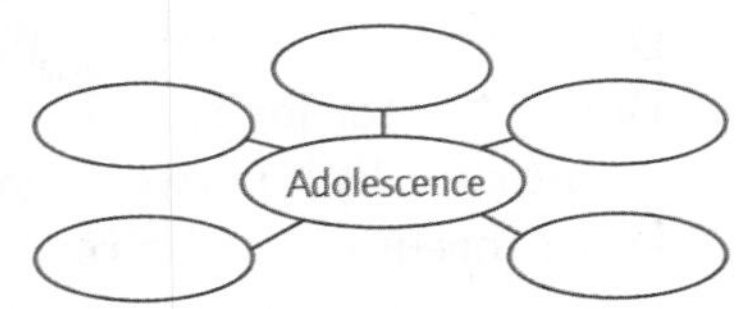

The Adolescent Brain: A Work in Progress

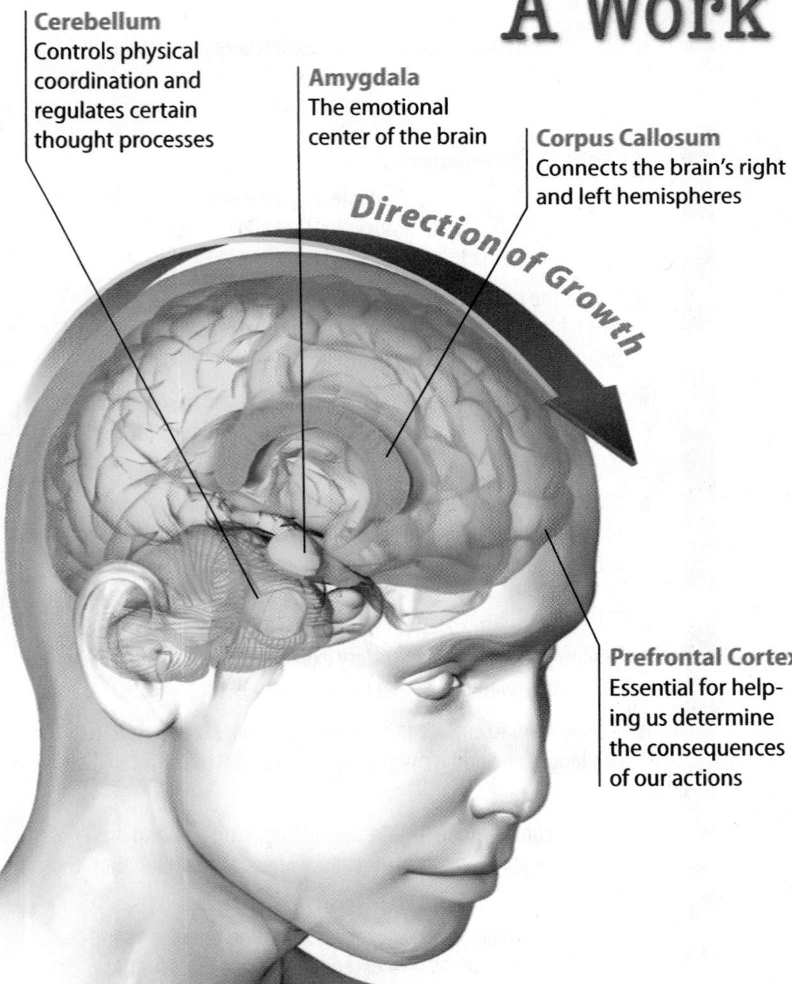

SOCIOLOGY CLOSE UP ***How is a teenager's brain different from an adult's brain?*** Before 2012, most neuroscientists believed that the human brain is fully developed by age 12. However, recent studies of the brain using magnetic resonance imaging, or MRI, have revealed that the adolescent brain continues to mature. The teenage brain can be likened to a giant construction project, with millions of connections being assembled and hooked up.

Areas of the brain that develop during the teen years include the cerebellum, corpus callosum, and prefrontal cortex. In the cerebellum, the number of neurons and their connections increase dramatically. In the corpus callosum, the fibers thicken and function more efficiently, which improves problem solving. The prefrontal cortex, an area that helps us plan ahead and think about the consequences of our actions, continues to develop well into the 20s. Until the prefrontal cortex is fully developed, teenagers must rely on the less-rational amygdala to make certain decisions.

Neuroscientists believe that the development of the adolescent brain helps to explain why some teens are impulsive, more susceptible to peer pressure, and may be prone to poor decision making. In addition, this new understanding of brain development helps mark adolescence as a distinct stage in life. ■

The Concept of Adolescence

Adolescence is a unique stage in a person's life. Adolescents are caught between two worlds. They are no longer children, yet they are not adults in the eyes of society. **Adolescence** is defined as the period between the normal onset of puberty and the beginning of adulthood. **Puberty** is the physical maturing that makes an individual capable of sexual reproduction. Adolescence as a distinct life stage is the creation of modern industrial society. It is not a universal phenomenon. The concept of adolescence simply does not exist in many parts of the world. However, puberty occurs in all human societies.

In American society, adolescence is generally considered to run from the ages of 12 to 19. However, puberty and acceptance into the adult world occur at different times for different people. Therefore, the beginning and end dates of adolescence are somewhat blurred.

Adolescence is not universal. In many preindustrial societies, young people go directly from childhood to adulthood once they have taken part in formal coming-of-age ceremonies. These ceremonies, which usually take place around age 13 or 14, differ from society to society. Common ceremonies include demonstrations of strength or endurance, filing of the teeth, and tattooing or scarring of the skin. Young people who successfully complete these ceremonies immediately become accepted members of adult society. Even though they are in their early teenage years, they can take on all adult roles. For these people, adolescence is an unknown concept.

Adolescence as a life stage is a relatively recent phenomenon. In the United States, this stage did not exist prior to the Civil War. Before that time, young people were treated simply as small adults. The adolescent experience has become an acknowledged stage of development in industrialized countries in only the past century.

Three factors have been particularly important in the development of adolescence as a distinct life stage in the United States. The first factor is education. State laws make education mandatory up to the age of 16, and most young people stay in school until they are 18. Those who attend college usually are in their early 20s when they graduate. For those people who pursue graduate degrees, educational requirements lengthen the time spent in school even more. Education extends the period of adolescence because many students are dependent on others for their financial support. While in school, most students do not take on the other roles of adulthood, such as spouse, parent, and provider.

The second factor that distinguishes young people as a separate group is the exclusion of youth from the labor force. In most states, child-labor laws prevent people from working until age 16. When they do start working, most young people lack the training to compete for all but the most routine jobs. Working adolescents do not typically have full-time jobs. Most work part-time while continuing to go to school.

The third important factor in the rise of adolescence as a distinct stage of the life cycle is the development of the juvenile-justice system. By distinguishing between juvenile and adult offenders, American society has created a separate legal status for young people.

Reading Check **Summarize** What factors are important to the development of adolescence?

Characteristics of Adolescence

The experiences of adolescence are not the same for everyone. However, five characteristics generally apply to the lives of all adolescents. These five characteristics are biological growth and development, an undefined status, increased decision making, increased pressures, and the search for self.

Biological Growth and Development The beginning of adolescence is typically marked by the onset of puberty. It is the period of human development during which people become able to produce children. Puberty begins when specific hormones are released. The brain and the endocrine system—a group of glands that produce various hormones—control biological development. Puberty is the one aspect of adolescence that is found in every society, and it is universal because it is biological rather than cultural in origin.

During early adolescence, young teens undergo growth spurts, voice changes, and the development of sexual characteristics.

Quick Lab

Using Refusal Skills

Drinking alcohol is one of the most common and serious pressures many teens face. How can you use refusal skills to say no to peer pressure?

PROCEDURE

1. Read the list of refusal skills and sample responses in the table below.
2. In three groups of four students, take turns role-playing a scenario in front of the class. In each group, one student will practice using refusal skills to avoid the pressure from three friends to drink alcohol, following the scenario.
3. Scenario: you have a couple of friends over to play video games. Your parents went out to dinner, so you have the house to yourselves. One friend finds beer in the refrigerator. She suggests that you and your friends drink it.

ANALYSIS

1. Discuss with your classmates how effective each student was in using refusal skills.
2. Make suggestions to each other about how to improve the use of refusal skills.

Refusal Skill	Sample Response
1. Blame someone else	"My parents would ground me for life. Besides it's just not worth it."
2. Suggest something else to do	"Let's order pizza and watch a movie."
3. Give a reason	"No, thanks, I don't think that's cool."

Other teens may also develop complexion problems. According to the American Academy of Dermatology, almost all teenagers develop some form of acne. More than 40 percent of adolescents have cases of acne so severe that they seek medical advice and treatment. These various biological changes sometimes cause anxiety or embarrassment, which is particularly true when the physical development of the individual is much faster or slower than others of the same age.

Undefined Status Our society's expectations for children are quite clear. The expectations for adults are also known. The adolescent expectations are often vague, however. While some adults treat adolescents as children, others treat them as adults. It is often difficult for adolescents to determine their status. For example, many states in the U.S. allow young people to marry—with parental consent—at age 16. However, they must be 18 before they can vote and must be 21 to drink alcohol. Different people have different attitudes about adolescents. Some adults are youth-oriented and have adopted some of the values, language, and dress that are popular among teenagers. On the other hand, adults are often critical of the way some adolescents dress, the music they listen to, and the way they behave.

Increased Decision Making Young children have most of their decisions made for them by adults. When children reach adolescence, they must make many of their own decisions. What courses should they take in school? What sports should they participate in? What school clubs should they join? Should they consider a college education? What career should they follow? There seems to be no end to the decisions that must be made. Some of these decisions are of little long-term importance. Other decisions, such as choosing a career, have far-reaching consequences.

Increased Pressure Adolescents are faced with pressure from many sources. For example, parents generally make rules on what time their children must be home, whom they can see, and where they can go. Yet some parents also want their children to have an active social life. As a result, young people are under pressure to strike a balance between parental wishes and peer pressures. Adolescents also have pressures placed on them in school. For example, they are required to attend classes, complete assignments, pass tests, and participate in activities.

Perhaps the greatest pressures come from peers. Most teenagers want to be accepted by their peers and to be a part of the "in" group.

If their friends have cars, most teenagers will feel some pressure to have a car of their own. Teenagers are also pressured to go along with the latest fads and fashions. Each year, billions of dollars are spent designing and marketing clothes, cosmetics, sports equipment, movies, and music to teenage consumers. In most cases, the advertisements for these products attempt to utilize peer pressure.

Adolescents also face pressure to establish relationships. Acceptance and popularity are central concerns. What does it take to be popular? How can a meaningful relationship be established? What should be done to maintain relationships? Such questions are of great importance to adolescents.

Some adolescents also face job-related pressures. The first pressure is that of finding a part-time or summer job. Then there is the pressure of having enough time for family life, a job, schoolwork, and social activities. Adolescents often find themselves in situations where their various roles of son or daughter, employee, student, athlete, club member, and friend conflict with one another.

The Search for Self Adolescents are mature enough to think about themselves and about what they want out of life. Most teens can sort through their values and decide what things are really important to them. They can establish personal norms that will guide their behavior. They can also set priorities for their lives. Such abilities are extremely important. When people know who they are, what they want out of life, and which values will serve them best, they are in a better position to make the most of adulthood.

Preparing for future roles is one aspect of finding oneself. Thus, anticipatory socialization is quite an important part of adolescent development. **Anticipatory socialization** involves learning the rights, obligations, and expectations of a role to prepare for assuming that role in the future. For example, playing house as a child is a form of anticipatory socialization for adult family roles. During adolescence, the time for taking on adult roles is much closer at hand. Therefore, anticipatory socialization becomes much more important. A part-time job, club membership, and dating are three common forms of anticipatory socialization during adolescence.

These five characteristics of adolescence are quite general, and individual experiences may differ widely. Adolescents do not live solely in an adolescent subculture. For example, economic status, family composition, and place of residence can affect a teen's life. Similarly, race, ethnicity, religion, and cultural heritage can make a difference in the kinds of adolescent experiences a person has.

Reading Check **Draw Conclusions** What do you think is the most challenging characteristic of adolescence? Explain.

SECTION 1 Assessment

Reviewing Main Ideas and Vocabulary

1. **Recall** What are the three factors that are important to adolescent development?
2. **Contrast** How is peer pressure different from job-related pressure?

Thinking Critically

3. **Elaborate** Give an example of a form of anticipatory socialization that you have experienced in your own life.
4. **Rank** Which of the five characteristics of adolescence do you think is most challenging for teens? Why?
5. **Draw Conclusions** Using your notes and a graphic organizer like this one, explain one issue associated with each characteristic of adolescence.

Characteristics	Issues

FOCUS ON WRITING

6. **Descriptive** Write two paragraphs explaining how the experience of adolescence might differ from teenager to teenager because of individual circumstances such as economic status, cultural background, family structure, or region of residence.

Coming of Age

What does it mean to become an adult? To answer this question, sociologists have examined cultures throughout the world. They have found that most cultures mark an adolescent's entry into adulthood with a rite of passage, a ritual that signals a transition from one major life stage to another. A rite of passage associated with becoming an adult is often called a coming-of-age ceremony.

The reading of the Torah is traditionally a part of the Jewish bar mitzvah ceremony.

Think about your own life. What events or ceremonies have marked different stages in your maturity? When do you expect society to say to you, "Now you have entered adulthood, and you can have the rights and responsibilities of an adult"? Some of our rites of passage into adulthood are informal events. For example, obtaining a driver's license has great significance to many teenagers. Likewise, voting at age 18 indicates that you are adult enough to participate in the political process. Rites of passage may also be marked by more formal and elaborate ceremonies, such as a high school prom or a debutante presentation.

All over the world, young people just like you engage in rites of passage to become adults. Although some of these rites and ceremonies may seem unusual, each has the same significance and function—to recognize that a young person has entered adulthood.

Mexico When a girl reaches 15 years old in Mexico, many people mark that milestone with a rite of passage called a *quinceañera*. A girl of 15 arrives at a thanksgiving mass in a traditional white or pastel dress full of frills. Her friends, who act as attendants, may accompany the girl. After mass, there may be a birthday party, at which a dance with the girl's favorite boy highlights the day's festivities.

Navajo Nation When a Navajo girl comes of age, she participates in a ceremony called Kinaalda. This ceremony lasts for four days. It is based on a cycle of songs called the Blessing Way. The ritual ends on the fourth day with a traditional meal in which the girl serves a special corn cake to symbolize her acceptance of the hard work that comes with adulthood.

Maasai As part of elaborate coming-of-age ceremonies, Maasai boys from the East African nations of Kenya and Tanzania go to live in manyattas, camps built by adult women of the society. There, the boys practice ancient rituals, including using spears and shields, to become warriors.

Judaism Many coming-of-age rituals are religious in nature. When a young boy of the Jewish faith makes a transition into manhood, he participates in a ceremony called a bar mitzvah. Girls participate in a similar ceremony called a bat mitzvah. Each ceremony is held on a single day soon after the youth's 13th birthday. However, the ritual requires months of preparation and learning about the Jewish faith, and completion of the ritual signifies that one has become an adult in the Jewish faith.

One thing that characterizes all of these rituals is the society's emphasis on the importance of publicly acknowledging a youth's entry into adulthood. Although the message that one is becoming an adult is serious, the rites and rituals themselves can be exciting and show that the adults accept the young person as one of their own.

Thinking Critically

1. **Contrast** How do these coming-of-age ceremonies differ?
2. **Discuss** What impact do you think coming-of-age ceremonies have on society?

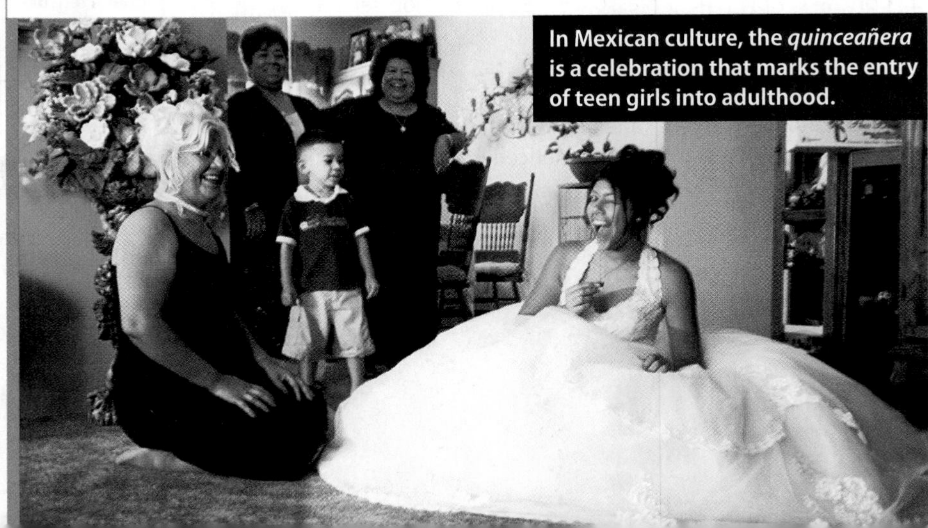

In Mexican culture, the *quinceañera* is a celebration that marks the entry of teen girls into adulthood.

SECTION 2

Teenagers and Dating

Before You Read

Main Idea

Dating, which has undergone many changes over time, serves important social functions for many teenagers.

Reading Focus

1. What are dating and courtship?
2. How did dating emerge as a form of social interaction?
3. What are some of the social functions of dating?
4. How are traditional and contemporary dating patterns different?

Vocabulary

dating
courtship
homogamy

TAKING NOTES As you read, use a graphic organizer like this one to take notes on dating.

Dating		
Traditional	Contemporary	Functions

SOCIOLOGY CLOSE UP ***How did a story of teenage love become one of the greatest romantic tragedies of all time?***

In *Romeo and Juliet,* a play by William Shakespeare, two young lovers in Verona, Italy, become victims of a bitter struggle between their rival families. As the feud between the families escalates, Romeo and Juliet fall in love and are secretly married. Eventually, however, they are engulfed by their families' conflict, and in the confusion both Romeo and Juliet commit suicide.

Romeo and Juliet is one of the most famous love stories of all time. It has been performed and retold many times and has influenced and inspired many great works of literature, art, music, film, and drama. In addition, the story's main characters have come to symbolize both young love and "star-crossed lovers" whose relationship, through fate, is doomed from the start.

Why has the story of *Romeo and Juliet* resonated so strongly with people for so long? There are many answers to this question, but one has to do with the nature of love, marriage, parental control, and social norms. *Romeo and Juliet* was written at a time when most young people were not free to choose their spouses. Instead, marriages were arranged by parents, and the idea of romantic love was not a primary concern. By falling in love and secretly marrying, Romeo and Juliet were defying the social customs of their time. ■

The story of Romeo and Juliet has inspired artists, poets, musicians, and writers for hundreds of years.

ACADEMIC VOCABULARY

continuum a coherent whole characterized as a collection, sequence, or progression

Dating and Courtship

Dating is a social behavior that is familiar to the vast majority of Americans—particularly teenagers. However, like adolescence, dating is not a universal phenomenon. **Dating,** or the meeting of people as a romantic engagement, is most commonly found in societies that allow individuals to choose their own marriage partners. In some societies, marriages are arranged by parents or a go-between who negotiates a formal marriage contract between families.

Because dating is so widespread in the United States today, it might seem as though it has been around forever. Actually, dating is a relatively recent phenomenon. It did not emerge as a form of social interaction between the sexes until after World War I. Moreover, only in the past 60 years have sociologists studied dating.

Prior to the rise of dating in the United States, interaction between young unmarried men and women was restricted to courtship. **Courtship** differs from dating in that courtship's express purpose is marriage. Dating, on the other hand, may eventually lead to marriage. The main purpose of dating is entertainment and amusement, at least in the casual stages. Dating is the means through which most individuals eventually do select their spouses in modern American society. Therefore, it might be helpful to view the process as a continuum. The continuum begins with casual dating, progresses to steady dating, and then moves on to engagement and, eventually, to marriage. As individuals move along the continuum, the degree of commitment given to the relationship increases. In the modern relationship system, the interaction may stop at any point along the continuum.

The courtship system that existed prior to dating was not this flexible. To understand courtship in modern terms, you might think of it as a point somewhere between steady dating and engagement on the continuum. Courtship was not casual, and roles were very strictly defined. To court a woman, a young man was expected first to meet her parents and ask their permission. It was also expected that the man's intentions would be honorable.

Courtship was usually conducted in the parlor of the woman's home under close supervision. Rarely was a couple left alone. If the relationship continued for some time, marriage was the expected outcome. Young people did have fun together during courtship, but its main purpose was to find a spouse. It was from this strictly structured base that the modern-day system of dating emerged.

Reading Check **Compare and Contrast** How are dating and courtship similar, and how are they different?

Courtship and Dating in the United States

For most of American history, young men and women socialized and selected spouses through courtship. Eventually, however, changing technologies and social patterns led to the decline of courtship and the development of dating. ***How have new technologies changed dating in the United States?***

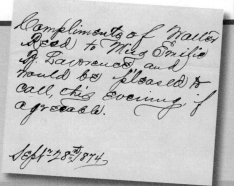

Compliments of Walter Reed to Miss Emilie B. Lawrence, and would be pleased to call, this Evening, if agreeable.

Sept 28th 1874

This letter from 1874 is an example of a request to visit in a formal courtship. It says "Compliments of Walter Reed to Miss Emile B. Lawrence, and would be pleased to call, this evening, if agreeable."

Early History Throughout the early history of the United States, most people were farmers, and men generally did not marry until their father gave them enough land to support a family. As a result, parents controlled the timing and circumstances of marriage.

Formal Courtship In formal courtship, roles were strictly defined, and the ultimate purpose was marriage. Young men had to ask permission to court a young woman. Couples usually met formally in the young woman's home, where they were closely supervised.

The Industrial Revolution During the Industrial Revolution, many young people left the farms and moved to cities to work. Free from their parents' economic control, young people began to interact more informally. Courtship declined, and dating began to develop.

The Emergence of Dating

The rise of industrialization contributed greatly to the development of dating in the United States. Prior to the Industrial Revolution, the economy of the United States was based primarily on agriculture. The timing of marriage was determined by the age at which a man acquired the property necessary to support a family. This requirement generally meant that marriage was delayed until a young man's father was willing to transfer a portion of the family land to the son. Because family property was involved, parents exercised considerable control over the marriage choices of their children.

During the Industrial Revolution many people moved away from farms and into the cities. As a result, young adults became less dependent on their parents for economic security. They could seek employment away from the family farm and establish their own households independent of their parents' assistance. This economic freedom reduced parental control over courtship and set the stage for the development of dating.

Free public secondary education also helped to pave the way for dating. By the beginning of the 1900s, the majority of secondary-school students were enrolled in public schools. Unlike many private schools, public schools were coeducational, which meant that young men and women spent a good portion of their day with one another.

The trend toward dating accelerated in the years after World War I. During this time, more and more Americans acquired telephones and automobiles. These two technological developments gave young people added freedoms. The 1920s also was a period of increased social and political equality for women. More women entered the workforce and took active roles in the community. As a result, the interaction between single adult men and single adult women increased. Under these changed social conditions, dating was a much more practical form of interaction than was the traditional courtship system.

Willard Waller conducted one of the earliest sociological analyses of American dating patterns. During the late 1920s and early 1930s, Waller studied the dating habits of students at Pennsylvania State University. Based on his findings, he concluded that casual dating was a form of entertainment that had little to do with mate selection. Status attainment and excitement were at the center of dating. Partners were selected on good looks, nice clothes, and popularity. Thus, dating contrasted sharply with the courtship process, in which the traits of dependability and honesty were most valuable.

ACADEMIC VOCABULARY

coeducational the education of students of both sexes at the same institution

Coeducational Public Schools By the early 1900s most high schools were coeducational, which increased social interaction between young men and women through events such as school dances.

The Telephone After World War I, telephone use increased dramatically, which allowed more opportunities for direct, informal contact between young men and women.

The Automobile The automobile increased dating among young people. By the 1950s, young couples commonly went in cars on unsupervised dates to drive-in movie theaters and other events.

Contemporary Dating Today, dating is more diverse than ever before. Young people have a range of new technologies that give them more flexibility to arrange informal meetings in a wide range of places.

Waller also found that dating on the Pennsylvania State campus was almost entirely limited to members of sororities and fraternities. Individuals dated people of similar social rank—members of the "best" fraternities dated members of the "best" sororities. Women ranked potential dates according to status characteristics such as fraternity membership, looks, money, clothes, cars, and dancing ability. The object was to be seen with the "right" people. To be seen with a person of lower status could damage an individual's social standing on campus.

Later research challenged Waller's picture of the "rating and dating" game. Status attainment and entertainment are certainly major factors that attract people to casual dating. However, character and personality factors are also important. Many similarities exist between the qualities that someone is looking for in a casual date and what he or she looks for in a marriage partner. For example, status attainment is important both in casual dating and in spouse selection. In fact, status attainment is a function of **homogamy**—the tendency of individuals to marry people with social characteristics similar to their own.

Reading Check **Identify Cause and Effect** What factors led to the emergence of dating in the United States?

Functions of Dating

Dating serves several important functions in adolescence. First, dating is a form of entertainment. Dating allows young people to get together to simply have fun. This goal is particularly true in the case of casual dating. Second, dating is a mechanism for socialization. It teaches individuals about other people and how to behave in social situations. It also helps individuals to learn appropriate role behaviors and to define their self-concepts. Third, dating fulfills certain basic psychological needs such as conversation, companionship, and understanding. Fourth, dating helps individuals attain status. In societies where individuals choose their own marriage partners, people are judged in part by whom they date. In some societies dating a person who is valued by others can raise one's own status. Finally, in the later stages of dating, spouse selection becomes an important issue.

All of these functions are not necessarily present at each stage of the dating continuum. If they are present, they may not carry the same weight. For example, in the case of casual dating, entertainment and status attainment may be, as Waller suggested, the most important functions. However, as the level of commitment in a relationship increases, socialization and companionship may be of primary concern.

Reading Check **Summarize** What are five important functions of dating?

Dating Patterns

Dating patterns, like dating relationships, can be viewed as a continuum. On one end are traditional dating patterns. These are the ones most closely associated with dating behavior prior to the 1960s. On the other end of the continuum are the informal patterns that are characteristic of dating today.

Traditional Dating Patterns Traditional dating patterns can still be found in small towns and rural areas of the United States. However, they are most characteristic of dating during the 1940s and 1950s. Under the traditional dating system, responsibility for arranging a date fell to the man. He was expected to contact his intended dating partner, suggest a time and place for the date, select the activity, and pay for any expenses that arose.

Dating behavior was quite ritualized. Both parties knew what was expected of them because the rules of conduct were well defined by the group to which they belonged. Peer pressure to conform to expected behavior was strong, and behavior that was not in line with group expectations met with sharp disapproval. In most cases, an established weekly timetable for setting up a date existed. If Wednesday was the designated day for arranging Saturday night dates, attempts by young men made later in the week often met with rejection. If a young woman accepted a date late in the week, this action was often seen as an acknowledgment that she was not a young man's first choice. Dating was so expected and so tied to social status that individuals who did not have dates on prime dating nights were known to hide in their rooms in shame.

TECHNOLOGY FOCUS

The Science of Attraction

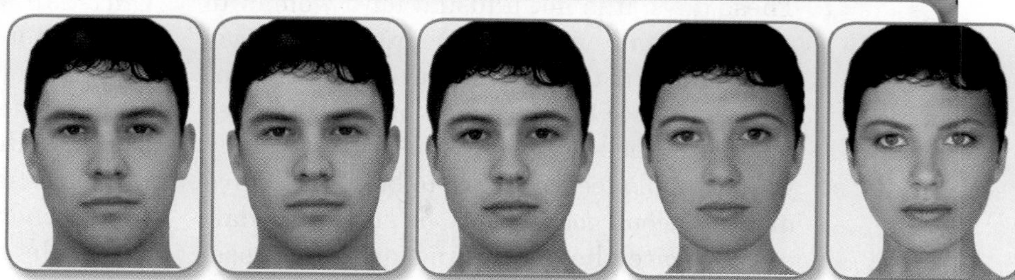

These photos show a male face morphed into a female face. Scientists use this advanced computer technology to study people's reactions to appearance.

Have you ever thought about why you are you attracted to someone? Using the latest technology to study the science behind attraction, scientists have discovered that most men and women prefer their partners' to have symmetrical faces. Other studies have also shown that people tend to be attracted to people who look very similar to themselves. In a study in Scotland, scientists used computer-graphic technology to morph photographs of college students' faces into the opposite sex. However, the students were not aware that they were viewing morphed photos of themselves. After viewing all of the photos of the opposite sex, most students preferred the morphed photos.

In addition to discovering that opposites do not usually attract, scientists have used technology to study other factors in attraction, such as the ability to "smell" genes. In one study, researchers gave t-shirts saturated with male sweat to female participants. The results astounded the researchers—the women preferred the odor of the men who shared genes similar to their own. Today, scientists continue to investigate the role of odors and certain chemicals humans may emit to attract the opposite sex. Science may one day determine whether the eyes or nose really knows who you should be attracted to.

Thinking Critically

Analyze Do you think most celebrities who are considered beautiful by society have faces that are symmetrical?

Particularly in the early stages of a relationship, dates revolved around set activities such as going to movies or sporting events. This type of activity often helped to lessen the stress felt by dating partners. For example, if interaction between the partners proved awkward, they could focus their attention on the activity.

If a couple continued to date casually over a period of time, the relationship often developed into one of steady dating. This type of dating carried with it a formal set of expectations and commitments. As a visible symbol of the commitment to "go steady", the young man often gave the young woman his class ring, identification bracelet, or letterman's jacket. Because of the level of commitment involved, steady dating acted as a form of anticipatory socialization for marriage. Even so, steady partners were not necessarily expected to get married. Individuals commonly had several "steadies" at different times throughout their adolescence before settling on a future marriage partner.

Contemporary Dating Patterns Since the 1960s, dating has not followed such formal patterns. Today there is greater opportunity for young men and women to interact with each other informally. There are no set stages of dating. In addition, there is now greater equality in dating, and both sexes actively initiate dates. Similarly, it is acceptable for either partner to pay for the date.

This tendency toward flexibility reveals some important differences between traditional and contemporary dating patterns. Under the traditional dating system, interaction was formal and the relationship centered on the couple. In order to obtain a date, some men thought they needed to have a good "line"—a method of selling themselves to a potential date. Today relationships are based more on friendship and the group than on the couple. Consequently, it is often not necessary to use a "line" to create a first impression. In addition, teens today have more opportunities to communicate with each other through text messaging and social media.

Contemporary society gives teenagers a lot more freedom than they had in the past. These days, it is not unusual for a woman to ask a man out on a date, something that was unthinkable in the past. However, today's teenagers can face enormous emotional stresses because of these freedoms. For example, many young people feel pressure to be cool, to have money, to look good, and to be successful daters. Despite the stress and awkwardness, however, dating is still an important step in adolescent development and socialization, and a way to test the waters of a relationship.

Dating in the Age of Social Media In the time before computers and the Internet, dating for young people was limited by the number of people with whom one had direct contact. Dating involved meeting people by chance encounter, the sharing of some physical space or event (such as a school or job), or through some common peer who might set up a meeting or date. In the digital age, however, the entire process of dating has changed considerably. In 2016, many young people can meet a potential mate through their digital technology, such as smartphones, computers, or computer tablets. Numerous dating Web sites have been developed to assist people in meeting potential romantic partners, making the process even simpler through the development of "apps" that can be used with mobile technology, such as smartphones. Some of the most popular dating sites include OkCupid, Match.Com, Plenty of Fish, Zoosk, E-Harmony, and MeetMe. Some sites, such as Christian Mingle (for Christian singles) and J-Date (for Jewish singles) even tailor their networking platforms to very specific groups. Others, like Match.Com and E-Harmony, use sophisticated algorithms to match potential mates, based on psychological research and the psychometrics of dating.

While many people have debated the net positives or net negatives of online dating, there is wide agreement that digital technology has had an impact on the process of dating. With online dating, it is easier to make contact with a potential mate. With the click of a mouse, one can easily search potential mates and schedule meetings. Also, online dating makes it easier to know considerably more about a potential mate before physically meeting them. Finally, it is imperative to mention the potential risks associated with engaging in social interaction with another person online. Sexual predators can use social media dating sites to stalk potential prey, and some social scientists have voiced concern over the possible effects of online dating's contribution to what has become known as a "hook-up" culture on many college campuses, where young people use social media dating sites to have casual sexual encounters.

Reading Check **Analyze** How have dating patterns changed in the United States over time?

SECTION 2 Assessment

Reviewing Main Ideas and Vocabulary

1. **Describe** What are some basic features of courtship and dating?
2. **Sequence** When did dating begin to emerge in the United States?
3. **Make Generalizations** How do the functions of dating differ as the level of commitment in a relationship increases?
4. **Compare** How are modern dating patterns similar to traditional dating patterns in the United States?

Thinking Critically

5. **Develop** How did the Industrial Revolution contribute to the development of dating in the United States? How have more modern technologies, such as the Internet and cell phones, affected dating patterns?
6. **Support a Position** Which of the functions of dating do you think is the most important? Why?
7. **Rank** Using your notes on dating and a graphic organizer like the one below, list the basic stages of dating on a continuum from Least Commitment to Most Commitment.

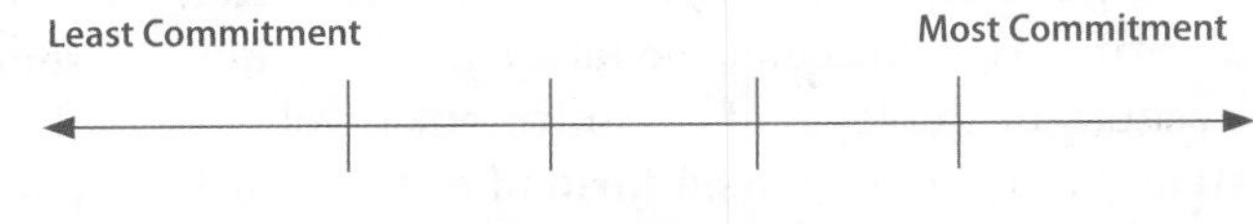

FOCUS ON WRITING

8. **Descriptive** Write two brief paragraphs comparing traditional dating patterns with dating patterns that are common today. Be sure to consider the ritualized nature of traditional patterns and the more informal nature of modern dating.

SECTION 3

Challenges of Adolescence

Before You Read

Main Idea

Adolescents face many difficult challenges, including issues related to sexual behavior, drugs, and suicide.

Reading Focus

1. What are some of the main concerns about teenage sexual behavior?
2. Why is teenage drug use such a problem in the United States?
3. What social factors contribute to teenage suicide?

Vocabulary

abstinence
sexually transmitted diseases (STDs)
drug
social integration

TAKING NOTES Use a graphic organizer like this one to take notes on the challenges of adolescence.

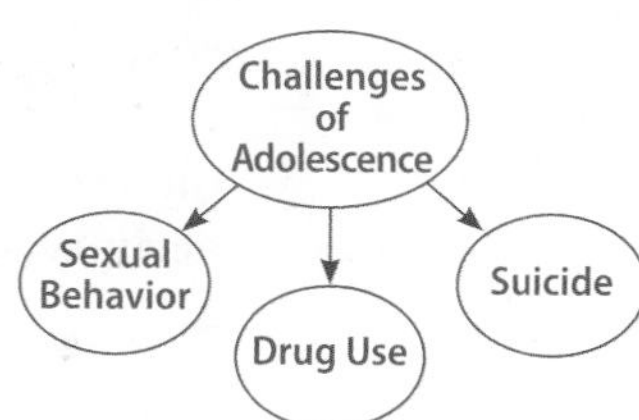

PROCEED WITH **CAUTION**

SOCIOLOGY CLOSE UP ***What are some of the difficult decisions that adolescents face in their lives?*** Adolescence can be a difficult and confusing time. Caught between the relative safety of childhood and the greater independence of adulthood, teenagers face major developmental challenges. These challenges include carving out an identity, becoming more independent, developing close relationships with other people, and planning for the future. Most teenagers accomplish these tasks without too much difficulty. However, others do not. For these teenagers, life can seem overwhelming at times.

As teenagers try to figure who they are and who they want to be, they are also confronted for the first time with important, life decisions—and their decisions can have serious long-term consequences. For example, many teenagers face situations involving sexual behavior, drug use, and other risky behaviors. They must learn to make responsible decisions, often under pressure from others. How teenagers make these difficult decisions shapes who they are, who they will become, and which way they will travel on the road of life. ■

Teenage Sexual Behavior

As with so many other social phenomena, the norms governing sexual behavior vary widely from society to society. Some small preindustrial societies permit adolescents to engage in sexual behavior before marriage. In some of these societies—such as the Trobrianders of the South Pacific Ocean—sexual experimentation is even encouraged. Such experimentation is viewed as preparation for marriage. In Western countries, on the other hand, traditional sexual values include strict norms against premarital sexuality. Traditional sexual values in the United States are an outgrowth of Puritan and Victorian views of sexual morality. According to these views, sexual activity should be confined to marriage.

The Sexual Revolution Until the 1960s, traditional sexual values had the support of the vast majority of Americans—at least in principle, if not always in practice. However, in the 1960s and 1970s the development of the birth-control pill, a youth counterculture, and the feminist movement led to what has been called the "sexual revolution."

During this revolution, the norms governing sexual behavior began to change. For many people, human sexuality became a topic that was openly discussed and explored. As a consequence, sexuality is a familiar feature of American culture today. For example, sexual references are common in the programs seen in the 98 percent of American households that own television sets. Similarly, varying degrees of physical intimacy are found in almost every film that does not carry a G rating. In addition, advertisers have been using the lure of sexuality to sell their products for years.

One of the unanticipated consequences of the changing norms concerning sexuality has been a dramatic increase in adolescent sexual behavior. As a result, social scientists now devote considerable time to measuring the rate of teenage sexual activity and to analyzing the factors that influence teenage sexuality consequences.

The Rate of Teenage Sexual Activity Survey data from the Centers for Disease Control and Prevention (CDC) indicate that 29 percent of unmarried American females between the ages of 15 and 19 were sexually active in 1970. By 1995 the rate of sexual activity had increased to 50 percent for the same category of teenagers. Teenage childbearing showed a similar pattern. In 1970 there were 22 births per 1,000 unmarried teenage females. By 1996 the birthrate for unmarried teenage females had risen to 43. However, these numbers have dropped since the early 1990s. In 2013 the birthrate for women aged 15–19 dropped to 26.5, a record low for U.S. teens.

The birthrate among American teenagers is considerably higher than it is among teenagers of other industrialized countries. During the 1990s the CDC established national health objectives to address this issue. CDC programs encouraged **abstinence,** or voluntarily not engaging in sexual behavior, among teenagers. For those unwilling to abstain, the CDC has encouraged the use of effective methods of birth control. Surveys conducted in the late 1990s indicate that CDC programs have had some success. Sexual activity among teenagers declined during the decade, teenagers' use of birth control increased, and the teen-pregnancy rate decreased.

Influences on Early Sexual Activity Social scientists have developed a number of explanations for why adolescents engage in sexual activity. Most often, these explanations focus on social and economic factors or on subcultural factors.

Among the social and economic factors found to influence early sexual activity are family-income level, parents' marital status, and religious participation. In general, teenagers from higher-income two-parent families have lower rates of sexual activity than teenagers from low-income one-parent families. Similarly, some teenagers who actively practice their religion tend to hold less-permissive attitudes and are less experienced sexually than some nonreligious teenagers.

Explanations that focus on subcultures suggest that teenage sexual activity is influenced by subgroup norms concerning sexual behavior. Generally, teenagers whose friends engage in premarital sex are more likely to be sexually active than those whose friends are not sexually active. Early sexual behavior is also associated with other risk-taking behaviors such as drug use and delinquency.

Consequences of Early Sexual Activity Sexual activity has consequences. For teenagers, these consequences are often negative. Some social scientists who study teenage sexuality focus on the social and health consequences of early sexual activity.

According to CDC statistics, less than one third of American teenage women who are sexually active use birth-control methods on a regular basis. Thus, it is not surprising that each year about 1 million teenage women become pregnant.

Teenage pregnancy has been found to have a number of negative consequences. Chief among them are the following:

- Babies born to teenage mothers have lower birth weights and are more likely to die within the first year of life than are babies born to women older than 20.
- Teenagers who become mothers and fathers are less likely to finish high school and college than teenagers who do not become parents. This outcome is particularly true for teenage mothers.
- Due in large part to lower levels of education, individuals who become parents during adolescence have lower lifetime earnings than individuals who delay parenthood until later in life.
- Children of teenage parents are more likely to experience learning difficulties than children of older parents.
- Children of teenage parents have an increased risk of becoming teenage parents themselves.
- Teenage mothers often face significant emotional stress.

Even when pregnancy does not occur, early sexual activity can have negative health effects. Sexual contact exposes teenagers to **sexually transmitted diseases (STDs),** such as the human papillomavirus (HPV), syphilis, gonorrhea, chlamydia, genital herpes, and acquired immune deficiency syndrome (AIDS). Studies indicate that some 4 million American teenagers contract a sexually transmitted disease each year. According to data released by the Centers of Disease Control in 2008, one in four women between the ages of 14 and 19 in the United States is infected with either HPV, chlamydia, or genital herpes.

Statistically Speaking...

Teen Pregnancy Since 2012 the birthrate among 15- to 19-year-old women in the United States has dropped by 10 percent. In 2014 Arkansas had the highest teen birthrate—3.95 percent. New Hampshire had lowest teen birthrate at just 1.1 percent. The birthrate among Hispanic teens was 4.17 percent—one-and-a-half times the national average.

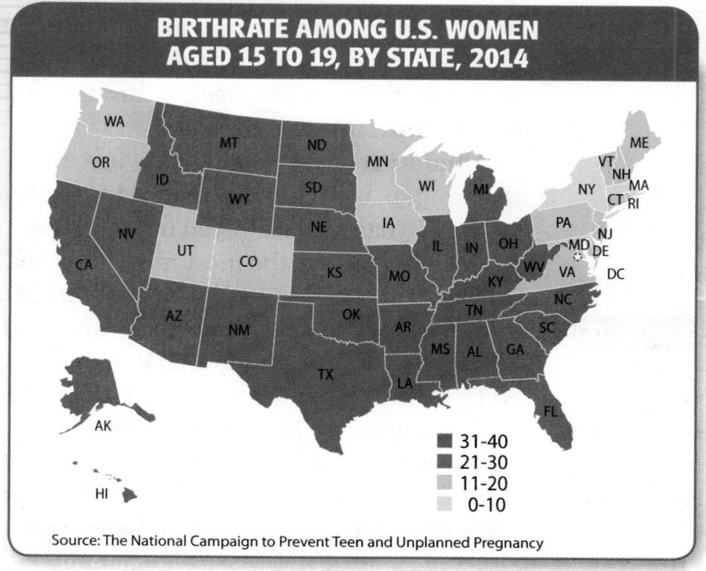

Source: The National Campaign to Prevent Teen and Unplanned Pregnancy

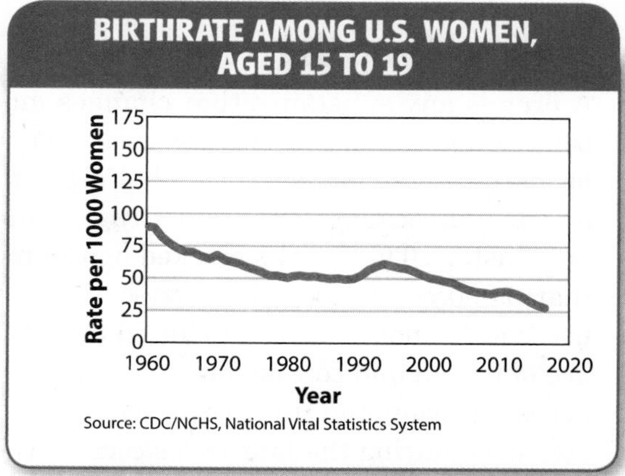

Source: CDC/NCHS, National Vital Statistics System

Thinking Critically What do you think accounts for the high birthrate in Texas and New Mexico?

The most common STD among teens in this age group is HPV infection. As a result, the Federal Drug Administration (FDA) quickly approved a vaccine for HPV. The FDA recommends this vaccine be given to women aged 9 to 26 years old before they become sexually active.

Another threat to the teenage population is the fatal disease AIDS, which is caused by a virus that attacks the human immune system, leaving the person vulnerable to a host of deadly infections. HIV is the virus that causes AIDS. High rates of sexual activity combined with low rates of condom use put teenagers at risk of contracting the disease through sexual contact with infected partners.

Studies show that teenagers are aware of the dangers of HIV/AIDS. Some 44 percent of 15- to 17-year-olds surveyed in 1998 said that HIV/AIDS is one of the most important health issues facing teenagers. Yet, at the same time, few teenagers say they think they are personally at risk of contracting HIV or any other STD. However, according to the CDC, at least 25 percent of new HIV infections occur among people younger than 25. More significantly, in 2010, about 60 percent of all youth with HIV were unaware of being infected and were not receiving treatment.

CASE STUDY CONNECTION

Teen Violence In the United States, school shootings and drug-related violence among teens are serious problems.

Reading Check **Find the Main Idea** What are some basic facts about teenage sexual behavior?

Teenage Drug Use

A **drug** is any substance that changes mood, behavior, or consciousness. Drugs exist in many forms, including medicines, alcohol, cigarettes, marijuana, cocaine, and heroin. Drug use has a long history. The Greeks smoked opium more than 3,000 years ago, and the Aztecs commonly used hallucinogens. In the United States the use of heroin and cocaine for nonmedical purposes was common until the early 1900s. In fact, even during the late 1800s cocaine could be found as an ingredient in a wide variety of products, including soft drinks, cough medicines, and nasal sprays. Today, drugs such as marijuana, methamphetamines, and prescription pain killers have become prevalent in American society. In 2013, about 9.4 percent of Americans 12 years and older had used an illicit drug in the past year. However, there are social consequences to drug use.

Drug Violence In recent decades, the public has become increasingly alarmed over the social consequences of drug abuse. This alarm is primarily a result of the dramatic increase in drug-related crime beginning in the 1980s and 1990s. Muggings, robberies, and burglaries committed by addicts in search of drug money have become a common occurrence. Even more frightening is the growth in violence associated with drug trafficking. In 2005 there were 589 drug-related murders in the United States. This violence was largely the result of turf wars between rival gangs engaged in drug trafficking. Adult criminal gangs control the drug trade in the United States. However, the foot soldiers are often children and teenagers. Children as young as 9 or 10 are hired first as lookouts. In time, they rise in the gang hierarchy to become runners and eventually drug dealers.

Crack cocaine is the principal cause of the dramatic rise in drug-related violence. Crack is a highly addictive smokable form of cocaine. With the introduction of crack in the early to mid-1980s, drug-related juvenile arrests skyrocketed. Although these numbers dropped in 1998, more than 200,000 juveniles were arrested in the United States for drug-abuse violations. This number represents an 86 percent increase over 1990 figures.

The Rate of Teenage Drug Use Since 1975, the University of Michigan's Institute for Social Research has conducted an annual survey of high-school seniors. The bar graph on the next page of drug use among 12th graders shows changes in the rates of use for various drugs from 2012 through 2015.

Usage patterns vary by type of drug. Marijuana use increased in the mid-1990s then gradually declined in the last several years. Marijuana remains the most widely used illegal drug among high-school seniors. Cocaine use has followed a similar pattern, but the use of hallucinogens such as LSD peaked in the mid-1990s. Use of new drugs such as MDMA, or ecstasy, has increased in the late 1990s and early 2000s. Cigarette smoking has dropped significantly since the 1990s— partly because of repeated health warnings about the negative effects of smoking. However, the survey indicates that 11.4 percent of high-school seniors are regular smokers.

Alcohol use among teenagers has declined in recent years, but it remains a widespread problem. In 2015 about 64 percent of the high school seniors surveyed reported having used alcohol at some point. In addition, 35.3 percent reported having had a drink as recently as a month before the survey was taken. About 2 percent of the seniors surveyed said that they drank daily. These findings are particularly significant in light of the fact that it is illegal for virtually all high-school students to buy alcohol.

Any downward trend in drug use, however slight, is encouraging. Nevertheless, two factors should be kept in mind when analyzing the University of Michigan data. First, even with the recent declines, the United States has the highest rate of drug use among adolescents of any industrialized country. Second, the survey does not measure drug use among the approximately 25 percent of young Americans who do not graduate from high school. Research has indicated that high-school dropouts have much higher rates of drug use than do high-school seniors. Thus, it is likely that the survey underestimates the scope of the drug problem among teenagers.

Influences on Teenage Drug Use Why do teenagers use drugs? Social scientists have found a number of factors associated with the regular use of drugs by teenagers. Chief among these factors are the following:

- having friends who regularly engage in drug use
- having social and academic adjustment problems
- living in a hostile and rejecting family setting

Teenage Attitudes Toward Drug Use The University of Michigan surveys also monitor changes in the attitudes of teenagers toward drug use. At the peak of marijuana use in 1979, only 42 percent of the twelfth graders surveyed believed that regular marijuana use was harmful to one's health. By 2007 that figure stood at about 55 percent. This jump can be attributed to a better awareness and education of marijuana's harmful effects. However, by 2015 this number had dropped to 31.9 percent, possibly owing to national changes in attitudes about marijuana due to the recent legalization in Colorado and Washington state. Similarly, in the late 1970s approximately 69 percent of the seniors surveyed thought that regular cocaine use was harmful. By 2015 more than 79 percent of the twelfth graders surveyed reported that regular cocaine use was harmful to one's health.

The view that cigarette smoking is harmful has increased over the years of the survey. In 1975 slightly more than 51 percent of the seniors believed that smoking one or more packs of cigarettes a day was harmful to one's health. By 2015 that figure had increased to about 75.9 percent. However, attitudes toward the health dangers presented by alcohol have remained fairly constant—and low—over the course of the surveys. Less than 25 percent of seniors believe that taking one or two drinks nearly every day was harmful.

Statistically Speaking...

Teen Drug Use According to the results of a national survey conducted by researchers at the University of Michigan's Institute for Social Research, the use of alcohol and cigarettes among twelfth graders has gradually declined between 2005 and 2015. However, during this 10-year period, illegal drug use by twelfth graders overall has remained about the same.

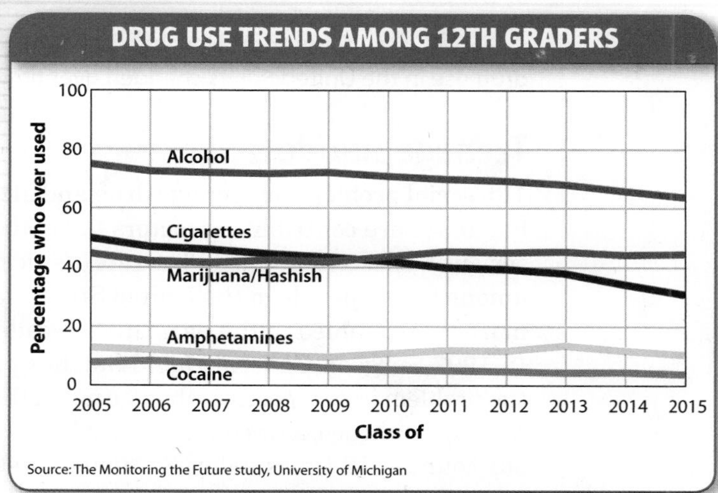

Skills Focus **INTERPRETING GRAPHS** Which drug showed the largest decline in usage between 2005 and 2015? Why do think fewer twelfth graders are using this drug?

The disapproval ratings for the use of marijuana among twelfth graders peaked and declined, while during the same time period the disapproval ratings for smoking among twelfth graders has remained relatively stable. For example, in 1977, more than 65 percent of the seniors surveyed disapproved of regular marijuana use. By 2005 about 58 percent of those surveyed disapproved. By 2015, however, that number had dropped to about 32 percent. However, the disapproval rate in the case of cigarette smoking has remained more constant. In 1977 about 66 percent of high-school seniors disapproved of smoking one or more packs of cigarettes a day. By 2005 that figure had increased to about 78 percent, and in 2015 was about 76 percent. Negative attitudes toward regular use of drugs such as LSD, cocaine, heroin, amphetamines, and barbiturates have remained fairly constant over the course of the surveys. Heavy daily use of alcohol received about a 60 percent negative response through the years of the survey.

Negative attitudes toward regular use of drugs such as LSD, cocaine, heroin, amphetamines, and barbiturates have remained fairly constant over the course of the surveys. Depending on the drug, disapproval ratings have ranged from 90 percent to 98 percent. Heavy daily use of alcohol received about a 90 percent negative response through the years of the survey.

Reading Check **Sequence** How has teenage drug use in the United States changed over time?

Teenage Suicide

The social problems of teenage drug and alcohol abuse are contributing factors to another serious adolescent problem. The rate of suicide among young people in the United States has more than doubled in the past three decades. In 1997 Surgeon General David Satcher put the problem in perspective when he noted that "a youth suicide occurs once every 2 hours in our country, 12 times a day, 84 times a week . . . well over 4,000 times a year." The suicide rate for young people now exceeds the rate for the general population. Suicide is third only to accidents and homicides as the leading cause of death among people age 5 to 24. It is the third leading cause of death among 10- to 14-year-olds.

Studies suggest that the actual number of suicides is higher than official statistics indicate. Many suicides are misreported as accidents. Deaths recorded as resulting from undetermined cause may actually be suicides. Researchers argue that suicide rates among the young would be much higher if certain accidental drownings, drug overdoses, and other similar deaths were taken into consideration.

In 2006 the CDC questioned a sample of high-school students on the topic of suicide. Some 8 percent of the students reported they had attempted suicide. Almost 17 percent said that they had seriously considered suicide. Two percent of them had even made a suicide attempt. While these findings may be startling, suicide is a much more serious problem among elderly people. The rate of suicide for adults aged 65 and older is almost twice as high as it is among the young.

The Sociological View of Suicide When you think of the causes and consequences of suicide, you probably think in terms of individuals. You most likely see suicide as a personal act that results from psychological factors such as depression. Sociologists acknowledge that suicide is an act committed by individuals, but they are more interested in the social factors that affect suicide rates. According to the sociological perspective, variations in suicide rates can be understood by studying the structure of society and people's experiences.

Émile Durkheim's classic study *Suicide* is still the most comprehensive sociological analysis of suicide to date. Durkheim was interested in why some societies or groups within a society have higher rates of suicide than others. According to Durkheim, variations in suicide rates can be explained by the level of social integration in a group or society. **Social integration** is the degree of attachment people have to social groups or to society as a whole. Durkheim predicted that groups or societies with particularly high or particularly low levels of social integration will have high rates of suicide.

In Durkheim's view, high levels of social integration can lead to increased rates of suicide because group members place the needs of the group above their own personal needs. For example, in the traditional Inuit society of

Arctic North America, elderly people walked into the snowy wild to die once they became a burden on the group. Strong community bonds made the elderly value the welfare of the group over their own welfare.

Suicides resulting from low levels of social integration are much more common than those resulting from high levels of integration. Low levels of integration occur in periods of social disorganization, which can result from many factors. Some common factors are rapid social change, increased geographic mobility, war or natural disasters, and sudden changes in economic conditions.

Suicide rates increase during periods of social disorganization because the norms that govern behavior during this time weaken or become less clear. In addition, the social bonds that give individuals a sense of group solidarity—such as family ties and religion—tend to weaken during periods of social disorganization. Some people turn to suicide when deprived of behavioral guidelines and social support. Suicide caused by low levels of social integration is found in modern societies.

Teenage Suicide As teenagers move from the role of child to that of adult, they are

Predictors of Teenage Suicide

Suicide cuts across all social categories. There are cases of teenage suicide among both sexes, every economic level, and all races, religions, and nationalities. Nevertheless, certain social factors appear to affect the rates of teenage suicide.

Alcohol or Drug Use The risk of suicide increases along with an adolescent's use of alcohol and drugs. Social scientists offer three explanations. First, teenagers who are heavy users of alcohol and drugs typically have low levels of self-control and are easily frustrated. Second, teenagers under the influence of drugs or alcohol are more likely to act on impulse. Third, teenagers often use drugs and alcohol as the method by which to commit suicide.

Triggering Events In most teenage suicides, a specific event or the anticipation of a specific event triggers the suicide attempt. Common triggers include fear of punishment, loss of or rejection by an important person, unwanted pregnancy, family crisis, poor school performance, and a fight with a friend or family member.

Age The risk of suicide increases with age. Although children under the age of 13 do commit suicide, rates are much higher for older teenagers and young adults.

Sex Females are three times more likely than males to attempt suicide. However, males are much more likely to succeed. This outcome is partially a result of the fact that teenage men often choose guns and other weapons as the means to commit suicide.

Population Density Recent studies indicate that underpopulated areas have higher rates of teenage suicide than do heavily populated areas. Researchers believe that the higher rate may be a result of social isolation, which is more likely in underpopulated areas. In addition, teenagers in underpopulated areas generally have access to fewer social services.

Family Relations Suicide rates are higher for teenagers from families in which violence, intense marital conflict, or the recent loss of a parent through divorce or death is evident. In addition, suicide is more common in those families in which parents show hostility or rejection toward their children.

Cluster Effect A teenage suicide sometimes results in other suicide attempts among adolescents in a community. This phenomenon is more likely to occur when a member of the community takes his or her life. In some instances, a well-publicized suicide can trigger "copycat" attempts in other communities as well. Mental-health officials suggest that the news of suicide acts as a fuse that ignites self-destructive behaviors in already unstable adolescents.

Skills Focus INTERPRETING CHARTS

How do social scientists explain the correlation between teen suicide and alcohol and drug use?

Warning Words

Recognizing the warning signs of suicide in yourself or in others could help save your life or someone else's life. If you notice yourself or another person making the following statements, talk to a parent or trusted adult.

"I wish I were dead."
"I just want to go to sleep and never wake up."
"I won't be a problem for you much longer."
"I can't take it anymore."
"This pain will be over soon."
"Nothing matters."

faced with new freedoms and responsibilities, as well as new restrictions. Many of the norms that governed proper behavior during childhood no longer apply. Yet many adult behaviors are still considered inappropriate for teenagers. At the same time, friends and the larger society have more and more influence over teenagers' beliefs and actions. As the control of the family lessens, teenagers begin to take increasing responsibility for their own actions.

Most teenagers adapt to these changing expectations. For some, however, the confusion and self-doubt common in adolescence are often blown out of proportion. Because teenagers tend to focus so much on the present, they often do not realize that most problems can be solved with time and patience. In some cases, social isolation and self-doubt lead to frustrations that may push adolescents toward suicidal behavior.

As the list of factors you've learned about indicates, teenage-suicide rates are influenced by the same sociological factors that affect rates of suicide in the adult population. Chief among these factors are social isolation and the weakening of social bonds.

Getting Help From Society Suicide is not the solution to a temporary problem. Everyone goes through hard times. Everyone has experienced loneliness. Learning to cope and manage pain and sadness is an important part of human development. Usually, the first step is to ask someone for help. Remaining silent can only cause isolation and further withdrawal from daily life.

When you or someone you know is thinking of suicide, do not ignore the problem. Warning signs include feelings of hopelessness, withdrawing from family and friends, neglecting basic needs, loss of energy, taking more risks, abusing alcohol and drugs, and giving away personal items. Anyone who is suicidal needs professional help and cannot fix the problem by himself or herself. It is very important that you get help for a friend who is suicidal. Thoughts of suicide are a cry for help. Likewise, if you or anyone you know are feeling depressed, don't delay asking a trusted adult for help.

Most cities have a variety of health organizations that offer services to people in need. Suicide hotlines staffed with trained counselors are available 24 hours a day.

Reading Check **Identify Supporting Details** What are three factors that can contribute to teenage suicide?

SECTION 3 Assessment

Reviewing Main Ideas and Vocabulary

1. **Cause and Effect** According to social scientists, what are some of the causes and consequences of teenage sexual activity?
2. **Identify** What are some of the main drugs used by teenagers, and what are their rates of use?
3. **Explain** According to Durkheim, how can variations in suicide rates be explained by levels of social integration?

Thinking Critically

4. **Analyze** Why might teenagers whose friends engage in sex be more likely to be sexually active?
5. **Elaborate** What are some possible explanations for the fact that the United States has the highest rate of drug use among adolescents in the industrialized world?
6. **Evaluate** Using your notes and a graphic organizer like the one below, identify what you think are the three most important facts about each of the challenges of adolescence.

Challenges of Adolescence

Sexual Behavior	Drug Use	Suicide
1. 2. 3.	1. 2. 3.	1. 2. 3.

FOCUS ON WRITING

7. **Persuasive** Write a brief public service announcement warning against the dangers of teenage sexual behavior or suicide. Use facts to highlight the seriousness of your topic. Then include a persuasive message designed to change teenage attitudes and behaviors.

Bullying

Distraught, afraid, and wondering why no one likes him, Evan sits at a table in his high school's cafeteria—alone. Evan is a 12th grader with average looks, a great sense of humor, and a loyal friend. Unfortunately, for some reason that Evan nor his parents or teachers understand, Evan has been singled out by his peers. His classmates call him names, punch him, and send him abusive e-mails. Like thousands of other adolescents, Evan is a victim of bullying.

THE STATS ON BULLYING

The #1 most common form of violence is bullying.

20% of high school students reported being bullied at school in 2013.

Nearly 160,000 young people miss school every day because of fear of attack or intimidation by other students.

9% of 10- to 17-year-olds say they were abused at least once by "cyber bullies."

Sources: Center for Disease Control (CDC); National Center for Education Statistics

Bullying is more than simply teasing. It is an intentional behavior that is meant to hurt and dominate another person. We used to think bullying was just verbal and physical abuse. In recent years, however, cyberbullying—using electronic means to torment, threaten, harass, humiliate, embarrass or otherwise target another—has grown. As a result of teenagers spending a lot of time online, bullies are using the Internet as their public space to torment their victims. In response to this problem, popular social networking Web sites such as Facebook have recently put safety measures in place to try to prevent cyberbullying.

"Fighting back only engages bullies, who want a reaction," says counselor Mary Worthington for the Network of Victim Assistance. "Handling bullying online is different than staring down someone in the schoolyard and asking them to stop." Unlike face-to-face bullying, cyberbullying allows bullies to unleash put-downs, nasty rumors, and embarrassing pictures in e-mail and blogs that reach victims at home and at any time. Even though it is not always obvious to parents and teachers, the damage to the victims can be devastating. "Bullying, like other forms of aggression and violence, have a cumulative effect on the social world. It leads to a decline in social standards of behavior and relationships with other people," states sociologist Roberto Hugh Potter.

What steps are being taken to discourage bullying? Many schools around the country hold a "Bully Awareness Week," which focuses on identifying the bullies and helping the victims of bullying. Nonprofit organizations in the United States and around the world have launched media campaigns to stop all forms of bullying. Because many parents are more aware of the problem, they are communicating with teachers and school officials to help alleviate bullying. Most importantly, more teens are realizing that bullying is a serious violent behavior that needs to be reported to parents or teachers.

Thinking Critically

1. **Explain** How is bullying more than teasing?
2. **Discuss** What else do you think school officials should do to prevent bullying?

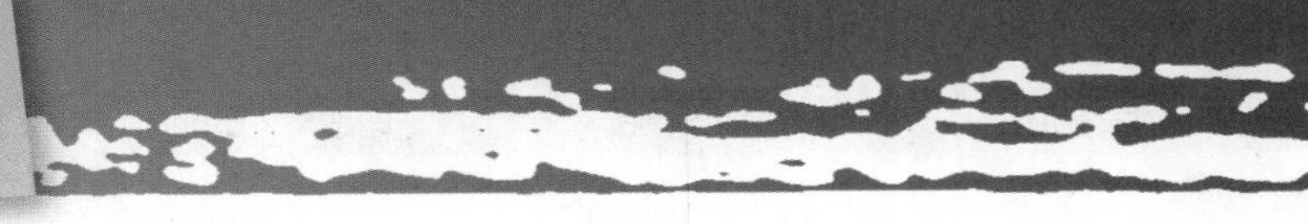

Lab
Applying What You've Learned

Creating a Drug Awareness Campaign

What is the best way to educate adolescents about the dangers of drug use?

Reading and Activity Workbook

Use the workbook to complete this lab.

1. Introduction

In this lab, you will create a drug awareness campaign designed to raise public awareness about the harmful effects of teenage drug use. You will work in small groups to gather material about a particular drug, create a drug profile, and create an anti-drug poster to educate and warn teenagers about the dangers of the drug. To complete this lab, follow the steps below.

- Following your teacher's instructions, organize the class into groups of four to six students.
- Your teacher will assign each group one of the drugs listed in the table at the bottom of this page.
- Work with the students in your group to review the chapter material on adolescent drug use. Write down any main points about drug use or details about your assigned drug that you think are important.
- Conduct library or Internet research to gather more information about your assigned drug. Your group is now ready to write a drug profile.

2. Writing a Drug Profile

Working as a group, write a profile for your assigned drug that will provide teenagers with basic information about the drug and its short- and long-term effects. Each drug profile should be written on a single sheet of paper and should include the items listed below.

- Name of drug
- Common street names
- Description of the drug
- How the drug is taken
- Short-term effects and dangers
- Long-term effects and dangers
- Three key statistical findings or general trends related to the drug's use
- One chart, graph, or table that summarizes data about the drug's use or effects, such as prevalence or relationship to other social problems

TEENAGE DRUG USE, 2015*

Grade	Marijuana	Methamphetamines	K2/Spice (Synthetic Marijuana)	Cocaine	Crack Cocaine	Heroin	Steroids	Cigarettes	Smokeless Tobacco	Alcohol
8th	15.50	1.30	3.10	1.60	1.00	0.50	1.00	13.3	8.60	26.1
10th	31.10	1.30	4.30	2.70	1.00	0.70	1.20	19.9	12.3	47.1
12th	44.70	1.00	5.20	4.00	1.70	0.80	1.90	31.1	13.2	64.0

*Percentage of teenagers who have tried a drug at least once in their lifetime.
Source: Monitoring the Future: Overview of Key Findings 2015; National Institute on Drug Abuse, U.S. Department of Health and Human Services

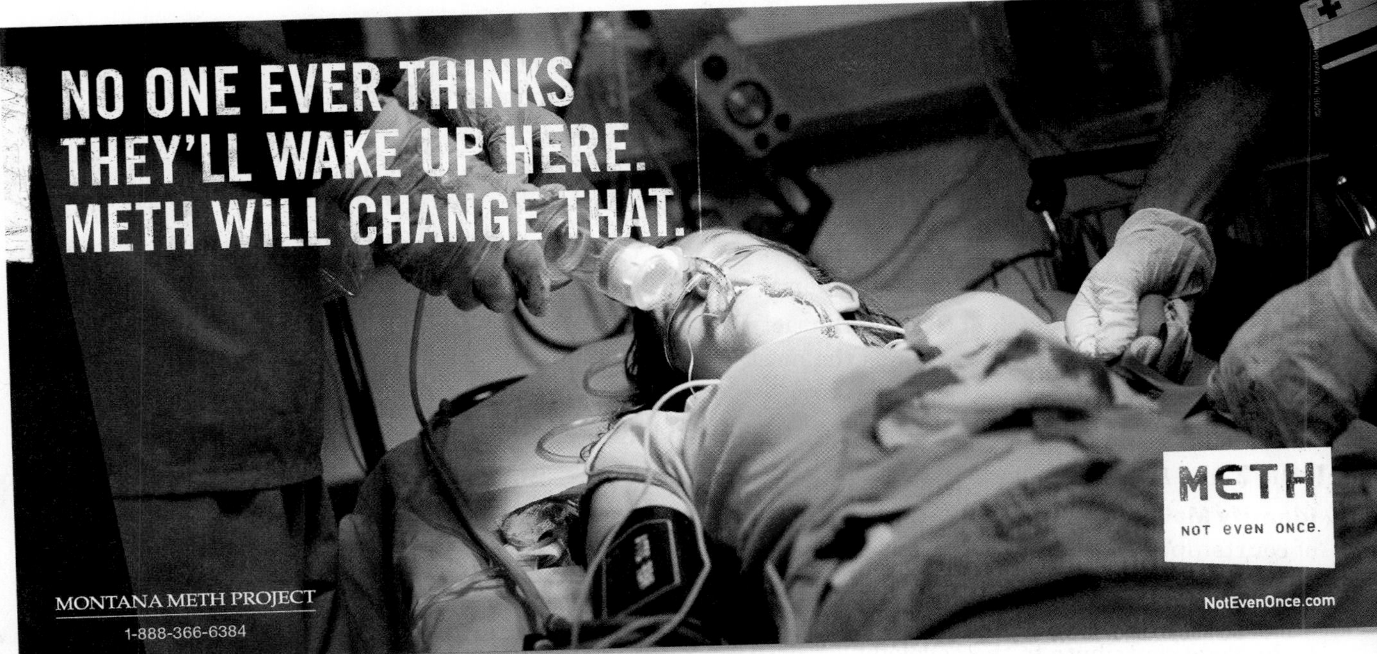

This poster from the Montana Meth Project uses powerful imagery and a strong statement to warn people about the dangers of meth.

3. The Anti-Drug Poster

Work with your group to create an anti-drug poster that illustrates the harmful effects of your assigned drug. Decide on a theme for your drug awareness campaign. For example, you may wish to discourage drug use by focusing on the effects of the drug on the life of a user. Be sure to include the following in your poster:

- a theme that tells how drugs impact individual lives or society
- a catchy slogan or message
- strong visuals that show the dangers of drug use
- key information from your data file

4. Presenting Your Poster

Review with your group the most important points of the drug profile and the anti-drug poster. Then present your drug profile and poster to the class. Be sure to give a good overview of the particular drug you were assigned, and explain what you chose to emphasize in your poster, and why.

5. Discussion

What did you learn from this lab? Hold a group discussion that focuses on the following questions:

- Overall, how successful was the class at creating posters that would prevent teenagers from using drugs?
- What methods did your group use to choose information and images for your presentation?
- Which elements from each group's presentation do you think are most effective?
- What information from the drug profiles could sociologists use to inform drug enforcement agencies and policy makers?
- Which drugs do you think present the greatest challenge to adolescents in the United States? Which do you think will be hardest to combat in the general population? Why?
- What other forms of media do you think should be used in a drug awareness campaign designed to reach teenagers?

CHAPTER 5 Review

Comprehension and Critical Thinking

SECTION 1 *(pp. 110–113)*

1. a. Describe How did the concept of adolescence as a distinct stage of life develop in the United States?

b. Compare and Contrast What are the main differences between adolescence and puberty?

c. Support a Position Which of the five characteristics of adolescence do you think has the most influence on an adolescent's transition into adulthood? Why?

SECTION 2 *(pp. 115–120)*

2. a. Identify Main Ideas What is the main purpose of courtship? What is the main purpose of dating?

b. Summarize How did industrialization and new technology contribute to the development of dating in the United States?

c. Make Judgments Which forms of technology do you think are most significant to changing dating patterns in the United States today? State whether you think these changes are positive or negative.

SECTION 3 *(pp. 121–128)*

3. a. Recall What are the consequences of pregnancy on a teen parent's education and lifetime earning potential?

b. Identify Cause and Effect Why did the introduction of crack cocaine in the mid-1980s cause an increase in drug-related violence?

c. Elaborate How might sociologists use Durkheim's ideas about high and low levels of social integration to understand teenage suicide?

INTERNET ACTIVITY

4. What social problems affect teenagers? Choose one of the problems discussed in this chapter, such as teenage pregnancy, drug use, violence, or suicide, and use the Internet to research how this problem affects teenagers. Look for information on how common the problem is among teens, recent statistics and data, contributing social factors, and prevention efforts. Write a short report that summarizes your findings.

Reviewing Vocabulary

Fill in each blank with the term that correctly completes the sentence.

5. The period between the normal onset of puberty and the beginning of adulthood is called ________.

6. ________ is the physical maturing that makes an individual capable of sexual reproduction.

7. Playing house is a form of ________ because it helps children learn about the expectations and roles that they will have as adult family members.

8. ________, the meeting of people as a romantic engagement, is most commonly found in societies that allow individuals to choose their own marriage partners.

9. In the United States, a system for interaction between unmarried men and women that existed before dating with the purpose of marriage was called ________ .

10. Dating in American society may be thought of as a(n) ________ of behavior that begins with casual dating and progresses to steady dating and then to engagement and marriage.

11. ________ is the education of students of both sexes at the same institution.

12. A ________ refers to any substance that changes mood, behavior, or consciousness.

13. The sociological term that refers to the degree of attachment people have to social groups or to society as a whole is ________.

Sociology in Your Life

14. Most sociologists agree that popular music is a powerful tool that shapes teenagers' ideas about the world. Concerns, however, have been raised that popular music often sends unrealistic messages, especially about love and romance. Select a popular song that does not have explicit lyrics and that you think presents unrealistic views about romance. Research the lyrics online, and write a paragraph analyzing the content of the song. What messages does the song send about romantic relationships? How might the lyrics influence people's thinking? Why do you think the song appeals to teenagers? Be sure to include a copy of the lyrics, as well as the name of the song and the artist, in your paragraph.

SKILLS ACTIVITY: INTERPRETING GRAPHS

Study the pie graphs below. Then use the information to help you answer the questions that follow.

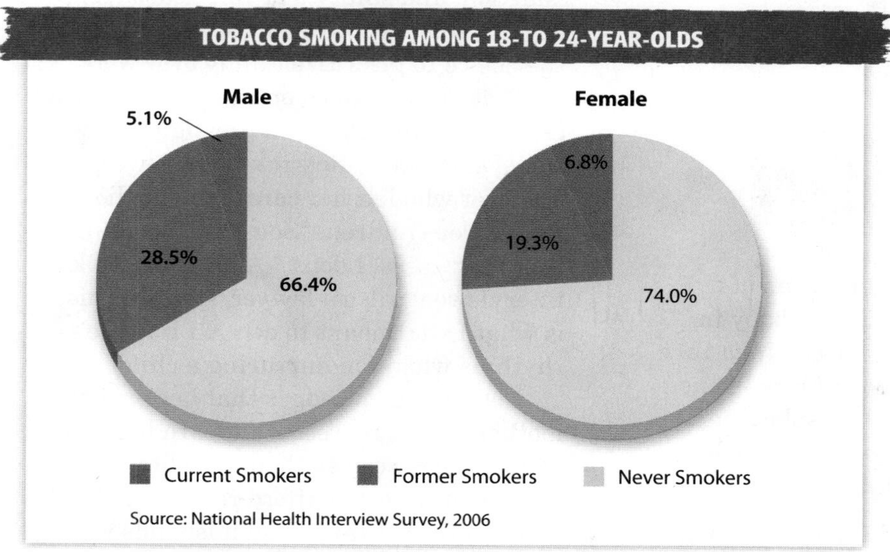

15. **Identify** Which group of young people, males or females, has a higher percentage of people who have never smoked?
16. **Compare** How does the percentage of male smokers from age 18 to 24 compare with the number of female smokers?
17. **Predict** Based on the information in the graphs, which group do you think would be more likely to experiment with marijuana? Why?

WRITING FOR SOCIOLOGY

Use your knowledge of adolescence to answer the question below. Do not simply list facts. Present a clear argument based on your critical analysis of the question, using appropriate sociological terminology.

18. Briefly describe each of the terms below from a sociological perspective. For each term, include a general description and a review of major characteristics and trends. Then use real-world examples to help explain the term within the context of U.S. society.
    - Adolescence
    - Dating
    - Teen suicide

Connecting Online

Go online for review and enrichment activities related to this chapter.

KEY TOPICS VIDEOS
View compelling clips on issues in the field.

KEEP IT CURRENT
Link to the Current Events site for regularly updated stories on sociology as well as other social studies topics.

QUICK LAB
Reinforce a key concept with a short lab activity.

CASE STUDY

The Opt-OUT REVOLUTION

On October 26, 2003 a photograph of a sophisticated woman cradling a baby in her arms graced the cover of *The New York Times Magazine*. "Why Don't More Women Get to the Top?" the headline splashing across the cover asked. The magazine's answer: "They Choose Not To."

The Pull of Motherhood Inside the magazine, journalist Lisa Belkin examined what she called the "Opt-Out Revolution," or many women's decision to "opt out"—choose to leave—the paid labor force to become stay-at-home parents. For her story, Belkin interviewed a dozen women, all high achievers. Eight were Princeton graduates and members of the same Atlanta book club. Belkin also interviewed four mothers from a San Francisco playgroup, three of whom had MBAs. All had "opted out" of successful careers to raise their children.

"There is nothing wrong with money or power," Belkin argues, but for women "they come at a high price." According to Belkin, women are becoming more inclined to define success in terms of balance, satisfaction, and sanity. For this reason, she argues, some working mothers are making the choice to prioritize family over work.

"I don't want to be on the fast track leading to a partnership at a prestigious law firm," said one of Belkin's interviewees, a lawyer who left her career to stay home with three children. "Some people define that as success. I don't." Another of Belkin's interviewees, also a lawyer, stated "This is what I was meant to do . . . I like life's rhythms when I'm nurturing a child."

Belkin acknowledges that her pool of mothers is not representative. In her own words, she describes them as "elite, successful women who can afford real choice." All had health insurance and husbands who earned substantial salaries. To be sure, this sample does not represent the majority of American mothers.

Still, "the Opt-Out Revolution" initiated a storm of news articles reinforcing the idea that women were increasingly choosing family over work. The articles left many people wondering if personal choice and the pull of family were enough to explain why some women decide to stay home.

Opting Out or Pushed Out? According to sociologist Pamela Stone, professional women who leave the workforce may have fewer options than it seems. Stone conducted in-depth interviews with 54 high-achieving women from a variety of professions—such as law, medicine, and publishing. She found that the reasons that women return home are far more complex than "the Opt-Out Revolution" suggests.

In addition to the pull of family, Stone found that mixed messages from husbands and employers often effectively pushed women from the workplace. For example, many women reported that their husbands

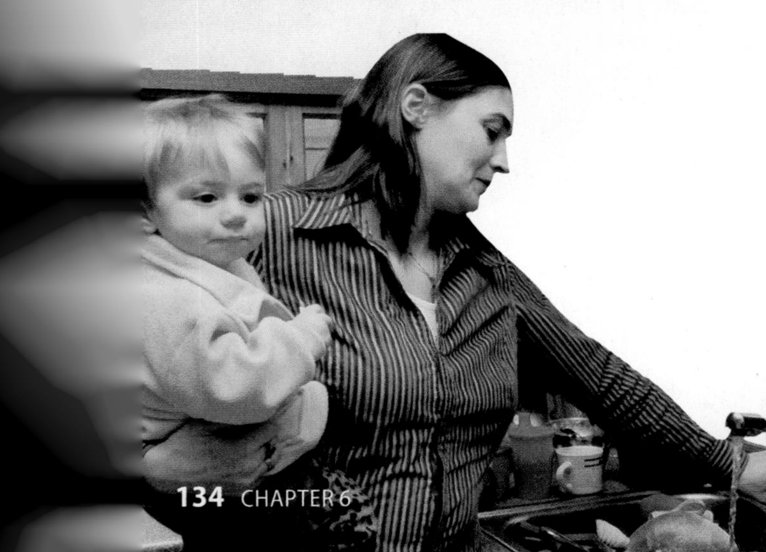

The vast majority of American women struggle to balance their life at home with the demands of work.

CHAPTER 6

THE ADULT IN SOCIETY

Over the last 30 years, women's career advancements have been crucial to achieving gender equality and narrowing the wage gap between men and women.

offered emotional support but did not contribute equally to household chores. Nor did husbands scale back their own careers for the sake of family.

Likewise, many of Stone's interviewees reported that their workplaces claimed to be "family friendly" but were really "all or nothing" work environments. For example, many workplaces offered a variety of supports, such as flexible workweeks, but women felt that taking full advantage of such benefits carried significant penalties in career advancement. Moreover, all but seven of Stone's interviewees cited features of their jobs, such as long hours and travel, as major motivating factors for quitting. As one marketing executive put it, her full-time workweek was "really 60 hours, not 40. Nobody works nine-to-five anymore."

Balancing work and family is one of the most challenging aspects of being an adult in American society, for both men and women. In this chapter, you will learn more about how these and other major factors shape adult roles and experiences.

What do you think?

1. What are some of the reasons that mothers leave the workplace? Why do they stay?
2. In what ways do you think men and women might experience the struggle to balance work with family life differently?

Chapter at a Glance

SECTION 1: Early and Middle Adulthood

- In American society, adult stages of development are experienced differently by men and women.
- Every adult has a life structure that is characterized by a combination of statuses, roles, activities, goals, values, beliefs, and life circumstances.
- Daniel Levinson developed a theory of adult male development based on three main eras: early, middle, and late adulthood.
- The stages of adult female development are heavily influenced by marriage, work, family, and raising children.

SECTION 2: The World of Work

- American workers often spend nearly 50 years in the labor force, making the world of work one of the most important components of adult life.
- The composition of the labor force and the nature of work have changed greatly over the last 100 years.
- According to opinion polls and social science research, most Americans report being satisfied with their jobs.

SECTION 3: The Later Years

- Social development continues throughout adulthood and well into the final stages of life.
- People age 65 and older make up the fastest growing segment of the world's population.
- Older Americans face many challenges, including physical and mental decline, dependency, and death.
- For many aging Americans, retirement opens up a new world full of freedom and new opportunities for growth and change.

SECTION 1

Early and Middle Adulthood

Before You Read

Main Idea
Men and women progress through adult development in different ways.

Reading Focus
1. What are the main eras in Daniel Levinson's theory of adult male development?
2. How does adult female development differ from adult male development?

Vocabulary
life structure
early adulthood
middle adulthood
late adulthood
novice phase
mentor

TAKING NOTES Use a graphic organizer like this one to take notes on adult male and adult female development.

Adult Development	
Male	Female

Quarter-Life Crisis

SOCIOLOGY CLOSE UP ***What if being an adult doesn't answer all of life's questions?*** Imagine the not-too-distant future: you are a twenty-something. You are college educated, independent, and living on your own. In fact, you have accomplished everything you set your mind to. Perhaps you have even landed your dream job and found your ideal mate. You should be having the time of your life, but you're not. You are totally confused. You are in the throes of a quarter-life crisis, and you are not alone.

Tales of teen angst and midlife crises are common in American culture, but until recently few people have talked about the difficulties associated with the period of adulthood in between. The term *quarter-life-crisis* was coined to describe a pattern of frustration, self-doubt, and identity crisis experienced by people in their twenties. Rather than breezing through the best years of their lives, many twenty-somethings find being in the "real world" isn't easy. They must decide where to live, how to best manage finances, what career to pursue, and how to establish new relationships. In facing these overwhelming choices and responsibilities, some feel helpless and indecisive. Others panic.

One truth that the quarter-life crisis illustrates is that socialization does not end in childhood. Rather, the quest for self-knowledge and the learning of new roles continues throughout life and into the final stages of adulthood. ■

Adult Male Development

The life courses of adult males and females in American society are somewhat different. Many women enter the labor force, take time out to have children, and then go back to work. Men, on the other hand, generally remain continuously in the labor force for most of their adult lives. The split employment pattern of women may be changing as more women choose to combine full-time careers with parenting. Nevertheless, the traditional pattern is still prevalent enough to merit looking at male and female adult development as two separate processes.

Psychologist Daniel Levinson and his colleagues at Yale University undertook an intensive long-term study to determine the adult male developmental stages. A research team of psychologists, sociologists, and psychiatrists conducted in-depth interviews with 40 men who were between the ages of 35 and 45 at the beginning of the study. Levinson and his colleagues selected study participants from four broad occupational categories.

The researchers interviewed each man for 10 to 20 hours over a two to three month period to determine how each had experienced personal development as an adult. The interviews focused on such issues as education, work, leisure, politics, and personal relationships. From these interviews, Levinson and his colleagues determined each man's life structure. A **life structure** is the combination of statuses, roles, activities, goals, values, beliefs, and life circumstances that characterize an individual. Through the analysis of these life structures, the research team was able to distinguish patterns that appear to be characteristic of most men.

After analyzing the patterns, Levinson and his colleagues concluded that there are three basic eras of adulthood. They named these eras **early adulthood, middle adulthood,** and **late adulthood.** The diagram at right shows how each era is divided into several distinct periods. Each era begins with a transitional period, which is then followed by alternating stable and transitional periods. The transitional periods last from four to five years, and the stable periods last from six to eight years. Levinson placed the greatest stress on the first five periods of adulthood.

QUICK FACTS

LEVINSON'S DEVELOPMENTAL STAGES OF ADULTHOOD

Daniel Levinson developed a theory of adult development to describe a general pattern in the life experiences of men.

17, 18, 19, 20, 21, 22	Early Adult Transition	The Novice Phase (17–32); Early Adulthood Era
23, 24, 25, 26, 27	Entering the Adult World	The Novice Phase; Early Adulthood Era
28, 29, 30, 31, 32	Age 30 Transition	The Novice Phase; Early Adulthood Era
33, 34, 35, 36, 37, 38, 39	Settling Down Period	Early Adulthood Era
40, 41, 42, 43, 44	Midlife Transition	Middle Adulthood Era
45, 46, 47, 48, 49	Entering Middle Adulthood	Middle Adulthood Era
50, 51, 52, 53, 54	Age 50 Transition	Middle Adulthood Era
55, 56, 57, 58, 59	Culmination of Middle Adulthood	Middle Adulthood Era
60, 61, 62, 63, 64	Late Adult Transition	Late Adulthood Era
65, 66, 67, 68, 69, 70, 71, 72, 73, 74, 75+	Late Adulthood	Late Adulthood Era

Skills Focus **INTERPRETING CHARTS** According to Levinson, at what age do men begin a midlife transition?

The Early Adult Transition Early adulthood begins with the early adult transition period—ages 17 through 22. This period represents the bridge between adolescence and adulthood. According to Levinson, the most important task of this period is leaving home, both physically and psychologically. The process begins when young adults go away to college or take full-time employment and move out of their childhood homes. However, the break with parents is seldom abrupt or total. In fact, many young adults are staying at home longer or returning home after a brief attempt to live independently.

Entering the Adult World The next stage in early adulthood is called entering the adult world—ages 23 through 27. The chief tasks of this period involve two slightly contradictory objectives. On one hand, the individual is expected to explore a variety of relationships and career opportunities. This expectation means that he must avoid strong commitments. On the other hand, the young adult is expected to become a responsible member of society and to form a stable life structure.

ACADEMIC VOCABULARY

apprentice
a person acquiring a trade or skills under supervision

This period is also characterized by the development of a dream of adult accomplishment. The dream is almost always phrased in terms of occupational goals. For many, the dreams are very specific, such as becoming a Nobel Prize winner or a great athlete. Although these dreams often prove to be unrealistic, they provide a sense of purpose.

The Age 30 Transition For many people, the age 30 transition—ages 28 through 32—is a difficult period. It is a time to look back on one's choices. Divorces are common during this period as individuals examine their commitments. Levinson considered the age 30 transition to be crucial because it often involves shifts in direction. Sound choices provide a firm foundation for future development. Bad choices can have far-reaching consequences.

Levinson referred to the first three periods of the early adulthood era as the **novice phase.** It is the time when men prepare for entry into full adulthood. Their major task during this phase is to make a place for themselves in the adult world and to construct a life structure that fits them and works in the adult world.

The Settling Down Period The last stage of early adulthood is the settling down period—ages 33 through 39. The major task of this period is what Levinson called "making it" in the adult world. Individuals try to establish themselves in society, usually by advancing in their occupations. During this period, individuals commit to things that are important to them, such as work, family, leisure, friendship, or community. They also work to fulfill the dreams they established previously.

Near the end of the settling down period, men come to realize how much they are relying on others for guidance. Feeling constrained by these influences, they begin a conscious effort to form their own identities. The first step in this process often involves separating oneself from a mentor. A **mentor** fosters a person's development by believing in the person and helping the person achieve his or her dreams. The break with a mentor is important because it allows individuals to see themselves as more than "apprentice adults."

The Midlife Transition The first stage in the middle adulthood era is the midlife transition—ages 40 through 44. This period serves as a bridge between early and middle adulthood. During the midlife transition, as in the age 30 transition, individuals question their life structures. In most instances, they come to realize that the dreams they formed in early adulthood are beyond fulfillment. Escaping the pressure of unattainable dreams is one of the major tasks of the midlife transition.

For about 80 percent of the men in Levinson's study, the midlife transition was a period of moderate to severe crisis. These men experienced both internal conflict and conflict with those around them. One way that many of the men worked through the crisis was by becoming a mentor. For those who successfully completed the transition, middle adulthood was a fulfilling period.

Support for Levinson's theory can be found in the fact that all the study participants went through the various periods in the same order and at about the same age. The research also indicates that the degree of difficulty that an individual experiences in a period depends on his success in mastering the previous period.

Reading Check **Compare** How are the age 30 transition and the midlife transition similar?

Becoming an Adult

Sociologists develop models to understand and explain broad patterns of behavior and experiences in society. How well do real lives fit sociological models for adult development?

Quick Lab

PROCEDURE

1. Choose one of the models of adult development discussed in this section. Then select a man or a woman to interview.
2. Develop a list of five interview questions. For example, you may wish to ask: How did you prepare for adult roles and responsibilities? When did you first feel like an adult? If you could pick the five most significant events of your adult life, what would they be? The five biggest challenges?
3. Conduct your interview. Be sure to take detailed notes and ask follow up questions, such as "How old were you when that happened?," that will help you compare your adult's responses to the sociological model that you chose.
4. Create a three-column chart to record your results. In the first column, list the stages of the model you chose, creating a row for each stage. In the second column, list the major characteristics of each stage. In the third column, record details from your interview that correspond with each stage.

ANALYSIS

1. Discuss with your classmates how well your adult's life pattern matched the sociological model you chose. Did your interview results support the model? Could the model be used to help explain your adult's life pattern?
2. How can one person's story help sociologists understand broader patterns?

Adult Female Development

Levinson suggested that his findings were equally valid for women. Later, he repeated his life-structure study using women to test his thesis. Employing the same interview method, he studied 45 women drawn from three broad categories—homemakers, college professors, and corporate executives. Comparing his findings to those of his earlier study, he concluded that men and women go through basically the same stages of adult development. Levinson did, however, find that men and women differed greatly in terms of their social roles and identities. Therefore, Levinson concluded that men and women also dealt differently with the developmental tasks associated with each stage of adult development.

Levinson's ideas on the similarity of male and female adult development have been a subject of some debate since he first made the suggestion in the 1970s. Some people argue that the differences he noted exist because the developmental processes for men and women are different. Irene Frieze and Esther Sales have both done work that lends support to this argument. Their research led to a suggestion of three phases in adult female development. These phases include leaving the family, entering the adult world of work and starting a family, and returning to the labor force.

Leaving the Family Women's entry into the adult world begins much the same way as that of men. It involves leaving home, making a psychological break from family, and developing a life plan. Some women focus more on marriage than their careers. In these cases, the specifics of the life plan are often shaped by the marriage relationship, for example, the husband's career may take priority. This emphasis on marriage over career is one factor that distinguishes female development from male development during adulthood.

Entering the Adult World Age at first marriage in the United States has been rising since the 1960s. In 2013, the Census Bureau reported the average for women was 26.6 years and for men, 29 years. However, most women still marry and become mothers in their twenties. Although many women find motherhood and a career to be a workable combination, dual roles tend to put an added strain on women. Consequently, about 62.1 percent of new mothers who were in the labor force return to work before their children reach one year of age.

CASE STUDY CONNECTION

The Opt-Out Revolution In the United States, many women struggle with balancing the demands of work and family.

According to Sales, remaining out of the labor force while their children are young can limit women's career advancement possibilities. This break in employment is another factor that distinguishes adult female development from adult male development.

Statistically Speaking...

Work and Motherhood Most American women juggle work and family. The career paths of working mothers are rarely straightforward. Most American mothers alternate between working full time and part time in an attempt to balance work and family life. Many take time out—often only a few months—to have children. Meanwhile, millions of other American women have their hands full as stay-at-home moms.

50.7% Percentage of working mothers with children younger than age one

64.4% Percentage of working mothers with children age one and older

80% Percentage of new mothers who return to the workforce within twelve months after childbirth

6.5 million Total number of stay-at-home parents in the United States, including 4.5 million moms and 2 million dads

14% Percentage of American families that have a wage-earning dad and a stay-at-home mom

Skills Focus INTERPRETING CHARTS Which statistic do you find most surprising? Explain.

Sources: U.S. Census Bureau; U.S. Bureau of Labor Statistics

Re-entering the World of Work Once their children reach school age, many mothers who left the labor force return to the world of work. According to Sales, these women—most of whom are in their early thirties—find themselves in a situation similar to that of men in their twenties. Fewer obligations at home make it possible for them to actively pursue their career goals. Sales describes this as "re-entering the adult world," and notes that women often commit to their careers at a time when their husbands begin to have serious doubts about their own career choices.

American attitudes on marriage and gender roles seem to be changing. Americans are delaying marriage or choosing not to get married at all. The marriage rate has dropped by more than 44 percent since the 1960s. Couples are delaying parenting as well. The age of mothers at the birth of their first child has risen slowly but steadily since the 1970s. Furthermore, the number of women in full-time executive, administrative, and managerial positions is increasing. In nearly one-fourth of all working couples, the wife earns more than the husband does. Such changes may signal that the developmental patterns of adult men and women are merging.

Reading Check **Find the Main Idea** What factors make adult female development different from adult male development?

SECTION 1 Assessment

Reviewing Main Ideas and Vocabulary

1. **Define** What is a life structure?
2. **Identify** According to Daniel Levinson, what are the three basic eras of male adulthood?
3. **Recall** When do adult men make a conscious effort to form their own identities and break from their mentors?
4. **Sequence** According to Irene Frieze and Esther Sales, what pattern does adult female development typically follow?

Thinking Critically

5. **Explain** In what ways do the developmental patterns of adult men and women appear to be merging?
6. **Evaluate** Why might using a model developed on the experiences of men present a problem for understanding the experiences of both men and women?
7. **Compare and Contrast** Using your notes and a graphic organizer like the one here, compare and contrast adult male development and adult female development.

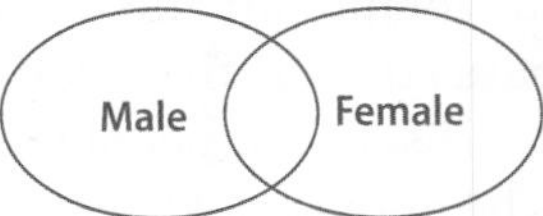

FOCUS ON WRITING

8. **Descriptive** Write a paragraph agreeing or disagreeing with the idea that there is little difference between adult female and adult male development. Consider changing attitudes toward marriage and changing views about gender roles.

SECTION 2

The World of Work

Before You Read

Main Idea
The world of work is a major component of adult life. In the last 100 years, major changes have transformed the organization of work and the composition of the labor force.

Reading Focus
1. How has the labor force in the United States changed?
2. In what ways has the nature of work changed?
3. What factors contribute to job satisfaction?

Vocabulary
work
labor force
profession
unemployment
unemployment rate
outsourcing

TAKING NOTES As you read, use a graphic organizer like this one to take notes on the world of work.

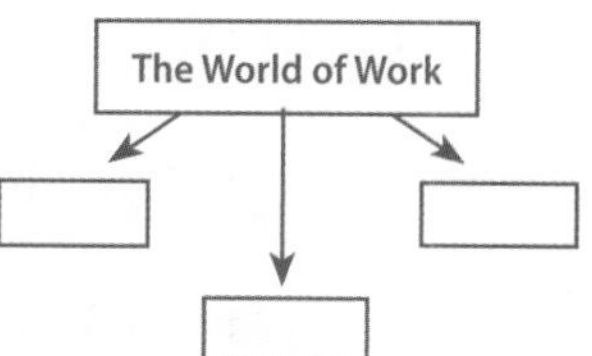

SOCIOLOGY CLOSE UP ***How far would you be willing to go for your dream job?*** On April 20, 2008, Danica Patrick made history when she crossed the finish line at the Indy Japan 300 in Motegi, Japan. The 26-year-old driver became the first woman to win an IndyCar race, a sport long dominated by men. However, it hasn't been all trophies and victory laps.

Patrick's racing career began at the age of nine when her father bought her a go-kart. During weekends at the track with her sister, she raced against men twice her age. Her father pushed her to learn all she could about driving and maintaining her vehicle.

Finally, at age 16, Patrick was given the opportunity to further her racing career—by quitting high school, leaving her family and friends behind, and moving to England. It wasn't easy. She rented space on a woman's living room couch, suffered from homesickness, and was still not succeeding on the racetrack. In the end, though, it was worth it. In 2005 Patrick joined the Indy Racing League as a driver for the Rahal Letterman team. That year, she became the first female driver to lead a lap at the Indianapolis 500, one of the most famous races in motor sports. Three years later she earned her first win. After 17 years of doggedly preparing for her racing career, Patrick was at the top of her chosen profession, proving that anything is possible if you set your mind to it. ■

Patrick finished 5.8594 seconds ahead of her competition to triumph at Indy Japan 300 in 2008.

The Labor Force

Danica Patrick's racing career may not sound like work, but it is. **Work** involves performing all of the tasks necessary to produce goods and provide services that meet human needs. The service Patrick's hard work provides, for example, meets a human need for entertainment. It also shows that work can be much more than tiresome, difficult, and dull. In all societies, work—both paid and unpaid—is the basis for the economy. In American society, many view work as an outlet for individual passion, a source of self-esteem, and an avenue for individual achievement.

It should come as no surprise then that work is an important aspect of adult life. If you begin working at age 18 and retire at 65, you will have spent 47 years in the labor force. Even if you go to college and graduate school or spend several years at home raising children, you will still be in the labor force for a long time. What will your years in the labor force be like? An examination of the labor force, the types of jobs workers hold, and the degree of job satisfaction among workers can provide answers to this question.

ACADEMIC VOCABULARY

informal economy unofficial economic activities that take place without government approval and outside of mainstream business and industry

By definition, the **labor force** consists of all individuals age 16 and older who are employed in paid positions or who are seeking paid employment. People who are not paid for their services, such as homemakers, are part of what is called an informal economy and are not considered part of the labor force. In 2015 approximately 62.7 percent of the United States population older than age 16 was in the labor force. Who are these workers, and what types of jobs do they hold?

Composition The composition of the American labor force is changing. One of the biggest changes involves the number of working women and the types of jobs they hold. In 1970 women made up 38 percent of the labor force. In 2015 women made up 53.7 percent. Women now hold just over 72 percent of the professional jobs in the United States. A **profession** is a high-status occupation that requires specialized skills and knowledge obtained through formal education. Professional occupations include jobs such as engineer, lawyer, teacher, dentist, and writer.

Another changing aspect of labor-force composition is the rise of minority workers as a percentage of the total labor force. Hispanics, who are now the fastest-growing population group among American workers are a major part of this trend. In 2011 Hispanics made up 15 percent of the country's labor force. This figure is expected to increase to more than 19 percent by the year 2020.

In addition, American workers now have a higher level of education. In 1940 most workers barely had more than an eighth-grade education. Today approximately 90 percent of labor-force workers age 25 and older have graduated from high school. And almost one-third of the labor force has a college degree.

Occupations What types of jobs do American workers hold? The chart on the next page shows the major categories of occupations in the United States. Below are some more detailed examples of occupational categories and jobs within the U.S. economy.

- *managerial, executive, and administrative:* business executives, office managers, sales managers, credit managers, personnel managers, public relations supervisors, and store managers
- *professional specialty:* doctors, lawyers, dentists, pharmacists, librarians, nurses, engineers, artists, veterinarians, psychiatrists, social workers, nurses, teachers, and accountants
- *service occupations:* private household workers—maids, cooks, butlers, and nursemaids; protective service workers—

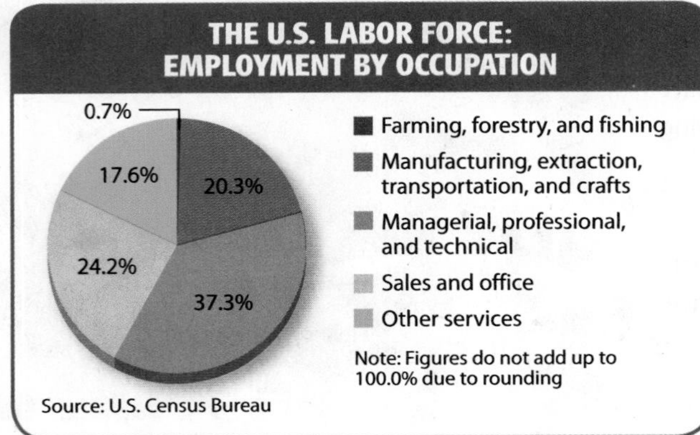

Skills Focus **INTERPRETING GRAPHS** Which category employs the smallest percentage of Americans?

police officers and firefighters; other service workers—waitpersons, cooks, dental and nursing assistants, janitors, hairdressers, airline attendants, and child-care workers

- *technical occupations:* laboratory technicians, dental hygienists, medical assistants, and X-ray technicians
- *sales workers:* manufacturers' representatives, retail salespeople, insurance salespeople, and real estate agents
- *administrative support occupations:* business machine operators, bookkeepers, office clerks, secretaries, receptionists, cashiers, telephone operators, postal workers, and bank workers
- *precision production, craft, and repair workers:* mechanics, television repairers, shoemakers, dressmakers, tailors, printers, carpenters, plumbers, electricians, concrete workers, and skilled precision production workers
- *operators, fabricators, and laborers:* packagers, assemblers, welders, heavy equipment operators, freight handlers, warehouse workers, and laborers
- *farming, forestry, and fishing:* farm owners and operators, farm laborers, lumberjacks, fishers, hunters, and trappers
- *transportation and material moving:* truck and bus drivers

Unemployment One way to understand the employment patterns in society is to look at unemployment. **Unemployment** is the situation that occurs when a person does not have a job but is actively seeking employment. The **unemployment rate** is the percentage of the civilian labor force that is unemployed but actively seeking employment. The unemployment rate varies according to such factors as age, gender, race, and cultural background.

It is nearly impossible to employ every adult member of society. There are always some people who are in the process of seeking employment. Other people cannot or do not want to work. Consequently, society sets a level of unemployment that is generally considered acceptable. In the United States, that level hovers around 5 percent. Thus, the U.S. economy is considered to have achieved full employment when about 95 percent of the labor force is employed.

MAJOR CATEGORIES OF OCCUPATIONS

QUICK FACTS

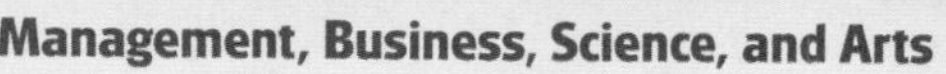

Management, Business, Science, and Arts
Total Employed*: 41,904,175
Percentage: Male 51.3% **Female** 48.7%

Sample Job: Physician or Surgeon
Median Salary: $194,521
Education Required: 4-year college degree, 4-year medical degree, 3 to 7 years of internship and residency

Service
Total Employed*: 14,170,926
Percentage: Male 50.9% **Female** 49.1%

Sample Job: Chef or head cook
Median Salary: $30,912
Education Required: 2 to 4 year college degree

Sales and Office
Total Employed*: 22,980,042
Percentage: Male 41.6% **Female** 58.4%

Sample Job: Real estate broker or sales agent
Median Salary: $52,124
Education Required: High school diploma

Natural Resources, Construction, and Maintenance
Total Employed*: 9,807,518
Percentage: Male 96.1% **Female** 3.9%

Sample Job: Roofer
Median Salary: $29,618
Education Required: High school diploma, 3-year apprenticeship

Production, Transportation, and Material Moving
Total Employed*: 13,333,361
Percentage: Male 80.4% **Female** 19.6%

Sample Job: Air traffic controller or airfield operations specialist
Median Salary: $89,236
Education Required: 4-year college degree, 12-week training program, 1 to 2 years on-the-job training

Sources: U.S. Census Bureau; Bureau of Labor Statistics, *Occupational Outlook Handbook*
*Number of full-time, year-round workers

Reading Check **Summarize** What major trends characterize U.S. employment patterns?

The Changing Nature of Work

There have also been changes in the nature of work in the United States. In 1900 about 35 percent of the labor force worked in farming. About 45 percent were employed in manufacturing and other jobs that required physical labor, such as construction. Only about 20 percent of the labor force worked in jobs that primarily involved intellectual work and interacting with people, such as the professions, management, office work, and sales.

By midcentury, manufacturing jobs dominated the labor force. Today the situation is dramatically different. Farming and manufacturing together now account for nearly 13 percent of the jobs in the United States. Considerable growth, on the other hand, has occurred in the number of people with professional, office work, sales, and service jobs. People holding such jobs make up just over 76 percent of the labor force.

Much of this increase can be attributed to the growth of bureaucracies and professional occupations. Managerial, professional, and administrative support positions account for almost 35 percent of the labor force. Technological developments, particularly the computer, have also contributed to this growth in the service-producing sector.

Moreover, in the 1990s, new technologies such as e-mail and the Internet intensified globalization, which is the development of economic, political, and social relationships that stretch worldwide. Globalization benefits companies by giving them new opportunities to maximize profits. For example, U.S. companies have saved money by **outsourcing,** a practice that involves moving business units and jobs across national boundaries, where operating and labor costs are less expensive. U.S. Department of Commerce figures reveal that U.S. multinational corporations, which employ one-fifth of the American workforce, added 2.4 million overseas jobs, while at the same time decreasing U.S. employment by 2.9 million over the last decade.

Reading Check **Identify Cause and Effect** What has caused the loss of U.S. manufacturing jobs?

TECHNOLOGY FOCUS

Surfing the Web on Company Time

In recent years, no technology has transformed the workplace more than the Internet. It has made possible telecommuting, new jobs, and 24-hour access to the office. It has also changed how workers take breaks and how they goof-off on the job.

In a 2008 study of 1,700 workers, researchers at Goldsmith College in London found that "ebreaks," or 10-minute Web surfing sessions, could increase employee performance. Their findings suggest that workers felt more focused after ebreaks than after cigarette or tea breaks. According to Dr. Tomas Chamorro-Premuzic, the study's lead researcher, banning access to Web sites is bad for employee morale, which leads to decreased productivity that could be costing British firms nearly $8 billion a year.

For employers, however, ebreaks are not the problem. Companies are concerned about employees who waste company time and money. A 2014 survey found that 89 percent of American workers admitted to wasting time at work each day, and much of that time is spent surfing the Web, instant messaging, and using social-networking sites. To prevent such abuse many U.S. companies use "time-tracking apps," such as Toggl, RescueTime, ATracker, Eternity, and others, to track the time their employees spend on the Internet.

Thinking Critically

Analyze Do you think employers should ban Internet access or encourage workers to take ebreaks? Explain.

Job Satisfaction

Opinion polls and social science research indicate that the vast majority of workers in the United States, regardless of what they do, are satisfied with their jobs. For example, in 2014, 86 percent of U.S. employees reported overall satisfaction with their current job, an improvement of five percentage points since 2013. However, the level of satisfaction varied according to such factors as income and age. For example, workers earning more than $35,000 a year reported greater satisfaction with their work than people with lower incomes. Similarly, older workers were more satisfied with their jobs than younger workers were.

What factors contribute to job satisfaction? According to a 2015 poll, the top five factors rated as "very important" by employees relating to job satisfaction were as follows:

- Respectful treatment of all employees at all levels: 72%
- Trust between employees and senior management: 64%
- Benefits, overall: 63%
- Compensation/pay: 61%
- Job security: 59%

The conditions that workers are unhappy with provide a better measure of what drives job satisfaction. In the same 2015 poll, workers expressed dissatisfaction with job stress, recognition of accomplishments, and commitment to professional development by management. They were also less satisfied with possibilities for advancement, networking opportunities, and management/employee communication.

One solution for dissatisfied workers is to look for new jobs. Even people who express high levels of satisfaction with their jobs do not stay in those jobs for their entire working lives. For example, about one in five workers in a CareerBuilder Survey said it was very likely that they would change jobs in 2014. Statistics also suggest that moving from job to job is a well-established pattern among American workers. A long-term study conducted by the U.S. Bureau of Labor Statistics (BLS) found that, on average, American workers hold nine jobs between the ages of 18 and 34. Another BLS study found that employee tenure—the median number of years that workers have been with their current employer—is 3.5 years.

Career changes are also becoming a common occurrence among American workers. Changing careers means that workers go into a new field for which their previous experience does not directly qualify them. Statistics indicate that the average worker will change careers from five to six times in a lifetime.

Reading Check **Identify Supporting Details** What statistics indicate a high level of job satisfaction among U.S. workers?

SECTION 2 Assessment

Reviewing Main Ideas and Vocabulary

1. **Define** What is work?
2. **Identify** Who makes up the labor force, and who is excluded from the labor force?
3. **Cause and Effect** What factors cause variation in the unemployment rate?

Thinking Critically

4. **Draw Conclusions** What features of professional jobs do you think contribute to making them high-status jobs?
5. **Make Generalizations** In what ways has technology changed the nature of work?
6. **Predict** How might employers use statistics concerning job satisfaction to improve the experiences of workers?
7. **Cause and Effect** Using your notes and a graphic organizer like this one, explain the causes and effects that have changed the world of work in the United States.

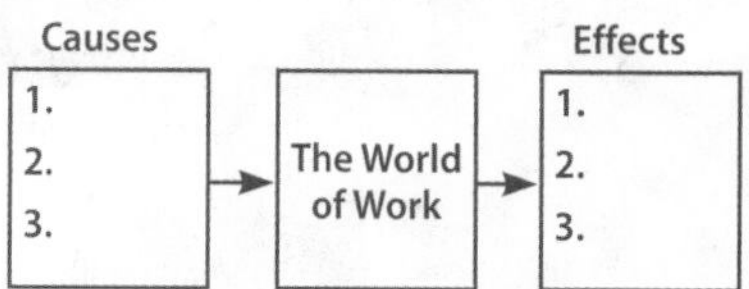

FOCUS ON WRITING

8. **Narrative** Over the last 100 years, the American labor force has experienced important changes. Choose one change discussed in this section and write a paragraph describing its effects on the labor force or on the nature of work from the point of view of a worker.

SECTION 3

The Later Years

Before You Read

Main Idea

Americans entering the later years, or old age, face a new set of life transitions, challenges, and opportunities.

Reading Focus

1. What changes characterize late adulthood?
2. What new opportunities do older Americans enjoy?

Vocabulary

gerontology
social gerontology
young-old
middle-old
old-old
Alzheimer's disease
dependency

TAKING NOTES As you read, take notes on the changes and opportunities that characterize the later years.

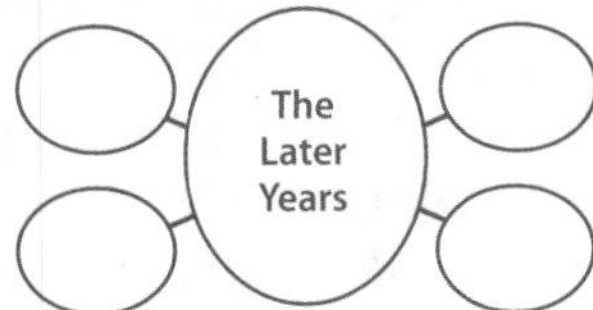

From the Top of the World

SOCIOLOGY CLOSE UP ***Why are seventy-somethings braving frostbite and altitude sickness to conquer Earth's highest peak?*** On May 25, 2008, Min Bahadur Sherchan, a 76-year-old Nepalese grandfather, became the oldest man to climb Mount Everest, the world's highest mountain. Early in the morning, Sherchan reached Everest's 29,035-foot summit with his climbing guides. Remarkably, Sherchan was just 25 days away from celebrating his seventy-seventh birthday.

Scaling Everest was a lifelong dream for Sherchan, a retired soldier. In realizing his dream, he beat a record set one year earlier by a 71-year-old Japanese teacher. Following close on Sherchan's trail was 75-year-old Yuichiro Miura, a Japanese skier who reached the summit on May 26—his second ascent since turning 70 and recovering from two heart operations.

Sherchan and his climbing peers have also done much to conquer stereotypes about old age as a time of failing health and loneliness. On his 2008 expedition Web site, Sherchan said he wanted his climb to the top of the world to inspire others "to achieve a better life even in old days." Likewise, Miura has expressed a desire to "challenge the limit of humans." As the world's population grows older and older, these are important messages, offering a vision of old age that is full of possibilities, rewarding experiences, and new achievements.

After setting a world record as the oldest person to scale Everest, Min Bahadur Sherchan (left and inset) poses with fellow climber Yuichiro Miura (right).

Changes in Late Adulthood

Improved health care has enabled more people around the world to live longer than ever before. People age 65 and older are the fastest-growing segment of the world's population. In the United States, people age 65 and older made up just over 11 percent of the population in 1980. This figure was more than 12 percent in 2000. Some estimates indicate that by the year 2030, some 20 percent of the population will be age 65 and older.

What is the period of late adulthood like? The field of **gerontology**—the scientific study of the processes and phenomena of aging—provides answers to this question. Sociologists are most interested in **social gerontology,** the study of the nonphysical aspects of the aging process. This section examines what social gerontologists have discovered about the characteristics of late adulthood.

People are now living longer. Thus, it has become impossible to view the late adulthood era as a single period of development. Life at age 65 is very different from life at 85. In recognition of this fact, gerontologists place individuals aged 65 and older into three groups. These groups are the young-old, the middle-old, and the old-old.

The topics of interest to gerontologists differ depending on the age group they are studying. Among the **young-old**—ages 65 through 74—adjustment to retirement is a key developmental issue. When the **middle-old**—ages 75 through 84—and the **old-old**—ages 85 and older—are considered, issues surrounding physical and mental decline and death take on added importance. This shift in emphasis is related to health and physical well-being. The young-old generally are in good health and can care for themselves. However, the body wears out eventually. For most senior citizens, physical and mental functioning declines with age, although the level of decline varies widely. Therefore, health and death issues become major areas of concern for the middle-old and the old-old.

Adjustment to Retirement In American society we tend to identify individuals by their jobs. When two people meet for the first time, the question of what each does for a living is likely to arise. In light of the importance placed on an individual's role in the labor force, it is reasonable to assume that people have difficulty adjusting to retirement. But is this actually the case?

For some people, the loss of the work role is a great shock. This shock is particularly evident in those who strongly identify with their jobs or who do not want to retire. However, research indicates that work-role loss affects a much smaller number of retired people than is generally assumed. In fact, one study found that elderly people consider retirement one of the least stressful events that they have experienced. Most gerontologists feel that the level of adjustment to retirement reflects a person's earlier attitudes and behavior. People who were happy and well adjusted in their working lives will generally enjoy retirement. Conversely, people who were unhappy or unfulfilled in their work rarely find retirement satisfying.

Young-Old

Age Range 65 to 74 years old

Population in the United States (2010 est.) 21,713,429

Percentage of U.S. Population 7%

Major Concerns

- adjustment to retirement
- maintaining social networks
- pursuing new opportunities
- positive mental health

Middle-Old

Age Range 75 to 84 years old

Population in the United States (2010 est.) 13,061,122

Percentage of U.S. Population 4.3%

Major Concerns

- physical health
- mental functioning
- dependency
- death issues

Old-Old

Age Range 85 years and older

Population in the United States (2010 est.) 5,493,433

Percentage of U.S. Population 1.8%

Major Concerns

- physical health
- mental functioning
- dependency
- death issues

Studies have found that such factors as income, health, social networks, and identity affect adjustment to retirement. Retirees need enough income to live comfortably. If they constantly struggle to make economic ends meet, retirees will have little time to enjoy retirement. Similarly, retirees need to have good health. Sickness makes adjustment to any stage of life, not just retirement, difficult. Income and health are related to one of the strongest desires of senior citizens—to remain independent. Retirees quickly lose this feeling of independence if their comfort, both economic and physical, depends on the help and generosity of others.

Retirees also adjust better to their new situation if they remain linked to the larger social world to which they belong. Maintaining social networks—both with friends and with family—greatly contributes to retirees' quality of life. Remaining active in the community helps retirees adjust because it bolsters their sense of identity within society. For example, contributing to the community through volunteering can help retirees develop a new identity to replace the identity they lost when they left the labor force.

Failure to adapt to retirement can have negative consequences. Suicide rates are high among people over the age of 65, particularly among white men. Some sociologists suggest that suicide is more prevalent among white male retirees because their identity is more directly tied to their work.

ACADEMIC VOCABULARY

dementia progressive deterioration of the cognitive and intellectual functions of the brain, such as memory loss

Physical and Mental Functioning As an individual ages, body cells begin to die. As a result, muscles and tissues shrink. The skin develops wrinkles. The entire body slowly loses weight. The weakened muscles lessen the individual's strength and endurance. The nervous system functions more slowly and less accurately. Hair gradually turns to gray or white as the cells in the roots produce less and less pigment. All the organs and functions of the body slow down. As a result, elderly individuals do everything more slowly than they did when they were younger.

Although people tend to slow down as they age, most remain mentally alert. Recent research has shown that most elderly people retain their intellectual abilities throughout life. This finding runs counter to the earlier assumption that loss of intellectual ability is an unavoidable part of aging. The earlier assumption was based on the results of intelligence tests given to people of different ages. Young people always achieved better scores. Researchers took this as an indication that intellectual ability declines with old age.

Psychologists now believe that two factors influenced the test results. First, the items on the tests related mainly to the youth and young-adult cultures. Second, young people tend to have more formal education than people age 65 and older. New testing techniques and revised test items have produced different results. These results indicate that there is a less-marked decline in intellectual ability among elderly people.

Now psychologists are also looking at changes in an individual's test scores over time, rather than comparing test results of people of different ages. For example, a person's score at age 70 might be compared with his or her score at age 50. This approach reveals that intelligence may be more stable than had been previously thought. Studies have found that intelligence, learning, and memory often decline with aging. However, the extent of loss is not so great as originally believed and varies greatly from individual to individual. Some aspects of intelligence and learning improve. Vocabulary, for example, increases until people are in their seventies. Certain kinds of intelligence can be improved with training in thinking skills.

Nonetheless, for some people aging is accompanied by marked mental decline, or dementia. The most common form of dementia among elderly people is **Alzheimer's disease**—an organic condition that results in the progressive deterioration of brain cells. The progress of this disease is slow but steady, usually lasting about 8 to 10 years from first symptoms to death.

One of the early symptoms of Alzheimer's disease is the inability to remember current events even though memories from the past can be recalled quite clearly. As the disease progresses, Alzheimer's sufferers may also have trouble performing simple tasks. For example, they may be unable to perform their work duties or drive a car. In time, many Alzheimer's sufferers become hostile and disoriented. Eventually, their eyesight, speech,

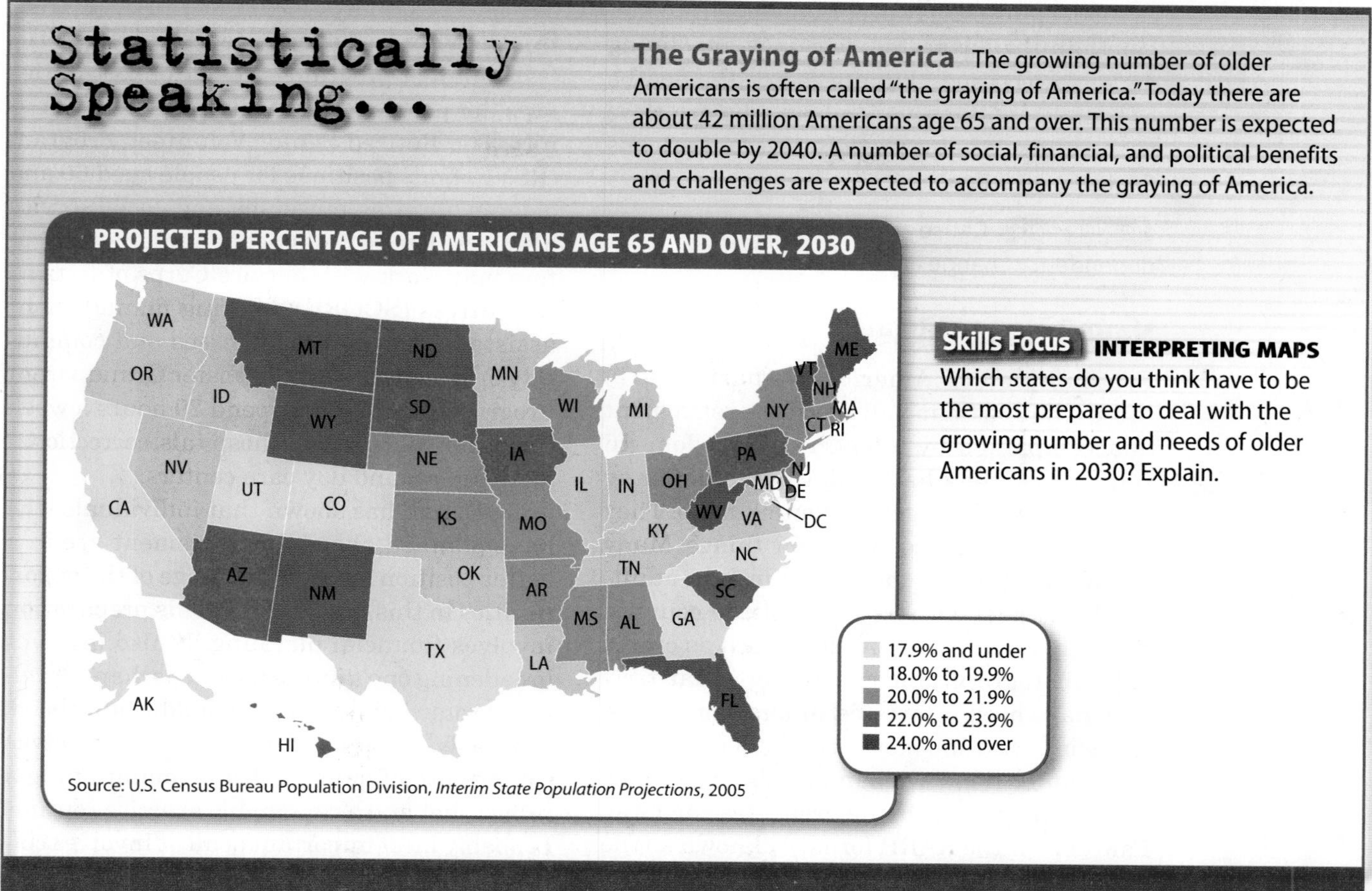

Statistically Speaking...

The Graying of America The growing number of older Americans is often called "the graying of America." Today there are about 42 million Americans age 65 and over. This number is expected to double by 2040. A number of social, financial, and political benefits and challenges are expected to accompany the graying of America.

Skills Focus INTERPRETING MAPS Which states do you think have to be the most prepared to deal with the growing number and needs of older Americans in 2030? Explain.

and muscle coordination begin to fail. In the final stages of disease, people with Alzheimer's often regress into a childlike state to the extent that they are no longer able to control their bodily functions.

Only about 1 in 9 Americans age 65 and older suffers from Alzheimer's disease. However, after age 60 the incidence of dementia nearly doubles with every five years of age. Dementia will become a greater challenge in the future because the American population is aging and people are living longer.

Dealing with Dependency and Death For the middle-old and the old-old, the issues of dependency and death take on increasing significance. In this context, **dependency** is the shift from being an independent adult to being dependent on others for physical or financial assistance. As you have already read, remaining independent is one of the greatest desires of elderly people. Dependency changes an individual's status in society, necessitating new roles and behaviors. For example, when an aged parent is forced to live with a grown child because of dependency, the parent-child relationship often becomes reversed. The child takes over the role of the caregiver and authority figure. The aged parent is expected to be grateful for the assistance and to follow the wishes of the child. This change in roles can be very difficult for a person who has become accustomed to making his or her own decisions. Consequently, dependency often strains the parent-child relationship.

Although elderly people fear dependency, they do not appear to fear death. In fact, the fear of death is much more common among middle-aged people. The lack of this fear among people in late adulthood is interesting when one considers that their likelihood of dying in the near future is much greater. Researchers believe that several factors contribute to lower levels of fear of death among senior citizens. First, elderly people are at the end of their lives. They see fewer prospects for the future; thus, people in late adulthood may feel that they have less to lose by dying.

Second, many elderly people, having lived longer than they expected, feel they are "living on borrowed time." Finally, facing the deaths of friends and family members who are close to them in age helps prepare older Americans for their own deaths.

Reading Check **Cause and Effect** How does dependency change an older person's life?

New Opportunities

For many older Americans—particularly those who are financially secure—retirement is accompanied by a feeling of freedom. In retirement, they have the time to do many of the things they always wanted to do. They also have the chance to try new things. Many people use part of their time in late adulthood to travel. Others take college courses. Still others pursue activities—such as crafts, golf, photography, or gardening—that they may have been interested in for many years. Some may become more active in politics and community life. For example, they may participate in such lobbying groups as the Gray Panthers or the AARP, formerly known as the American Association of Retired Persons.

Some elderly Americans begin a second career, either for pay or as volunteers. In recent years, part-time employment opportunities have increased for senior citizens. Many businesses, particularly those in the service sector, have attempted to draw from this growing pool of experienced workers.

Volunteer programs provide opportunities for older people to get involved in the community. The Retired Senior Volunteer Program (RSVP) finds positions for people aged 60 and older in libraries, museums, and social service agencies. Retired managers and administrators may work with Service Corps of Retired Executives (SCORE), offering management assistance to small businesses and community organizations. In the Foster Grandparent Program, older adults spend 20 hours a week caring for youngsters in hospitals, correctional institutions, and day care centers.

Research has shown that individuals who have planned ahead for retirement are in a better position to take advantage of the opportunities in this period of life. This preparation involves financial planning. It also involves broadening one's interests and perhaps developing some hobbies during middle adulthood. Similarly, planning for retirement involves taking care of one's health by maintaining a proper diet and a reasonable exercise routine. Probably most important of all, it involves cultivating patterns of living that make the most of life in every growth period.

Reading Check **Draw Conclusions** What social factors contribute to the ability of older Americans' to volunteer in their community?

SECTION 3 Assessment

Reviewing Main Ideas and Vocabulary

1. **Contrast** What distinguishes social gerontology from the broader field of gerontology?
2. **Recall** What are the major characteristics of the three age groups that gerontologists use to study the aging process?
3. **Define** What is Alzheimer's disease?

Thinking Critically

4. **Explain** What factors make the transition into retirement challenging for many Americans?
5. **Elaborate** Give an example of dependency and how it affects social roles at another stage of the life cycle.
6. **Rank** What do you think is the most difficult change for aging Americans to face? Why?
7. **Summarize** Using your notes and a graphic organizer like this one, explain the physical and social changes that affect the life course of Americans in late adulthood.

The Later Years	
Physical	Social

FOCUS ON WRITING

8. **Expository** Write two short paragraphs explaining the social dimensions of the aging process. In your first paragraph, be sure to discuss the four major changes described in this section. In the second paragraph, summarize the opportunities open to aging Americans.

Challenging Stereotypes about the Aging

"You can't teach an old dog new tricks." At some point in your life you have probably heard this saying, but have you ever stopped to think about what it really means? In a nutshell, this saying expresses one of the most basic stereotypes that Americans hold about elderly people—older people are resistant to change. According to popular wisdom, as people grow older, they grow more rigid in their habits and more conservative in their social and political thinking. But is this true?

Old people are stodgy—stubborn, old-fashioned, and unwilling to change. Not so, says a new study published in the *American Sociological Review*. According to this study, the idea of older people growing increasingly conservative bears no weight at all. In fact, the study found that old people grow more open-minded and that, on occasion, they are more liberal in their thinking than younger people (Danigelis et al., 2007).

Sociologists Nicholas Danigelis and Stephen Cutler of the University of Vermont worked with Melissa Hardy of the Pennsylvania State University to analyze data from the U.S. General Social Survey that measured changes in attitudes at different life stages. In all, the researchers studied the social and political beliefs reported by 46,510 people over a 32-year period. They divided the group into two cohorts, or age-based groups: one for ages 18 to 39 and the other for age 60 and older.

For each cohort, the researchers studied three areas of beliefs. The first area concerned attitudes toward historically disadvantaged groups, such as African Americans and women. The second area explored opinions about the civil liberties of groups outside of mainstream American society, such as communists and atheists. The third area focused on privacy issues, including beliefs about sex outside of marriage and right-to-die issues.

Contrary to stereotypes of older people being "set in their ways," the researchers found that people in the older cohort changed their attitudes significantly over time and did so at a higher rate than people under age 40. What is even more fascinating is that older people grew noticeably more tolerant in their attitudes over time, not more conservative.

Nicholas Danigelis, the study's lead researcher, has suggested one possible explanation for these surprising results. Because older people often start from a more conservative position, changes within their cohort appear more obvious. For example, while both young and old may have become more open-minded about race relations over the last 30 years, the change is more obvious in the older population.

In some cases, however, younger people were even more conservative in their thinking than people in the older cohort. For example, people under 40 held more-conservative opinions about communists and atheists than did people over 60. Over time, however, both cohorts became increasingly conservative about sex outside of marriage.

Such results show that people's attitudes grow and change throughout their lives, sometimes in unexpected ways. More importantly, they challenge us to rethink commonly held assumptions about older people and the aging process.

For many Americans, such as the yoga practitioners above, the aging process offers plentiful opportunities for growth and change.

Thinking Critically

1. **Draw Conclusions** Why do you think stereotypes of aging Americans as conservative persist?
2. **Discuss** Do you think it is possible to use people's age to predict their attitudes on topics? Explain.

Simulation
Applying What You've Learned

Trading Places: Becoming Your Parent's Parent

How would you cope with becoming your parent's caregiver?

Use the workbook to complete this simulation.

1. Introduction

This simulation will help you review the stages of adulthood by examining the effects of dependency on elderly people and their adult children. You will work in small groups to write a case study that describes the symptoms an aging person might experience that would lead to a loss of independence. Your group will use its case study as the basis for a simulation in which you will take on the role of either an adult child or an aging adult. Finally, the class will discuss of how dependency changes the status of adults in American society. To complete this simulation, follow the steps below:

- Following your teacher's instructions, form groups of four to six students. Each group should have at least one male student and one female student.
- Your teacher will invite one volunteer from each group to play an aging father or mother who is losing his or her independence. The other students in the group will play the roles of adult children.
- Work with the students in your group to review the chapter material on the stages of adulthood for both men and women, as well as the characteristics of late adulthood. Write down a few main points about late adulthood, paying careful attention to the concept of dependency and the changes in physical and mental functioning that might lead to dependency.
- Conduct additional research on dependency and caring for adult parents, if your teacher instructs you to do this. Your group is now ready to write the case study.

2. Writing the Case Study

Working as a group, select at least two specific changes in physical and mental functioning that might lead to an adult child becoming the caregiver to an aging parent. Then write a scenario based on these changes. Your scenario should be written on a single sheet of paper and should include each of the four items listed below.

1. A fictional name and age for the parent and for each child;
2. A brief description of the adult child's current roles or responsibilities;
3. A description of the parent's physical and mental symptoms, with any relevant details;
4. A description of how the parent's physical and mental symptoms are changing his or her life and the lives of his or her children.

Sample Case Study

1 At age 42, Margaret Perry is slowly becoming her mother June's caregiver. June, age 74, is a widow and a retired schoolteacher. She had always been fiercely independent and had raised four children of her own. 2 Lately, however, June has been making strange phone calls to Margaret, a busy stay-at-home mother of three children.

3 In the first call June said, "I'm quitting my senior's activity club. They think I'm stealing from them." A week later, June called again insisting her high school sweetheart, the one who died in the Korean War, was coming over to take her out dancing.

Then the police called. June had been pulled over for reckless driving. The police said it would be safer for June—and everybody else—if June did not drive anymore. June disagrees. "They can take away my driver's license," she says, "but I'm still going to drive."

4 At this point, Margaret suspects the worst. The forgetfulness and the fantasies could be signs of dementia. June needs care, so Margaret is pleased when June agrees to move in with her. Still, Margaret knows it will be a big role reversal for both of them.

3. Reversing Roles

Imagine what it would be like to be a child "in charge" of his or her parents. What issues would you have to deal with? How would a parent respond to being "ordered around" by his or her child? Work with your group to brainstorm what life would be like when the parent and child roles reverse. As you brainstorm, be sure to address who should make decisions about each of the areas below and identify why these areas might be a source of conflict.

- Driving privileges
- Independent trips and outings
- Diet and exercise
- Medical information and decisions
- Living situation
- Finances

4. The Simulation

Review with your group the case study you wrote and the results of your brainstorming session. Then write a short script that focuses on a conflict that arises between an aging parent who is losing his or her independence and the adult-child caregivers. Be sure to write at least four lines for each person in your group. Your teacher will invite each group to perform its script for the class.

5. Discussion

What did you learn from this simulation? Hold a group discussion that focuses on the following questions:

- Overall, how successful were the simulations in communicating the challenges faced by families?
- Would you rather be placed in the position of the aging parent or the adult child who must become a caregiver? Explain.
- In what ways are the reversed roles similar to the relationship between a parent and a child?
- How would you react if someone placed you in a nursing facility against your wishes?
- Do you think involving an outside professional, such as a doctor, nurse, or lawyer, would make it easier or more difficult to make decisions about a dependent parent?

The person most likely to be a family caregiver to a person age 65 or over is an adult child. More than 70 percent of caregivers care for a parent, step-parent, mother-in-law, or father-in-law.

CHAPTER 6 Review

Comprehension and Critical Thinking

SECTION 1 *(pp. 136–140)*

1. a. **Identify** During which stage in Levinson's model of adulthood do most men leave their childhood homes?
   b. **Compare and Contrast** According to Frieze and Sales, what patterns distinguish adult female development from adult male development?
   c. **Make Judgments** Do you think the theory of adulthood developed by Daniel Levinson in the 1970s still applies to adults today? Explain.

SECTION 2 *(pp. 141–145)*

2. a. **Recall** What factors cause variation in the unemployment rate of American workers?
   b. **Summarize** How has the nature of work changed since the 1900s?
   c. **Rank** What three changes in the composition of the labor force do you think are most important? Explain.

SECTION 3 *(pp. 146–150)*

3. a. **Recall** What challenges and opportunities are associated with the later stages of life?
   b. **Explain** What factors have sociologists identified that help explain why elderly people fear dependency more than death?
   c. **Predict** How do you think the aging of the U.S. population will influence the perception of age in American society?

INTERNET ACTIVITY

4. Use the Internet to research a group that works to protect the rights of older Americans, such as the AARP or the Gray Panthers. Then design a table outlining the goals of the group you select. Write a brief introduction that explains the history of your group and its mission to serve elderly people. In your chart, be sure to identify and describe the goals of your group and how they relate to issues that concern older people. Use at least three statistics to help explain why specific issues are of concern to your group.

Reviewing Vocabulary

Match the terms below with their correct definitions.

5. life structure
6. novice phase
7. mentor
8. work
9. labor force
10. informal economy
11. gerontology
12. social gerontology
13. Alzheimer's disease
14. dependency

A. an organic condition that results in the progressive deterioration of brain cells

B. a condition in which an adult shifts from living independently to being physically or financially dependent on others

C. the scientific study of aging

D. all individuals age 16 and older who are paid for their work or who are seeking paid employment

E. the combination of statuses, roles, activities, goals, values, beliefs, and life circumstances that characterize an individual

F. a person who helps others develop into adulthood and achieve their dreams

G. the first three periods of early adulthood during which a person prepares for the adult world

H. the study of the nonphysical aspects of aging

I. unofficial economic activities that take place outside of government regulations and mainstream business and industry

J. the tasks that people perform to make goods and provide services that meet human needs

Sociology in Your Life

15. What is the future of work in the United States? Identify three careers that interest you. Conduct Internet research on the Bureau of Labor Statistics Web site to find information about the future of employment in the United States and in your career choices. Then write two paragraphs summarizing the results of your research. In your first paragraph, tell whether the U.S. job market is expected to grow, what the fastest-growing jobs and industries are, and what occupations will add the largest number of workers. In your second paragraph, describe the employment outlook for each of your career options. Be sure to describe the level of training or education you will need and the salary you can expect for each career.

Skills Activity: Interpreting Graphs

Study the bar graph below. Then use the information to help you answer the questions that follow.

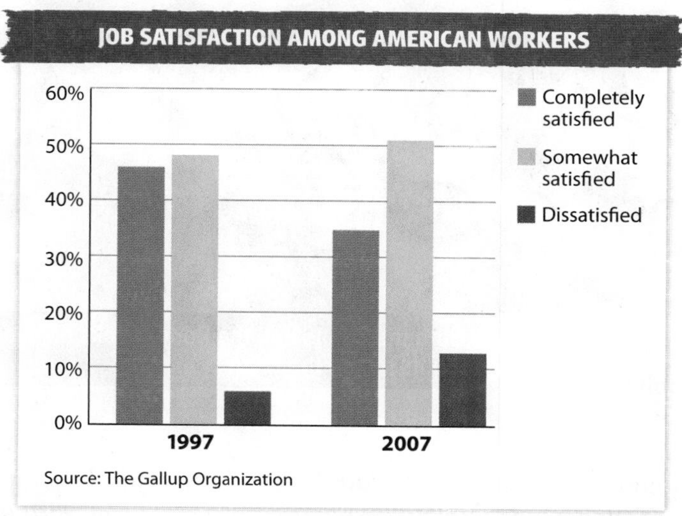

Source: The Gallup Organization

16. Identify In what year did a higher percentage of employees report that they were dissatisfied with their jobs?

17. Analyze Between 1997 and 2007, was there an overall increase or decrease in job satisfaction among American workers?

18. Make Judgments What job characteristics do you think contribute most to job satisfaction?

Writing for Sociology

Use your knowledge of adulthood to answer the question below. Do not simply list facts. Present a clear argument based on your critical analysis of the question, using appropriate sociological terminology.

19. Briefly describe each of the terms below from a sociological perspective. For each term, include a general description and a review of major characteristics and trends. Then use real-world examples to help explain the term within the context of American society.
- middle adulthood
- labor force
- Alzheimer's disease

Connecting Online

Go online for review and enrichment activities related to this chapter.

KEY TOPICS VIDEOS
View compelling clips on issues in the field.

KEEP IT CURRENT
Link to the Current Events site for regularly updated stories on sociology as well as other social studies topics.

QUICK LAB
Reinforce a key concept with a short lab activity.

CASE STUDY

The Saints and the Roughnecks

Both the Saints and the Roughnecks enjoyed rowdy nights out on the town.

In 1973 sociologist William Chambliss published "The Saints and the Roughnecks," an article documenting the two years he spent observing two groups of delinquent teenage boys. One group, which he called the Saints, was made up of young men from upper-middle class families. Despite frequently skipping school, the Saints got good grades, participated in school activities, and were liked by students and teachers. The local police saw the Saints as good boys and leaders in the youth community. Chambliss described his observations.

> *Eight promising young men . . . were some of the most delinquent boys at Hanibal High School. While community residents knew that these boys occasionally sowed a few wild oats, they were totally unaware that sowing wild oats completely occupied the daily routine of these young men. The Saints were constantly occupied with truancy, drinking, wild driving, petty theft, and vandalism . . .*
>
> *Every Friday and Saturday night most of the Saints would meet . . . and would go into Big Town. Big Town activities included drinking heavily in taverns or nightclubs, driving drunkenly through the streets, and committing acts of vandalism and playing pranks . . .*
>
> *Abandoned houses, especially if they were located in out-of-the-way places, were fair game for destruction and spontaneous vandalism. The boys would break windows, remove furniture to the yard and tear it apart, urinate on the walls, and scrawl obscenities inside.*

Unlike the Saints, the other group that Chambliss observed, the Roughnecks, had a reputation for being delinquents. They were less well-to-do than the Saints, and their grades were not as good. Although they attended school more often than the Saints and were not particularly disruptive, teachers saw them as troublemakers. According to Chambliss, the police shared this view.

> *Hanibal townspeople never perceived the Saints' high level of delinquency. The Saints were good boys who just went in for an occasional prank. After all, they were well dressed, well mannered, and had nice cars. The Roughnecks were a different story. Although the two gangs of boys were the same age, and both groups engaged in an equal amount of wild-oat sowing, everyone agreed that the not-so-well-dressed, not-so-well-mannered, not-so-rich boys were heading for trouble . . .*
>
> *The community's impression of the degrees to which this group of six boys (ranging in age from 16 to 19) engaged in delinquency was somewhat distorted. In some ways the gang was more delinquent*

than the community thought; in other ways they were less . . .

Although community members perceived that this gang of kids was delinquent, they mistakenly believed that their illegal activities were primarily drinking, fighting, and being a nuisance to passersby. Drinking was limited among the gang members . . . and theft was much more prevalent than anyone realized.

Chambliss explored why the community saw the Roughnecks as troublemakers but did not see the Saints that way. He explained that the Saints' delinquent behavior was less visible because access to cars allowed them to leave the community. The Saints were also more contrite and respectful when caught. Perhaps most important was that once a group had been labeled as "good" or "bad," the labels stuck:

Selective perception and labeling—finding, processing, and punishing some kinds of criminality and not others—means that visible, poor, nonmobile, outspoken, undiplomatic "tough" kids will be noticed, whether their actions are seriously delinquent or not. Other kids, who have established a reputation for being bright . . . , disciplined, and involved in respectable activities, who are mobile and monied, will be invisible when they deviate from sanctioned activities. They'll sow their wild oats—perhaps even wider and thicker than their lower-class cohorts—but they won't be noticed.

In this chapter, you will learn more about how society typically responds to such delinquent behavior.

What do you think?

1. How did community members view the Saints and the Roughnecks differently?

2. What factors do you think influenced their views?

CHAPTER 7

SOCIAL CONTROL AND DEVIANCE

Chapter at a Glance

SECTION 1: Social Control

- People generally follow social norms—and expect others to as well—because they have internalized the norms that they feel are useful and appropriate.
- When a person has not internalized a norm, society uses sanctions to motivate his or her conformity.
- Sanctions can be positive or negative, formal or informal.
- Social control is necessary to ensure that a society functions smoothly.

SECTION 2: Deviance

- Deviance is any behavior that violates significant social norms.
- Deviance can serve positive functions, such as clarifying norms, unifying the group, diffusing tension, promoting social change, and providing jobs.
- Functionalists, conflict theorists, and interactionists offer different theories to explain deviance.

SECTION 3: Crime

- Crime affects everyone in the United States, some as victims, some as criminals, and some as observers.
- Crimes are grouped into five general categories: violent crime, property crime, victimless crime, white-collar crime, and organized crime.
- Crime statistics are gathered and reported by two main sources, the *Uniform Crime Reports* and the National Crime Victimization Survey.
- The criminal-justice system—made up of the police, the courts, and corrections—deals with crimes that have been committed and reported.

SECTION 1

Social Control

Before You Read

Main Idea
Norms must be followed for a society to run smoothly, and they are enforced through internalization and sanctions.

Reading Focus
1. How do social norms become internalized?
2. What are the differences between positive and negative sanctions and between formal and informal sanctions?
3. What is social control?

Vocabulary
internalization
sanctions
positive sanction
negative sanction
formal sanction
informal sanction
social control

TAKING NOTES Use a graphic organizer like this one to take notes on the different kinds of sanctions.

Types of Sanctions	Positive	Negative
Formal		
Informal		

The Virtual Pillory

SOCIOLOGY CLOSE UP ***What if your every misdeed were posted on a Web site?*** The idea of public shaming as a means of social control is not new. Until the early 1800s, communities across Europe used devices called pillories that restrained and displayed criminals in public places to punish and humiliate them. The criminal was locked in place, and people gathered to hurl abuse—along with rotten food, dead animals, and even rocks—at him or her. This type of punishment also sent a message to the rest of the community: Behave badly and this could be you.

Today people have found a less-physical way to punish and discourage violations of cultural norms. A number of Web sites encourage users to expose petty criminals and rude people. For example, at one site used primarily by bicycle commuters, cyclists and other concerned citizens send in photographs of drivers who endanger cyclists by parking in designated bicycle lanes. Vehicles' license plate numbers are displayed, and repeat offenders are shown in a special "Top Offenders" section. Another Web site is designed to expose the entire range of socially offensive behavior. Stories posted on the site range from office food thieves and rude customer service workers to loud cell phone talkers and reckless drivers. Posters to the Web site often identify their targets by name, location, or license plate number. Does the idea of bad behavior on display make you nervous? If it does, these Web sites are having the effect their creators are hoping for. ■

Internalization of Norms

Every society develops norms that reflect the cultural values its members consider important. For a society to run smoothly, these norms must be upheld. Norms are enforced through two basic means—internalization and sanctions.

When people come to believe that a particular norm is good, useful, and appropriate, they generally follow it and expect others to do the same. People do this because they have internalized the norm. **Internalization** is the process by which a norm becomes a part of an individual's personality, thus conditioning that individual to conform to society's expectations. For example, when you go to the movies, you automatically sit in a chair, not on the floor. When the traffic signal ahead turns red, you stop without thinking. You do not take these actions because you fear being punished. Rather, you have internalized society's norms concerning movies and driving.

Reading Check **Identify Supporting Details** What characteristics describe a norm that is likely to be internalized?

Sanctions

Most members of society follow norms without conscious thought. However, not everyone internalizes all of society's norms. Some people must be motivated by **sanctions.** These are rewards or punishments used to enforce conformity to norms.

Positive Sanctions Sociologists call an action that rewards a particular kind of behavior a **positive sanction.** Usually people are introduced to positive sanctions early in their lives through interaction with their families. Most parents praise their children for good behavior. Positive sanctions are also a common form of control outside of the family. Teachers react favorably to students who turn in good work, giving them good grades. Positive sanctions continue into adulthood. Employers may give pay raises to workers who show initiative and dedication. Cheers from teammates and the crowd at sporting events are used to push athletes to try even harder. In all areas of life, rewards such as ceremonies, ribbons, badges, and awards are used to encourage conformity to society's norms.

Negative Sanctions Positive sanctions alone do not always ensure conformity. Society uses negative sanctions to discourage undesired behavior. A **negative sanction** is a punishment or the threat of punishment used to enforce conformity. The mere threat of punishment is often enough to ensure acceptable behavior. The possibility of getting a parking ticket and having your car towed is usually enough to persuade you not to park in a "no parking" zone. However, if the threat of punishment is not enough, the actual punishment is there to remind you that conformity to the "no parking" rule is expected.

Quick Lab

Observing Norms in Social Interaction

Have you ever thought about the norms you obey when carrying on a conversation? Most of us follow certain guidelines for social interactions without realizing it.

PROCEDURE

1. Read the questions about conversational behaviors below.

   Social Distance: How close or far apart do people stand or sit when talking to one another?

   Hand Gestures: Do some people use hand gestures when they speak? Do these gestures clarify or distract from their points?

   Eye Contact: Do the individuals maintain eye contact? Is eye contact important?

   Facial Expressions: What kinds of facial expressions do individuals make during conversation? How does the other person react?

2. Observe your friends and family during conversation, paying close attention to the behaviors mentioned above.
3. Record your observations in a chart.

ANALYSIS

1. Think about what you saw. What can you conclude about the norms that govern these behaviors?
2. Were these norms followed, or did some people violate them? How did other people react to the violation?
3. Discuss your observations and conclusions as a class.

ACADEMIC VOCABULARY

rebuke sharp criticism or expression of disapproval

Negative sanctions can range from frowns, ridicule, and rejection to fines, imprisonment, and even death. In general, the more important the norm is to social stability, the more serious the negative sanction.

Neither positive nor negative sanctions work if people are not sure that rewards or punishment will follow particular behavior. If you are rarely or never rewarded for good behavior nor punished for bad behavior, then sanctions quickly become meaningless to you. In other words, they lose their power to encourage or enforce conformity.

Formal Sanctions In addition to being positive or negative, sanctions can also be either formal or informal. A **formal sanction** is a reward or punishment given by a formal organization or regulatory agency, such as a school, business, or government. Negative formal sanctions include low grades, suspension from school, termination from a job, fines, and imprisonment. Graduation certificates, pay raises, promotions, awards, and medals are examples of positive formal sanctions.

Informal Sanctions Formal sanctions play a major role in maintaining social stability. However, the majority of norms are enforced informally. An **informal sanction** is a spontaneous expression of approval or disapproval given by an individual or a group. Positive informal sanctions include standing ovations, compliments, smiles, pats on the back, and gifts. Negative informal sanctions include frowns, gossip, rebukes, insults, ridicule, and ostracism—exclusion from a particular group. Informal sanctions are particularly effective among teenagers, who consider group acceptance to be important. Few teenagers, for example, want to be told that their clothes are out of style.

Reading Check **Find the Main Idea** What is the purpose of sanctions?

Social Control

Enforcing norms through either internal or external means is called **social control.** The principal means of social control in all societies is self-control, which is learned through the internalization of norms. Various agents of social control perform external enforcement through the use of sanctions. These agents include authority figures, the police, the courts, religion, the family, the peer group, and public opinion.

Individuals must follow certain rules of behavior if society is to function smoothly. Behavior that violates society's basic norms jeopardizes the social order. When a society's methods for ensuring conformity break down, social stability is lost. No society can survive for long without an effective system of social control.

Reading Check **Analyze** Why is social control important to society?

SECTION 1 Assessment

Reviewing Main Ideas and Vocabulary

1. **Define** What is internalization?
2. **Recall** Are most norms enforced with formal or informal sanctions?
3. **Identify** What is the principal means of social control in all societies?

Thinking Critically

4. **Categorize** Give an example of each of the following kinds of sanctions: positive formal, negative formal, positive informal, and negative informal.
5. **Predict** What do you think society would be like if it used only informal sanctions to enforce norms?
6. **Compare and Contrast** Using your notes and a graphic organizer like the one below, analyze the similarities and differences between positive and negative sanctions.

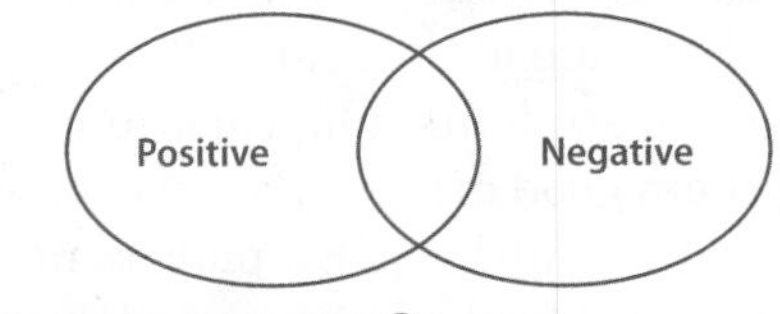

FOCUS ON WRITING

7. **Persuasive** Write two paragraphs supporting the need for government involvement in social control. Consider how violations of norms affect social order.

Death Penalty: The Ultimate Sanction

Capital punishment, or the death penalty, is the ultimate negative formal sanction. Used since ancient times to punish murderers and other criminals, the death penalty is much debated today. The United States still uses the death penalty, but many other countries have abolished it.

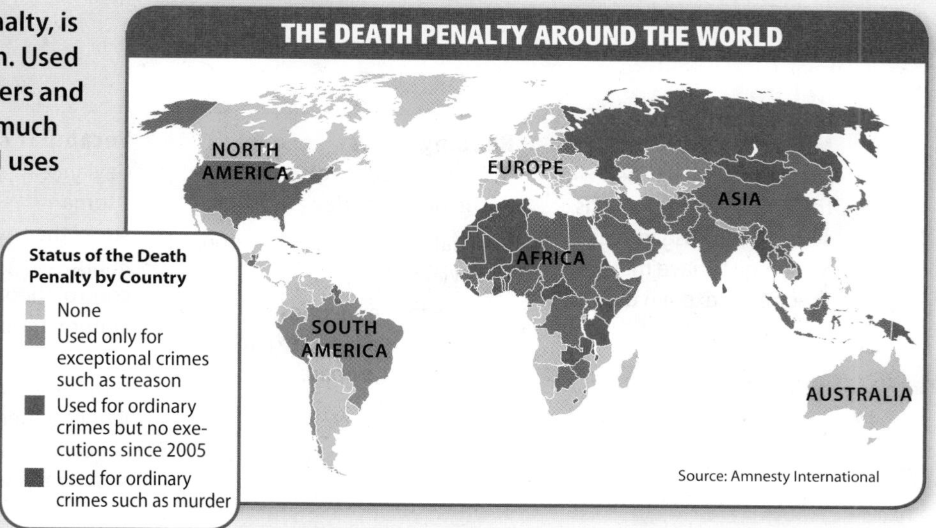

For centuries, the death penalty has been used as a form of social control. In the late 1700s, the Enlightenment ideal of an individual's natural right to life encouraged some governments to limit its application to major crimes, such as treason or murder. Before this shift, a wide variety of crimes had been punishable by death in many jurisdictions.

In 1863, Venezuela became the first country to abolish capital punishment. During the early 1900s, other nations followed. Since 1967, an average of three countries per year have abolished the death penalty (Amnesty International, 2007). According to the human rights organization Amnesty International, by 2012, more than two-thirds of the world's nations had abolished the death penalty in law or practice. By the end of that year, 141 countries had abolished the death penalty for all crimes. Ten countries had abolished capital punishment for "ordinary crimes," such as murder, but were still able to use it for "exceptional crimes," such as treason (Amnesty International, 2012).

There were also 33 countries that Amnesty International classified as "abolitionist in practice." These are countries that have not legally abolished the death penalty, but that have not had an execution for 10 years and are believed to be committed to a practice of not carrying out executions. This category also includes nations that have made a formal international commitment not to execute criminals (Amnesty International, 2012).

Death sentences jumped by more than 500 in 2013 due to the conflicts in Egypt and Nigeria with 2,466 deaths in 2014, up by 28 percent from the previous year (Amnesty International, 2015). Only 22 countries carried out executions in 2014, down from 41 countries in 2004. Amnesty International has seen a slow movement away from the death penalty as punishment and more toward life imprisonment, and the organization advocates for the elimination of the death penalty worldwide.

Whether to abolish the death penalty is a topic of much debate in the United States. Public opinion on the subject has fluctuated over the years. Critics of capital punishment argue that it is immoral and hypocritical to punish murder by taking life. In 2011, when asked why Americans oppose the death penalty they cite doubts raised about the death penalty and the imperfect justice system (Lipka, 2014).

Still, polls indicate that 63 percent of Americans support the death penalty. About the same number, 66 percent, believe it is "morally acceptable." Yet, when pollsters separate the groups into Democrats and Republicans the numbers change dramatically. Almost half of Democrats support the death penalty, down from 75 percent in 1994. More than three-quarters of Republicans support the death penalty, down from 85 percent in 1994 (Gallup, 2014).

Thinking Critically

1. **Define** What does it mean when a country is considered "abolitionist in practice"?
2. **Discuss** Why do you think the death penalty is a focus of such debate in the United States?

SECTION 2

Deviance

Before You Read

Main Idea
Deviance, which is behavior that violates social norms, serves a purpose in society. Sociologists have many theories to explain deviant behavior.

Reading Focus
1. How do sociologists identify the nature of deviance?
2. What are the social functions of deviance?
3. How do the theories that have been proposed to explain deviance compare?

Vocabulary
deviance
stigma
strain theory
anomie
control theory
cultural transmission theory
differential association
labeling theory
primary deviance
secondary deviance

TAKING NOTES Use a graphic organizer like this one to take notes about deviance.

Deviance		
Definition	Functions	Explanations

SOCIOLOGY CLOSE UP ***Why would a teenage boy lock himself in his room and hide from society?*** They don't go to school. They don't go to work. Some don't even leave the rooms that they've retreated to. They are *hikikomori*, sufferers of a Japanese syndrome of the same name, which means "withdrawal." The term refers to a person who confines himself or herself to the home for at least six months, with no outside social life. Some experts estimate that 1 million Japanese youth, about 80 percent of them male, have become hikikomori.

Psychologists are not sure what causes hikikomori. Some think it is the pressure to succeed, a cultural expectation made difficult by Japan's sagging economy, which has made full-time work harder to find. Instead of facing possible failure, hikikomori abandon the goals and norms of Japanese society and retreat, a behavior the culture at large cannot understand. ■

Retreating from Society

The Nature of Deviance

Read through and consider the following list of behaviors. What do you think these behaviors have in common?

- continually talking to oneself in public
- drag racing on a public street
- regularly using illegal drugs
- using a weapon to attack another person

Most people internalize the majority of their society's norms. However, individuals do not internalize every norm. Even sanctions—the rewards and punishments used to enforce conformity to norms—cannot bring about complete social control. There are always individuals who break the rules of their society or the group. Behavior that violates significant social norms is called **deviance.** The behaviors listed to the left are examples of deviant behavior in American society.

Violating Norms Every society has countless norms that govern behavior. Some norms deal with fairly insignificant behaviors, such as personal cleanliness or table manners. Other norms are vital to the smooth operation of a society and the safety of its members. For example, norms governing the taking of a person's life or property are essential.

Because there are so many norms governing behavior, occasional violations are unavoidable. Not all norm violations are considered deviant acts. An act considered deviant in one situation may be considered acceptable in another, even within the same society. For example, to kill someone is generally seen as deviant. However, if a soldier or a police officer kills someone in the line of duty, the action is usually judged quite differently.

What is considered deviant also varies from society to society. For example, divorce is accepted in the United States. However, it is prohibited in the Philippines. Similarly, an act might be considered deviant during one period of time but not in another. Throughout much of the 1900s, it was illegal for stores to do business on Sunday. Today, however, many stores are open each Sunday.

How do people come to be considered deviant? Suppose a person gets a speeding ticket. That person would not be considered deviant on the basis of this one event. However, if that person were continually caught driving at high speeds, such reckless behavior would be considered deviant. Repeating an offense is not the only way a person comes to be labeled a deviant. A person who commits an act that has serious negative consequences for society—such as murder, sexual assault, or robbery—is likely to be labeled as deviant because of his or her single act.

The Label of Deviance The labeling of someone as deviant involves two components. To be considered deviant by society, an individual must first be detected committing a deviant act. A person will not be labeled as deviant unless his or her deviant behavior is in some way known to other people. Next, the individual must be stigmatized by society. A **stigma** is a mark of social disgrace that sets the deviant apart from the rest of society. Stigmas have been used as a form of social control throughout history. For example, the ancient Greeks cut or burned signs into the bodies of criminals to warn others to avoid those people.

The power of the outward sign as a form of social control is still used today. For example, prison inmates in the United States are forced to wear special clothing and are assigned numbers as a visual sign of stigma. Some people have suggested that the cars of convicted drunk drivers should be marked in some way. This visual sign would serve as a warning to others and as a form of public humiliation.

When sociologists speak of the stigma resulting from the label of deviance, they usually do not mean outward signs. Rather, they are referring to the negative social reactions that result from being labeled deviant. According to sociologist Erving Goffman, a person labeled as deviant has a "spoiled social identity." He or she is no longer seen as being normal or whole.

Reading Check **Analyze** How does behavior that is considered deviant change based on context?

Social Functions of Deviance

A society without deviance is an impossibility. As Émile Durkheim observed in *The Rules of Sociological Method,* deviance has some uses in social life. Deviance, Durkheim suggested, helps to clarify norms, unify the group, diffuse tension, and promote social change. Deviance also serves another positive function not mentioned by Durkheim—it provides jobs in fields such as law enforcement.

Deviance serves to define the boundaries of acceptable behavior. When rules are broken and the guilty parties are caught, members of society are reminded of the norms that guide social life. The punishment of norm violators serves as a warning to others that society will not tolerate certain behaviors. For example, harsh prison sentences are intended to discourage crime. People may not commit deviant acts if they are aware of how severe the consequences of those acts will be.

Deviance also draws a line between conforming members of society and "outsiders," or the nonconforming members. This "us against them" attitude reinforces shared values and a sense of community. Deviance helps maintain group unity—a function so important that Durkheim suggested deviance would have to be invented if it did not already exist.

People who are unhappy with their lives or social conditions may want to strike out at society. In such situations, minor acts of deviance can serve as a safety valve. These acts allow individuals to relieve tension without disrupting the basic fabric of society. For example, participating in unauthorized demonstrations allows people to express political or social discontent without destroying the social order.

Deviance can help prompt social change by identifying problem areas. When large numbers of people violate a particular norm, it is often an indication that something in society needs to be changed. Once alerted to the problem, individuals in positions of authority can take steps to correct the situation.

Deviance also provides legitimate jobs for a wide range of people. Judges, lawyers, police officers, prison personnel, and parole officers have jobs related to one form of deviant behavior—crime. So too do crime reporters and criminologists, or the social scientists who study criminal behavior. In addition, many other jobs are based in part on the existence of deviance. For example, workers at clothing manufacturers might make prison uniforms as well as other types of clothes.

Reading Check **Summarize** How can deviance benefit society?

Explaining Deviance

Why do people commit deviant acts? You can better understand the answers to this question by considering how the three sociological perspectives explain deviance. The functionalist perspective views deviance as a natural part of society. The conflict perspective explains deviance in terms of power and inequality. The interactionist perspective looks at how interaction among individuals influences deviance.

Functionalist Perspective The major functionalist explanation, strain theory, was developed by sociologist Robert K. Merton. **Strain theory** views deviance as the natural outgrowth of the values, norms, and structure of society. According to Merton, American society places a high value on certain goals, such as economic success. However, not everyone in society has access to the accepted means to achieve these goals. For example, individuals may be prevented from finding a job because of social conditions or because they lack an adequate education. Nevertheless, they are expected to meet this goal, and society judges them according to how well they do so.

Under the strain of incompatible goals and means, these individuals fall victim to anomie. **Anomie** is the situation that arises when the norms of society are unclear or are no longer applicable. Anomie leaves people without sufficient guidelines for behavior, causing confusion both for individuals and for society. The concept was originally proposed by Émile Durkheim to explain high rates of suicide in countries undergoing industrialization.

Merton suggested that individuals respond to the culturally approved goals and the legitimate means of achieving these goals in five ways, which he called modes of adaptation. Merton labeled them conformity, innovation, ritualism, retreatism, and rebellion. The first and most common response is conformity. Many individuals in a society accept both the culturally approved goals and the means for achieving these goals. Whether people succeed or fail in reaching these goals, the effort always involves legitimate means. The other four modes of adaptation employ deviant behavior.

People who use the mode of adaptation that Merton called innovation accept the cultural goals of their society but do not accept the approved means for reaching these goals. For example, people may want to acquire wealth but reject the acceptable means to obtain it. Therefore they innovate, or devise new means for achieving the goals, and consequently violate accepted norms. Such people become deviants. Criminals such as drug dealers and burglars fit into this category.

Ritualists also find it impossible to achieve cultural goals by acceptable means. Instead of violating the norms for achievement, they abandon the goals while continuing to observe the expected rules of behavior. For example, a worker may pass up opportunities for promotion rather than face possible failure. A bureaucrat may make a ritual of upholding the rules of the organization while abandoning personal goals. The ritual of upholding the norms becomes an end in itself.

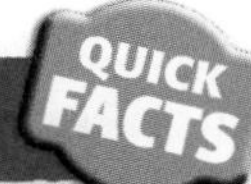

MERTON'S STRAIN THEORY OF DEVIANCE

Merton suggested five responses to the strain that individuals feel when they attempt to meet the cultural goal of economic success through the approved norm of hard work.

Mode of Adaptation	Method of Adaptation	Seeks Culture's Goals	Follows Culture's Norms
Conformity	Accepts cultural goals and pursues them through culturally approved ways	Yes	Yes
Innovation	Accepts cultural goals but uses disapproved ways of achieving them	Yes	No
Ritualism	Abandons cultural goals but continues to follow society's norms	No	Yes
Retreatism	Abandons cultural goals and the approved ways of achieving them	No	No
Rebellion	Challenges cultural goals and norms and substitutes new ones	No—tries to replace	No—tries to replace

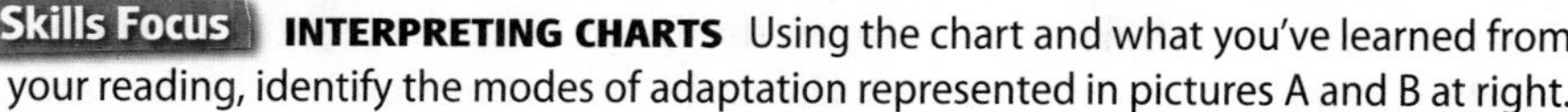

Skills Focus **INTERPRETING CHARTS** Using the chart and what you've learned from your reading, identify the modes of adaptation represented in pictures A and B at right.

Some individuals, whom Merton called retreatists, reject both the cultural goals and the socially acceptable means of attaining them. Unlike innovators and ritualists, retreatists make no effort to appear to share their society's goals and norms. Instead, they may simply drop out of society. Examples of retreatists may include drug addicts, beggars, and hermits.

Not all individuals who reject the cultural goals and the socially acceptable means to attain them follow the path of retreatism. Some people rebel. Rebels want to substitute a new set of goals and means for the currently approved set. To achieve their alternate goals, rebels may use violent or nonviolent tactics. Members of any revolutionary movement fall into this category of deviant adaptation.

The four categories of deviant adaptation are not considered equally deviant. Innovators and rebels obviously pose a threat to society. Retreatists also are perceived as a serious problem because they lead what society considers to be an unproductive life and often rely on the support of others. However, ritualists are generally not regarded as a serious threat to social order.

Conflict Perspective Conflict theorists believe that competition and social inequality lead to deviance. These theorists see social life as a struggle between the ruling classes who possess power and the lower classes who do not. People with power commit deviant acts to maintain their position. People without power commit deviant acts to obtain economic rewards or to improve their low self-esteem and stop feeling powerless.

According to conflict theorist Richard Quinney, the ruling classes label as deviant any behavior that threatens their power. Because the lower classes have limited opportunities, they are often forced to commit acts defined as deviant. To keep power, the ruling classes then establish ideologies that explain deviance as a problem found among the lower classes. Thus, most law enforcement efforts are directed toward the types of crimes committed by the lower classes. As a result, these groups have higher arrest and conviction rates. People without power do not necessarily commit more crimes. Rather, they commit the types of crimes that are most likely to be detected and punished.

ACADEMIC VOCABULARY

ideology a belief system

Interactionist Perspective Interactionists have proposed three major explanations for deviance—control theory, cultural transmission theory, and labeling theory. Like strain theory, **control theory** explains deviance as a natural occurrence. However, the focus of control theory is somewhat different. Control theorists are interested in why people conform rather than in the causes of deviance. Social ties among individuals, control theorists propose, determine conformity. Control theorists suggest that individuals who are integrated into the community are likely to conform. Conversely, those who have weak ties to the community are likely to commit deviant acts. Communities in which most members have strong social bonds will have lower rates of deviance because community members are able to exert stronger social control over those who deviate.

According to Travis Hirschi, a leading control theorist, people develop bonds to their communities in four ways. First, they form attachments with others—parents, teachers, and friends—who accept the norms of society. Second, they have a strong belief in society's moral codes, accepting that some behavior is simply wrong. Third, they show commitment to traditional societal values and goals, such as getting a good education or job. Finally, they are fully involved in nondeviant activities, leaving no time for deviant behavior. People who display strong attachment and commitment to, belief in, and involvement with their community are likely to conform. People who lack these qualities are more likely to engage in deviant acts.

In a recent study, criminologists Travis Hirschi and Michael Gottfredson have suggested that conformity is the result of strong self-control. Socialization—particularly during childhood—helps determine one's level of self-control. Children may develop more self-control if their parents punish them for deviant behavior and reward them for conformity.

Socialization is also central to **cultural transmission theory.** This sociological theory explains deviance as a behavior learned in much the same way that nondeviant behavior is learned—through interaction with others. However, in interactions among individuals engaging in deviance, the norms and values being transmitted are deviant. As a result, the individual is socialized into deviant behavior rather than into socially acceptable behavior.

The concept of **differential association,** proposed by Edwin Sutherland, is at the heart of the cultural transmission theory. This concept refers to the frequency and closeness of associations a person has with deviant and nondeviant individuals. If the majority of a person's interactions are with deviant individuals, the person is likely to be socialized into patterns of deviant behavior. On the other hand, if the person's associations are primarily with individuals who conform to society's norms, that person is more likely to conform. Sutherland suggested that the learning of deviant behavior occurs in primary groups.

Cultural transmission theory views all individuals as conformists. The difference between the deviant and the nondeviant lies in the norms to which each chooses to conform. The deviant individual conforms to norms that are not accepted by the larger community. The nondeviant conforms to socially accepted norms.

Perspectives on Deviance

Functionalist Perspective Deviance is a natural part of society. It serves positive functions, such as clarifying social norms, as well as negative ones. Deviance results from the strain of goals incompatible with the available means of achieving them.

Conflict Perspective Deviance is a result of competition and social inequality. People with power commit deviant acts to hold on to power. They also label as deviant behavior that threatens them. Those without power commit deviant acts to obtain economic rewards or to relieve their feelings of powerlessness.

Interactionist Perspective Interaction among individuals influences deviance. Control theory suggests that strong social bonds make people conform to norms and refrain from deviance. Cultural transmission theory proposes that deviance is a learned behavior. Labeling theory examines how individuals are identified as deviant.

Gresham Sykes and David Matza offered an extension to Sutherland's concept of differential association. They noted that some people show strong commitment to society's norms yet still engage in deviance. Through techniques of neutralization, people suspend their moral beliefs to commit deviant acts. These techniques, which are learned through the process of social interaction, are denying responsibility, denying injury, denying the victim, condemning the authorities, and appealing to higher loyalties.

When accused of a deviant act, some people deny responsibility. A person might claim that the act was an accident or that it was the result of a force beyond his or her control, such as a lack of parental supervision. Other people accept responsibility for their behavior, but they deny that it caused any harm. Such a person may ask "If no one was hurt, has a crime really been committed?" Similarly, people sometimes accept responsibility but deny the victim. A person may claim that "he had it coming" or "she got what she deserved." On occasion, people try to justify their actions by condemning the authorities. "The police and the courts are corrupt," someone may claim, "so they have no right to accuse others." Finally, some people claim that their loyalties to a particular group are more important than loyalty to society. They might say they committed the acts "to protect family" or "to help friends."

Instead of focusing on why people perform deviant acts, **labeling theory** focuses on how individuals come to be identified as deviant. Labeling theory is heavily influenced by Edwin Lemert and Howard Becker. Labeling theorists note that all people commit deviant acts, yet not everyone is labeled as deviant. Labeling theorists suggest that there are two types of deviance. **Primary deviance** is the occasional violation of norms. Individuals who commit acts of primary deviance do not see themselves as deviant and neither does society. **Secondary deviance** refers to deviance as a lifestyle and results in the individual being labeled as deviant and believing the label.

Once someone is labeled as deviant, people judge his or her actions in light of that label. The deviant label often restricts an individual's options and forces him or her into a deviant lifestyle. For example, of William Chambliss's Saints, all but one went to college and had successful careers. However, among the Roughnecks, only two attended college. Two dropped out of high school, were later involved in separate murders, and went to prison. One became a bookie. Another's whereabouts are unknown. The deviant label is a self-fulfilling prophecy. Treating people as deviants may encourage them to commit deviant acts.

CASE STUDY CONNECTION

The Saints and the Roughnecks The deviant label applied to the Roughnecks determined how the community saw them and limited their life chances.

Reading Check **Contrast** How do the sociological perspectives view deviance differently?

SECTION 2 Assessment

Reviewing Main Ideas and Vocabulary

1. **Identify Main Ideas** What are the two components involved when society labels an individual as deviant?
2. **Explain** How can deviance help prompt social change?
3. **Recall** Which type of deviance results in the individual being labeled as deviant, primary or secondary?

Thinking Critically

4. **Identify Cause and Effect** Why does society use stigmas to mark deviant individuals?
5. **Rank** Which social function of deviance do you think is the most important? Why?
6. **Support a Position** Which of the theoretical explanations of deviance do you find most convincing? Why?
7. **Categorize** Using your notes and a graphic organizer like the one below, identify the functions that deviance serves.

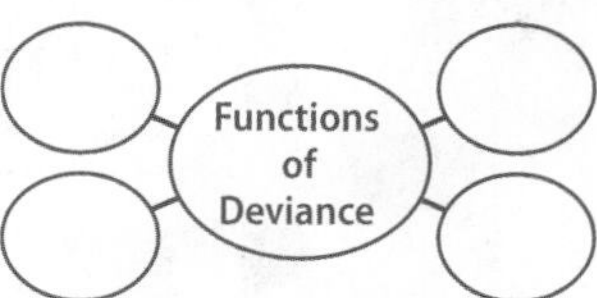

FOCUS ON WRITING

8. **Descriptive** Write a brief essay describing an act of deviance and how the three sociological perspectives would explain that act.

SECTION 3

Crime

Before You Read

Main Idea
There are several different types of crimes. The U.S. criminal-justice system investigates, prosecutes, and punishes criminals.

Reading Focus
1. What are crimes, and who commits them?
2. What are the principal types of crime in the United States?
3. How are crime statistics gathered and reported?
4. What are the characteristics of the criminal-justice system?

Vocabulary
crime
white-collar crime
crime syndicate
criminal-justice system
police discretion
racial profiling
plea bargaining
corrections
recidivism

TAKING NOTES Use a graphic organizer like this one to take notes on crime in the United States.

That's Illegal!

SOCIOLOGY CLOSE UP ***How does the definition of crime change with time and circumstance?*** In Missouri, it is against the law to carry an uncaged bear down the highway. In Savannah, Georgia, citizens are prohibited from placing laundry out in the street to dry. And in Wilbur, Washington, it is illegal to ride an ugly horse. These laws may have made sense when they were passed, but as times have changed, there is no longer a need for them. Industrialization, the shift from a mostly rural to a mostly urban society, and advancing technology are major changes that can make legal codes obsolete. Sometimes, the laws take a while to catch up. In Texas, for example, a law forbids people to carry pliers or wire cutters around with them. Legislators originally passed this law in the 1880s to prevent the cutting of barbed wire fences, either by cattle thieves or by farmers who felt that ranchers' fences made it difficult to access their own lands. These concerns are less pressing today, and the law is probably not enforced. That it is still on the books, along with many others like it, reminds us how the definition of crime can change. ■

Crime and Criminals

Crime affects everyone in the United States. Some people are victims. Some people are criminals. Some people are both. However, the majority of Americans are affected by crime as bystanders. Newspapers, radio, television, and movies bombard us daily with information about and images of crime. As a result of our experiences and exposure through the mass media, many consider crime a serious social problem.

A **crime** is any act that is labeled as such by those in authority and is prohibited by law. For example, a person who robs a bank—an act that is labeled criminal and is prohibited by law—has committed a crime. On the other hand, a champion swimmer who stands by and watches a friend drown instead of attempting a rescue has not necessarily committed a crime. The swimmer may have violated society's moral code but has not necessarily broken any laws.

Who commits crimes? The graphs on this page show a breakdown of arrests by the offenders' sex, race, and age. Note that men are much more likely than women to be arrested. In terms of race, more than two-thirds of all people arrested are white. However, African Americans, who make up approximately 13 percent of the population, account for nearly 30 percent of the arrests. Even so, many factors lead an individual to commit a crime, and there is no causal link between race and crime. The percentages for age are particularly dramatic. About 44 percent of all arrests involve people under 25. Moreover, people younger than 35 account for just over two-thirds of all arrests.

Reading Check **Find the Main Idea** What criteria are used to determine if an act is criminal?

Types of Crimes

The Federal Bureau of Investigation (FBI) organizes crimes into 29 separate classifications with two levels of severity. In this discussion, crimes are grouped into five broad categories: violent crime, property crime, victimless crime, white-collar crime, and organized crime.

Violent Crime Violent crimes—murder, forcible rape, robbery, and aggravated assault—make up a very small percentage of all crimes committed. Nonetheless, violent crime statistics are quite alarming. According to the FBI, a violent crime occurs every 22 seconds in the United States. Every 37 seconds, an aggravated assault is committed. A robbery occurs every 1 minute and 12 seconds. A forcible rape takes place every 5 minutes and 42 seconds, and a murder occurs every 30 minutes and 54 seconds. Violent crimes increased in the early 1990s. Since then, they have steadily declined.

Most victims of violence are African American. In the case of murder, young African American men are much more likely to be victims. African American men between the ages of 18 and 24 have a victimization rate that is 8 times that of African American women and white men and more than 30 times that of white women of the same age.

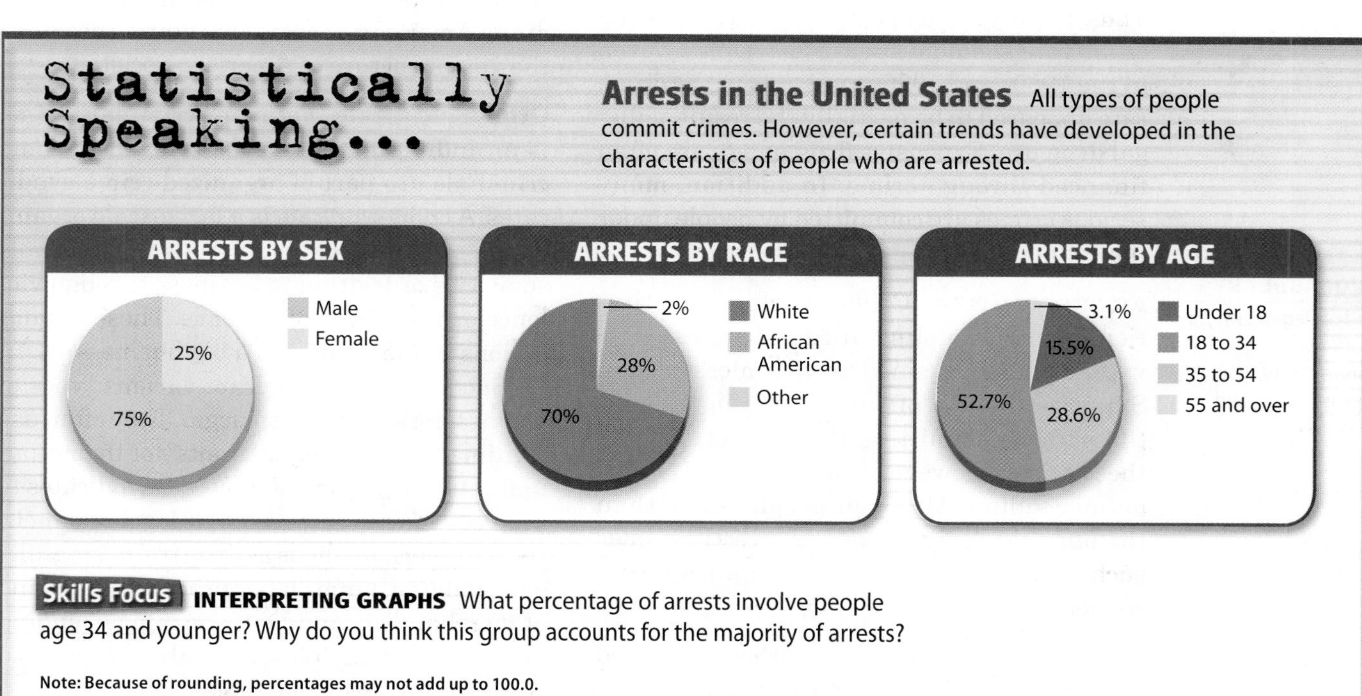

Statistically Speaking...
Arrests in the United States All types of people commit crimes. However, certain trends have developed in the characteristics of people who are arrested.
ARRESTS BY SEX
Male
Female
25%
75%
ARRESTS BY RACE
2%
White
African American
Other
28%
70%
ARRESTS BY AGE
3.1%
Under 18
18 to 34
35 to 54
55 and over
15.5%
52.7%
28.6%
Skills Focus INTERPRETING GRAPHS What percentage of arrests involve people age 34 and younger? Why do you think this group accounts for the majority of arrests?
Note: Because of rounding, percentages may not add up to 100.0.
Source: Department of Justice, Arrest in the United States, 1990–2010, 2012

According to the Centers for Disease Control, homicide was the leading cause of death among African American males between the ages of 16 and 35 in 2013.

The majority of murders are committed with guns. Guns are used in about 69 percent of all murders, with handguns being the weapon used about 47 percent of the time. The rate of handgun use in homicides is higher in the United States than in any other industrialized country in the world.

Property Crime All property crimes involve either stealing or intentionally damaging someone else's property. Crimes against property—burglary, larceny (theft other than auto), motor vehicle theft, and arson—are much more common than crimes of violence. FBI estimates suggest that a property crime is committed every three seconds in the United States. The crime rate for burglary declined throughout the 1990s but leveled off somewhat in the first few years of the 2000s. The crime rate for larceny has continued to decline gradually since the early 1990s.

Sociologists generally tie variations in the crime rate to changes in the population. People under the age of 25 commit a large percentage of crimes. As the size of this group changes, the crime rate varies in the same direction. Thus, as the younger population decreases, the crime rate should decrease as well. However, in the 1980s and 1990s increases in the crime rate appeared to be partially the result of illegal drug use. Expensive drug habits are often financed through crime. In addition, many serious crimes are committed by people under the influence of drugs.

ACADEMIC VOCABULARY

vice legal term for offenses involving immorality, such as prostitution and gambling

Victimless Crime Crimes such as prostitution, illegal gambling, illegal drug use, and vagrancy are classified as victimless crimes. Supposedly, such offenses harm no one but the person committing the act. For some of these crimes, however, this classification may be misleading. Although people other than the offenders may not suffer directly, crimes such as drug abuse can have significant consequences for society.

White-Collar Crime Edwin Sutherland coined the term **white-collar crime** to describe offenses committed by people of high social status in the course of their professional lives. Politicians, employees of corporations, and corporations themselves sometimes commit crimes of this type. Misrepresentation, fraud, tax evasion, embezzlement, price-fixing, toxic pollution, insider trading, and political corruption are examples of white-collar crime. Traditionally, the public and the press have played down white-collar crime even though it is a serious social problem. Yet in recent years crimes such as insider trading on Wall Street, political corruption, corporate crimes, and computer-related crimes have received much attention.

Charging a corporation—rather than the officials or employees who actually committed the offense—with a white-collar crime may seem odd. However, corporations can be charged with offenses because these businesses are considered "legal persons" under the laws of incorporation. Once incorporated, a business becomes subject to the same laws as any person in the United States.

Estimates suggest that white-collar crimes cost the United States from $300 billion to $660 billion each year. The Department of Justice recovered $6.4 billion in 2015 through non-prosecution and deferred prosecution agreements. Some people feel that the nonfinancial costs of white-collar crimes are far greater. When political and corporate leaders break the law, they abuse the trust and confidence of the American people. This abuse threatens the very structure of American society.

Organized Crime For many criminals, crime is an individual enterprise. However, some criminals are part of organized crime syndicates. A **crime syndicate** is a large-scale organization of professional criminals that controls some vice or legitimate business through violence or the threat of violence. These organizations pursue crime as a big business.

Such syndicates operate various types of businesses, many of them legal. They often use legitimate businesses as "fronts" for their criminal activities. Fronts enable the syndicates to reinvest their money through legal channels. By using such methods as drug trafficking, illegal gambling, unfair labor practices, hijacking of merchandise, and loan-sharking—lending money at very high interest rates—organized crime syndicates make huge profits.

Reading Check **Analyze** Pick one type of crime and analyze its cost to society.

FBI CLASSIFICATIONS OF CRIME

The Federal Bureau of Investigation (FBI) classifies crime into 29 categories. The eight Part I offenses, also called index crimes, are more serious than the Part II offenses. This dividing line varies somewhat from state to state.

PART I OFFENSES (More Serious)	**1. Murder and Nonnegligent Manslaughter** willful killing of one human being by another
	2. Forcible Rape sexual violation of a person by force and against the person's will
	3. Robbery use of the threat of force to take anything of value from a person
	4. Aggravated Assault unlawful attack on another person for the purpose of causing great bodily injury
	5. Burglary (breaking and entering) attempted or actual unlawful entry of a structure to commit a felony or theft
	6. Larceny (theft, except auto) unlawful taking of property without using force or fraud, such as pocket picking
	7. Motor Vehicle Theft unlawful stealing or driving away and abandoning of a motor vehicle
	8. Arson attempted or willful burning
PART II OFFENSES (Less Serious)	**9. Other Assaults** attacks of a less-serious nature than aggravated assault
	10. Forgery and Counterfeiting attempting to or making or possessing anything false that seems true to deceive
	11. Fraud use of false pretenses to obtain money or property
	12. Embezzlement misappropriation or misuse of money or property entrusted to an individual's care or custody
	13. Stolen Property attempting to or buying, receiving, or possessing stolen property
	14. Vandalism willful or vicious destruction, injury, disfigurement, or defacement of property
	15. Weapons all violations of regulations related to manufacturing, carrying, possessing, or using firearms
	16. Prostitution and Commercialized Vice sex offenses of a commercialized nature
	17. Sex Offenses attempts at or consensual sex with someone underage or offenses against common decency
	18. Drug Abuse Violations unlawful possession, sale, or use of narcotics
	19. Gambling promoting, permitting, or engaging in illegal gambling
	20. Offenses Against Family and Children nonsupport, neglect, desertion, or abuse of family and children
	21. Driving Under the Influence driving or operating any motor vehicle while under the influence of alcohol or drugs
	22. Liquor Laws violations of state or local liquor laws
	23. Drunkenness intoxication
	24. Disorderly Conduct breach of the peace
	25. Vagrancy includes vagabondage, begging, and loitering
	26. Suspicion arrests for no specific offense, followed by release without placing charges
	27. Curfew and Loitering Laws (juveniles) violations of local curfew and loitering laws, where such laws exist
	28. Runaways (juveniles) limited to juveniles taken into custody under local statutes as runaways
	29. All Other Offenses all violations of state and local laws except traffic laws and those listed here

Source: Federal Bureau of Investigation

Crime Statistics

There are two major sources of crime statistics in the United States. Administered by the FBI since 1929 and published annually, the *Uniform Crime Reports* (*UCR*) is one of the major sources of information concerning crime in the United States. The FBI uses data provided by local police departments to compile nationwide statistics. However, these statistics have certain limitations. Sociologist Donald Black identified the following characteristics that limit the filing of formal crime reports.

- Not all of the complaints that citizens make to the police find their way into the official statistics. The responding officer decides whether to file a formal report. Officers are more likely to file reports in the case of serious offenses.
- Individuals are less likely to report a crime if family or friends are involved.
- The police are more likely to file formal reports when the victims are members of the higher social classes and when the victims show the officer respect.

In addition, victims are less likely to report certain crimes, such as sexual assault. The National Crime Victimization Survey (NCVS), conducted by the Bureau of Justice Statistics since 1973, gathers data from crime victims about reported and unreported crimes. Twice a year, researchers interview a representative sample of approximately 50,000 households. The NCVS makes up for the underreporting of certain crimes and provides a more personal look at crime victimization in the United States. As a result, it can be a useful supplement to the *UCR*.

Reading Check **Summarize** What circumstances may limit the filing of formal crime reports?

The Criminal-Justice System

Once a crime has been committed and reported, it falls under the jurisdiction of the **criminal-justice system.** The most important components of the criminal-justice system are police, courts, and corrections. Most states have a special section of the criminal-justice system, called the juvenile-justice system, that deals with young offenders.

Police The police hold the most immediate control over who is arrested for a criminal act. It might seem reasonable to assume that the police arrest everyone who is accused of committing a crime. In reality the police have considerable power to decide who is actually arrested. This power is called **police discretion.** The size of the U.S. population, the number of criminal offenses, and the number of full-time police officers make it necessary for the police to use their own judgment in decisions involving arrest.

Research has indicated that police officers consider several factors when deciding whether to make an arrest. First, they consider the seriousness of the offense. Less serious offenses are more likely to be ignored. Second, the wishes of the victim are taken into consideration. If the offense is serious or if the suspect is male, victims generally press for an arrest. Third, the police consider the suspect's attitude. An uncooperative suspect is more likely to be arrested than one who is polite or apologetic. Fourth, the police are more likely to make an arrest if bystanders are present. In doing so, the police reinforce that they are in control.

TECHNOLOGY FOCUS

Futuristic Crime Fighting

Police departments and security agencies in the United States are already using technology to detect and prevent crime. For example, millions of video cameras monitor our activities in public spaces. Researchers are already working on improving the capabilities of video surveillance. One recently developed software uses a complex equation to analyze streaming video and detect suspicious activities. The software's ability to flag activity that may be criminal addresses the difficulty of monitoring several screens of video footage at the same time.

As technology advances, however, the potential applications seem to stray into the realm of science fiction. What if authorities could see beyond what is visible to a video camera and read someone's mind? Government and university researchers are working on technology that would allow them to remotely detect brain activity. And scientists have already made progress toward decoding what they might find there. In a 2007 study, neuroscientists were able to look at brain scans and determine whether an individual given two numbers intended to add or subtract them. It was the first time scientists were able to determine intentions. As the technology continues to progress, some believe that police may one day be able to apply it to detect thoughts of criminal behavior.

Thinking Critically

Make Generalizations What are some of the ethical implications of these technologies and their application as crime-prevention tools?

Finally, police are more likely to arrest—and use force against—African Americans than white Americans. Many people charge that the higher arrest rate among African Americans results from **racial profiling** by the police. This is the practice of assuming that nonwhite Americans are more likely to commit a crime than white Americans. The issue of racial profiling has become an important political topic, particularly in the aftermath of the events such as the shooting of Michael Brown in Ferguson, Missouri.

Courts Once arrested, the accused becomes the responsibility of the courts. The courts' role is a twofold process. First, a court holds a trial to determine whether the accused person is guilty. Second, if there is a guilty finding, the court assigns some form of punishment. In reality, however, more than 90 percent of all criminal cases are settled through plea bargaining before going to trial.

Plea bargaining is the process of legal negotiation that allows an accused person to plead guilty to a lesser charge in return for a lighter sentence. This process allows courts to reduce their huge volume of cases while avoiding the risk of expensive and time-consuming jury trials that may not produce a guilty verdict.

Corrections People found guilty of crimes are punished. Sanctions used to punish criminals are called **corrections.** These sanctions—which include imprisonment, parole, probation, and community service—serve four basic functions in society.

- *Retribution.* The punishing of a criminal serves as a socially acceptable act of revenge for the victim and society.
- *Deterrence.* Corrections are intended to discourage offenders from committing future crimes and to make the rest of society think twice before breaking laws.
- *Rehabilitation.* During the 1800s, prisons emerged as places in which to reform criminals so that they could return to society as law-abiding citizens.
- *Social protection.* By limiting the freedom of offenders, society protects itself from additional crimes they might commit. In the case of the death penalty, the threat of an offender committing future criminal acts is eliminated.

Statistically Speaking...

The American Prison System Despite having less than 5 percent of the world's population, the United States has almost 25 percent of the world's prisoners. Compared to other industrialized nations, the United States has a high rate of violent crime. Also, people convicted of nonviolent crimes in the United States are more likely to be sentenced to prison than those convicted in other countries. In addition, American prison sentences tend to be longer, which drives up the incarceration rate. This rate varies by state due to several factors, such as the crime rate, the effectiveness of law enforcement, and variations in state laws.

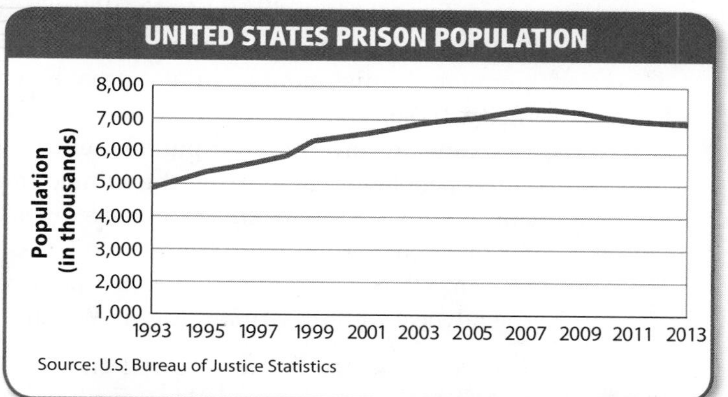

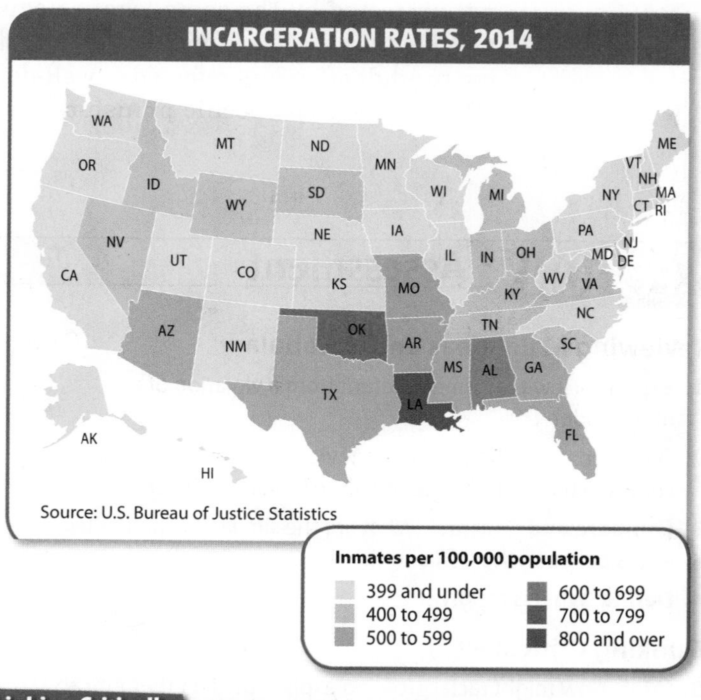

Thinking Critically **INTERPRETING GRAPHS** About how much did the prison population increase between 1993 and 2013?

The effectiveness of corrections is a topic of heated debate. One indication that corrections are not always effective is the rate of recidivism among convicted criminals. **Recidivism** is the term for repeated criminal behavior. According to a U.S. Department of Justice study, 68 percent of released prisoners will be charged with new crimes and 50 percent will return to prison within three years of their release.

Courts can assign punishments ranging from fines to probation to imprisonment. The majority of convicted criminals are punished through fines and probation. However, in the case of serious crimes—particularly murder, rape, and robbery—prison sentences are common. Punishments can also vary by ethnicity. In some cases, African Americans and Hispanics receive harsher punishments than white people for committing the same crimes. For example, African Americans are arrested for drug possession more than three times as often as whites, according to a 2009 report from the advocacy group Human Rights Watch.

Juvenile-Justice System Until the 1960s, juveniles—people under 18—who were charged with crimes had few rights and were not protected by the same legal safeguards provided for adult offenders. Laws pertaining to adult offenders referred to well-defined offenses, carried specific punishments, and applied to all offenders more or less equally. However, the laws for juvenile offenders were much less specific. For example, they contained vague provisions about "incorrigible, ungovernable" children who associated with "immoral or vicious persons." A juvenile offender could remain in custody longer than an adult convicted of the same offense.

The reasoning behind having separate regulations was that juvenile offenders, because of their age, could not be expected to be as responsible as adults. Thus, it was thought that juveniles needed special, more considerate treatment. Sometimes, however, the result was that they were denied equal protection under the law. Consequently, they were not usually granted any special care or attention.

To guard against such abuses, the courts now must guarantee juvenile defendants the same legal rights and privileges as adult defendants. At the same time, juveniles are still regarded as a special kind of offender. Juvenile courts try, in principle at least, to provide many more services for offenders than do adult criminal courts. Yet some areas of the country, particularly large cities, are establishing tougher laws governing juveniles. For example, in some places juveniles—even very young suspects—can be tried as adults for certain serious offenses, such as murder.

Reading Check **Summarize** What role does each component of the criminal-justice system serve?

SECTION 3 Assessment

Reviewing Main Ideas and Vocabulary

1. **Explain** How is a crime different from a violation of a moral code?
2. **Describe** Describe the trends in violent crimes and property crimes in the United States over the last several years.
3. **Compare and Contrast** What are the similarities and differences between the *UCR* and the NCVS?
4. **Define** What is recidivism?

Thinking Critically

5. **Infer** How might racial profiling explain the fact that African Americans make up 13 percent of the population but about 30 percent of arrests?
6. **Elaborate** What do recent trends in the crime rate suggest about the composition of the American population?
7. **Summarize** Using your notes and a graphic organizer like the one below, identify and describe the characteristics of the five types of crimes discussed in this section.

Type of Crime	Characteristics

FOCUS ON WRITING

8. **Expository** Write two paragraphs explaining why the effectiveness of corrections is a subject of debate. Consider the functions of corrections as well as recidivism rates.

SOCIOLOGY IN TODAY'S WORLD

Identity Theft

A man bought two cars and two motorcycles. His purchases of these items and others ended up costing $265,000. Unfortunately, when he did it, he was using someone else's name and credit. His victim has spent more than 2,000 hours trying to reclaim his identity and repair his finances. This victim is still hounded by creditors seeking to collect more than $140,000 in debts. Identity theft, a growing concern for many Americans, can change the victim's entire life in a matter of minutes.

THE STATS ON IDENTITY THEFT

12.7 million American adults fell victim to identity theft in 2014.

$16 billion was stolen in identity theft crimes in the United States in 2014.

2.5 million complaints of identity theft and fraud were made in 2014.

65% of students in 2014 said they were not very concerned about fraud.

Source: Insurance Information Institute, *Identity Theft and Cybercrime, 2015*

Identity theft occurs when someone uses another person's identifying information—such as his or her name, Social Security number, or credit card number—without permission to commit fraud or other crimes. Sometimes identity thieves use this information to obtain a credit card and make purchases or set up telephone accounts. In other instances, they may rent an apartment, get medical services, or even use a victim's personal information instead of their own during an arrest.

The experience of the victims can vary dramatically. In some cases, victims may be able to resolve the issue quickly with little cost. In others, victims may have to spend countless hours and hundreds of dollars to get the problem resolved, as in the case of the victim described above.

The Federal Trade Commission estimates that more than 12 million Americans have their identities stolen each year. Other reports place estimates as high as 15 million victims annually. Identity theft is the fastest-growing crime in the United States.

Identity thieves have several methods of obtaining someone's personal information. Some methods are old-fashioned, such as stealing wallets, combing through trash for papers containing personal information, or looking over someone's shoulder when he or she enters a personal identification number at the ATM. The Internet has increased instances of identity theft by providing new ways of acquiring personal information. For example, some identity thieves use a method called phishing, or using e-mail spam or pop-up messages to get someone to reveal personal information.

The Internet has also made personal information more accessible in general. One important piece of personal information thieves often seek is Social Security numbers, because they can be used to find other personal and financial information. It is difficult to protect these numbers because they are used for so many purposes. Today Web sites exist that—for a small fee—will provide a person's Social Security number to anyone, including identity thieves.

How can you protect yourself from identity theft? Shred documents containing personal information. Protect your wallet, and keep your Social Security card in a secure location. Watch out for online scams. Also, monitoring your bank statements and checking your credit report regularly will help you detect identity theft early, which may limit the damage.

Police discovered these stolen identification cards and credit cards during a raid.

Thinking Critically

1. **Identify** In which category of crime does identity theft belong?
2. **Discuss** How might the different theoretical perspectives on deviance explain identity theft?

Experiment
Applying What You've Learned

How to Be an Ethnomethodologist

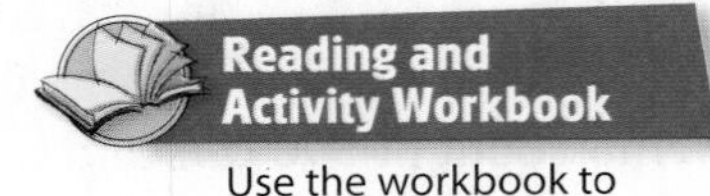

Use the workbook to complete this experiment.

What role do norms play in your everyday life?

1. Introduction

Norms are an important part of culture. They help us decide what behaviors are proper and improper in various settings. In many cases, you may have internalized society's norms and be following them without even realizing it.

Given that, how can sociologists determine exactly what these norms are? In the late 1960s, sociologist Harold Garfinkel came up with an interesting technique to find out. He coined the term *ethnomethodology*, which means "the study of how people do things." More specifically, ethnomethodology is a technique for studying norms by breaking them. The premise is that social interaction is based on norms that most people accept and follow. You cannot just walk up to people and ask what norms they follow, because they will not be able to explain what the norms are and may not even be aware of them. Instead, ethnomethodologists deliberately violate social norms to reveal people's expectations about how social interaction is supposed to occur.

In this experiment, you will choose a norm to break in order to experience the effect of violating an established social norm. You will also observe and record other people's responses to your deviation from expected social behavior. Finally, you will share your experience and discuss your observations with the class.

2. Choosing a Norm

Identify a social norm or expectation that you can break in order to study the reactions of others. The main requirement is that breaking the norm must result in unique but harmless behavior that is atypical for you. Do not choose behavior that is dangerous, or you will get in trouble with the school administration, the police, your family, or other authority figures. Also, avoid behavior that a teacher would consider disruptive in the classroom. Remember, the behavior must be something that you would not typically do. Some examples are listed below:

- Give away flowers at a shopping center.
- Wear formal attire to an informal event or to school.
- Ask a teacher to give you more homework.
- Stand facing the rear of an elevator.
- Stand up in class each time you are called on by a teacher.
- Begin singing on a street corner.

Once you have chosen your norm, violate it. While you are breaking your norm, observe the people around you and their reactions. If possible, repeat your norm violation in a few different settings among different groups of witnesses. This will allow you to experience and compare a wider variety of reactions. In each case, jot down some notes as soon as possible after violating your norm so that you do not forget important details that will help you write your report.

3. Record Your Observations

Using your notes, write a report describing how people reacted to your norm-violating behavior. Elaborate with as many details as you can recall. The questions below might help you to focus and shape your report:

- What norm did you choose to violate?
- What was the setting for your norm violation?
- What kinds of people witnessed you break your chosen norm?
- How did people respond to your behavior?
- Why do you think people reacted as they did?
- What consequences do you think would result from continuing the behavior or repeating it on a daily basis?
- How did you feel while breaking the norm?

4. Role-play Your Experience

Once you have completed your experiment and written your report, you and your classmates will use role-play as a tool to share one another's experiences. Follow the steps below:

- Follow your teacher's directions for organizing into small groups.
- Share and discuss your report with the other members of your group. Include details and describe your experience as completely as possible.
- Working as a group, decide whose experience is best-suited to a role-play exercise.
- Work up a brief skit to act out your group's chosen norm violation for the class. Every person in the group must participate. Some members will act out the norm violation itself, while others will have roles as observers who show their reactions to the norm violation.
- Elect a spokesperson to
  - briefly summarize the written report
  - explain why your group chose this norm violation
  - describe what would happen if this behavior spread

5. Discussion

What did you learn from this experiment? Hold a group discussion that focuses on the following questions:

- Which norm violations shared by your classmates do you think were the most interesting?
- How did you feel while performing your norm violation? What emotions were you experiencing?
- What was the reaction of those observing your norm violation?
- Was your behavior observed by anyone in a position of authority (such as a teacher or an administrator)? If so, what was his or her reaction?
- Do you think ethnomethodologists are right in the belief that this kind of experiment is the most effective way to uncover social norms?
- Did you experience any type of sanction for your behavior? Describe how the sanction was enforced. Was it a positive or negative sanction? Was it a formal or informal sanction?
- If you experienced a sanction, do you think it was the most effective means of controlling your behavior? Might a different type of sanction have been more effective?
- While you were violating your norm, did you think of yourself as deviant? Why or why not?
- Why do you think the people observing you responded as they did?
- What do you think the consequences would be for you personally if you continued the behavior? How would continuing this behavior affect society?
- What social norms have changed in the last 20 years? Do you think this change has been for the best? Are there any norms that haven't changed that you think should? Are there any norms that have changed that you wish had not?

CHAPTER 7 Review

Comprehension and Critical Thinking

SECTION 1 *(pp. 158–160)*

1. a. **Identify** What are the two methods through which society enforces norms?
   b. **Summarize** Explain the two ways that negative sanctions work to enforce social norms.
   c. **Evaluate** Which kind of sanction do you think is more effective, positive or negative? Explain your answer.

SECTION 2 *(pp. 162–167)*

2. a. **Define** What is deviance?
   b. **Contrast** How does labeling theory differ from other theories of deviance?
   c. **Elaborate** How might the label of deviance serve as a self-fulfilling prophecy?

SECTION 3 *(pp. 168–174)*

3. a. **Recall** What are the five general categories of crime? List the types of crimes in each category.
   b. **Explain** What purposes does the corrections system serve? How does the juvenile-justice system meet these same purposes?
   c. **Support a Position** Do you think the term *victimless crime* is valid? Explain your answer.

INTERNET ACTIVITY

4. Do you think theoretical perspectives can be combined to explain deviance? Use the Internet to locate and read the full text of the article featured in the Case Study, "The Saints and the Roughnecks" by William Chambliss. Then write a short essay discussing how Chambliss used the control perspective to explain why the Roughnecks were labeled as deviant but the Saints were not.

Reviewing Vocabulary

Identify the term from the chapter that best fits each of the following descriptions.

5. the situation that arises when the norms of society are unclear or are no longer applicable
6. the practice of assuming that nonwhite Americans are more likely to commit a crime than white Americans
7. rewards or punishments used to enforce conformity to norms
8. occasional nonconformity based on which the nonconforming individual is not considered deviant
9. the frequency and closeness of associations a person has with deviant and nondeviant individuals
10. the process by which a norm becomes a part of an individual's personality, thus conditioning that individual to conform to society's expectations
11. repeated criminal behavior
12. behavior that violates significant social norms
13. sharp criticism or expression of disapproval
14. offenses committed by individuals of high social status in the course of their professional lives
15. the enforcing of norms through either internal or external means

Sociology in Your Life

16. Have you ever heard the saying "Let the punishment fit the crime"? Choose a social norm that you would like to see enforced. It could be anything, from a pet peeve that annoys you to an important social issue. Design a system of social control to enforce your chosen norm. Determine what kinds of sanctions would be appropriate to enforce the norm and whether they should be formal or informal, positive or negative, or a combination. Also decide what authorities would be responsible for enforcing the norm. Write a short report identifying the norm you selected and describing your system of social control.

Skills Activity: Interpreting Graphs

The pie graph below lists the percentage of each of the eight Part I offenses in the FBI's classification of crime that were committed in 2005. They are commonly referred to as index crimes. Use the graph to answer the questions that follow.

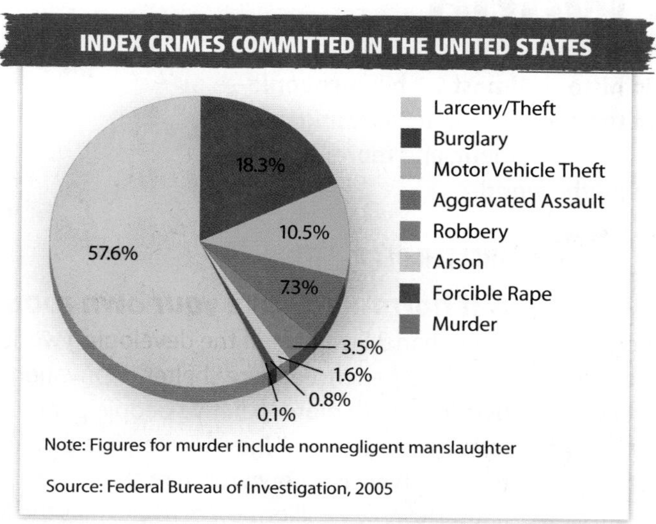

17. **Categorize** Which of the crimes in the graph are violent crimes, and which are property crimes?
18. **Compare** What percentage of the total is made up of property crimes? What percentage of the total is made up of violent crimes?
19. **Make Judgments** Why do you think property crime occurs more frequently than violent crime?

Writing for Sociology

Use your knowledge of deviance to answer the question below. Do not simply list facts. Present a clear argument based on your critical analysis of the question, using appropriate sociological terminology.

20. Do minor acts of deviance serve as a safety valve for society? Why or why not? Choose a position and use details to support your argument. Consider the topics listed below.
    - The importance of social control to society
    - Durkheim's belief that deviance is necessary
    - Control theory

Connecting Online

Go online for review and enrichment activities related to this chapter.

KEY TOPICS VIDEOS
View compelling clips on issues in the field.

KEEP IT CURRENT
Link to the Current Events site for regularly updated stories on sociology as well as other social studies topics.

QUICK LAB
Reinforce a key concept with a short lab activity.

Adolescent Issues Around the World

Today's generation of young people is the largest in history. Almost 1.2 billion people—16 percent of the world's population—are between the ages of 15 and 24. Young people around the world face issues involving family, shelter, employment, and more. These issues strongly impact life in different societies around the world.

TEENAGE MOTHERHOOD

Is it normal to be a teenage mother?

About 1 out of 10 babies born in the world today is born to a teenage mother. In the United States, teenage motherhood is not very common, but it is in many other areas of the world. In these places, motherhood among teens is not unusual because many people get married and start having families much earlier than in the United States. As you can see from the graph below, by far the greatest number of teenage mothers is found in Southern Asia. In fact, India is home to about one third of all teenage mothers. Africa also has a large number of teenage mothers. Just how common teenage motherhood is in any given place depends on social and economic factors, as well as customs, traditions, and values.

TOP TEN COUNTRIES WITH TEENAGE MOTHERS

Country	Women aged 20–24 who gave birth by 18
Niger	51%
Chad	48%
Mali	46%
Guinea	44%
Mozambique	42%
Bangladesh	40%
Sierra Leone	38%
Liberia	38%
Central African Republic	38%
Madagascar	36%

Sources: UNFPA Open Data; United Nations Population Division, 2010

SHELTER DEPRIVATION

Is it normal to have your own room?

More than 34 percent of the developing world's young people experience severe shelter deprivation—living in dwellings with more than five people per room or with mud flooring. In the United States, it is common for teens to either have their own room or share a room with siblings. However, millions of teens, such as the Moroccan boy in the photo below, do not have their own room. This young man only has a mattress in the corner of his family's kitchen. Sub-Saharan Africa has the world's highest rate of severe shelter deprivation for young people. In contrast, only 8 percent of young people in East Asia and the Pacific suffer from severe shelter deprivation.

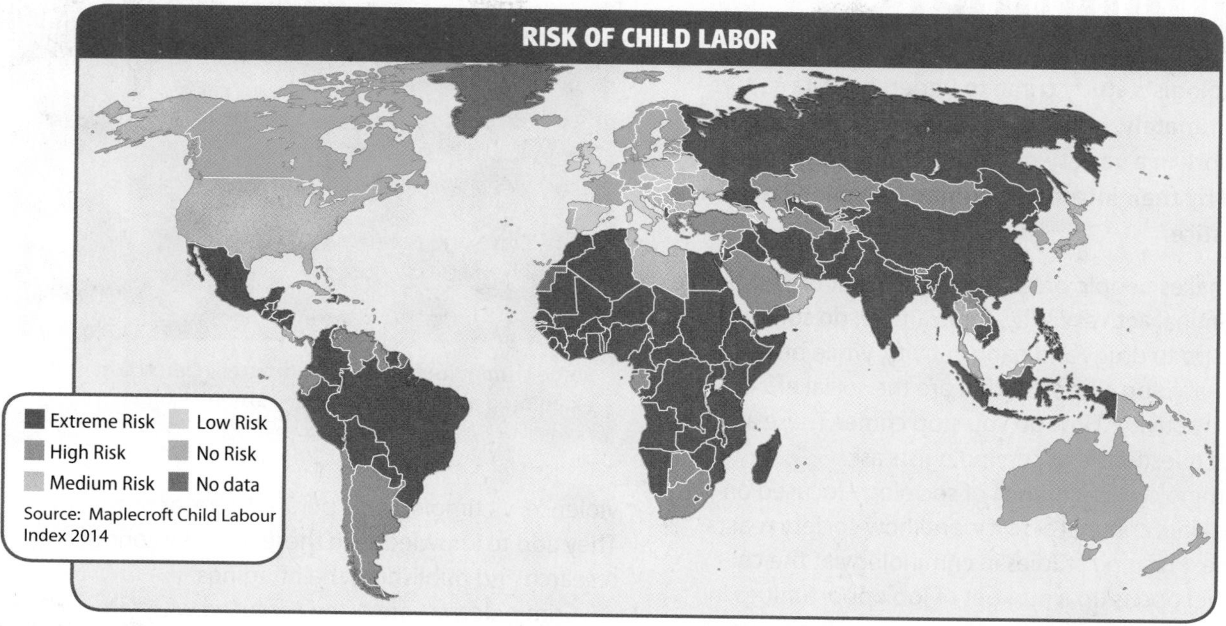

EMPLOYMENT

Is it normal for teenagers to work? What is a normal job for a teen?

Young people make up 25 percent of the global working-age population but account for 43.7 percent of the world's unemployed. One out of every three young people in the world today is either seeking but unable to find work, has given up the job search entirely, or is working but still living on less than $2 a day. East and Central Africa have the highest percentage of young people in the workforce (see map above). In Burundi, 82 percent of teens—the most in the world—are employed. Unlike teens in the United States who usually only work part-time in mostly service-related jobs, most working teens around the world work full-time in agriculture. Some teens work on their family farms, but other jobs are labor intensive and dangerous. For example, in El Salvador children and teens working in sugarcane fields are frequently injured by the sharp machetes they use to cut the cane. Other jobs for teens include work in trade, services, and domestic labor.

THINKING LIKE A SOCIOLOGIST

What other issues do adolescents around the world face today?
In addition to these issues, young people around the world face many other challenges. Member states of the United Nations have agreed to combat issues related to young people by the year 2030. They have set forth seventeen goals, including the following six:

1. End poverty in all its forms everywhere
2. End hunger, achieve food security and improved nutrition and promote sustainable agriculture
3. Ensure healthy lives and promote well-being for all at all ages
4. Ensure inclusive and quality education for all and promote lifelong learning
5. Achieve gender equality and empower all women and girls
6. Ensure access to water and sanitation for all

Research one of these six goals as it relates to young people. You can start by going to the United Nations-supported Web site, "Sustainable Development Goals." After you have completed your research, write a report on the issue you selected. In your report, address the steps you think must be taken to meet the goal by 2030.

CAREERS IN SOCIOLOGY

Criminologist

Criminologists study crime to understand its causes and, ultimately, how best to prevent it. Although they work in a variety of fields, criminologists are united by their interest in human behavior, law, and justice.

Some criminologists study computer-related crimes by examining and extracting computer files.

What makes people break the rules? What draws people into criminal activity? Why, for example, do some teenagers turn to drugs and gang activity, while others are law-abiding citizens? What are the social effects of criminal activity? How do you stop crime? These are the kinds of questions that criminologists ask.

Criminology is a branch of sociology focused on law-making, criminal activity, and how society reacts to crime. Pursuing studies in criminology at the college level opens up a number of job opportunities in the criminal justice system. Many criminologists work for police and law enforcement agencies, such as the Federal Bureau of Investigation. Others work as parole and probation officers or as counselors in substance-abuse, rehabilitation, and victim-services programs. Criminologists also work in the corrections system, assessing problems and setting policies.

Many criminologists with doctoral degrees become college professors. They pass on their expertise and knowledge to others through teaching. Criminology professors often specialize in specific areas of study, such as juvenile justice, cybercrime, corrections, violence, victimology, corporate crime, or terrorism. They add to knowledge in these areas by conducting research and publishing their findings.

Criminologists are often confused with forensic scientists, another group of scientists concerned with criminal investigation and law enforcement. One main difference between criminologists and forensic scientists is the scope of their study. Criminologists measure and study the characteristics of criminals and crime to explain broad patterns of behavior in society as a whole. In contrast, forensic scientists engage in crime scene investigations, collecting evidence related to a single crime. In recent years, media attention to crime and public perceptions about rising crime rates have led to growth in both fields.

Applying ASA Style

Many criminologists publish articles in professional journals, magazines, and other publications. In keeping with guidelines from the **American Sociological Association (ASA)**, these articles follow a similar style for citing source materials. The papers you write for your sociology class should follow these guidelines, too.

The ASA prefers in-text citations for referencing the source material used for direct quotes and paraphrased information. These citations appear in the body of the text and include the author's last name and the year of publication: (Goode 1994). For direct quotes, page numbers are also included in the citation: (Newman 2008: 46). Used properly, in-text citations are a sign of solid sociological scholarship. They help authors avoid plagiarism and allow readers to locate source materials for additional information.

Through Think Central you can access the ASA Quick Style Guide for more information on using in-text citations. Review the ASA guidelines that you find at the Web site. Then make a list of different types of in-text citations, and provide an example for each type.

Citation Type	Example
one author	(Hammond, 2003)
two authors	
three authors	
direct quote	

UNIT 3 Social Inequality

CHAPTER 8
Social Stratification

CHAPTER 9
Racial and Ethnic Relations

CHAPTER 10
Gender, Age, and Health

CASE STUDY

RURAL POVERTY

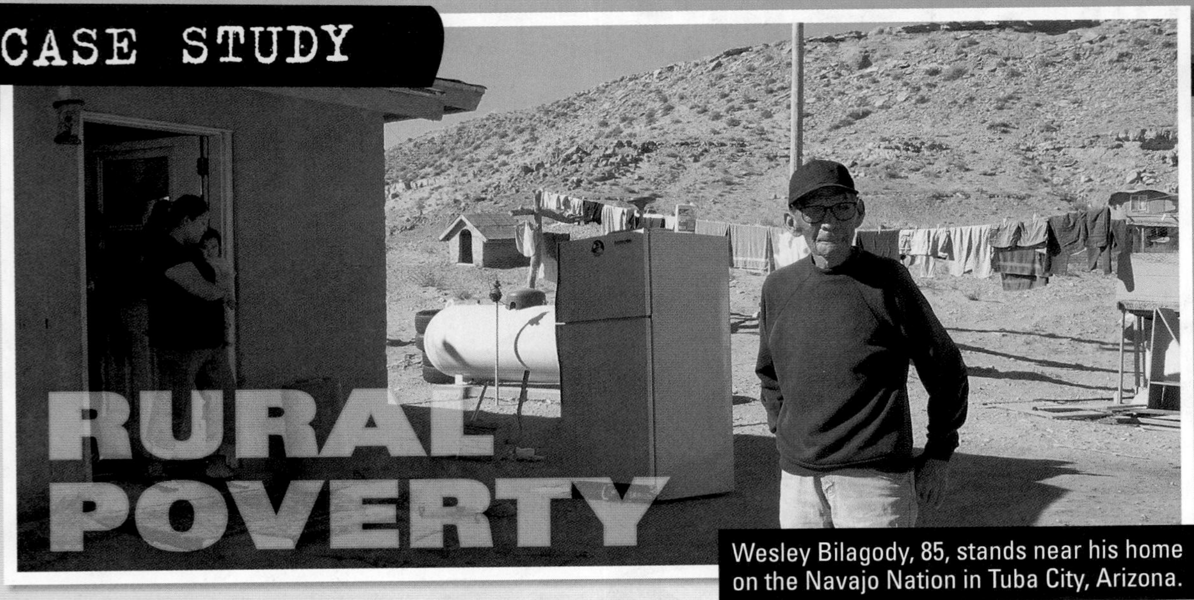

Wesley Bilagody, 85, stands near his home on the Navajo Nation in Tuba City, Arizona.

For many Americans, poverty statistics bring to mind images of urban areas. They conjure up mental pictures of single mothers and their children living in dark and dingy tenements. Or people might visualize crime-infested city streets controlled by drug dealers and street gangs. For others, images of the homeless sleeping on park benches and begging on street corners come to mind. However, urban poverty is just one part of a larger picture.

Characteristics of Rural Poverty About 20 percent of poor Americans—more than 7 million people—live in rural areas. In fact, the poverty rate in rural areas has exceeded the level found in big cities. According to government statistics, 18.4 percent of rural Americans are poor. In contrast, the poverty rate for urban areas stands at 15.1 percent. However, the characteristics of poverty are much the same in rural areas as elsewhere. Poverty rates are much higher among rural minorities than among rural whites. African American, Hispanic, and Native American families are more than twice as likely as white families to be poor. Rural young people are also more likely to be poor than are members of other age groups. In fact, one out of every four rural Americans under the age of 17 is poor. Families headed by single women are more likely to be poor than are married-couple families.

Special Challenges The poor people living in rural areas face many challenges. They seldom have easy access to government services. Social-welfare offices, public health clinics, job-training programs, and federally funded day-care centers are rare in rural areas. Poor people in rural areas are at particular risk in terms of health care. Many rural hospitals have closed, and registered nurses are in short supply at those that remain open. In addition, the ratio of physicians to residents in small communities is less than the national average. Rural counties had on average 1.2 active doctors for every 1,000 residents in 2007, compared with 3 active doctors for the same number of residents in urban areas. Urban counties also had more than 3 times as many specialists, 1.1 for every 1,000 residents compared with only 0.3 for every 1,000 residents in rural counties. Some rural communities in the United States do not have any primary-care physicians at all.

Changes in the economy have worsened the already difficult employment situation of poor people in rural areas. Many of the industries that traditionally supported the rural economy, such as farming, mining, timber, and manufacturing, suffered declines during the 1980s and 1990s. Some businesses relocated factories to other countries to take advantage of cheap labor. This relocation has led to a general economic decline. Many rural jobs have also been lost to automation.

CHAPTER 8

SOCIAL STRATIFICATION

Roxie Hurt, of Hemphill, West Virginia, and her husband Rex work hard to raise their three children on only $724 per month.

A Hidden Problem Urban poverty is visible. Americans are often confronted by news reports about its effects. Although the reality of rural poverty is largely hidden, it is no less a problem than urban poverty. Both types of poverty are examples of how people around the world are affected by the unequal distribution of a society's resources and rewards. As you will read in this chapter, a person's social status plays a role in determining how those resources are distributed.

What do you think?

1. How are the characteristics of rural poverty similar to and different from the characteristics of urban poverty?
2. The "invisibility" of rural poverty intensifies the problem. What steps would you take to bring this issue to the public's attention?

Chapter at a Glance

SECTION 1: Systems of Stratification

- Most societies divide their members into ranks based on selected characteristics, which can lead to social inequality.
- Two basic types of stratification systems exist today: caste systems and class systems.
- Systems of stratification range from closed, in which movement between ranks is difficult, to open, in which individuals are able to move between ranks.
- Members of a social class have similar levels of wealth, power, and prestige.
- Functionalists and conflict theorists offer differing explanations of the causes and consequences of stratification, while other sociologists attempt to blend the two theoretical approaches.

SECTION 2: The American Class System

- Sociologists use three techniques to determine social class: the reputational method, the subjective method, and the objective method.
- Most sociologists use a system that identifies six social classes in the United States: the upper class, the upper middle class, the lower middle class, the working class, the working poor, and the underclass.
- Because the United States has an open class system, social mobility—movement between social classes—is possible.
- Sociologists are more interested in the structural causes of social mobility than in the individual causes.

SECTION 3: Poverty

- About 37 million Americans live in poverty, or below what society considers to be the minimum adequate standard of living.
- The government calculates the poverty level annually based on the cost of an adequate diet.
- Characteristics such as age, sex, and race affect poverty.
- Poor and wealthy members of society have different life chances and behavior patterns.
- Government welfare programs attempt to reduce inequality.

SECTION 1

Systems of Stratification

Before You Read

Main Idea
Many societies rank their members based on certain criteria, a process called social stratification.

Reading Focus
1. What are the characteristics of the two types of stratification systems?
2. What are the three dimensions of social stratification?
3. How do the major theories explaining social stratification differ?

Vocabulary
social stratification
social inequality
caste system
exogamy
endogamy
class system
bourgeoisie
proletariat
social class
wealth
power
prestige
socioeconomic status

TAKING NOTES Use a graphic organizer like this one to take notes on systems of stratification.

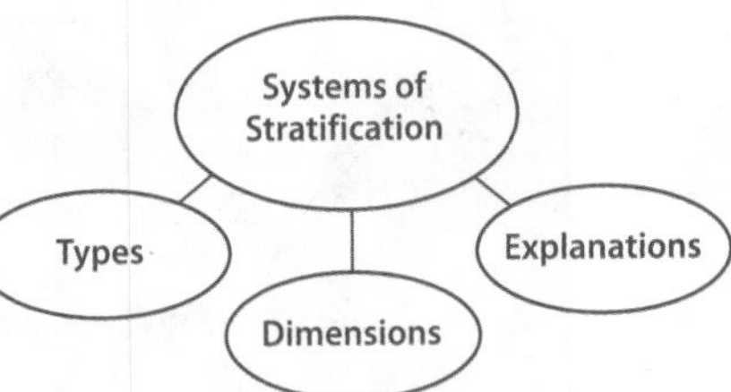

THE POWER OF POPULARITY

SOCIOLOGY CLOSE UP ***Do some groups at your school seem to have more power than others?*** They are the students who decide what's cool. The clothes that they wear become the clothes that everyone wants to wear. The parties that they go to become the events that everyone wishes they hadn't missed. And if you hang out with them, you are probably considered cool, too.

Maybe they're the school's top athletes. Perhaps they're heavily involved in student government. In your school they might even be the president of the drama club or the best speaker on the debate team. For whatever reason, certain characteristics distinguish these students from the rest of the school and make them popular. Along with their popularity, they gain power—the power to set trends and to determine the popularity of others.

These students are at the top of the school's social hierarchy. They form one layer of an informal system of social stratification, or the division of a society into ranks. Other groups with varying degrees of popularity and power form the remaining layers. Perhaps without even realizing it, your school plays out a phenomenon that sociologists study in societies around the world. ■

Types of Stratification Systems

Almost every society throughout history has separated its members on the basis of certain characteristics. Sociologists call this division of society into categories, ranks, or classes **social stratification.** The levels of stratification and the characteristics used have varied. Such ascribed statuses as ancestry, race, age, physical appearance, and gender are among the most common distinguishing characteristics. Achieved statuses—such as education and occupation—can also be used to determine social standing. Factors such as talent and effort may also play a part. Divisions based on individual characteristics and abilities lead to **social inequality**—the unequal sharing of scarce resources and social rewards.

The level of social inequality in a society depends on the degree to which that society's stratification system is open or closed. In a closed system, movement between the strata, or status levels, is impossible. A person is assigned a status at birth and remains at that level. In an open system, movement between strata is possible. The openness of the system determines the ease of movement.

Sociologists recognize two basic types of stratification systems in today's societies: caste systems and class systems. Picture a continuum with closed systems to the left and open systems to the right. Caste systems would fall at the far left of the continuum. In a caste system, a person's status is assigned at birth. In all but the rarest cases, the individual remains in that status. Class systems, on the other hand, would fall somewhere on the right of the continuum. The actual location depends on the society, because class systems range from slightly open to very open.

Caste Systems In a **caste system,** resources and social rewards are distributed on the basis of ascribed statuses. A newborn child's lifelong status, or caste, is determined by the status of his or her parents. Effort and talent may affect someone's position within a caste, but they cannot move the person to a higher status.

Because status is inherited, a caste system has elaborate norms governing interaction among the different castes. For example, marriage between members of different castes would make it difficult to assign a status to children. Which parent's status would be used? To avoid this problem, caste systems traditionally have forbidden the practice of **exogamy,** or marriage outside one's social category. Caste systems generally have practiced **endogamy,** or marriage within one's social category, instead.

Caste systems were once common in South Asia. India provides one of the best examples of this system of stratification. Developed more than 3,000 years ago, the Indian caste system assigned individuals to one of four castes: Brahmans, Kshatriyas (kuh-SHA-tree-uhz), Vaisyas (VISH-yuhz), and Sudras. These castes were subdivided into thousands of subcastes based on specific occupations. Below these four castes was a class of outcasts, Harijans—or Dalits, as they now call themselves. Harijans were considered unclean and were given only the most undesirable tasks to perform. Other castes avoided all contact with them because being touched by a Harijan made a higher-caste person unclean. The only way to remove this "stain" of uncleanness was to go through special cleansing rituals.

The Indian constitution, which was adopted in 1950, outlawed the discrimination against the Harijans. It also declared that all Indians, regardless of background, were equal. In addition, government programs set aside places in schools and government jobs for lower caste members and Harijans. But dismantling the caste system has proved extremely difficult. Some blurring of distinctions among the castes has taken place in the cities. There, modern transportation systems and work arrangements force mixing among the castes. However, in the rural areas—where most Indians live—caste still plays a major role in organizing everyday life.

THE CASTE SYSTEM IN INDIA

Caste	Typical Occupations
Brahmans	Priests, scholars
Kshatriyas	Rulers, nobles, soldiers
Vaisyas	Merchants, bankers, businesspeople
Sudras	Laborers, artisans
Harijans	Outcasts, limited to the most undesirable tasks

Class Systems In a **class system** the distribution of scarce resources and rewards is determined on the basis of achieved statuses. This linking means that individuals have some control over their place in the stratification system. Given talent, effort, and opportunity, individuals can move up the social-class ladder. However, the reverse is also true. Circumstances can reduce an individual's standing in a class system.

Sociologists have defined social class in various ways. For those who base their work on the theories of Karl Marx, society is divided into two basic groups—those who own the means of production and those who own only their labor. According to the followers of Marx, the owners of the means of production in a capitalist society are called the **bourgeoisie.** The workers who sell their labor in exchange for wages are called the **proletariat.** The bourgeoisie reaps all of the profits, even though the proletariat does the work. According to Marx, the only determining feature of class is the ownership of property.

ACADEMIC VOCABULARY

means of production the materials and methods used to produce goods and services

Max Weber expanded Marx's ideas. Weber believed that class consists of three factors—property, prestige, and power. Weber accepted that property plays a significant role in determining people's places in society. However, he suggested that prestige and power also greatly affect social standing. For example, inheritance taxes and the costs of maintaining their estates have reduced the wealth of many English nobles. However, they still may hold a position of power in the community. On the other hand, a wealthy individual who made his or her money through illegal means may be shunned by the established upper class.

Reading Check **Contrast** Describe the continuum of open and closed stratification systems.

The Dimensions of Social Stratification

Today many sociologists adopt Weber's view of social stratification. They define **social class** as a grouping of people with similar levels of wealth, power, and prestige. For sociologists, these three terms mean very specific things.

Wealth An individual's **wealth** is made up of his or her *assets*—the value of everything the person owns—and *income*—money earned through salaries, investment returns, or other capital gains. In the United States, wealth is concentrated overwhelmingly in the hands of a small minority of the population. The richest 1 percent of the population controls nearly half of the country's wealth.

Income is also distributed unequally in the United States, although not as strikingly as total wealth. The top 1 percent of the population earned over 22 percent of the total national income in 2012. Recent studies suggest that this income gap has been growing. In 1982, the top 1 percent of families received 10.8 percent of all income, while the bottom 90 percent received 64.7 percent. In 2012, the top 1 percent received 22.5 percent of pretax income, while the bottom 90 percent's portion had fallen to 49.6 percent.

Power People with substantial wealth usually also possess considerable power. **Power** is the ability to control the behavior of others, with or without their consent. Power can be based on force, the possession of a special skill or type of

Statistically Speaking...

Distribution of Wealth and Income In the United States, wealth is unequally distributed. About four-fifths of the country's wealth is in the hands of the richest fifth of the population. The lowest fifth is in debt and has negative wealth. Income is also distributed unequally. The top one-fifth of income earners receives approximately half of the total national income.

SHARES OF HOUSEHOLD INCOME AND NET WORTH BY QUINTILES IN THE UNITED STATES IN 2014

	Income	Wealth (household net worth in dollars)
Lowest fifth	3.1%	$-6,029
Second fifth	8.2%	$7,263
Third fifth	14.3%	$68,839
Forth fifth	23.2%	$205,985
Highest fifth	51.2%	$630,754

Sources: *Statista*, "Household Income in the U.S. — Shares of Quintiles 1970–2014"; *Forbes*, "Census Bureau Finds the Obvious about US Wealth Inequality"

Skills Focus **THINKING CRITICALLY** What do you think is the significance of the lowest fifth having negative wealth?

Quick Lab

Rating Prestige

These occupational prestige ratings from a Harris poll show the percentage of people who find these occupations prestigious. How would your ratings compare?

TOP 10 MOST PRESTIGIOUS PROFESSIONS IN 2014

Occupation	Percentage of people who find the occupation prestigious
Doctor	88%
Military officer	78%
Firefighter	76%
Scientist	76%
Nurse	70%
Engineer	69%
Police officer	66%
Priest/Minister/ Clergy	62%
Architect	62%
Teacher	60%

Source: *Business Insider*, "The 10 Most Prestigious Jobs in America"

PROCEDURE

1. Working in pairs, survey a sample of students in your school to create your own occupational prestige ratings. First, list the 10 occupations from the chart in alphabetical order on a piece of paper.
2. Then ask each student in the sample to assign a prestige value from 1 to 100 to each occupation.
3. Calculate a rating for each occupation by adding up the values that each student assigned and dividing by the number of students in the sample. Rank the occupations in order of their rating.

ANALYSIS

1. Compare your results with the ratings in the table at left and discuss your findings as a class.
2. How might you explain the similarities or differences? What factors might influence the values each person assigned?

knowledge, a particular social status, personal characteristics, or custom and tradition.

Prestige Individuals can also be ranked according to prestige. **Prestige** is the respect, honor, recognition, or courtesy an individual receives from others. Prestige can be based on any characteristics a society considers important. Occupation, education, family background, and area of residence are among the factors that often determine prestige.

In the United States, occupation tends to be the most important determinant of prestige. When asked to rate occupations according to levels of prestige, Americans consistently place jobs that require higher levels of education at the top of the list. Also, jobs with higher prestige ratings tend to produce higher incomes.

To rank people according to wealth, power, and prestige, sociologists often calculate people's **socioeconomic status** (SES). This rating combines social factors such as educational level, occupational prestige, and place of residence with the economic factor of income. The SES is then used to determine an individual's relative position in the stratification system.

Reading Check **Summarize** How do wealth, power, and prestige affect social rankings?

Explaining Stratification

Sociologists are interested not only in the nature of social stratification but also in its causes and consequences. Functionalists and conflict theorists have offered explanations. Other sociologists, seeing weaknesses in both approaches, have tried to blend the two.

Functionalist Theory Functionalists view stratification as a necessary feature of the social structure. The functionalist explanation assumes that certain roles in society must be performed if the system is to be maintained. Higher rewards for the performance of these roles ensure their fulfillment—the more important the role and the more skill needed to perform the role, the higher the reward. Functionalists claim that without varying rewards, many jobs would not be filled, and society could not function smoothly. For example, why would someone take the time and expense to become a physician if the reward for being a salesclerk were the same?

ACADEMIC VOCABULARY

synthesize to blend

Critics suggest that the functionalist explanation has weaknesses. The theory fails to consider that not everyone in society has equal access to such resources as education. Without this access, people are unlikely to obtain high-status occupations. The functionalist approach also assumes that positions that offer higher rewards are more important. A heart surgeon may earn more money, but is he or she more important to society than the garbage collector whose work prevents the spread of contagious diseases?

Conflict Theory Conflict theorists see competition over scarce resources as the cause of social inequality. Conflict theorists who base their work on Marxist theory say that stratification comes from class exploitation. The owners of the means of production control the working class in order to make profits and maintain their power in society.

Many American conflict theorists—such as C. Wright Mills, Irving Louis Horowitz, and G. William Domhoff—take a broader view of inequality. According to their view, various groups within society compete with one another for scarce resources. Once a group gains power, it is able to shape public policy and public opinion to its own advantage. In that way, it maintains its position of power.

Critics have found shortcomings in conflict theory as well. One of its major weaknesses is that it fails to recognize that unequal rewards are based, in part, on differences in talent, skill, and desire. Not everyone is suited for every position in the social structure. Consequently, society must have some way to urge the proper individuals into positions that are vital to its operation. One approach is to offer different rewards.

Efforts at Synthesis Some sociologists, noting that neither approach fully explains stratification, have tried to synthesize the two. Ralf Dahrendorf suggests that each approach might be used to explain specific aspects of stratification. For example, functionalist theory helps explain why people spend years training to become doctors or lawyers. Conflict theory helps to explain why the children of the wealthy tend to go to the best colleges.

Gerhard Lenski takes a similar approach. However, he asserts that the usefulness of the theory depends on the society under study. He notes that functionalists state that a stratification system functions because members of society accept it. Such a view would apply to simple societies—such as hunter-gatherer societies—where survival depends on cooperation. Lenski suggests that the conflict theory would apply to more complex societies, in which people struggle to control wealth and power. A ruling group emerges from the struggle, and social inequality develops as this group takes steps to maintain its position.

Reading Check **Find the Main Idea** How have sociologists synthesized the functionalist and conflict approaches to social stratification?

SECTION 1 Assessment

Reviewing Main Ideas and Vocabulary

1. **Explain** How does social stratification lead to social inequality?
2. **Define** How do sociologists define social class?
3. **Recall** What are the criticisms of the functionalist and conflict approaches to explaining social stratification?

Thinking Critically

4. **Compare and Contrast** How are caste systems similar to and different from class systems?
5. **Evaluate** Which of the three dimensions of social stratification—wealth, power, and prestige—do you think should have the most weight in determining social class?
6. **Interpret** Using your notes and a graphic organizer like this one, explain the functionalist and conflict theories of social stratification and which factors form a synthesis of the two.

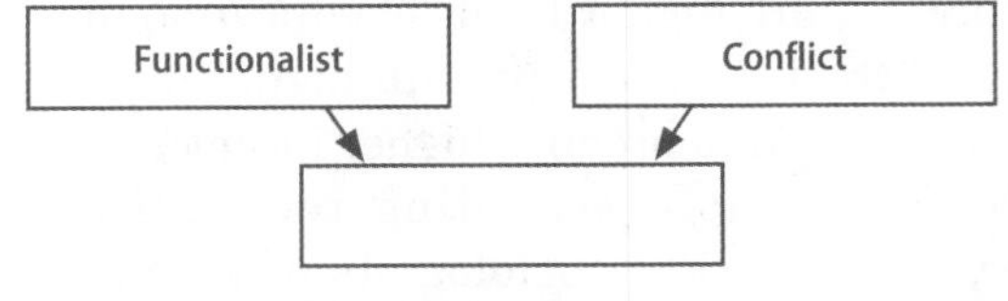

FOCUS ON WRITING

7. **Descriptive** Some sociologists believe that the functionalist and conflict theories of stratification are complementary rather than contradictory. Write two paragraphs describing how such sociologists explain the complementary relationship between the two theories. Consider the ideas of Ralf Dahrendorf and Gerhard Lenski.

Social Stratification Around the World

These Maasai prepare for an initiation ceremony that will make them young warriors of the tribe.

All societies have found ways to stratify their members based on specific characteristics. Ascribed statuses such as race, gender, and age are among those most commonly used to divide a society's members into ranks. Even achieved statuses such as occupation or education may be used.

Kiwai Papuans Even simple societies experience social stratification. Anthropologist Gunnar Landtman at first observed little social inequality among the Kiwai Papuans of New Guinea. Most villagers did the same work and lived in similar dwellings. Eventually, however, Landtman observed that men who were warriors, harpooners, and sorcerers were considered "a little more high" than others. Women and the unemployed were described as "down a little bit" and were not allowed to own land.

Mosuo The Mosuo are a minority ethnic group of about 56,000 people in southwest China. Some scholars consider Mosuo society a matriarchy, or a society in which women have authority over men. Mosuo society is matrilineal, meaning that women carry on the family name and lineage is traced through the mother. Women also run Mosuo households, which often consist of several families with one woman elected as the head. The female leaders of each village govern the region by committee.

Democratic Republic of the Congo Historically, Congolese society has been stratified by gender. Women are seen as lower in the social ranks than men. The result is a society plagued by social inequality. Legally, men are considered the head of the household. Women are expected to obey their husbands. They do not have the legal right to choose where they live or to file for divorce. Because they are underrepresented in government, women's opportunities to change these policies are limited.

Women are at the core of Mosuo culture. These Mosuo tribeswomen wear traditional dress. Women receive their skirts in a coming of age ceremony around ages 12 to 14.

Maasai The Maasai, a nomadic group in East Africa, use a system of age-sets to organize their society. Boys of the same age go through the rite of passage initiating them into adulthood at the same time, forming a permanent age-based group. These groups move up through a system of ranks, each lasting about 15 years. Ultimately they reach the rank of senior elder and gain the authority to make decisions for the tribe.

South Africa For decades, South Africa presented a prime example of a society stratified by race. The white minority practiced a policy of apartheid, or apartness. People were divided into four racial groups: white, black, Colored (mixed race), or Asian. Whites and nonwhites were segregated in housing, education, employment, and transportation. Nonwhites also faced political and economic discrimination. A new constitution in 1994 ended apartheid but not its effects on the nonwhite population.

Thinking Critically

1. **Identify Cause and Effect** How do these systems of stratification lead to social inequality?
2. **Discuss** Do you think that societies around the world should allow social stratification to continue? Explain your answer.

SECTION 2

The American Class System

Before You Read

Main Idea

Most sociologists use six class divisions when describing the American class system. Because it is an open system, people are able to move between classes.

Reading Focus

1. How do sociologists determine social class?
2. What are the characteristics of social classes in the United States?
3. What are the types of social mobility?

Vocabulary

reputational method
subjective method
objective method
social mobility
horizontal mobility
vertical mobility
intragenerational mobility
intergenerational mobility

TAKING NOTES Use a graphic organizer like this one to take notes about the American class system.

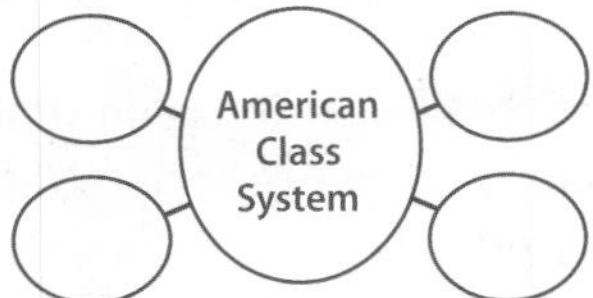

SOCIOLOGY CLOSE UP ***Does everyone have access to the nation's best universities?*** In the last decade and a half, Harvard University has made significant changes to its financial aid policy. In 2004, the university announced the Harvard Financial Aid Initiative, which eventually made it possible for students from families earning less than $60,000 per year to attend Harvard without paying tuition. In 2007, Harvard revised its policies again, this time reducing the amount of tuition families earning $180,000 per year or less will have to pay so that tuition costs do not exceed 10 percent of their income. These changes will benefit over half of Harvard's 6,600 undergraduates. Several Ivy League schools followed suit and revised their own financial aid policies.

The goal of these revisions was to make Harvard and the other Ivy League schools affordable for lower-class and middle-class students as well as the wealthy. In 2004 only about 8 percent of Harvard's undergraduates came from low-income families. Harvard says that their new financial aid policy has increased the number of students from families with incomes of less than $80,000 by 33 percent. However, at the nation's 59 wealthiest private colleges, an average of 14 percent of students come from low-income households. And in 2008 Harvard only accepted 7 percent of a record 27,426 applicants. Low-income students—who tend to have lower standardized test scores and are more likely to have part-time jobs, leaving them less time for activities sought after by college admissions boards—still face a monumental task in trying to get accepted by an Ivy League school. Most low-income students continue to attend public colleges and universities. ■

Determining Social Class

By definition, social inequality exists in all class systems. What form inequality takes varies from society to society—the fewer the number of ascribed characteristics used to determine access to rewards, the more open the class system. The United States has a fairly open system. The law forbids discrimination based on ascribed characteristics such as race, religion, ancestry, or sex.

In theory, Americans have equal access to the resources needed for social advancement. However, the United States has a wide range of social classes, and the rate of social mobility is not equal for every segment of American society. To understand why such conditions exist, one needs to look at the characteristics of social class and the patterns of social mobility in the United States.

Sociologists do not agree on the number of class divisions that exist in the United States. Most sociologists use a six-class system. The divisions in this system are upper class, upper middle class, lower middle class, working class, working poor, and underclass.

Sociologists rely on three techniques to rank individuals according to social class—the reputational, subjective, and objective methods. In the **reputational method,** individuals in the community are asked to rank other community members based on what they know of their characters and lifestyles. This method is suitable only when studying small communities in which everyone knows almost everyone else. The findings from these studies cannot be used to make conclusions about other communities.

In the second technique, the **subjective method,** individuals are asked to determine their own social rank. When the choices are limited to upper, middle, and lower class, most people say they are middle class. Researchers have found that people do not like to place themselves in the upper or lower classes. This problem can be partially eliminated by including the upper middle class and working class in the list of choices.

The third classification technique is the **objective method.** In this approach, sociologists define social class by income, occupation, and education. The statistical basis of this method makes it the least biased. However, it is not without its shortcomings. This technique's major problem involves the selection and measurement of social factors. Each combination of factors produces a slightly different picture of social-class membership.

Reading Check **Find the Main Idea** Explain the three techniques that sociologists use to determine social class.

Social Classes in the United States

ACADEMIC VOCABULARY

social advancement the process of moving up through the ranks of a class system

Regardless of the method used to identify class membership, sociologists generally agree on the basic characteristics of the American social-class system. Many of them also agree on the relative distribution of the population within the system. Estimates suggest that about 1 percent of the population of the United States belongs to the upper class. Another 14 percent of Americans are part of the upper middle class, while about 30 percent belong to the lower middle class. Another 30 percent comprise the working-class category. Another 22 percent of Americans are members of the working poor, and 3 percent are members of the underclass. However, recent figures suggest that the underclass may be shrinking.

One major difference between the classes is income. Classes also differ in terms of lifestyle and beliefs. A brief look at the general characteristics of each class will help you understand how social class affects life patterns.

The Upper Class Although the upper class is a small segment of the population, it controls a sizable proportion of the country's wealth. Generally, the upper class can be divided into two groups—"old money" and "new money."

America's old money includes such families as the Rockefellers, Vanderbilts, and Kennedys. The term *old money* refers to the fact that these families have been wealthy for generations. Much of their wealth comes from inheritance. Yet in terms of social rank, the family name and the accomplishments of previous generations are as important as the size of the family fortune. Members of this class are born into an atmosphere of wealth and power. They are able to attend prestigious schools, eat at the best restaurants, and vacation at the most exclusive resorts. Most have some of the world's richest and most famous people among their friends.

The term *new money* refers to the newly rich. They generally have acquired wealth through their own efforts rather than through inheritance. New money is less prestigious than old money. Some of those with old money look down on the newly rich for their conspicuous consumption. This term was coined by economist Thorstein Veblen in 1899 to describe the purchase of goods for the status they bring rather than for their usefulness.

Not surprisingly, membership in the upper class sometimes carries with it great power and influence. Members often fill top positions in government and private enterprise. Frequently, upper-class members also use their wealth to support charities.

The Upper Middle Class Members of the upper-middle class are primarily high-income businesspeople and professionals such as doctors and lawyers. Most have a college education, and many have advanced degrees. Their money buys them large houses, expensive cars, yearly vacations, a college education for their children, and many added luxuries. Class membership is generally based on income rather than on assets. Consequently, many in the upper middle class are career-oriented. Many people in this class are politically and socially active. However, their power and influence are limited to the community level and do not extend to the national level.

The Lower Middle Class Like the majority of the upper middle class, most members in the lower middle class hold white-collar jobs, which do not involve manual labor. Many of their jobs require less education and provide a lower income than the jobs held by the upper middle class. Lower middle class jobs include nursing, middle management, and sales. Owners of small businesses also belong to the lower middle class. Members of this class live a comfortable life but must work hard to keep what they have achieved.

The Working Class Many members of the working class hold jobs that require manual labor. Factory workers, tradespeople, less skilled workers, and some service workers fall into this category. Such jobs have traditionally been labeled blue-collar jobs, named after the color of the coveralls worn by many manual laborers. Some of these jobs pay as much or more than many of the positions held by members of the lower middle class. However, these jobs carry less prestige. Other working-class people hold clerical, lower-level sales, and various service jobs that do not require manual labor. These types of jobs are sometimes called pink-collar jobs because traditionally women have held them. Many members of the working class have few financial reserves. Unexpected crises, such as the loss of a job, can push working-class individuals into lower classes.

Social Classes in the United States

Upper Class

Percent of U.S. Population 1%

Education prestigious universities

Occupations owners and executives of large businesses; investors; heirs

Upper Middle Class

Percent of U.S. Population 14%

Education college or university

Occupations business executives; professionals

Lower Middle Class

Percent of U.S. Population 30%

Education high school, some college

Occupations lower-level managers; skilled craftsworkers; supervisors

The Working Poor Members of the working poor work at the lowest-paying jobs. These jobs are often temporary or seasonal, such as housecleaning, migrant farmwork, and day laboring. Even though the working poor work hard, they rarely make a living wage. Many depend on government-support programs. Most are high-school dropouts and, because of their lack of education, their future prospects are often bleak. Most are not involved politically. They believe their situation will remain the same regardless of who is in power.

The Underclass Families that have experienced unemployment and poverty over several generations are considered part of the underclass. Some members of the underclass do work, but usually only at undesirable, low-paying jobs. Their chief source of income is often public assistance. Life for people in the underclass is a day-to-day struggle for survival. Typically, only 50 percent of children in the underclass make it into a higher class.

Reading Check **Analyze** How do American social classes reflect social inequality?

Social Mobility

The United States has an open class system, which makes social mobility possible. **Social mobility** is the movement between or within social classes. Sociologists study two types of social mobility: horizontal and vertical.

The term **horizontal mobility** refers to movement within a social class or stratum. When an individual moves from one job to another of equal social ranking, that individual experiences horizontal mobility. An accountant may consider a move from one firm to another an important step up the career ladder. However, if the move does not involve any major change in the accountant's wealth, power, or prestige, sociologists view it as horizontal mobility.

Vertical mobility, on the other hand, is the movement between social classes or strata. The monetary and social rewards of promotion from a secretarial to a management position may move an individual from the working class to the lower middle class. This type of mobility can be either upward or downward.

There are two kinds of vertical mobility. When sociologists focus on changes in social position during one person's life, they are studying **intragenerational mobility.** With **intergenerational mobility,** however, the focus is on status differences between generations in the same family. For example, the child of a mechanic who becomes a doctor experiences intergenerational mobility.

Most Americans believe that all people in the United States are free to reach their own particular level of achievement. They believe that people will rise or fall to various levels according to their efforts and abilities. Although this theory appears to be true, the reality is somewhat different.

Working Class

Percent of U.S. Population 30%

Education high school

Occupations factory workers; clerical workers; lower-level salespeople

Working Poor

Percent of U.S. Population 22%

Education some high school

Occupations laborers; service workers such as gardeners and house cleaners

Underclass

Percent of U.S. Population 3%

Education some high school

Occupations undesirable, low-paying jobs; unemployed; on welfare

Research indicates that even though the majority of Americans reach a higher occupational status than their parents, most remain in the same social class. When individuals do undergo vertical mobility, they rarely move up or down more than one social class.

Structural Causes of Upward Mobility While individual effort often plays a role in social mobility, sociologists are more interested in the structural causes. These causes include advances in technology, changes in merchandising patterns, and increases in the population's general level of education.

When technologies change, the jobs available to workers also change, which can result in downward mobility for individuals caught in the shift. However, it often means upward mobility for the next generation of workers. For example, the disappearance of millions of factory jobs due to mechanization has forced some new workers into higher-status jobs, primarily in the service industry.

Changes in merchandising patterns have also affected social mobility. Recent changes include an explosion in the credit industry, a greater emphasis on insurance, increased real-estate transactions, and an extraordinary growth in personal services. These changes have increased the white-collar workforce from approximately 31 percent of all workers in 1940 to 77 percent today.

Another factor that has promoted upward mobility is an increase in the general level of education. The percent of the population aged 25 and older without a high school diploma has shrunk from 75 percent in 1940 to 15 percent today. Also, more Americans are going to college. Today 26 percent of people 25 and older have earned a bachelor's degree or higher, compared to less than 5 percent in 1940.

Structural Causes of Downward Mobility Although upward mobility is more common, movement down the class ladder also occurs. Personal factors such as illness, divorce, and retirement can cause downward mobility. Once again, sociologists are more interested in the structural causes of this movement.

Changes in the economy are the primary structural causes of downward mobility. Breakthroughs in technology can alter the demand for labor. Workers may suddenly find themselves without jobs. If these workers are unable to find new jobs with comparable salaries, they may experience downward mobility. For younger workers, the drop in social status is often temporary. However, for older workers the shift may be permanent.

Economic changes also can affect intergenerational mobility. In times of economic growth and low unemployment, individuals entering the job market have less difficulty finding desirable employment. However, jobs are less plentiful during an economic recession. As a result, even highly qualified graduates sometimes cannot find jobs in their chosen fields.

Reading Check **Contrast** What are the two types of vertical mobility, and how do they differ?

SECTION 2 Assessment

Reviewing Main Ideas and Vocabulary

1. **Recall** In what kind of situation is the reputational method the most useful for determining social class?
2. **Categorize** What are the general characteristics of the six social classes in the United States?
3. **Define** What is social mobility?

Thinking Critically

4. **Evaluate** Do you think there is a relationship between occupational achievement and social class? Explain.
5. **Make Judgments** Which do you think occurs most often, horizontal mobility or vertical mobility?
6. **Identify Cause and Effect** Using your notes and a graphic organizer like the one below, list and explain the structural causes of upward mobility.

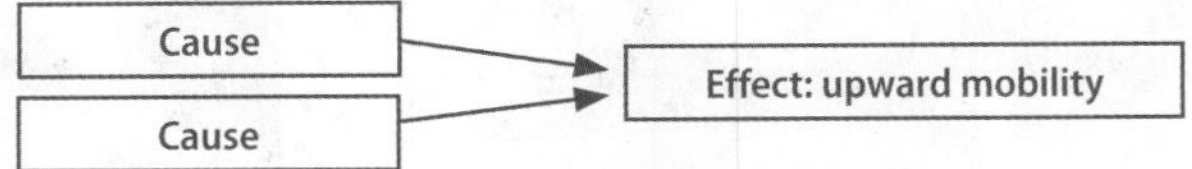

FOCUS ON WRITING

7. **Expository** Write three short paragraphs evaluating the methods of measuring social class. Consider the applicability of the results, the personal feelings of respondents, and the social factors selected for measurement.

SECTION 3

Poverty

Before You Read

Main Idea
Americans living below the poverty level have fewer opportunities. Government welfare programs attempt to remedy this situation.

Reading Focus
1. How is poverty defined in the United States?
2. What groups of Americans are affected by poverty?
3. What are the effects of poverty on poor Americans?
4. What steps have been taken by the federal government to reduce the effects of poverty?

Vocabulary
poverty
poverty level
life chances
life expectancy
transfer payments

TAKING NOTES Use a graphic organizer like this one to take notes on American poverty.

A Penny Per Pound

SOCIOLOGY CLOSE UP ***Can you imagine having to struggle for a one-cent raise?*** That is exactly what the Coalition of Immokalee Workers—an advocacy group composed largely of tomato pickers in the Immokalee area of southwest Florida—has been doing since 2001. For decades, the Immokalee tomato pickers have been working 12-hour days for substandard wages and living in rundown shacks and trailers. They spend each day on their hands and knees filling 32-pound buckets of tomatoes. To earn even $50 a day, each worker must pick enough tomatoes to fill 125 buckets—two tons of tomatoes!

In an effort to improve the workers' situation, the Coalition of Immokalee Workers began a campaign of protests and boycotts against the major fast-food chains that purchase their tomato harvest. Since 2005, the tomato pickers have gotten Burger King, McDonald's, and Yum! Brands, the parent company of Taco Bell, to agree to pay an additional penny per pound of tomatoes. This increase means that a worker will earn 77 cents per bucket instead of 45 cents, the first substantial raise in decades. The group plans to continue its quest to provide a living wage for its workers by targeting other fast-food chains and grocery suppliers. ■

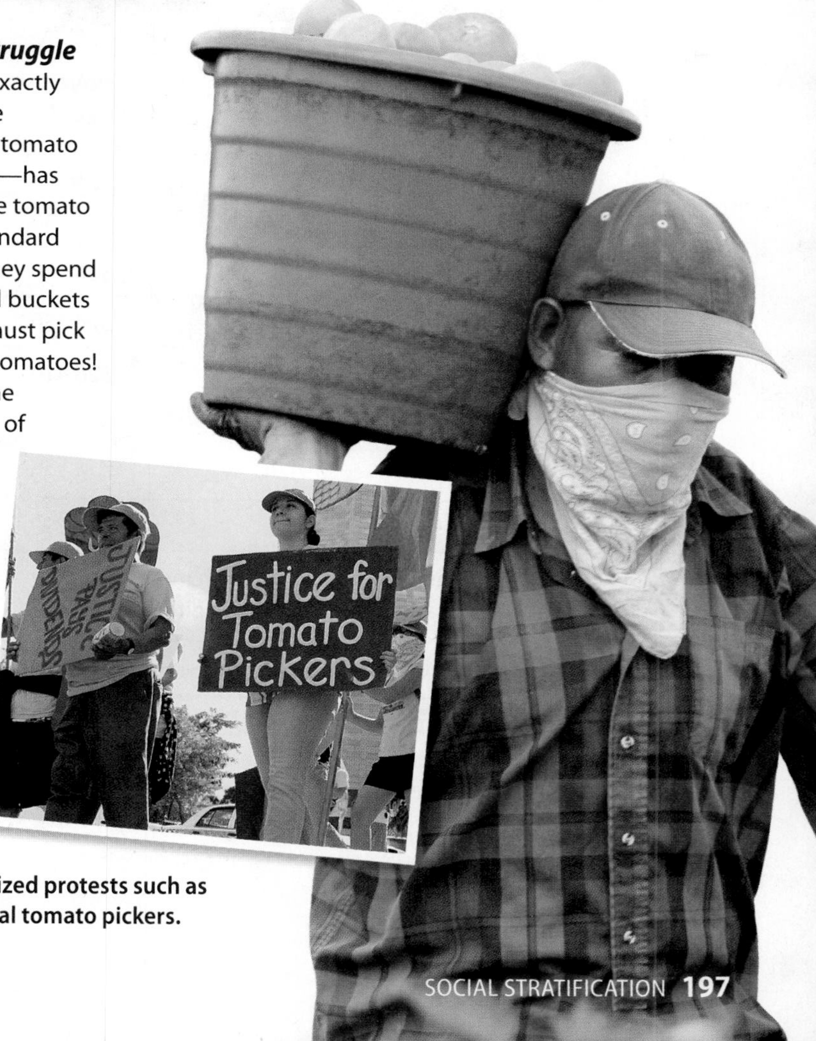

The Coalition of Immokalee Workers organized protests such as this one in an effort to secure a raise for local tomato pickers.

Defining Poverty in the United States

The United States is one of the richest countries in the world. However, not everyone in American society shares equally in this prosperity. Almost 46.7 million people—about 14.8 percent of the population—live below the poverty level. Many millions more make incomes that are too low to meet their basic needs. However, they make too much money to qualify for public assistance. For all of these people, daily life is often a struggle.

Who is classified as poor depends on how poverty is defined. In general, **poverty** is seen as a standard of living that is below the minimum level considered adequate by society. Thus, poverty is a relative measure. What one society considers poverty might be seen as an adequate standard of living in another. For example, many poor Americans live more comfortable lives than the majority of people in some industrializing nations. This fact does not mean there are no poor people in the United States. Rather, it means that the standard of living in the United States is high.

What does it mean to be poor in the United States? To answer this question, you need to look at the characteristics of poverty in the United States and at the effects that poverty has on people's lives. You also need to examine some of the ways that the government responds to the problem of poverty.

The U.S. Census Bureau defines poverty in terms of the minimum annual income needed by a family to survive. This minimum income is called the **poverty level.** The government considers families with income levels below this amount to be poor.

The poverty level is determined by calculating the cost of providing an adequate diet, based on the U.S. Department of Agriculture's minimum nutritional standards. This figure is then multiplied by three because research has indicated that poor people spend one-third of their income on food. Each year, the government adjusts the poverty level to reflect increases in the cost of living. The poverty level most often quoted in news stories is for a family of four. The government actually establishes a series of poverty levels that takes into account the number of people in a family. The table on this page lists the poverty levels for various family sizes.

Recently, poverty researchers have questioned the usefulness of the government's poverty levels. They point out that the method for calculating poverty was developed in the 1960s. Since then, eating and spending habits have changed greatly. In response to this criticism, the Census Bureau has begun to experiment with different definitions of poverty. One definition bases the poverty level on spending for the basic necessities, which include food, clothing, housing, and "a little bit more"—other personal expenses. Using this definition would raise the poverty level for a family of four by a few thousand dollars. As a result, several million more Americans would be added to the ranks of those in poverty.

Reading Check **Identify Supporting Details**
How is the poverty level determined?

QUICK FACTS

POVERTY LEVEL BY FAMILY SIZE, 2015

Family Size	Poverty Level
1	$11,770
2	$15,930
3	$20,090
4	$24,250
5	$28,410
6	$32,570
7	$36,730
8	$40,890

For families/households with more than 8 persons, add $4,160 for each additional person.

Source: U.S. Department of Health & Human Services

Skills Focus **INTERPRETING TABLES** Why do you think there are different poverty levels for people aged 65 and older?

Statistically Speaking...

Poverty in America Poverty affects Americans of all races, ethnicities, and age groups. However, because of a history of discrimination and many other factors, certain groups suffer from greater percentages of poverty. As you can see in the table at right, the poverty rate for whites averages 2 percentage points lower than the rate for the overall population. African Americans and Hispanics, on the other hand, have poverty rates that are almost twice that of the nation as a whole.

Although the poverty level is uniform across the country, the percentage of people below the poverty level varies by state. In Mississippi—the state with the highest percentage of residents living in poverty—22.5 percent of the population is below the poverty level. In contrast, only 9.0 percent of New Hampshire residents are below the poverty level. Economic factors such as the strength of local industries or education programs can cause these variations. Cost of living, a local measure, may also play a role. For example, urban areas tend to have high costs of living. In New York City the cost of living is among the highest in the nation, and one in five people there live below the poverty level.

Skills Focus **INTERPRETING MAPS** What region suffers the most from poverty? Why do you think this is so?

PERCENT OF POPULATION BELOW POVERTY LEVEL BASED ON SELECTED CHARACTERISTICS, 2014

Age	All Races	White	African American	Hispanic American
Total Population	14.8	12.7	26.2	23.6
Under 18	21.1	17.9	37.1	39.1
18 to 64	13.5	11.9	22.6	19.8
65 and over	10.0	8.7	19.2	18.1

Source: U.S. Census Bureau, 2015

POVERTY LEVELS ACROSS THE UNITED STATES

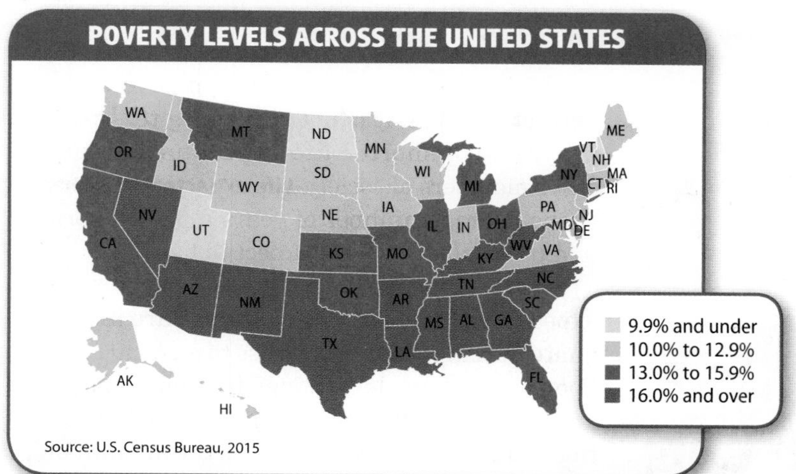

Source: U.S. Census Bureau, 2015

Variations in American Poverty

Not every American runs an equal risk of being poor. Characteristics such as age, sex, and race and ethnicity affect poverty.

As an age group, children have the largest percentage in poverty. Children under age 18 form 25 percent of the population, but they represent 33 percent of those living in poverty. Not all children have an equal likelihood of being poor. The level of poverty among African American and Hispanic children is more than twice the level among white children.

About 57 percent of the poor are women. Also, women head about one-half of all poor families. As in the case of children, not all female-headed households are at equal risk. Almost 40 percent of households headed by African American and Hispanic women live in poverty. This compares to a rate of 25 percent for families headed by white women.

As the statistics above indicate, poverty varies by race and cultural background. Regardless of age or sex, African Americans and Hispanics are more likely than whites to live in poverty. As you can see in the table above, African Americans and Hispanics have poverty rates that are almost twice that of the United States as a whole.

Reading Check **Infer** What characteristics make it more likely that someone will live in poverty?

Effects of Poverty

The lives of poor Americans differ markedly from the lives of society's wealthier members. Poor and wealthy members of society have different life chances and behavior patterns.

Life Chances By **life chances,** sociologists mean the likelihood that individuals have of sharing in the opportunities and benefits of society. Life chances include such things as health, length of life, housing, and education. Research has shown that life chances vary by social class. The lower their social class, the less opportunity individuals have to share in the benefits of society.

Poor Americans are at a serious disadvantage in two important life chances—health and length of life. Rates of heart disease, diabetes, cancer, arthritis, pneumonia, and tuberculosis are highest among those living in poverty. In light of this fact, it is not surprising that poor people have shorter life expectancies than other members of society. **Life expectancy** refers to the average number of years a person born in a particular year can expect to live.

Two reasons for ill health and a shorter life expectancy among poor Americans are inadequate nutrition and less access to medical care. Poor people have less money to spend on food and are often less informed about good nutrition. A lack of money also limits the amount of health care that poor people receive. A significant number of poor Americans do not have health insurance because it is too expensive. Uninsured people are less likely to get routine physical checkups and other preventive care. They are also more likely to postpone medical treatment and to not fill prescriptions.

CASE STUDY CONNECTION

Rural Poverty Poor Americans in rural areas must also overcome the low ratio of physicians to the population as a whole.

The environment that poor Americans work and live in has negative effects on health. The working poor often have jobs that involve considerable health and safety risks. The housing that poor people are able to afford is often inadequate and unsafe. As a result, poor children are more likely to be exposed to environmental hazards such as lead paint.

Educational opportunities are also limited for poor Americans. School funding is based in part on local property taxes. As a result, schools in low-income areas are often inadequately funded because of low tax revenues. These limitations negatively affect future life chances.

Patterns of Behavior Certain behaviors also vary depending on social class. For example, divorce rates are higher among low-income families than among other segments of the population. Poor Americans are also more likely to be arrested, convicted, and sent to prison for crimes than are Americans from higher social classes. This situation results, in part, from the fact that people living in poverty are more likely to commit crimes that the police pursue more aggressively. Among these are violent crime and crimes against property, such as burglary and auto theft. Because criminals usually commit offenses in or near their own communities, poor people are more likely to be the victims of crime.

Reading Check **Contrast** How do the poor's life chances differ from those of wealthy Americans?

Government Responses to Poverty

In 1964 President Lyndon B. Johnson declared a "war on poverty." Since then, the federal government has taken an active role in attempting to reduce inequality in the United States. The results have been mixed.

Almost 46.7 million Americans still live in poverty. In addition, the poverty rate is about the same as it was in the early 1970s. Nevertheless, the situation has improved in some ways. In 1966, for example, poverty among elderly Americans was almost three times as high as among the general population. Today the poverty rate for people 65 and older is lower than the rate for the country as a whole. This improvement is due mainly to increased Social Security benefits and the introduction of Medicare, the government-sponsored health-insurance program for people 65 and older.

The government tries to reduce inequality through various social-welfare programs. These programs use one of two methods—transfer payments or government subsidies. The government uses **transfer payments** to redistribute money within society by funneling a percentage of tax revenues to groups that need public assistance. These groups include people who are poor, unemployed, elderly, or disabled. The major transfer-payment programs include Supplemental Security Income (SSI) and Temporary Assistance for Needy Families (TANF).

SSI provides income support for people 65 years of age and older and for blind and disabled adults and children. TANF gives cash payments to poor families with children.

The second approach used by the government to assist poor Americans is subsidies, which transfer goods and services rather than cash. The Food Stamp program is, perhaps, the best-known government subsidy. Under this program, poor people receive coupons or cards that can be used to buy food. Other subsidies include those for housing, school lunches, and Medicaid—a health-insurance program for the poor.

From the 1980s onward, calls for reform of the social-welfare system grew louder. Critics charged that the system had created a permanent "welfare class" who chose to live off government assistance rather than to work. In 1996 the federal government responded by passing the Personal Responsibility and Work Opportunity Reconciliation Act. This act turned the administration of some welfare programs over to the states. It also changed the rules for payment of assistance. Before, people could receive payments indefinitely. Now most people receive payments for no more than five years and are required to work after two years in the program.

Some observers have hailed welfare reform as a success, pointing out that it has greatly reduced the number of people on welfare. How well the people who have moved from welfare to work are doing is less clear, however. One study found that nearly a third of those who had left welfare were back on the rolls within two years. Those who remained off welfare reported facing considerable economic problems. About half said they sometimes ran out of food and could not afford to buy more. More than a third reported that at least once during the year they could not pay their rent or utility bills. Some observers suggest that such statistics show that the success of welfare reform should be judged as much on "income and poverty outcomes" as on welfare-roll reductions.

MILESTONES IN WELFARE LEGISLATION

Date	Legislation	Significance
1935	Social Security Act	Established Aid to Families with Dependent Children (AFDC), requiring states to assist eligible families
1964	Economic Opportunity Act	Cornerstone of Johnson's war on poverty; provided job training, adult education, and small business loans
1996	Personal Responsibility and Work Opportunity Reconciliation Act	Replaced AFDC with Temporary Assistance to Needy Families (TANF), changing the criteria for determining eligibility and delivering benefits
2006	Deficit Reduction Act of 2005	Revised TANF, changes designed to promote work and support children

Skills Focus **INTERPRETING CHARTS** How long did Aid to Families with Dependent Children (AFDC) operate before being replaced?

Reading Check **Summarize** Describe the two methods used by government welfare programs.

SECTION 3 Assessment

Reviewing Main Ideas and Vocabulary

1. **Define** What is the poverty level?
2. **Recall** How do characteristics such as age, sex, and race affect poverty?
3. **Identify** What are two reasons for ill health and a shorter life expectancy among poor Americans?
4. **Explain** Why did critics call for welfare reform?

Thinking Critically

5. **Predict** What effect do you think the changes to welfare programs might have on the recipients' self-esteem? Explain.
6. **Summarize** Using your notes and a graphic organizer like the one below, describe the effects of poverty on life chances and behavior patterns.

Effects of Poverty	
Life Chances	Behavior Patterns

FOCUS ON WRITING

7. **Descriptive** Write a short essay on what effects you think welfare reform will have on poverty in the United States in the future.

Simulation
Applying What You've Learned

Only What You Can Afford

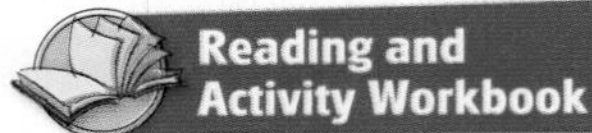

Use the workbook to complete this simulation.

What are the significant, everyday lifestyle differences between people of different classes in the United States?

1. Introduction

Social stratification is a system by which society places its members into social classes. The ranking of people into a hierarchy is practiced by most of the societies in the world. This simulation will give you a glimpse of what some of the American social classes look like from within. It is based on three imaginary families who belong to various social classes in the United States. They live in a major metropolitan area with a high cost of living. For this simulation, the families are

- **The Van Horns** An upper middle class couple who work as a doctor and a lawyer. Their annual income is $160,000, which leaves them $96,000 after taxes.
- **The Johnsons** A lower middle class couple who work as a teacher and a librarian. They make $75,000 a year, which leaves them $57,000 after taxes.
- **The Drakes** A single mother with one child from among the working poor whose job as a nursing aide pays $17,000. After taxes are deducted, she has $16,000 to spend each year.

You will work in small groups to create monthly budgets for these families to live on based on estimated average costs. To complete this simulation, follow the steps below.

- Following your teacher's instructions, organize into groups of at least six students.
- Create a budget worksheet for each of the three families. Divide the work among your group members, so that two students do the research for and complete one of the families' budget worksheets.
- Once you have filled out your budget worksheets, work as a group to make a pie graph that represents each family's budget. Use the pie graphs to compare the three budgets. You will turn in the worksheets and pie graphs.
- As a class, discuss how you made your budgets and what you noticed when you compared your pie graphs.

2. Creating Your Budget

Use the Budget Worksheet on the next page to create your budget. First, divide your family's after-tax income by 12 to determine how much they can spend each month. Then consider the categories below. Figures listed are per month.

1. **Housing** You should spend about 35 percent of your monthly income on housing. Review the options below. If you choose to purchase your residence, you will need to budget 3 percent of your mortgage payment each month for maintenance. Also note the appropriate utilities cost on your budget worksheet.

4-Bedroom house (mortgage, insurance, taxes)	$3,300
2-Bedroom house (mortgage, insurance, taxes)	$2,200
2-Bedroom apartment (rent, insurance)	$1,000
1-Bedroom apartment (rent, insurance)	$600
Utilities for houses (energy, water, sewer)	$150
Utilities for apartments (energy)	$90

2. **Transportation** The cost of an automobile should not exceed about 25 percent of your monthly income. The figures below include loan payment, insurance, and gas. You may not be able to afford a car at all and be forced to rely on public transportation. Choose one of the options below.

Two luxury cars	$2,200
One luxury car	$1,100
Two economy cars	$1,000
One economy car	$500
Public transportation	$100

3. **Food** Research indicates that the poor spend about 30 percent of their income on food. Review the grocery options below and choose the one your family can afford. Also decide if they will eat out and how often. Add the appropriate figure to your budget worksheet.

Groceries, Tier 1 (fresh, organic, lots of variety)	$350
Groceries, Tier 2 (mostly packaged, less variety)	$300
Groceries, Tier 3 (limited to discount options)	$250
Dining Out, Tier 1 (specialty restaurant, per visit)	$60
Dining Out, Tier 2 (family restaurant, per visit)	$30
Dining Out, Tier 3 (fast-food chain, per visit)	$10

❹ **Health Care** Choose one of the options below for your health care coverage, based on how much you think your family can afford.

Excellent coverage	$400
Good coverage	$300
Moderate coverage	$200
Minimal coverage	$100

❺ **Personal Care** This category includes clothing and grooming products. Consider what kind of clothing your family's jobs require when selecting one of these options.

From a high-end department store	$150
From a discount department store	$100
From a uniform or thrift store	$50

❻ **Miscellaneous** Do you have anything left over for these miscellaneous expenses? Are you able to spend anything on entertainment? If so, decide how your family should spend its remaining funds.

Phone, landline	$70
Phone, cellular	$70
Basic cable	$20
High-speed internet access	$40
Annual vacation, one week in another city	$100
Pet supplies and care	$60
Entertainment (movies, amusement parks, etc.)	Varies

3. Discussion

What did you learn from this simulation? Hold a group discussion that focuses on the following questions:

- How did the options available to each family differ?
- Which families bought property and which had to rent? What are the long-term consequences of these choices?
- How did the amount of money available for unnecessary expenses such as dining out and entertainment vary among the families? Was spending less in some areas in order to have more "fun money" an option for all families?
- Did your families have any money left over for emergencies? How about for savings? Did this vary by social class and income level? How?
- The poverty level is national, but cost of living varies by city. How do you think this situation affects poor families in areas with a high cost of living, such as the Drakes?
- This simulation ignored solutions to poverty, such as charities and welfare programs. How might these options change the Drake family budget?

Sample Budget Worksheet

Total Net Annual Income $________
Total Net Monthly Income $________

Housing
Mortgage or Rent $________
Maintenance (applies to houses only) $________
Utilities $________
TOTAL $________

Transportation
Car Payment $________
Cost of mass transit (if car not possible) $________
TOTAL $________

Food
Groceries $________
Dining Out (total cost of meals chosen) $________
TOTAL $________

Health Care
TOTAL $________

Personal Care
TOTAL $________

Miscellaneous
Phone, landline $________
Phone, cellular $________
Basic cable $________
High-speed Internet access $________
Vacation $________
Pet supplies and pet care $________
Entertainment $________
Other $________
TOTAL $________

TOTAL EXPENSES $________
SURPLUS OR SHORTAGE $________

CHAPTER 8 Review

Comprehension and Critical Thinking

SECTION 1 *(pp. 186–190)*

1. a. Recall According to functionalist theory, why is social stratification necessary?

b. Analyze How has the caste system in India changed since the 1800s? What factors have contributed to these changes?

c. Support a Position What factors do you think should be used to measure social class? Why?

SECTION 2 *(pp. 192–196)*

2. a. Identify What are the six social classes recognized by most American sociologists?

b. Identify Cause and Effect In what ways do technological advances affect upward and downward mobility?

c. Evaluate Do you think social class affects social mobility? Explain.

SECTION 3 *(pp. 197–201)*

3. a. Recall Who calculates the poverty level for the nation?

b. Infer Why might the welfare-reform programs introduced in 1996 be called welfare-to-work?

c. Rank Which of the effects of poverty do you think has the most significance for poor Americans? Explain.

INTERNET ACTIVITY

4. How does the welfare system work? Use the Internet to research the government's welfare program. Who qualifies to receive assistance? What process must applicants follow? What are the requirements to continue to receive welfare? Create a fact sheet that would explain the system to needy Americans.

Reviewing Vocabulary

For each of the following questions, choose the letter of the best answer.

5. What do sociologists call the division of society into categories, ranks, or classes?

A. caste system
B. exogamy
C. social inequality
D. social stratification

6. What term refers to the materials and methods used to produce goods and services?

A. bourgeoisie
B. proletariat
C. means of production
D. socioeconomic status

7. What is the respect, honor, recognition, or courtesy an individual receives from others called?

A. power
B. prestige
C. socioeconomic status
D. wealth

8. Which of the following involves asking individuals to determine their own social rank?

A. objective method
B. social mobility
C. subjective method
D. reputational method

9. Which type of mobility relates to status differences between generations of the same family?

A. horizontal
B. vertical
C. intergenerational
D. intragenerational

10. What term do sociologists use to describe the likelihood that individuals have of sharing in the opportunities and benefits of society?

A. life chances
B. life expectancy
C. poverty
D. poverty level

Sociology in Your Life

11. Social stratification occurs throughout the United States to varying degrees. You may witness its effects on a daily basis. Write an essay analyzing how social stratification has affected your community. Consider its effects on community institutions such as neighborhoods, schools, and jobs. Provide detailed examples to support your analysis.

SKILLS ACTIVITY: INTERPRETING CARTOONS

The phrase "the haves and the have nots" is often used to informally describe the gap between the rich and the poor in the United States. Study the cartoon below. Then use the information to answer the questions that follow.

12. **Describe** How has the cartoonist chosen to visually represent social stratification?
13. **Analyze** What is the significance of the fact that the bridge is crumbling?
14. **Make Judgments** Who do you think is the intended audience for this cartoon? What is the cartoonist trying to say to them?

WRITING FOR SOCIOLOGY

Use your knowledge of social stratification to answer the question below. Do not simply list facts. Present a clear argument based on your critical analysis of the question, using appropriate sociological terminology.

15. Write a dialogue between a functionalist and a conflict theorist explaining social stratification. Include the following topics in the dialogue.
    - Causes of social stratification
    - Consequences of social stratification
    - Wealth, power, and prestige

Connecting Online

Go online for review and enrichment activities related to this chapter.

KEY TOPICS VIDEOS
View compelling clips on issues in the field.

KEEP IT CURRENT
Link to the Current Events site for regularly updated stories on sociology as well as other social studies topics.

QUICK LAB
Reinforce a key concept with a short lab activity.

CASE STUDY

A Class Divided

What if you lived in a society where blue-eyed people were considered inferior? How do you think blue-eyed people would feel and behave? What about brown-eyed people? Third-grade teacher Jane Elliot conducted a unique experiment to find the answers to these questions.

The Experiment On April 5, 1968, Elliot assigned her 28 students to one of two groups, depending on whether their eyes were blue or brown. Blue-eyed students, she told the class, were inferior. Elliot made up a list of rules that both groups would have to follow. Brown-eyed children would be given five extra minutes of recess. They could go to lunch first and could go back for second helpings. In addition, they could drink from the water fountain in the room. In contrast, the blue-eyed children got a shorter recess period, had to wait to go to lunch, and they had to use paper cups.

With the rules in place, Elliot took every opportunity to praise the brown-eyed students and to criticize those with blue eyes. For example, when a brown-eyed student missed a word while reading, she helped him or her. When a blue-eyed child did likewise, Elliot shook her head in disapproval. Then she asked a brown-eyed student to read the passage correctly. Elliot made sure to treat each group differently for the sake of her experiment.

How did the students react to the experiment? Elliot noted that by lunchtime, it was easy to tell if a child was blue- or brown-eyed. The brown-eyed children were happy and alert. Their work was much better than before. The blue-eyed children, on the other hand, looked miserable and defeated. Their work had deteriorated. More frightening, Elliot said, was the way the brown-eyed children behaved. Everything they said and did suggested that they truly believed they were superior.

In 1968 teacher Jane Elliott devised an exercise to teach her class what it feels like to be discriminated against.

The Roles Reversed On the second day of the experiment, the roles were reversed. The blue-eyed students were now told that they were superior and that brown-eyed students were inferior. How did the students react this time? Elliot expected that since the brown-eyed students knew this was a one-day experiment, they would not react so intensely. Surprisingly, they behaved exactly as the blue-eyed children had. In a very short time they began to look miserable, resentful, and defeated. Interestingly, however, the blue-eyed children—now the dominant group—were far less unpleasant to the brown-eyed group than the latter had been to them.

The Ethics Issue Although it provides insights into the power of discrimination, most researchers today would consider Elliot's classroom exercise unethical. Sociologists, like all researchers, must follow strict guidelines for experiments that involve people, and even stricter ones for children. For example, an experiment cannot hurt a human participant in any way. Because Elliot's original experiment had the potential for severe psychological consequences, it would not be allowed today under most research ethics guidelines.

Long-retired from teaching school, Elliot continues to teach about discrimination and how it feels. Today she travels frequently throughout the United States, conducting lectures and training seminars. In some of her sessions, she still conducts her "brown-eyed, blue-eyed" exercise, but only with informed, consenting adults.

What do you think?

1. What were students' reactions on the first day of the experiment? On the second day?
2. What can you learn from Elliot's classroom experiment about relations between dominant and minority groups?

CHAPTER 9
RACIAL AND ETHNIC RELATIONS

Chapter at a Glance

SECTION 1: Race, Ethnicity, and the Social Structure

- Like other scientists and social scientists, sociologists reject the idea that races are biologically distinct.
- Ethnicity is a social category based on a set of cultural characteristics, not physical traits.
- Sociologists acknowledge that a society's dominant groups enjoy a position of power and privilege in comparison to minority groups, or groups who are singled out and treated unequally.

SECTION 2: Patterns of Intergroup Relations

- Discrimination and prejudice are common features of the minority group experience worldwide.
- Discrimination can occur at a societal level, as legal discrimination and institutional discrimination, and at an individual level.
- Prejudice is supported by the use of stereotypes, simplified, exaggerated, and unfavorable generalizations about groups of people.
- Sociologists draw upon sociological, psychological, and economic explanations to identify the source of racism.
- The most common patterns of minority-group treatment exist along a continuum that ranges from cultural pluralism to assimilation, legal protection, segregation, subjugation, population transfer, and extermination.

SECTION 3: Minority Groups in the United States

- Minority groups in the United States have achieved varying levels of social and economic success.
- The major minority groups in the United States include African Americans, Hispanics, Asian Americans, and Native Americans.
- Other minority groups in the United States include white ethnics, Jewish Americans, and Arab Americans.

SECTION 1

Race, Ethnicity, and the Social Structure

Before You Read

Main Idea
Race, ethnicity, and minority groups are important factors that shape the social structure of the United States.

Reading Focus
1. To what extent is race both a myth and a reality?
2. Which cultural characteristics help define ethnicity?
3. What is a minority group?

Vocabulary
race
ethnicity
ethnic group
minority group
dominant group

TAKING NOTES As you read, use a graphic organizer like this one to take notes about how race, ethnicity, and minority groups influence the social structure of the United States.

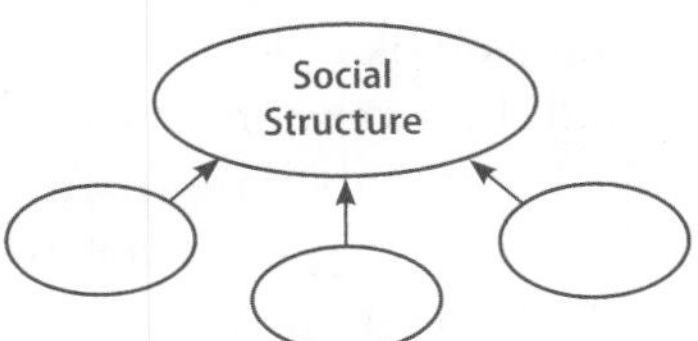

SOCIOLOGY CLOSE UP

Is race in the eye of the beholder? For a number of years, Tiger Woods dominated the sport of golf and is still one of the most recognizable golfers in the world. When it comes to race, however, Woods is not so easily pinned down. In fact, he openly challenges how many Americans think about race. In 1999, Woods was asked if it bothered him to be called African American. Woods responded that he wasn't actually black. He was "Cablinasian." As a child, Woods came up with *Cablinasian* to explain who he was and to honor his multiracial ancestry. The term, like Woods himself, is a combination of *Caucasian*, *black*, *American Indian*, and *Asian*.

At the time, most Americans looked at Woods, saw his golden-brown skin, and believed him to be African American. This is not surprising given the number of attempts by people and the government to establish racial categories based on observable physical differences. For example, until recently, the U.S. Census offered respondents a choice of only four boxes to indicate their race: American Indian/Alaska Native, Asian and Pacific Islander, black, and white.

For years, Americans complained these categories did not accurately reflect their identities. In 2000 the census added new options and, for the first time, asked Americans to select "one or more races" that they consider themselves to be. Nearly 7 million Americans checked more than one box, identifying themselves as multiracial. As you read this section, you will see why such a small change allowed the census to better reflect how Americans experience race. ■

Race as Myth and Reality

What is race? In the minds of many Americans —and many people the world over—it is the idea that humankind can be sorted into biologically distinct groups called races. One of the key assumptions underlying this view is that biologically "pure" races can exist. People can be assigned to one racial category, separate from all the others, based on observable physical characteristics, such as skin color, hair texture, and facial features. They can be African American or Hispanic, white or Asian, Native American or Arab American. Using this view of race, a person would have to belong only to one group or the other.

Biologists, geneticists, and social scientists overwhelmingly reject this view of race. Some go as far as to call biological race a myth, a product of the human mind and a story long told. At the most basic level, biologists sort living creatures into groups called species, not races. The dividing line between species has to do with reproduction. Organisms from different species cannot produce offspring. Because all people belong to the same species, the human species, no such barrier divides the over 7 billion people who inhabit Earth.

Moreover, contemporary studies of genetics suggest that inherited traits, such as skin color and hair texture, are superficial indicators of genetic similarity. Geneticists have found that far more genetic variation exists within racial groups than between racial groups. For example, imagine two sets of men. In one set there is a tall man and a short man of the same race, and in the other there is an African American man and an Asian American man. If you could examine their genetic code, their DNA, which set do you think would be most genetically different? The result may surprise you. There is far more genetic variation between the tall man and the short man. While each cell of the human body has about 100,000 genes, only about 6 of those control for skin color. By contrast dozens of genes affect a person's height.

Biologically speaking, race may be a myth, but the idea of race is still very much a reality. How can this be so? Race is real in a social sense. Assigning people to racial groups has tremendous social significance, and racial distinctions are powerful because people attach meaning to them. In other words, racial differences become real and important because people believe they are so. Later, you will read about some of the more severe consequences of racial thinking, which vary from prejudice and discrimination to slavery and genocide.

For these reasons, almost every sociologist looks at race from a social perspective. In sociological terms, a **race** is a category of people who share observable physical characteristics and whom others see as being a distinct group. For sociologists, the important issue is not that a person has a specific color of skin or hair of a certain texture. Rather, sociologists are concerned with how people react to these physical characteristics and how these reactions affect individuals in society.

This cover of a 1993 special edition of *Time* magazine featured a computer-generated image of a woman's face to represent what a multiracial United States might look like. *Time*'s "New Eve" blended features from six different racial and ethnic groups.

Reading Check **Summarize** Why do scholars argue that race is a myth?

Quick Lab

Race and the U.S. Census

What can U.S. Census classifications tell us about changing views of race in the United States?

PROCEDURE

1. Conduct library or Internet research to find the racial classifications used in the U.S. Census across time. Use one census from the 1800s, one from the 1900s, as well as the classifications used in the census beginning in 2000.
2. Create a three-column table comparing the racial categories from each census form. Record the census data for each year in a separate column. Be sure to record the correct census year in the top row of each column.
3. Look at the image of the woman on the *Time* magazine cover on the previous page. Based on her physical appearance, how would you identify her race on each census? Circle your response for each year.
4. How would you categorize yourself? Underline your responses for each census year.

ANALYSIS

1. Before 1960, the census taker was responsible for identifying the race of each person taking the census. What do you think census takers based their classifications on?
2. Did you find it easy or difficult to categorize the woman from the *Time* magazine cover or yourself? Explain.
3. Why do you think these categories have changed over time? What factors might cause the categories to change in the next 50 years?

Ethnicity

ACADEMIC VOCABULARY

arbitrary determined by personal preference, notion, or whim

Although the terms *race* and *ethnicity* are often used interchangeably, sociologists assign each term a different meaning. They use the term **ethnicity** to refer to the set of cultural characteristics that distinguishes one group from another group. Like most other societies, American society consists of people of different cultural backgrounds. People who share a common cultural background and a common sense of identity are known as an **ethnic group.** Ethnicity is generally based on such cultural characteristics as national origin, religion, language, customs, and values.

If an ethnic group is to last over time, its cultural beliefs and practices must be passed from generation to generation. Some ethnic groups in the United States have been more successful than others in keeping their heritage alive. For example, Asian Americans and Hispanics tend to have strong ethnic roots. In contrast, many generations of German Americans who were raised in the United States no longer feel deep ties to their ancestral homeland or its cultural traditions. Consequently, they share few cultural characteristics with people in Germany.

In some cases, ethnic identity crosses racial or national boundaries. Jews worldwide are thought to form an ethnic group. This ethnic-group status is based on a shared religious and cultural heritage. Even Jewish people who no longer firmly hold to the religious beliefs of Judaism are linked by factors such as a common history.

Ethnicity and *race* refer to two separate sets of characteristics. Ethnicity is based on cultural traits. On the other hand, race is associated with physical traits. Nevertheless, some ethnic groups are also racially distinct. For example, African Americans are viewed as a racially distinct group in the United States. Many African Americans also share a common ethnic heritage that includes particular foods, types of music, forms of speech, and cultural traits. Similarly, groups such as Mexican Americans, Japanese Americans, Chinese Americans, and Native Americans can be classified both ethnically and racially.

Reading Check **Compare** How does ethnicity differ from race?

Minority Groups

Of course, no particular physical feature or ethnic background is superior or inferior to any other. However, many sociologists recognize that people who hold power in a society may place an arbitrary value on specific characteristics. By establishing the values and norms of society, dominant-group members consciously and unconsciously create a social structure that operates in their favor. Speaking the language most common in a society is one position of power held by the dominant group. Using a conflict theory approach, many sociologists argue that a dominant group's position of power allows its members to enjoy certain privileges, such as better housing, better schools, and higher incomes.

The resources and rewards found in society are limited. Consequently, the privileged position of the dominant group is often gained at the expense of minority groups within the society. In the 1940s, sociologist Louis Wirth defined a **minority group** as a group of people who—because of their physical characteristics or cultural practices—are singled out and unequally treated. As a result, minority group members view themselves as objects of collective discrimination.

You should be aware that, used in this sense, the term *minority* has nothing to do with group size. For example, in South Africa, white people made up about 15 percent of the population during the second half of the 1900s. Yet, for much of that time, they dominated the lives of the other racial groups in the country. Similarly, in many countries across the globe, women are a minority group.

Minority status, then, is not related to group size but to the group's unequal standing in society in relation to a dominant group. Sociologists use the term **dominant group,** not majority, to refer to the group that possesses the ability to discriminate by virtue of its greater power, privilege, and social status in a society. For example, in American society, white people with northern European ancestry, often called white Anglo-Saxon Protestants (WASPs), are the dominant group.

Certain characteristics distinguish minority groups from other groups in society.

- The group possesses identifiable physical or cultural characteristics that differ from those of the dominant group.
- Group members are the recipients of unequal treatment at the hands of the dominant group.
- Membership in the group is an ascribed, or assigned, status.
- Group members share a strong bond and a sense of group loyalty.
- Members tend to practice endogamy—marriage within the group.

To be considered a minority group, a group must exhibit all of the above characteristics. Exhibiting only one or two of the characteristics is not enough. For example, blue eyes are an identifiable physical characteristic, and having blue eyes is an ascribed status. However, blue-eyed people do not face challenges because of their eye color. Consequently, they are not considered a minority group. Haitian Americans in the United States or Aborigines in Australia, on the other hand, are often treated differently because of their ethnic and racial backgrounds. Therefore, they are considered to be minority groups.

Reading Check **Find the Main Idea** What makes a minority group less powerful in society than a dominant group?

CASE STUDY CONNECTION

A Class Divided To teach about discrimination and inequality, Jane Elliot created within her classroom a minority group based on a physical feature—blue eyes.

SECTION 1 Assessment

Reviewing Main Ideas and Vocabulary

1. **Recall** Why do sociologists and scientists reject the notion of biological races?
2. **Identify** Which cultural characteristics form the basis for ethnicity and ethnic groups?
3. **Analyze** How is it possible for a minority group to be in the numerical majority in a society?

Thinking Critically

4. **Explain** Why do sociologists study race if it is a myth?
5. **Draw Conclusions** What might happen to an ethnic group if its members are not allowed to practice their culture?
6. **Summarize** In what ways are minority groups distinguished from the dominant group in a society?
7. **Analyze** Using your notes and a graphic organizer like the one below, discuss the similarities and differences between the concepts of race, ethnicity, and minority groups.

Similarities	Differences
1.	
2.	
3.	

FOCUS ON WRITING

8. **Persuasive** Given the mounting evidence that biological race has little meaning, should sociologists continue to study race? Take a position on this question. Then write a paragraph to persuade sociologists to continue their study of race or to turn their attention elsewhere.

SECTION 2

Patterns of Intergroup Relations

Before You Read

Main Idea

Understanding the concepts and causes of discrimination and prejudice are key to understanding major patterns of minority group treatment.

Reading Focus

1. How do discrimination and prejudice differ?
2. Which approaches do sociologists use to explain the sources of discrimination and prejudice?
3. What are the most common patterns of minority group treatment?

Vocabulary

discrimination
prejudice
legal discrimination
institutionalized discrimination
stereotype
self-fulfilling prophecy
racism
scapegoating
cultural pluralism
assimilation
segregation
subjugation
genocide
ethnic cleansing

TAKING NOTES As you read, use a graphic organizer like this one to take notes on the features and patterns of intergroup relations.

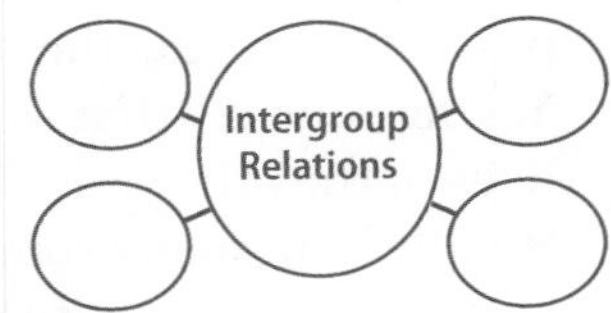

FIGHTING for Social Equality

Elizabeth Eckford, followed by an angry mob, makes her way to an integrated high school in Little Rock, Arkansas, in 1957.

Two men drink from segregated water fountains.

Rosa Parks sits on a bus in 1956 in Birmingham, Alabama, one year after she refused to give up her seat to a white passenger.

SOCIOLOGY CLOSE UP ***What does inequality feel like?*** Picture this: You walk into a restaurant with your friends, and the manager says that you have to sit in a different section simply because you are a member of a certain racial group. That would be unfair, illegal discrimination, right? What if you were prevented from voting, denied a seat on a public bus, fired from your job, or denied an education? You would probably go to court to protect your rights and to hold those who violated them accountable. But what if the courts ruled that it was legal for the government and private businesses to treat you and other people unfairly?

The unfair treatment described above was once a common pattern of intergroup relations in the United States. Some racial and ethnic groups, women, and others were denied basic civil rights for much of U.S. history. They were prevented from voting, denied equal access to education, discriminated against by the government and by businesses, and were kept in an inferior position in society.

So what has changed? Over time, some minority group members joined movements to demand equality and civil rights. To end unfair treatment, they fought for new laws and challenged old, discriminatory ones in court. Their efforts changed social conditions and official government policies that allowed for the unfair treatment of minority groups. In short, these groups proved that unequal and unjust patterns of relations between minority and dominant groups can be changed for the better. ■

Discrimination and Prejudice

The inequality experienced by minority groups is not unique to the American experience. In fact, sociologists have identified a number of common features and patterns of interaction that characterize relationships between dominant and minority groups across the globe. Discrimination and prejudice, for example, are two features common to the minority group experience worldwide. Although these terms are often used interchangeably, discrimination and prejudice are two separate but related conditions. **Discrimination** is the denial of equal treatment to individuals based on their group membership. By definition, discrimination involves *actions.* **Prejudice** is an unsupported generalization about a category of people. Prejudice refers to the *attitudes* that one group holds toward other groups.

Discrimination Discrimination can occur on an individual level or on a societal level. Discriminatory acts by individuals range from name-calling and rudeness to acts of violence. In their most extreme forms, such acts lead to physical harm or even death. For example, between 1882 and 1970, more than 1,170 African Americans were lynched by white mobs in the United States. In many cases, those lynched had committed no crime. Rather, they were attempting to vote, use the same public facilities as white Americans, or had become financially successful.

Societal discrimination can take one of two forms—legal discrimination or institutionalized discrimination. **Legal discrimination** is upheld by law. The apartheid system in South Africa is an example of legal discrimination. South Africa had an elaborate system of laws that distinguished the political, economic, and legal rights of white South Africans from nonwhite South Africans.

Many other countries, including the United States, have had systems of legal discrimination. For example, the Jim Crow laws passed in southern states during the late 1800s required African Americans, and white Americans to use separate public facilities and to attend separate schools. This so-called separate-but-equal doctrine was upheld as constitutional by the U.S. Supreme Court in the 1896 case of *Plessy* v. *Ferguson.*

In 1954, the Court reversed its decision with the *Brown* v. *Board of Education of Topeka, Kansas* decision. Because legal discrimination is based on laws, it can be stopped by changing the offending laws.

Institutionalized discrimination, on the other hand, is an outgrowth of the structure of a society. Over time, unequal access to resources can push minority groups into less-powerful positions in society. Once this occurs, it is not necessary for the dominant group to intentionally discriminate against minority groups. Rather, discrimination and inequality become a part of the social structure to the extent that they become self-perpetuating. This makes institutionalized discrimination extremely difficult to change.

For example, consider what can happen when minority groups are denied access to jobs and housing. Over time, group members may become concentrated in low-income communities. If schools in these communities are poorly funded, students may not acquire the skills needed to compete effectively in the labor market and, as a result, they may have fewer opportunities for advancement. In such a case, inequality becomes a cycle that is difficult to break.

Prejudice Negative forms of prejudice often involve stereotypes. A **stereotype** is an oversimplified, exaggerated, or unfavorable generalization about a group of people. When stereotyping, a person forms an image of a particular group and then applies that image to all members of the group. For example, saying all Irish people are hot-tempered is a stereotype. If individuals are found to differ from the stereotype, they are thought to be exceptions to the rule, rather than proof that the stereotype is wrong.

Stereotyping can have grave consequences for society. If people are told often enough and long enough that they or others are socially, mentally, or physically inferior, they may come to believe it. It does not matter whether the accusations are true. American sociologist W. I. Thomas recognized this phenomenon in his famous theorem: "If [people] define situations as real, they are real in their consequences." In other words, people often act based on what they believe to be true, not necessarily on what is true.

Building on Thomas's work, sociologist Robert K. Merton proposed that a stereotype could become a **self-fulfilling prophecy,** a prediction that results in behavior that makes the prediction come true. If members of a minority group are considered incapable of understanding technical information, they may not be given technical training. As a result, they will lack the skills needed to gain employment in highly technical occupations. This lack of employment in technical fields will then be taken as proof of the group's inability to understand technical information.

For the dominant group in society, prejudice serves as a justification for discrimination. Once people come to believe negative claims about a minority group, they may find it easier to accept open acts of discrimination against the group's members. At times, these prejudicial beliefs can take the form of **racism**—the belief that one's own race or ethnic group is naturally superior to other races or ethnic groups. Throughout history, racism has been used as a justification for atrocities such as slavery and genocide.

Reading Check **Analyze** How is discrimination related to prejudice?

Merton's Patterns of Prejudice

Robert K. Merton argued that prejudice and discrimination are related, but do not always go hand-in-hand. According to Merton, people could combine discrimination and prejudice in four possible ways.

The Active Bigot

- The *active bigot* is prejudiced and openly discriminatory.

The Timid Bigot

- The *timid bigot* is prejudiced, but is afraid to discriminate because of societal pressures.

The Fair-Weather Liberal

- The *fair-weather liberal* is not prejudiced but discriminates anyway because of societal pressure.

The All-Weather Liberal

- The *all-weather liberal* is not prejudiced and does not discriminate.

Sources of Discrimination and Prejudice

Various explanations have been offered for the development of discrimination and prejudice. Sociologists often organize these explanations into three broad categories: sociological, psychological, and economic.

Sociological Explanations Most sociological explanations of discrimination and prejudice focus on the social environment. This environment includes the accepted norms of a society and the process through which these norms are learned—socialization. In some societies, prejudices are embedded in social norms that describe how members of society are expected to relate to members of certain out-groups. People become prejudiced simply by internalizing these norms.

Even if prejudice is not a part of the culture of society at large, it may be a norm of groups within society. People often become prejudiced to maintain their group membership. They may also become prejudiced through their identification with a reference group that encourages and supports such beliefs.

Psychological Explanations By studying individual behavior, psychologists hope to gain a better understanding of prejudice and discrimination. One psychological explanation suggests that people are prejudiced because they have a specific personality type. In a survey of American society, a team of psychologists lead by Theodor Adorno found that prejudiced people often show characteristics of what Adorno called an authoritarian personality. Authoritarians are strongly conformist, have a great respect for authority, and are likely to follow the orders of an authority figure. They also exhibit a great deal of anger and tend to blame others for their problems.

Another psychological explanation suggests that prejudice may be the product of frustration and anger. When individuals have problems but cannot confront the real causes of those problems, they often turn their frustration and anger on innocent groups. The practice of placing the blame for one's troubles on an innocent individual or group is called **scapegoating.** The process of scapegoating sometimes gives people a sense of superiority when they are feeling powerless.

A number of social conditions make it likely that racial and ethnic minority groups will become the objects of scapegoating. First, they are easily identified as different because of physical features, language, style of dress, or religious practices. Second, they often lack power in society and may be unlikely to fight back. Third, they may be concentrated in a specific geographic area and therefore are easily accessible and an easy target. Finally, minority groups may have been the target of past scapegoating, so a certain amount of hostility toward them may already exist among members of the dominant group.

Economic Explanations According to economic explanations, prejudice and discrimination arise out of competition for scarce resources. For example, during the second half of the 1800s large numbers of Chinese work ers immigrated to the West Coast of the United States. In the beginning, they were welcomed as an inexpensive labor source. When jobs became scarce many white workers began to view Chinese workers as economic competitors. Many white Americans reacted with violence, and in time, laws were passed to restrict Chinese immigration.

Conflict theorists suggest that the dominant group, to protect its position, encourages competition for resources among minority groups. This competition creates a split labor market, in which workers are set against each other along racial and ethnic lines. In the struggle for jobs, the various minority groups may come to fear, distrust, and hate one another.

Reading Check **Identify Supporting Details**
What are the key points of the three explanations for the sources of discrimination and prejudice?

Patterns of Minority Group Treatment

Official policies toward minority groups within a society vary widely. The most common patterns of minority treatment include cultural pluralism, assimilation, legal protection, segregation, subjugation, population transfer, and extermination. Look at the visual display on the following page and note that these patterns may be placed on a continuum that runs from acceptance to rejection.

Cultural Pluralism One response to ethnic and racial diversity is **cultural pluralism.** This policy allows each group within society to keep its unique cultural identity. Switzerland provides an example of cultural pluralism in action. Switzerland has three official languages—French, German, and Italian—one language for each of its three major ethnic groups. These groups live together peacefully and are extremely loyal to Switzerland. Furthermore, none of the groups has taken on a dominant or minority role in Swiss society.

Assimilation In many societies, racial and ethnic minorities attempt to hold on to some of their unique cultural features. However, official policies do not always favor such efforts. For example, at one time in the United States, it was hoped that the various groups that make up American society could be blended into a single people with a common, homogeneous culture. This hope formed the basis of the image of the United States as a "melting pot." The blending of culturally distinct groups into a single group with a common culture and identity is called **assimilation.**

In most societies, some assimilation occurs voluntarily. Over time, different groups within a society exchange many cultural traits as a result of daily interaction and intermarriage. On the other hand, attempts to force assimilation often lead to conflict. For example, in the 1980s the Bulgarian government waged a long campaign to forcibly assimilate the country's large Turkish minority. This campaign involved forbidding the Turks from practicing their religion, from using their language, and from celebrating their culture. Thousands of Turks were reportedly killed or tortured in conflicts over these assimilation policies.

Legal Protection Many countries have taken legal steps to ensure that the rights of minority groups are protected. The Civil Rights Act of 1964 and the Voting Rights Act of 1965 are examples of such legislation in the United States. The United Kingdom adopted similar legislation in 1965 with the passage of the Race Relations Act. Affirmative action programs in the United States are another example of legal efforts to achieve equal rights. These programs are designed to correct past imbalances in educational and employment opportunities available to minority groups.

Affirmative action programs generally give preference to racial and ethnic minorities and women for jobs and school admission. In recent years, criticism has grown over affirmative action policies. Critics charge that they are a form of "reverse discrimination." Recent legal challenges have been made against affirmative action, and government institutions have been reconsidering their policies.

ACADEMIC VOCABULARY

ghettos sections of a city where minority groups live, often because of economic or social pressure

Segregation Policies that physically separate a minority group from the dominant group are referred to as **segregation.** Under segregation, the minority group is forbidden to live in the same areas as the dominant group and cannot use the same public facilities. Sociologists recognize two types of segregation. De jure segregation is based on laws. Segregation based on informal norms is called de facto segregation.

History provides many examples of segregation. For example, during the Middle Ages, European Jews were forced to live in walled-off communities called ghettos. Segregation was practiced legally in the United States until the 1960s. As a result of earlier segregation policies, many American minority groups are still concentrated in specific areas of cities.

Subjugation Some countries maintain control over groups through force. This practice is called **subjugation.** The most extreme form of subjugation is slavery, the ownership of one person by another. Examples of slavery can be found throughout history.

South Africa's system of apartheid is a recent example of subjugation. Apartheid, which literally means "apartness," called for the legal segregation of all groups within the country. Political and economic power rested with the smaller white population and was rigidly maintained through force. International opposition eventually brought about the dismantling of the system in the mid-1990s.

Population Transfer Sometimes the dominant group in a society separates itself from a minority group by transferring the minority population to a new territory. This policy can be carried out indirectly or directly. With indirect transfer, the dominant group makes life for minorities so miserable that they simply leave. By contrast, direct transfer involves using force to move people to new locations, sometimes within the same country. Two examples of direct transfer from U.S. history are the resettlement of Native Americans on reservations during the 1800s and the placement of nearly 120,000 Japanese Americans in internment camps during World War II.

Direct population transfers may also involve expelling a group from a nation. For example, in the 1750s the British authorities in Canada expelled the Acadians, a French-speaking minority, from Nova Scotia. A more recent example is the forceful removal of the Asian population from Uganda in 1972.

INTERGROUP RELATIONS

QUICK FACTS

The patterns of intergroup relations can be seen as a continuum of behavior and treatment that ranges from acceptance to rejection.

Acceptance

Cultural Pluralism	Ethnic, religious, and racial variety encouraged (Example: Switzerland) 
Assimilation	Culturally distinct groups blended into a single group with a common culture (Example: United States)
Legal Protection	Minority rights protected by law (Example: United States after the passage of the Civil Rights Act of 1964)
Subjugation	Dominant group controls every aspect of minority group life through force (Example: South Africa under apartheid)
Segregation	Minority group physically separated from the dominant group (Example: United States until the 1960s)
Population Transfer	Dominant group moves minority group to new locations within or outside of the country (Example: Relocation of Native Americans to reservations) 
Extermination	Dominant group attempts to destroy minority group (Example: The Holocaust) 

Rejection

Extermination The most extreme pattern of intergroup relations is the extermination, or elimination, of a minority group. When the goal of extermination is the destruction—in whole or in part—of a national, racial, ethnic, or religious group, it is referred to as **genocide.** The phrase "in whole or in part" is significant. Perpetrators of genocide need not intend to destroy an entire group. The intent to destroy a substantial segment of a group, such as all of the group members that live in a particular region, still qualifies as genocide.

The twentieth century's most notorious case of genocide occurred in Europe. Soon after gaining power over Germany in 1933, Adolf Hitler and his Nazi Party began to persecute German Jews. During World War II, German conquests brought nearly all of Europe's 9 million Jews under Nazi control. In the largest genocide in world history, the Nazis attempted to exterminate the entire Jewish population of Europe. This atrocity became known as the Holocaust. In all, Hitler's Nazi forces murdered some 6 million Jews. The Nazis also murdered as many as 5 million other people from groups they viewed as inferior and undesirable, such as Slavs, Roma (Gypsies), Jehovah's Witnesses, Communists, and people with mental or physical disabilities.

Another notorious twentieth century genocide occurred in the African nation of Rwanda. In 1994 long-simmering tensions between Tutsi and Hutu ethnic groups erupted in violence. In just three months, the Hutus killed more than 800,000 Tutsis and moderate Hutus. Some 2 million people became refugees and fled Rwanda, where food shortages and diseases killed thousands, despite international humanitarian aid.

In the 1990s, some dominant groups combined population transfer and extermination in a practice called **ethnic cleansing.** This practice involves removing a group from a particular area through terror, expulsion, and mass murder. For example, in 1998 the government of the European nation of Serbia began a campaign to drive out or kill about 1.7 million ethnic Albanians in the province of Kosovo. Within a year, more than 1.5 million ethnic Albanians had been expelled from their homes. As many as 10,000 had been killed. Only armed intervention by North Atlantic Treaty Organization (NATO) forces prevented Serbian forces from achieving their goal.

Unfortunately, genocide is not a thing of the past. In July 2007 the International Criminal Court charged Sudanese president Omar Hassan al-Bashir with carrying out genocide against African peoples living in the Darfur region of western Sudan. Despite the efforts of an African Union peacekeeping force, the brutal campaign killed an estimated 400,000 people and forced another 2.5 million to flee from their homes.

Reading Check **Draw Conclusions** What features of cultural pluralism do you think are missing in a society where extermination occurs?

SECTION 2 Assessment

Reviewing Main Ideas and Vocabulary

1. **Identify** What are the major forms of discrimination?
2. **Describe** What is a stereotype, and how do stereotypes influence prejudice?
3. **Contrast** In what ways is cultural pluralism different from assimilation?

Critical Thinking

4. **Explain** What are the key points of the economic explanations for discrimination and prejudice?
5. **Draw Conclusions** What is scapegoating, and what functions does it serve?
6. **Develop** What are some measures that people in a society could take to prevent genocide?
7. **Analyze** Using your notes and a graphic organizer like this one, identify the key features of the seven patterns of minority group treatment discussed in this section.

Pattern	Key Features

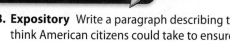

FOCUS ON WRITING

8. **Expository** Write a paragraph describing the steps you think American citizens could take to ensure that a positive form of cultural pluralism develops in the United States over the next 50 years.

SECTION 3

Minority Groups in the United States

Before You Read

Main Idea
The United States is home to a remarkable number of diverse minority groups, each with its own distinctive history and challenges.

Reading Focus
1. What is the American dilemma?
2. How did the civil rights movement affect African Americans?
3. What major challenges face Hispanics?
4. Why have Asian Americans been called a "model minority"?
5. How have government policies affected Native Americans?
6. What unique problems do other minorities face?

Vocabulary
environmental racism
pan-Indianism
white ethnics
anti-Semitism

TAKING NOTES As you read, use a graphic organizer like this one to take notes on minority groups in the United States.

Minority Group	
Group	Conditions

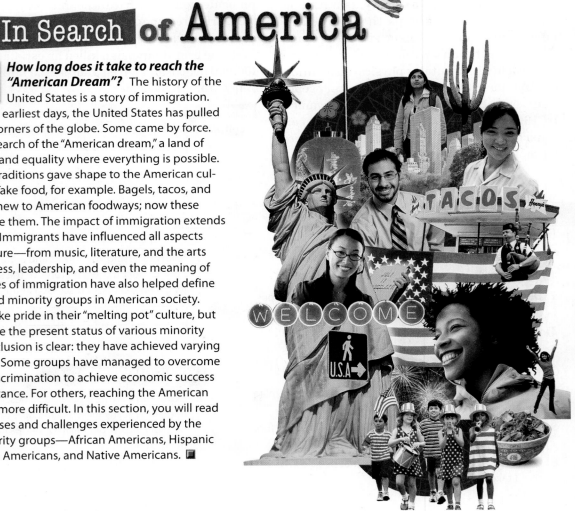

In Search of America

SOCIOLOGY CLOSE UP ***How long does it take to reach the "American Dream"?*** The history of the United States is a story of immigration. From the nation's earliest days, the United States has pulled people from all corners of the globe. Some came by force. Others came in search of the "American dream," a land of freedom, justice, and equality where everything is possible.

Immigrants' traditions gave shape to the American cultural landscape. Take food, for example. Bagels, tacos, and pizza were once new to American foodways; now these dishes help define them. The impact of immigration extends far beyond food. Immigrants have influenced all aspects of American culture—from music, literature, and the arts to science, business, leadership, and even the meaning of democracy. Waves of immigration have also helped define the dominant and minority groups in American society.

Americans take pride in their "melting pot" culture, but when we examine the present status of various minority groups, one conclusion is clear: they have achieved varying levels of success. Some groups have managed to overcome prejudice and discrimination to achieve economic success and social acceptance. For others, reaching the American dream has been more difficult. In this section, you will read about the successes and challenges experienced by the largest U.S. minority groups—African Americans, Hispanic Americans, Asian Americans, and Native Americans. ■

The American Dilemma

In 1944 Swedish sociologist Gunnar Myrdal examined the issue of race relations in the United States. He came to the conclusion that the American people faced a great psychological and cultural conflict. He called this conflict "an American dilemma." A gap existed, he said, between what Americans claim to believe and how they actually behave. Although they express support for equality, freedom, dignity of the individual, and inalienable rights, Americans have not always lived up to these ideals. The enslavement and segregation of African Americans, the establishment of American Indian reservations, and the internment of Japanese Americans during World War II are but a few examples of the denial of these ideals.

The conflict between ideals and actions has been part of the American experience since the arrival of white settlers on the North American continent in the late 1500s. When the original English colonists came to this land, they brought with them the cultural values of English society. As the colonists established dominance in the new land, their values became the standards for a new society.

These early settlers also provided an image for the dominant group in American society—white, of Anglo-Saxon (northern European) descent, and Protestant. This white Anglo-Saxon Protestant, or WASP, image does not reflect the country's multicultural reality. Yet this image has been the yardstick against which some have compared other groups in the United States.

For the most part, minority groups have prospered in relation to how closely they adapt to the WASP image. Those who can more easily adapt are accepted into mainstream American society relatively quickly. Immigrants from heavily Protestant countries such as Sweden, the Netherlands, and Germany generally gained dominant status within one generation. Other groups—such as African Americans, Hispanic Americans, Native Americans, and Asian Americans—have had more difficulty gaining acceptance. The remainder of this section focuses on the current conditions under which various minority groups live in the United States.

Reading Check **Draw Conclusions** How does the American dilemma affect minorities?

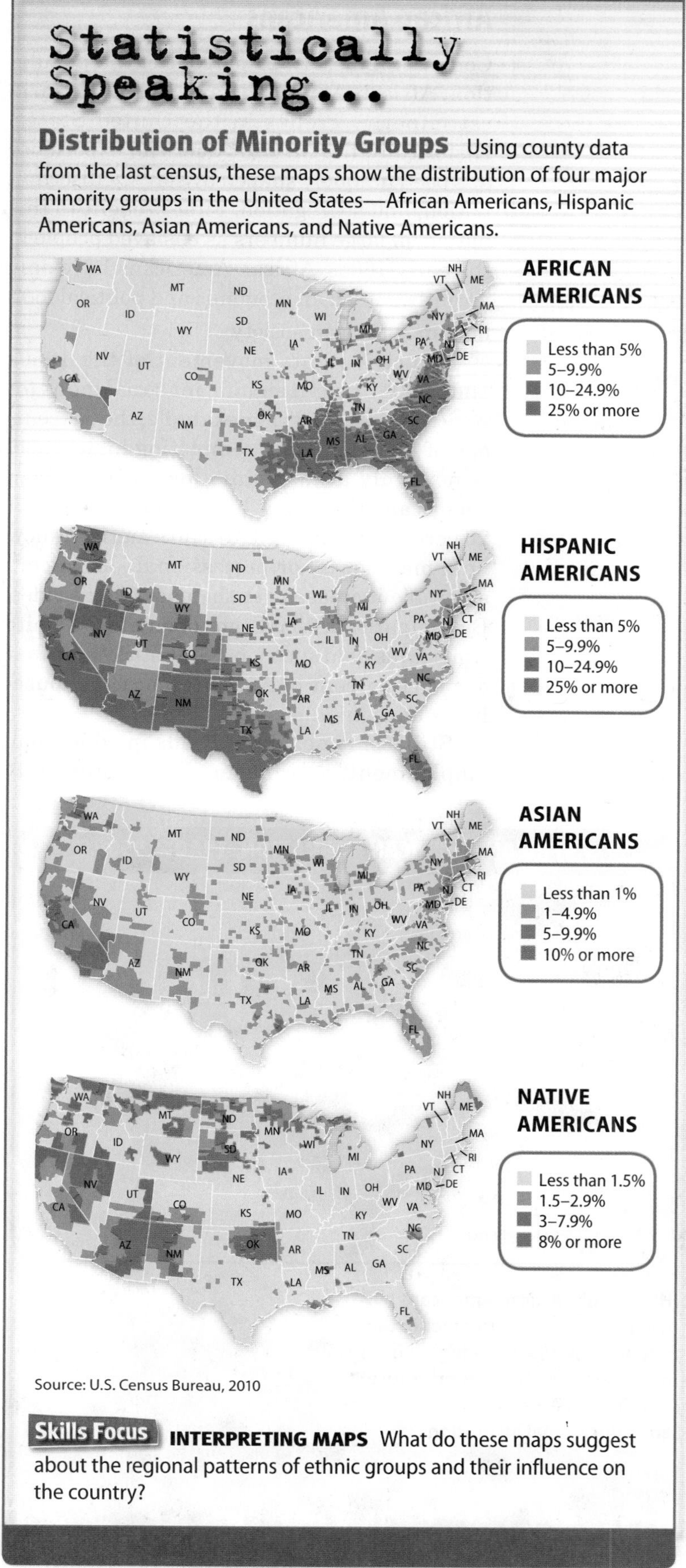

Statistically Speaking...

Distribution of Minority Groups Using county data from the last census, these maps show the distribution of four major minority groups in the United States—African Americans, Hispanic Americans, Asian Americans, and Native Americans.

Source: U.S. Census Bureau, 2010

Skills Focus **INTERPRETING MAPS** What do these maps suggest about the regional patterns of ethnic groups and their influence on the country?

African Americans

Comprising nearly 14 percent of the population, African Americans are one of the largest minority groups in the United States. Historically, the African American experience has been uniquely shaped by slavery, discrimination, and segregation. First brought to this nation in large numbers as enslaved people in the early 1600s, African Americans have only recently gained an economic and political foothold in American society.

The civil rights movement of the 1950s and 1960s brought significant social gains for African Americans. For example, the percentage of the population completing high school is now only a few points lower for African Americans than for white Americans. About 26 percent of employed African Americans now hold managerial or professional jobs, a considerable increase over the past two decades. By comparison, 35 percent of employed white Americans hold such jobs. Statistics show that some 41 percent of African American households have middle-class incomes.

Still, some negative trends in education, employment, and income have potentially far-reaching consequences. For example, although more African Americans attend college today than in the 1960s, the percentage of African Americans graduating from college is slightly more than half that of white Americans. This disparity contributes to an income and employment gap between African Americans and whites. The average African American family income is about 60 percent of white family income, and the percentage of African American families living below the poverty level is three times that of white families. This has a significant effect on African American children, 31 percent of whom live in poverty. Finally, the unemployment rate among African American workers is more than twice as high as that of white workers.

These statistics represent a serious social problem, and solutions are being sought. The process is being aided by the active role that African Americans are taking in the political process. Since the passage of the Voting Rights Act in 1965, the number of elected African American officials has jumped from 200 to more than 9,000 in 2000. For example, in 2004 Barack Obama of Illinois became the fifth African American elected to the U.S. Senate. In 2008, Obama became the first African American president of the United States. He was reelected in 2012 to his second term.

Many of today's African American leaders are working to improve the black community. Organizations such as the National Urban League strive to empower African Americans through leadership and education programs. Some African Americans are also working to improve education, health care, and the criminal justice system. Others are leading grassroots efforts to stop **environmental racism,** or racial bias in environmental policies and practices, such as targeting minority communities as sites for toxic waste disposal and polluting industries.

Reading Check **Summarize** What challenges face African Americans today?

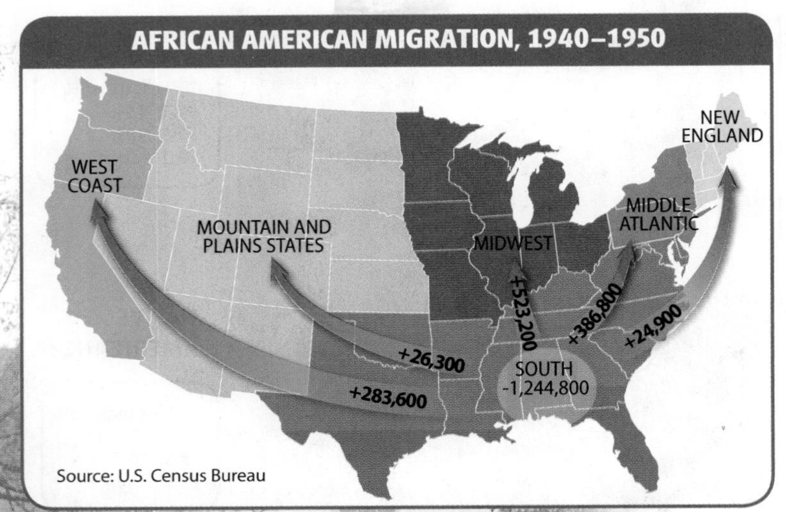

Historically, African Americans have used a number of strategies in the struggle for equality, ranging from moving in search of opportunity to the founding of African American colleges and educational institutions.

Hispanic Americans

Hispanic Americans trace their heritage to Spain or Spanish-speaking Latin America, regardless of race. According to the U.S. Census Bureau, more than 55 million Hispanics and Latinos called the United States home in 2015. This figure represents a 2.1 percent increase between 2013 and 2014. The Hispanic population has grown so fast that Hispanics have replaced African Americans as the country's largest minority group.

Until the 1960s the Hispanic population in the United States consisted primarily of people of Mexican, Puerto Rican, and Cuban ancestry. Today these three groups make up the largest Hispanic groups in the United States. Close to 64 percent of Hispanics are of Mexican descent. With 9 percent of the total Hispanic population, Puerto Ricans are the second-most-populous Hispanic group. More than 1.5 million Cuban Americans make up the third-largest group of Hispanics.

In the 1960s immigrants from Central and South America and the Caribbean began to swell the number of Hispanics living in the United States. A smaller portion of the Hispanic population trace their roots to nations such as Guatemala, El Salvador, Nicaragua, Costa Rica, Argentina, Honduras, and the Dominican Republic. The pie graph on this page shows the percentage of the Hispanic population by area of origin.

Like other immigrant groups, many Hispanics came to the United States in search of political freedom and economic opportunities. Since the 1960s, many Hispanic immigrants have entered the United States through legal means. Others have arrived illegally. The U.S. Department of Homeland Security estimates that as of 2015, there were more than 11 million unauthorized immigrants in the United States. The vast majority of these immigrants are Hispanic. The actual number of unauthorized immigrants—both Hispanic and non-Hispanic—is likely much higher today.

By 2020 the number of Hispanics in the United States is estimated to reach 60.4 million. With their rising numbers, Hispanics have gained increasing political power in recent years. Hispanics currently hold more than 6,000 elected and appointed offices and control large voting blocs in several states. These states include California, New York, Texas, Illinois, and Florida.

Despite these gains, Hispanics struggle in areas such as employment and education. The poverty rate among Hispanics is more than twice that among white Americans. Moreover, Hispanics have the highest high school dropout rate of any minority group in the United States. Such distressing trends are due, in part, to the poor English language skills of recent immigrants. For these Hispanics, addressing educational and language needs is central to making the American dream a reality.

Reading Check **Identify Main Ideas** Why are Hispanics becoming more politically powerful?

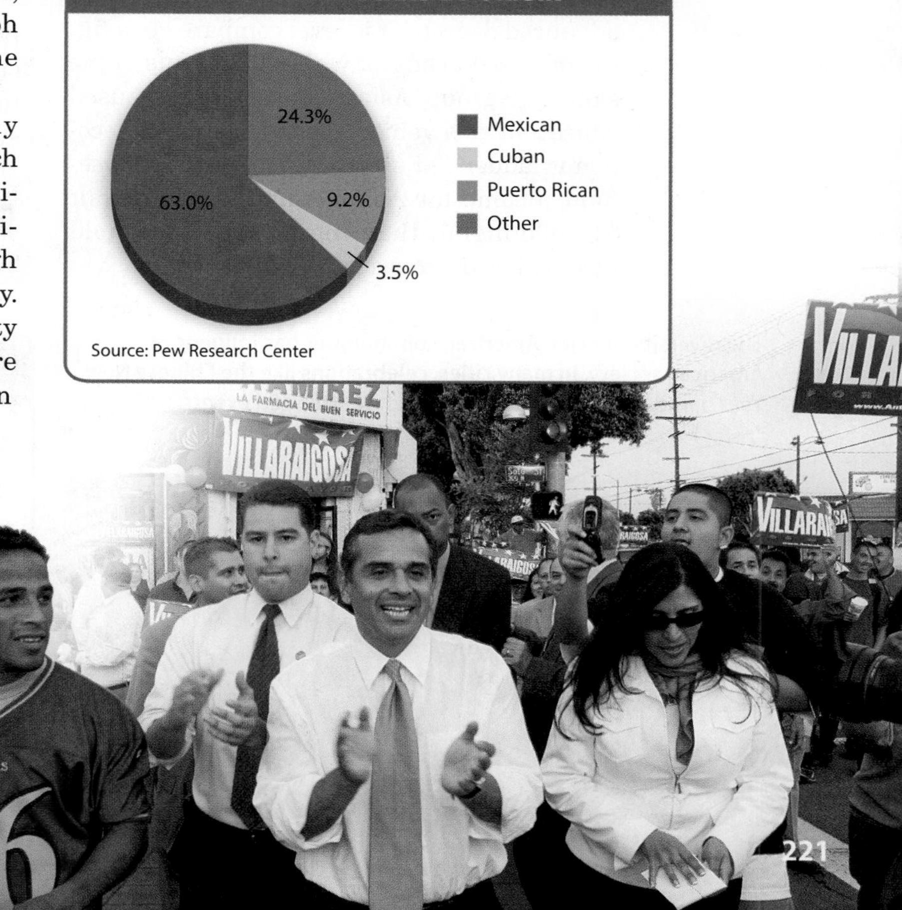

Hispanic Americans come from a variety of national backgrounds. In recent years, their growing numbers have led to increased political power.

Asian Americans

Like Hispanics, Asian Americans come from a variety of national backgrounds. Immigrants from almost every Asian nation have settled in the United States over the past 150 years. The earliest to arrive were from China and Japan. More recent immigrants have come from the Philippines, Korea, Vietnam, Cambodia, Laos, India, and Pakistan.

Representing close to 6 percent of the total U.S. population, Asian Americans are the country's third-largest ethnic minority group. These Americans are also the fastest-growing ethnic group in the United States. In 1990 the U.S. census placed the size of the Asian American population at more than 7 million. By the 2000 census, that figure had grown to more than 14.9 million. Based on current growth rates, the U.S. Census Bureau projects that Asian Americans will make up 8 percent of the U.S. population by the year 2050.

Much has been written about the commitment to education exhibited by many Asian Americans. For example, Asian American students consistently achieve high scores on both the verbal and mathematical sections of the SAT Reasoning Test. Moreover, 2012 figures show that 49 percent of Asian Americans over the age of 25 have a bachelor's or more advanced degree. This level compares to a figure of 28.6 percent for white Americans in the same age group. Asian Americans have used education as a vehicle for moving up the economic ladder. For example, the median household income for Asian Americans is about $16,000 higher than the median household income for all Americans.

The success of Asian Americans in achieving economic security and social acceptance has led some to call them a "model minority." But many Asian Americans resent this label. It hides the fact that the group has faced severe hardships in its quest for acceptance. The path to economic success has been complicated by anti-Asian laws, open violence, and discrimination. Perhaps the most notable of these incidents was the forced relocation of more than 110,000 Japanese Americans to special prisons called internment camps during World War II. Many lost their homes, jobs, and businesses, in addition to their freedom.

Asian Americans argue that the label "model minority" masks huge differences in the cultures and experiences of the various national groups that make up the Asian American population. Poverty, for example, does not affect all Asian American groups in the same way. Today poverty is unusual among Chinese and Japanese Americans. By contrast, Americans from Southeast Asian nations, such as Laos and Cambodia, experience high levels of poverty. Like many new arrivals to the United States, immigrants from Southeast Asia who arrived in the 1980s and 1990s faced language barriers that confined them to low-paying jobs.

For Asian Americans struggling with poverty, the "model minority" stereotype can be emotionally damaging. Compared to other minority groups, Asian Americans suffer from higher rates of stress, depression, mental illness, and suicide attempts.

Reading Check **Summarize** Why do Asian Americans reject the label "model minority"?

The diversity of Asian American communities has influenced American society. In many cities, celebrations like the Chinese New Year parade below, have become widely attended events.

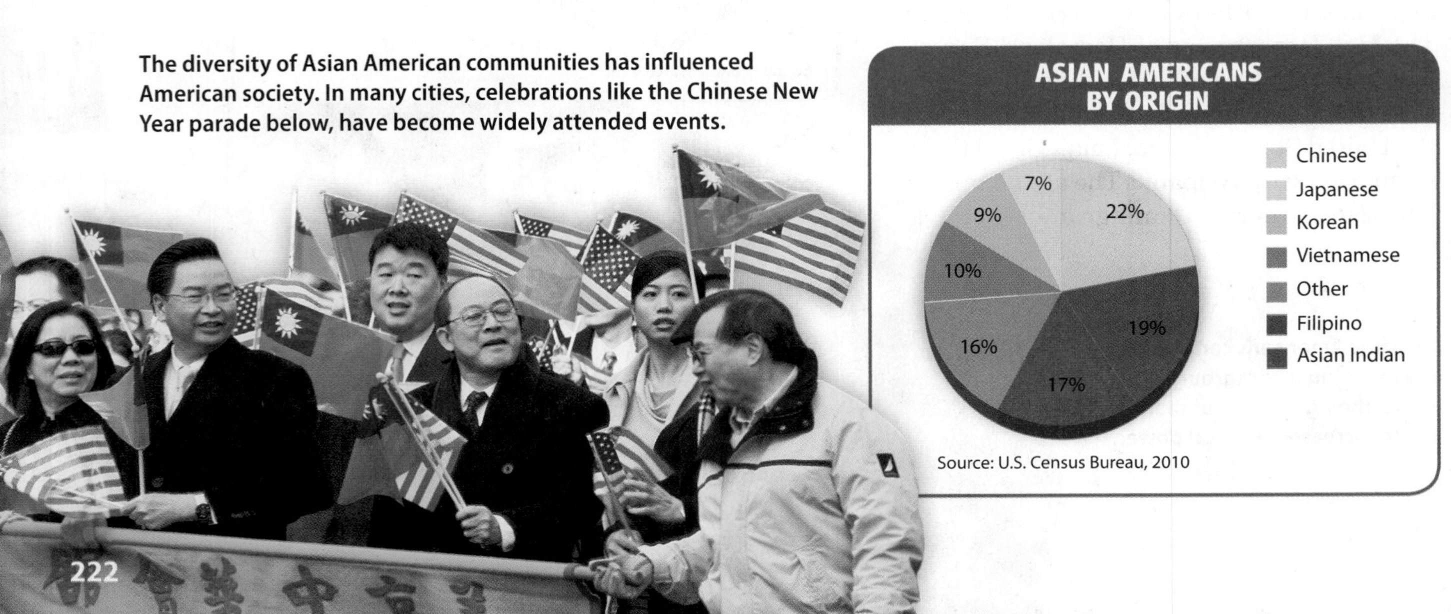

Native Americans

When Europeans first set foot on the shores of what is now the United States, the Native American population numbered in the millions. These people, the ancestors of Native Americans today, were divided into hundreds of nations, each with its own history and culture. However, disease, warfare, and the destruction of traditional ways of life reduced the Native American population to about 228,000 by 1890.

The challenges now faced by Native Americans, in large part, are the legacy of a history of changing U.S. government policies. During our nation's early years, the government took Native American lands by force and through treaties. In the late 1800s a new policy made Native Americans wards of the U.S. government and they were moved to reservations.

Government policies also aimed to assimilate Native Americans into white society. Native American men were encouraged to become farmers, even though many were traditionally hunters or herders. Tribal lands were redistributed to male heads of households, thus disrupting the communal nature typical of many Native American societies. Children were separated from their parents and sent to boarding schools. Native Americans who lived away from the reservations and adopted the ways of white society were rewarded with U.S. citizenship. However, the rest of the Native American population—about one-third of the total—did not gain citizenship until Congress passed the Indian Citizenship Act in 1924.

Today about 5.1 million Native Americans live in the United States. About 55 percent of Native Americans live on reservations. Another 45 percent live in or near urban areas. Of all the nation's minority groups, Native Americans—both on and off of the reservations—face the greatest challenges.

Statistics concerning Native American employment, poverty, health, and education reflect the dire nature of these challenges. For example, about 50 percent of the Native American workforce on or near the reservations is unemployed, and some 25 percent of all Native Americans live below the poverty level. In terms of health, the rate of alcohol-related deaths among Native Americans is about 7 times higher than among the general population and suicide is the second leading cause of death among Native Americans aged 15 to 24 years old. Finally, although about 76 percent of Native Americans aged 25 and over have graduated from high school, less than 14 percent have graduated from college.

In spite of such obstacles, Native Americans continue to fight to retain their cultures and improve their communities. Toward this end, one significant trend is **pan-Indianism,** a social and political movement that unites culturally distinct Native American nations to work together on issues that affect all Native Americans. Economic changes are also benefitting Native Americans. A reinterpretation of federal law in the 1990s has made it possible for Native American nations to open lucrative businesses on their reservations. Top among these are cigarette shops, bingo halls, and casinos.

Reading Check **Draw Conclusions** How might pan-Indianism enable Native Americans to address economic and social challenges?

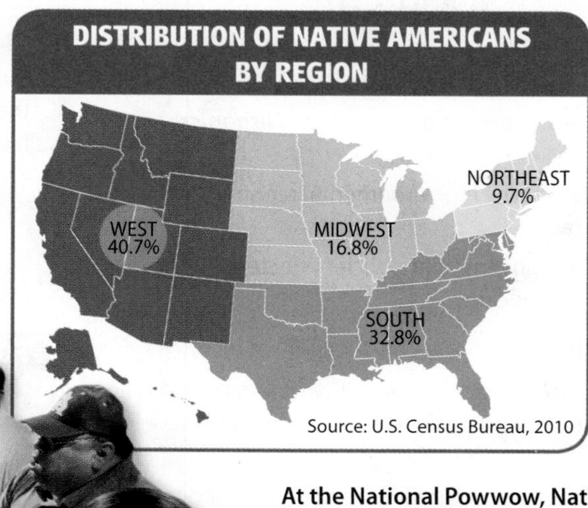

At the National Powwow, Native Americans from across the country celebrate their cultures with music, dance, and educational programs.

Other Minorities

The United States is home to a great many other minority groups, including white ethnic groups, Jewish Americans, and Arab Americans. Each has faced similar challenges in American society.

White Ethnics During the 1800s and 1900s, **white ethnics**—immigrants from the mainly Catholic countries of Ireland, Italy, France, and Poland, and Greece—entered the United States in great numbers. Once on American soil, they faced open discrimination at the hands of the white Protestant majority.

Many white ethnics responded to discrimination by assimilating rapidly into mainstream society. Some adopted American-sounding names and required their children to speak English at home as well as in public. Other white ethnics banded together in ethnic neighborhoods in an attempt to hold on to their ethnic identities.

Jewish Americans American Jews differ from other ethnic groups in that many focus their ethnic identity on their religion, Judaism. In 2012 about 5.5 million Jews lived in the United States. Many trace their ancestry to the more than 2 million Jews who arrived in the United States between 1880 and 1920 from countries in Eastern Europe, such as Russia, Poland, and Hungary. Others trace their heritage to Germany. German Jews arrived in two phases—just prior to Eastern European Jews and just after Adolf Hitler's rise to power in the late 1930s.

Because many German Jews were highly-educated and spoke English, they assimilated quickly into American society. Still, Eastern European and German Jews alike faced long periods of **anti-Semitism,** or discrimination and prejudice against Jews. In spite of anti-Semitism, Jewish Americans have achieved success in many areas—the arts and sciences, education, medicine, business, and politics.

Arab Americans The more than 3.6 million Arab Americans living in the United States trace their heritage to one of 22 Arab nations, including Egypt, Iraq, Lebanon, Morocco, and Syria, as well as the region of Palestine. Arab Americans are remarkably diverse, speaking a variety of languages and following no single religion. Many are Catholic, some are Protestant, and many others are Muslim.

Arab Americans have been a part of the American story since the 1880s. Recently, times have brought challenges, however. Following the terrorist attacks on the World Trade Center and the Pentagon on September 11, 2001, many Arab Americans became unjustly suspect in this country. Hate crimes and other forms of discrimination against Arab Americans escalated.

Reading Check **Summarize** What challenges have faced other minorities in the United States?

SECTION 3 Assessment

Reviewing Main Ideas and Vocabulary

1. **Recall** What groups of people does the term *Hispanics* refer to?
2. **Identify Main Ideas** Why is environmental racism an issue for African Americans?
3. **Describe** How have government policies affected the life chances of Native Americans?

Thinking Critically

4. **Compare and Contrast** In what ways have the historical experiences of minority groups been similar, and how have they differed?
5. **Predict** How might current trends in immigration and the growth of minority groups change the minority group experience in the United States?
6. **Summarize** Using your notes and a graphic organizer like the one below, summarize the gains made and challenges faced by minority groups in the United States.

Minority Group	
Gains	Challenges

7. **Descriptive** Write a paragraph describing what you think Americans would have to do both individually and collectively to resolve the so-called American dilemma.

CURRENT RESEARCH IN SOCIOLOGY

Being Arab American after the 9-11 Attacks

For Arab Americans, the trauma caused by the September 11, 2001, terrorist attacks on the United States was heightened by personal assaults on some Arab American communities. Within hours of the attacks, hate crimes and other forms of discrimination were directed at Arab Americans. Although only a handful of individuals committed such acts, the acts highlighted the unfortunate fact that most other Americans knew very little about Arab Americans.

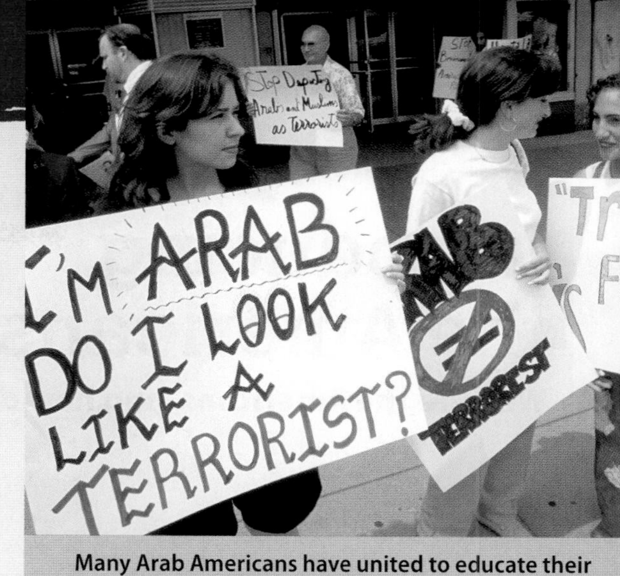

Many Arab Americans have united to educate their fellow citizens about Arab American culture and to dispel stereotypes of Arab Americans as terrorists.

What has life been like for Arab Americans living in the United States since September 11, 2001? To answer this question, the Detroit Arab American Study surveyed Arab Americans living in the Detroit, Michigan, metropolitan area. Detroit is the home of one of the oldest and largest Arab American communities in the United States.

The study was a collaborative project conducted by researchers from the University of Michigan–Dearborn with the help of more than 20 secular, religious, and social service organizations. Together, they aimed to build a body of accurate information about the Arab American experience, which could be used to correct misinformation and stereotypes about Arab Americans.

On January 23, 2007, vandals defaced a mosque at the Islamic Center of America in Dearborn, Michigan, with graffiti.

In all, the researchers completed face-to-face interviews with 1,016 Arab Americans and Chaldeans (Iraqi Christians) between July and December 2003. They also interviewed 508 members of the general population in and around Detroit.

Fifteen percent of Arab Americans said they had experienced discrimination following the September 11 attacks. Verbal insults—"Go back to where you came from!" or "How's Osama doing?"—were the most common forms of abuse. Other study participants reported workplace discrimination, unfair targeting by law enforcement or airport security, and vandalism (Baker, et al., 2004).

Acts of physical violence, however, were rare. Only 3 percent reported having experienced a "serious negative event." Such events included a relative being badly beaten or a family's being threatened at gunpoint. Some of the study's other findings about the Arab American community may also interest you.

- The study's respondents were deeply religious; 58 percent identified themselves as Christian and 42 percent as Muslim.
- The majority of respondents were naturalized U.S. citizens; 75 percent were born outside of the United States, and 79 percent were U.S. citizens.
- A similar percentage of Arab Americans (48 percent) and the general population (44 percent) reported feeling less secure after the September 11 attacks.
- Compared to 11 percent of Christian Arabs, 42 percent of Muslim Arabs reported feeling like their religion was not respected by mainstream American society.

Thinking Critically

1. **Analyze** Which of the study's findings do you find most interesting? Explain.
2. **Discuss** How do you think the study's findings could be used to fight stereotypes or misinformation?

Lab
Applying What You've Learned

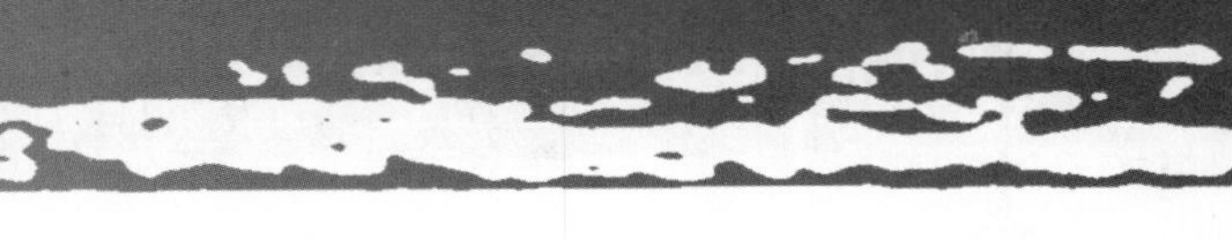

Introducing the Americans

Who are the Americans, and how did we get here?

Reading and Activity Workbook
Use the workbook to complete this lab.

1. Introduction

This lab will help you better understand the concepts of race and ethnicity in the United States. You will work in small groups to research and create an exhibit tracing the immigration history of one of the eight ethnic and racial populations discussed in this chapter. One group will be challenged to create an exhibit documenting "The Newest Americans" to show current trends in immigration.

Each exhibit will consist of an illustrated time line and two posters. Once you have completed both parts of the assignment, you will be asked to present your exhibit to the class. To complete this lab, follow the steps below.

- Following your teacher's instructions, organize the class into nine student groups.
- Your teacher will assign eight groups one of the ethnic and racial groups discussed in this chapter: African Americans, Hispanics, Asian Americans, Native Americans, white Anglo-Saxon Protestants, white ethnics, Jewish Americans, and Arab Americans. The last group will be assigned "The Newest Americans," and asked to research and report on issues facing two immigrant or refugee groups in the United States today.
- Work with students in your group to review the chapter material on race, ethnicity, and minority groups. Take notes on key concepts and on any main points about the ethnic or racial group you were assigned.
- Read the entire lab with your group. Brainstorm a list of topics that require additional research and develop a plan for creating your exhibit.
- Conduct additional Internet or library research on your assigned ethnic and racial group and topics.
- Collect the following materials: butcher-block paper, pens, colored pencils, scissors, and tape. Your group is now ready to create your exhibits.

2. Illustrating Your Time Line

Working as a group, create an illustrated time line documenting major dates, groups of people, and events surrounding the immigration history of the group you have been assigned. Be sure to indicate major phases of immigration and use complete sentences to clearly label dates. Use illustrations, photographs, and maps to illustrate your time line.

3. Creating an Immigration Poster

Choose one of the groups from your time line and create a poster that explains why and how that group arrived in North America. If you have been assigned Native Americans, be sure to discuss different theories about how Native Americans populated North America. For other groups, be sure to describe what factors pushed them from their places of origin or pulled them to a new land. For example, did your group come by their own choice or did historical circumstances force their migration to North America? Did they come to escape violence or oppression? Were they looking for religious freedom or economic opportunity? Use the Sample Immigration Poster Worksheet on the next page to help you select information for your poster.

4. Creating a Culture Poster

Immigrant groups are changed by living in the United States and, in turn, they change American culture. How has your group contributed to American society and culture? Work with your classmates to create a poster that answers this question. Pick four of the areas listed below to include on your poster. For each area, describe the unique contribution of your group with a specific example. Illustrate your poster with photographs, illustrations, charts, graphs, or other images.

- **Art**
- **Music**
- **Food**
- **Language**
- **Politics**
- **Science**
- **Religion**

5. Presenting Your Exhibit

Following your teacher's instructions, display your time line and posters for the class to see. When called upon, present your exhibit to the class as a group. Make sure that each person in your group is assigned a part of the exhibit to explain.

6. Discussion

What did you learn from this lab? Hold a group discussion that focuses on the following questions:

- In what ways were the various immigration histories illustrated on the time lines similar? How were they different?
- What push and pull factors that caused immigration did you find most compelling? Why?
- Were you aware of the cultural contributions of all of the ethnic and racial groups presented, or did some of the contributions surprise you? Explain.
- Do you know how your ancestors arrived in the United States? Where did they come from and why?
- Based on the information presented by "The New Americans" group, how do you think American culture will change over the next 50 years?

Sample Immigration Poster Worksheet

Who came?

____

____

Where did they come from?

____

____

Why did they come?

____

____

____

Did they come by their own choice or were they forced to immigrate?

____

____

____

When did they first arrive?

____

____

____

How many came?

____

____

____

Where did they settle?

____

____

____

What challenges did they face when they arrived?

____

____

____

CHAPTER 9 Review

Comprehension and Critical Thinking

SECTION 1 *(pp. 208–211)*

1. a. Describe In what ways can categories of race and ethnicity overlap?

b. Explain Why can race be viewed as both a myth and a reality?

c. Contrast What makes minority groups different from the dominant group in a society?

SECTION 2 *(pp. 212–217)*

2. a. Define What is cultural pluralism?

b. Identify Cause and Effect How can a stereotype become a self-fulfilling prophecy?

c. Support a Position Do you agree with sociologist Robert K. Merton's idea that some people—fair-weather liberals—can discriminate without being prejudiced? Explain.

SECTION 3 *(pp. 218–224)*

3. a. Recall What challenges face Native Americans today?

b. Draw Conclusions Why do you think many white ethnics were able to assimilate quickly into the dominant culture?

c. Evaluate What did Gunnar Myrdal mean by the term "American dilemma"? Do you think that this term can still be applied to the United States today? Explain.

INTERNET ACTIVITY

4. Choose three of the patterns of minority group treatment discussed in this chapter. Then conduct Internet research on how each pattern has been used by an actual society. Your research may focus on historical or present-day patterns of group interactions in societies. Summarize your findings in a table titled "Patterns of Minority Group Treatment." Be sure to record information about the dominant and minority groups, relevant dates, and a brief description of each pattern's effects on minority groups.

Reviewing Vocabulary

Match the terms below with their correct definitions.

5. race
6. ethnicity
7. minority group
8. stereotype
9. scapegoating
10. assimilation
11. subjugation
12. ethnic cleansing
13. ghettos
14. environmental racism

A. the set of cultural characteristics that distinguishes one group from another

B. a pattern of racial bias in environmental practices and policies

C. the practice of blaming one's troubles on an innocent person or group

D. a group of people who because of their physical characteristics or cultural practices are singled out and treated unequally

E. sections of a city where minority groups live, often because of economic or social pressure

F. a pattern of group interaction that combines population transfer and extermination

G. a pattern of group interaction in which a dominant group maintains control by using force

H. a group of people who share observable physical traits and whom others see as belonging to a distinct group

I. the blending of culturally distinct groups into a single group with a common culture and identity

J. an oversimplified, exaggerated, and unfavorable generalization about a group of people

Sociology in Your Life

15. Select and watch a television program that depicts the experiences of a person or persons from a racial or ethnic minority in the United States. Write a brief essay that answers the following questions: What stereotypes are supported by the program? What stereotypes does the program break?

SKILLS ACTIVITY: INTERPRETING GRAPHS

Study the pie graphs below. Then use the information to help you answer the questions that follow.

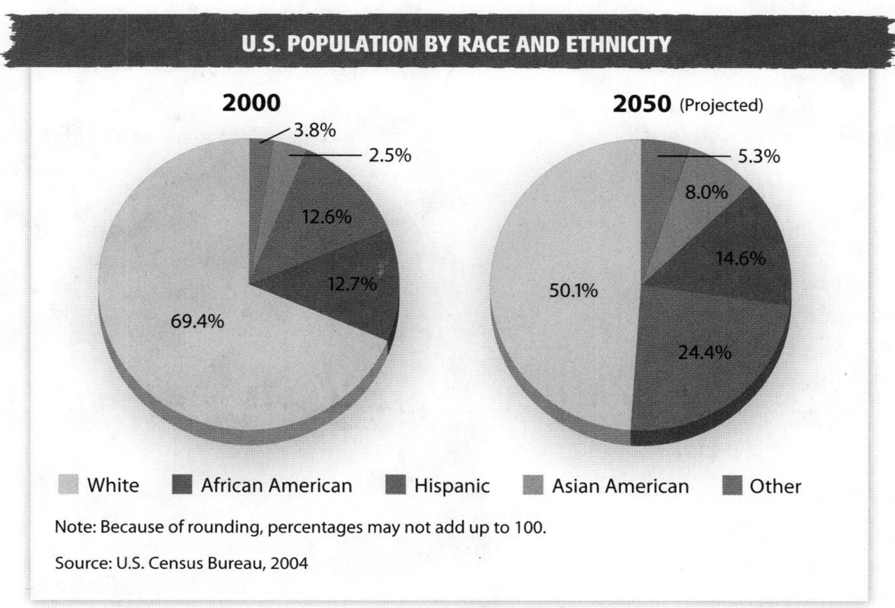

16. Identify Based on information from the graphs, the percentages of which ethnic and racial groups are projected to decline by 2050?

17. Contrast How does the percentage of Hispanics in 2000 compare to the percentage of Hispanics in 2050?

18. Predict What are some of the possible social consequences of the changing racial and ethnic composition of the U.S. population?

WRITING FOR SOCIOLOGY

Use your knowledge of race and ethnicity to answer the question below. Do not simply list facts. Present a clear argument based on your critical analysis of the question, using appropriate terminology.

19. Briefly describe each of the terms below from a sociological perspective. For each term, include a general description and a review of major characteristics and trends. Then use real world examples to help explain the term within the context of U.S. society.

- dominant group
- institutionalized discrimination
- "model minority"

Connecting Online

Go online for review and enrichment activities related to this chapter.

KEY TOPICS VIDEOS
View compelling clips on issues in the field.

KEEP IT CURRENT
Link to the Current Events site for regularly updated stories on sociology as well as other social studies topics.

QUICK LAB
Reinforce a key concept with a short lab activity.

CASE STUDY

HE SAID, SHE SAID

In her career as a sociolinguist, Deborah Tannen has studied how men and women communicate differently and how these differences affect their interactions. Although generalizing about whole groups of people can be ill-advised, Tannen believes that the dangers of ignoring these gender-based communication differences justify the risk.

Cross-Cultural Communication According to Tannen, boys and girls are essentially raised in different cultures, which makes interaction between genders an exercise in cross-cultural communication. Tannen argues that people speak differently to boys and girls, even within the same family. She also states that "children learn how to talk, how to have conversations, not only from their parents but also from their peers."

Anthropological studies show that children spend most of their time playing in same-sex groups. Boys tend to play in large groups based on a hierarchy with a dominant leader. Boys are typically encouraged to be competitive. In contrast, girls often play in pairs or small groups. A best friend is at the center of a girl's social life. Girls are typically encouraged to be cooperative. Tannen concludes that how children play influences how they communicate—both as children and as adults.

Gender Differences Tannen suggests that many men view themselves as one individual within a hierarchy. She states, "In this world, conversations are negotiations in which people try to achieve and maintain the upper hand if they can . . . Life, then, is a contest, a struggle to preserve independence and avoid failure." On the other hand, many women see themselves as one individual within a social network. According to Tannen, "In this world, conversations are negotiations for closeness in which people try to seek and give confirmation and support . . . Life, then, is a community, a struggle to preserve intimacy and avoid isolation." When men and women talk to each other, they tend to approach their conversations from these two worldviews.

Men's and women's different communication styles occasionally can lead to conflict. Understanding these differences can make social interaction more pleasant.

One classic example of these differences is the willingness to ask for directions. Tannen suggests that the reason many men are unwilling to stop and ask for directions is that they value the independence they display by finding the way themselves. In addition, to ask another person would place them below that individual in the social hierarchy. Many women, however, see the exchange of information as another opportunity to connect. They may ask directions of a local resident as a way to create intimacy and initiate a bond in a community with which they are unfamiliar.

Communication Problems Because both the struggle for independence and status and the negotiation of connection and intimacy are present in all conversations, men and women are able to focus on different elements in the same conversation. Often the result is miscommunication, which can lead to frustration and resentment. This can cause problems in relationships between men and women who blame each other as individuals instead of the different conversational styles that may be at fault.

Gender-based communication differences can also put women at a disadvantage. Many women worry about being seen as different from the norm, which tends to be established by men. When studies like Tannen's reveal that men and women have different styles, more often than not women are expected to change. However, both conversational styles are valid. Understanding these differences can ease interaction between men and women.

What do you think?

1. How do men and women approach conversation?
2. What kinds of problems might these communication differences cause?

CHAPTER 10

GENDER, AGE, AND HEALTH

Chapter at a Glance

SECTION 1: Gender

- The specific behaviors and attitudes that a society establishes for men and women are called gender roles.
- Individuals learn appropriate gender-role behavior through socialization.
- Gender roles are both different and unequal. In general, to be female is to be in a position of lesser power in society.
- Women have worked hard to overcome inequality in education, work, and politics.

SECTION 2: Age and Disability

- While age discrimination still exists, many Americans are attempting to change the stereotypical image of people aged 65 and older.
- The populations of the United States and the world are aging.
- Elderly Americans have become both a political force and a topic of debate.
- Many people with disabilities, some of whom are also elderly, face discrimination and prejudice in addition to dealing with their health problems.

SECTION 3: Health

- Many Americans are concerned about three aspects of the nation's health-care system: cost, quality, and access.
- Health care costs are rising, but many Americans are concerned that the same health insurance plans that allow them to pay their medical bills may not provide the highest quality of care.
- The distribution of physicians, both geographically and within the medical profession, affects Americans' access to health care.
- The health-care system faces such issues as health insurance, inequality and health, alternative medicine, and the global challenge of AIDS.

SECTION 1

Gender

Before You Read

Main Idea
Individuals learn appropriate gender behavior through socialization. In many societies, gender roles lead to social inequality.

Reading Focus
1. How are gender roles and identity formed?
2. How does gender play into social inequality in the United States?

Vocabulary
gender
gender roles
gender identity
patriarchy
sexism
suffrage
wage gap
glass ceiling
second shift

TAKING NOTES Use a graphic organizer like this one to take notes on gender.

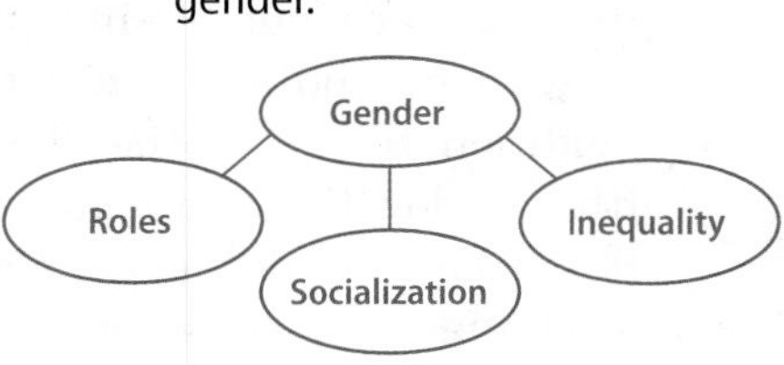

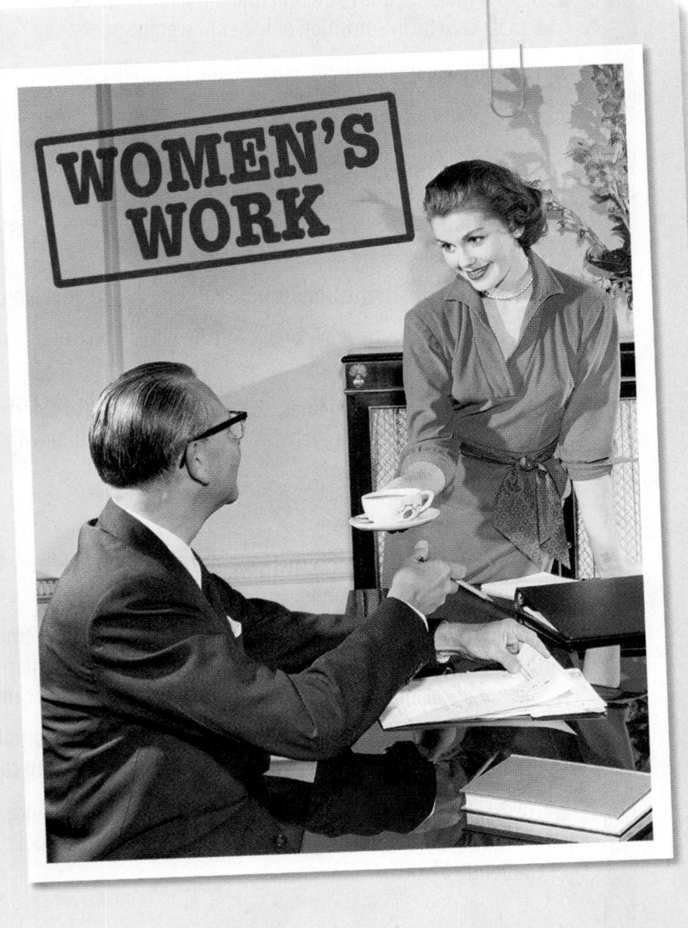

SOCIOLOGY CLOSE UP ***How did expectations about women in the workplace change over time?*** In the later half of the 1800s, the division of labor between American men and women was clearly defined. Men worked and supported the family, while women primarily restricted their activities to the home. In the early 1900s, more women began entering the workforce. By 1930, 10 million women were earning wages. However, their male coworkers argued that women were just temporary workers whose real job was at home. Between 1900 and 1930, the patterns of discrimination and inequality for women in the workforce began.

During World War II, over 6 million women entered the workforce. In many cases, expectations about their abilities were still rooted in the traditional roles of the past. For instance, a list of rules for hiring women published in 1943 included gems such as, "Give every girl an adequate number of rest periods during the day. You have to make some allowances for feminine psychology. A girl has more confidence and is more efficient if she can keep her hair tidied, apply fresh lipstick and wash her hands several times a day." Or, "Be tactful when issuing instructions or in making criticisms. Women are often sensitive; they can't shrug off harsh words the way men do. Never ridicule a woman—it breaks her spirit and cuts off her efficiency." After the war, many men still believed women did not belong in the workforce. Not until the 1960s did women make great strides in overcoming discrimination in the workplace. ■

Gender Roles and Identity

How would you answer this question: In what ways do men and women differ? You might mention biological characteristics. Certainly, men and women do differ in such physical traits as average height and weight, amount of body hair, and muscle-to-fat ratio. However, most of the ways you might mention would refer to gender differences. **Gender** comprises the behavioral and psychological traits considered appropriate for men and women. A person's sex refers to the biological identity of that person. The variety of biological characteristics is the same in all societies. In contrast, gender traits are socially created and may vary from culture to culture.

The consequences of gender differences are far-reaching. It is gender, not biology, that determines the majority of the roles men and women play in society. Equally as important, it is primarily beliefs about gender that determine the distribution of power between the sexes. In this section, you will examine the social significance of gender.

What do people mean when they say that a man is being masculine or a woman is being feminine? These labels simply mean that the person exhibits behaviors and attitudes considered appropriate for his or her gender. All societies have norms governing how men and women should act. The specific behaviors and attitudes that a society establishes for men and women are called **gender roles.** In most societies, men and women do specific kinds of work. In a division of labor based on gender, women are generally assigned child-care and domestic duties. Men are often charged with providing economic support and physical safety for the family.

What does it mean to be a boy or a girl, and how does gender affect behavior? Sociologists are concerned with how gender identity is formed and how this identity influences social behavior. **Gender identity** is the awareness of being masculine or feminine as those traits are defined by culture. However, the cultural values that influence gender identity and roles are not static and have changed in recent decades. The degree to which a person takes on a gender identity affects his or her response to the gender roles established by society as a whole.

Between Cultures Variation exists in the psychological characteristics considered appropriate for men and women. Anthropologist Margaret Mead's study of three New Guinea societies indicates how gender roles can differ between cultures. In one of these societies, the Tchambuli, Mead found that the women were bossy and efficient, while the men were gossipy and artistic.

The other two societies Mead studied showed comparable gender-role variations. Among the Mundugumor, aggressiveness—a traditionally masculine trait—was the norm for men and women alike. However, both men and women of the Arapesh were expected to be passive and emotionally warm. Such traits are considered feminine in most cultures.

Sociologists interpret cross-cultural variations as evidence that gender roles are socially created rather than biologically based. They argue that if gender roles were based primarily on biology, there would be little variation in gender behavior from society to society.

Gender Identity and Socialization Individuals learn appropriate gender-role behavior through socialization. As you already read, socialization is the interactive process through which people learn the basic skills, values, beliefs, and behavior patterns of their society. In most societies, gender socialization begins at birth and continues throughout life.

In the United States a person's gender role is often reinforced at birth. The newborn is usually given sex-specific clothes and toys. Such gender-typing is not as widespread as it was in the past. Change is more evident in the treatment of girls. For example, most people no longer discourage girls from playing with traditionally male toys, such as trucks and airplanes. Although girls have taken up many traditionally male activities, few boys are encouraged to play with dolls or other traditionally feminine toys.

CASE STUDY CONNECTION

Gender Differences Different styles of play as children lead to different styles of communication as adults.

Even more important than the physical trappings of gender are the different expectations that most people hold for girls and boys. Traditionally, little boys were expected to be adventuresome, aggressive, and physically active. Little girls were expected to be polite, gentle, and passive. The traditional understanding of the proper roles and behaviors of boys and girls has begun to change.

Gender in Advertising

Quick Lab

During adulthood, mass media play an important role in gender socialization. Advertising is a medium that most Americans confront on a daily basis. How do advertisements in various publications represent and reinforce established gender roles in American society?

PROCEDURE

1. Flip through a variety of magazines and look at the advertisements. Make sure that you have magazines directed at male, female, and gender-neutral audiences. You may look at Internet ads if you cannot access any magazines.
2. Choose 10 advertisements to examine in detail. These ads should represent a range of products and audiences.
3. Analyze the ads for their portrayal of gender roles. Which products are geared toward each gender? Do advertisers use different techniques to sell their products to men as opposed to women? Record your observations.

ANALYSIS

1. Compare the advertisements that you selected with the ones chosen by your classmates. Discuss your observations.
2. How do the advertisements represent traditional American gender roles? Are certain roles more commonly addressed than others?
3. Do you think that advertising helps to perpetuate, or prolong the existence of, specific gender roles? If so, what are the possible consequences of this situation?

Differing gender expectations have extended to school as well. Boys were expected to be good at math and science and mechanically inclined. Girls were expected to excel in reading and the social sciences and to be creative in the arts. Boys were encouraged to prepare for a career, while girls were encouraged to look to marriage and a family as their future. Today, more and more young women are being encouraged to pursue careers.

The family is the most powerful agent of gender socialization. Parents, siblings, and other relatives all act as role models for young children. Through family members' actions, children quickly learn what gender behaviors are expected of them. Schools, peer groups, and the media all reinforce these gender expectations. During adulthood, peer groups and the media take on increasingly important roles in the gender-socialization process.

Gender Roles and Social Inequality Gender roles are both different and unequal. In most societies, gender is the primary factor used to determine a person's social standing. In general, to be female is to have less power in society. Sociologists are interested in how this inequality between men and women arose.

One widely held view is that gender inequality is related to human reproduction. To grow, primitive societies depended on the birth and survival of children. Women spent many of their adult years pregnant or nursing. As a result, they took on roles that allowed them to stay close to home. However, men took on the roles that required strength and travel away from home. They became hunters, traders, and warriors who risked their lives for the group. The prestige of these roles provided men with a source of power. In time, the power relationship between men and women developed into a **patriarchy,** a system in which men are dominant over women.

Families in industrial societies are generally small, and most people live well into their seventies. As a result, women in industrial societies spend much of adulthood free from the duties of child care. Women still generally bear more of this responsibility than men. In addition, few jobs in industrial societies require such physical strength that they preclude women from performing them. Yet women still occupy a secondary position in many industrial societies.

The conflict perspective provides an explanation for this situation. According to conflict theory, gender roles are a reflection of male dominance. Through their control of the economic and political spheres of society, men have established laws and customs that protect their dominant position. In so doing, men have blocked women's access to power.

Another explanation for the persistence of gender roles is institutionalized discrimination. Over time, certain discriminatory customs based on gender have become part of the social structure. **Sexism**—the belief that one sex is by nature superior to the other—is at the heart of gender-based discrimination. The long history of male economic and political dominance has led some people to believe that men are inherently superior to women. This view has been used as a justification for continued male dominance.

Sexism becomes a self-fulfilling prophecy. People who believe that women are in some way incapable of occupying positions of power make choices based on this belief. Men who see women as inferior oppose their entrance into powerful positions in business and politics. Women who accept this stereotype do not pursue careers in traditionally male fields. Consequently, there are not enough women in positions of power to push for greater access.

Reading Check **Sequence** How have gender roles changed over time?

Gender Inequality in the United States

In the mid-1800s, women in the United States were very much second-class citizens. They had few rights and limited opportunities. They could not vote. Very few women had the opportunity to get more than a basic education. Many jobs were closed to them. Women who did work were paid less than men. When women married, their possessions became their husbands' property. Many Americans accepted this situation. However, some women took steps to end gender discrimination. They were the founders of the American women's movement, which held that the sexes were socially, politically, and economically equal.

The Women's Movement In July 1848, delegates at a women's rights convention in Seneca Falls, New York, issued a call for reforms to strengthen women's standing in society. These reforms included allowing married women to control their own property and earnings independently of their husbands. However, the most important reform they demanded was **suffrage**—the right to vote.

The Women's Movement

After many years of fighting for gender equality, women have made great strides in their struggle to be given the same treatment and opportunities as men. ***How has the women's movement achieved these gains?***

1848 Elizabeth Cady Stanton and Lucretia Mott organized the first women's rights convention in Seneca Falls, New York. Attendees approved the Declaration of Sentiments, a document detailing social injustice toward women.

1920 With the adoption of the 19th Amendment, suffragists finally succeeded in gaining women the right to vote.

1941 When the United States entered World War II, millions of women joined the labor force to fill jobs vacated by male soldiers. Women also found new roles in the military, joining special divisions of the army and navy.

1963 Betty Friedan published *The Feminine Mystique*, a criticism of the limits society placed on women, which galvanized the women's movement.

1964 The passage of the Civil Rights Act of 1964 prohibited discrimination based on gender and created the Equal Employment Opportunity Commission (EEOC).

1966 Friedan and a group of women formed the National Organization for Women (NOW) to pursue the goals of the women's movement, including equal pay for equal work, child care for working mothers, and abortion rights.

1972 Congress passed the Equal Rights Amendment (ERA) which would guarantee men and women the same rights and protections under the law. The amendment was never ratified.

Today The gender gap in achievement and pay continues to shrink gradually. More women are elected to political office.

ACADEMIC VOCABULARY

civil disobedience the nonviolent refusal to obey the law as a way to advocate change

Although some states passed laws giving women greater rights, suffrage was not so easily won. Women leaders undertook a program of civil disobedience to achieve their goal. They chained themselves to public buildings and harassed public officials. When imprisoned, they went on hunger strikes. At one point, they picketed the White House for six months. Finally, their efforts proved successful. The Nineteenth Amendment, adopted in 1920, gave women the right to vote.

For the most part, the women's movement was inactive for the next 40 years. However, Betty Friedan's book *The Feminine Mystique* sparked the movement into action once more. Friedan rejected the popular notion that women were content with the roles of wife and mother. She argued that the glorification of these roles—which she called the "feminine mystique"—was a ploy to keep women in a secondary position in society. Friedan's ideas struck a chord with many women. They soon began to demand greater educational opportunities and fairer treatment at work.

Statistically Speaking...

The Gender Gap Prior to 1979, men outnumbered women on college campuses across the country. Since then, however, women have made great strides in narrowing the gender gap in the number of advanced degrees awarded, and since 2009, have exceeded men in the number of doctoral degrees received.

DOCTORAL DEGREES, BY FIELD AND GENDER, 2012

Field	Male	Female
Arts and Humanities	46.4%	53.6%
Biological, Agricultural Sciences	47.6%	52.4%
Business	56.8%	43.2%
Education	32.4%	67.6%
Engineering	77.8%	22.2%
Health Sciences	29.2%	70.8%
Mathematics and Computer Sciences	74.8%	25.2%
Physical Sciences	66.6%	33.4%
Public Administration	43.6%	56.4%
Social, Behavioral Sciences	38.9%	61.1%
Other Fields	46.4%	53.6%

Source: American Enterprise Institute

Skills Focus **INTERPRETING GRAPHS** Which field awarded the largest percentage of doctoral degrees to women?

Many feminists argued that the only way to ensure such changes was a constitutional amendment ending discrimination based on sex. Congress approved the Equal Rights Amendment (ERA) in 1972. To become part of the Constitution, the ERA had to be ratified by 38 states. However, it fell three states short in the ratification process. Yet women made other important gains during the last few decades of the 1900s. For example, Congress passed several acts outlawing gender discrimination in education and in the workplace.

Progress toward gender equality has been made in almost every area of American social life. However, equality has not been fully achieved. A review of women's standing relative to men in education, work, and politics will illustrate this point.

Education Prior to 1979, women were underrepresented among college students. Since then, women have outnumbered men on college campuses. Today women make up about 71 percent of the total college population and earn 57 percent of all bachelor's degrees. However, there are strong gender distinctions in degree majors. Men more often pursue degrees in engineering, physical science, and architecture. Women tend to concentrate on education and the humanities. Women earn only about 21 percent of the engineering bachelor's degrees awarded. However, 79 percent of education bachelor's degrees go to women.

More and more women are attending graduate school. Women make up 60 percent of those enrolled in graduate courses. They earn 59 percent of the master's degrees awarded each year. Women are also narrowing the gap in doctoral or professional degrees. About 49 percent of the doctorates and professional degrees awarded go to women. As the bar graph on this page shows, these percentages are a marked improvement over the past.

Work Since the 1960s, more women have entered the workforce. One thing that has changed little is the **wage gap**—the level of women's income relative to that of men. During the 1960s, female workers earned between 58 and 61 cents for every dollar earned by male workers. Today the wage gap is about 77 cents to the dollar. The difference in the yearly median earnings of female and male full-time workers is nearly $10,000.

When the incomes of men and women working in the same occupations are examined, women consistently earn less. A wage gap exists in all age groups and education levels.

The number of women in full-time executive, administrative, and managerial positions is increasing. These increases may indicate that the "glass ceiling" is beginning to crack. The **glass ceiling** is the invisible barrier that prevents women from gaining upper-level positions in business. Recent studies also suggest that cracks are appearing in the ceiling. A 2007 study found that women accounted for over 15 percent of corporate officers in America's 500 largest companies, up from 10 percent in 1995. However, the study also showed that women occupy few "line officer" positions—the jobs that lead to top leadership positions. Interestingly, men in traditionally female occupations—such as nursing, social work, and library administration—do not face a glass ceiling. Rather, they often quickly rise to high-level positions with top salaries.

Married women who work face a particular kind of gender inequality. Sociologist Arlie Hochschild noted that working wives work a **second shift.** After their day at work, they also have household duties such as cooking, cleaning, and child care. Even when husbands share in the second shift, wives still do more work. Women in the United States have on average about 6 hours per week less leisure time than men. Wives face not only a wage gap at work, but also a "leisure gap" at home.

Politics There is also a political gender gap in the United States. Women make up 52 percent of the voting-age population, outnumbering men by 7.6 million. They are more likely than men to vote in elections. Yet men dominate the political arena. For example, in 2016 women made up approximately 19.4 percent of the 535 seats of both the U.S. Senate and the U.S. House of Representatives. Women held 24.5 percent of state legislative seats. These figures represent large increases over previous years. In 1981 women made up only 4 percent of the U.S. Congress and 12 percent of state legislators. Even so, women are still hugely underrepresented in government.

One development on the political scene is that many Americans seem open to the idea of women occupying public office—even the presidency. In a 2015 Gallup poll, 91 percent of the respondents said that they would vote for a woman as president. A more perceptible change is that women are being appointed to high office in growing numbers. Several women have held leadership roles in Congress. President Obama appointed a number of women to high-level positions, including Hillary Clinton as secretary of state, Loretta Lynch as attorney general, and Sonia Sotomayor and Elena Kagan as Supreme Court justices.

Reading Check **Analyze** How do gender roles affect the opportunities available to men and women in American society?

SECTION 1 Assessment

Reviewing Main Ideas and Vocabulary

1. **Define** What is gender identity?
2. **Sequence** Describe the major milestones in the women's movement and their significance.

Thinking Critically

3. **Summarize** How does Margaret Mead's research suggest that gender roles are socially created?
4. **Explain** How do gender expectations differ for men and women in the United States?
5. **Develop** What do you think might be done to eliminate the glass ceiling and the wage gap?
6. **Categorize** Using your notes and a graphic organizer like the one below, identify examples of gender inequality in education, work, and politics.

Area	Example of Gender Inequality
Education	
Work	
Politics	

FOCUS ON WRITING

7. **Persuasive** Write a brief essay agreeing or disagreeing with the viewpoint that as more women enter and stay in the workforce, differences in gender roles will fade. Consider why gender inequality exists and progress already made.

SECTION 2

Age and Disability

Before You Read

Main Idea
As society ages, the concerns of the elderly take on increasing importance. Many elderly people have disabilities, as do many other Americans.

Reading Focus
1. What is ageism?
2. What are the population trends of the aging world?
3. How do the politics of aging affect elderly Americans?
4. What issues do Americans with disabilities face?

Vocabulary
ageism
graying of America
baby-boom generation
dependency ratio
Medicare
Medicaid

TAKING NOTES Use a graphic organizer like this one to take notes on age and disability.

Age	Disability

[Living in the Zone]

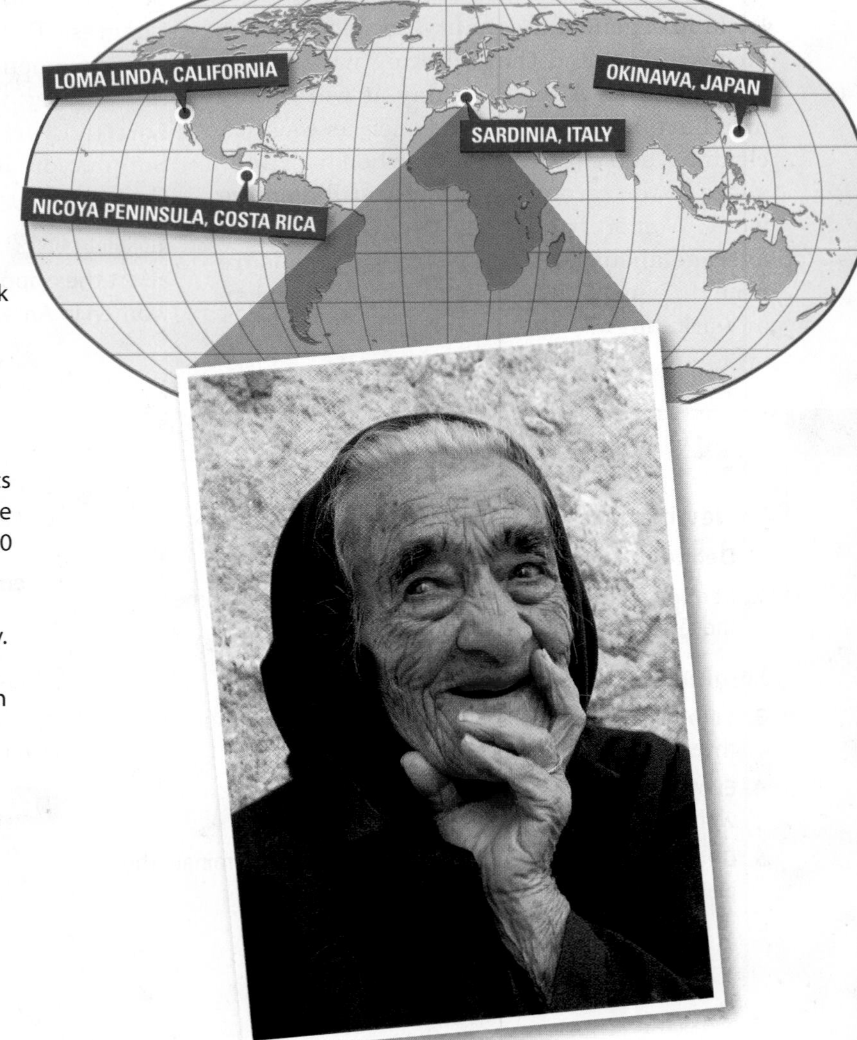

SOCIOLOGY CLOSE UP ***What's the secret to living to be 100 years old?*** Some researchers think they may have found it. They have discovered four far-flung places, which they call "Blue Zones," where people live longer lives than anywhere else. These Blue Zones are Loma Linda, California; Okinawa, Japan; Sardinia, Italy; and the Nicoya Peninsula in Costa Rica. The residents of these areas have up to three times the chance of becoming centenarians—people who are 100 years of age or older—than most Americans. Blue Zone residents also make up part of a growing segment of the population: the elderly. Despite living in different corners of the globe, many of these Blue Zone residents share certain characteristics: they eat sensibly; they incorporate physical activity into their daily lives; they have a sense of purpose; and they surround themselves with the right people. Perhaps they can teach us why so many people are living longer—and how we might as well. ■

Ageism

Different societies place different values on age. In preindustrial societies, the social standing of individuals increased with age. The older members of society were viewed as sources of knowledge and as the enforcers of social customs. In industrial societies, middle-aged people hold the greatest social power. Employment is one of the major indicators of social status in industrial societies, and employment opportunities decline with age. The closer people get to retirement age, the more difficult it is for them to find re-employment in the event of job loss. Job-retraining programs are seldom geared toward older workers.

Ageism—the belief that one age category is by nature superior to another age category—is at the heart of age-based role loss. Although ageism can apply to any age group, it is most often directed against elderly people in industrial societies. One way in which ageism can be seen is in the stereotypes used to portray elderly citizens. They are often shown as unproductive, cranky, and physically or mentally impaired. In reality, the vast majority of people aged 65 and older are self-sufficient, active members of society with much to contribute.

In American society, the media reinforces ageism. For example, in television commercials elderly people are seldom used to sell household products, cosmetics, clothing, or automobiles. Instead, they endorse products such as over-the-counter medications, health-related devices, denture preparations, or insurance and burial plans. Moreover, news coverage of senior citizens often focuses on the negative aspects of aging, such as poor health, poverty, and loneliness.

Efforts are now being made to change the image Americans have of people aged 65 and older. In the United States, more television programs, movies, and children's books that present older adults as positive role models are beginning to appear. Nevertheless, much age discrimination still exists. This ageism is particularly significant in light of current world population trends.

Reading Check **Identify Supporting Details** How can ageism be seen in American society?

The Aging World

The world's population is aging. Today there are approximately 705 million people aged 60 and older worldwide. By the year 2050, this number will have grown to an estimated 2 billion. Japan—with a median population age of 42.9—is the oldest country in the world. In contrast, Uganda is the world's youngest country, with a median population age of 14.8.

In Europe, projections suggest that over the first half of the 21st century the population will continue to age. By 2050 the median age will be 49.5, and close to 40 percent of Europeans will be age 60 and older. People age 60 and older will outnumber children under the age of 15 by nearly three to one in Europe. While Africa's population will also age, it will remain the world's youngest region.

Population trends in the United States reflect what is happening worldwide. In 2012 about 14 percent of the population in the United States was aged 65 or older. Projections are that the U.S. elderly population will reach 20 percent by 2030. Sociologists refer to the phenomenon of the increasing number of elderly Americans as a percentage of the total U.S. population as the **"graying of America."**

There are two primary reasons for the graying of America. First, advances in health care and better living conditions have resulted in more people surviving into old age. Second, variations in birthrates have changed the age structure of the United States. Birthrates in the United States rose sharply in 1946 and stayed about the same until the 1960s when they noticeably declined. The approximately 76 million children born during this period are known as the **baby-boom generation.** After the early 1960s the birthrate began to drop and has remained relatively low ever since. This rise in the birthrate, followed by a decline, made the baby-boom generation the largest segment of the American population. Today baby boomers are in their mid-forties to early sixties. By the year 2030, all of the baby boomers will have reached at least 65 years of age, thereby swelling the ranks of the elderly population to nearly 70 million.

Reading Check **Summarize** What are the two primary reasons for the graying of America?

Statistically Speaking...

Age Around the World Populations are aging across the globe. In the United States, the percentage of people aged 65 and older tripled in the 1900s.

AGE OF POPULATION IN MAJOR REGIONS

Region	Percent of Population: Under 15	Aged 15 to 44	45-64	65 and Over
Africa	39.8%	45.2%	11.4%	3.6%
Asia	25%	47.9%	20.1%	7.1%
Europe	15.6%	40.3%	27.3%	16.8%
Central America	29.6%	47.4%	16.7%	6.3%
North America	19.7%	39.9%	26.4%	14.0%
Oceania	23.8%	43.0%	21.9%	11.3%

Source: GeoHive, 2013

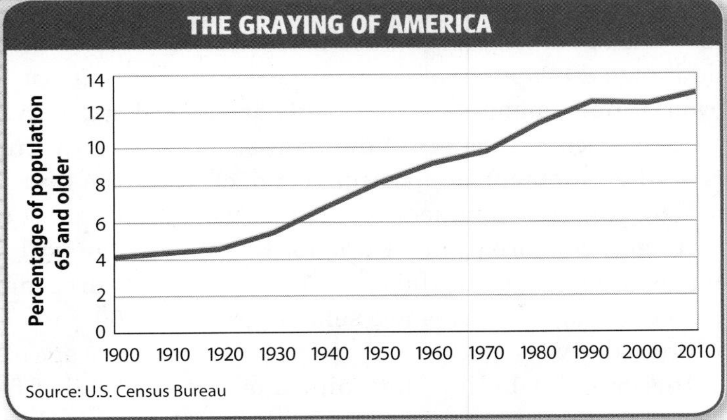

Skills Focus **INTERPRETING CHARTS** Which world region has the youngest population? Which region has the oldest? What do you think the consequences will be for these regions?

The Politics of Aging

The changing age structure of the United States has thrust elderly people into the center of American politics. In short order, they have become both a political force and a topic of debate. Recently, the image of the elderly population has changed from one of an underprivileged and forgotten segment of society to one of a powerful and effective voting bloc. Exactly how organized a voting bloc senior citizens represent is unclear. What is clear is that few politicians are willing to risk ignoring the needs of older Americans. The political influence of elderly people is likely to continue to grow as their ranks swell with the aging of the baby boomers.

ACADEMIC VOCABULARY

voting bloc a group whose shared concerns motivate how they vote in elections

Several groups work to bring the special needs of the elderly to national attention. Among the largest are AARP, the National Council of Senior Citizens, the National Council on Aging, and the Gray Panthers. AARP is one of the most successful of these organizations. With 35 million members, AARP is the largest special-interest group in the United States. In addition to its political lobbying efforts, AARP provides many services for its members. These services include financial advice, health-insurance plans, and travel discounts. In addition, AARP publishes a magazine, produces weekly radio programs, and operates a Web site.

Challenges to Government One of the major issues of concern for older Americans is the Social Security system. Some people have expressed fears that the system is not up to the task of caring for future generations of elderly people. The Social Security system is funded by payroll or income taxes on workers, employers, and the self-employed. Current payroll taxes fund the benefits paid to current retirees. However, declining birthrates and longer life expectancies mean that there are fewer workers available to support growing numbers of retirees. In 1960 the **dependency ratio**—the number of workers for each person receiving Social Security benefits—stood at 5 to 1. By 1998 the ratio had declined to just more than three workers for every retiree. In 2030 when all the baby boomers reach retirement age, the ratio will have dropped to 2 to 1.

Longer life expectancies have created another challenge for the Social Security system. Because of increasing life expectancies, the fastest growth in the elderly population is among the old-old—individuals aged 85 and older. For example, in 1970 there were approximately 1.4 million Americans aged 85 or older. By 2006 the number had reached 5.3 million. Projections show that by 2050 there will be about 20.9 million old-old—about 24 percent of the elderly population. Thus, not only is the number of people receiving Social Security benefits increasing, but they receive the benefits for a longer period of time.

Ideas about how to ensure the future of Social Security have stirred debate. Some people have suggested raising the retirement age, reducing benefits, or increasing the contributions of workers who pay Social Security taxes. Others have suggested investing Social Security funds in the stock market. However, none of these solutions has received the enthusiastic backing of a majority of Americans.

The old-old present another challenge, because they are most likely to be in poor health. This challenge places an added strain on government transfer-payment programs, particularly Medicare and Medicaid. **Medicare** is the government-sponsored health-insurance plan for elderly Americans and Americans with disabilities. **Medicaid** is the state and federally funded health-insurance program for low-income individuals. These programs are the sole sources of health insurance for close to one-quarter of elderly Americans.

Age Inequality in the United States Some people claim that government transfer payments like Social Security have made older Americans financially secure at the expense of younger generations. They base this claim on the falling poverty rate among Americans aged 65 and older. In 1959, 35 percent of older Americans lived in poverty. In 2014 the poverty rate for the elderly was 10 percent. In comparison, the poverty rate is 15 percent for the general population and 21 percent for children under the age of 18.

On the surface, these statistics paint a positive picture for older Americans. However, they mask a great deal of variation in living conditions among the different segments of the elderly population. When viewed from the perspective of race and gender, poverty among older Americans looks very different. For example, more than 23 percent of elderly African Americans live in poverty. For older Hispanics, the figure is about 20 percent. Poverty among elderly white Americans, on the other hand, is about 9 percent. Women are harder hit by poverty than are men. About 12 percent of women aged 65 and older are poor, compared to 7 percent of elderly men. The figures rise among elderly African American and Hispanic women. Poverty levels are also higher among the old-old.

Social Security benefits and other government transfer payments may have managed to pull most elderly individuals above the poverty level, but often by only a few hundred dollars. Thus, many elderly people are living their lives in conditions of near-poverty.

Reading Check **Analyze** What are the major political issues of concern to elderly people?

Americans with Disabilities

Disabilities affect many older Americans. There were about 56.7 million people, or 19 percent of the population, that had a disability in 2010. The term disability covers a variety of conditions, including physical disabilities; chronic health impairments; mental retardation; mental illness; and visual, hearing, or speech impairments. Disabilities vary in severity. The severest disabilities include blindness, deafness, and paralysis. About 33 million people have severe disabilities.

Prejudice and Discrimination In addition to dealing with their health problems, many Americans with disabilities have to deal with prejudice and discrimination. A particular problem for people with disabilities is the stereotypical belief that their disabilities make them incapable of doing productive work. As a consequence, people with disabilities often have difficulty finding meaningful employment. Unemployment rates are high, particularly among those with severe disabilities. Those who do work usually receive lower-than-average wages. Not surprisingly, many Americans with disabilities receive some form of government assistance but still struggle to make ends meet. For example, some 28.6 percent of Americans with severe disabilities lived below the poverty line in 2010.

THE AMERICANS WITH DISABILITIES ACT

QUICK FACTS

Passed in 1990, the Americans with Disabilities Act (ADA) addresses four main areas in the lives of people with disabilities.

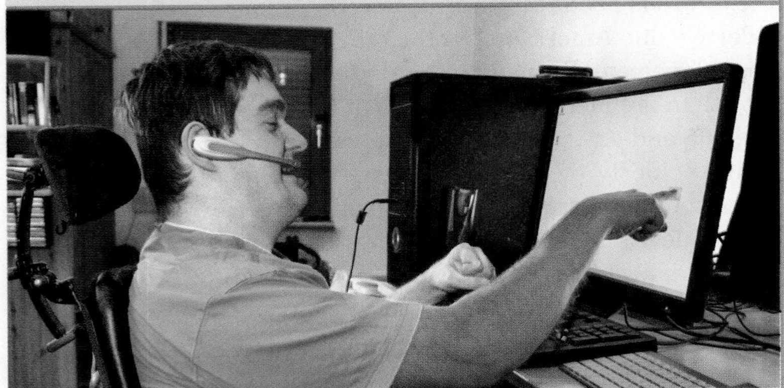

Employment
The ADA makes it illegal to discriminate against people with disabilities in hiring, promotion, and pay. It also requires companies to provide job training and aids such as interpreters to improve opportunities.

Public Services
The ADA also makes it illegal to deny Americans with disabilities the benefit of public services, including transportation. All new public buses and trains have to be made accessible to people with disabilities.

Public Accommodations
Hotels, restaurants, theaters, and other businesses that serve the public must make their facilities accessible to people with disabilities.

Telecommunications
Telephone companies must provide telecommunications relay services (TRS), which allow the text telephones used by the hearing-impaired or speech-impaired to communicate with regular telephones.

Disability rights activists have struggled for decades to gain the civil rights afforded to other groups in society. Over the years, they have had some success. For example, the Education for All Handicapped Children Act of 1975 guaranteed children with disabilities a public education geared toward their needs and abilities. In 1988 the Fair Housing Amendments Act gave persons with disabilities protection from discrimination in housing.

The ADA The Americans with Disabilities Act (ADA) of 1990 has perhaps brought the most sweeping changes in the lives of people with disabilities. The ADA addresses four main areas: employment, public services, public accommodations, and telecommunications. The ADA makes discrimination against people with disabilities illegal. It also requires that state and local government programs, public transportation vehicles, and businesses that serve the public be made accessible to Americans with disabilities.

The ADA has improved the lives of people with disabilities but much remains to be done. One of its goals was to increase employment opportunities for Americans with disabilities. However, employment rates among Americans with disabilities have risen only slightly. Finding meaningful employment remains a problem for those with disabilities.

Reading Check **Find the Main Idea** What efforts have been made to guarantee civil rights for Americans with disabilities?

SECTION 2 Assessment

Reviewing Main Ideas and Vocabulary

1. **Define** What is ageism?
2. **Summarize** How has the aging of the population affected American society?
3. **Identify Cause and Effect** How does social inequality affect elderly Americans?
4. **Recall** What stereotype often makes it difficult for people with disabilities to find employment?

Thinking Critically

5. **Elaborate** How might the stereotypical image of elderly people affect their life chances?
6. **Explain** Explain the dependency ratio and its significance.
7. **Identify Cause and Effect** Using your notes and a graphic organizer like the one below, identify and describe the factors that led to the graying of America.

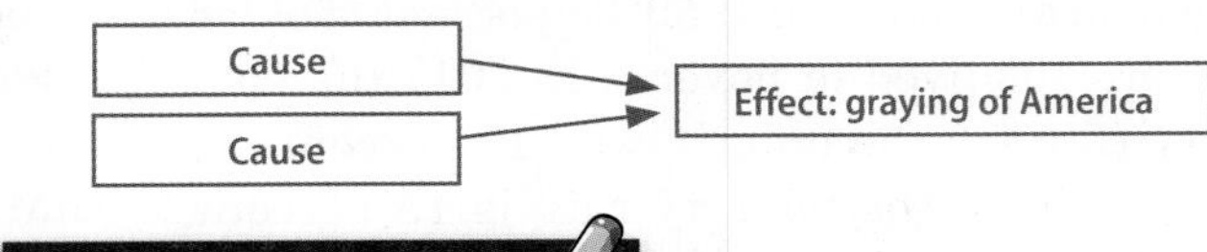

FOCUS ON WRITING

8. **Expository** Write two paragraphs explaining how the Americans with Disabilities Act and other legislation have changed the lives of people with disabilities.

SECTION 3

Health

Before You Read

Main Idea
Americans are concerned about the cost and quality of health care. Not all Americans have equal access to the health-care system.

Reading Focus
1. What are the three main concerns about health care in the United States?
2. What are the major issues facing the American health-care system today?

Vocabulary
managed care
alternative medicine
acquired immune deficiency syndrome (AIDS)

TAKING NOTES Use a graphic organizer like this one to take notes on health care.

Health Care in the United States			
Cost	Quality	Access	Issues

Express Checkup

SOCIOLOGY CLOSE UP ***Do you have a health clinic in your grocery store?*** If not, you could have one soon. Walk-in health clinics have been springing up inside drugstores, supermarkets, and big-box retailers across the country. By mid-2008, over 900 such clinics were operating in stores such as CVS, Walgreens, Target, and Wal-Mart. Currently there are about 1,900 clinics across the United States, a sevenfold increase since 2007.

These retail-based clinics, with names like MinuteClinic, appeal to busy shoppers. Staffed mostly by physician assistants and nurse practitioners, who have the necessary training and licensing to interpret tests and prescribe drugs, they offer a convenient and inexpensive alternative for treating minor health issues. Their weekend and evening hours, short wait times, and posted price lists attract patients. And they are cheaper than a trip to the emergency room or urgent care center, which satisfies insurance companies and the uninsured alike. Whether an individual has health insurance through their employer or a health exchange, more people are having to pay out-of-pocket costs, which makes retail clinics appealing. As demand for more health care professionals exceeds the supply, retail clinics provide a cheaper and more convenient alternative to traditional health care clinics. ■

Health Care in the United States

In a 2007 Gallup poll, respondents rated health care among the top ten priorities for elected officials. Another 2007 Gallup poll found that only 17 percent of Americans are satisfied with the country's health-care system. In the same poll, 30 percent of Americans named health-care costs as the most urgent health problem facing the nation, over diseases such as cancer and heart disease. People's worries about the American health-care system focus on three major issues: the cost of health care, the quality of the health care that people receive, and access to health care.

Cost of Health Care The United States spends a higher percentage of its gross domestic product (GDP) on health care than any other country in the world. In 2013 health-care expenditures in the United States exceeded $2.9 trillion, almost four times as much as in 1990. Estimates suggest that health-care costs will top $4 trillion by 2017. Everything from the cost of a stay in the hospital to health-insurance premiums has increased steadily in recent years. For example, American health-insurance companies paid approximately $61 billion for health care in 1980. By 2006 this figure had increased to almost $635 billion. Similarly, Medicare payments increased from about $107 billion in 1990 to about $401 billion in 2006. Group health-insurance plans also have shown marked cost increases. In 2007, health-insurance costs for large American companies rose by over 6 percent.

Many factors have contributed to the rapid rise in health-care costs. At the top of the list is hospital care, which accounts for nearly 32 percent of all medical expenditures. In recent years, hospitals have been attempting to contain costs through shorter hospital stays and increased treatment on an outpatient basis. Even with those efforts, hospital care cost the country more than $611 billion in 2005.

Advances in medical technology have also affected health-care costs. Doctors now have at their disposal more than 1,000 diagnostic tests, ranging from simple blood tests to high-technology techniques. Some of these tests, such as magnetic resonance imaging (MRI) and computerized axial tomography (CAT) scanning, are very expensive to administer. Nevertheless, many doctors rely heavily on such testing in their efforts to provide the best health care possible. Fears of malpractice lawsuits have also played a part in the increased use of these expensive diagnostic techniques. Doctors—particularly those in high-risk specialty areas—often order batteries of tests simply as a precaution against possible lawsuits. As a result, many of the diagnostic tests involved in defensive medicine, as it is called, may be unnecessary. Estimates suggest that somewhere between 5 and 9 percent of health-care spending goes toward defensive medicine.

Statistically Speaking...

Health-Care Spending Health care costs in the United States are climbing. Most Americans rely on insurance companies and the government to pay their medical expenses.

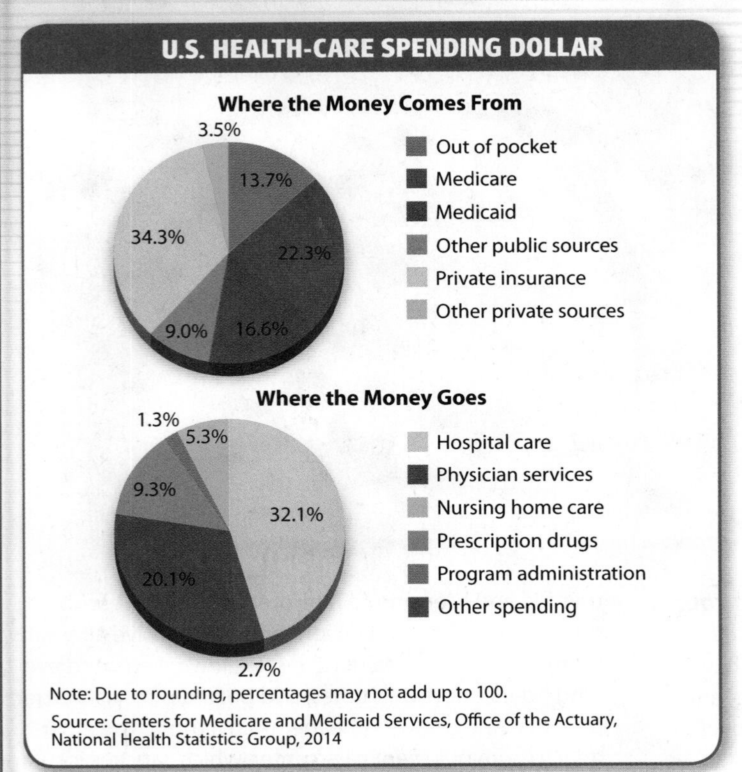

Skills Focus **INTERPRETING GRAPHS** Who is the largest provider of health-care dollars? What service requires the largest portion of those dollars? Why do you think that is the case?

Another reason for rising health-care costs is increased spending on prescription drugs. Prescription-drug costs have been rising at double-digit rates in the past decade compared to single-digit rates for hospital and physician services. For many group health-insurance plans, prescription drugs are the fastest-rising cost item. Drug costs have risen for several reasons. First, drug companies have increased their spending on advertising and marketing, driving up prices. Second, drugs are becoming the preferred form of treatment for many illnesses. Third, the number of elderly Americans—the leading consumers of prescription drugs—is rapidly increasing.

Escalating medical costs affect all sectors of society. Medicare and Medicaid account for 33 percent of the country's medical expenditures. Medical costs account for a sizable chunk of the federal budget. A share of medical expenditures comes from business in the form of health-insurance premiums. Businesses can ask their employees to share increased health-insurance costs, or they can cover the costs themselves by accepting lower profits or raising prices. American consumers also share the burden of increasing medical costs. About 12 percent of annual health-care spending—about $257 billion—comes directly out of consumers' pockets. The effects of such expenditures can be seen in the fact that many personal bankruptcies are caused by huge medical bills.

Quality of Health Care One popular method of controlling health expenditures is the use of alternative health-insurance plans called **managed care.** Although there are several types of managed-care plans, they generally follow the same pattern. In return for a set monthly or annual charge, plan members receive health-care services. The plan limits costs by requiring patients to choose approved doctors who have agreed to reduced rates, requiring approval for treatments, and setting limits on some prescription drugs. According to estimates, 75 percent of Americans with private health insurance—over 200 million—are members of managed-care plans.

TECHNOLOGY FOCUS

Smaller than Small

That's nanotechnology. It is the application of research conducted on the nanoscale, which ranges roughly from 1 to 100 nanometers. A nanometer is defined as one billionth of a meter. A sheet of paper is about 100,000 nanometers thick. When things get that small, they begin to exhibit new behaviors and properties. By working at the nanoscale, at the molecular level, scientists can create new materials and get familiar ones to behave in new ways.

After two decades of working with nanoscale materials, scientists and engineers have begun to apply their knowledge. Nanotechnology is already used to make sunscreen transparent, to make clothing stain-resistant, and to make tennis balls last longer. It has also been applied to the world of medicine. New anti-bacterial wound dressings use nanotechnology. Researchers are using nanotechnology to improve the usefulness of biochips like the one shown in the photo on this page. These biochips can test human proteins for infectious diseases in less than 15 minutes.

A biochip used to identify infectious diseases

Current research in nanomedicine is focused on finding new ways to diagnose and treat diseases. Supporters of nanomedicine argue that earlier detection and more effective treatments will cause health care costs to decline. Others, however, wonder if nanomedicine will be another expensive therapy that only certain people can afford. Researchers in nanotechnology recognize that their product will need to be affordable in order to be most useful.

Thinking Critically

Predict What ethical issues might nanomedicine bring up?

Managed care has brought down costs. However, Americans feel that the savings have come at a price. Polls conducted in the mid-2000s by the Kaiser Family Foundation found that 49 percent of respondents said that managed care had decreased the quality of health care. In addition, 60 percent said that managed care had cut the time doctors spend with patients, and 56 percent believed these plans made it harder for the sick to see specialists. Alarmingly, 61 percent said that they worried that if they became sick, their health plans would be more concerned about saving money than about providing them with the best treatment. Yet 63 percent of people thought these plans made no difference toward reducing health care costs.

In 1999, Congress began to develop a "patient's bill of rights" to address public concerns about managed care. This bill would allow patients to use hospital facilities and doctors not included in their plans and to have easier access to specialists. The bill of rights would also enable patients to gain more information on available treatments and to appeal any denials of treatment or coverage. The bill has been introduced repeatedly but never passed, despite continued public discontent.

Access to Health Care Studies of the American medical workforce estimate that there is a surplus of somewhere between 100,000 and 150,000 doctors. In spite of this oversupply of doctors, access to health care is a problem for many Americans. One of the major factors affecting access to health care is the distribution of physicians, both geographically and within the medical profession.

Geographically, most physicians concentrate in wealthy urban and suburban areas. In such areas, doctor-to-population ratios are low. In poor inner-city and rural areas, on the other hand, ratios are high. For example, in the exclusive Beverly Hills area of Los Angeles there is one doctor for every 254 people. In some poverty-stricken areas of south-central Los Angeles, however, there is approximately one doctor for every 24,500 people. This shortage of doctors is problematic because underserved areas usually have a greater number of people with chronic diseases. These areas are also usually home to many elderly people, who have an array of health-care needs.

Professionally, many physicians concentrate in specialty fields such as cardiology, internal medicine, and obstetrics. It is among specialists, not general practitioners, that surpluses are developing. Of the more than 850,000 government and private physicians in the United States, only about 89,000 are in general and family practice. This shortage is partially a result of doctors' pay structures. For example, the median annual income for a cardiologist is about $370,000. Doctors in family medicine earn about $186,000 a year.

Reading Check **Identify Cause and Effect** What trends cause Americans to be concerned about the cost and quality of and access to health care?

Health-Care Issues Today

Health-care issues—costs, quality, and access—are major concerns for the United States. Several other health-care issues are also at the center of political debates. These issues include health insurance, inequality in the health-care system, the search for alternative treatments, and the AIDS epidemic.

Health Insurance The majority of medical costs in the United States—84 percent—is covered by private or public insurance. With private insurance, people pay set periodic fees. When they are sick, the insurance companies pay the medical bills. Most people obtain private insurance through group plans offered by their employers. Public insurance includes government programs such as Medicare and Medicaid, which provide coverage for elderly, disabled, and poor people.

Critics note that the Medicare-Medicaid system has created very uneven health-care delivery. The kinds of procedures and treatments covered, and the levels to which they are covered, vary among private health-insurance plans. Some doctors and hospitals will not accept Medicare and Medicaid patients. Many private health-insurance companies are reluctant to offer coverage to people with pre-existing medical conditions. The working poor also find it difficult to get coverage. The companies they work for often do not offer group plans, and they do not earn enough to pay for their own coverage. About 16 percent of the population—more than 47 million people—are uninsured.

Some people have suggested that such problems could be overcome by the creation of a centrally planned national health system. In many industrialized nations, the government actually owns and operates the health-care system. Medical care is provided free or nearly free of charge to all citizens, regardless of their income levels. For example, in the United Kingdom all citizens have access to the National Health Service (NHS). Hospitals in the NHS system are controlled and funded by the government, and NHS physicians are government employees. People in the United Kingdom are also free to seek health care from private physicians and hospitals. However, the government will not assist people with the costs for such services. Moreover, critics of the NHS have argued that the quality of health care in the United Kingdom has been negatively affected by the program.

In other industrialized nations—such as Canada—the government finances health care through national health insurance. Under such a system, the government pays for health services, but physicians are not government employees. Critics have also challenged the quality of the Canadian health-care system. Early in his first term, President Bill Clinton suggested setting up a system similar to that of Canada. However, strong opposition from the American Medical Association (AMA) and the public led Clinton to abandon the plan. Whether it is the government's responsibility to ensure that every American has health insurance remains a hotly debated topic.

Statistically Speaking...

Uninsured Americans The cost of health care varies by state, which affects how many people can purchase health insurance.

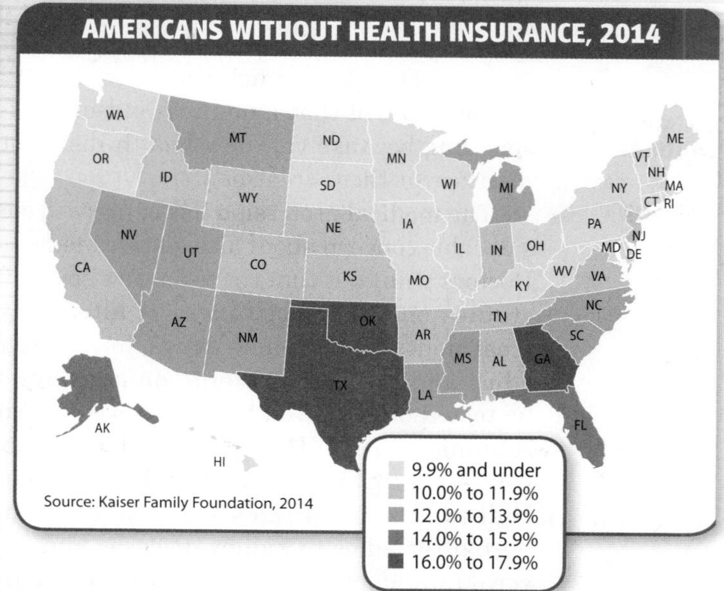

Source: Kaiser Family Foundation, 2014

Skills Focus **INTERPRETING MAPS** What characteristics might the states with the highest rates of uninsured residents share?

Inequality and Health Access to health care is just one way in which health is directly related to social status. Poor people are less likely to receive adequate medical care. The effects of poverty—such as malnutrition, lack of health insurance, and lack of access to health services—lead to greater health problems for many Americans.

- Children born to poor families are more likely to die within the first year of life than children born to wealthier families.
- Some 36 million Americans face hunger and cannot afford to buy the food needed for a healthy diet. Undernourishment during critical growth periods can affect a child's behavior, school performance, and overall cognitive development.
- Approximately 22 percent of poor children have no health insurance.
- About 32 million Americans, mostly among the working poor, did not have health insurance in 2014. Uninsured people are less likely than those with insurance to get routine physical checkups and other kinds of preventive care. In addition, the uninsured are more likely to delay or postpone medical treatment—even for serious conditions.
- People with lower incomes are more likely to characterize their health as fair or poor than people with higher incomes.

The poor also suffer disproportionately from diseases such as influenza, pneumonia, tuberculosis, alcoholism, and heart disease. Therefore, it is not surprising that poor Americans have a much lower life expectancy than wealthy Americans.

ACADEMIC VOCABULARY
disproportionate in greater or lesser numbers than an equal share

Alternative Medicine Many Americans have become interested in **alternative medicine** in recent years. Alternative medicine uses unconventional methods such as acupuncture, acupressure, biofeedback, massage, meditation, yoga, herbal remedies, and relaxation techniques to treat illness. About 48 % of Americans who have used some kind of alternative treatment. Estimates set yearly spending on alternative medicine at more than $27 billion. Most of that amount is out-of-pocket spending because very few health-insurance plans cover these treatments.

ACADEMIC VOCABULARY

diagnoses more than one diagnosis

The medical profession has expressed considerable concern about alternative medicine. Doctors point out that there are few scientific studies on the effectiveness of alternative treatments. Unlike new drugs, herbal remedies and diet supplements do not have to be tested or approved by the Food and Drug Administration (FDA). The result, some doctors suggest, may be harmful to patients. Indeed, recent studies have linked some herbal remedies to kidney diseases and cancer. Many doctors have urged that, for the safety of patients, herbs and supplements should undergo the same FDA testing-and-approval process required for other drugs.

AIDS—A Pressing Health Problem In 1981 when the first few cases of a strange new ailment were reported in the United States, very few could have imagined the potential effects on society. However, in just two decades that ailment has become one of the most serious public-health problems in the United States and around the world.

Acquired immune deficiency syndrome (AIDS) is a disease that attacks the immune system, leaving a person vulnerable to a host of deadly infections. The number of AIDS diagnoses in the United States has grown from a few hundred in 1981 to more than a million. About 50,000 Americans are diagnosed with human immunodeficiency virus (HIV)—the virus that causes AIDS—each year. Researchers believe that virtually all people who test positive for HIV eventually will develop AIDS if a cure is not found. They almost certainly will die from the disease. An estimated 13,712 people with an AIDS diagnosis died in 2012, and approximately 658,507 people in the United States with an AIDS diagnosis have died overall.

HIV is transmitted through sexual contact with an infected individual, contaminated blood and human tissue, and the use of contaminated hypodermic needles. The virus does

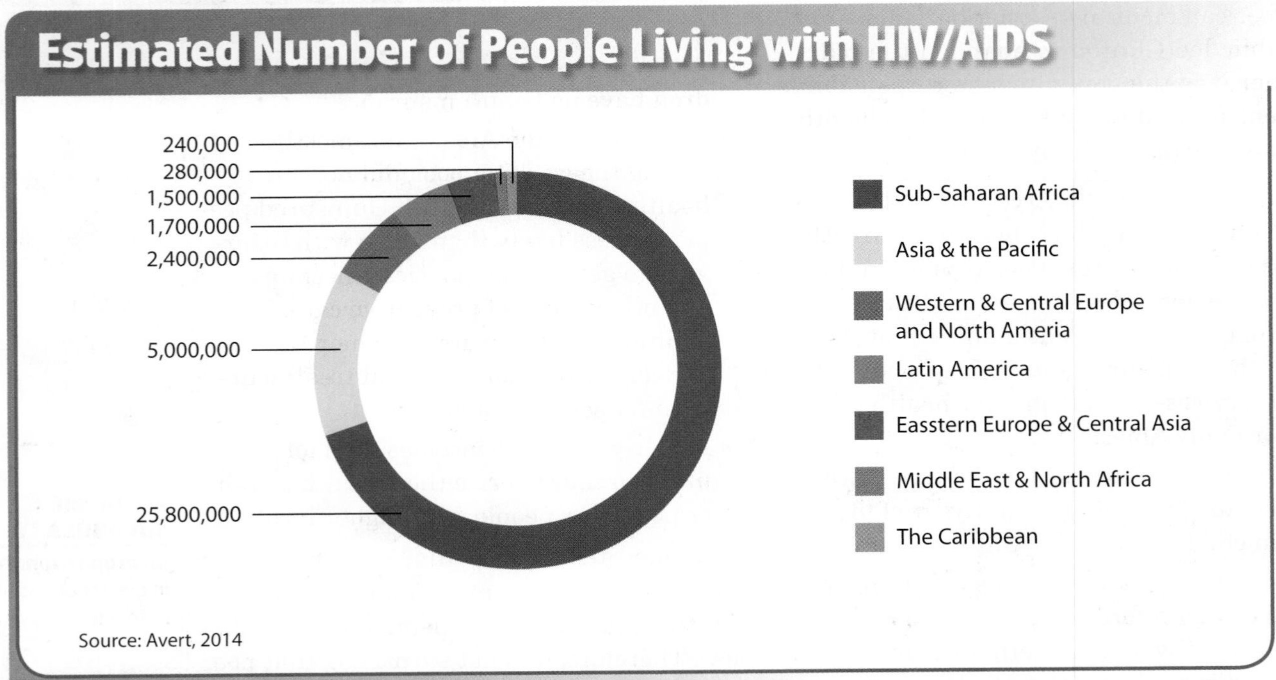

In 2014, an estimated 36.9 million people were living with HIV (including 2.6 million children) – a global HIV prevalence of 0.8%. ***What percentage of people living with HIV/AIDS reside in Sub-Saharan Africa?***

not threaten every segment of society equally. Homosexual and bisexual men account for the largest percentage of AIDS sufferers (45 percent). The next largest category is sexual partners of high-risk persons (27 percent). Intravenous drug abusers, persons receiving blood transfusions, and the babies of high-risk mothers are also at high risk. However, patterns of HIV transmission have changed somewhat in recent years. The number of new AIDS cases among homosexual and bisexual men has decreased. In contrast, the proportion of AIDS cases contracted through heterosexual sex has increased. Heterosexual contact is the primary method of HIV infection among women.

Many AIDS activists claim that the U.S. government has not responded adequately to the HIV/AIDS crisis. However, in recent years the government has made major efforts to combat this deadly disease. It has enacted several laws establishing AIDS research, education and prevention, and treatment programs. Over the years, the government has increased its spending on these programs. The proposed 2016 budget included $25.3 billion for domestic efforts and $6.3 billion for global efforts. Most of the money goes to domestic care and treatment (58%). HIV/AIDS treatments are very expensive. Researchers estimate that an HIV/AIDS patient may spend as much as $2,100 a month on health care.

Medical treatments and government programs finally seem to be having an effect. The numbers of new HIV/AIDS diagnoses have begun to decline. Also, since the mid-1990s powerful new drugs have been used to slow the progress of HIV. As a result, AIDS deaths have decreased, and the numbers of people living with AIDS have increased. However, AIDS is the sixth-leading cause of death among Americans between the ages of 25 and 44. Among African Americans in the same age group, it is the fourth-leading cause of death.

HIV/AIDS is not simply an American problem. The disease is a global epidemic. Since the late 1970s, more than 34 million people have died of AIDS worldwide. In 2012, the estimated death toll was 1.2 million. In 2014, some 2 million new HIV infections were reported. This brought the worldwide total of people living with HIV/AIDS to 36.9 million. Such figures, experts say, indicate that the death toll is bound to rise.

Sub-Saharan Africa, where AIDS is the leading cause of death, is the hardest hit of the world's regions. Some 68 percent of adults and nearly 90 percent of children infected with HIV live in this part of the world. Approximately 4,400 people die of AIDS each day in Africa. The life expectancy in sub-Saharan Africa has fallen to 47 years. Without AIDS, the life expectancy would be 62 years. HIV/AIDS is also having devastating effects on the economy of Africa. The disease is rapidly reducing the number of available workers. At the same time, the cost of caring for HIV/AIDS patients is rising. As a result, economic growth is slowing at an alarming rate. Economists fear that as HIV/AIDS takes hold in Asia, its economy could share the same fate.

Reading Check **Infer** How are these four issues affecting the American health-care system?

SECTION 3 Assessment

Reviewing Main Ideas and Vocabulary

1. **Identify** What factors contribute to rising health-care costs in the United States?
2. **Explain** What is HIV/AIDS, and why is it such a pressing health issue?

Thinking Critically

3. **Develop** What kinds of rights do you think a patient's bill of rights should include? Explain.
4. **Summarize** Describe the problems with health insurance in the United States.
5. **Support a Position** Should insurance plans cover the costs of alternative medicine? Why or why not?
6. **Rank** Using your notes and a graphic organizer like the one below, list the major issues facing the American health-care system today from Least Significant to Most Significant.

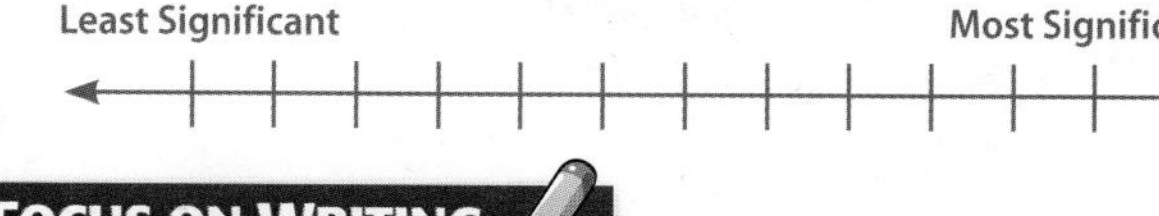

FOCUS ON WRITING

7. **Descriptive** Write a paragraph describing the ways that social status helps determine health. Consider the cost of health care, access to health care, and the relative health of wealthy and poor people.

Experiment
Applying What You've Learned

Testing Gender Differences

Use the workbook to complete this experiment.

Are men and women really that different from each other?

1. Introduction

Most of us assume that there are great differences between men and women. Some of these differences are biological. Others, however, are the result of gender socialization. And some of these differences may not be as dramatic as stereotypes would have us believe.

The purpose of this activity is to find ways to determine how different men and women really are. You will design an experiment that is meant to test society's assumptions regarding the differences between men and women. You will work in small groups and follow the scientific method as you design your experiment. To complete this experiment, follow the steps below.

- Following your teacher's instructions, organize into groups of 3 to 4 students.
- Once in your group, review the seven-step process that most sociologists use when conducting empirical research.
- Brainstorm and discuss some of the ways that men and women are different. You will choose one of these differences upon which to base an experiment.
- Form a hypothesis and create an experiment to test it.
- Present your experiment to the class and respond to their comments. Use their feedback to improve your experiment. Write a revised description of your experiment and hand it in to your teacher.

2. Review the Research Process

How do sociologists and other social scientists use the scientific method to test their assumptions? Review each of the following steps of the research process listed below. (You can find a more detailed explanation of each step in Chapter 1.) Consider what actions you will need to take at each step to design a useful and scholarly experiment.

THE RESEARCH PROCESS
Step 1 Define the Problem The researcher selects a topic for study and develops operational definitions of key concepts.
Step 2 Review the Literature The researcher reviews existing literature on the topic.
Step 3 Form a Hypothesis The researcher develops a testable hypothesis on the research topic.
Step 4 Choose a Research Design The researcher develops a plan for collecting, analyzing, and evaluating data.
Step 5 Collect the Data The researcher gathers and carefully records data.
Step 6 Analyze the Data The researcher objectively analyzes the data to determine whether the data support the research hypothesis.
Step 7 Present Conclusions The researcher presents the research findings to other sociologists.

3. Discuss Gender Differences

Before designing your experiment, spend some time brainstorming and discussing how men and women may be different. During your discussion, you should focus primarily on social characteristics. Consider any possible differences, no matter how obvious. When discussing different characteristics, try to focus on what kind of effect they have on socially accepted gender roles. Use the following prompts to make a list of the ways men and women may be different:

- What are some of the stereotypes that exist regarding men and women?
- What are some of the ways that men and women may potentially be different (such as leadership style, intelligence, expressing emotion, etc.)?
- How do we measure these different areas? For instance, how do we know if someone is a good leader or an intelligent person?

Select one of the differences that your group has come up with to base your experiment on. For example, you might decide to test whether men spend more time watching sports than women or if women gossip more than men do. Choose a gender difference that is potentially in question and can be proven.

4. Design Your Experiment

Your task is to design an experiment that tests whether or not the difference your group has selected actually exists. Follow the steps below to develop your experiment.

1. Form a hypothesis. Your hypothesis should propose that your selected gender difference does or does not exist.
2. Determine what data you need to prove your hypothesis.
3. Design an experiment to help you gather the necessary information to test your hypothesis. Be creative and scientific. Develop clear operational definitions. Set up your experiment carefully, with an experimental group, a control group, an independent variable, and a dependent variable. You are looking for control in the scientific sense. How you design your experiment is very important.
4. Consider what results you expect. What concerns might someone have upon reading about your experiment?
5. Assume that your hypothesis will be proven correct. What conclusions might you draw about human behavior?

5. Present Your Experiment

All good science must undergo and withstand the scrutiny of others who are knowledgeable about the subject. Describe your group's experiment to the class, and address the following points:

- What concerns do your classmates have? Do they have comments about design, sample/population, or control?
- How would your classmates improve on the design of your experiment?
- Sociologists are expected to provide enough information to allow their research to be replicated by their colleagues. Do your classmates have any concerns about your results?
- If your classmates were an ethical review board, would they approve your study?

As a group, use your classmates' comments to revise and improve your experiment's design. Prepare a written description of your experiment to give to your teacher.

6. Discussion

What did you learn from this experiment? Hold a group discussion that focuses on the following questions:

- Overall, how successful was the class at designing experiments that would test how different men and women really are?
- What did the best experiments have in common?
- What were some common weaknesses in the various experimental designs?
- How did you define the characteristics you tested for?
- Why do you think stereotypes about sex and gender persist?
- If your experiment were conducted in another country, do you think researchers there would get the same results? What if your experiment were conducted 50 years ago or 50 years from now?

CHAPTER 10 Review

Comprehension and Critical Thinking

SECTION 1 *(pp. 232–237)*

1. a. **Recall** What factors have helped to create a "leisure gap" between men and women?
   b. **Summarize** How are gender roles and gender identity related to the different experiences of boys and girls?
   c. **Support a Position** Do you agree with the theory that suggests that gender inequality is related to human reproduction? Why or why not?

SECTION 2 *(pp. 238–242)*

2. a. **Identify Main Ideas** What differences between segments of the elderly population affect social inequality?
   b. **Draw Conclusions** How has the aging of the population affected the opportunities available to elderly people?
   c. **Evaluate** Why do you think that the Americans with Disabilities Act has not been more successful in fulfilling its goal of helping Americans with disabilities find meaningful employment?

SECTION 3 *(pp. 243–249)*

3. a. **Identify** What is managed care, and what opinions about it do most Americans hold?
   b. **Summarize** What health-care issues have been at the center of public debate recently?
   c. **Elaborate** Why do you think many Americans have faced challenges using the health-care system in the United States?

INTERNET ACTIVITY

4. Doctors and scientists confronted many challenges in their efforts to identify and explain HIV/AIDS when patients first began exhibiting the disease. Use the Internet to research the history of the disease. Create a time line highlighting the major milestones in the identification and treatment of HIV/AIDS.

Reviewing Vocabulary

Match the terms below with their correct definitions.

5. gender
6. gender roles
7. gender identity
8. sexism
9. ageism
10. dependency ratio
11. Medicare
12. Medicaid
13. voting bloc
14. managed care
15. alternative medicine

A. the awareness of being masculine or feminine as those traits are defined by culture
B. the use of unconventional methods such as acupuncture, acupressure, biofeedback, massage, meditation, yoga, herbal remedies, and relaxation techniques to treat illness
C. the belief that one sex is by nature superior to the other
D. a group whose shared concerns motivate how they vote in elections
E. alternative health-insurance plans used to help control health-care costs
F. the government-sponsored health-insurance plan for elderly Americans and Americans with disabilities
G. the number of workers for each person receiving Social Security benefits
H. the specific behaviors and attitudes that a society establishes for men and women
I. the belief that one age category is by nature superior to another age category
J. the behavioral and psychological traits considered appropriate for men and women
K. the state and federally funded health-insurance program for low-income individuals

Sociology in Your Life

16. Gender socialization continues throughout life. How have you learned the appropriate behaviors for your gender? Think about the toys you played with and clothing you wore as a child, the mass media, and the attitudes of your parents, teachers, and friends. Write an essay examining your gender role socialization. Include an analysis of how you think you compare to the typical American student.

Skills Activity: Interpreting Cartoons

Study the political cartoon below. Then use it to help you answer the questions that follow.

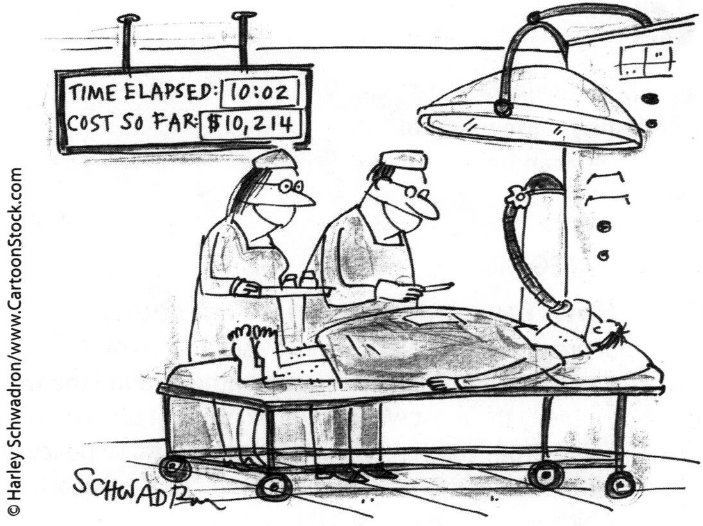

© Harley Schwadron/www.CartoonStock.com

17. Identify About how much is this man's surgery costing per minute?

18. Explain What point do you think the cartoonist is making about the American health-care system?

Writing for Sociology

Use your knowledge of the concerns facing elderly Americans to answer the question below. Do not simply list facts. Present a clear argument based on your critical analysis of the question, using appropriate sociological terminology.

19. Describe the steps you would take to ensure the future of the Social Security system. Consider:

- The problems facing the Social Security system, such as the growing number of recipients and the changes in the dependency ratio
- Solutions already offered and their possible effects
- New ideas

Connecting Online

Go online for review and enrichment activities related to this chapter.

KEY TOPICS VIDEOS
View compelling clips on issues in the field.

KEEP IT CURRENT
Link to the Current Events site for regularly updated stories on sociology as well as other social studies topics.

QUICK LAB
Reinforce a key concept with a short lab activity.

Social Inequality Around the World

Societies all around the world separate people into groups, both formally and informally. This separation provides the basis for social inequality—the unequal sharing of wealth, resources, and social rewards. Social inequality can be reflected in income, segregation, gender, and other areas.

INCOME

How unequal are incomes within countries?

Income inequality varies greatly around the world. In some countries, a small percentage of people holds much of the wealth, while in others, resources are more evenly distributed. One of the most common measures of inequality is called the GINI index. On this scale, zero corresponds to perfect income equality (everyone has the same income) and 100 corresponds to perfect income inequality (one person has all the income). The graph below shows income inequality in selected countries. In general, developing countries tend to have more income inequality than developed countries. Countries can alter their inequality with policies such as taxes and education.

SEGREGATION

How does segregation affect countries?

Segregation is one of the most visible types of social inequality, and it has affected countries around the world. Probably the most well known example of segregation comes from South Africa, which had an official policy of racial segregation from 1948 until 1993. Called apartheid, which means "apartness," this policy separated South Africans into four racial groups: White, Black, Colored (mixed ancestry), and Asian. White South Africans had full economic and political rights, while the other groups faced legal restrictions in many areas. Many Black South Africans, for example, were forced to live in townships, such as the one below, under extremely poor conditions.

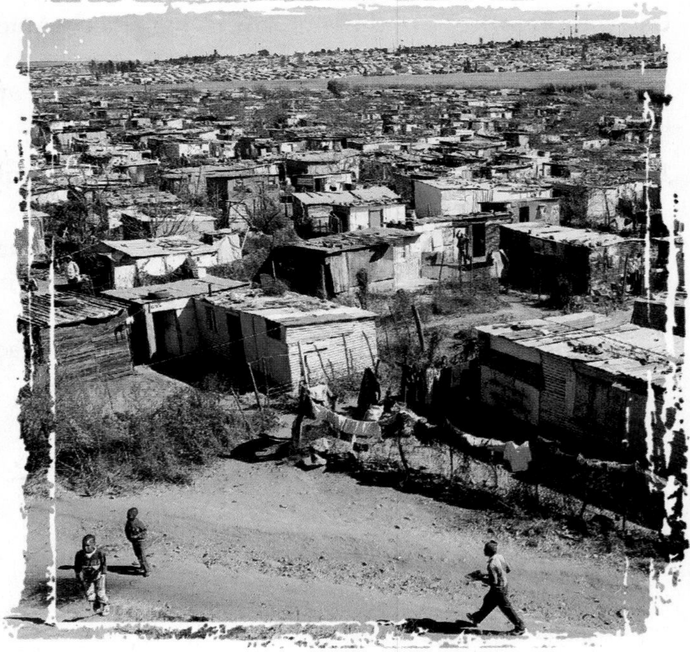

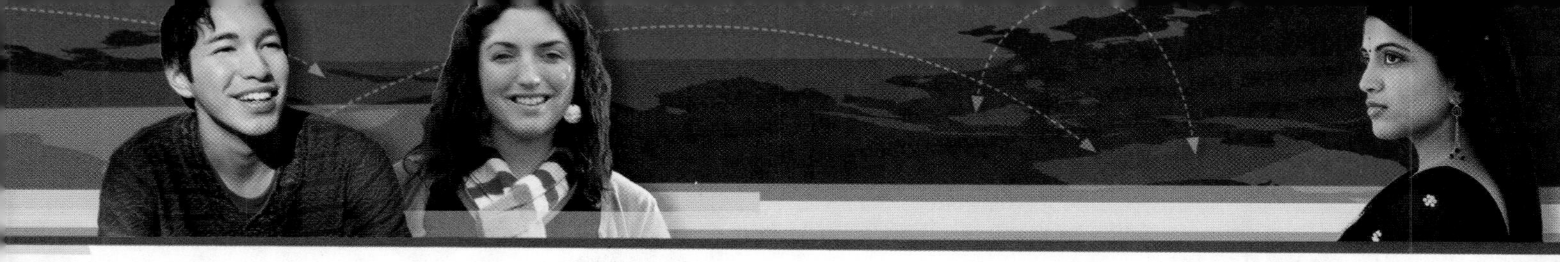

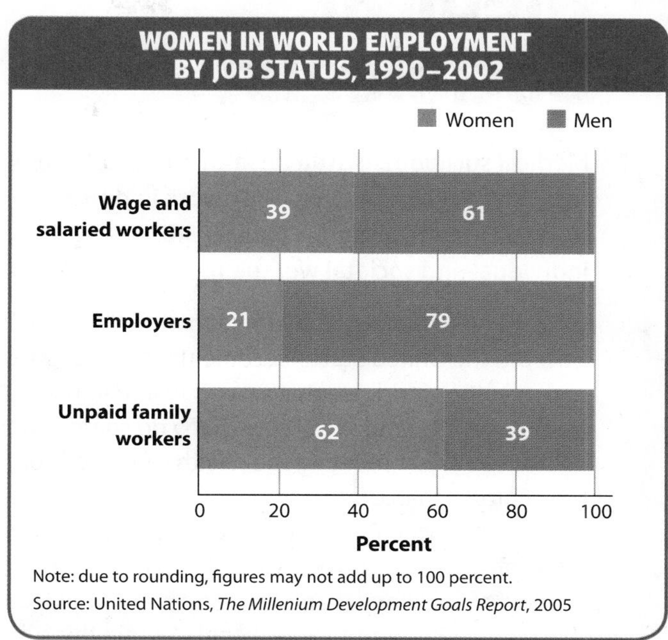

Note: due to rounding, figures may not add up to 100 percent.

Source: United Nations, *The Millenium Development Goals Report*, 2005

GENDER

How does gender inequality affect women around the world?

Gender inequality is a truly global issue. It is caused by a variety of factors, including discrimination, devaluing women's work, and the fact that women typically have greater family responsibilities than men and are therefore more limited in their career options. In countries around the world, women earn less than men for the same work. In addition, women are underrepresented in government and in certain high-status careers, such as law and medicine. They are also less likely than men to own their own businesses. As a result, women are more likely to be poor and to work in low-status jobs. Gender inequality tends to be worse in developing countries, where women often face inferior working conditions as well. In the photograph above, two women in India sift through broken light bulbs to sort glass from aluminum sockets. They earn about 90 cents a day and work without any protective equipment. Overcoming gender inequality is seen as a key to meeting global challenges such as reducing poverty and promoting sustainable development.

THINKING LIKE A SOCIOLOGIST

How does social inequality affect life in two different countries?

Social inequality is reflected around the world in many different ways. Select two countries that you would like to compare and contrast. For each country, use library or Internet resources to research the level of social inequality and how it affects society. Focus your research on one of the following areas:

1. Income
2. Status of minorities
3. Gender
4. Class
5. Opportunities for social mobility
6. Discrimination and prejudice
7. Politics
8. Education

After you have completed your research, write a short paper comparing and contrasting social inequality in your selected countries. How is social inequality in these two countries similar? How is it different?

CAREERS IN SOCIOLOGY

Medical Sociologist

Medical sociologists study health and health care from a social perspective. They work in different fields and share a commitment to improving individual and societal well-being.

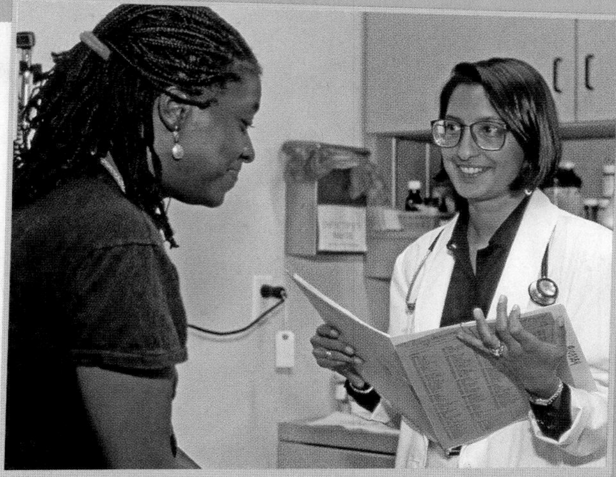

Medical sociologists study many issues related to the quality of health care within a community.

Why are women more vulnerable to AIDS than men? How did the United States become the second fattest nation in the world? In what ways is health impacted by race, gender, and social class? Why do some nations do a better job at meeting the health care needs of their citizens than others?

Medical sociologists are trained to answer such questions. Broadly speaking, medical sociology is a subfield of sociology that focuses on how social factors shape individual and societal health. Within this subfield, sociologists specialize in a number of areas. Some study inequalities in health care that are associated with race, ethnicity, gender, or social class. Others study relationships within health care systems, such as the relationship between doctor and patient, or how health and well-being are affected by individual choices, such as smoking, drinking, taking drugs, and engaging in risky sexual behavior. Still other medical sociologists study global health and disease patterns.

A four-year college degree is important for students who want to pursue a career in medical sociology. Some colleges offer students majoring in sociology a concentration in medical sociology coursework. Medical sociology courses are designed to prepare undergraduates for work in health care institutions and social service agencies, and are helpful for students in pre-medicine, pharmacy, nursing, and social work. Many students pursue medical sociology at the graduate level, completing a master's degree or a Ph.D. program.

Should you choose to specialize in medical sociology, you can enjoy a rich and rewarding career that will have important and far-reaching impact on the lives of others, and on society. People with a background in medical sociology find work in hospitals and nursing homes, as well as in social service agencies that provide help to people with medical problems and disabilities. They are also employed as researchers, college professors, patient advocates, intervention specialists, hospice workers, health administrators, and policy planners. If you are passionate about improving people's health and the health care system, a future in medical sociology may be high on your list of career options.

Applying ASA Style

Many medical sociologists publish articles in professional journals. In keeping with the guidelines from the **American Sociological Association (ASA)**, these articles follow a similar style for citing sources in a reference list. The papers you write for your sociology class should follow these guidelines, too.

A reference list is similar to a bibliography. It is a list of sources that follows the text in a section headed ***References***. The author is responsible for ensuring that all sources cited in the text are correctly listed in the reference list. For this reason, it is important to double-check the accuracy of all publication information, especially titles and the spelling of names.

Through Think Central you can access the ASA Quick Style Guide for more information on compiling a reference list. Review the ASA guidelines that you find at the Web site. Then practice writing a reference list with different types of sources, such as a book, a journal article, and an e-resource. An example of a book entry has been provided for you.

Mills, C. Wright. 1959. ***The Sociological Imagination***. New York: Oxford University Press.

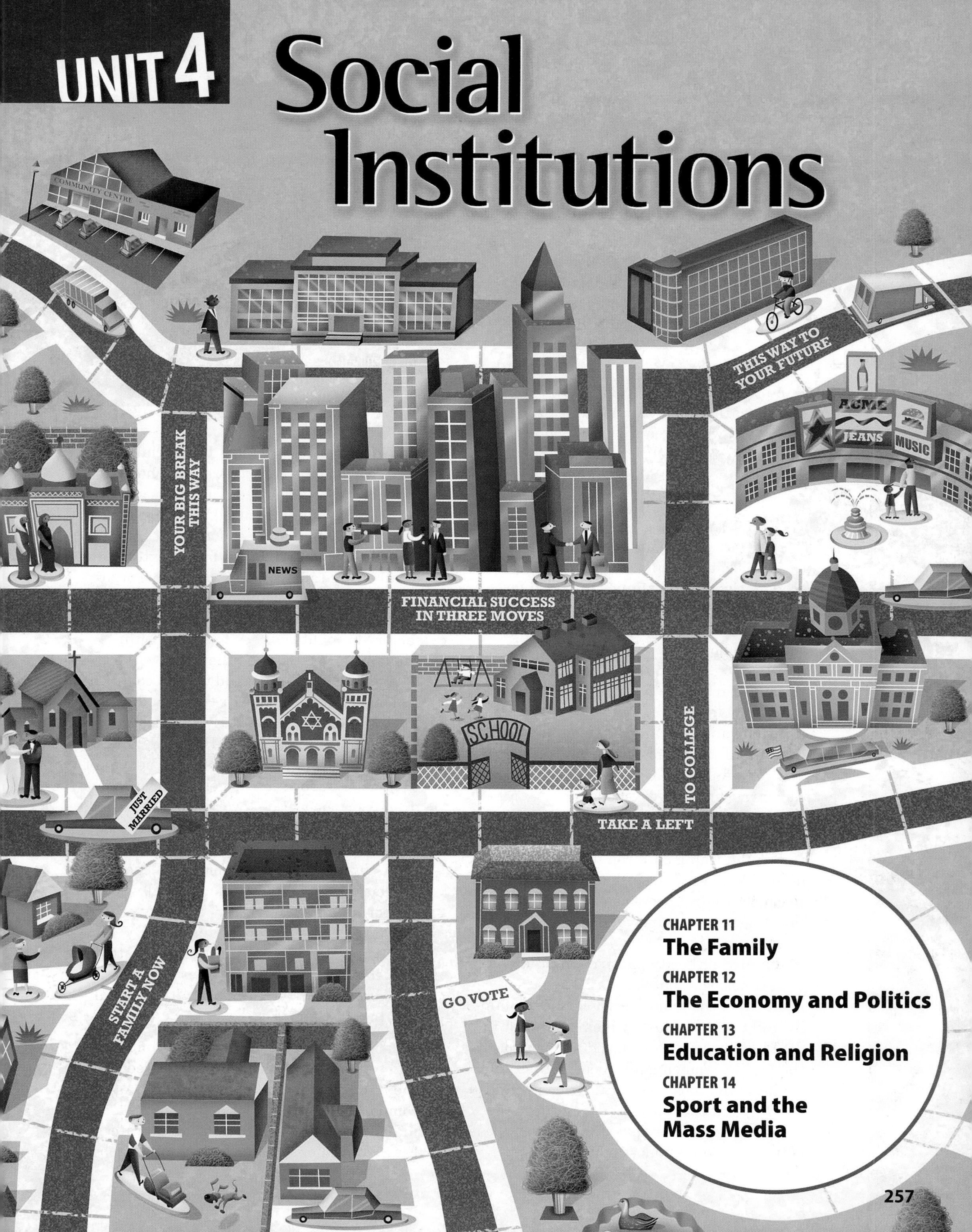

UNIT 4 Social Institutions

CASE STUDY

THE MYTH OF THE *Traditional Family*

This family from the early 1900s works together sewing clothing. Many families of that era had little time for anything but work.

Pundits and politicians often decry the decline of the "traditional" family, the type where dad works, mom stays at home, and the kids go to school. This model has been an ideal since the 1800s. In reality, though, it has rarely been the prevalent family structure in the United States.

The Preindustrial Family In preindustrial times, the family was the center of economic activity. Families provided for their own needs by growing their own food, making their own clothes, and building their own houses. What goods and services families could not produce, they acquired through barter.

Family life and economic life were essentially one and the same because the home was where work was done. Even skilled artisans in urban areas usually practiced their trades from workshops next to or inside the home. Work was a family activity, and all family members had a role to play. Even young children were expected to do simple work tasks or household chores. Because children were considered important to economic survival, families tended to be large.

Family authority patterns in preindustrial times were patriarchal. The father made all of the major decisions for the family and told other family members what to do. However, mothers played a major role in the family. Women made food, clothes, and candles, and took the leading role in child rearing. But they also produced goods to be sold or traded, or they provided services outside the home that produced income.

The Industrial Era Family Industrialization shifted economic activity from the home to the factory. The family became less self-sufficient as manufactured goods took the place of homemade ones. Over time, many services formerly handled by the extended family were taken over by charitable organizations and government agencies.

The shift of work from the home to the factory brought changes to roles within the family, too. Because they now worked outside the home, men and women could no longer watch over their children during the workday. Until the early 1900s, many children took factory jobs. However, laws that restricted child labor and the advent of compulsory education largely removed children from the world of work. This separation of children from work helped give rise to adolescence as a life stage.

As unions grew stronger, they began to push for a "living wage," one that would support a family. A healthy economy produced more and better-paying jobs. By the 1950s, most men in the United States earned enough to support their families. The family we now think of as "traditional" had taken shape.

The Postindustrial Family The economic and social trends of the late 1900s reduced the number of "traditional" families. As companies closed factories and moved manufacturing jobs outside the United States, they cut millions of high-paying union jobs.

Fathers who lost these jobs found that their new jobs often did not pay as much as their old ones. Many mothers had to go to work in order to help their families meet expenses.

At the same time, the women's movement led many mothers to seek employment after their children had entered school. However, women regularly received lower wages and fewer promotions than men.

In addition, inflation in the 1970s and recession in the 1980s led many families to need additional sources of income to make ends meet. By the late 1900s, the two-earner family had become the norm.

Many sociologists predict that the technological revolution will bring even more changes to the family. The growing practice of telecommuting—working at home using a computer—may make the home a major center of economic activity once again.

Today, most paying work takes place outside the home. Families spend much time away from each other.

What do you think?

1. How did industrialization change the institution of the family?
2. How might future technological advances change the family?

CHAPTER 11

THE FAMILY

Chapter at a Glance

SECTION 1: Family Systems and Functions

- Families throughout the world follow similar patterns.
- Family organization is determined by how societies answer questions of authority and relationships.
- The family's most important functions include reproduction, socialization, and economic security.

SECTION 2: Families in the United States

- Most families in the United States begin with courtship followed by marriage.
- The way families in the United States handle responsibilities has changed.
- Violence within families remains one of the leading forms of disruption.
- Many marriages end in divorce, which also disrupts families.
- Families face other disruptions later in life.

SECTION 3: Recent Trends in Marriage and Family

- People have begun to delay getting married for economic reasons.
- Some women choose to postpone having children so that they can pursue their careers.
- Many married couples choose to never have children.
- In most American families, both the mother and the father work.
- About a quarter of families in the United States are led by a single parent.
- Many divorced people get remarried, and new families are formed as a result.

SECTION 1

Family Systems and Functions

Before You Read

Main Idea
Families follow a variety of organizational patterns, but they all fulfill common functions.

Reading Focus
1. What are the three major family systems?
2. Do all societies use the same marriage and kinship patterns?
3. What are the basic functions of the family?

Vocabulary
family
nuclear family
family of orientation
family of procreation
extended family
kinship
monogamy
polygamy

TAKING NOTES Use a graphic organizer like this one to take notes on family systems and functions.

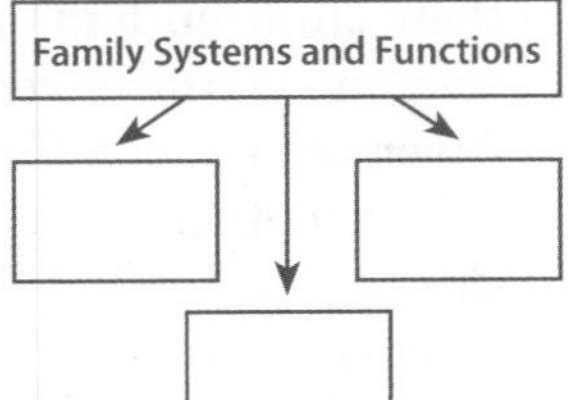

Learning to Love a Perfect Stranger

SOCIOLOGY CLOSE UP ***Should love come before or after two people marry?*** Families begin with two people falling in love. At least, that's the way it usually happens here in the United States. You meet the perfect man or woman, fall in love, get married, and start a new life together.

But some parts of the world follow a different order. Two people meet, get married, start a family, and only then have a chance to fall in love. This is how arranged marriages usually work. In India, China, and many other countries, arranged marriages are the norm.

Generally, parents find suitable spouses for their children. "Suitable" might include someone who practices the same religion, has a profitable job, or comes from a family with a good reputation. Often, the two prospective spouses have some say in the matter. They might meet in person a few times before agreeing to the marriage. However, in some cases the marriage is entirely up to the parents.

To those of us accustomed to the rituals of dating, marrying someone without a courtship might seem scary. How could you agree to spend the rest of your life with someone you barely know?

But many arranged marriages are successful. People in arranged marriages don't expect the romantic love that we count on as a basis for wedded bliss. They focus on practical details: earning a living, raising children, caring for aging parents. They expect to work at the relationship and hope to earn the love and respect of their partners. ■

An elaborate ceremony celebrates this couple's arranged marriage.

Family Systems

As you have learned, a social institution is a system of statuses, roles, values, and norms organized to satisfy one or more of the society's basic needs. The most universal social institution is the family—every society organizes its members into families. However, what constitutes a family varies widely from culture to culture. Despite this variety, families throughout the world follow similar organizational patterns and fulfill common functions.

A **family** is a group of people who are related by marriage, blood, or adoption and who often live together and share economic resources. How would you answer the question, What is a typical family? You would probably describe what sociologists call the nuclear family. A **nuclear family** consists of one or both parents and their children. The nuclear family is the family form most recognizable to people in the United States.

A person often is a member of two different, overlapping nuclear families. An individual's **family of orientation** is the nuclear family into which the person is born or adopted. This family is composed of the individual and his or her siblings—brothers and sisters—and parents. When an individual marries, a new nuclear family is formed. The new nuclear family is now a **family of procreation,** consisting of the individual, his or her spouse, and their children.

In many societies the nuclear family is embedded in a larger family group. Sociologists refer to this family unit as the **extended family.** An extended family consists of two or more generations. In an extended family, grandparents, parents, children, uncles, aunts, and cousins may all live in one house or group of houses or even in different countries.

Nuclear families and extended families are often part of a much larger kinship system. **Kinship** refers to a network of people who are related by marriage, birth, or adoption. Kinship systems can be quite large. In fact, in some kinship systems there are close to 200 possible categories of relatives. These categories can be organized into three broad groupings—primary, secondary, and tertiary—depending on relationships among individual family members.

An individual's closest relatives are called primary relatives. They are the members of an individual's families of orientation and procreation. The seven possible categories of primary relatives are mother, father, sister, brother, spouse, daughter, and son.

Family Systems

Families are people related by blood, marriage, or adoption. This diagram shows the three major family systems for the person in purple.

Extended family two or more generations of relatives

Family of orientation the family into which a person is born or adopted

Family of procreation a person's spouse and children

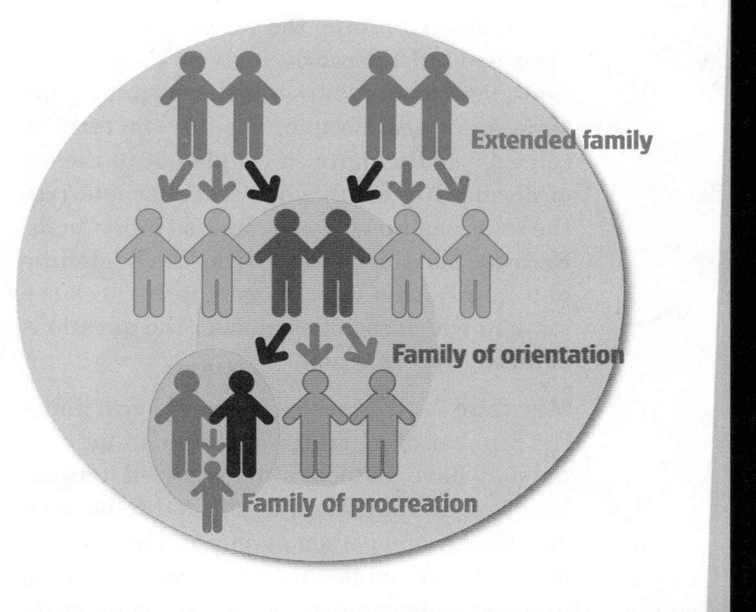

Skills Focus INTERPRETING CHARTS

Who belongs to the family of procreation for the two dark green people?

An individual's next closest relatives are called secondary relatives. Secondary relatives are the primary relatives of an individual's primary relatives. Secondary relatives consist of over 30 more categories of people, including grandparents, grandchildren, in-laws, aunts, uncles, nephews, and nieces.

When the primary relatives of an individual's secondary relatives are considered, some 150 other categories of people are added to the kinship system. Individuals at this level are called tertiary relatives, and include great-grandparents, great-grandchildren, great-aunts, great-uncles, and cousins. These nearly 200 categories can translate into literally hundreds of relatives because several people can occupy each category.

ACADEMIC VOCABULARY

enable make possible or supply an opportunity

Reading Check **Find the Main Idea** What is the most universal social institution?

Marriage and Kinship Patterns

Some form of family organization exists in all societies. However, the exact nature of the family varies from society to society and even within societies. Family organization is determined by how a society or group within a society answers four questions:

- How many marriage partners may a person have?
- Who lives with whom?
- How is family membership determined?
- Who makes the decisions in the family?

Before examining the ways in which societies around the world answer those questions, you should know what is meant by the term *marriage*. Sociologists use the term to refer not to the married couple but to the set of norms that establishes and characterizes the relationship between married individuals. Because marriage often marks the beginning of a family, this set of norms influences the ways in which societies answer the questions of family organization.

Marriage Partners No universal norm limits the number of marriage partners an individual may have. In most industrialized nations, however, an individual is allowed to be married to only one person at a time. The practice of being married to only one spouse at a time is called **monogamy.** However, in the majority of pre-industrial societies around the world, individuals are permitted to have multiple marriage partners. Marriage with multiple partners is called **polygamy.**

Polygamy can take either of two forms. The most common form of polygamy is poly-gyny, in which a man is permitted to marry more than one woman at a time. The practice of polygyny in preindustrial societies generally occurs when there are large areas of land available for cultivation. A husband who has two or more wives gains additional workers for the land. With multiple wives, the husband is likely to produce more children. These factors enable the man to attain higher status and gain more wealth.

Polyandry—in which a woman is permitted to marry more than one man at a time—is a much rarer form of polygamy. Polyandry, which is found primarily in parts of Asia, appears to arise in response to extreme poverty and a shortage of women. For example, the Toda of India once practiced female infanticide—the killing of female babies. As a result, there were not enough women to provide monogamous partners for all of the men in the society. Because of this shortage the Toda developed a system of polyandry. When a woman married a man, she became a wife to all of his brothers. This practice also served to keep the birthrate down, which was important in a poverty-stricken society that could not afford to support a large population.

Polygamy is the more common marital system in preindustrial societies around the world. Nevertheless, most people in polygamous societies take only one spouse. The main reason for this practice is that it is very expensive to have more than one marriage partner. In all polygamous societies, individuals are expected to marry only the number of spouses that they can support. Few people can support two or more spouses and their children. Therefore, polygamy is limited mostly to the wealthy few in a society and serves to increase their status and prestige.

Historically, marriage has been understood to be strictly between a man and a woman. In recent years, however, marriage between partners of the same sex has gained wider social acceptance and legal recognition. In an increasing number of countries, mostly in Europe and the Americas, gay and lesbian couples can marry.

Residential Patterns Rules of married residence vary from society to society. In some societies the newly married couple is expected to live with or near the husband's parents. This residential pattern is called patrilocality—*patri* means "father" in Latin, *locality* means "location." Patrilocality is the most common rule of residence. In some societies, though, the couple is expected to live with or near the wife's parents. This pattern is called matrilocality—*matri* means "mother." One residential pattern, called bilocality—*bi* means "two"—allows the newly married couple to choose whether they will live near the husband's or the wife's parents. Patrilocal, matrilocal, and bilocal rules of residence encourage the development of extended-family living.

In most industrial societies the newly married couple is free to set up a residence apart from both sets of parents. This residential pattern is called neolocality—*neo* means "new." Neolocal residence is most commonly associated with nuclear-family living.

Descent Patterns In some societies, people trace their kinship through the father's side of the family. In other societies, kinship is traced through the mother's side. In still other societies, kinship is traced through both parents.

Societies that trace kinship through the father's family follow the rule of patrilineal descent. Patrilineal descent is common in preindustrial societies in which men produce the most valued resources. In a patrilineal society, property is passed from father to son. Matrilineal descent—the tracing of kinship through the mother's family—is much less common. In matrilineal descent, property is passed from mother to daughter. Most industrial societies practice bilateral descent. In bilateral descent, kinship is traced through both parents, and property can be inherited from either side of the family.

Rules for descent are important for the smooth operation of society because they establish who is eligible to inherit property from whom. However, the need to maintain lines of descent can lead to interesting practices. For example, in a few patrilineal societies a father can declare one of his daughters a "son" if he does not have male heirs. This "son" takes a bride who then bears children by various men. These children are considered members of the "son's" kinship group. The marriage between the two women is in name only, however. The women never live together. In fact, the "son" may already be married to a man from another village. The only purpose of the marriage is to produce children who will qualify as legitimate members of the "husband's" kinship group, thereby ensuring that the group will continue.

Authority Patterns In theory there are three possible patterns of authority in families. A family may be a patriarchy, in which the father holds most of the authority. It may be a matriarchy, in which the mother holds most of the authority. Or it may be egalitarian, meaning that the mother and the father share authority.

The vast majority of societies around the world are patriarchal. Matriarchal societies are rare. Even in societies that practice matrilineal descent, true authority usually rests with the mother's brothers.

MARRIAGE AND KINSHIP TERMS

Sociologists use special terminology to describe families.

Marriage Partners
Monogamy Marriage of one man to one woman
Polygamy Marriage with multiple partners
Polygyny Marriage of one man to multiple women
Polyandry Marriage of one woman to multiple men

Residential Patterns
Patrilocality Couple lives with or near the husband's parents
Matrilocality Couple lives with or near the wife's parents
Bilocality Couple decides which parents to live with or near
Neolocality Couple lives apart from both sets of parents

Descent Patterns
Patrilineal descent Kinship traced through father's family; property passed from father to son
Matrilineal descent Kinship traced through mother's family; property passed from mother to daughter
Bilateral descent Kinship traced through both parents; property inherited from either side of family

Authority Patterns
Patriarchy Father holds most authority
Matriarchy Mother holds most authority
Egalitarian Authority shared between mother and father

Skills Focus **INTERPRETING CHARTS** What is the name for the marriage of one woman to multiple men?

TECHNOLOGY FOCUS

Wired Genealogy

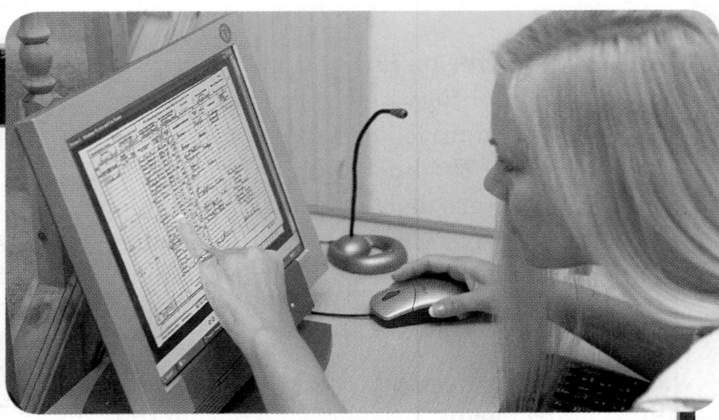

Genealogy—tracing a family's ancestors and history—has long been a popular hobby. In the past, it required travel to libraries, courthouses, and other places where ancestors had lived. Researchers would dig through musty files and record books in search of birth certificates, census records, and other documents.

With the advent of the Internet, much of the research has moved online. Thousands of Web sites specialize in genealogical research. There are so many of these sites that people have created online genealogy directories, sites that contain lists and descriptions of genealogical Web sites. There are also genealogy-specific search engines. Results from typing a family name into a general-purpose search engine would include mostly pages with irrelevant information. The genealogy-specific search engines restrict the search to genealogy sites and produce much better results.

Many sites have electronic copies of documents important to genealogical research. Social security records, census forms, and other documents are all available online. However, some significant records are not yet available online and still require old-fashioned methods of research.

Genealogy is an extremely popular hobby, and many of the sites charge fees. But millions of people are willing to pay for easy access to family records.

Thinking Critically

Infer Why are there so many genealogy Web sites?

Many industrialized societies—such as the United States—are moving toward more egalitarian authority patterns. However, patriarchal authority is still the cultural norm for most of these societies. The new egalitarian authority patterns have greatly altered domestic life in many American families. American couples are increasingly sharing the demands of domestic chores, earning income, and raising children.

Reading Check **Identify Supporting Details** What are the two forms of polygamy?

The Functions of the Family

All families perform similar functions, although the ways these functions are fulfilled may differ from culture to culture. Among the family's most important functions are the regulation of sexual activity, reproduction, socialization, and the provision of economic and emotional security.

Regulation of Sexual Activity All societies regulate the sexual activities of their members to some degree. At the very least, they enforce some type of incest taboo. An incest taboo is a norm forbidding sexual relations or marriage between certain relatives. The incest taboo is found universally, but the relatives that are included in this taboo vary from society to society.

For example, in the United States a person cannot marry his or her parents, siblings, grandparents, aunts, uncles, nieces, or nephews. However, about half of the states allow marriages between first cousins. Marriages between first cousins are also allowed among the patrilineal Yanomamö of South America. These marriages are restricted to cross cousins—the children of an individual's paternal aunt or maternal uncle. The Yanomamö consider marriages between parallel cousins—the children of an individual's maternal aunt or paternal uncle—incestuous.

The labeling of biologically related individuals as nonrelatives is common in patrilineal and matrilineal societies because ancestry is traced only through one side of the family. For example, among the Lakher of Southeast Asia individuals can marry their maternal half-siblings but not their paternal half-siblings.

Because the Lakher are a patrilineal group, they do not consider their maternal half-siblings to be relatives.

Reproduction To survive, societies must replace members who die or move away. In every society the family is the approved social unit for the performance of this function. Consequently, societies establish norms governing childbearing and child rearing. These norms determine such things as who is eligible to marry and to bear children, the number of children that is considered appropriate, and the rights and responsibilities of parents.

Socialization A society's survival also depends on teaching its children the ways and values of the society. The family is the first agent of socialization that most children encounter. As a result, most children first learn about the customs and norms of society from the family. Parents, siblings, and other relatives usually serve as the earliest role models for children.

Economic and Emotional Security The family acts as the basic economic unit in society. In most societies, labor is divided on the basis of gender—some tasks in the family fall to males while others fall to females. Most societies also have a division of labor based on age; tasks are divided within the family depending on the ages of the family members. Through this division of labor, the family ensures that its members are fed, clothed, and housed. However, not every family meets these needs.

Although most societies divide labor within the family, specific roles vary from society to society. For example, in some societies that rely on horticulture—simple gardening—for food production, the men tend plants. In other societies, the same task often falls to women. In most industrialized nations, both men and women work and earn money for the family.

In addition to economic support, the family also provides emotional support for its members throughout their lives. As the basic and most intimate primary group in society, the family is expected to guide the individual's psychological development and to provide him or her with a loving and caring environment. In practice, not all families provide such an environment.

In industrialized societies, many of the traditional functions of the family have been taken over, in part, by other social institutions. For example, the educational system plays a major role in socializing young people. Similarly, the government fulfills many of the economic functions that would be the task of families in traditional societies.

Reading Check **Summarize** What are the four basic functions of every family?

SECTION 1 Assessment

Reviewing Main Ideas and Vocabulary

1. **Define** What is a family?
2. **Identify** What is the name for a network of people related by marriage, birth, or adoption?
3. **Recall** How does the incest taboo vary in different societies?

Thinking Critically

4. **Compare** How is the nuclear family related to a person's family of orientation?
5. **Explain** How do industrial and preindustrial societies differ in terms of marriage partners?
6. **Draw Conclusions** How do families help societies to survive and to grow?
7. **Evaluate** What marriage and kinship terms describe your family? Use one term from each of the four groups—marriage, residential, descent, and authority—and explain how each term describes your family.
8. **Categorize** Using your notes and a graphic organizer like the one below, categorize these relatives as primary, secondary, or tertiary.

Relative	Kinship type
aunt	
brother	
mother	
cousin	
grandfather	

FOCUS ON WRITING

9. **Descriptive** What would it be like to live in a true matriarchal society with matrilineal descent? How would it compare to the current society of the United States?

SECTION 2

Families in the United States

Before You Read

Main Idea
In the United States, families usually begin with marriage. They are also subject to many different forms of disruption.

Reading Focus
1. How have courtship and marriage changed?
2. How do most U.S. families distribute responsibilities?
3. Is family violence increasing?
4. What is the divorce rate?
5. What disruptions do families experience later in life?

Vocabulary
heterogamy
dual-earner families

TAKING NOTES Use a graphic organizer like this one to take notes on families in the United States.

How families begin	How families end

SWITCHED AT BIRTH

SOCIOLOGY CLOSE UP ***What counts as your real family?*** When nine-year-old Arlena Twigg got sick and died in 1988, routine testing revealed that she was not her parents' biological child. She had been accidentally switched at birth with another child. Ernest and Regina Twigg's biological daughter had been taken home by the Mays family and raised as Kimberly Mays.

The Twiggs decided to try to establish a connection with Kimberly. Bob Mays, whose wife Barbara had died when Kimberly was two, allowed the Twiggs to spend time with Kimberly. But Kimberly felt uncomfortable around her biological parents, and she became more distressed after each visit. After only five visits, Bob Mays decided it would be best for his daughter if she stopped seeing the Twiggs.

The Twiggs thought otherwise, and they went to court to establish custody over Kimberly. Years of legal battles ensued, pitting the Twiggs' rights as biological parents against Kimberly's desire to stay with the father who had raised her. Finally, in 1993, a judge ruled that Kimberly could stay with Bob Mays and not see the Twiggs anymore.

A happy ending? Not so simple. Six months later, Kimberly left the Mays home and moved in with the Twiggs and their seven other children. More legal proceedings gave the Twiggs custody but also granted visitation rights to Bob Mays. Kimberly later ran away from the Twiggs.

Families face many potential disruptions, but few this strange. This section will discuss some of the more common issues encountered by families in the United States.

A hospital mistake sent Kimberly Mays home with the wrong family. After a five-year court battle, she won the right to stay with the family that raised her.

Courtship and Marriage

Traditionally the popular image of the "typical" American family included a working father, a stay-at-home mother, and two or three children. However, families in the United States are much more diverse. Some families consist of a married couple who have decided not to have children. Other families have just one parent present. In still other families, no parents are present—the children live with their grandparents or other relatives.

However American families are arranged, most begin in the same way—with marriage. The majority of adults in the United States marry at least once during their lifetime. In 2011 about 51 percent of Americans over 18 years of age were married. However, marriage rates are declining, particularly among younger people. For example, about 20 percent of Americans over the age of 17 have never been married. Among Americans between the ages of 25 and 34—the prime years for marriage—this figure is about 25 percent.

Why do people marry? In the United States romantic love is often the basis of marriage. People marry because they are emotionally and physically attracted to one another. Yet love is neither blind nor random. Americans overwhelmingly marry individuals who have social characteristics similar to their own. This kind of marriage is called homogamy. Homogamy is based on characteristics such as age, socioeconomic status, religion, and race.

In general, people in the United States marry spouses who are close to them in age, with the husband slightly older than the wife. Americans also marry within their own socioeconomic class. When differences between a couple do exist, it is most often the woman who is of a lower socioeconomic standing.

In the case of religion, marriages between individuals from different Protestant denominations are relatively common. However, it is much less common for Protestants to marry non-Protestants. The same is true for Catholics, Jews, and people of other faiths. When individuals from different religious backgrounds do marry, one partner sometimes adopts the other partner's religion.

Homogamy is even stronger when it comes to race. Only about 10 percent of all marriages in the United States are between individuals of different races. Nevertheless, the number of interracial marriages has grown by about 28 percent since 2000. As recently as the 1960s, at least a dozen states had laws that made interracial marriages illegal. In 1967 a Supreme Court ruling struck down those laws.

Although homogamy is still typical in the United States, an increasing number of marriages are heterogamous. **Heterogamy** is marriage between individuals who have different social characteristics. This increase in heterogamy is a function of changing social conditions. As contact between people of differing social backgrounds increases, the likelihood of heterogamous marriages also increases. Some of the factors that have contributed to heterogamy are higher college enrollments, more geographical mobility, and the increased participation of women in the workforce.

Reading Check **Identify Supporting Details** How do most U.S. families begin?

Distribution of Responsibilities

In order to survive, families need to provide shelter, food, and clothing for all members. Caring for children is another important task for most families. As described in this chapter's Case Study, the way families meet these needs has changed as societies have evolved.

In the mid-1900s, most American families followed a similar pattern. The father earned money outside of the home that paid for shelter, food, and clothing. The mother tended the home, bought and prepared food, and took care of the children. The children often assisted their parents in household chores.

CASE STUDY CONNECTION

The Myth of the Traditional Family The responsibilities of family members have changed through the years.

In the late 1900s more mothers began working, and **dual-earner families**—families in which both husband and wife have jobs—became the norm. With this change responsibilities shifted. Day-care centers have taken the place of stay-at-home moms to care for younger children. Many fathers began to do more of the household chores. In practice, the new division of labor places more of a burden on women. Even though both husbands and wives work full-time jobs, most women still do the majority of housework.

Reading Check **Summarize** What responsibilities do all families need to fulfill?

Child-Care Arrangements

Options for Child Care In the United States, about half of children younger than three years of age are cared for by their parents. The majority of children from three to five years of age receive care from someone other than a parent.

When a relative takes care of children, it is usually a grandparent. People caring for unrelated children include nannies, neighbors, and informal day care based in homes. Over half of children from three to five years of age attend day-care centers or preschools, including Head Start programs.

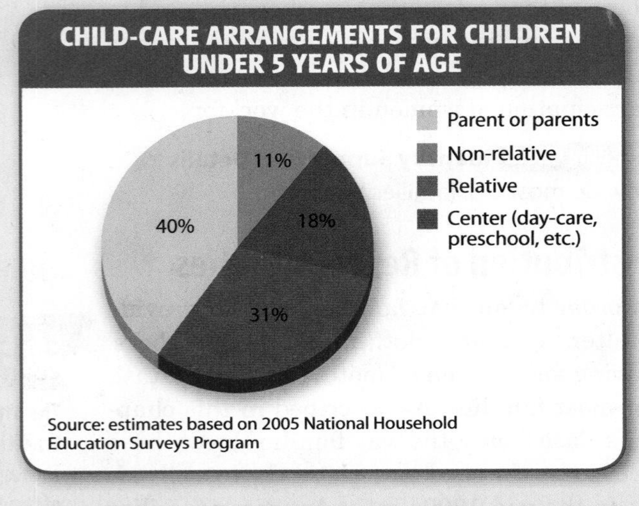

Family Violence

Most families experience disruption in one form or another. Some disruptions are very serious—threatening or even destroying family stability. Others are simply a part of the family life cycle.

Some sociologists argue that family violence is the most devastating family disruption. Until relatively recently, family violence was considered a rare phenomenon. However, sociologists now know that family violence is a serious problem among all social classes and racial and ethnic groups.

One reason family violence was at first considered a problem of the lower classes was the way in which statistics were collected. Most early research was based on police and hospital reports. Because the police and hospitals were more likely to be involved in cases of domestic violence involving lower-income families, these families were overrepresented in the statistics. Cases of violence among middle- and upper-income families generally went unreported.

The widespread nature of family violence was confirmed in a 1975 nationwide study. The researchers found that nearly one-third of the people they interviewed had experienced some form of family violence. Moreover, almost three-fourths of the people interviewed reported hitting their children, usually more than once. The study also revealed that wives were as likely as husbands to commit violent acts within the family. However, the acts committed by wives were less violent in nature and less damaging to spouses and children.

Since that study, family violence has decreased, according to studies done by various government and private agencies. Statistics collected by the U.S. Department of Justice suggest that the number of female victims of abuse and murder has dropped while the number of male victims has stayed the same. Surveys by child-advocacy groups suggest that child abuse is also decreasing. However, the following statistics show that family violence remains a serious problem.

- A woman is assaulted or beaten every 9 seconds in the United States.
- A third of women and a quarter of men have been physically assaulted by an intimate partner.
- In the United States, 19.3 million women and 5.1 million men have been victims of stalking.
- 72% of murder-suicides involve killing an intimate partner.
- About 6.6 percent of children are exposed to violence between intimate partners.

Reading Check **Compare** Which social classes does family violence affect?

Divorce

Divorce is another significant family disruption. The media often quote an estimate that half of all marriages in the United States eventually end in divorce. However, sociologists suggest that the actual figure probably ranges from 40 to 45 percent. The United States divorce rate—the number of divorces per 1,000 population—remains one of the highest in the world at 3.2.

The rate of divorce varies among different segments of the population. For example, couples who marry during their teenage years have a greater likelihood of divorce than couples who marry after the age of 20. Education also influences the rate of divorce. Couples with college educations are less likely to divorce than couples who have not attended college. However, women who have attended graduate school are more likely to divorce than less-educated women.

Divorce also varies by race and ethnicity. African American women are more likely than white women to be separated or divorced. Hispanic women, on the other hand, are slightly less likely than white women to experience divorce. The higher rate of divorce among African American women is partially explained by the fact that a higher percentage of African American women are young and have low incomes when they marry.

Divorce has major consequences for former partners. Economically, divorce has greater effects on women than on men. Because children typically reside with the mother, divorced women usually suffer a decrease in economic resources, whereas divorced men see an increase. Conversely, women seem to make better emotional adjustments to divorce. Rates of suicide, alcoholism, drug abuse, depression, and anxiety are all higher among divorced men than among divorced women.

Adults are not the only ones affected by divorce. Each year, more than 1 million children under the age of 18 witness the breakup of their parents' marriages. Like their parents, children of divorce often struggle to adjust to their new situations. Studies suggest that children of divorced parents have more emotional problems than children of parents who have not divorced. Many children still struggle to adjust 10 years after their parents divorced.

Sociologists suggest several reasons for the high divorce rate. First, laws governing the divorce process have become less complicated, and the cost of obtaining a divorce has decreased. In the past for divorce to be granted one spouse had to be "at fault" of marital misconduct. Most states now have some form of no-fault divorce, in which neither party has to state a reason for seeking divorce. Second, the increase in the number of dual-earner families and the growth of day care facilities has decreased the economic dependence of women. It now is financially possible for more women to remove themselves from unhappy marriages. Third, society in general has become

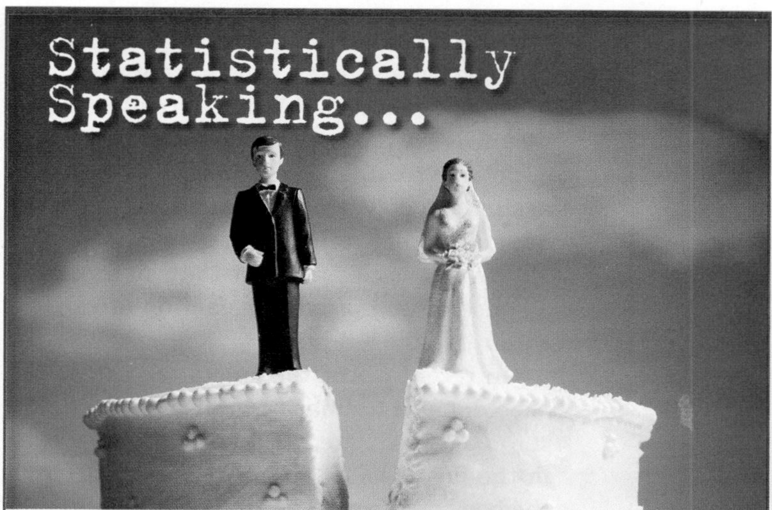

Divorce, USA As divorce became more socially acceptable in the United States, the divorce rate skyrocketed. Although the rate has begun to decrease, close to half of all marriages end in divorce.

1 in 5 Number of adult Americans who have ever been divorced

38% Marriages in which one or both of the partners had been previously divorced

8 years Average length of first marriages that end in divorce

5.3 per 1,000 Divorce rate in the United States at its peak in 1981

6.4 per 1,000 Divorce rate in Nevada in 2004

Skills Focus **INTERPRETING DATA** Does divorce stop people from getting married again? What statistic shows this?

Sources: National Center for Health Statistics; Census Bureau more tolerant of divorce. It no longer carries the same social stigma it did in the mid-1900s and before. Finally, many people expect more of marriage and are less ready to accept marital problems. When these problems become overwhelming, people often see divorce as an acceptable alternative to staying in an unsatisfactory marriage.

Reading Check **Identify Supporting Details** What is the rate of divorce in the United States?

Disruptions Later in Life

Most parents spend a good part of their lives raising their children. When the children grow up and leave home, parents are left with what sociologists call an empty nest. Some people assume that parents, particularly mothers, have difficulty adjusting to this disruption. However, studies suggest that mothers feel a sense of increased satisfaction after their children have left home.

In recent years, the empty-nest stage has been delayed for many families. Children, for the most part, are leaving home later than in the past. Over half of Americans between the ages of 18 and 24 still live at home. Some children are returning to their parents' homes after living independently for several years. About 12 percent of 25- to 34-year-olds now live with their parents.

The final disruption that families face is family dissolution that follows the death of a spouse. Because women statistically have a longer life expectancy than men, they are more likely to experience this disruption. About 13 percent of men aged 65 and older are widowers. However, over 40 percent of all women over the age of 65 are widows.

Widowhood creates identity problems for some women. This is particularly true for women who have defined themselves primarily in terms of being a wife. Such women often continue to judge their own actions and life choices against the values of their dead husbands. In essence, these women continue to use the wife role as a guide to behavior long after they become widows.

Widowed women also frequently face economic problems. The loss of employment income or the decrease in Social Security benefits that accompanies the death of a husband may push some widows into poverty. Less money means that it is more difficult for these women to enjoy activities outside of the home. This change in circumstances translates into increased levels of loneliness for many widowed women.

Reading Check **Find the Main Idea** What are the two main sources of disruption later in life?

SECTION 2 Assessment

Reviewing Main Ideas and Vocabulary

1. **Define** What is a dual-earner family?
2. **Compare** What is the difference between homogamy and heterogamy?
3. **Recall** What is the marital status of most adults in the United States?

Thinking Critically

4. **Make Generalizations** How are responsibilities shared in most dual-earner families?
5. **Support a Position** Family violence seems to be decreasing. Should governments and social service agencies turn their attention elsewhere?
6. **Interpret** Why do many widows experience difficulties after their husbands die?
7. **Explain** Using your notes and a graphic organizer like the one below, explain why the divorce rate in the United States is so high.

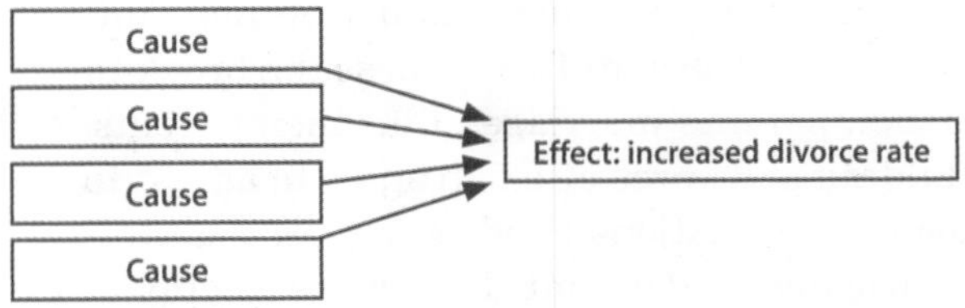

FOCUS ON WRITING

8. **Narrative** How does divorce change a family? Tell a story about a family that goes through a divorce. Focus the story on one particular event or character rather than telling the entire history.

SECTION 3

Recent Trends in Marriage and Family

Before You Read

Main Idea
Marriage and family arrangements that once seemed unusual have become the norm in the United States.

Reading Focus
1. Is delayed marriage new?
2. Why do some couples delay childbearing?
3. Why are there more dual-earner marriages?
4. How many one-parent families are there?
5. What are the consequences of remarriage?

Vocabulary
sandwich generation
voluntary childlessness

TAKING NOTES Use a graphic organizer like this one to take notes on recent trends in marriage and family.

Trend	Characteristics

Till DEATH Do Us Part

Many marriages that began in the mid-1900s lasted much longer than historical averages.

SOCIOLOGY CLOSE UP ***Are marriages lasting as long as they used to last?*** We often hear that marriages don't last as long as they used to. Anecdotally, it seems that might be right. Almost everyone knows some people who have been divorced, others who have been divorced and remarried, and possibly some who have been divorced and remarried several times. So it certainly seems like marriages must not be lasting as long.

But does the data support the hypothesis? At first glance, it seems that way. About 70 percent of couples who got married in the 1950s reached their 25th wedding anniversaries, whereas only about 50 percent of couples who got married in the 1970s did.

However, some sociologists point out that it all depends on what eras you compare. Marriages begun in the mid-1900s certainly lasted longer than those begun in the late-1900s. But compared to historical averages—from the 1800s and before—marriages today last about the same amount of time.

Surprised? The difference is modern medicine. In the past, most marriages ended when one of the spouses died. As health care improved in the 1900s, median length of marriage peaked. Then divorce took the place of death in ending marriages, and median marriage longevity returned to historical norms.

Delayed Marriage

Dual-earner families, one-parent families, childless couples, and stepfamilies are common features of American family life. Sociologists are particularly interested in these and other developments, such as delayed marriage, delayed childbearing, and remarriage.

In 1890 the median age at first marriage in the United States was 22.0 years for women and 26.1 years for men. By 1950 the median age at first marriage had dropped to 20.3 years for women and 22.8 years for men. However, in recent years this trend toward earlier marriages has reversed. In 2010 the median age at first marriage was 25.8 years for women and 28.3 years for men. As you can see in the graph on this page, these ages are among the highest recorded since the Bureau of the Census first began collecting this information in 1890.

Some sociologists view this tendency toward later marriage as an indication that being single has once again become an acceptable alternative to being married. Relatively common in the early part of the last century, being single lost ground in the marriage-minded years following World War II. By 1970 only 6.2 percent of American women between the ages of 30 and 34 had never been married. This number was down from 16.6 percent in 1900. Then in the 1970s and 1980s, the marriage rate began to slow. By 2006 the proportion of women between the ages of 30 and 34 who had never been married had increased to about 24 percent. Demographers estimate that more than 15 percent of today's young adults will never marry.

Sociologists note that most young people today are delaying marriage in order to finish their education and to launch their careers. This trend is particularly notable among women. Sociologists also note that the increase in the number of unmarried people may partially be the result of more couples living together outside of marriage. Sociologists refer to this practice as cohabitation. In 2005 there were almost 6 million cohabiting couples in the United States. Cohabitation is particularly common among the young. Estimates suggest that about 10 percent of unmarried women between the ages of 25 and 29 are currently cohabiting and an additional 15 percent have cohabited at some time in the past. Cohabitation now precedes more than half of all first marriages. Although most individuals who cohabit eventually marry someone—not necessarily their current partner—the practice usually delays marriage.

Reading Check **Draw Conclusions** Is delayed marriage a new trend? Why or why not?

Statistically Speaking...

Age at First Marriage This graph shows the median age at first marriage for men and women in the United States from 1890 to 2000. "Median" is a type of statistic that shows the middle value of any group of figures. From 1890 to 1950, the median age at first marriage generally followed a downward trend. An exception to the trend occurred from 1920 to 1940, as the median age for women rose slightly. From 1960 to 2000, the median age at first marriage for both men and women followed an upward trend.

Skills Focus **INTERPRETING GRAPHS** When was the median age of first marriage the lowest?

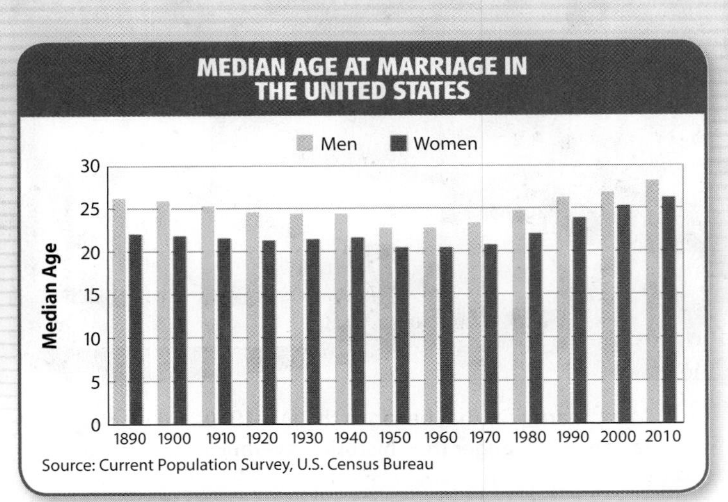

Delayed Childbearing and Childlessness

Two other trends in family life in the United States that sociologists have noted in recent years are delayed childbearing and childlessness. In the past, having children was a primary purpose of marriage. Now, many couples have other priorities.

Delayed Childbearing In the 1960s the average length of time between marriage and the birth of the first child was 15 months. By the 1970s that interval had increased to 27 months. Today it is not at all uncommon for women to have their first child after the age of 30. Women older than 30 accounted for about 40 percent of all births in 2004. The reasons for delaying childbearing are similar to the reasons for delaying marriage—to allow time for one or both spouses to complete education and to establish a career.

Some couples who delayed having children until their thirties are now facing a particularly challenging situation. They have young children to raise at the same time that they have aging parents who need care and assistance. These couples have been labeled the **sandwich generation** because they are caught between the needs of their children and those of their parents. Worn down by family duties and the demands of work, members of the sandwich generation often feel overwhelmed.

Childlessness There has also been an increase in the number of married couples who never have children. Some couples who at first plan to delay parenting find later that they have waited too long. Other married couples discover that they cannot have children because of infertility. Still others consciously choose never to have children.

Sociologists call the conscious choice to remain childless **voluntary childlessness.** The number of voluntarily childless couples has increased markedly in recent years. In 2004, about 20 percent of married or divorced women had no children. Among childless married women in their late thirties, a little more than 40 percent had no plans to have children in the future.

Studies have found that married couples who choose to remain childless often have high levels of education and income. Career success is a priority for many voluntarily childless women. Many voluntarily childless couples place great value on the woman achieving success. These couples also value the freedom, financial security, and the opportunity to spend time together that childlessness allows.

Reading Check **Make Generalizations** Why do some couples choose to remain childless?

Dual-Earner Marriages

Another trend in American family life is an increase in the number of dual-earner marriages because of the increased numbers of married women entering the labor force. The percentage of married women who worked outside the home increased steadily until the mid-1990s. In 1940 about 17 percent of married women were employed outside the home. By 1960 the number of married women in the labor force had grown to 31 percent. The growing number of married working women in the labor force helped to lessen the stigma once attached to working wives and mothers. This favorable climate encouraged more women to seek work outside the home. Today about 74.7 percent of all married women work outside the home at least part-time.

ACADEMIC VOCABULARY

interval space or time between points

Married women work for the same basic reason that married men work—economic necessity. Few families today can survive or live as comfortably as they want on a single salary. In about one quarter of all dual-earner couples, the wife earns more than the husband does.

The labor market itself has been a factor in the increase of dual-earner families. After World War II, there was a tremendous rise in the number of available jobs in service industries. Women also entered many occupations that had been held primarily by men. Women today make up about 18 percent of the computer scientists, and 48 percent of the college and university teachers in this country.

Women's participation in the labor force is influenced by the ages of their children. In 2015 about 64 percent of married women with children under the age of 6 were employed outside the home, compared to about 74 percent of married women with children between the ages of 6 and 17.

Single Parenting

"Fathers lead 12 to 20 percent of single-parent households."

Many single-parent households are run by dads. ***What trends may have contributed to the rise of single-parent households?***

Many women with newborn children in the home leave the labor force for a period of time. However, in 1993 Congress passed the Family and Medical Leave Act to help parents care for their newborn children without having to quit working. The law requires companies with more than 50 workers to give up to 12 weeks of unpaid leave to parents of newborns. The law also covers workers who need to take time to arrange for the adoption of a child or to care for a sick spouse, child, or parent. Federal government officials estimate that about three million people take advantage of the Family and Medical Leave Act each year.

Some people have expressed concern that the participation of married women in the labor force may have negative consequences for their children. However, research has failed to establish any meaningful negative effect. In fact, some studies suggest that daughters of working women may benefit. Daughters of working mothers often have a better self-image, are more independent, and are higher achievers than daughters of nonworking mothers.

Reading Check **Find the Main Idea** Why are there so many dual-earner families?

One-Parent Families

Another trend in American family life that has gained the attention of social scientists in recent years is the increase in one-parent families. One-parent families are formed through separation, divorce, death of a spouse, births to unwed mothers, or adoption by unmarried individuals. However, in the United States most one-parent families are the result of divorce or of births to unwed mothers. One-parent families account for about 27 percent of the families in the United States with children under the age of 18. Women head about 87 percent of these one-parent families.

Although all families experience problems, single parents are subject to a special set of stresses and strains. Sociologist Robert S. Weiss identified three problems common to the single-parent experience. Weiss labeled one source of stress found among single parents as "responsibility overload." In two-parent households, husbands and wives share the responsibility of making plans and decisions. Single parents, on the other hand, often make their plans and decisions alone. They are also generally alone in providing the care needed by their families.

Weiss called a second source of stress among single parents "task overload." Single parents must handle all of the tasks usually divided between two people—such as maintaining the home, caring for children, and earning a living. They spend so much time handling those tasks that they often have little or no time for themselves.

Single parents also experience "emotional overload," Weiss noted. Single parents must often cope with the emotional needs of their children by themselves. Handling this task, along with everything else, generally means that their own emotional needs go unmet.

The major source of stress for most single parents, particularly single mothers, is lack of money. The poverty rate among children in female-headed families with no spouse present was 45.8 percent in 2013. Many of the women who lead poor families are young unwed mothers or divorced mothers who did not work when they were married. For the most part, the only positions open to these women are low-skilled, low-paying jobs. As a result, they find it very difficult to climb out of poverty.

Single parenthood affects not only adults but also children. In 2011 about 20.6 million children under the age of 18 lived in single-parent families. Some studies suggest that these children are much more likely than children who live in two-parent families to experience negative life outcomes. School drop-out rates, teen pregnancy rates, and arrest rates tend to be higher for children of single-parent families. However, some sociologists point out that these problems arise from economic disadvantage, not from single parenthood.

Reading Check **Summarize** What three problems do most single parents face?

Remarriage

Another trend in American family life that is of interest to sociologists is the increase in the rate of remarriage. In over one-third of the marriages occurring today, one or both of the partners have previously been married. The majority of the people who get divorced eventually remarry.

The high rates of divorce and remarriage in the United States have led to a large number of stepfamilies. Stepfamilies, also called blended families, arise when one or both of the marriage partners bring children from their previous marriages into their new family. The majority of families created by remarriage involve children from prior marriages. About 17 percent of children under the age of 18 now live in stepfamilies.

Becoming part of a stepfamily may involve a period of adjustment. The marital partners take on the parenting roles formerly held by biological parents. This process is sometimes a source of conflict in the family. Children may resent stepparents who appear to be trying to take the place of a biological mother or father. Similarly, stepparents may resent not being treated with the love and respect usually given to parents. Studies have shown that it takes approximately four years for children to accept a stepparent in the same way that they accept a biological mother or father.

Learning to accept new stepparents is not the only adjustment that children in a stepfamily have to make. They may also have to adjust to having new stepbrothers or stepsisters living in the home with them. This adjustment often involves learning how to share a parent's affections with their new siblings.

Adjusting to life in a stepfamily takes patience, understanding, and a willingness to work together. The reward can be a strong family unit. However, the pressures of family life sometimes prove too much for these marriages as well. Many remarriages eventually end in divorce.

Reading Check **Identify Supporting Details** What is another name for a stepfamily?

SECTION 3 Assessment

Reviewing Main Ideas and Vocabulary

1. **Define** What is the sandwich generation?
2. **Describe** What are some reasons for voluntary childlessness?
3. **Recall** What is one consequence of the high rates of divorce and remarriage?

Thinking Critically

4. **Explain** Why do most young people delay getting married?
5. **Draw Conclusions** How are delayed marriage and delayed childbearing related?
6. **Analyze** Are all married couples without children voluntarily childless? Why or why not?
7. **Support a Position** Do one-parent families cause children to have problems? Explain.
8. **Analyze** Using your notes and a graphic organizer like the one below, analyze the changes that led to dual-earner marriages becoming the norm.

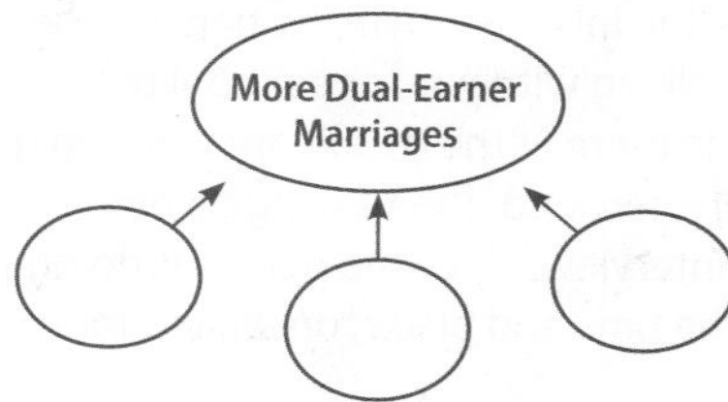

FOCUS ON WRITING

9. **Expository** Should people be encouraged to stay married if they have children? Write a short essay explaining your answer to this question.

Lab

Applying What You've Learned

Changes in Family Life in the Recent Past

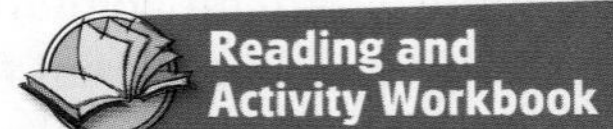

Reading and Activity Workbook

Use the workbook to complete this lab.

How have families changed over the past 40 years or so?

1. Introduction

You might have heard an older person say, "Back in my day, my folks were too busy working to take me to school. I had to walk a mile to get to school, and a lot of days that was through a foot of snow!"

Television shows and other popular media have turned this grumpy older person into a cliché. He or she remembers the way things used to be and looks skeptically on the way things are today—especially family life. To the grump it seems that parents are much too relaxed and not strict enough. You might also hear older people say things like, "If my parents had ever caught me doing some of things you get away with, I'd be in big trouble!"

But what was family life really like in the past? Did children respect their parents more? Were responsibilities at home different for some family members? Were families similar in different parts of the country or the world?

2. Conducting an Interview

In this lab, you will try to learn what family life used to be like by conducting an interview. To see if the crotchety old person was right or not, follow these steps:

- Interview one person who is at least 60 years old. Try to think of a few people who are that old who might be willing to talk with you for 20–30 minutes. They don't have to be related to you, but they do need to be at least 60 years old.
- Next, arrange the interview. Ask the person if he or she would mind talking with you for a school project. If he or she agrees, explain more of the details and confirm that your subject is still interested. Then arrange a time and place to conduct the interview. Since the person is doing you a favor, try to make the time and place convenient for him or her.
- Ask the interview subject the questions below. In addition, think of three more questions you would like to learn about.

1. Where did you grow up?
2. What was your neighborhood like?
3. What was your home like?
4. What people made up your immediate family?
5. How did your parents or guardians make a living?
6. What were your responsibilities around the house? Did you get an allowance for completing chores?
7. Did you have a job? If so, what kind of work did you do?
8. How often did you get in trouble with your parents? How did they discipline you?
9. What was the most important lesson your parents or guardians taught you?
10. How do you think family life has changed since you were 18?

- Being a good interviewer requires both good preparation and good listening. The most important thing is to listen carefully and to record what the person says. Take notes, use an audio recorder, or use a video camera with a microphone. If you are writing notes, be sure to finish writing down the answer before moving on to the next question.
- In order to get complete answers to your questions, you may sometimes need to ask follow-up questions. Just make sure to let the interviewee finish what he or she has to say before asking a follow-up question.
- Be courteous throughout the interview. Make sure to begin and end the interview by thanking the person for taking the time to talk with you.
- You may want to do a trial run of the interview with a classmate or friend before conducting the actual interview. That will allow you to test the phrasing of your questions as well as to practice your interviewing techniques.

3. Documentation and Analysis

After the interview, you will need to organize your notes. As you do so, see if you find common themes.

- If you took notes, transcribe them into an electronic document. (See the sample transcript below.) The sooner you do this, the better. You may need to add information that you remember but did not write down.
- If you made an audio or video recording, listen to it and transcribe it into an electronic document. Again, the sooner you do your transcription, the better. If parts of the interview are unclear, you will have an easier time remembering what was said.
- Now review your notes and recall the conversation with the person you interviewed. What did you learn about family life in the past? Are there any questions that didn't get answered completely? Have new questions occurred to you based on what you learned?
- Prepare to present your findings to the class. You shouldn't read the entire transcript of the interview to the class. Choose the most interesting parts to quote directly. Summarize the rest.
- Also prepare a brief description of the person you interviewed. Include his or her name, age, and other important information.

Sample Interview Transcript

Transcript of conversation with Mr. Evan Jones
Conversation took place on April 10 from 7:00 to 7:30 PM

Me: Thank you for meeting with me, Mr. Jones. To begin the interview, could you just tell me a little about yourself?

Mr. Jones: Well, sure. I'm 68 years old, and I've lived in Maryland my entire life. I'm married to a wonderful woman, and I have three children and four grandchildren.

Me: Where in Maryland did you grow up?

Mr. Jones: My family lived on the Eastern Shore near Chestertown . . .

4. Presentation and Discussion

When all students have completed their interviews and documented them, share the findings with the class. Then hold a discussion about how family life has changed and how it has remained the same.

Have each student present his or her findings. Begin with a brief description of the person you interviewed. Then present the highlights of the interview and what you learned. When all students have shared their findings, hold a discussion about family life:

- Did all of the interviewees present the same picture of family life? How did they differ?
- How has family life changed? Cite specific examples to support your assertions.
- How is family life the same? Again, cite specific examples.
- Would you rather live in a family in the past or today?
- What was the most surprising thing you learned about family life in the past?
- How did families in the past perform the functions described in Section 1?

CHAPTER 11 Review

Comprehension and Critical Thinking

SECTION 1 *(pp. 260–265)*

1. **a. Describe** What functions does the family fulfill?

   b. Summarize What four basic questions help to determine how a society or group within a society organizes families?

   c. Support a Position Why is polygamy relatively rare even in the societies where it is an acceptable marital system?

SECTION 2 *(pp. 266–270)*

2. **a. Recall** How do sociologists explain the high rate of divorce in the United States?

   b. Explain If family violence is decreasing, why is it still considered a serious problem?

   c. Elaborate What is more common in the United States, homogamy or heterogamy? Why?

SECTION 3 *(pp. 271–275)*

3. **a. Identify Main Ideas** Why has the number of married women in the workforce increased?

   b. Compare How are the reasons for delaying childbearing similar to the reasons for delaying marriage?

   c. Explain What led to the increase in the number of dual-earner marriages?

INTERNET ACTIVITY

4. How different was family life in the past? Use the Internet to find historical studies on marriage and the family in colonial America. Look for information on courtship, roles within the family, and the treatment of children. Use what you find to prepare a brief research paper describing what marriage and family life were like in colonial times.

Reviewing Vocabulary

Fill in each blank with the term that correctly completes the sentence.

5. A __________ is a group of people related by marriage, blood, or adoption.
6. A __________ consists of one or both parents and their children.
7. An __________ consists of two or more generations of relatives.
8. In some __________ systems there are close to 200 possible categories of relatives.
9. The __________ between when people get married and when they have children has increased.
10. The marriage of one man to one woman is called __________.
11. Marriage with multiple partners is called __________.
12. Most Americans practice __________ by marrying individuals who have social characteristics similar to their own.
13. Marriage between individuals who have different social characteristics is called __________.
14. In __________ both the husband and the wife have jobs.
15. Couples who have young children to raise at the same time that they have aging parents who need care have been labeled the __________.

Sociology in Your Life

16. Watch several television programs, some that feature one-parent families and others that feature two-parent families. Make a list of the problems encountered by these families and the methods they use to solve them. Prepare a brief report comparing and contrasting the problems faced by the two types of families and the way they solved the problems.

SKILLS ACTIVITY: INTERPRETING GRAPHS

Study the bar graph below. Then use the information in the graph to help you answer the questions that follow.

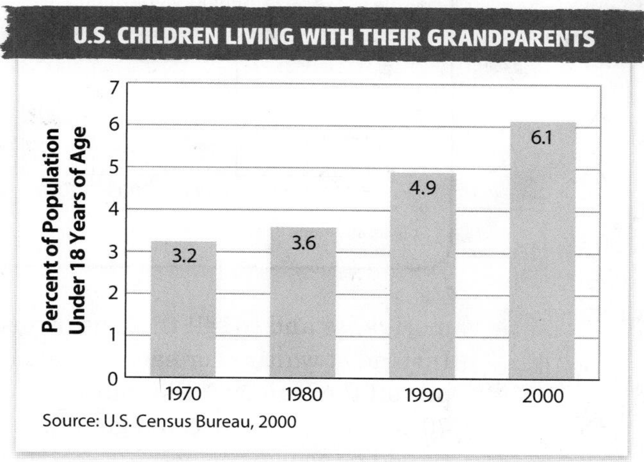

17. Identify In what year was the largest percentage of the population under age 18 living with grandparents?

18. Interpret Describe the trend shown in the graph.

19. Make Judgments What other trends in family life coincide with the trend shown in this graph? Do any of them have a cause and effect relationship with the trend in this graph?

WRITING FOR SOCIOLOGY

Use your knowledge of the family to answer the question below. Do not simply list facts. Present a clear argument based on your critical analysis of the question, using the appropriate sociological terminology.

20. How have the following trends changed family life in the United States?

- decline in manufacturing
- increase in workers living in suburbs but working in the city
- increase in use of cellular telephones

Connecting Online

Go online for review and enrichment activities related to this chapter.

KEY TOPICS VIDEOS
View compelling clips on issues in the field.

KEEP IT CURRENT
Link to the Current Events site for regularly updated stories on sociology as well as other social studies topics.

QUICK LAB
Reinforce a key concept with a short lab activity.

CASE STUDY

LIAR'S LOANS

Why would someone take out a loan they might not be able to repay? Why would a bank loan someone hundreds of thousands of dollars without checking that person's income? Why would investors buy these same risky loans from banks—hundreds of billions of dollars worth?

The answers to these questions help to explain the financial crisis that gripped the United States at the end of the first decade of the 2000s. The subprime mortgage crisis, as it became known, affected every level of the economy, stretching from Wall Street to Main Street. All of the levels were interrelated, so there was no single culprit responsible for the mess.

Let's begin the investigation by examining the U.S. housing market. Usually when a home buyer applies for a loan, a banker requires the buyer to prove his or her ability to repay the loan. When a bank hands the buyer hundreds of thousands of dollars from its own reserves, it wants assurance that the home buyer will be able to make regular payments on the loan.

In the early 2000s, something shocking happened. Banks became much less concerned about verifying the financial status of the home buyer. Why? Because of an innovation at the next level of the financial world: mortgage-backed securities. Banks began to bundle hundreds or thousands of mortgages and to sell them as investments. Instead of waiting for each home buyer to pay off the loan over the course of 15 to 30 years, the banks could get those loans repaid as soon as they could sell them.

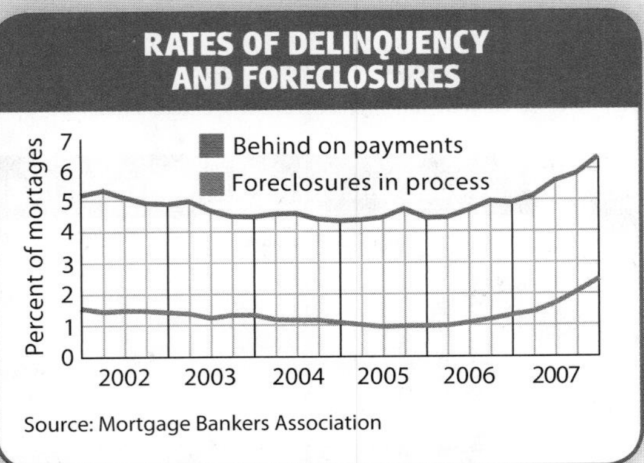

And it turned out that banks could sell the loans as quickly as they could package them. The global pool of capital—money from such sources as central banks, pension funds, and wealthy investors—reached record levels early in the 2000s. Investors ran out of standard investments for all this cash, so they turned to bundled mortgages.

The demand for mortgage-backed securities outstripped the ability of banks to find credit-worthy home buyers. So the banks and other financial companies lowered their standards for who could qualify for a home loan.

Which leads us back to Main Street. Lenders developed the "stated income loan," which has come to be known by the less flattering name "liar's loan." Borrowers no longer needed to prove their income; they just had to show proof of employment. The banks didn't care what the applications said, because they sold off the risky loans before the borrowers got into trouble.

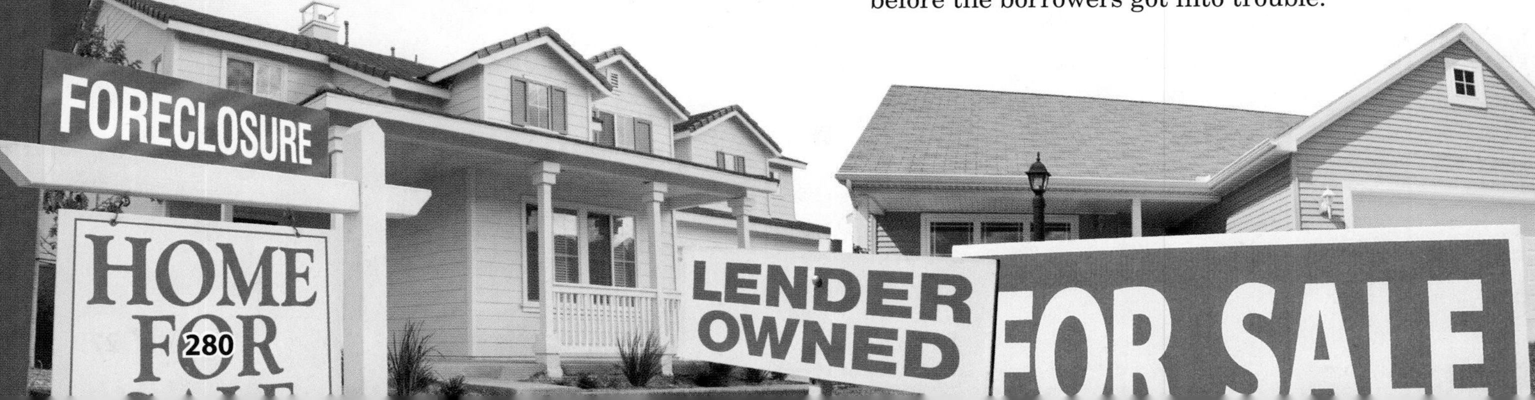

Given the new leeway, many people signed up for loans they had no way of repaying. Some of them may have known up front that they would have a hard time repaying their loans. Others may have had plans to increase their income. All of them wanted their part of the American dream: to own their own home.

In the past, when banks carefully verified a borrower's ability to repay a loan, only a small percentage of homeowners defaulted on, or failed to repay, their loans. But by 2008, the percentage of defaults rose to record levels, as the graph on the previous page shows. As a result, millions of new homeowners lost their homes.

As more and more homeowners stopped making payments on their mortgages, the bundled mortgage investments started to fail. Investors stopped buying mortgage-backed securities, but they also grew cautious about making similar investments. The pool of available capital dried up, wreaking havoc on the financial system. The federal government stepped in to try to stabilize the crisis. This crisis led to the near collapse of the U.S. stock market and resulted in the Great Recession.

What do you think?

1. What is a stated income loan? How is it different from a traditional mortgage?
2. What could have been done to prevent the subprime mortgage crisis?

CHAPTER 12

THE ECONOMY AND POLITICS

Chapter at a Glance

SECTION 1: The Economic Institution

- Societies develop economic institutions to decide how to allocate their resources.
- Economic systems have three basic sectors: primary, secondary, and tertiary.
- The two main economic models are capitalism and socialism.

SECTION 2: The United States Economy

- The United States economy became the strongest in the world in the 1900s.
- New economic developments have changed the way the U.S. economy works.

SECTION 3: The Political Institution

- Societies exercise power over their members through political institutions.
- Legitimate power is authority; power exercised through force is coercion.
- The two basic types of government are democratic and authoritarian.

SECTION 4: The United States Political System

- The United States is one of the few countries with a two-party system.
- Politicians are influenced by more than just the voters.
- People develop political beliefs through political socialization.

SECTION 1

The Economic Institution

Before You Read

Main Idea
Societies develop economic institutions in order to distribute limited resources.

Reading Focus
1. How do economic basics affect society?
2. What three sectors do all economic systems have?
3. What are the two main economic models?

Vocabulary
economic institution
factors of production
primary sector
secondary sector
tertiary sector
capitalism
socialism
law of supply
law of demand
laissez-faire capitalism
free-enterprise systems
communism

TAKING NOTES Use a graphic organizer like this one to take notes on the economic institution.

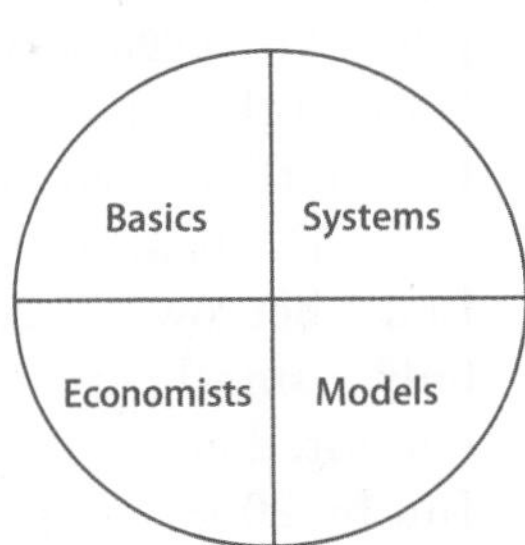

Urban Foraging

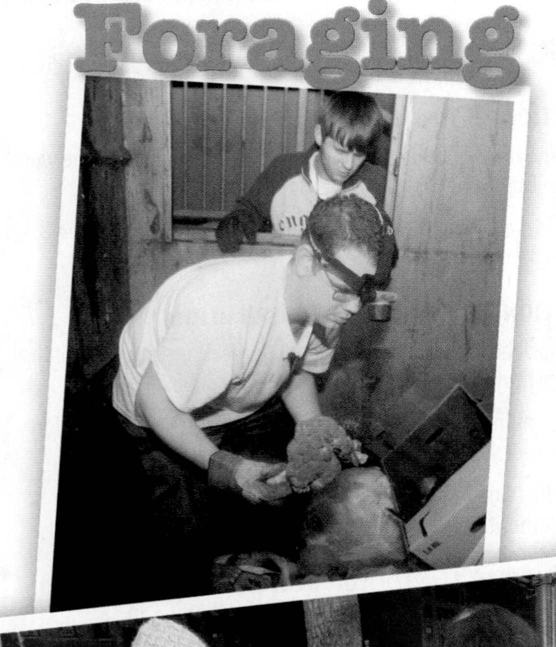

Freegans search trash for free food and other items, then hold swap meets where they exchange the goods they don't need.

SOCIOLOGY CLOSE UP ***Do you think you could survive without money?*** In many urban centers around the world, a new economic subculture has developed. They call themselves Freegans, and they live on what the rest of the world throws away.

Freegans see the mainstream economic system as corrupt and unsustainable, and they try to avoid participating in the system. As a result, Freegans do not spend money unless absolutely necessary. Instead of going shopping Freegans go foraging, as the hunter-gatherers did thousands of years ago. Freegans search the city for their clothes, their furniture, even their food.

Food may be the easiest thing for Freegans to find. Most grocery stores throw away expired dairy products, bruised fruits and vegetables, and many other kinds of food. Freegans are also aware that bakeries frequently toss unsold bread after a day or two.

Besides food, Freegans try to forage for all their other material needs. If they can't find what they need in the trash, they can trade items with other Freegans at swap meets and bartering websites.

With a little effort and a lot of ingenuity, most Freegans live fairly well. They may not have the latest fashions or the coolest techno-gadgets, but they do not lack for any necessity. And it all comes from what the rest of us throw away.

Economic Basics

In every society people have certain needs and wants. Needs—such as food, clothing, and shelter—are basic to survival. Wants—such as new cars, stereo systems, and personal digital assistants—are not necessary for survival, but they often add to the quality of life. To satisfy people's needs and wants, every society develops a system of roles and norms that governs the production, distribution, and consumption of goods and services. This system is called the **economic institution.**

The need for economic institutions is rooted in the problem of scarcity. People's needs and wants are unlimited. However, the resources available to satisfy these needs and wants are limited. Consequently, societies must decide how best to use their limited resources to satisfy the most needs and wants. Societies do that by answering three basic questions:

- What goods and services should be produced?
- How should these goods and services be produced?
- For whom should these goods and services be produced?

How a society answers these questions is determined in large part by the society's factors of production and its level of technology. The **factors of production**—resources needed to produce goods and services—include land, labor, capital, and entrepreneurship. Land refers to natural resources such as soil, water, minerals, plants, animals, sunlight, and wind. Labor, also called human resources, involves anyone who works to produce goods and services. Capital refers to all the manufactured goods used in the production process—such as tools, machinery, and factories. Capital also refers to the means to purchase goods, stock, or other items. Entrepreneurship includes the organizational skills and the risk-taking attitude required to start a new business or develop a new product. In economic terms, technology is the use of science to produce new products or to make the production process more efficient. A society's ability to use technology to exploit the factors of production shapes that society's economic system.

Reading Check **Find the Main Idea** What three questions must every society answer?

Economic Systems

All economic systems comprise three basic sectors—the primary sector, the secondary sector, and the tertiary sector.

- The **primary sector** deals with extracting raw materials from the environment—for example, fishing, mining, and farming.
- The **secondary sector** concentrates on the use of raw materials to manufacture goods. Examples of such activities include turning wood into furniture or manufacturing a computer.
- In the **tertiary sector** the emphasis shifts to providing services, such as retail sales or auto repair.

The degree to which any one of the sectors is emphasized over the others depends on a society's subsistence strategy. A subsistence strategy is the way a society uses technology to provide for the needs of its members.

Preindustrial Societies In preindustrial societies, there is very little technological development. All economic activity is carried out using human labor and animal power. One major consequence of this low level of technology is that the majority of the population must engage in producing food.

In all preindustrial societies, labor is heavily concentrated in the primary sector. However, the degree of concentration varies by type of society. There are four types of preindustrial societies—hunting and gathering, pastoral, horticultural, and agricultural. As the subsistence strategy progresses from hunting and gathering to agriculture, the economic system becomes more complex.

In the simplest preindustrial societies, providing sufficient food to feed the population demands the efforts of the entire population. Consequently, the secondary and tertiary sectors of the economy are very small. People are involved in these sectors on just a part-time basis. Even essential secondary-sector activities, such as the production of tools, take second place to food production.

As technology improves, food production becomes more efficient. More people can transfer their labor to the secondary and tertiary sectors without affecting food supplies. Even so, the number of people in secondary and tertiary positions remains relatively small.

ACADEMIC VOCABULARY

administrative type of job that organizes and assists, such as a secretary

Industrial Societies In industrial societies, the main emphasis in the economy shifts from the primary sector to the secondary sector. Advances in technology—machines and new sources of energy—make this shift possible. As agricultural productivity increases, industrial societies can support larger populations. Higher agricultural productivity also causes fewer workers to be needed in the primary sector. Consequently, the labor pool for the secondary and tertiary sectors swells.

Technological advances also change the nature of work—jobs become specialized. The Scottish economist Adam Smith first analyzed job specialization in his 1776 book *The Wealth of Nations*. Smith described how production greatly increases when a manufacturing process is divided into a series of tasks and each task assigned to a different individual. Each person becomes more efficient at completing his or her task. Job specialization cuts the time needed to make each product, thereby increasing productivity.

Job specialization also increases the variety of jobs in the secondary and tertiary sectors. In industrial economies people make few of the goods and services they need for their own daily lives. Instead, they perform jobs in return for wages, then use their wages to buy goods and services created by other workers.

Postindustrial Societies In postindustrial societies, the tertiary sector becomes the most important area of the economy. Several factors lead to this shift. First, technological innovations such as automation lead to more efficient production techniques. As a result, the number of jobs available in the secondary sector begins to decline. Second, postindustrial economies place greater emphasis on knowledge and on the collection and distribution of information. These emphases create a demand for administrative, managerial, professional, technical, and service personnel. Finally, the higher standard of living that is characteristic of postindustrial societies increases the demand for services.

Reading Check **Analyze** What type of economic society is the United States?

Economic Models

Industrial and postindustrial societies are categorized by the type of economic model they follow. Sociologists recognize two basic economic models: capitalism and socialism. In reality, most countries have characteristics of each of these models. The differences between the two models hinge on who owns the factors of production and on how economic activity is regulated. In **capitalism** the factors of production are owned by individuals. The forces of profit and competition regulate economic activity. In **socialism**, though, most of the factors of production are owned by the government, which regulates economic activity.

Keep in mind that the descriptions of capitalism and socialism are ideal types—that is, they are descriptions of the essential characteristics of the systems in their purest forms. In reality, no society has a purely capitalist or purely socialist system, but some societies lean heavily toward one or the other. For example, the United States follows the capitalist model. Cuba, on the other hand, follows the socialist model.

Between those extremes are a host of countries that combine the elements of capitalism and socialism to various degrees. France and Sweden, for example, fall in the middle of the

Adam Smith

- Wrote *The Wealth of Nations*, the founding work of modern economics
- Argued in favor of free trade between nations
- Showed how when individuals pursue their economic self-interest, everyone benefits

Karl Marx

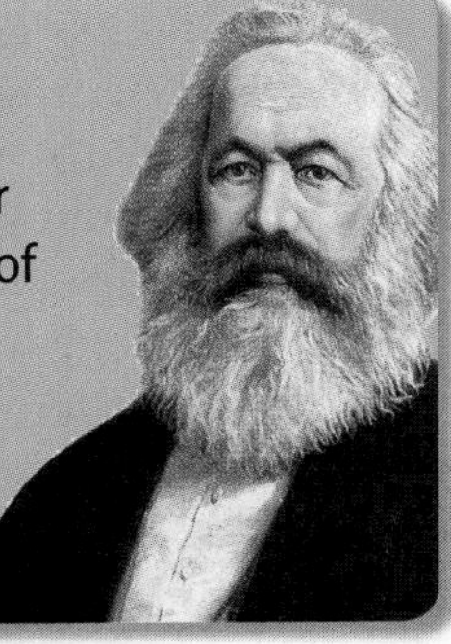

- Wrote *Capital* and *The Communist Manifesto*
- Argued that owners make their profits by exploiting the labor of workers
- Believed a class struggle between owners and workers would lead to revolution

spectrum. In those countries the government controls certain essential services and industries, such as health care, energy production, and the manufacture of industrial goods. However, individuals own a wide range of businesses in both countries.

Capitalism In a purely capitalist system, only self-interest and market competition regulate the economy. Self-interest regulates the economy by guiding the actions of consumers and producers. It leads consumers to try to purchase the goods and services they desire at the lowest prices possible. Self-interest also guides producers to undertake only those business ventures that have the potential for profit.

Market competition regulates the economy by ensuring that businesses produce goods or services wanted by consumers at prices consumers are willing to pay. Businesses that do this will be successful. Businesses that do not will soon fail. For competition to be effective, however, it must not be constrained either by government interference or by businesses dominating a market.

Prices in a purely capitalist system are regulated not by the government but by the laws of supply and demand. The **law of supply** states that producers will supply more products when they can charge higher prices and fewer products when they must charge lower prices. The **law of demand** states that consumers will demand more of a product as the price of the product decreases. On the other hand, consumer demand for a product decreases as the price increases.

Adam Smith compared the effect of this interplay between the forces of supply and demand to an "invisible hand." According to Smith, if competition is not restricted, the invisible hand of market forces will keep the economy in balance. This pure form of capitalism is sometimes referred to as **laissez-faire capitalism.** Laissez-faire is a French term translated as "let people do as they choose."

In practice, pure capitalism does not necessarily lead to the greatest good for everyone. All capitalist systems have government regulations that protect the consumer and ensure fair business competition. These regulations do not prevent individuals from setting up and running their own businesses with limited government interference. This commitment to limited government control of business operations has resulted in the labeling of capitalist economies as **free-enterprise systems.**

Socialism In a pure socialist system, economic activity is controlled by social need and by the government through central planning. Thus, the three basic economic questions are answered quite differently under pure socialism than they are under pure capitalism.

What to produce is determined by the needs of society. If the members of society need a good or service, it is provided regardless of whether it can be produced profitably. However, need is not determined by consumer demand. Rather, economic planners in the central government determine it.

Central planners also determine how to produce goods. These central planners decide which factories will produce which items and in what quantities. Rather than a range of similar products from which to choose, government planners provide consumers with one type of each good. Thus, market competition is not a factor in regulating supply and demand in a purely socialist economy.

John Maynard Keynes

- Wrote *The General Theory of Employment, Interest, and Money*
- Argued that it is sometimes more important for government to stabilize the economy than to maintain a balanced budget
- Established modern macroeconomics (large-scale economics)

Milton Friedman

- Wrote *Capitalism and Freedom*
- Started the movement for low taxes and smaller government
- Believed that government monetary policy led to the Great Depression

In socialism, for whom to produce is determined by need rather than by the ability to pay. It is for this reason that the government owns the means of production in a socialist system. Supporters of the socialist system claim that equal access to goods and services cannot be guaranteed if the means of production are owned by individuals.

For some socialists the ultimate goal of socialism is communism. Ideally **communism** is a political and economic system in which property is communally owned. In such a system, social classes cease to exist, and the role of the government declines as individuals learn to work together peacefully and willingly for the good of all.

Karl Marx argued that the imbalance of economic power between workers (the proletariat) and capitalists (the bourgeoisie) would lead to conflict. This class conflict would end only when the proletariat united to overthrow the bourgeoisie. After the revolution, a temporary dictatorship of the proletariat would be established to assist in the transformation to communism.

Communism has never been achieved in practice. In theory, on the way to establishing communism, the government should "wither away." In practice, governments in countries that adopted strong socialist economic models grew stronger. Even though they do not meet the communist ideal outlined by Karl Marx, such societies are called communist.

Changes in Capitalism and Socialism Over time, both the capitalist and socialist economic systems have undergone changes. The United States, a capitalist country, has adopted economic programs and practices that are socialist in nature. For example, tax revenues fund programs that benefit people with low incomes, such as Medicare, Medicaid, and Social Security.

The socialist economic system did not so much change as collapse. In the late 1980s and early 1990s, the Soviet Union and other communist-bloc countries abandoned the socialist economic model. They replaced the system of central planning, which was riddled with corruption and inefficiency, with a market system. Many of the countries have experienced economic booms, but corruption remains a problem in some places.

Even countries that retained socialism introduced elements of free enterprise. In the People's Republic of China the government allowed local managers of state-owned factories to make more decisions on how business should be run. Further, it privatized—sold off to private businesses—some large state-owned industries. Reflecting these changes, China adjusted its constitution in 1999 to note that private business was an important part of the economy.

Reading Check **Find the Main Idea** What are the two main economic models?

SECTION 1 Assessment

Reviewing Main Ideas and Vocabulary

1. **Define** What are factors of production?
2. **Identify Main Ideas** What are the three sectors that define all economic activities?
3. **Recall** What does the law of supply state?

Thinking Critically

4. **Sequence** What are the three basic types of societies, as defined by industrialization?
5. **Explain** Why are capitalist economies described as free-enterprise systems?
6. **Draw Conclusions** Capitalism is based on doing what's best for yourself. How does this help everyone else?
7. **Compare** Using your notes and a graphic organizer like the one below, compare how capitalism and socialism answer the basic economic questions.

	Capitalism	Socialism
What to produce?		
How to produce?		
For whom to produce?		

8. **Expository** Describe how Marx expected socialism to evolve into communism, and give some possible reasons why this never happened.

SECTION 2

The United States Economy

Before You Read

Main Idea
The United States has one of the world's richest and most diverse economies.

Reading Focus
1. Why are the 1900s sometimes called "the American Century"?
2. What recent developments have transformed the American economic system?

Vocabulary
corporation
oligopoly
protectionism
free trade
multinational
e-commerce

TAKING NOTES Use a graphic organizer like this one to take notes on the United States economy.

Corporations → Multinationals → U.S. Jobs

An Immigrant's Dream of Prosperity

SOCIOLOGY CLOSE UP ***What does the United States economy offer that so many immigrants want?*** Throughout the history of the United States, immigrants have flocked to the country's shores in search of a better life. The vibrant economy of the United States frequently offers immigrants a better chance for success than they would have in their homelands.

The story of Fernando Salazar epitomizes the dream of success that draws immigrants to the United States. In 1971, at the age of 15, he came to the United States from Ecuador to join his parents, who had previously immigrated. At his first job, Salazar operated the service elevator at a hotel in New York City. Soon promoted to a position at the front desk, Salazar continued to advance. He went on to establish a career managing the food and beverage operations of hotels and hotel chains. In 2007 Salazar became a vice president of Wyndham Hotels and Resorts. He is the most senior person responsible for the bars, restaurants, and other food and beverage services throughout the company's world-wide chain of hotels.

Salazar's story is an example of how the United States economy rewards talent, hard work, and dedication, regardless of one's background. Had Salazar and his family stayed in Ecuador, it is unlikely that he could have achieved so much. ■

The smaller picture shows Fernando Salazar (kneeling, blue suit) on the day he left Eduador for the United States. He built a successful career in the hotel industry, as shown in the larger picture.

The American Century

The twentieth century is sometimes called the American Century because the United States was the world's most powerful nation for most of that period. At the beginning of the 1900s, the United States was one of several large economies in the world. But the two world wars left the other great economies in ruins. At the same time, two trends added to the power of the U.S. economy: the rise of corporate capitalism and globalization.

Rise of Corporate Capitalism In Adam Smith's time, economic activities were controlled by the efforts of individual capitalists. However, by the late 1800s corporations had become the moving forces behind the economy. A **corporation** is a business organization that is owned by stockholders and treated by law as if it were an individual person. Because it has the same legal rights as a person, a corporation can enter into contracts, negotiate bank loans, issue stocks and bonds, and buy and sell goods and services.

ACADEMIC VOCABULARY

domestic produced in a particular country; opposite of foreign

The rise of corporate capitalism has changed the relationship between business ownership and control. Like the owners of most small businesses and privately held companies today, early stockholders managed the day-to-day affairs of their businesses. Today management by stockholders is practiced only by the smallest corporations. Few stockholders participate in daily business operations. In many cases, stockholders are not even individuals. Other corporations, Wall Street financial firms, foreign governments, and pension and mutual funds own the stocks of most large corporations in the United States.

Corporations account for only about 5 percent of the businesses in the United States, yet they generate over 62 percent of business sales. Corporations also employ the majority of American workers. However, a few big companies exercise most of this tremendous economic power.

One of the chief consequences of corporate capitalism is the growth of oligopolies. An **oligopoly** is the market situation in which a few large companies control an industry. The American automobile, oil, and breakfast-cereal industries are examples of oligopolies. The many mergers among companies in recent years have resulted in these and other American industries becoming more oligopolistic.

Because of its hold on an industry, a company in an oligopoly has more control over pricing and product quality than companies in more competitive markets. In addition, it can protect its hold on the industry by making it difficult for competing companies to enter the market. Also, oligopolistic companies often use their wealth and power to push through legislation that maintains or increases their share of the market.

For example, since the 1970s, American automobile companies have faced stiff competition from Japanese carmakers. They have often urged the government to impose protectionist policies. **Protectionism** is the use of trade barriers to protect domestic manufacturers from foreign competition. Common trade barriers include quotas—limits on the amount of goods that may be imported—and tariffs—surcharges on goods entering the country. American automakers faced opposition from supporters of **free trade**—trade that is not restricted by trade barriers between countries.

Globalization of Corporate Capitalism In recent years, the debate between protectionists and supporters of free trade has been complicated by the globalization of corporate capitalism. Many of the larger corporations are also multinationals. A **multinational** is a corporation that has factories and offices in several countries. Generally, a multinational has its head office in one country and operates businesses in one or more other countries. For example, a multinational with headquarters in the United States might make products in its factories in Mexico with materials from its offices in several European countries. The finished products might then be shipped for sale in countries throughout the Americas. Similarly, a foreign multinational might make products in its U.S. factories, use American labor and materials, and sell the product in the United States.

Some multinationals are huge. Several have economies that are bigger than many national economies. Wal-Mart, for example, has a bigger economy than 157 individual countries! The graphs on the next page compare the economies of several American multinationals with certain national economies.

Great power comes with such wealth. The board members of one corporation often serve on other boards or in political organizations, which adds to the power of the original corporation. Indeed the world's largest multinationals, many of which are American, help to set the economic, social, and political policies of many countries. Multinationals have led the drive to reduce trade barriers around the world. For some sociologists, the growing power of multinational corporations signals the end of the old world order of nation-states. They suggest that in the future, international affairs will be driven less by national loyalties than by market forces.

Reading Check **Find the Main Idea** What two trends have increased U.S. economic power?

Recent Developments

At the outset of the 21st century, the U.S. economy faces many challenges. Globalization and other trends have changed the types of work available in postindustrial America. In addition, doing business over the Internet has opened up new avenues for profit.

The Changing Nature of Work Work in the United States has steadily shifted from an industrial base to a service base. This shift is due in part to advances in technology. Automation and increased efficiency have reduced the number of workers needed to meet the demand for manufactured goods. The globalization of the economy has played an equally important role in the shift. In recent years American workers have faced competition from workers in the newly industrializing countries (NICs), particularly in Latin America and Asia. Some American multinationals, attracted by tax breaks and lower wage rates, have moved their manufacturing operations to NICs. Other American companies, to streamline operations and boost profits, have cut costs by reducing their workforces.

The service sector has not been able to absorb the large numbers of displaced workers. Technological advances eliminated many less-skilled service jobs. Further, many new service jobs require a relatively high level of education but do not always pay high wages. Many of the manufacturing jobs that remain require higher-level skills. Yet studies indicate that about 40 percent of American workers have limited reading and writing skills. To ensure that workers can handle future jobs, government and business leaders have called for a strong commitment to education.

E-commerce Another important recent development in the U.S. economy—e-commerce—has also brought great changes. The computer completely transformed the way people store and access information.

Statistically Speaking...

Companies vs. Countries The revenues of multinational corporations rival the gross domestic products of many countries. For example, in 2011, Wal-Mart earned about $420 billion. If Wal-Mart were a country, that would make it the 25th largest economy in the world.

Source: *Business Insider*, "25 US Mega Corporations: Where They Rank If They Were Countries"

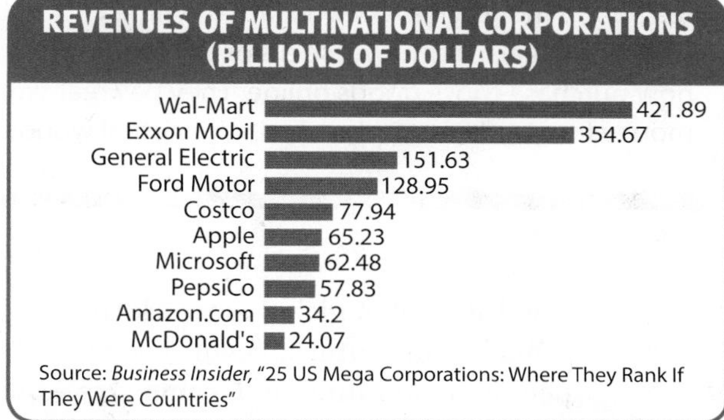

Source: *Business Insider*, "25 US Mega Corporations: Where They Rank If They Were Countries"

Skills Focus **INTERPRETING GRAPHS** Which country's economy generated about as much economic activity as McDonald's?

TECHNOLOGY FOCUS

The Economics of Online Worlds

With millions of players worldwide, massively multiplayer online games (MMOGs), such as EverQuest, have thriving internal economies. Players earn points or game currency for tasks such as slaying a monster. They use their earnings to buy goods within the game.

Many of the MMOGs allow players to run businesses within the virtual world. Some virtual entrepreneurs create restaurants or amusement parks. Others design and sell clothing, furniture, or other virtual goods. Some real-world companies have established virtual versions of themselves within the games.

The companies who run the MMOGs find themselves confronting economic problems similar to those faced by real-world countries. For example, if players have too much in-game currency, inflation results.

Many imaginary currencies have become worth real-world money. Players who lack the time or patience to earn high-level spells or equipment can now purchase those goods online. They pay real-world money for goods that only exist in the virtual worlds.

This has led real-world entrepreneurs to satisfy the demand. Low-paid employees, known as gold farmers, spend hours playing the games to collect goods and currency (shown above). The businesses then sell the virtual goods for real profits. Most MMOG companies disapprove of the practice. So do many devoted players, who resent those who simply purchase what they had to earn through skill and effort.

Thinking Critically

Analyze How does the law of supply explain why so many businesses want to be involved in MMOGs?

The Internet, a global network that links millions of computers, revolutionized the way people communicate. **E-commerce**—business conducted over the Internet—is not based on the traditional factors of production but instead is based on information. The most widely used service provided by the Internet is the World Wide Web. The Web is a set of computer programs that makes multimedia presentations—combinations of text, sound, pictures, animation, and video—possible on the Internet. The Web helps businesses to directly reach both consumers and suppliers.

The largest sector of e-commerce is business-to-business activity. In the past, ordering products from a supplier involved meetings, telephone calls, and paperwork. However, now the Internet allows companies to automate many of these purchases. As a result, businesses in the United States exchange about $1 trillion in goods and services each year.

The Internet also transformed the way businesses sell to consumers. Before the Internet, most businesses relied on physical stores to sell their products. Now, company Web sites sell products directly to consumers. Many companies, such as Amazon, exist only on the Internet. In addition, businesses can draw consumers' attention to products by advertising on the Web.

The Internet represents not so much a new location to do business as a new way of doing business. Computer links between businesses and suppliers streamline communication and other activities between the two. For example, tasks such as resupplying and billing can be handled automatically. This technology allows businesses to track, store, and analyze consumers' buying practices. Using this information, businesses can quickly respond to changes in buying trends. They can also "package" goods and services to meet the exact requirements of individual consumers.

While consumers appreciate the level of service available through e-commerce, some worry about the loss of privacy it creates.

Many express concern about what businesses might do with all the personal information they collect. Others worry that businesses will not be able to keep sensitive information—such as credit card numbers—secure. Such fears arise from continued problems with data security. In 2014, the number of U.S. data breaches tracked hit a record high of 783. But businesses understand that consumer confidence is necessary for e-commerce to succeed, and they have devoted many resources to making Internet shopping more secure.

Trouble Ahead? The U.S. economy faces many challenges. These include massive amounts of government debt, future funding of the Social Security system, a slow-growing economy from the Great Recession, and unstable international markets.

In 2014, the United States had a debt-to-GDP ratio of 101 percent, as the national debt approached $18 trillion. Each year that the federal government spends more than it receives in taxes, more debt is accumulated. Just paying the interest on the national debt accounts for about 6.23 percent of all federal spending—or about $222.75 billion in 2013.

The U.S. government is not alone in running up massive amounts of debt. About half of all U.S. households carry debt on their credit cards. The average household has $129,579 in debt, with $15,355 of it on credit cards. Credit card debt alone in the United States totals $712 billion.

One key U.S. government program may run short of funds unless action is taken. The Social Security system, which pays benefits to retirees and the disabled, is funded by payroll taxes. It depends on a balance between the number of workers and the number of recipients. As the Baby Boom generation begins to retire, this balance will begin to tip in the wrong direction. Fixing the imbalance may require raising taxes or cutting benefits.

In the late 1900s, rising house prices gave consumers confidence and fueled enormous growth in the housing industry. But speculators began buying and selling houses simply for profit, and lenders offered risky mortgages. As a result, house prices became unreasonably high. When the market cooled after 2006, prices dropped and foreclosures rose, slowing the entire U.S. economy.

CASE STUDY CONNECTION

The Housing Crisis Rising foreclosures and falling house prices threatened the entire U.S. economy in the first decade of the 2000s.

The U.S. economy depends heavily on oil. People drive their cars to work, school, and shopping, many industries are fueled by oil and gas, and many products are derived from petroleum. When oil prices rise, each of these elements becomes more expensive, people and businesses reduce their use of oil and oil products, and the economy slows.

Reading Check **Analyze** What three factors led to a reduction in U.S. manufacturing jobs?

SECTION 2 Assessment

Reviewing Main Ideas and Vocabulary

1. **Define** What is a corporation?
2. **Describe** How does an oligopoly work? Use a real example in your description.
3. **Recall** What new kind of commerce uses the Internet?

Thinking Critically

4. **Explain** What allows corporations to enter into contracts, take out loans, and issue stocks and bonds?
5. **Compare** How are protectionism and free trade related?
6. **Draw Conclusions** You are the head of a small country. A large multinational company wants to discuss expanding its presence in your country. Diplomats from another small country want to discuss trade relations. You only have time for one meeting. Which would you pick and why?
7. **Identify Cause and Effect** Using your notes and a graphic organizer like the one below, indicate what effect each trend has had on jobs in the United States.

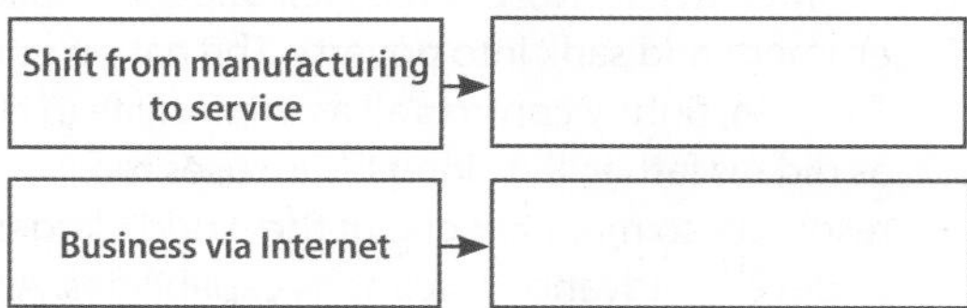

FOCUS ON WRITING

8. **Persuasive** Write a letter to your congressperson about one of the challenges facing the U.S. economy. Begin by defining the problem, then offer a possible solution.

SECTION 3

The Political Institution

Before You Read

Main Idea
Political institutions around the world exercise power in many different ways.

Reading Focus
1. How does sociology view politics?
2. What gives legitimacy to a person or group in power?
3. What types of government do sociologists recognize?

Vocabulary
political institution
legitimacy
traditional authority
rational-legal authority
charismatic authority
constitutional monarchy
authoritarianism
absolute monarchy
dictatorship
junta
totalitarianism

TAKING NOTES Use a graphic organizer like this one to take notes on the political institution.

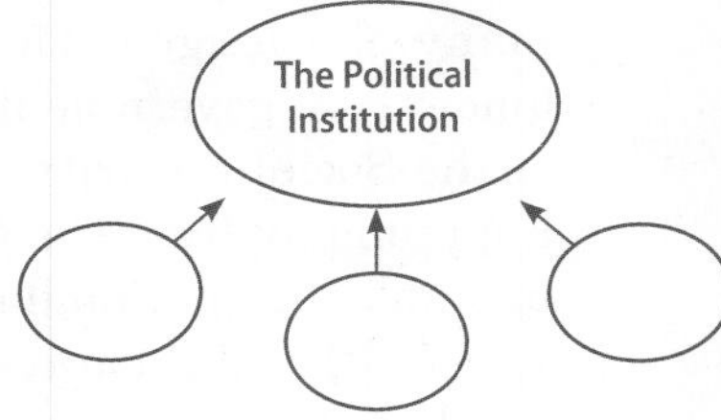

Two Koreas Two Political Systems

SOCIOLOGY CLOSE UP ***Can a country's politics really make a difference?*** Following World War II (1939–1945), Korea split into two parts. Communists allied with the Soviet Union dominated North Korea; Korean nationalists allied with the United States controlled South Korea. During the Korean War (1950–1953), neither side was able to defeat the other, and the division became permanent.

In the years since, the two countries have followed dramatically different paths. South Korea became one of the world's largest economies and a leading exporter of cars and personal electronics. In the 1980s, it developed a vibrant multiparty democracy. More recently, South Korea has become one of the most digitally-connected countries in the world, with a proliferation of wireless Internet access, cell phones, and online gaming.

Meanwhile, North Korea fell under a totalitarian government and sank into poverty. The nation's dictator, Kim Jong Un, tightly controls all aspects of life in North Korea—as did his father, Kim Jong Il. Kim uses most of the country's resources to maintain one of the world's largest armies and to develop advanced weapons capabilities. Although information about life in North Korea is closely guarded, reports of mass famine, torture, slave labor, prison camps, and public executions have reached the outside world.

The divide between the two Koreas shows just how deeply politics affects people's lives. Put simply, it matters a great deal who rules a nation and what form of government is in place. ■

A barren street in North Korea dominated by propaganda posters (top) stands in contrast to a busy street scene typical of South Korea's thriving economy (bottom).

Sociological View of Politics

No society can survive for long if each person in the society does exactly as he or she pleases. For society to run smoothly, people must often act together for the common good. Thus, all societies exercise some degree of power over societal members. Power is the ability to control the behavior of others with or without their consent. The family holds power in very simple societies. In more complex societies power is exercised by the state—the primary political authority in society. The nature of a state's power is shaped by its **political institution**—the system of roles and norms that governs the distribution and exercise of power in society.

Political institutions have evolved over time. Early hunter-gatherer societies had no formal political institution. However, a successful hunter might have served as a tribe's leader. As agriculture developed and people began settling in villages, more structured political systems emerged. Castes of religious leaders guided their communities to success in planting, and warrior-kings helped to defend or to expand the territory. City-states developed, and written laws came into use. With them, a class of people emerged whose primary role was political leadership.

The different sociological perspectives view the political institution differently. Functionalists analyze the political institution in terms of the functions of the state. These functions include creation and enforcement of laws, settling of conflicts between individuals, provision of services, establishment of economic and social policies, and maintenance of relations with other countries. All of these functions center on the task of maintaining order in society.

Conflict theorists, on the other hand, focus on how the political institution brings about social change. According to this view, different groups in society compete with one another for power. Although the political institution generally favors the wealthier segments of society, ongoing conflict causes the distribution of power to shift enough to result in varying degrees of social change.

Reading Check **Find the Main Idea** What are two sociological views of politics?

Legitimacy of Power

All sociologists, regardless of their perspective, are interested in the legitimacy of power. **Legitimacy** refers to whether those in power are viewed as having the right to control, or govern, others. When power is exercised with the consent of the people being governed, it is considered legitimate. Power is considered illegitimate when it is exercised against the will or without the approval of the people.

Authority Max Weber referred to legitimate power as authority. Weber was particularly interested in why people accepted the idea that leaders had the legitimate right to exercise power over others. According to Weber, this right to govern is based on one of three types of authority: traditional, rational-legal, or charismatic.

Traditional authority is power that is based on long-standing custom. In other words, people accept the exercise of power as legitimate because people in the past considered it so. Traditional authority is usually hereditary and is passed down from one generation to the next. Kings, queens, and tribal chieftains are examples of leaders who rely on traditional authority for their right to rule.

Until the rise of the modern political state, traditional authority was the most common form of legitimate power. Kings and queens asserted that their power was a divine right, and they sometimes served as head of the state religion. This authority usually descended to one of the ruler's children, but in some cases another relative claimed power. Establishing a clear line of succession was essential to government stability.

Formal rules and regulations provide the basis for **rational-legal authority.** These rules and regulations describe the rights and obligations of those in power. Frequently, they are part of a written constitution or a set of laws. Rational-legal authority is the most common form of authority in modern societies.

Rational-legal authority rests not with a particular individual but in the office or position that he or she holds. Thus, the authority to govern is lost when an individual leaves or is removed from office. For example, the president of the United States has the right to govern only while in office.

TYPES OF AUTHORITY

QUICK FACTS

Sociologists recognize three types of authority: traditional, rational-legal, or charismatic. Each has unique characteristics.

Traditional	Rational-Legal	Charismatic

Power based on long-standing custom	Power based on formal rules and regulations	Power based on characteristics of person in power
Authority lasts for the life of the leader	Authority belongs to the office, not the person	Authority depends on people's belief in leader
Usually, a child or other relative inherits the authority	Each person holds power only for as long as he or she holds office	Leader may lose following, or new leaders may emerge
Examples include king, queen, tribal leader	Examples include president, prime minister	Examples include dictator, supreme leader

Skills Focus **INTERPRETING CHARTS** Which type of authority is the least predictable?

By the same token, rational-legal authority limits the power of individual leaders. Each office has well-defined roles and responsibilities. When a leader oversteps the boundaries of the office, legal measures call the leader to account.

One famous example is what happened to U.S. President Richard Nixon for his role in the Watergate scandal. Nixon's staff orchestrated illegal monitoring of their political rivals, which included breaking into a room at the Watergate hotel. Nixon faced charges that included obstruction of justice and abuse of power, but he resigned rather than face impeachment.

Charismatic authority is based on the personal characteristics of the individual exercising the power. People accept the authority of a charismatic leader because they believe that he or she possesses special qualities that merit devotion and obedience. Charismatic leaders often emerge during periods of social unrest. At such times people are searching for leaders who promise a better life.

Some examples of famous charismatic leaders include Adolf Hitler, Mohandas Gandhi, Mao Zedong, the Reverend Martin Luther King Jr., Ayatollah Khomeini, and Saddam Hussein. As this list shows, charismatic leaders are not always people whom you would consider "good." Charismatic leadership, then, can have positive or negative consequences for society.

In addition, charismatic leadership is limited by being tied to a particular person. The authority lasts only as long as the charismatic leader. Eventually, governments led by charismatic leaders must adopt some other form of authority.

Coercion The opposite of authority is coercion, power exercised through force or the threat of force and based on fear. The use of armed troops to maintain order is one example of coercion. Leaders who have seized power through a military takeover or a revolution often use troops to maintain their hold on power. However, coercion is not limited to the use or threat of physical violence. Placing restrictions on the press or denying citizens the right to hold public meetings are also examples of coercion.

All political systems use force to some degree to maintain order. For example, the threat of being sent to prison for breaking a law is a form of coercion. Yet in a legitimate political system, coercion is used as a last resort. In an illegitimate system, on the other hand, coercion is the main method of maintaining order.

The more that a government relies on coercion, the less stable it will be. The more people are subjected to coercive power, the more they will view the government as illegitimate, and the more likely they will be to take action against the government.

Reading Check **Draw Conclusions** What type of authority is the most difficult to sustain from one leader to the next?

Types of Government

Although people often use the words interchangeably, the terms *state* and *government* are not the same thing. The combined political structures of a society, such as the presidency, Congress, and Supreme Court in the United States, form the state. The government on the other hand, consists of the people who direct the power of the state.

In the United States, the federal government includes the president, the members of Congress, and the Supreme Court justices. The individuals who make up the government come and go, but the state gives a society's political system continuity by providing an underlying structure.

How power is exercised by a state varies by its type of government. Sociologists recognize two basic types of government: democratic systems and authoritarian systems. As in the case of economic models, these systems are ideal types. Actual governments vary widely in their characteristics. However, all governments can be roughly categorized as one of those types.

Democratic Systems In a democracy, power is exercised through the people. The central feature of a democracy is the right of the governed to participate in the political decision-making process. In practice modern democratic systems are representational democracies. Voters elect representatives who undertake the task of making political decisions. If the elected officials do not perform to the people's liking, they can be voted out of office.

For most of history, democracies were rare. It was much more common for states to be ruled by monarchies, a type of government in which one person rules. The ruler—known as the monarch—inherits power. However, of the few remaining monarchs in the world today, most have limited power. True political power rests primarily with elected officials. This system is called **constitutional monarchy.** Constitutional monarchies are considered democratic because ultimate power rests with elected officials. In many instances, the monarch is nothing more than the symbolic head of state. The United Kingdom is an example of a constitutional monarchy.

Today democracies have become more common because more societies possess the conditions needed for a democracy to thrive. These conditions include the following:

- **Industrialization** Although industrialization does not necessarily lead to democracy, most democratic societies are industrialized. According to sociologist Gerhard Lenski, one reason for this relationship is that the educated urban populations found in industrial societies expect to have a voice in the political process.
- **Access to information** Democracy requires well-informed voters. Thus, democracies are strongest in those societies where the public and the media have open access to information and the media are free to publish.
- **Limits on power** All governments exercise power. However, in democracies clear limits are placed on the scope of government power. One way to limit power is to spread the power among many different groups. When power is divided between the branches of government and among nongovernmental organizations, such as labor unions and businesses, it reduces the amount of power concentrated in the hands of any person or group of people.
- **Shared values** Although the right to hold opposing views is a cornerstone of democracy, a shared set of basic values is essential. Without some agreement among voters on basic values, it would be difficult to reach the compromises necessary for a functioning democratic system.

ACADEMIC VOCABULARY

scope range or room in which to function

Democratic governments can be distinguished by the type of economic model they adopt. Many democracies have capitalist economies. The United States is the leading example of a democratic country with a capitalist economy.

Some other democracies have socialist economies. The combination of a democratic government and a socialist economy is called democratic socialism. Under democratic socialism, the government owns some of the factors of production. However, individuals maintain control over economic planning through the election of government officials. The Scandinavian countries of Sweden, Denmark, and Norway are examples of democratic-socialist states.

Authoritarian Systems In a government based on **authoritarianism,** power rests firmly with the state. However, this is not Weber's authority of legitimate power. Members of society have little or no say in the political decision-making process. In most cases, government leaders cannot be removed from office through legal means.

Authoritarian governments exist in a variety of forms. An **absolute monarchy** is an authoritarian system in which the hereditary ruler holds absolute power. Absolute monarchs rule several states in the Persian Gulf. An authoritarian system in which power is in the hands of a single individual is called a **dictatorship.** Many Latin American countries, at one time or another, have been ruled by dictators.

A **junta** is an authoritarian system in which a small group has seized power from the previous government by force. Juntas have been common in Africa and Latin America, where many countries have unstable governments.

The most extreme form of authoritarianism is totalitarianism. Under **totalitarianism,** those in power exercise complete authority over the lives of individual citizens. Public opposition to government policies is rarely allowed, and most personal freedoms are greatly restricted. Leaders of totalitarian governments accept few limits on their authority. Nazi Germany under Adolf Hitler, the Soviet Union under Joseph Stalin, and Cambodia under the Khmer Rouge present some striking examples of totalitarianism.

Sociologists study the question of why individuals submit to totalitarian rule. Psychoanalyst Erich Fromm attempted to provide an answer in *Escape from Freedom,* his classic study on totalitarianism in Germany under Adolf Hitler. Fromm wondered why the German people supported the Nazi government. According to Fromm, people succumb to totalitarianism because they want to escape feelings of isolation and powerlessness. By submitting to the will of those more powerful or by dominating those less powerful, people achieve a sense of security. Fromm labeled the personality structure that gives rise to this response as the "authoritarian character."

Reading Check **Summarize** What are the two basic types of government?

SECTION 3 Assessment

Reviewing Main Ideas and Vocabulary

1. **Define** What is a political institution?
2. **Describe** What does it mean for a government to have legitimate power?
3. **Recall** Why do people accept the authority of a charismatic leader?

Thinking Critically

4. **Interpret** How is the office of president of the United States a blend of rational-legal authority and charismatic authority?
5. **Explain** Why is access to information important to a healthy democracy?
6. **Support a Position** Do you see political institutions from a functionalist perspective or a conflict perspective? Pick one level of government and use it to explain your stance.
7. **Compare** Using your notes and a graphic organizer like the one below, compare democratic systems of government to authoritarian systems.

Similarities	Differences

FOCUS ON WRITING

8. **Descriptive** Choose one of the democratic forms of government discussed in this section. Imagine a situation in which the democratic government wields its power illegitimately, and describe how that might happen.

SECTION 4

The United States Political System

Before You Read

Main Idea
The United States is a democracy, but American voters are not the only group that influences the government.

Reading Focus
1. How does the number of political parties influence a country's political system?
2. How do sociologists analyze who rules the United States?
3. What is political socialization?

Vocabulary
political party
proportional representation
interest group
power-elite model
pluralist model

TAKING NOTES Use a graphic organizer like this one to take notes on the U.S. political system.

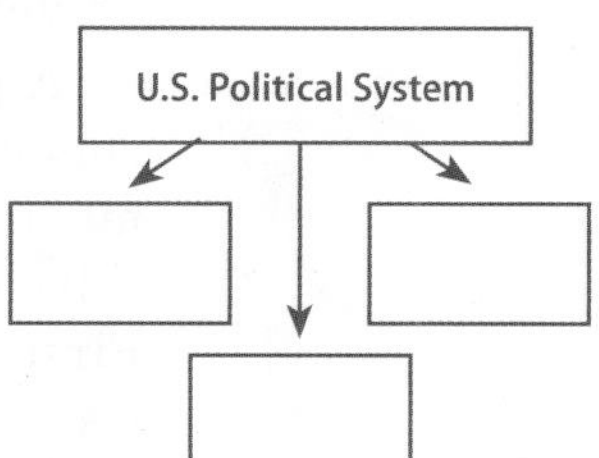

FIGHTING the SYSTEM

SOCIOLOGY CLOSE UP ***Why aren't third parties more successful?*** In the United States, the Democrats and Republicans hold the vast majority of political offices at every level of government. Only a handful of offices are held by members of other parties, which are commonly called "third parties." In a nation as diverse as the United States, why do only two parties dominate politics?

Part of the answer lies in the design of the political system. In the United States, all politicians represent, and are elected by, specific districts. Unless there are more third-party supporters in a district than either Democrats or Republicans, one of the major party candidates will win.

Take a state representative election as an example. A third party could have the support of 30 percent of the people in a state, but it would only win seats in districts where its supporters outnumbered those of both of the two major parties. Instead of winning 30 percent of the seats in the state legislature, the third party would be lucky to win 10 percent of the seats.

Another factor is that the two major parties each represent a wide range of viewpoints. Republicans generally agree with other Republicans, and Democrats with other Democrats. But few politicians hold exactly the same views, and each must represent the concerns of his or her particular constituency. As a result, most of the issues that voters care about find a voice through a representative of one of the two major parties.

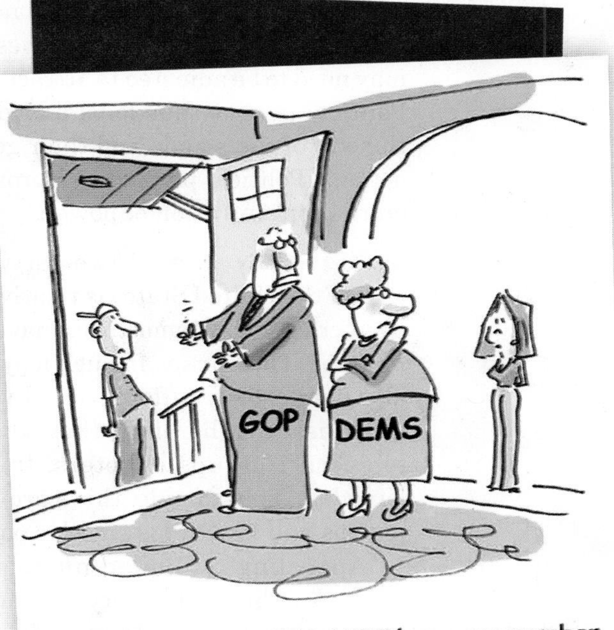

"I'm sorry, but I WILL NOT have any member of my electorate flirting with a THIRD PARTY such as him!"

Political Parties

Since the time of Max Weber, sociologists have devoted considerable attention to the analysis of political systems. Topics of special interest to sociologists who study the American political system include:

- political parties
- special-interest groups
- voter participation
- political models
- political socialization, or how people develop their political views

A **political party** is an organization that seeks to gain power through legitimate means. Political parties distinguish themselves from one another in two basic ways. First, they adopt specific points of view on issues of interest to voters. Second, they formulate programs for legislative action based on these points of view.

By supporting candidates from the party that most closely represents their views, voters directly influence government decision making. A party that cannot get enough of its candidates elected to office will not be able to put its programs into effect. These programs may need to be adjusted to attract more voters. Political parties thus form a bridge between the will of the people and their government's actions. Political parties also provide a check on the concentration of power.

ACADEMIC VOCABULARY

policy plan or guiding principle

Multiparty Systems A two-party system like that of the United States is relatively rare in a democracy. Most democracies have multiparty systems. The parties in such a system generally hold clearly differentiated views on the major issues. Therefore, they tend to appeal to specific groups of voters. In the United Kingdom, for example, there are three major parties and numerous smaller parties.

Appealing to limited numbers of voters works in the multiparty systems of other countries because of the way legislative seats are assigned. For example, if a party receives 10 percent of the popular vote on the national level, it will receive 10 percent of the seats in the national legislature. This system is called **proportional representation.** Proportional representation ensures that minority parties—and thus minority viewpoints—receive a voice in the government.

The Two-party System In the United States, voters have a choice among candidates from the Democratic Party, the Republican Party, and several third parties. These third parties regularly run candidates for local, state, and national office. However, nearly all elected officials since the Civil War have been members of either the Democratic Party or the Republican Party. The United States is considered to have a two-party system.

Except for the president, in the United States candidates are elected to office on the basis of a simple plurality, meaning that whichever candidate receives the most votes wins. Critics charge that minority-party candidates have little hope of winning a majority of votes. Therefore, this winner-takes-all rule discourages the formation of minority parties. Further, it prevents citizens who hold minority views from having a voice in the government.

Critics also argue that the winner-takes-all rule discourages sharp differences between the policy positions of the Republican and Democratic parties. According to this view, the two parties fear that adopting "extreme" positions on issues might cost them votes. Therefore, to avoid alienating voters, the parties adopt positions that are only slightly different from each other.

In the 1992 presidential election, voter disenchantment with the "sameness" of Democratic and Republican policy positions helped a third-party candidate make an unusually strong showing. In that election, independent H. Ross Perot vied with Democrat Bill Clinton and Republican George Bush. Perot's share of the popular vote—some 19 percent—was the highest of any third-party candidate since Theodore Roosevelt took 27 percent in 1912.

Reading Check **Compare** What type of political party system do most democratic countries have?

Who Rules the United States?

In theory, the voters have all the power in a democracy. In practice, the system can be manipulated by other groups. Low voter turnout, among other features of the American political system, has led sociologists to question who actually rules the United States.

Interest Groups People with minority views can join together to get their voices heard through interest groups. An **interest group** is an organization that attempts to leverage political power in order to influence the political decision-making process. There are thousands of such groups in the United States. They represent a variety of interests—such as business, labor, medical practitioners, patients, environmentalists, and senior citizens. (See the list of leading interest groups on this page.)

Interest groups use a variety of techniques to win political and public support for the issues of interest to their members. Most groups employ lobbyists—people paid to meet directly with government officials in order to win their support. Lobbyists have greater access to elected officials than the average citizen. Federal reports suggest that there are 11,465 political lobbyists registered to work in Washington, D.C. In the first decade of the 2000s special-interest groups spent over $2 billion per year on lobbying the federal government.

Another common pressure technique used by interest groups is contributing money to the campaigns of political candidates. Most interest groups use political action committees (PACs) to collect and distribute political-campaign contributions. So-called "Super PACs" are a relatively new type of committee that arose following the July 2010 federal court decision in a case known as *SpeechNow.org v. Federal Election Commission*. As of 2016, more than 2,221 Super PACs operate in the United States. In the 2014 elections, Super PACs contributed almost $235 million to congressional candidates.

Other methods that interest groups use to apply political pressure include collecting petitions, organizing letter-writing campaigns, and promising to have their members vote for candidates sympathetic to their causes. Many large interest groups—such as the National Rifle Association (NRA), the National Education Association (NEA), and the National Organization for Women (NOW)—also launch expensive media campaigns to sway public opinion.

Political Interest Groups

Leading Lobbying Groups	2016 Spending
U.S. Chamber of Commerce:	$1,225,115,680
National Association of Realtors:	$351,247,463
American Medical Association:	$347,792,500
General Electric:	$334,220,000
American Hospital Association:	$295,951,424

Leading Political Action Committees (PACs)	2016 Contributions
Right To Rise USA:	$86,534,118
Conservative Solutions PAC:	$42,977,642
America Leads:	$18,500,097
Keep the Promise I:	$9,327,573
New Day For America:	$8,442,489

Source: Center for Responsive Politics

Political Participation Public participation is at the heart of the democratic process. Yet the United States has one of the lowest rates of voter participation among the democratic countries of the world. About 35 percent of voting-age Americans are not registered to vote. Among registered voters, an average of about 80 percent vote in most presidential elections. But that's only about 60 percent of the voting-age population.

The percentage of registered voters who cast ballots in nonpresidential elections is always lower than the percentage in presidential elections. Winning candidates often speak of landslide victories and of having the mandate of the people. However, they generally only receive the support of about one third of potential voters.

Voter participation varies among different groups of Americans. For example, white Americans and African Americans are much more likely to vote than are Hispanics. Similarly, employed people are far more likely to vote than are people who are unemployed. Voter participation also varies by level of education—people with college educations have a higher voter-participation rate than do people who have never attended college.

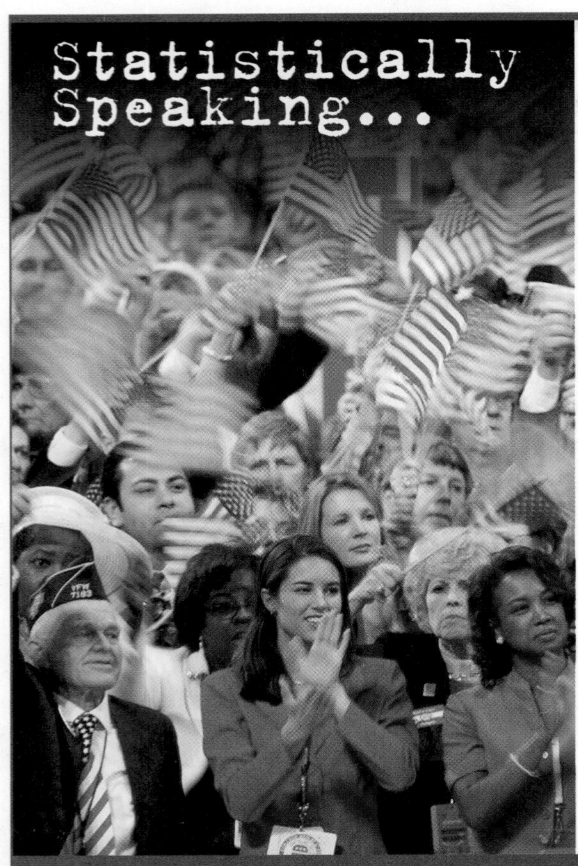

Statistically Speaking...

Voter Participation Voter participation in the United States fell to historically low levels in the late 1900s. Although participation levels began to rebound in the 2000s, they remained below those of most democratic countries. The following data are from the 2012 election.

235 million Number of U.S. citizens who were eligible to vote in the 2012 elections

153 million Number of U.S. citizens who were registered to vote

133 million Number of U.S. citizens who actually voted

74% Percentage of citizens aged 65–74 years who voted in the 2012 elections

41% Percentage of 18- to 24-year-olds who voted

Skills Focus **INTERPRETING DATA** Why might politicians pay more attention to the problems of senior citizens than they do to the problems of college students?

Source: U.S. Census Bureau

Age is also associated with voter participation. Generally, voter participation increases with age. People under the age of 25 are the least likely to vote, and people aged 55 or older have the highest voter-participation rate. In recent elections, people aged 65 to 74 years old have been the group most likely to vote.

Since the 1980s voter participation among senior Americans has shown an overall increase in presidential-election years and has held steady in congressional-election years. Participation among all other age groups declined until the 2000 presidential election. Since then, voter participation, particularly among the young, steadily increased through 2008, but fell off in 2012.

Political Models To answer the question of who actually rules America, sociologists generally adopt one of two models: the power-elite model or the pluralist model. The **power-elite model,** first presented by sociologist C. Wright Mills, states that political power is exercised by and for the privileged few in society. According to Mills, the top ranks in America's political, economic, and military organizations are controlled by people who are linked by ties of family, friendship, and social background. In his studies on the ruling class, G. William Domhoff came to a similar conclusion. Domhoff found that while they make up just 1 percent of the American population, members of the ruling class are heavily represented in the top levels of business, politics, and the military.

The **pluralist model,** on the other hand, states that the political process is controlled by interest groups that compete with one another for power. Pluralists do admit that power is distributed unequally in society and that this asymmetry has led to such social problems as poverty, unemployment, and racial inequality. However, they argue that competition among interest groups prevents power from becoming concentrated in the hands of a few people.

Reading Check **Summarize** What methods do interest groups use to gain politicians' support?

Political Socialization

As you have learned, socialization is the process through which people learn a society's basic skills, values, beliefs, and behavior patterns. Political socialization focuses on how people develop political beliefs. The same agents of socialization that influence other aspects of socialization also contribute to shaping political ideas.

Family Children begin learning political beliefs from their parents and other relatives. Political socialization begins as unintended socialization. Children may begin to develop political opinions when they overhear family members discussing politics or witness a family member's reaction to political news.

Parents may also conduct deliberate socialization activities. For example, they may take a child with them when they go to vote. As children grow up, family members might invite them to take part in political discussions. The majority of people in the United States belong to the same political party as their parents.

Mass Media Television, movies, the Internet, and the other forms of mass media carry vivid political messages. However, the political viewpoint is not always announced directly.

For example, consider how two different television news programs—with two different viewpoints—might handle a story about capital punishment. One program might begin by showing a picture of a child who was murdered before interviewing a death penalty advocate. The other program might begin by telling the story of a person released from prison after DNA evidence proved his innocence. Each story is covering the same subject—capital punishment—but with two very different political messages.

Political messages become explicit during a campaign season. News stories, advertisements, and debates all present political views for public consideration.

School In the United States, public education plays a major role in political socialization. Children recite the Pledge of Allegiance every school day. In their social studies courses, they learn the political histories of the country and of their states. Government courses further political socialization by deepening student understanding of how government works.

Peer Groups People with similar characteristics tend to share political beliefs. Economic status and age are two of the major factors that influence a person's political views. Generally, older, wealthier people tend to favor Republican candidates; younger, less well-to-do people tend to favor Democrats.

Reading Check **Draw Conclusions** How is reciting the Pledge of Allegiance a form of political socialization?

SECTION 4 Assessment

Reviewing Main Ideas and Vocabulary

1. **Describe** How does proportional representation work?
2. **Identify** What does PAC stand for, and what is a PAC?
3. **Recall** How do political parties distinguish themselves from one another?

Thinking Critically

4. **Identify Cause and Effect** How are candidates elected in the United States, and how does this make it more difficult for third parties?
5. **Explain** How do politicians use money from PACs?
6. **Compare** What's the difference between the power-elite model and the pluralist model?
7. **Make Judgments** Which form of political socialization has the strongest influence? Explain.
8. **Compare and Contrast** Using your notes and a graphic organizer like the one below, compare multiparty systems to the two-party system.

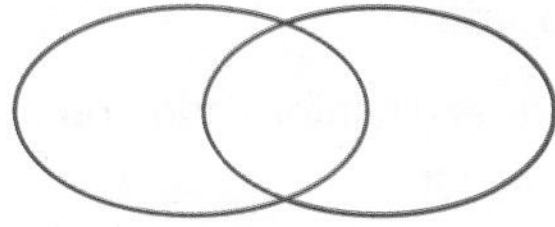

FOCUS ON WRITING

9. **Expository** Does lobbying distort the democratic process? Write a short essay explaining your answer to this question.

Simulation

Applying What You've Learned

There Should Be a Law!

How do special-interest groups influence the creation of laws?

Use the workbook to complete this simulation.

1. Introduction

Laws are types of norms that are formally defined and enforced by officials. These laws reflect the values of a society. Your role in this activity is to role-play a member of a special interest group and to write a bill to be presented to members of Congress. This simulation should give you some insight into how compromise and conflict play a part in ensuring that our laws reflect society and not just certain segments of society.

The class will be divided into groups that will each represent a specific special interest group. The job of each group is to write a piece of legislation that is self-serving. Write one that will benefit your group and your members. Use the Internet to learn about your group and to compare your legislation to actual legislation.

Once each group has completed their bill they will present it to the class. Each of the groups will have a chance to critique and comment on the legislation of the other groups. Your teacher will act as moderator. The goal will be to see if a compromise can be reached so that the bill can be amended to gain the support of the entire class. The final version will be turned in along with the original version of the legislation.

2. Simulation

❶ Following your teacher's instructions, divide into 6 to 8 groups. Each group should have someone to perform the following tasks:

- Moderator—keep everyone on task
- Secretary—record information and put the group's legislation into writing
- Researchers—research information on the group's issues and sponsored legislation
- Presenter—present the group's legislation to the class for discussion and debate

❷ Now the teacher will help each group choose a special interest group to represent. The special interest groups should have some conflicting interests. For example, if one group represents People for the Ethical Treatment of Animals, another group could represent the American Cattlemen's Association. Consider choosing groups that have active issues in your part of the country. For ideas, see the list of groups with opposing viewpoints on the next page.

Use the library and the Internet to learn more about your group. Try to become an expert on what matters to your group. Also learn about the group's history and past legislative efforts.

❸ Each group will draft a piece of legislation that serves their group's special interest. It should address a specific issue that the special interest group would find important and suggest a way to deal with the issue.

For guidance, each group should use the Search Bill Text feature on the Library of Congress Thomas webpage (http://thomas.loc.gov/) to find a piece of legislation similar to the topic of their bill. Save a copy of the actual legislation to turn in with the final product.

Pay attention to both the style and content of your draft legislation. Try to follow the format and style of the legislation you find through the Library of Congress. But also give some thought to how your law might be enforced, how much it would cost to enforce, and who might object to it.

❹ Once all bills are completed, each group will present its proposed law to the class. Hold a discussion in which the other groups can voice opposition or support for the legislation. The goal is to see if the legislation can be amended to overcome any opposition but still maintain the support of the original authors.

Remember: While you are expected to defend your position and legislation vigorously, it should also be done in a respectful manner. Stick to the issues and avoid personal attacks.

At the end of the exercise each group will turn in the following:

- A copy of the legislation they researched through the Library of Congress Thomas webpage.
- A copy of the legislation originally written by their special interest group.
- A copy of the revised final copy of their legislation as approved by the class.
- A group analysis of the final version. This analysis should include comments such as the following:

  What changes did you agree with?

  Which changes did you not agree with?

  What caused you to give in on some issues and not others?

  How satisfied are you with the final version compared to your original vision?

3. Discussion

What did you learn from this lab? Hold a group discussion that focuses on the following questions.

- How difficult was it to originate an idea for a law you wanted to create?
- How did that compare with the actual process of putting that idea into writing? What do you think caused one to be harder than the other?
- What do you think causes society to rely on governments to create laws and sanctions to reflect our values? Why do folkways and mores not always work for this purpose?
- What is your opinion of some of the bills that become laws every year? Are they all necessary?
- Do special interest groups help or hurt the lawmaking process?
- How does the concept of conflict affect the lawmaking process? How does the concept of cooperation affect the lawmaking process? Which is more useful in helping society reach a consensus on laws that reflect their values, conflict or cooperation?
- Should the lawmaking process be simplified? Should it be made more difficult? Why?

SPECIAL INTEREST GROUPS

AFFIRMATIVE ACTION

Pro

- Affirmative Action & Diversity Project
- American Association for Affirmative Action
- Americans United for Affirmative Action

Anti

- American Civil Rights Institute
- Center for Equal Opportunity
- Center for Individual Rights

EUTHANASIA ("RIGHT-TO-DIE")

Pro

- Choice In Dying
- Compassion in Dying
- Euthanasia Research & Guidance Organization

Anti

- Citizens United Resisting Euthanasia (CURE)
- Physicians for Compassionate Care

GUN CONTROL

Pro

- Children's Defense Fund: Safe Start!
- Coalition to Stop Gun Violence

Anti

- Citizens Committee for the Right to Keep & Bear Arms
- National Rifle Association (NRA)
- National Center for Policy Analysis: Crime
- Second Amendment Foundation

CHAPTER 12 Review

Comprehension and Critical Thinking

SECTION 1 *(pp. 282–286)*

1. a. Identify Who wrote *The Wealth of Nations*?

b. Compare How do capitalism and socialism differ in terms of ownership of the factors of production?

c. Identify Cause and Effect How do the laws of supply and demand help to regulate a capitalist economy?

SECTION 2 *(pp. 287–291)*

2. a. Define What is a corporation?

b. Make Generalizations How has e-commerce changed the American economy?

c. Make Judgments How might oligopolies undermine the self-regulatory features of the free-enterprise system?

SECTION 3 *(pp. 292–296)*

3. a. Recall How did Max Weber define authority?

b. Contrast How do democratic and authoritarian governments differ in the ways they use power?

c. Draw Conclusions Why did some countries that adopted strong socialist economic models also adopt authoritarian forms of government?

SECTION 4 *(pp. 297–301)*

4. a. Identify What are the two major political parties in the United States?

b. Explain What methods do interest groups use to win political support for their issues?

c. Analyze Why does voter participation vary according to age?

INTERNET ACTIVITY

5. Choose one of the corporations in the graph "Revenues of Multinational Corporations" in Section 2. Use the Internet to find the corporate website—not the consumer website, but the site for investors. Use the website and news sources to research the corporation. Write a brief report describing how extensive the company's operations are outside the United States.

Reviewing Vocabulary

Match the terms below with their correct definitions.

6. factors of production
7. capitalism
8. socialism
9. communism
10. protectionism
11. free trade
12. domestic
13. constitutional monarchy
14. dictatorship
15. totalitarianism

A. economic model in which the factors of production are owned by individuals
B. political and economic system in which property is communally owned
C. type of government in which one person rules but true political power rests with elected officials
D. manufactured within a country instead of imported from another country
E. authoritarian government in which a single individual holds all the power
F. resources needed to produce goods and services
G. trade that is not restricted by tariffs and other barriers between countries
H. use of trade barriers to protect domestic manufacturers from foreign competition
I. economic model in which the factors of production are owned by the government
J. authoritarian government that exercises complete control over the lives of its citizens

Sociology in Your Life

16. Could you get involved in party politics? Find a local office for the Democratic, Republican, or other political party. Contact the office and tell them you are researching volunteer opportunities for high school students. Create a table showing the different volunteer opportunities and what each involves.

Skills Activity: Interpreting Primary Sources

The following excerpt is taken from Erich Fromm's study of authoritarian governments, *Escape from Freedom*. Read the excerpt and then answer the questions that follow.

> "The feature common to all authoritarian thinking is the conviction that life is determined by forces outside of man's own self, his interest, his wishes. The only possible happiness lies in the submission to these forces . . . The authoritarian character does not lack activity, courage, or belief. But these qualities for him mean something entirely different from what they mean for the person who does not long for submission. For the authoritarian character activity is rooted in a basic feeling of powerlessness which it tends to overcome. Activity in this sense means to act in the name of something higher than one's own self . . . The authoritarian character wins his strength to act through his leaning on superior power . . .
>
> He has belief in authority as long as it is strong and commanding . . . For him the world is composed of people with power and those without it, of superior ones and inferior ones . . . He experiences only domination or submission. Differences, whether of sex or race, to him are necessarily signs of superiority or inferiority. A difference which does not have this connotation is unthinkable to him."
>
> —Erich Fromm, *Escape from Freedom* (Farrar & Rinehart, 1941)

17. Recall According to Fromm, what feature is common to all authoritarian thinking?

18. Explain Why might feeling powerless lead someone to become authoritarian?

19. Develop How is North Korea under Kim Jong Un an example of the authoritarian character?

Writing for Sociology

Use your knowledge of economics and politics to answer the question below. Do not simply list facts. Present a clear argument based on your critical analysis of the question, using the appropriate terminology.

20. Are capitalism and socialism converging? Write a brief essay on this question. Consider the following:

- social programs in the United States
- the transformation of the Chinese economy
- trade between the United States and China

Connecting Online

Go online for review and enrichment activities related to this chapter.

KEY TOPICS VIDEOS
View compelling clips on issues in the field.

KEEP IT CURRENT
Link to the Current Events site for regularly updated stories on sociology as well as other social studies topics.

QUICK LAB
Reinforce a key concept with a short lab activity.

CASE STUDY

RELIGION in Public Schools

In the United States, as in nearly all societies, the family is the most fundamental social institution. Parents have the primary responsibility of caring for their children, and along with that responsibility, they have the right to raise their children according to their judgments and values. For most people, this means sharing religious worship and celebration with their children and generally raising them to be part of their religious community.

Yet you are probably familiar with news stories describing police or child welfare officers removing children from the home of a parent who has neglected or mistreated them. These examples show how the government overrides parental authority to prevent harm to children. By common belief, failing to educate a child to fully participate in society constitutes harm, so the government requires parents to send their children to school. In addition, most schools in the United States are public institutions—owned by state-established school districts, funded by taxes, administered by elected officials—and their actions are government actions.

An entire classroom prays together at Boys Town, a private organization that cares for and educates at-risk youth.

So what should happen when the government, in the form of a public school, attempts to teach lessons that parents or students object to on religious grounds?

In 1940 the U.S. Supreme Court ruled that students could be expelled for refusing to salute the flag (*Minersville School District* v. *Gobitis*). The students in the case were Jehovah's Witnesses who, along with their parents, believed saluting the flag was a blasphemous worship of graven images.

That decision was overturned in 1943 in a similar case (*West Virginia Board of Ed.* v. *Barnette*) in which Jehovah's Witnesses refused to salute the flag. In the majority opinion, Justice Robert Jackson wrote

> *If there is any fixed star in our constitutional constellation, it is that no official, high or petty, can prescribe what shall be orthodox in politics, nationalism, religion, or other matters of opinion or force citizens to confess by word or act their faith therein.*

The *Barnette* decision has guided American law concerning school prayer. The First Amendment clearly prohibits the government from establishing a state religion, but courts have ruled that it also prohibits public schools from conducting or even permitting so-called voluntary prayer at school events.

In addition to the concern about establishing religion through government-sponsored religious practices, another reason courts have rejected "voluntary" prayer is that psychological pressure to conform, from both peers and from school authorities, calls into question whether any officially

U.S. SUPREME COURT RULINGS ON PRAYER IN PUBLIC SCHOOLS	
***Engel* v. *Vitale* (1962)**	A public school may not conduct a voluntary, "nondenominational" prayer.
***School District of Abington Township* v. *Schempp* (1963)**	A public school may not conduct public Bible readings, even if student participation is optional.
***Wallace* v. *Jaffree* (1985)**	A public school may not conduct a silent meditation or voluntary prayer.
***Lee* v. *Weisman* (1992)**	A public school may not conduct a prayer at a graduation ceremony, even if attendance is voluntary.
***Santa Fe Independent School Dist.* v. *Doe* (2000)**	A public school may not permit individual students to conduct public prayers at extracurricular events.

conducted prayer can in fact be voluntary. Not all American schools are public. American private schools offer a huge variety of religious perspectives (although the options in sparsely populated areas may be limited). American courts have ruled that children cannot be required to attend a public school (*Pierce* v. *Society of Sisters*, 1925). However, private schools can be regulated to ensure that they provide the basic education required of all citizens. In this chapter you will learn more about education and religion, two important institutions in any society.

What do you think?

1. What religious education can be required in a public school?
2. How can schools in a pluralistic society teach a common culture?

CHAPTER 13

EDUCATION AND RELIGION

Chapter at a Glance

SECTION 1: The Sociology of Education

- Education consists of the norms and roles involved in transmitting knowledge, values, and patterns of behavior from one generation to the next.
- Sociologists have gained insight into education by studying it from functionalist, conflict, and interactionist perspectives.

SECTION 2: Issues in American Education

- Americans have tried to reform education in order to achieve broad and important social goals.
- Alternatives to the traditional public school system include private and charter schools, school choice, and homeschooling.
- Violence in schools is a serious social concern.
- Methods and curricula for teaching English to non-native speakers are highly controversial.

SECTION 3: The Sociology of Religion

- A religion is a system of roles and norms organized around the sacred, which binds people together in groups.
- Religions can provide social cohesion, social control, and emotional support.
- Religions are characterized by their rituals, symbols, belief systems, and organizational structures.

SECTION 4: Religion in American Society

- A vast majority of Americans believe in God and consider themselves affiliated with a religion.
- American religions are organized into more than 400 denominations.
- About half of Americans consider themselves religious and consider religious teachings when making decisions.

SECTION 1

The Sociology of Education

Before You Read

Main Idea
Sociologists use differing analytical perspectives to understand the nature and functions of education.

Reading Focus

1. How does society define education?
2. What is the functionalist perspective on education?
3. How do sociologists view education through the conflict perspective?
4. How do interactionist sociologists look at education?

Vocabulary
education
schooling
hidden curriculum
tracking

TAKING NOTES Use a graphic organizer like this one to take notes on differing sociological perspectives on education.

Functionalist	Conflict	Interactionist

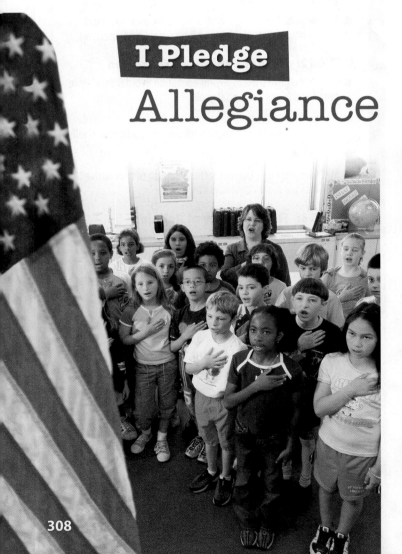

I Pledge Allegiance . . .

SOCIOLOGY CLOSE UP ***How do we learn what it means to be American?*** Americans have been saluting the flag for over 100 years. In the early 1900s the flow of immigrants to the United States led to a great increase in the responsibilities of the nation's schools. Schools were charged with teaching immigrants not only basic English, math, science, and so on, but also to accept and defend American beliefs and values.

For example, the purpose of the flag salute is to teach patriotism. There has always been controversy about saluting the flag because there has always been controversy about what is patriotic: patriotism means different things to different people. For some, patriotism means standing up for their country and their government, no matter what. For others, patriotism means trying to change their country when they believe it is wrong. For some, it means shared traditions going back to colonial days; for others, it means picking and choosing a variety of traditions from the world's cultures.

Does the flag salute express reverence for the flag as a symbol of freedom? Is it simply a convention that breeds conformity? If the flag salute means different things to different people, how would you teach a newcomer what is essential to U.S. society? ■

Defining Education

A society's future largely depends on the successful socialization of new members. Young members must be taught their society's norms and values and the skills necessary to continue the work of the older generation. In other words, children must acquire the knowledge, skills, behavior patterns, and values necessary to become functioning members of their society. To accomplish this goal, every society has developed a system of **education.** Education consists of the roles and norms that ensure the transmission of knowledge, values, and patterns of behavior from one generation to the next.

In some small preindustrial societies, education is largely informal and occurs mainly through a process of socialization that occurs within the family. Family members teach children the norms and values of their society as well as certain basic skills. Parents may teach young sons and daughters the skills of cooking, pottery making, food gathering, hunting, and fishing. In this way children learn the ways of society, mainly by participating in adult activities. As societies become more complex, the family shares the process of educating the young with more formally established organizations. Formal education, which involves instruction by specially trained teachers who follow officially recognized policies, is called **schooling.** Sociologists who study the institution of education typically focus more on schooling than on the informal education that takes place within the family.

As with many topics in sociology, functionalist, conflict, and interactionist sociologists approach the study of educational institutions differently. The functionalist sociologist studies the ways in which education contributes to the smooth operation of society. The conflict sociologist looks at how education serves to limit certain individuals' and groups' access to power. The interactionist sociologist is interested in the face-to-face relationships in the classroom. Each sociological perspective provides valuable insight into education, yet no one perspective gives a complete explanation of this institution.

Reading Check **Find the Main Idea** What is the purpose of education?

The Functionalist Perspective on Education

Functionalist sociologists believe that the functions performed by education work to maintain and perpetuate the stability and smooth operation of society. The most important of these functions include the teaching of knowledge and skills, the transmission of culture, social integration, and occupational placement.

Teaching Knowledge and Skills The basic function of education is to teach children the knowledge and skills they will need as independent adults. Schools fulfill this function through a core curriculum—or a set of courses—that includes such subjects as English language and literature, civics, history, geography, mathematics, science, and foreign languages.

In addition to transmitting existing knowledge and skills to students, education also serves to generate new knowledge. All societies must be able to adapt to changing conditions. Education makes this possible by providing the means through which individuals can develop approaches and solutions to new problems. Schooling develops the intellectual and critical-thinking skills that enable future adults to contribute to existing knowledge.

The creation, testing, and sharing of new knowledge and technology are central to the development of society. For this reason, much of the research conducted in colleges and universities worldwide is funded by governmental agencies. In many societies, the funds for research also come from private corporations eager for innovations and inventions that can be used to increase their profits.

Transmission of Culture For societies to survive over time, they must pass on to following generations not only useful skills and knowledge but also the core values of their culture, such as responsibility and respect for others' differences and rights. After families, schools are perhaps the most important and obvious means through which children learn social norms, values, and beliefs. Within the core curriculum, schools also teach students patriotism, loyalty, and socially acceptable forms of behavior.

Quick Lab

Observing American Values in the Classroom

A classroom is a place for learning values as well as skills and knowledge. What values does your classroom teach?

PROCEDURE

1. Review the text in this section on "Transmission of Culture" and "Social Integration."
2. Observe all the items—posters, quotations, lists, art—on the walls of your classroom. What values do they express? Besides the U.S. flag, what other objects are in your classroom to promote patriotism? Write your answers.
3. Think about how the school day is scheduled and how you spend your time. What values does this reflect? Write your answers.

ANALYSIS

1. In what ways does your classroom contribute to social integration?
2. In what ways does your classroom transmit American culture and support American values?
3. How much of your classroom space is devoted to material that promotes some American values?

Schoolchildren learn about patriotism through songs, rituals, plays, and stories. For example, in the United States young children are taught to salute the flag, recite the Pledge of Allegiance, and stand when the national anthem is played. Children may not understand the words of the pledge or the national anthem. However, they learn very early that these are important rituals that produce feelings of pride. Their sense of pride in the country is strengthened through studying subjects such as U.S. history and civics. American schools also emphasize the benefits of the free-enterprise system, individualism, and democracy—values on which the United States is based.

ACADEMIC VOCABULARY

sanction penalty, punishment

All societies use education to support their communities' own social and political systems. For example, Japanese education emphasizes conformity, cooperation, group loyalty, and respect for elders—qualities that are highly valued in Japan. Before the former Soviet Union collapsed, schoolchildren there were taught the principles of Communism.

Socializing the young to accept the superiority of their own political and social systems is sometimes accomplished by teaching them that other systems are inferior. This approach serves to create a bond of unity and loyalty among members of a society. Loyalty to one's nation is reinforced by emphasizing the country's accomplishments in history books while downplaying or ignoring the less positive aspects of the country's history.

Schools also help to teach socially acceptable forms of behavior. Children are taught to be punctual, to obey rules, and to respect authority by encountering a series of rewards and punishments designed to encourage these behaviors. Teachers may award gold stars, certificates, and badges to students both for good academic performance and for good behavior. Because teachers and other school officials are such visible authority figures, the school is a powerful agent of social control. However, schools do not rely solely on the strength of sanctions to enforce acceptable behavior. Their ultimate goal is to produce citizens who have internalized cultural norms and thus have learned to control their own behavior in the social world.

Social Integration Functionalist sociologists also believe that education serves to produce a society of individuals who share a common national identity. Modern societies very often consist of a number of different religious, ethnic, and racial groups. This situation exists in the United States, which has admitted large numbers of immigrants from around the world for many years. American schools are expected to provide a common set of cultural values and skills to all members of society, regardless of their national origin.

This expectation formed the basis of the "melting pot" view of American society. In this "melting pot," immigrant identities were to be melted down and blended to form a new, American identity. During the first two decades of the 1900s, immigrants poured into the country at a rate of about 725,000 a year. The schools were expected to assimilate and "Americanize" immigrant students by eliminating all traces of their cultural backgrounds.

Today many people view American society as a mosaic—a picture formed by putting together many small pieces of tile. Each tile is separate and distinct from the others, yet together the tiles create a larger picture. In keeping with this view of society, many schools around the country teach a curriculum designed to help students understand how their racial and ethnic heritages contribute to a richer American culture. At the same time, schools continue to foster social integration and national unity by teaching a core set of skills and values common to the American way of life.

Occupational Placement All societies must have some system for differentiating young people and preparing them for their future occupations. Education often serves to screen and select the members of society for the work they will do as adults. Some societies assign adult positions on the basis of ascribed statuses, such as family background or wealth. Others assign these positions on the basis of achieved statuses.

According to the functionalist perspective, schools in industrialized countries such as the United States identify students who show special talents and abilities at an early age. The schools then train these students to occupy the important positions in society. Beginning in elementary school and continuing throughout their educational lives, children are tested and evaluated. Based on these tests and evaluations, some students are steered toward college-preparatory courses while others are steered toward vocational courses or other noncollege programs.

The occupational selection function of education is particularly prominent in Japanese society. In Japan, students are admitted into universities only if they pass the entrance examinations. These examinations are very demanding and require students to undertake an incredible amount of studying. Japanese parents often hire tutors to supplement the classroom instruction their children receive. They also send their children to "cram schools" that prepare students for the examinations. Most high school students spend much of their free time preparing for what the Japanese call the "examination war."

The college entrance examinations are a national event in Japan, and they gain wide media coverage. A student's high score results in his or her admission to one of the top universities. Future employment greatly depends on the university that a student attends. On the day that the results are released, families, friends, and observers wait for hours for university officials to post the names of successful students.

The effects of the "examination war" have come into question. Many Japanese worry about the pressure it places on students. They also wonder whether it identifies the best students. In response the Japanese Ministry of Education has proposed that other methods of evaluation—such as interviews, essays, and grade-point averages—might be used along with examinations. However, few parents or students are willing to give up the "examination war."

ACADEMIC VOCABULARY

differentiate to identify or create difference between

Reading Check **Identify Supporting Details** What facts about schools seem to be explained by the functionalist perspective?

The Conflict Perspective on Education

While the functionalists believe that the educational system functions to maintain the stability and smooth operation of society, conflict sociologists believe that the educational system serves to sort students into social ranks and to limit the potential of certain individuals and groups to gain power and social rewards. Conflict sociologists typically point to two factors as evidence that education helps to maintain inequality: social control and tracking. Additionally, conflict sociologists note that a student's achievement or failure in school tends to reflect existing inequalities in society.

Statistically Speaking...

Educational Achievement and Race Conflict theorists argue that the opportunity for educational success is distributed unequally across society. To illustrate this, conflict theorists point out that minority students are more likely to drop out of high school than are white students, and they are less likely to graduate and go on to college.

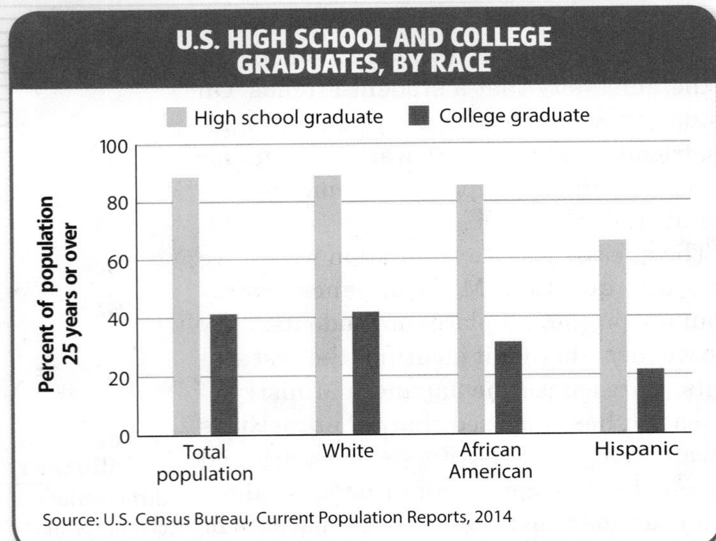

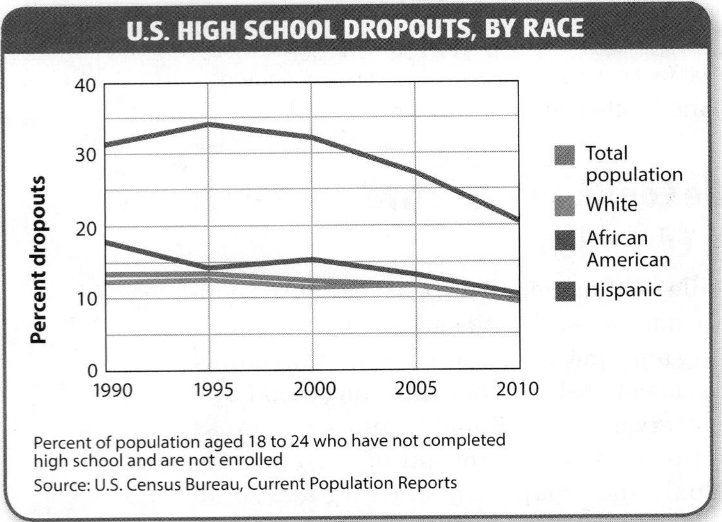

Skills Focus **INTERPRETING GRAPHS** How do the data on achievement for each group compare to the national average?

Social Control In the views of both functionalist and conflict sociologists, the schools are an agent of social control. However, the two disagree on the effects of this control. Functionalists propose that the purpose of social control is to produce citizens who share a common set of values. Conflict sociologists, on the other hand, believe that this control serves to produce unquestioning citizens who accept the basic inequalities of the social system. Conflict sociologists further propose that most individuals are unaware of this process.

Sociologists use the term **hidden curriculum** to describe schools' transmission of cultural goals that are not openly acknowledged. The hidden curriculum embodies a conservative set of values that centers on obedience to authority and acceptance of the status quo. According to conflict sociologists, these values serve the dominant groups in society by helping them maintain their position of power.

From the time of their earliest experiences in school, children are taught to be punctual, to stand in line, to be quiet, and to obey. Students who do not meet these expectations often have difficulties in school, no matter how well they perform academically. Once students are identified and labeled as having behavioral problems, teachers and administrators often watch them closely. Conflict sociologists believe that the hidden curriculum, and the tight control associated with it, produces cooperative adult workers who willingly accept the demands of those in power.

Tracking According to conflict sociologists, tracking is another way that the educational system maintains inequality. **Tracking** involves the assignment of students to different types of educational programs, such as general studies, vocational training, and college-preparatory studies. Students are assigned to tracks on the basis of test scores, teacher evaluations, and grades. The stated goal of tracking is to allow students to progress at their own pace.

Functionalist sociologists view tracking as a way to fulfill the occupational placement function of education. Conflict sociologists, on the other hand, view tracking as a means by which the wealthy and powerful maintain their position in society. Conflict sociologists point out that members of the lower social classes and minority groups are typically assigned to the lower, less academically demanding tracks. These tracks are geared toward blue-collar, clerical, or menial jobs in which opportunities for advancement, income, and prestige are limited. Middle-class students, on the other hand, are more likely to be assigned to college tracks.

Conflict theorists further suggest that the methods of classroom instruction used in the different tracks serve to reproduce the status quo. Educational sociologist Jeannie Oakes maintained this view in her study of 300 high school English and mathematics classes in the United States. She found that higher-track classes, which generally contained large numbers of higher-status students, encouraged the development of skills related to critical thinking, problem solving, and creative writing. Lower-track classes, which generally contained large numbers of low-income, minority, and lower-status students, focused instead on classroom drills and memorization. Lower-track classes also tended to emphasize obedience, conforming behavior, cooperation, and getting along with other people.

Conflict sociologists believe that the type of instruction students receive in the different tracks is designed to mold their behavior to fit their future occupations. For example, students in the higher tracks learn creativity, independence, and self-motivation. Such qualities are desirable in managerial and professional jobs. Students in the lower tracks, on the other hand, learn to work under supervision, follow a routine, and obey instructions. These traits are typically called for in lower-paying and menial jobs.

Education and Socioeconomic Status

Many Americans point to education as the key to social mobility. For example, in a recent survey the vast majority of respondents said that a college education is the key to a good job and a comfortable lifestyle. Statistics show a strong relationship between education and income, with income increasing as education increases. Functionalist sociologists view education as a system that gives individuals the chance to succeed according to their own abilities and talents. Conflict sociologists, in contrast, argue that the opportunities for educational success are distributed unequally. In this way, achievement in school reflects existing inequalities in society.

Educational achievement appears to be tied strongly to socioeconomic status. Generally, higher-status students are more likely to attend and graduate from college. Sociologist Samuel Bowles found that among the highest-achieving high-school students, 90 percent of those from wealthy families attended college. In contrast, college attendance among high achieving students from low-income families was only 50 percent. Bowles noted that this inequality was even more marked among students who did not perform well in high school. Among low-achieving students, those from wealthy families were four times more likely to attend college than those from poor families.

Because socioeconomic status and race overlap to a great extent, minority groups tend to have less educational success. For example, African American and Hispanic students are more likely to drop out of high school than are white students. Hispanic and African American students are also less likely than white students to go on to college and to earn a degree.

Conflict theorists propose that socioeconomic status affects the distribution of educational achievement in a number of ways. First, they hold that the expectations families have for their children's achievement differ by socioeconomic class. Higher-status families tend to assume that their children will succeed at school; they believe that success in school leads to success outside school; and they encourage their children to do well in school. Conflict theorists argue that lower-status families are less likely to hold these beliefs about school. Thus, they may stress the value of getting a good job over higher education.

Second, conflict theorists suggest that higher-status parents are both better able and more motivated than are lower-status parents to provide out-of-school experiences and a home environment that enrich their children's learning. For example, the homes of higher-status students are more likely to contain books and toys that stimulate independent thought and creativity.

Higher-status children are also more likely to be exposed to cultural events that broaden their horizons and to values that emphasize independence and long-term goal setting. Lower-status families are generally less able to offer these experiences; many are barely able to provide the basic necessities of life.

Finally, higher-status families are better able to pay the expenses of putting their children through college. Conflict theorists hold that these opportunities destine higher-status children to become higher-status adults.

Reading Check **Summarize** What are some ways schools prepare young people for different futures?

The Self-Fulfilling Prophecy

Students tend to accept the labels that teachers place on them and behave accordingly. The students' behavior thus confirms the teachers' original expectations. ***How might a sociologist use the self-fulfilling prophecy to illustrate the conflict perspective on education?***

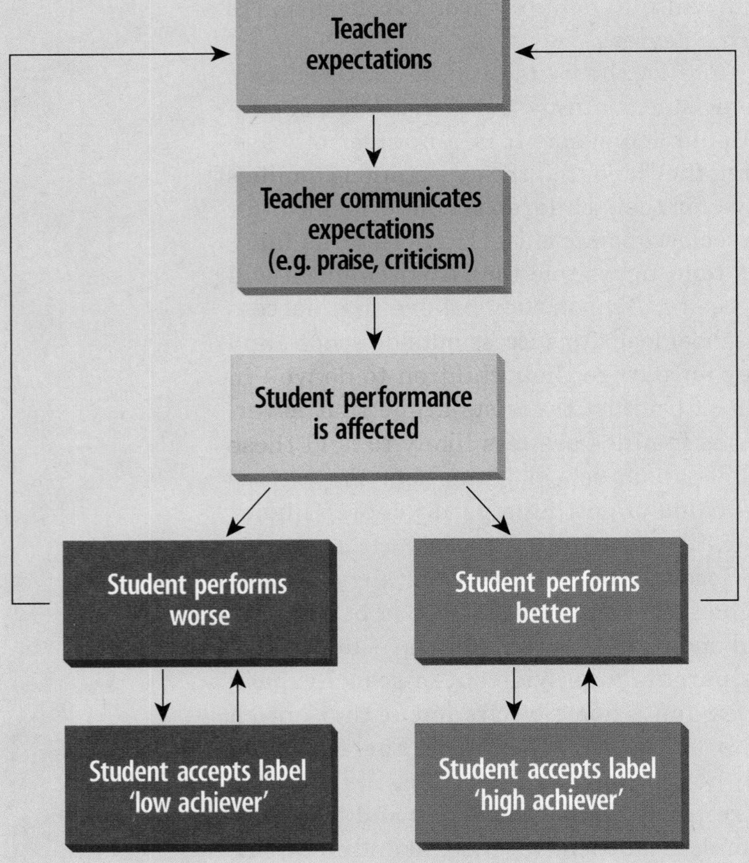

The Interactionist Perspective on Education

Interactionist sociologists seek to explain social phenomena in terms of the interactions among the individuals involved. To explain educational achievement, they observe how people in schools relate to one another and how they share meanings.

Student-Teacher Interaction Sociologist Ray Rist studied a kindergarten classroom in which the teacher divided students into three work groups—fast learners, average learners, and slow learners. This grouping was not based on measured ability, for the students had not taken any tests; rather, students were grouped by social class. Those labeled fast learners were mostly middle class, and those labeled average or slow learners were mostly children of working-class or working-poor parents. The fast learners received most of the teacher's attention and praise, while the slow learners were placed at the table farthest from the teacher's desk and received little attention. At the end of the school year, the fast learners were performing at a high level, but the slow learners had made little progress. Rist found that these differences in kindergarten affected the students throughout their education.

In another study Eigil Pedersen and Terese Annette Faucher examined how teacher expectations affect disadvantaged high school students. They found that most of the highest achievers in their study had been taught by the same first-grade teacher. Examining this teacher's classroom methods, they learned that she stressed the importance of both education and hard work. She gave as much or more time to slow learners than she did to better students. She also expected much from her students and assumed that all would succeed, regardless of background or ability.

Social psychologists Robert Rosenthal and Lenore Jacobson took a different approach to studying the role of teacher expectations. They administered a test to elementary school students and identified a small group of students as likely to succeed. In actuality, Rosenthal and Jacobson ignored the test results and selected the group at random. Nevertheless, those students did perform better than other members of the class.

All three of these studies provide examples of the self-fulfilling prophecy—a prediction that leads to behavior that makes the prediction come true. When teachers treat students as if they are bright and capable, the students come to think of themselves as bright and capable; when teachers expect students to do poorly, those students come to think of themselves as inferior. Once students believe that they are intellectually superior or inferior, they behave in ways that confirm that belief. Thus, they fulfill the prophecy of their teachers' expectations.

Interactions among Students Interactionist sociologists have also studied the learning that occurs through interactions among students. The role of student interaction was brought to prominence by James S. Coleman in his study of inequality in schools. Coleman found that the most significant factor in explaining why some students are more successful than others—more important than anything the teacher does, more important than even the individual student's race or family income—was the socioeconomic status of fellow students. The Coleman Report spurred the shift in U.S. education policy from school desegregation to school integration.

A more recent study by econometrician Eric Hanushek and several colleagues found that peers' achievement has a positive effect on student achievement. A partial explanation for this fact is that peer pressure strongly influences students' achievement motivation. That is, students may be encouraged or discouraged to study and work for good grades because they want to be accepted by a particular social group.

Reading Check **Find the Main Idea** Why are interactionist sociologists interested in the self-fulfilling prophecy?

Perspectives on Education

Functionalist Perspective Education maintains social stability by transmitting culture, teaching knowledge and skills, and preparing individuals for the world of work.

Conflict Perspective Education perpetuates a social system that limits the potential of certain individuals and groups to gain social rewards and power.

Interactionist Perspective Face-to-face interactions between students and teachers profoundly affect student educational achievement.

SECTION 1 Assessment

Reviewing Main Ideas and Vocabulary

1. **Contrast** Describe the difference between education and socialization.
2. **Compare and Contrast** Compare and contrast the core curriculum and the hidden curriculum.
3. **Elaborate** How would a conflict sociologist and a functionalist sociologist explain academic and vocational tracking?

Thinking Critically

4. **Interpret** How is education important for equality of opportunity?
5. **Explain** Give an example of how a self-fulfilling prophecy works in a classroom.
6. **Make Judgments** What else happens in schools besides instruction?
7. **Explain** Explain the role of education in making America a "melting pot."
8. **Summarize** Using your notes and a graphic organizer like this one, describe the nature of education from the functionalist, conflict, and interactionist perspectives.

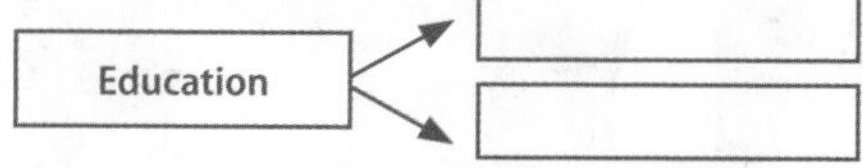

FOCUS ON WRITING

9. **Narrative** Try to imagine a society without an education system. Write a story about an event or a day in that society, describing what life in that society would be like.

SECTION 2

Issues in American Education

Before You Read

Main Idea
Americans devote much attention and money to education because they want education to remedy social problems.

Reading Focus
1. What are some key conflicts in educational reform?
2. What alternatives are there to traditional public schools?
3. How have schools tried to prevent violence?
4. What options have been proposed for teaching English as a second language?

Vocabulary
charter schools
school choice
homeschooling
zero tolerance
bilingual education

TAKING NOTES Use a graphic organizer like this one to take notes about current issues in education.

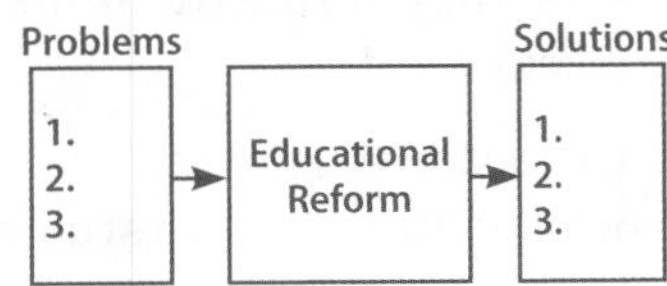

Equal Opportunity and the Schools

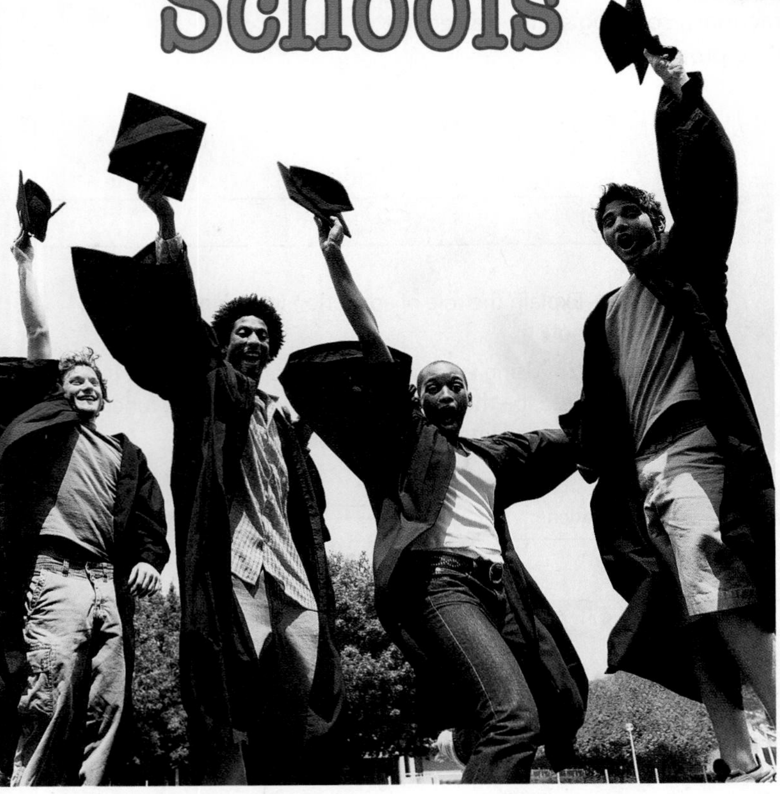

SOCIOLOGY CLOSE UP ***How do schools contribute to social justice?*** The job of the schools is not only to educate, but also to prepare young people for the challenges of adult life. In the United States, adult life is a competition. And key to fair competition are equal rights, equal protection of the laws, and equal life chances. What you make of your chances is up to you.

But is the competition fair if some people are purposely put at a disadvantage? The U.S. Supreme Court said "no." In the 1954 *Brown v. Board of Education* decision on segregation, Chief Justice Earl Warren wrote: "In these days, it is doubtful that any child may reasonably be expected to succeed in life if he is denied the opportunity of an education." Warren's statement attests to the importance of education in our society. It is no wonder that education has been a battleground for all sorts of social conflicts. ■

Educational Reform

Americans have always had a great deal of faith in the institution of education. There is a strong belief among Americans that education is the key to such issues as economic competitiveness, national security, and racial injustice. Many Americans also see education as a major tool in upholding democracy and free enterprise around the world.

History of Reform In the early part of the 1900s concerns about American education centered on the assimilation of immigrants. In the mid-1900s Americans looked to education to help them win the space race.

Attention was refocused after 1983, when *A Nation at Risk* warned that the declining quality of American education "threatens our very future as a nation and as a people." The report charged that United States students had fallen behind those of other industrialized countries and were not prepared for jobs in the new technological age. The commission also made specific recommendations for reform, including a more demanding curriculum, more emphasis on achievement, more homework, more discipline, and a longer school year.

Subsequently, many states and school districts overhauled their educational systems and raised graduation requirements. To attract and keep better teachers, most districts raised teacher salaries, and many states required new teachers to pass strict competency exams. But according to most observers, these reforms brought little progress.

In 1994 Congress enacted the Goals 2000: Educate America Act. This legislation provided grants to states for developing school reform plans and established a series of goals for schools to meet by the year 2000, such as improving school readiness and high school graduation rates. In 1999 the governing panel admitted that American schools would not meet the goals by the 2000 deadline. However, it noted that some progress had been made.

No Child Left Behind Reform efforts continued with the 2001 No Child Left Behind Act (NCLB). The act required each state to deliver standards-based tests in reading, math, and (by 2005) science every year from grades 3 through 8 and tied federal school funding to success on those tests.

To ensure that no child was left behind, test scores would not be averaged across entire schools; instead, traditionally disadvantaged groups were to be tracked separately. The scores of every group had to improve, or a school could be defunded. In severe cases, the state would be forced to take over the school. Further, all scores would be made public, so parents would be informed. Parents in underperforming schools would be able to send their children to a different school. The law also expanded opportunities for individuals and private companies to operate schools.

Extra emphasis was given to early reading instruction. Extra funds were made available to schools that adopted a comprehensive preschool through grade 3 reading program. Other provisions required teachers to use methods that had been "proven effective" by "scientifically based research" and required states to certify that all teachers in core academic subjects are "highly qualified."

The law proved quite controversial, and in 2015, it was replaced with the Every Student Succeeds Act, which shifted the responsibility for implementing most NCLB provisions from the federal government to the states. In addition, the 2009 American Recovery and Reinvestment Act created the Race to the Top grant program to reward states for meeting federal educational goals such as performance-based teacher evaluations and the adoption of common standards.

ACADEMIC VOCABULARY

assimilate
to integrate or fit into

Reading Check **Infer** What have been the purposes behind education reform since the 1980s?

Declining Achievement

"My teacher said the school has tough new standards and I need to improve my vocabulary. What's 'vocabulary'?"

Skills Focus INTERPRETING CARTOONS

What is the cartoonist's opinion about the need for education reform?

TECHNOLOGY FOCUS

Schools Without Walls

The increasing use of technology is changing how we view the classroom. Students in different locations can participate in a course run by a teacher using podcasts, shared electronic whiteboards and message boards, and real-time audio and video chats. Small and rural schools have been using these methods for many years to share courses with each other and expand their offerings. But there are further advantages. Technology like that which enabled engineers in California to control a vehicle on the surface of Mars now enables a middle school student in Virginia to control a camera mounted on an undersea vehicle deep in the Pacific Ocean. Simultaneously, he or she can converse with a scientist in Scotland, while students all over the world watch and listen.

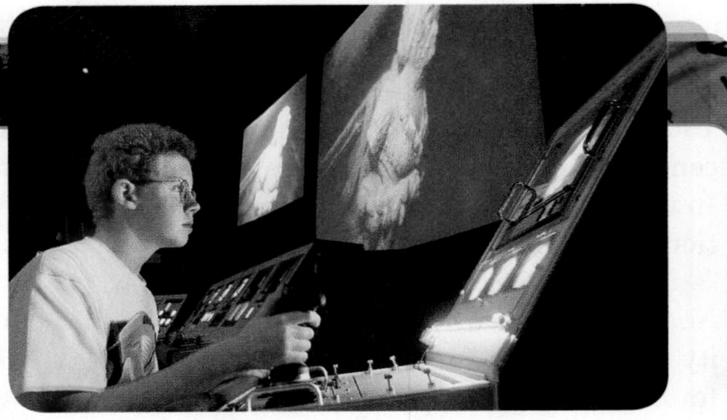

A student directs observations through the National Geographic Society's JASON Project, which allows students to "join real expeditions without leaving their classrooms."

Thinking Critically

Infer What questions might an interactionist sociologist ask about the effects of modern technology on the process of education?

Alternatives to Public Schools

Some Americans think that reforming the public schools is not enough. They believe that alternative approaches to education should also be adopted. One popular alternative to the public school system is the charter school.

Charter Schools **Charter schools** are funded with public money but are privately operated and run. A charter school receives a charter of operation from the state education department or the local school board. The charter establishes the school's educational philosophy, budget, staffing plans, and student goals. In addition, the charter establishes the amount of public funding the school will receive and how long the school will receive it. The charter gives the school considerable freedom in the way it operates and frees it from many regulations that public schools must follow. However, the state or school board can cancel the charter if the school violates charter conditions or fails to meet its goals.

The first charter school in the United States was established in Minnesota in 1991. By 2013 4.6 percent of all public school students nationwide attended charter schools, and there were 6,100 charter schools in 42 states and Washington, D.C.

School Choice Charter schools are a part of a broader educational alternative known as **school choice.** With school choice, parents may receive a voucher equal to the amount their state spends on education for their child. Parents are then free to use the voucher to pay tuition at the school of their choice—charter, private, religious, or public.

Homeschooling An alternative to public schools, **homeschooling** is a system in which a child's main education is undertaken by parents at home. The number of homeschooled students increased greatly in the 1990s, but growth has slowed. In 2012 it was estimated that 1.8 million students—about 3.4 percent of the total student population—were being homeschooled.

Some parents homeschool their children because they are dissatisfied with the quality of education offered by the public schools. Others homeschool because they feel that their public school does not meet the individual needs or interests of their children. Other parents choose homeschooling for ideological or religious reasons.

Critics of homeschooling argue that it may not provide a broad enough curriculum. They also assert that, because of their relative isolation, homeschooled students do not learn about getting along with others and following rules. In addition, critics argue that most parents do not have the teaching skills necessary to provide children with a solid education. Nevertheless, most homeschooled students score as well as or better than public school students on standardized tests like the SAT. Also, homeschooled students are just as likely to attend college as are public-school students.

Reading Check **Summarize** What alternatives to traditional public schools have been proposed?

Violence in the Schools

Many Americans worry that the country's schools are unsafe. A 2006 Harris poll found only 75 percent of parents believed that their public schools were "very" or "somewhat" safe. A Gallup poll the same year found that 35 percent of parents feared for their children's safety at school.

Such fears are generated by violent incidents such as the Columbine High School shootings. In April 1999, two students at this school in Littleton, Colorado, shot and killed a teacher and 12 students and wounded more than 20 others before killing themselves. In 2012, 26 people, including 20 students, were killed in a shooting at Sandy Hook Elementary School in Newtown, Connecticut. While such deadly rampages are rare, violence in American schools is a real problem. In 2005, about 10 percent of boys and 3 percent of girls were threatened or injured by a weapon at school.

The occurrence of all types of crime in schools has declined from a peak in the mid-1990s. In terms of violent crime, students are far more likely to be victims of violent crime off campus than at school, and schools may be some of the safest places for children. According to the National Center for Educational Statistics, in 2011–2012 there were 26 school-associated homicides, among over 58 million students. Most students do not appear to feel threatened in school. In a 2005 poll, 5 percent reported a fear of being attacked or harmed either at school or on the way to or from school.

To combat on-campus violence, a growing number of schools have been instituting strict security measures, such as requiring visitors to sign in before entering. Some have taken more drastic measures, including metal detectors, school guards or other law enforcement officers, closed campuses, and controlled access to school grounds. Most schools have also adopted **zero tolerance** policies. These involve set punishments—often expulsion—and no leniency for serious offenses such as carrying a weapon, committing a violent act, or possessing drugs or alcohol.

Some educators believe that the best way to curb school violence is to teach young people how to resolve disputes peacefully. They advocate lessons in communications skills such as active listening and using "I" statements. The expectation is that young people who learn such skills will be more likely to resolve disputes by negotiation and thus less likely to resort to

Statistically Speaking...

Making Schools Safe School safety has become a major concern for students, their parents, and teachers. As a result, administrators have taken steps to make schools safer.

8% Percentage of students in grades 9–12 who have been involved in a physical fight at school

23% Percentage of public schools that reported bullying occurring on a daily or weekly basis

44% Percentage of public schools in which a theft was reported in the 2009–2010 school year

88% Percentage of public schools that control access to school buildings

64% Percentage of public schools that use security cameras

3% Percentage of public schools that require students to pass through metal detectors on a daily basis

Skills Focus **INTERPRETING CHARTS** What is the most prevalent security measure used in public schools?

Source: National Center for Education Statistics

violence. More than 75 percent of American public schools offer some kind of school-violence prevention program.

Reading Check **Make Generalizations** What solutions to school violence have been proposed?

English as a Second Language

One of the more long-standing and controversial issues in American education concerns **bilingual education,** a system in which non-English-speaking students study science, math, and other subjects in their native languages until they gain fluency in English. Congress enacted several laws concerning bilingual education in the 1960s and 1970s. However, bilingual education did not become solidly established until the U.S. Supreme Court decided in *Lau* v. *Nichols* that schools must provide language programs for students with limited English skills.

Bilingual education has had the support of many educators. But the plan has been opposed by those who believe that it interferes with cultural assimilation. Critics argue that it may take four to five years under the bilingual program for students to learn English. During this time students may lose critical language-development skills, as facility for language learning decreases through adolescence. Many critics also point to the sink-or-swim philosophy that governed education in the early 1900s, when millions of non-native speakers immigrated to the United States. Those immigrants who made it through school got jobs and succeeded through hard work. But proponents of bilingual education point to the many immigrants who dropped out and remained uneducated. They also note that the early twentieth century in this country was a time of great difficulty and social unrest.

According to the U.S. Department of Education, in 2013 about 4.4 million students were classified as English language learners. Spanish was the first language of more than 73 percent of these students. Thus, the debate over bilingual education tends to be most intense in states that have large Hispanic populations, such as California, Florida, Texas, New York, and Illinois.

In 1998 a citizens' initiative made bilingual education illegal in California. Around the country, several groups have organized against bilingual education and against other measures that provide assistance to non-English speakers. As of 2016, 31 states have laws making English their officially recognized language.

Reading Check **Find the Main Idea** Why are bilingual education programs controversial?

SECTION 2 Assessment

Reviewing Main Ideas and Vocabulary

1. **Recall** Describe three alternatives to traditional public schools.
2. **Explain** Explain the theory behind bilingual education.
3. **Contrast** What are the differences between a charter school and a purely private school?

Thinking Critically

4. **Evaluate** Identify everything that is done in your school to prevent and contain violence. Which measures do you think are most effective?
5. **Make Judgments** Should individual teachers be held accountable for the success of their students on basic math and reading tests? Explain your reasons.
6. **Evaluate** What are some pros and cons of homeschooling?
7. **Compare and Contrast** Compare and contrast the reforms proposed by *A Nation at Risk* and No Child Left Behind.
8. **Interpret** Using your notes and a graphic organizer like this one, use the functionalist, conflict, and interactionist perspectives to analyze the issue of English as a second language.

	Problem	Solution
Functionalist		
Conflict		
Interactionist		

9. **Expository** Select one educational issue and explain how you think it might be addressed or resolved.

Alternative Education

Twice each day, all students and teachers at the Nixyaawii Charter School in Mission, Oregon, meet to discuss rules and make agreements.

Interest in alternative approaches to traditional schooling methods took root in the United States in the 1890s, promoted by such figures as Francis W. Parker and John Dewey. Since the 1960s, three distinctive styles of alternative education have developed in the United States.

The first style, or what became known as the free school movement, was driven by the view that traditional schools were suppressing children's natural urge to learn. Proponents said that schools should encourage creativity by allowing students to learn through exploration and experimentation. Various types of schools were set up with this aim in mind. Some free schools maintained aspects of the traditional school setting but had open classrooms where grade levels and subjects were completely integrated. Others took a far more radical approach. In these "democratic schools," faculty, staff, and students had an equal say in the running of the school, and classes were optional.

The second style, which emerged in the mid- to late-1960s, hoped to give parents and students greater choice. Supporters of this style felt that students learned better in situations where they felt comfortable. Therefore, they said, a wide variety of choices in school settings and teaching styles should be available to students. This led to the creation of magnet schools—schools with distinct features intended to attract students from across a district.

The third style, which developed in the 1970s, was very different from free schools and magnet schools. This style focused on students who were considered at risk—those with difficult family circumstances, learning disabilities, or behavior problems. For advocates of this style, the problem was not the school but the students. The programs in these modern alternative schools—back-to-basics curricula, teacher-directed instruction, and strict discipline—were chiefly designed to prepare failing or at-risk students for their return to mainstream schools. Unlike the other types of alternative education, this third style was designed as a substitute for traditional schooling, not as a way to change it. Still, for most people today, this third style has come to symbolize alternative education, which they see as little more than special classes for bad kids.

Some longtime supporters of alternative schools are concerned that the third style has become dominant. For them, alternative education has a much broader meaning. According to educator Dr. Robert Fizzell,

> ***[Alternative education is] a perspective, not a procedure or program. It is the belief that there are many ways to become educated, many possible environments and structures within which this may occur. Further, it is the belief that all people can be educated, and that it is in society's interest to ensure that all are educated . . . . To accomplish this requires that we provide a variety of structures and environments such that each person can find one that is sufficiently comfortable to facilitate progress.***

Thinking Critically

1. **Compare and Contrast** What three movements in alternative schooling developed in the 1960s and 1970s? How were they similar? How were they different?
2. **Discuss** Do you think alternative education as defined by Dr. Robert Fizzell is needed in the United States?

SECTION 3

The Sociology of Religion

Before You Read

Main Idea
Religion is a socially created set of practices that embody and define a group's idea about the sacred.

Reading Focus
1. What is a sociological definition of religion?
2. What are the functions of religion?
3. How do sociologists analyze the nature of religion?

Vocabulary
sacred
profane
religion
ritual
animism
theism
monotheism
polytheism
ethicalism
ecclesia
denomination
sect
cult

TAKING NOTES Use a graphic organizer like this one to note the functions of religion and examples of how religions serve those functions.

Functions	Examples

Angels and Aliens

What does religion mean to you? Not only do people hold different religious beliefs, but they also have different beliefs about what religion is. In her book *From Angels to Aliens*, professor Lynn Schofield Clark describes how teens who identify themselves as "religious" tend to have a broad notion of which beliefs count as religious. For the young people Clark interviewed, religious beliefs included any beliefs about supernatural beings and events—anything outside the realm of science. This included beliefs about alien visitations, angels, and ESP. In contrast, Clark found that older people's ideas of religious beliefs were more limited to ideas about worship, faith in a higher power, creation, life after death, and sin. In this section you will learn how sociologists define religion and interpret its functions in society. ■

Religion—A Sociological Definition

Throughout every time period and in every place humankind has lived, human beings have searched for answers to two basic questions—why do we live, and why do we die? Societies have struggled with the need to give meaning to human existence and to provide people with the motivation for survival.

According to sociologist Émile Durkheim, all societies have attempted to satisfy these needs by making a sharp distinction between the sacred and the profane. The **sacred** is anything that is considered to be part of the supernatural world and that inspires awe, respect, and reverence. The **profane,** on the other hand, is anything considered to be part of the ordinary world and, thus, commonplace and familiar.

This distinction between the sacred and the profane is at the heart of all religions. **Religion** may be defined as a system of roles and norms that is organized around the sacred realm and that binds people together in social groups. As are all basic institutions, religion is a universal phenomenon. Yet religion exists in many different forms because different societies give sacred meaning to a wide variety of objects, events, and experiences. No one thing is considered to be sacred by everyone.

According to sociologists, religion is a social creation. Things take on sacred meaning only when they are socially defined as such by a group of believers. Things that are sacred in one society may be profane in another society. For example, in Hindu society the cow is revered as holy. To most Christians a cow is regarded as a mere animal. Similarly, many Christians believe that a wafer given in the Mass is sacred, but Hindus might regard it only as something to eat. Some religions worship their ancestors; other religions honor animals and trees.

Religions focus on the supernatural world, and thus belief in a particular religion is based on faith rather than on science. Sociologists are not concerned with the truth or falseness of any religion. Rather, they focus on the social characteristics of religion and the consequences that religion has for society. One of the topics of interest to sociologists is the functions of religion.

Reading Check **Analyze** What are the essential features of religion?

The Functions of Religion

Since religion is a universal phenomenon, sociologists assume that it serves certain essential functions in all societies. The most important functions of religion that are recognized by sociologists include social cohesion, social control, and emotional support.

The Functions of Religion

From the functionalist perspective, religion promotes social stability by integrating society, serving as an agent of social control, and offering emotional support. ***How do conflict theorists view these functions of religion?***

Social Cohesion
Religion encourages the strengthening of bonds among people. Participating in religious ceremonies such as the hajj—a pilgrimage to Mecca—strengthens Muslims' bonds to the wider Islamic world.

Social Control
Religion encourages conformity to the norms and values of society. For example, their simple, uniform robes remind Buddhist monks that they must replace individual desires with total dedication to their faith.

Emotional Support
Religion often provides comfort in times of personal suffering or natural disaster. The support of clergy may lend strength to those confronting difficult times.

Social Cohesion One of the most important functions of religion is that it encourages social cohesion—the strengthening of bonds among people. For individuals, both participating in religious ceremonies and sharing beliefs create a sense of belonging, which makes them feel less alone in the world. In his study of suicide, Durkheim found that suicide rates were lowest among those people who had strong attachments to religious groups. These attachments served to anchor people to society, providing them with support and purpose.

However, conflict theorists suggest that social cohesion based on religion may create problems in societies where more than one religion is practiced. Indeed, some societies have been plagued for years or even centuries with continuous conflict. For instance, Pakistan was split off from India in 1947 due to tensions between Muslims and Hindus. The Middle East has been the scene of great strife between Muslims and Jews.

Social Control Religion also serves as a powerful agent of social control by encouraging conformity to norms. In some societies, norms and values may not only be formalized in laws but may also be supported by religious doctrine. Religious followers' belief in the sacredness of writings such as the Bible, the Torah, and the Qur'an give a divine purpose to social conformity. In addition, religion may serve to stabilize society by presenting the traditional social order as commanded by a supreme being.

Some religions also provide formalized means through which individuals may rid themselves of the guilt associated with straying from their societies' norms. Rituals such as confession and communion serve as emotional releases for individuals while contributing to the unity of the group. Religion thus maintains a control over behavior by providing a standard by which individuals may judge themselves and be judged by others.

Some conflict sociologists suggest that a religion's emphasis on conformity to an existing social order may inhibit innovation, freedom of thought, and social reform. When a society gives sacred meaning to its norms and values, it may deny individuals the freedom to question or change unjust practices that support inequality. Obedience to religious doctrine may leave little room for ideas and beliefs contrary to that doctrine.

Emotional Support A third function of religion is to provide emotional support for people during difficult times. Religion helps people endure disappointment and suffering by providing a comfort in believing that harsh circumstances have a special purpose. This belief can motivate people to survive even when happiness appears out of reach and life seems hopeless.

Religion also attempts to provide answers to the ultimate questions concerning life and death—questions that cannot be answered adequately by science or common sense. These answers have lent strength and calm to people as they approached the unknown and the unexpected.

However, conflict sociologists argue that the emotional support given by religion may block social and political change. Karl Marx suggested that religion acts as "the opium of the people." In Marx's view, faith in the mysteries of a benevolent God and the promise of rewards in the afterlife prevent people from seeking out the sources of their hardships and from taking action to better their lives.

Reading Check **Summarize** What basic human needs does religion serve?

The Nature of Religion

Religion exists in varied forms around the world. However, all religions contain certain basic elements. Among these elements are rituals and symbols, belief systems, and organizational structures.

Rituals and Symbols In terms of religion, a **ritual** may be defined as an established pattern of behavior through which a group of believers experiences the sacred. The particular religious rituals found around the world exhibit an enormous variety, but ritualistic behavior is a part of every religion.

Religious rituals are often used to mark changes in status, such as birth, marriage, and death. In most societies, namings, weddings, and funerals are conducted in sacred places by acknowledged religious leaders.

Rituals are also used to unite believers and reinforce faith. Prayer meetings, worship services, and religious feasts allow believers to express their devotion to their religion while contributing to the unity of the group.

Some rituals involve asking or giving thanks for divine intervention in human affairs. These rituals often include sacred symbolic objects—such as particular clothing, herbs, chalices, books, or other symbolic items—which are used only in special places on special days to emphasize their sacred character.

Belief Systems Religions around the world vary considerably in the content of their belief systems. In general, belief systems can be organized into three basic types: animism, theism, and ethicalism.

Animism is a belief that spirits actively influence human life. Animals, plants, rivers, mountains, and even the wind are believed to contain spirits. Societies with animistic religions do not worship these spirits as gods. Rather, they see these spirits as supernatural forces that can be used to human advantage. Rituals such as fasting, dancing, or purifying the body may be used to win the good will of the spirits or to thank them for gifts.

In one type of animism—called shamanism—it is believed that spirits communicate with only one person in the group. This person, called the shaman, is believed either to speak directly to the spirits or to make his or her soul leave the body and enter the spirit world. Followers believe that shamans can communicate with spirits, cure sickness, predict the future, and see events happening far away. Shamanism is practiced in small preindustrial societies in northern Asia and North and South America.

Another type of animism, called totemism, is most commonly found in Australia and some Pacific islands. Totemism involves a belief in kinship between humans and animals or natural objects. The animal or object, called a totem, is thought to represent a family or clan and their ancestors and is considered sacred. The totem is seen as a helpful protector who watches over the group. Because of its supposed supernatural quality, the totem is treated with awe and respect. No one is allowed to hurt, eat, kill, or even touch it.

A second belief system found around the world is **theism** (THEE-i-zuhm)—the belief in a god or gods. In theism, the god is considered a divine power worthy of worship. Generally, there are two types of theism: monotheism and polytheism.

Monotheism is the belief in one god, who is usually seen as the creator and moral authority. Judaism, Christianity, and Islam are examples of monotheistic religions. All monotheistic religions contain an organizational structure, sacred writings, worship rituals, and an organized priesthood or ministry.

Polytheism refers to the belief in a number of gods. The best-known polytheistic religion is probably Hinduism. Polytheistic religions usually center on one powerful god who has control over a number of lesser gods. The lesser gods are thought to have their own separate spheres of influence, controlling such things as harvests, childbirth, and earthquakes.

The third type of religious belief system, **ethicalism,** is based on the idea that moral principles have a sacred quality. Ethical religions are based on a set of principles such as truth, honor, and tolerance that serve as a guide to living a righteous life. Some examples of ethical religions, which are found mainly in Asia, are Buddhism, Confucianism, and Shinto. Ethicalism involves meditation and purity of thought and action. The goal for followers of ethical religions is to reach their highest human potential.

Organizational Structures The organizational structure of religion can be categorized into four types: ecclesiae, denominations, sects, and cults. These categories apply mainly to religions found in the West, and they are so-called ideal types: even Western religious organizations may deviate in various ways from these categories.

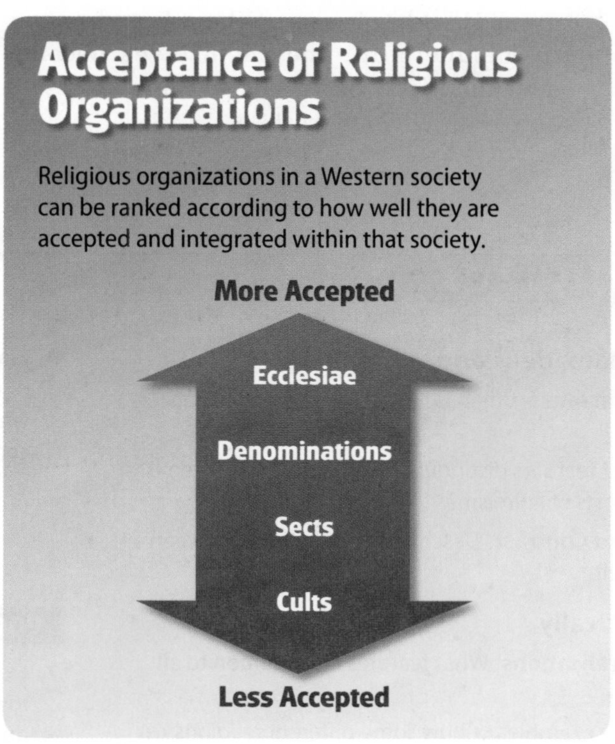

Acceptance of Religious Organizations
Religious organizations in a Western society can be ranked according to how well they are accepted and integrated within that society.
More Accepted
Ecclesiae
Denominations
Sects
Cults
Less Accepted

An **ecclesia** is a structured bureaucratic organization, closely allied with the government, whose officials are highly trained and wield considerable power. Essentially, an ecclesia is the state church. Most people in the society are members by virtue of their birth, and membership is commonly a matter of law. Worship ceremonies tend to be very formal and follow well-established procedures. Ecclesiae do not tolerate religious differences. Fundamentalist Islam in Iran resembles this type of organization.

ACADEMIC VOCABULARY

disillusion to free someone from a naïve or idealized belief

A **denomination** is a well-established religious organization in which a substantial number of the population are members. Examples of denominations include the Presbyterian Church and the Baptist Church. Like ecclesiae, denominations are formal bureaucratic structures with trained officials. Denominations hold strongly to their beliefs, although in comparison to ecclesiae, denominations tend to be more tolerant, acknowledging the rights of others to hold beliefs that differ from their own. Although many members are born into denominations, these organizations also welcome converts.

A **sect** is usually a small organization by comparison to a religious denomination. Sects typically have split off from a denomination over differences in beliefs or practices. Some groups that began as sects have lasted, grown in membership, and themselves become denominations. Sects tend to claim exclusive access to religious truth.

Sects often view other faiths as being in error. They tend to be hostile toward the existing power structure, seeing it as corrupt and worldly. As a result, sects are often viewed negatively by people in the "mainstream." Sects also actively recruit new members. Despite this, many sects are short-lived.

A **cult** is a new religion whose beliefs and practices differ markedly from those of the society's major religions. Cults are typically led by a charismatic figure who claims extraordinary qualities. Often, the cult's beliefs are based on the revelations or visions of this leader. Followers tend to be people who are disillusioned by traditional religion and by life in general. More often than not, followers are initially attracted to the leader as much as to his or her message. After accepting the leader, they may give themselves totally to the cult and reject the rest of society, including family and friends.

Most cults are short-lived. For the most part, their beliefs are too different for very many people in a society to accept. In 1997 in California, 39 members of the Heaven's Gate cult committed mass suicide. In videotapes they left behind, they explained that they were "shedding their containers" and would be transported to a higher existence by a spacecraft that was trailing the Hale-Bopp comet. Such incidents cause many to view cults as dangerous groups with strange ideas.

Reading Check **Identify Supporting Details** What are the four basic elements of all religions?

SECTION 3 Assessment

Reviewing Main Ideas and Vocabulary

1. **Identify Main Ideas** What are three social functions of religion?
2. **Define** What features distinguish shamanism and totemism from other sorts of animism?
3. **Compare and Contrast** Describe the difference between a sect and a cult.

Thinking Critically

4. **Make Generalizations** What features are common to all religions?
5. **Explain** Give examples of how some different religions exercise social control.
6. **Elaborate** Using your notes on the nature and functions of religion and a graphic organizer like the one here, explain why societies with multiple religions might experience conflict.

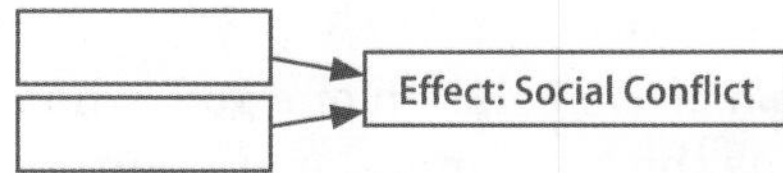

FOCUS ON WRITING

7. **Expository** Why do you think societies have found it useful to distinguish between the sacred and the profane? How does this distinction help religion to serve its functions? Write your answers in a paragraph or two.

SECTION 4

Religion in American Society

Before You Read

Main Idea
Americans' religious beliefs and practices vary along several dimensions.

Reading Focus
1. What are the main religions in the United States?
2. How many Americans participate in religion?
3. How is fundamentalist Christianity important in American society?

Vocabulary
religiosity
secular
fundamentalism

TAKING NOTES Use a graphic organizer like this one to note features of religion in American society.

More than 57,000 people attended services at Lakewood Church during the grand opening weekend of the Lakewood's Central Campus in 2005. The building seats 16,000.

SOCIOLOGY CLOSE UP ***Why do some church services look like rock concerts?*** Traditionally, a church service is an occasion for reflection and worship. Without giving up their seriousness of purpose, many churches have in recent years made more of an effort to entertain. If attendance is a measure of success, some of these churches have been outstandingly successful.

One result is today's "megachurch." There are over 1,300 U.S. churches that are defined as "mega," with an attendance that exceeds 2,000 at each service, and 50 churches have an average weekly attendance of over 10,000. One megachurch—Joel Osteen's Lakewood Church in Houston, Texas—attracts over 43,000 people to services each week. Many of these churches offer multiple services for different segments of their audience, such as youth, singles, and families. In many cases, both the churches and their leaders have become exceedingly wealthy.

Sociologists are interested in understanding these changes. Some look for underlying social trends that could explain why people's expectations of church have changed. Others investigate how the size of a church might affect its internal organization and the experiences of individual members. Sociologists also examine the role of the church within the larger community. In this section you will read about what sociologists know about how Americans meet their religious needs. ■

Religion in the United States

The United States has long been a haven for religious freedom. For centuries immigrant groups have come to America to gain sanctuary from religious persecution. Freedom of religion is protected by law and supported by popular opinion. As a result, the United States is now home to hundreds of different religious denominations, sects, and cults. Changing immigration patterns have added to this variety of religions. For example, the growth in immigration from Asia in the 1990s increased the numbers of Buddhists, Muslims, and Hindus living in the United States.

CASE STUDY CONNECTION

Prayer in Schools Americans value both religion and religious freedom. Religious freedom has been protected by prohibiting organized prayers in public schools.

Another feature of religion in the United States is that the majority of Americans hold it in high regard. The general opinion in the United States is that all people should hold some religious beliefs. A poll taken by the Gallup Organization in 2015 found that 52 percent of Americans feel that religion is very important in their lives. In another Gallup poll in 2011, 92 percent of Americans stated that they believe in God, and in 2014, some 57 percent said they believe that religion can solve all or most of today's problems.

Another feature of religions in the United States is the separation of church and state. This separation is a concept that has been derived by courts from the U.S. Constitution. For the protection of the freedom of religion in the United States, the government lacks the official power to either support or deny any religious beliefs or to favor or work against any religious organization. Hence, the United States, unlike many other countries, has no national religion.

Sociologists who study religion in the United States generally focus on people's religious affiliations and religious participation. Another topic that has gained the attention of sociologists in recent years is the rise of fundamentalist Christianity.

Although more than nine-tenths of Americans say that they believe in God, only about 79 percent are affiliated with some religious organization.

Statistically Speaking...

Religion in the United States Religious affiliation has a strong regional basis. Baptists dominate the South, while Methodists are strong through the Midwest. Lutherans are found mostly in the upper Midwest, and Catholics are numerous in the Northeast and Southwest.

DOMINANT RELIGIOUS AFFILIATION BY COUNTY

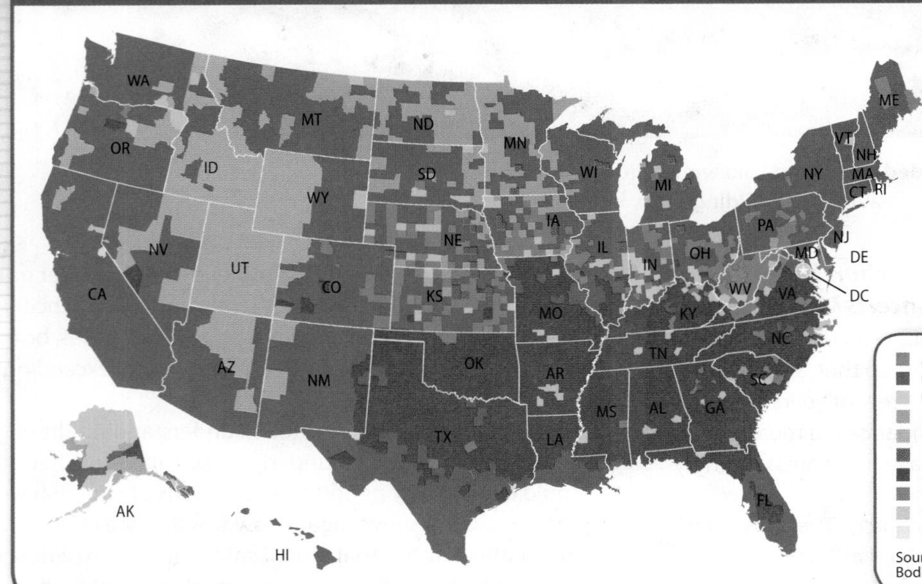

- American Baptist Churches in the USA (26 counties)
- Catholic Church (1,231)
- Christian Churches & Churches of Christ (33)
- Evangelical Lutheran Church in America (155)
- Latter-day Saints (115)
- Lutheran Church–Missouri Synod (25)
- Southern Baptist Convention (1,217)
- United Methodist Church (244)
- Other* (95)
- None Reported (2)

Source: Association of Statisticians of American Religious Bodies, 2010

Skills Focus

INTERPRETING MAPS

Why do you think Catholicism is the dominant religion in much of the southwestern United States?

Even though the United States has many religions, most people with a religious affiliation are members of the major faiths—Christianity, Judaism, and Islam. If you examine religious affiliation by looking at the major faiths, you will find that Christians are the most numerous category of believers in the United States.

Further breaking down the faiths into branches and denominations yields different findings. Christians who belong to Protestant churches far outnumber Catholics, but the Roman Catholic Church is the largest religious organization in the United States. Moreover, the Roman Catholic Church is a unified organization. In contrast, Protestant groups such as Baptists or Methodists may be thought of as families of denominations: Methodists, for instance, are affiliated with any one of nine distinct denominations, such as the African Methodist Episcopal Church, the Southern Methodist Church, and the United Methodist Church.

There are some notable demographic differences among religious groups. For example, Jews and Episcopalians tend to have higher educations and to have higher incomes than other religious groups. In terms of region, Baptists and Methodists reside mainly in the South and Midwest. The largest numbers of Catholics and Jews are found in the large cities. Catholics are also numerous in the West. Political differences also appear among the major faiths. Generally, Protestants have traditionally backed the Republican Party, while Catholics and Jews have given their support to the Democrats.

Reading Check **Summarize** Describe Americans' religious affiliations.

Religious Participation

Although the majority of Americans claim a religious preference, only about 39 percent of people attend religious services on a regular basis. This proportion has remained fairly stable over the past few decades. Women, African Americans, and older citizens are more likely to participate regularly in services. Among the major faiths, Catholics go to services more often than do Protestants or Jews.

However, regular attendance at worship services—whether at a church, synagogue, temple, or mosque—is a poor indicator of religious involvement. Sociologists generally find it difficult to measure **religiosity,** or the depth of people's religious feelings and how they translate these feelings into behavior. Frequent participation in religious services does not demonstrate religiosity because people attend services for a variety of reasons, including socializing and making business contacts. Likewise, nonattendance at formal services does not necessarily indicate a lack of feeling or belief.

However, Americans' attitudes about their own religious feelings and behaviors may provide some insight into religiosity. Only a little more than half of all Americans define themselves as "religious." When deciding how to conduct their lives, Americans are about equally split between paying attention to religious teachings and paying attention to their own views or the views of others. To some sociologists, such statistics indicate that American society is becoming more **secular.** In other words, religion is losing its influence in everyday life in the United States. In 2012, the Pew Research Center found that 18 percent of Americans consider themselves spiritual, but not religious; 15 percent of Americans identified as neither religious nor spiritual. Nonetheless, 71 percent of Americans think that religion as a whole is increasingly influential in American life, while 24 percent think it is becoming less influential.

Reading Check **Find the Main Idea** Why have some sociologists claimed that the United States is becoming more secular?

Fundamentalist Christianity

Membership in several mainstream denominations has been declining in recent years. In contrast, participation in fundamentalist and in evangelical Christian groups has been on the rise. Religious **fundamentalism** refers to a set of associated beliefs including strict adherence to the religion's rules and practices and the belief that religion should be the primary force in one's life. A variety of fundamentalist Christian groups exist in the United States, but they share many beliefs, including:

- that the Christian Bible is completely and literally true
- that Jesus Christ is divine

- that their faith will bring personal salvation—the "born-again" experience
- that they are obligated to bring Jesus Christ into the lives of all nonbelievers

Some 25 percent of Americans describe themselves as "born-again" or evangelical Christians. In recent years, they have organized to exert political influence in the United States. Religious conservative activists donate money to political causes, attend political meetings, and campaign for politicians who share their beliefs. These beliefs generally include opposition to abortion, homosexuality, gun control, and sexual permissiveness, and support for prayer in schools and for what they believe to be traditional family values.

In 1991 Professor James Hunter wrote about the increasing politicization of fundamentalist Christians and identified what he called "culture wars" over moral and religious issues, and ultimately over "the meaning of America." But a more recent study by the Pew Forum on Religion and Public Life concluded that the American public is not so generally polarized. Americans hold strong and divided opinions on values questions, but the public cannot neatly be divided into "liberal" and "conservative." Overall, Americans are conservative or restrictive on some issues and liberal or permissive on others. Nevertheless, fundamentalist Christians make up some of the more active and vocal participants in the culture wars.

Some fundamentalist Christian leaders have questioned the wisdom of involvement in the political system. They have urged fundamentalists to adopt a "strategy of separation" from the mainstream culture so that they may follow a Christian lifestyle. Some fundamentalists have followed this advice by becoming "selective separatists." They remain a part of the mainstream society by voting, working regular jobs, and paying taxes. However, they homeschool their children and avoid all elements of popular culture, such as television, pop music, and movies. Nonetheless, many fundamentalist Christians remain involved in politics, including in support of the Supreme Court's decision in the 2014 case *Burwell v. Hobby Lobby.* In its decision the Court found that the religious owners of Hobby Lobby stores were not required to comply with the Affordable Care Act's mandate that would have required them to cover certain contraceptives for their female employees.

America has experienced waves of religious fervor in the past. The nation has also experienced conflict, sometimes leading to violence, over how the public should control morality. Perhaps it is still too early to tell what will result from these latest waves.

Reading Check **Identify Supporting Details** What are the main beliefs of fundamentalist Christians?

SECTION 4 Assessment

Reviewing Main Ideas and Vocabulary

1. **Describe** What demographic differences exist among American religious denominations and groups?
2. **Define** How is Christian fundamentalism distinct from other Christian denominations?
3. **Recall** How many Americans believe in God? How many are affiliated with a church?
4. **Identify Supporting Details** In what ways is America a secular society?

Thinking Critically

5. **Elaborate** Why is it difficult to observe and characterize a society's religiosity?
6. **Infer** Why might some fundamentalist leaders advocate separatism?
7. **Explain** Why is it that, while most Americans believe that people should hold religious beliefs, they also do not want the government to enforce religious beliefs?
8. **Evaluate** Using your notes on the functions of religion and a graphic organizer like this one, rank what you know about religion in American society from most to least important.

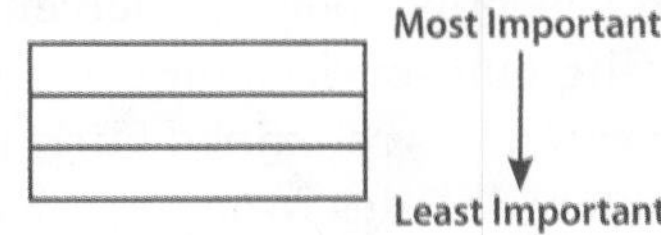

FOCUS ON WRITING

9. **Persuasive** Are public and political disputes about values issues "battles"? Do you believe there is a culture war in the United States? Defend your ideas in a short essay.

Religious Diversity in the United States

Daily prayer is an important part of life for Muslims in the United States.

Since colonial times, people have come to America to enjoy the freedom to worship how they please. Immigrants, particularly those who have arrived in the last 30 years, have helped to transform the United States into the world's most religiously diverse country. A brief review of the major religions in the United States illustrates this diversity.

Christianity The first Protestants came to America in the 1600s, and today the country remains predominantly Christian. As of 2014 more than 80 percent of Americans were Christians, and about one-fifth of Christians were Roman Catholics. Christianity is based on the life and teachings of Jesus of Nazareth as related in the Christian Bible.

People of various religions join Catholics in celebrating the blessing of the fleet.

Buddhism Chinese immigrants brought Buddhism to the United States in the mid-1800s. Since the 1950s, many non-Asian Americans have also adopted the teachings of Siddhartha Gautama, known as the Buddha (enlightened one). The Buddha taught that the source of all suffering is selfish desire and that the path to enlightenment is the Middle Way between desires and self-denial.

Hinduism Hinduism was born in the ancient Indus Valley civilization, on the Indian subcontinent. Today most American Hindus are of South Asian ancestry. As of 2014, the Hindu population in the U.S. was more than 2 million. Hindus believe that everything in the universe is part of the divine Brahman. In addition, Hindus worship deities such as Vishnu, Siva, and Shakti, each of whom represents an aspect of Brahman.

Judaism Judaism, one of the world's oldest monotheistic religion, was founded in western Asia by Abraham sometime after 2000 B.C. Today it is practiced by more than 5.5 million Americans—nearly as many as the Jewish population of Israel. Judaism is based on the belief in and obedience to God as described in the Torah—ancient writings that relate the laws and the early history of the Jews.

Hasidic Jews participate in popular culture but retain a degree of separation.

Islam Islam is the religion of Muslims. Muslims follow the teachings of Muhammad as laid out in the Qur'an, the sacred book of Islam. Most of the more than 3.3 million American Muslims are immigrants from Africa and Asia, as well as their descendants. Another sizeable portion of American Muslims are descendants of enslaved Africans who returned to Islam in the last century.

Other Religions Many other religions are practiced in the United States. These other religions include Sikhism, Baha'i, Taoism, Spiritualism, and diverse Native American and New Age faiths. Just as Americans have the freedom to follow the religion of their choice, they are also free not to worship. As of 2014, more than 55 million Americans stated that they follow no religion, and more than 7 million were atheists.

Thinking Critically

1. **Draw Conclusions** What effect has immigration had on religious diversity in the United States?
2. **Discuss** In what ways does the religious diversity of the United States affect society?

Lab
Applying What You've Learned

How One Society Dealt with Calamity

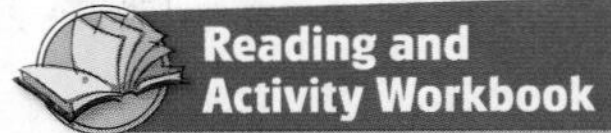

Use the workbook to complete this lab.

Investigate how Amish religious beliefs shape their norms and guide their behavior.

1. Introduction

In this lab you will investigate how one religiously based, highly separatist community adjusts their moral and religious education to accommodate their relations with the larger American society.

Amish began coming to the United States in the early eighteenth century. Amish believe in a literal interpretation of the Christian Bible. They live in self-sustaining agricultural communities isolated from the rest of American society and are forbidden to marry non-Amish. They prohibit the use of technologies such as electricity and automobiles. Each congregation is independent—there is no national or worldwide organization.

When disaster struck one Amish community in 2006, America was able to see how the Amish value system truly plays out in their lives. To complete this lab, follow the steps below.

- Read the case study at right.
- Following your teacher's instructions, organize the class into five student groups. Your teacher will assign each group one of the five group discussion activities A through E.
- Each activity focuses on one important sociological concept from the chapter. Work with students in your group to review the chapter material on this concept and discuss how it pertains to the case study.
- Answer the questions posed in the activity. Each member of the group should write her or his answers on a separate sheet of paper that can be handed in. Each group will also be presenting its findings and opinions to the class.

Case Study

Nickel Mines

Nickel Mines, Pennsylvania, is predominantly Amish—a pacifist religious community that practices a simple farming life without modern conveniences, much the same as their seventeenth-century Swiss-German forebears did. On October 2, 2006, a non-Amish resident of a nearby town went to a one-room Amish school in Nickel Mines and shot 10 students before killing himself.

The modern media world descended en masse on the tiny community. What they found astounded many. Coming from the community was not revenge or anger but a gentle, heartfelt insistence on forgiveness for the shooter, his widow, and his children. The widow was invited to the funeral of one of the victims. Half of the 75 attendees at the killer's funeral were Amish and included parents of the victims. The gestures of love and forgiveness included hugs and condolences from the victims' families as well as an offer to let the widow and her family live in the Amish community. Within a week of the tragedy, the Amish had set up two funds to help the surviving families, one for the families of the girls, and one for the children of the shooter. Herman Bontrager, a spokesperson for the Amish, explained, "The Amish believe that we must forgive because we ourselves need to be forgiven."

This would be a devastatingly difficult event for any community, but perhaps especially for one in which, according to CNN, "there's no crime." Yet it is not as though the Amish are ignoring their inner feelings and hurts. The old school has been torn down, and one year after the incident the Amish were still dealing with the pain. The local Family Resource and Counseling Center has provided therapy for adults and children of the community. The center's founder, Jonas Beiler, grew up and was married in Nickel Mines, and knows his own grief: some years ago, his and his wife Anne's infant daughter was killed. Jonas says, "We've talked to these people and they're all dealing with this one day at a time, the best they can. There are still nightmares."

2. Group Activities

Working as a group, address one of the following topics:

Topic A An important primary function of religion is social control. How does the Amish value of forgiveness serve as a social control? How does it shape the behavior of the Amish? Do you think their compassionate response is possible among people who do not value forgiveness as greatly?

Topic B One function of religion is to provide emotional support during difficult times. Describe the ways in which the Amish displayed emotional support for the members of their community and for others. How does this create a stronger, more close-knit community? Do you see any other benefits to the Amish of widespread emotional support?

Topic C Many in the general population have odd or interesting conceptions of Amish beliefs, practices, and personalities. Make a list of some of the generalizations or stereotypes you have heard concerning the Amish. After reading this case study, what actions, ideas, or values do you find surprising? Make a second list of surprises.

Topic D Religion attempts to provide answers to questions concerning the meaning of life and death, answers that cannot be provided by science. From what you know, do you think their religion gives meaning to Amish lives and makes the passing of loved ones easier for them to handle?

Topic E Social cohesion is "the strengthening of bonds among people." Based on the information in this case study, how do you think their religion helps the Amish community achieve social cohesion? More generally, how do you think religion might help members hold together in times of great tragedy? Are you familiar with other ways that the Amish work together to overcome adversity that comes their way?

3. Discussion

What did you learn from this lab? Hold a class discussion in which each group shares its findings and opinions. If you came to a shared opinion, explain how you came to agree. If members of your group disagreed with each other, explain what you disagreed about.

A year after the Nickel Mines school shootings, members of the Amish community comfort each other at a memorial service. An official statement said, "Forgiveness is a journey . . . [Y]ou need help from your community of faith . . . to make and hold onto a decision not to become a hostage to hostility."

CHAPTER 13 Review

Comprehension and Critical Thinking

SECTION 1 *(pp. 308–315)*

1. a. **Define** What are the functionalist, conflict, and interactionist perspectives on education?
   b. **Summarize** What are the four main functions of education?
   c. **Make Judgments** Using the functionalist perspective on education, what would you suggest to improve American schools?

SECTION 2 *(pp. 316–320)*

2. a. **Describe** Why do people disagree about whether schools should use bilingual education?
   b. **Evaluate** What are some of the pros and cons of alternatives to traditional public schools?
   c. **Predict** Would you expect public or private schools to do better at fulfilling the four main functions of education? Explain your thinking.

SECTION 3 *(pp. 322–326)*

3. a. **Identify** What purposes do religious rituals serve?
   b. **Compare and Contrast** How do animism and theism differ? How are they similar?
   c. **Make Judgments** Do you think it is insulting to label a religious group a cult?

SECTION 4 *(pp. 327–330)*

4. a. **Recall** What are the largest religious denominations in the United States?
   b. **Infer** What might be some advantages of living in a society with a single, dominant religion as opposed to one with a great many religions?
   c. **Evaluate** Based on information in this chapter and your experience, would you say that American society is too secular or too religious, or do you think there is a good balance between religiosity and secularism? Defend your view.

INTERNET ACTIVITY

5. More than most other populations, teenagers are vulnerable to the appeal of cults. Use the Internet to research how cults operate: how they attract new members, how they control people, and why teens are often targeted by cults. Write a short report describing some ways teens can be protected from cults.

Reviewing Vocabulary

Match the terms below with their correct definitions.

6. assimilation
7. charter school
8. cult
9. denomination
10. differentiate
11. education
12. ethicalism
13. fundamentalism
14. hidden curriculum
15. profane
16. sacred
17. sect
18. tracking
19. zero tolerance

A. a publicly-funded, experimental private school
B. imparting useful knowledge, skills, and values to the next generation
C. irreligious; mundane and ordinary
D. a new religion that differs markedly from a society's main religions, often led by a charismatic authority
E. aspects of the world deserving awe and reverence
F. values taught in school that are not publicly or openly acknowledged
G. to distinguish between or tell apart
H. split system of schooling intended to prepare people for different careers
I. adopting the language and culture of one's adoptive society
J. an offshoot religious group whose practices or beliefs differ from those of the main body
K. religious belief system that holds that moral rules are sacred
L. a large, well-established religious organization
M. strict policy prohibiting all weapons in schools
N. ideological movement based on literal interpretation and strict obedience to doctrine

Sociology in Your Life

20. How do school violence and school security affect you or people you know? For example, have violence or threats of violence occurred in your school? Does your school take extensive security measures? Think about how violence and security affect the education your school provides. Organize a few of your main thoughts on these topics into a short essay.

Skills Activity: Interpreting Graphs

The graph below shows the results of a Gallup survey in which Americans were asked how often they attend religious services. Read the graph. Then use the information to help you answer the questions that follow.

ATTENDANCE AT RELIGIOUS SERVICES IN THE UNITED STATES

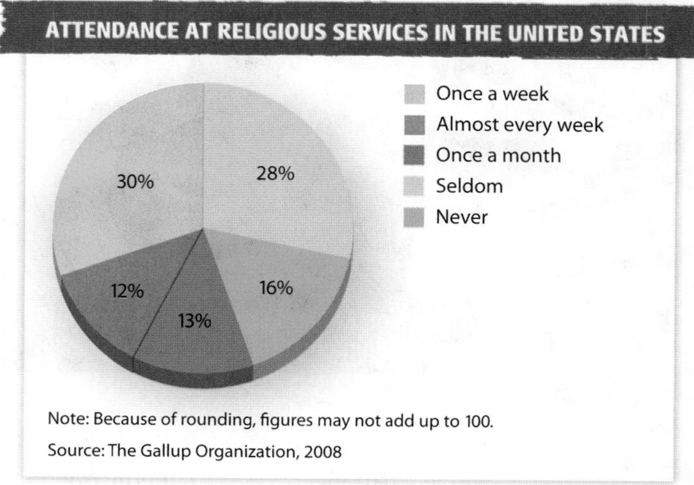

Note: Because of rounding, figures may not add up to 100.

Source: The Gallup Organization, 2008

21. Analyze What percent of Americans attend religious services once a month or more?

22. Make Generalizations Based on the data in the graph, write a simple statement about how frequently Americans attend religious services.

Writing for Sociology

Use your knowledge of education to answer the question below. Do not simply list facts. Present a clear argument based on your critical analysis of the question, using the appropriate sociological terminology.

23. Explain why you agree or disagree with the following quotation:

> "Society can survive only if there exists among its members a sufficient degree of homogeneity; education perpetuates and reinforces this homogeneity by fixing in the child . . . the essential similarities that collective life demands."
>
> —**Émile Durkheim**, ***Education and Sociology***

- Use information and concepts you have studied in this chapter.
- Provide examples to support your points.
- Be sure to include an introduction that sets out your position clearly.

Connecting Online

Go online for review and enrichment activities related to this chapter.

KEY TOPICS VIDEOS
View compelling clips on issues in the field.

KEEP IT CURRENT
Link to the Current Events site for regularly updated stories on sociology as well as other social studies topics.

QUICK LAB
Reinforce a key concept with a short lab activity.

CASE STUDY

SPORT and Television: A Love Affair?

Television cameras focus on a team huddle at the beginning of a basketball game.

Sociologist John Goldlust has suggested that the coming together of sport and television was a "match made in heaven." Some studies of this relationship show that in the early days it was something of a one-sided affair. For example, in their study *Sports for Sale,* David A. Klatell and Norman Marcus discuss the way television changed how, when, and where sports are played.

Today, Klatell and Marcus note, television time-outs are common in many professional sports. As often as not, the television producer rather than the coach calls these time-outs. Similarly, in professional football, the two-minute warning serves the needs of television advertisers, not coaches. Basketball also has bowed to the needs of television. Both professional and college basketball have a shot-clock rule that requires teams on offense to take a shot before a set time elapses. This rule is designed to keep the game moving for television audiences. Tennis, too, has changed to accommodate television coverage. Yellow balls have replaced white balls, because the yellow is easier to see on television.

The needs of television programming have influenced sports scheduling. Games on the West Coast often are delayed until 6 p.m. to accommodate viewers in the East. Similarly, football games scheduled to kick-off at 1 p.m. sometimes are delayed until 4 p.m. to enable television networks to attract larger audiences. In many cases the ticket holders do not learn of the scheduling changes until a few days before the game.

Even the distribution of professional teams has been affected by television. More often than not, teams are located in cities that have "television potential." In some cases concerns over television coverage have lured teams away from cities with loyal fans to new cities with higher viewer appeal. Television also has been the driving force behind team expansion. More teams mean more television coverage.

Perhaps the biggest change that television has produced in sports is the way Americans watch sporting events. According to Klatell and Marcus, the instant replays, slow-motion and close-up shots, in-depth interviews and commentaries, and nonstop action characteristic of television coverage of sports have made sporting fans lose faith in their ability to interpret games unassisted. As a result,

Klatell and Marcus note, fans often bring portable television sets to live games. In many stadiums and sporting facilities, giant replay screens are provided so that spectators in the stands can still enjoy the television experience.

How did television gain such a strong hold over sports? The answer is money. The money teams could earn from television rights and from advertisers far exceeds the money they could earn through ticket sales. The "match made in heaven" was, perhaps, really nothing more than a marriage of financial convenience.

Klatell and Marcus carried out their study in the late 1980s, when the major networks controlled the visual media. Since that time, however, the visual media have changed enormously. The introduction of cable channels such as ESPN has turned sports viewing from a weekend and occasional weeknight event into a 24-hours-a-day, seven-days-a-week preoccupation. At the same time, the development of the computer and the Internet changed the way sports-related news and entertainment are delivered to fans.

These changes, in part, have enabled sports teams to become their own media companies. Some teams have their own cable channel, radio station, print publications, and Web sites with video. Obviously, the connection between sports and television still exists. However, sports appears to be exerting a little more power in the relationship than it did in the past.

What do you think?

1. What brought about a change in the relationship between sports and television after the 1980s?
2. Do you think the relationship between sports and television has been of benefit to sports? Why or why not?

CHAPTER 14

SPORT AND THE MASS MEDIA

Chapter at a Glance

SECTION 1: Sport as a Social Institution

- In sociological terms sport involves games that are won or lost on the basis of physical skills and are played according to specific rules.
- Sport as a social institution is distinguished by characteristics such as secularization, equality, specialization, rationalization, bureaucratization, and quantification.

SECTION 2: Perspectives and Issues in American Sport

- The three sociological perspectives differ in how they view sport's impact on society. Functionalists concentrate on how sport helps to maintain stability in society. Conflict theorists are interested in the relationship between sport and social inequality. Interactionists focus on how sport influences everyday social behavior.
- Sports sociologists focus on issues such as the role of race, the role of gender, and deviant behavior in sport.

SECTION 3: Mass Media as a Social Institution

- The institutionalization of mass media has been driven by a series of intellectual and technological innovations, including writing and paper, the printing press, radio, television, and the computer.
- Americans are able to obtain information from a wide variety of media. These media can be grouped into four categories: print, audio, visual, and online.

SECTION 4: Perspectives and Issues in Mass Media

- The three sociological perspectives differ in the way they view mass media. Functionalists focus on the ways mass media help to preserve social stability. Conflict theorists focus on how mass media reinforce the existing social order. Interactionists look at the impact of mass media on social interaction.
- Sociologists are interested in the power of the media and the way mass media affects children and civic and social life.

SECTION 1

Sport as a Social Institution

Before You Read

Main Idea
In sociological terms, sport is a physical activity that is governed by a set of rules or customs and is played competitively. Sport became a distinct social institution with the rise of modern industrial society.

Reading Focus
1. How do sociologists define the term *sport*?
2. What characteristics distinguish sport as a social institution?

Vocabulary
sport
secularization
rationalization

TAKING NOTES Use a graphic organizer like this one to take notes on the institutionalization of sport.

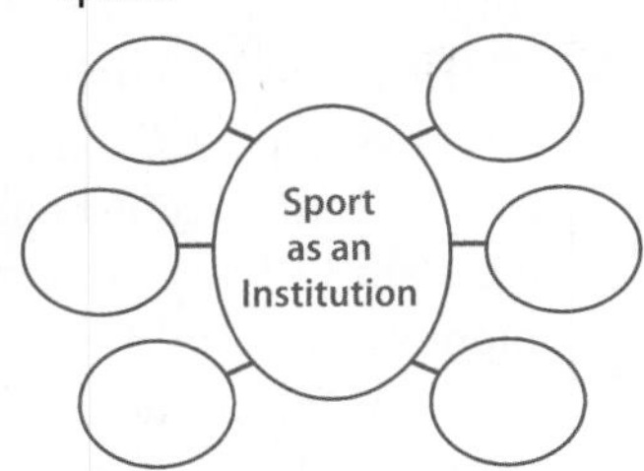

MORE Than Just a Game

Football fans celebrate during a Super Bowl party in San Leandro, California.

SOCIOLOGY CLOSE UP ***Why do some people consider Super Bowl Sunday a national holiday?*** The Super Bowl is a little more than just another football game. Of course, it settles which is the best team in the National Football League. Just as important for the millions of people who watch the game at home, it has become something of a national holiday—and an excuse for a big party.

One observer has suggested that the Super Bowl is "the world's biggest reunion . . . a time when you get together with people that maybe you haven't seen for a while—friends, family." When family and friends get together, they usually eat, and Super Bowl Sunday is no exception. It ranks second only to Thanksgiving Day in terms of the amount of food prepared and eaten. Estimates suggest that 12 million pounds of avocados are purchased to make the favorite party dish, guacamole dip, along with some 15,000 tons of tortilla chips.

The huge television audience, perhaps as much as half of the country's population, makes Super Bowl Sunday very important for advertisers. They spend more than $5 million for a 30-second spot during the game. Many party goers spend as much time discussing the merits of the commercials as they do watching the play on the field. ■

Defining Sport

The Super Bowl is obviously more than just a game, but is football, in sociological terms, a sport? For sociologists **sport** refers to competitive games that are won or lost on the basis of physical skills and played according to specific rules. Football certainly meets the three necessary conditions—competition, physical skill, and rules—set down in the definition. So, too, do baseball, basketball, hockey, tennis, swimming, track and field, gymnastics, skiing, and a host of other spectator sports.

For some sociologists competition is the most important aspect of sport. These sociologists see three distinct types of sporting competition. In direct competition, two individuals or teams engage each other physically. The Super Bowl, which pits two football teams against one another, is a perfect illustration of direct competition. So, too, are events that pit individuals against each other, such as track and swimming races. In indirect competition athletes take turns at the same skill. Field events, such as the shot put or the pole vault, involve indirect competition. In the third type of competition, individuals or teams compete indirectly, but their performances are measured against some preset standard. Figure skaters, for example, are awarded points for how well they perform certain moves and jumps. Gymnastics competitions are decided in a similar fashion.

Not all games that involve competition are considered sport. Dice and chess, for example, are competitions, but they require little or no physical skill. Sociologists also do not classify such childhood games as tag, leapfrog, or hide-and-seek as sport. Rather, they consider these activities as a form of play.

Reading Check **Identify Supporting Details** What three conditions are necessary for an activity to be called a sport?

SPORT AS COMPETITION

QUICK FACTS

Sociologists recognize three types of competition: direct, indirect, and against a standard.

Direct Competition In this form of competition, two individuals or teams engage each other physically. Examples: baseball, basketball, football, ice hockey, tennis, track, swimming

Indirect Competition In indirect competition, participants take turns at the same skill. Examples: bowling, ski jumping, field events

Against a Standard In this form of competition, individuals or teams may compete indirectly, but their performances are measured against a preset standard. Examples: diving, figure skating, gymnastics

The Institutionalization of Sport

Archaeological evidence indicates that physical games have been a part of human culture from the earliest times. Even so, sport as a social institution is a relatively recent phenomenon. The social changes brought on by the Enlightenment and the Industrial Revolution gave rise to modern sport. Thus, the rise of sport closely follows the rise of modern industrial society. It is not surprising, therefore, that modern sport first emerged in England and then spread to the United States, Western Europe, and the rest of the world.

According to sociologist Allen Guttmann, sport as a social institution is distinguished by the same characteristics that distinguish modern industrial society. These characteristics include secularization, equality, specialization, rationalization, bureaucratization, and quantification.

Secularization For sport to be considered an institution, it must have roles, norms, and values that distinguish it from other institutions. For much of history sport did not meet this criterion. Games of physical skill most often were part of religious festivals. Archaeological evidence indicates, for example, that the ball game played by the ancient Mayans was a life-or-death struggle in honor of the gods. Stone reliefs found at Chichén Itzá in Mexico clearly show players being sacrificed to the gods.

Quick Lab

But Is It Sport?

Are the physical activities you and your friends engage in considered sport by sociologists? Poll your classmates to discover the games they play and if these activities qualify as sport.

PROCEDURE

1. Read the paragraphs under the heading "Defining Sport" and take close note of the three conditions necessary for an activity to be classified as sport.
2. Select a representative sample of your classmates. Be sure that neither athletes nor nonathletes are over-represented.
3. Ask your subjects to each list all the activities they take part in that they consider sport. Then ask them to note how each activity meets each of the three conditions of the sociological definition.

ANALYSIS

1. Collate your results and present them in a chart showing the types of sport and nonsport that your subjects take part in and the most popular of these activities.
2. Use your chart as the starting point for a discussion on what are the most popular sport activities, what are the most popular nonsport activities, and who takes part in these different activities and why.

The religious nature of the game is reinforced by the fact that all the ball courts discovered to date have been located in temple complexes.

Even the ancient Greek Olympic games—the forerunners of modern sports—were carried out as part of a religious festival honoring Zeus. Other Greek athletic festivals also paid tribute to the gods. As long as sport remained a part of the religious institution, its influence was relatively minor. To become an institution in its own right, sport had to move from the realm of the sacred to that of the profane, a process that sociologists call **secularization.**

The ancient Greeks began this move when they provided pensions for winning athletes and built athletic facilities for the general population. Not until the eighteenth and nineteenth centuries, however, did sport completely separate from religion. With the Industrial Revolution came the overall secularization of society, which led to a wider social role for sport.

Equality In most past societies, participation in sporting events was based on ascribed rather than achieved characteristics. In medieval times, for instance, only people of noble birth were allowed to compete in organized sporting events. Wealth and social status thus determined eligibility but do not do so in modern sport—at least in principle. Two basic norms of modern sport are that competition is open to everyone and that the same rules apply to all contestants. However, sometimes expectations do not match reality.

ACADEMIC VOCABULARY

eligibility quality of being qualified or worthy of being chosen

Specialization The Olympic games of the ancient Greeks involved specialization. For example, some athletes specialized in running, others in wrestling, and still others in discus throwing. Today, however, specialization in sport is much more highly refined. A football player, for example, not only specializes in football but generally concentrates on playing a single position within the sport. In addition to having specialized players, a football team has owners, managers, coaches, trainers, scouts, doctors, and recruiters, each fulfilling a specific role.

According to sociologists, the high degree of specialization in modern sports results from the stress on achievement. The underlying assumption is that an individual who is allowed to concentrate on a single task will have a better chance of excelling in that task than will an individual who divides his or her talents among numerous sports.

Rationalization According to Max Weber, rationalization is the hallmark of modern capitalist society. **Rationalization** refers to the processes by which every feature of human behavior becomes subject to calculation, measurement, and control. Since sport is an important part of modern society, not surprisingly it also has become rationalized. Every major sport is played according to established rules that are subject to periodic modification. Because these rules are official and, therefore, widely accepted, sports are played in basically the same way everywhere in the world.

People playing basketball in China, for example, play the game according to the same general rules as people playing the game in the United States and around the world.

Bureaucratization Rationalization and bureaucratization go hand in hand. If a sport is to be played according to specific rules, a formal organization must be charged with the task of developing and enforcing those rules and settling disputes. In addition to carrying out these tasks, sports organizations generally organize competitions and keep official records against which to measure future athletic feats. The first athletic organizations appeared in Great Britain in the middle of the nineteenth century. Today every major sport, and many minor ones, has a national or international organization that serves as a final governing authority.

Quantification Modern sport focuses heavily on achievement. Athletes want to know where they stand in relation to other athletes, both past and present. Thus, quantification is an essential element in modern sports. Every year, the methods of measurement become more sophisticated. In recent years, for example, the stopwatch has been replaced by the computer. In today's high-tech world, sports records are achieved or missed by milliseconds.

The desire to achieve and set new records can create a "win-at-any-cost" mentality in some athletes. Such athletes may use steroids or other performance-enhancing drugs. Steroids supposedly increase muscle mass and strength, thereby improving an athlete's performance. Steroid users willingly risk heart, kidney, and liver damage—three common side effects of the drug—in exchange for a chance at glory. Health risks, including the possibility of death, become just another price to pay for the promise of a winning edge.

The Quest for Records Swimming competitors not only race against each other but also against the clock. Setting records is an important aspect of this and similar sports.

1:57.04 Men's 200-meter butterfly world record in 1984

1:51:51 Men's 200-meter butterfly world record in 2015

2:05.96 Women's 200-meter butterfly world record in 1984

2:01.81 Women's 200-meter butterfly world record in 2015

Skills Focus **INTERPRETING DATA** How have the men's and women's world records changed since 1984?

Source: FINA

Reading Check **Analyze** How is industrialization related to the rise of sport as a social institution?

SECTION 1 Assessment

Reviewing Main Ideas and Vocabulary

1. **Define** How do sociologists define sport?
2. **Identify** What term do sociologists use to describe the process of moving from the sacred to the profane?

Thinking Critically

3. **Explain** Why are children's games not considered sport by sociologists?
4. **Infer** How might the drive for achievement have a negative impact on athletes?
5. **Summarize** Using your notes and a graphic organizer like the one here, show how sport became a social institution.

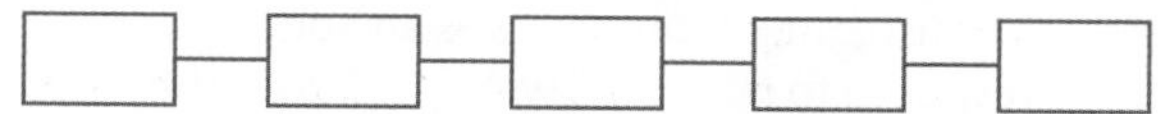

FOCUS ON WRITING

6. **Expository** Select a physical activity and write a brief essay explaining why it is or is not a sport. Consider the three conditions of sport when writing your essay.

SECTION 2

Perspectives and Issues in American Sport

Before You Read

Main Idea
The three sociological perspectives differ in how they view sport's impact on society. Sports sociologists focus on issues such as the role of race, the role of gender, and deviant behavior in sport.

Reading Focus
1. How do the three sociological perspectives view sport?
2. What are some of the issues in American sport?

Vocabulary
stacking
Title IX

TAKING NOTES Use a graphic organizer like this one to take notes on how the three perspectives view sport and major issues of sociological interest in sports.

Sport	
Perspectives	Issues

Dropping the Gloves

SOCIOLOGY CLOSE UP ***Does violence serve a purpose in sport?*** Fighting has been a part of hockey ever since the game began. The level of violence even became the subject of a joke by stand-up comedian Rodney Dangerfield: "I went to a fight the other night and a hockey game broke out." However, according to sociologist Kenneth Colburn, "violence . . . is in the eye of the beholder." Colburn admits that the fistfight certainly fits the definition of violence—physical assault with intent to do harm. Hockey players do not view fighting in this way, he states. Rather, they see the fistfight as a legitimate form of assault that is not a violent or a particularly dangerous act.

Colburn explains the players' attitude by suggesting that the fistfight is a social ritual, an action that has no apparent purpose but, through the behavior and symbols used, contributes to social solidarity. The fight begins with one player dropping his gloves and stick, signaling his intentions, and allowing his opponent ample time to respond. This behavior, Colburn suggests, affirms the norms of fairness and respect for opponents. The fistfight, he continues, is an honorable response to perceived wrongdoing on the ice. It also acts as an informal mode of social control. Without the ritual release of the fistfight, Colburn concludes, players might resort to more dangerous forms of assault, such as hitting each other with their sticks or slamming opponents into the boards that surround the ice. ■

Sociological Perspectives on Sport

Sport is a huge part of life in the United States. Annual attendance at Major League Baseball games averages more than 73 million people, while yearly attendance at professional football and basketball games tops 17 million and 21 million, respectively. Even more people attend college football and basketball games. Now, with the advent of sport stations on cable television, fans can enjoy sports 24 hours a day, seven days a week in the comfort of their own homes.

Given America's love affair with sports, it is not surprising that sociologists have devoted considerable attention to studying the institution. As they do for other social issues, sociologists examine the effect of sport on society from the three basic perspectives. Those who adopt the functionalist perspective concentrate on the ways in which sport helps to maintain stability in society. Conflict theorists are more interested in the relationship between sport and social inequality. Sociologists who view society from an interactionist viewpoint, however, focus on how sport influences everyday social behavior.

Perspectives on Sport

Functionalist Perspective By providing a common interest, sport helps to unite members of the community. Sport also reinforces important norms and values, such as hard work, competition, and patriotism. In addition, sport offers a socially acceptable means of getting rid of tension and aggression.

Conflict Perspective Sport perpetuates the power structure by distracting people from working for social change. Sport also tends to reinforce gender and racial inequality.

Interactionist Perspective The symbols, norms, and values of sport influence everyday social behavior. For example, adopting athletes as role models can influence behavior both positively and negatively.

Functionalist Perspective According to functionalists, sport serves at least three very important positive functions. First, sport encourages social integration. By providing a common interest for people of different racial, ethnic, and economic backgrounds, sport serves to unite members of society. Second, sport reinforces important social norms and values. With its emphasis on competition and winning, sport teaches people to value hard work, team spirit, and obedience to authority—traits that are important in a capitalist society. Finally, sport functions as a kind of societal safety valve since it provides athletes and spectators with a socially acceptable means of working off stress and aggression.

Conflict Perspective Rather than look at the functions of sport, conflict theorists focus on how sport reflects or serves to maintain social inequality in society. Some conflict theorists suggest sport maintains inequality through its ability to draw people's attention away from personal and societal problems. According to their view, sport serves to lessen people's unhappiness with their lot in life by providing a distraction. The bored worker, the low-income city dweller, and the unemployed adult or teenager can forget his or her troubles by watching or participating in sports. In addition, by reinforcing the idea that achievement comes through hard work, sport provides a justification for the unequal distribution of wealth. People who achieve wealth and power are seen as doing so through personal talent and effort, not through the social and economic advantages they may have. Finally, conflict theorists point out that sports such as football, boxing, and hockey serve to legitimate violence and make it more acceptable in other areas of life.

Interactionist Perspective Interactionist theorists are interested in the meaning and influence of the symbols, norms, and values of sport. For example, society honors athletes for their physical skill and prowess. As a result, many people adopt athletes as role models. Athletes, however, have a life beyond the field of play where their behavior may be less than admirable. Even so, some in society—most notably young people—accept this behavior as part of the role of athlete.

Interactionists also look at the ways the coach-player relationship affects behavior. Studies of youth sports suggest that the message that coaches are imparting to their players is not necessarily the same as that which the players receive. For example, coaches believe they are stressing the value of competition, hard work, and effort. Some players, however, hear a message that supports the use of aggressive, win-at-any-cost tactics. Parents, too, may send mixed messages to young players. For example, parents' unrealistic expectations for success may result in disappointment—even when players have performed well.

How being part of a team affects individual behavior is another subject that interests interactionists. For a team to be successful, all players must make a contribution. This experience of working together for a common goal, some studies suggest, may cause some players to discard previously held prejudices about teammates of different racial or economic backgrounds.

Reading Check **Find the Main Idea** How do the three sociological perspectives view sport?

Issues in American Sport

Sport is a growing area of interest in sociology. Three areas of great interest for sports sociologists are the role of race, the role of gender, and deviant behavior in sport, particularly drug use and violence.

Race and Sport Most studies on race and sport tend to focus on racial discrimination. One area of interest is **stacking,** or the practice of assigning people to central or noncentral athletic positions on the basis of race or ethnicity. Sociologists label positions as central or noncentral on the basis of leadership responsibility. Central positions are those positions that require leadership responsibility and that afford players greater opportunity to affect the outcome of the game. In football, for example, central positions tend to be on offense and special teams, such as quarterback, center, left and right guard, kicker, and punter. In baseball, central positions include pitcher, catcher, and infielder.

Studies conducted during the 1970s and 1980s found strong evidence of stacking in college and professional football. White players were predominant in positions considered central. African Americans, on the other hand, were concentrated in defensive positions—positions considered noncentral. Similar studies of baseball found white players concentrated in central positions, while African Americans and Hispanics usually occupied noncentral positions in the outfield.

Regular studies conducted by the Institute for Diversity and Ethics in Sport show that stacking is becoming less and less a part of sport on the playing field. African Americans have moved into central football roles such as quarterback. Similarly, in baseball African Americans and Hispanics fill many central positions. These studies also show that while some gains have been made, minorities still are underrepresented in the central roles of coaches, trainers, managers, front-office officials, and owners.

Sociological explanations for stacking suggest that coaches perceive minority players as lacking the skills needed to carry out the decision-making duties associated with central positions. Interestingly, since the increase of minorities in central positions, many of these duties have been taken over by coaches on the sidelines or in the dugout.

Another area of interest for sports sociologists is whether racial attitudes of fans influence who plays for a team. Most research on this topic focuses on the National Basketball Association (NBA), where approximately 75 percent of the players are African American but most fans are white. Studies show that even though some fans have expressed a preference for watching players of their own race, the number of white players in the NBA has been falling. However, when a skilled white player replaces an equally skilled African American player on a team, attendance increases slightly. In addition, star white players tend to play for teams located where the population is overwhelmingly white.

Women in Sport Early sociological studies of women's athletics often focused on participation in sports. Most found that women had few opportunities to take part because of lack of funding. Prior to the 1970s, funding for women's athletics was almost nonexistent at most coeducational colleges and

Statistically Speaking...

Stacking The practice of stacking on the playing field is much less an issue today than it was 15 or 20 years ago. However, it is still much in evidence among coaches, managers, and front-office officials, most of whom are white. The graphs to the right provide information on the racial makeup of head coaches and managers in professional baseball, basketball, and football. Women face stacking, too—even in women's college sports. A recent study of the top women's sports programs found the following:

38.6% Percentage of head coaches who are women

48.4% Percentage of assistant coaches who are women

Skills Focus **INTERPRETING GRAPHS** What trends in the racial makeup of head coaches and managers do the graphs show?

Source: The Institute for Diversity and Ethics in Sport

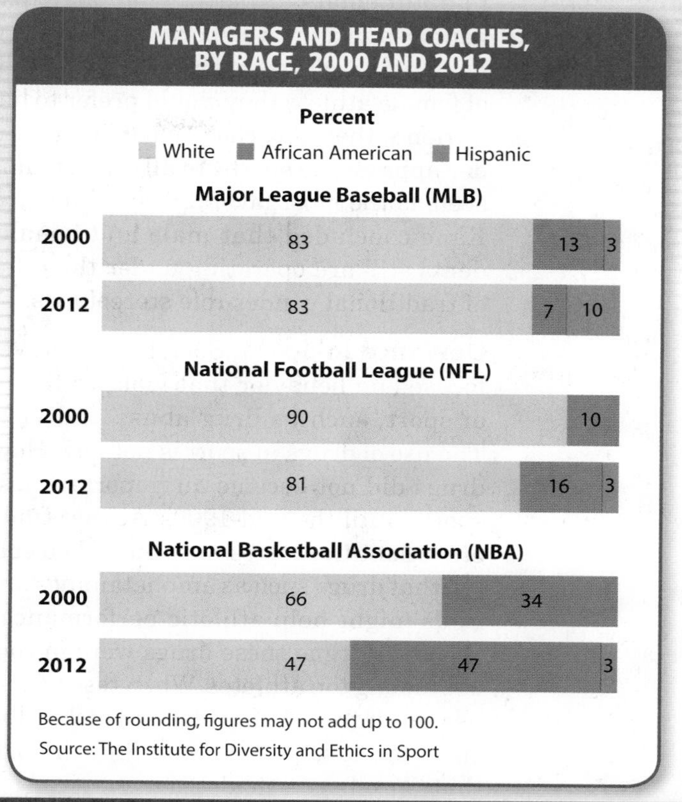

universities. In fact, women began receiving college athletic scholarships only in 1973. This situation began to change with the Education Amendment Act of 1972. **Title IX** of the act, which went into effect in 1975, bars discrimination on the basis of gender in any program—including athletics—at any educational institution receiving federal funds. As a result of Title IX, female participation in intercollegiate sports jumped from approximately 16,000 in 1972 to more than 43 percent of all college athletes today. Similarly, female participation in high school sports rose from 294,000 in 1971 to more than 3 million in 2014.

This major step forward in women's sports, one study suggested, is a revolution that "is not being televised." The study found that in 1989 only 5 percent of sports news coverage on television focused on women's sports. By 2004, that figure had barely changed—just 6 percent. By 2014, it had dropped to only 3.2 percent. Apparently, the relationship between sports and television has not benefited women's athletics.

In light of changing attitudes toward appropriate gender behavior for women, some recent studies have focused on whether athletic participation for female high school students is considered socially acceptable. The findings have been mixed. Some studies found that participation in sports increases a female's standing within the social stratification system of high school. Other studies found that students rate female athletic participation well down on the list of roles associated with high social standing.

In an attempt to determine whether these contradictory findings might be the result of lumping together all sports, sociologist Mary Jo Kane conducted a study that distinguished between five sports: tennis, golf, volleyball, basketball, and softball. Based on the amount of body contact, the weight of sports equipment, and the degree of face-to-face competition, Kane classified basketball and softball as gender-inappropriate sports for women, and tennis, golf, and volleyball as gender-appropriate sports.

CASE STUDY CONNECTION

Sport and Television: A Love Affair? Live coverage of women's athletic events is rare except for the Olympic Games and major competitions such as the U.S. Open Tennis Championship.

Kane found that male students preferred to date female athletes who participate in gender-appropriate sports. Similarly, when female students were asked to list which type of female athlete they would prefer to have as a friend, they, too, chose participants in gender-appropriate sports. In all cases, tennis was seen as the most favorable sport for females. Kane concluded that male and female students still are operating under the influence of traditional gender-role stereotypes.

Deviance in Sport Sociologists have also focused on behavior that violates the norms of sport, such as drug abuse and violence. The use of drugs in sport is not new. However, drugs did not become an important issue in sports until the mid-1900s. At that time, several scientific studies were published suggesting that drugs such as amphetamines and steroids might help athletic performance. In a very short time these drugs were in common use among top athletes. When testing for drug use was introduced, athletes switched to other substances, such as human-growth hormone, that were harder to detect.

Today the use of performance-enhancing substances is widespread. Many male and female athletes, from top professionals to high school athletes, use them to gain a competitive edge or simply to stay at their own level of performance. Even those who know that taking these drugs is morally wrong and physically dangerous still use them. Why are so many athletes willing to take such risks? Sports sociologist Jay Coakley suggests that they are overly committed to the sport ethic. That is, they are so committed to competing—to being an athlete—that they will do anything to ensure that they can continue.

Several studies of violence in sport have looked at sport's function as a safety valve. The hypothesis of these studies is that both players and spectators use sport as a way to relieve feelings of frustration and aggression. These studies found little evidence that athletes are less aggressive away from the sports arena. However, some seem to suggest that without the outlet of sport, some spectators might well commit violent crime. Still others suggest that sports may create frustration and anger among spectators, and the result may be more violence.

Some sociologists think that violence in sport reflects normal, not deviant, behavior. For example, anthropologist Richard Sipes made a comparison of 20 societies, 10 peaceful and 10 warlike. He found that combative sports, such as football, hockey, boxing, and wrestling, were popular in nearly all warlike societies but only in 2 peaceful societies. Violence in sport, he concluded, is simply an expression of established cultural patterns.

Reading Check **Summarize** On what social issues do sports sociologists focus their attention?

SECTION 2 Assessment

Reviewing Main Ideas and Vocabulary

1. **Define** What do sociologists mean by the term *stacking*?
2. **Explain** What is the purpose of Title IX?

Thinking Critically

3. **Elaborate** According to the functionalist perspective, how does violent sport help maintain social stability?
4. **Support a Position** Based on the discussion of the issue in this section, do you think that racial discrimination exists in sport? Explain your answer.
5. **Summarize** Using your notes and a graphic organizer like the one below, select one of the issues in sport and describe how each sociological perspective might view it.

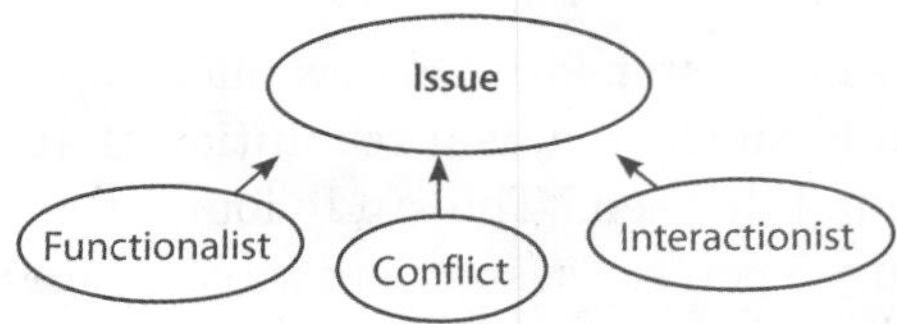

FOCUS ON WRITING

6. **Expository** Write two paragraphs describing how a feminist theorist would view the impact of Title IX on women's athletics.

SECTION 3

Mass Media as a Social Institution

Before You Read

Main Idea
The institutionalization of the mass media was driven by several technological developments. The media available in the United States fall into four categories: print, audio, visual, and online.

Reading Focus
1. How did the mass media develop as an institution?
2. What is the nature of mass media in the United States?

Vocabulary
information society
media convergence

TAKING NOTES Use a graphic organizer like this one to take notes on the institutionalization of mass media and on the types of mass media in the United States.

Institutionalization of Mass Media	Types of Mass Media

Can't Live Without Them

SOCIOLOGY CLOSE UP ***How important is the media in your life?*** Take a look at this list of activities that involve the media and identify which ones you have done recently.

Read a book, newspaper, or magazine
Listened to the radio
Watched a movie at the theater
Watched television
Bought or rented a DVD
Played a video game
Listened to an MP3 player
Downloaded special ring tones for your cell phone
Took a picture with your cell phone
Sent a text message
Chatted with friends on social networking Web site

How much time do you think you spend on these activities? If they take up a good part of your day, you are not alone. The average American spends four months of the year using media! If you are like the average American, you spend more time watching television than using any of the other types of media. The only activity that many teenagers spend more time doing than watching television is sleeping. Going through a day without using some type of media, then, is almost unthinkable. ■

The Institutionalization of Mass Media

As you recall, mass media are instruments of communication that reach large audiences with no personal contact between those sending the information and those receiving it. The emergence of mass media as a social institution is a fairly recent event. The institutionalization of mass media has been driven by a series of intellectual and technological innovations. The first major breakthrough came with the development of writing and paper. Hundreds of years passed before the next major step—the creation of the printing press. Developments during the Industrial Age transformed media into a central force in society. The computer—the most recent and, perhaps, far-reaching development—has also helped to create an information society.

Writing and Paper People in the earliest nomadic societies had little need for any form of media. They lived in small groups, constantly on the move in search of food. To convey information to one another, they relied on the spoken word. With the development of agriculture, societies became more complex. Individuals began to specialize in specific economic activities. For example, some people became craftworkers, producing tools and jewelry. This production of goods encouraged the development of trade. People soon became aware that they needed some form of written language to record business transactions.

The Sumerians, who flourished more than 5,000 years ago in what is Iraq today, produced a form of writing called cuneiform. This involved the use of pictograms—symbols that represent objects. The Sumerians scratched the pictograms into clay tablets. Over time, writing became more elaborate, and about 1800 B.C. people in the Middle East developed an alphabet. It consisted of a small number of symbols that represented sounds. These symbols could be combined to form thousands of words representing objects and ideas. Traders spread this alphabet around the Mediterranean, and it became the model for later Western writing systems.

During this time the materials on which people wrote changed too. Sometime between 3100 and 2500 B.C. the Egyptians developed papyrus, a type of paper made from reeds. In the 200s B.C. the Greeks began to use parchment, which was made from the skins of goats, sheep, and calves. Parchment was primarily used until the A.D. 1400s, when the printing press was developed and paper became more commonly used. The Chinese had developed the skill of papermaking as early as the A.D. 100s. However, more than 1,000 years passed before this skill reached Europe.

Development of the Media

The development of mass media was driven by a series of intellectual and technological innovations. These innovations include writing, printing, newspapers, radio, movies, television, computers, and the Internet.

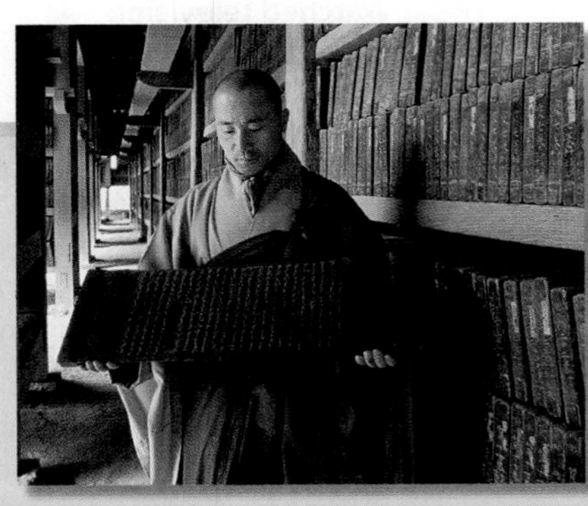

3000 B.C.

c. 3000 B.C. Sumerians develop a system of writing called cuneiform, which uses wedge-shaped symbols scratched into clay tablets.

1800s B.C. People in the Middle East develop an alphabet—a small number of symbols representing sounds that can be combined to form words.

A.D. 700s Koreans and Chinese develop wood-block printing. Later, Asian printers create wooden movable type.

The Printing Press Until the 1400s the principal mass medium in Europe was the handwritten book. Hand copying was a long, laborious, and costly process. As a result, the audience for this medium was mostly limited to society's wealthy and powerful elite.

During the 1450s Johannes Gutenberg, a German goldsmith, developed movable metal type. He also built a mechanical press that pushed and held paper against the blocks of type to create readable text. The combination of movable type and a reliable printing press revolutionized communication. The production of books became relatively inexpensive, which made the widespread distribution of information possible. Even so, for centuries the audience for media remained limited to rich, powerful people. During industrialization, however, this situation began to change.

The Industrial Age During the Industrial Revolution, factories became the chief setting for the production of goods. This shift encouraged people to move to cities, where most factories were located. With a rising standard of education and increasing requirements for factory work, more and more people learned to read and write. As these people earned higher wages, they had more disposable income. To ensure that some of this disposable income was spent on their products, many businesses started advertising. The forces of urbanization, rising literacy, and advertising contributed to the development of what many consider the first true mass medium—the newspaper.

For hundreds of years the transfer of information had depended mainly on the printed word. This changed with the Industrial Age and the development of electronic media, which used electric signals to transmit information. The telegraph and the telephone enabled people to communicate over long distances. Movies provided a new form of mass entertainment. In time the phonograph, radio, and television brought entertainment right into people's homes.

The Information Society The digital computer, which became widely available in the 1980s, completely transformed the way people store and access information. The information contained in thousands of books can now be stored on a handful of computer disks. Different kinds of software, the programs that instruct computers what to do, allow people to manipulate information in many ways. Furthermore, the Internet, introduced for commercial use in the 1990s, revolutionized the way people communicate and access information. With a few clicks of a mouse, people can send documents, pictures, sound recordings, and movies to locations around the world. Similarly, people can access information stored thousands of miles away.

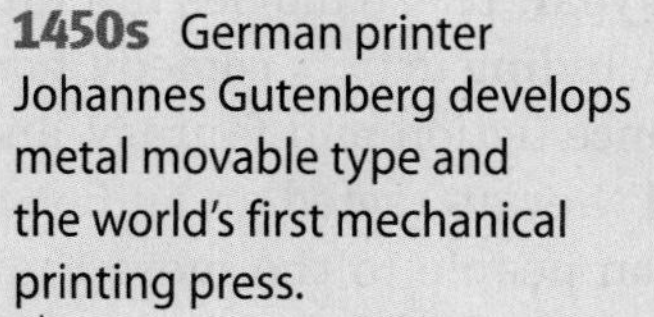

1450s German printer Johannes Gutenberg develops metal movable type and the world's first mechanical printing press.

1930s Radio and movies gain popularity.

1980s–2000s The development of the personal computer and the Internet leads to media convergence.

2000

1650s The first daily newspapers begin publication.

Late 1800s Newspapers become the primary method of communication.

1960s Television becomes the most popular medium.

Today in the United States, more and more workers are employed in information-related fields, such as computer programming, journalism, television-camera operation, and advertising copywriting. This trend is bound to continue because several of the occupations expected to experience the fastest growth in the coming years are computer related. The number of Internet-related jobs is also expected to increase rapidly. According to many media specialists, such trends show that the United States has become an **information society,** or a community in which the exchange of information is the main social and economic activity.

Reading Check **Identify Supporting Details** Which ideas and innovations led to the institutionalization of the mass media?

Mass Media in the United States

Americans are able to obtain information from a wide variety of media. These media can be grouped into four categories: print, audio, visual, and online. In recent years some media specialists have argued that separating the media in this fashion is artificial. They believe that various forces have caused the different media to converge.

Print Media The print media include newspapers, magazines, and books. The United States has about 1,300 daily newspapers—those published at least five times a week—which sell around 56 million copies a day. About 38 percent of American adults regularly read a daily newspaper. Magazines are published periodically—such as once a week or once a month. Over 7,000 magazines are published in the United States. Covering a wide variety of subjects, these magazines had a total circulation per issue of about 370 million in 2007. About 48 percent of Americans over the age of 16 read magazines regularly. The statistics on books in the United States are similarly impressive. Some 63,000 book publishers issue approximately 300,000 titles a year, and Americans spend about $14 billion annually on book purchases. Reading is a popular pastime—about 28 percent of Americans read more than 10 books a year.

As you can see, the print media have a substantial audience. However, that audience is declining. The number of daily newspapers, newspaper circulation, and newspaper readership have fallen steadily over the last few years. Those people who do read newspapers are spending less time on this activity than they did in the past. While magazine circulation is on the increase, people appear to be spending less time reading magazines. Falling readership has affected the book market, too. Some 16 percent of Americans admit that they do not read books at all.

Audio Media Sound recordings and radio are the two major categories of audio media. The sound-recording business is one of the country's major industries, with a value of about $15 billion dollars in 2014. Sound recordings come in physical formats (e.g., compact discs, vinyl records) and digital formats (e.g., MP3s). Physical and digital formats account for roughly equal shares of the market.

About 15,330 radio stations broadcast in the United States today. These stations broadcast a variety of formats—everything from news and talk to classic rock to religion. Radio broadcasts have a large audience. Some 99 percent of the homes in the United States have a radio, with an average of five radios per household. Americans over the age of 12 listen to about 2.5 hours a day of radio on average. Newer technologies, such as satellite radio, are gaining in popularity. In addition, listeners now have several choices of digital audio services, such as iTunes, Pandora, and Spotify.

Visual Media Movies, television, videocassettes, and DVDs make up the visual media. American movie studios release between 500 and 600 movies a year. These movies fall into various genres, including action, comedy, horror, romance, science fiction and fantasy, and westerns. In 2014 they attracted an audience of about 1.2 billion people to the more than 40,000 movie screens at 5,856 theaters across the country and generated box-office revenue of more than $10.36 billion.

Of all media, television reaches one of the largest audiences in the United States. Some 95 percent of American homes have television sets, with an average of 2.9 sets per home. About 84 percent of homes subscribe to paid television services, which provide nearly 200 channels for viewing. The average American household spends considerable time watching television—more than 34 hours a week. Americans are also spending more time than ever, over an hour a day, watching video on digital devices.

In the past the major broadcast networks dominated television in the United States. The networks offer a variety of programming, including comedies, dramas, quiz shows, "reality" shows, sports, children's programs, and news. Although some cable TV channels offer a mix of programming, many more focus on a particular genre, such as news, sports, cartoons, religion, music, or movies. Cable TV has grown in popularity, but the network-viewing audience has declined significantly.

About 91 percent of American households have DVD players, while 40 percent have Blu-ray disc players. Home video has greatly affected the movie industry. Revenues from the rental and sale of movies on video are more than two times the revenues from ticket sales at movie theaters. In 2014, DVD and Blu-ray sales totaled $6.93 billion, while spending on video-on-demand services, such as Netflix and Amazon Prime, totaled $7.53 billion.

Online Media The most recent media development is the Internet. It offers many services, including e-mail, online chat and discussion groups, social-networking sites, and online shopping. The billions of sites accessible through the Internet deal with practically every imaginable subject.

A recent study found that 74 percent of Americans have Internet access at home. The average adult now spends more than 20 hours online every week. More than one-fourth of people who use the Internet now regularly watch television and films online. Almost 70 percent of Americans shop online every month. Nearly half of Americans get their news online.

Convergence Some media specialists believe that the media are merging and are no longer separate entities. This **media convergence** is the result, in part, of the integration of the different media technologies. For example, the print media have adopted computer technology and the Internet. Newspapers are now laid out and typeset by computers. In addition, many daily newspapers have their own Web sites. Book publishers are also using computers for typesetting. Furthermore, e-books are

Types of U.S. Media

Print Media

Newspapers About 1,300 daily newspapers with a daily circulation of 56 million

Magazines About 7,000 magazines with total circulation per issue of 370 million

Books About 300,000 titles published per year

Audio Media

Radio 99 percent of American homes have a radio

CDs Account for 46 percent of sound-recording industry revenue

Music Downloads Valued at about $5.6 billion

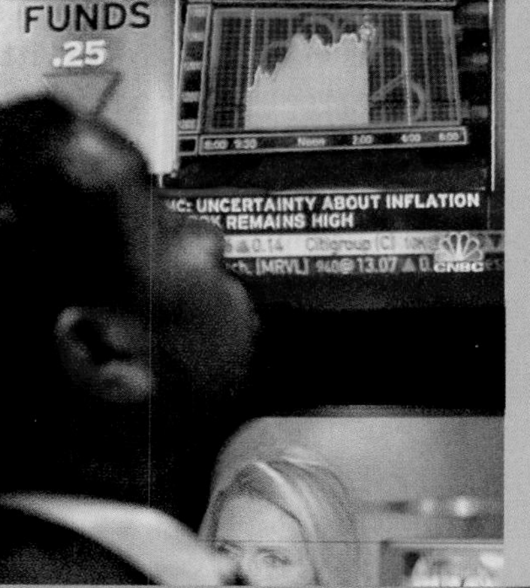

Visual Media

Movies About 5,900 theaters with some 40,000 screens

Television About 3 television sets per home; average family watches 34 hours per week

Online Media

Home Access 74 percent of Americans have Internet access in the home

Mobile Access About 53 percent of cell-phone users access the Internet via cell phone

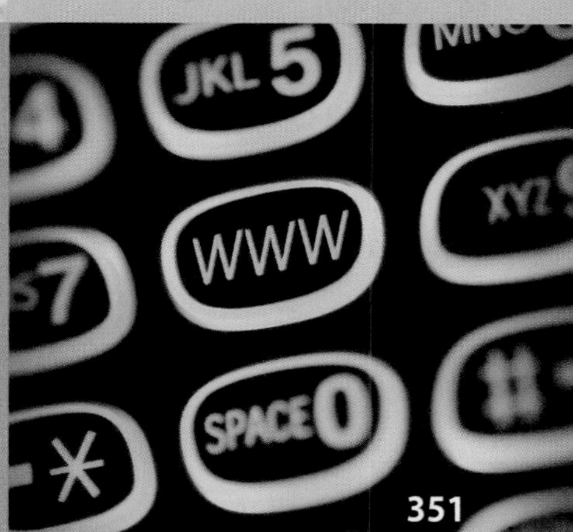

Using Media

"Why don't you get off the computer and watch some TV?"

Skills Focus INTERPRETING CARTOONS

What does this cartoon suggest about media consumption in the United States?

gaining in popularity. Radio stations use computer and online technology to make broadcasts available on the Internet, and most cable companies offer Internet access with television packages.

The merging of media companies has also contributed to this convergence. Movie companies have purchased book publishers, telephone companies have taken over cable television operations, and newspapers have bought Web search engines.

Some scholars think that this convergence may lead to the development of a single communications medium based on computer technology. However, others think that convergence will have the opposite result. The merging of computer technology with elements of existing media may create new media forms and broaden communications choices.

Media Consumption American media consumption is quite remarkable. On average, each American spends nearly 5,700 hours a year using the media! As of 2015, television was still the most popular medium, but the Internet had become a very close second.

Individual media usage varies and is strongly influenced by social factors such as age, education, and income. For example, young people are more likely to consume digital media. In 2013, Americans aged 18–34 spent an average of 35 hours a week consuming digital media, while Americans aged 70 or older averaged only 13 hours a week. However, younger people are less likely to read newspapers, magazines, and books than are older people. In addition, newspaper and book readership increases with education and income. People with higher incomes are also more likely to have access to cable television and the Internet.

Reading Check **Summarize** What types of mass media are available in the United States?

SECTION 3 Assessment

Reviewing Main Ideas and Vocabulary

1. **Explain** Why is the United States considered an information society?
2. **Describe** What is the process of media convergence?

Thinking Critically

3. **Draw Conclusions** Why do you think the newspaper is considered the first true mass medium?
4. **Make Judgments** What do you think will be the outcome of media convergence? Give reasons for your answer.
5. **Summarize** Using your notes and a graphic organizer like the one here, list the intellectual and technological innovations that led to the institutionalization of the mass media.

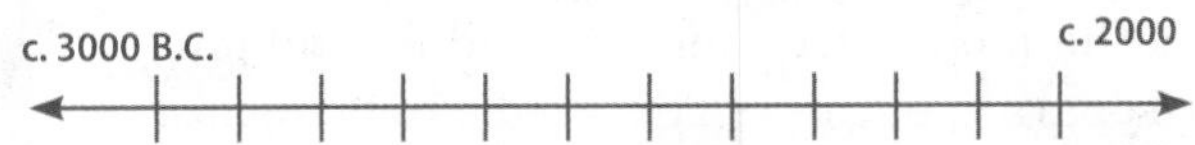

FOCUS ON WRITING

6. **Descriptive** Write a summary of your typical daily mass-media consumption. Include the categories of media you consume and the average amount of time you spend using each. Also, note if your media usage varies at different times of the day or week.

SECTION 4

Perspectives and Issues in Mass Media

Before You Read

Main Idea
The three sociological perspectives differ in how they view the purpose of mass media. Sociologists are concerned with the media's impact on social and civic life and on public opinion.

Reading Focus
1. How do the sociological perspectives of mass media differ?
2. What are some contemporary mass-media issues?

Vocabulary
knowledge-gap hypothesis
digital divide
social capital
spiral of silence
agenda setting
gatekeepers
opinion leaders

TAKING NOTES Use a graphic organizer like this one to take notes on sociological perspectives on and major issues in mass media.

Mass Media	
Perspectives	Issues

First on the Scene

SOCIOLOGY CLOSE UP ***Can anyone report the news?*** New communication technology is changing the way the news is reported and viewed. Ordinary people—everyone from high school students to retired army generals—have taken to the streets to provide their take on the news. Some use camera phones to capture events. They then post their photographs and videos to Web sites such as Flickr and YouTube. Other "citizen journalists," armed with laptop computers, post reports on events as they happen to weblogs, or online journals.

These photographs, videos, and weblogs can be viewed by anyone with Internet access. In addition, e-mails, text messages, and links on other Web sites can draw thousands of viewers in a matter of minutes. Total viewership of some of these postings often exceeds the audience that most national television newscasts can expect.

This "we" journalism, or moblogging (the first syllable is pronounced MOH, as in *mobile*), is in the early stages of development, and many people wonder if it will have a lasting effect on journalism. The major media companies certainly have taken notice. Television news programs often lead off reports on breaking events with photographs, videos, or eyewitness accounts provided by citizen journalists. Also, some media outlets have set up their own Web sites, both visual and written word, to report the news as it happens. ■

Sociological Perspectives on Mass Media

What purpose do mass media fulfill? Different sociological perspectives have contrasting views on this question. The functionalist perspective focuses on the ways in which mass media help to preserve social stability. The conflict perspective focuses on how mass media reinforce the existing social order. The interactionist perspective looks at the impact of mass media on social interaction.

Functionalist Perspective Functionalists believe that the mass media perform functions that support the stability and smooth operation of society. These functions include keeping track of what is happening in the world, interpreting information, transmitting cultural values, and entertaining people.

Who's on Television? Media critics have challenged producers and directors to be more aware of diversity when casting television programs. A recent study showed the racial and ethnic breakdown of broadcast television roles as follows:

81% White

10% Black

4% Asian

2% Latino

3% Mixed or Other Race

Skills Focus **INTERPRETING DATA** How might a conflict theorist use these statistics to argue that the media reinforce social inequality?

Source: UCLA, *2015 Hollywood Diversity Report*

To be productive members of society, people need to know what is going on around them. Through e-mail, text messages, and instant messages, family members and friends can let each other know what is happening in their lives. Newspapers, magazines, and news programs on television, radio, and the Internet keep people informed of local, national, and world events. In addition to providing information, the media also interpret it. Movies, television, and books—both fictional and factual—try to explain why events happen. Editorials and commentaries in the news media also discuss the importance and meaning of recent developments.

Mass media influence socialization. Some media, such as school textbooks, make a conscious effort to pass on society's basic values and beliefs. Other media transmit culture inadvertently. For example, the stated purpose of a television police drama may be to entertain. However, it may also remind viewers that the United States is a society of laws.

Entertainment is probably the most obvious function of mass media. The majority of TV channels and radio formats are designed to entertain rather than to inform. The same is true of movies. Most people go to the movies for entertainment, not for information.

Conflict Perspective Conflict sociologists believe that the purpose of social institutions is to maintain the present social order. Some conflict theorists believe that the role of mass media is to persuade people to accept the existing power structure. The media can accomplish this goal, these sociologists assert, because they are able to control the flow and interpretation of information. In other words, the media can decide what information is provided and how it is presented. Because the media are owned by members of the power elite, conflict sociologists argue, this information and its presentation represent the power elite's point of view.

Other conflict sociologists believe that mass media in the United States encourage the acceptance of the power structure by encouraging a culture of consumerism. According to this theory, if people are busy increasing their collection of material possessions, they have no time to think about society's inequalities.

Certain conflict sociologists suggest that the knowledge gap provides an example of how the media maintain social inequality. The **knowledge-gap hypothesis,** first advanced by Phillip Tichenor, George Donohue, and Clarice Olien, states that as new information enters society, wealthy and better-educated members acquire it at a faster rate than poor and less educated people. Therefore, a gap in knowledge widens between these two segments of society. This gap develops even if access to information is equal.

Studies show that a **digital divide**—the gap between those with access to new technologies and those without—exists and may be widening. Access to computers and online media is of particular concern. The groups that lack access include minorities, the children of single mothers, and people with lower incomes and less education. Steps are being taken to close this digital divide, most notably by providing schools with computers and Internet connections. However, such actions may not help to narrow the knowledge gap. Some studies indicate that the "information rich"—those who have better information skills and more resources—are likely to benefit more from greater access to the new technology than are the "information poor."

Some conflict theorists suggest that the misrepresentation and nonrepresentation of minorities in the media reinforce social inequality. Several studies of the print media have found that coverage of minorities is limited. One found that in day-to-day coverage, the mainstream media have few stories about minorities, except stories involving crime, sports, or entertainment. Some of these stories contain stereotypes and biased reporting.

Studies of the entertainment media have made similar findings. A review of prime-time television and movies in 2015 found that women, Hispanics, Asian Americans, low-income wage earners, senior citizens, and people with disabilities were all underrepresented. Also, where minorities are cast, they usually play minor roles. Some sociologists are concerned that the absence of minorities from the media may encourage minority children to be less ambitious and expect less from life. Others argue that stereotypical coverage of minorities may encourage white Americans to view minorities negatively. Attention

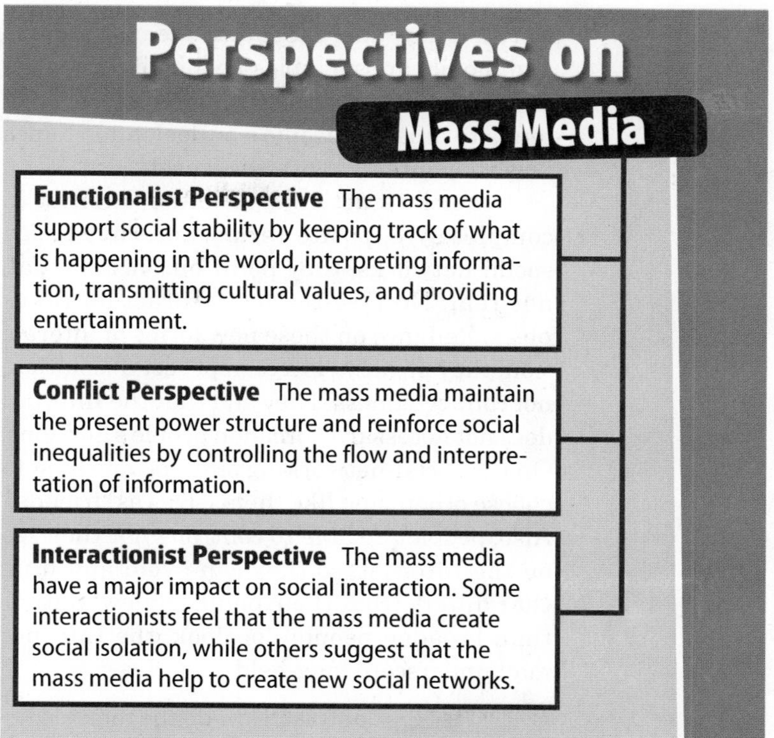

to this issue has begun to have an effect. Organizations such as the Screen Actors Guild (SAG) have pushed for an increase in the presence of minorities in positive television and movie roles.

Perspectives on
Mass Media
Functionalist Perspective The mass media support social stability by keeping track of what is happening in the world, interpreting information, transmitting cultural values, and providing entertainment.
Conflict Perspective The mass media maintain the present power structure and reinforce social inequalities by controlling the flow and interpretation of information.
Interactionist Perspective The mass media have a major impact on social interaction. Some interactionists feel that the mass media create social isolation, while others suggest that the mass media help to create new social networks.

Interactionist Perspective Interactionist sociologists are interested in how mass media shape everyday social interaction. As you read earlier, most Americans spend several hours a day using media. So, considerable opportunity exists for this shaping to take place.

Some interactionists point out that people often plan social events around the media. For example, families and groups of friends may gather to watch a major television program such as the Super Bowl, coverage of an election, or the season-ending episode of a drama or situation comedy. Watching television, then, becomes almost a primary-group activity. Other interactionists, however, characterize watching television as essentially a solitary activity that encourages social isolation.

The Internet has also produced conflicting views among interactionists. Some see the Internet, with its chat rooms and social networking Web sites such as Facebook and Twitter, as an avenue of new, creative, and exciting forms of social interaction.

Further, they add, the multitude of Web sites and mobile apps enables people to find information about practically any subject. This tends to broaden people's outlook and shapes how they interact with the world.

Other interactionists see the Internet in completely opposite terms. Internet-based social networks, they point out, are virtual, not real. No face-to-face interaction takes place. Reliance on these new forms of interaction, they suggest, is a sign of social isolation, not connectedness. They add that the Internet does not necessarily broaden people's horizons. On the social-networking sites, people tend to choose others just like themselves as "friends." Also, people are able to control what they see on the Internet, so they can avoid anything that differs from their point of view. Rather than broaden people's outlook, the Internet may underscore long-held prejudices.

Reading Check **Contrast** How do the three perspectives differ in how they view mass media?

Contemporary Mass-Media Issues

One of the major topics covered by mass media is the media themselves. Stories abound on the relationships between the media and a host of social issues—everything from teen suicide to the breakup of the family. Media critics have focused on the effect that the media have on children, the way the media affect civic life, and the power that the media wield.

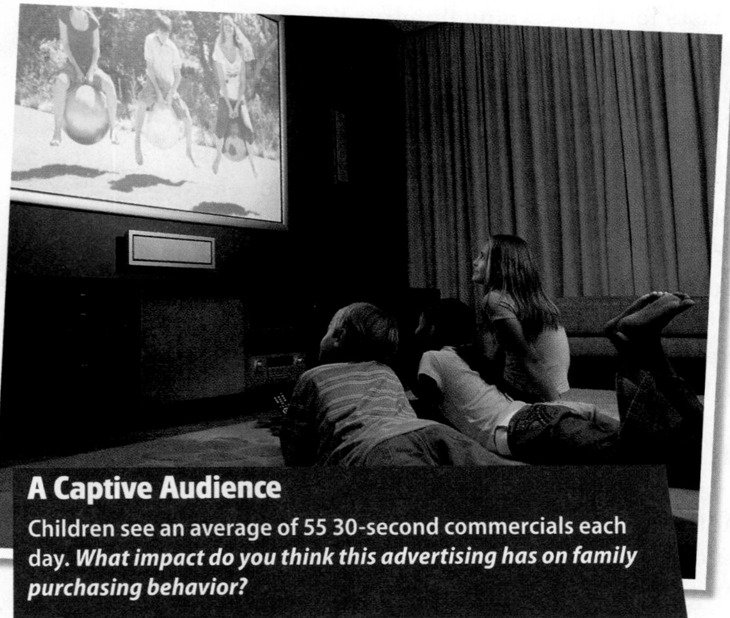

A Captive Audience

Children see an average of 55 30-second commercials each day. ***What impact do you think this advertising has on family purchasing behavior?***

Mass Media and Children Most children spend many hours each week watching television. It is the primary after-school activity for most students. Social scientists and the general public have a strong interest in how television affects children. One area of concern is the connection between television violence and aggressive behavior among young people. Dozens of studies have been conducted on this subject over the years. The findings of these studies include the following:

- Television depicts a great deal of violence.
- Television violence encourages viewers to act in aggressive ways and to see aggression as a valid way to solve problems.
- Television violence encourages viewers to be less sensitive to the suffering of others.
- Television violence appears to make viewers fearful of the world around them and less trustful of others.

During the 1990s the U.S. government and the American public began to pressure the television industry to do something about violent programming. In response, television networks established a rating system in 1997. The ratings provide parents with information about the content and age appropriateness of programs. In addition, the Telecommunications Act, enacted by Congress in 1996, requires all new televisions to have a V-chip. This V-chip allows the viewer to block reception of unwanted programming.

Another area of concern is the relationship between television and performance at school. A study of fourth-, eighth-, and eleventh-graders found a link between the amount of time spent watching television and test scores. Students who watched five or more hours per day of television scored lower than students who watched very little. Exactly what this link means is unclear. It may indicate that heavy television watching contributes to poor performance at school, or it may simply show that students who perform poorly in school watch a lot of television.

Regardless of the medium children use—magazines, radio, television, or the Internet—they are bombarded by ads. The average child sees more than 20,000 30-second commercials each year on television alone.

Businesses spend about $17 billion on advertising directly targeted at children. This figure is of great concern to many people who believe that children are a vulnerable audience. In other words, children do not have the information or skills to make objective decisions about advertisements, particularly those children who watch a lot of television, because they accept advertising claims more readily. In addition, many younger children cannot distinguish between advertisements and regular programming. Advertisers have been requested to take more care when developing commercials targeted at children. For example, the Telecommunications Act of 1996 encouraged advertisers to use a rating system similar to that used by the television networks.

Mass Media and Civic and Social Life In his book *Bowling Alone* political scientist Robert Putnam argues that since the 1960s Americans have become more and more disconnected from civic and social life. To illustrate this disengagement, Putnam offers an array of statistics. Voting and participation in political activities have fallen over the years. Membership in civic organizations such as the PTA has declined. So, too, has church attendance. In addition, people are entertaining family and friends less often than in the past. Putnam argues that this disengagement has resulted in a decline in the country's social capital. In essence, **social capital** refers to everything that makes up a community. It includes the social networks and the reciprocal norms associated with these networks that encourage people to do things for each other. Social capital includes everything from the civic, social, and religious organizations to which people belong to the friendship networks people develop through their neighborhoods, schools, and sports teams.

Putnam attributes a large part of the decline in social capital—perhaps as much as 25 percent—to television. He points out that television is everywhere. Practically every household in the country has a television set, and most have at least two. Americans spend a lot of time in front of these sets, perhaps as much as 50 percent of their free time. Watching television is the favorite nighttime activity of the vast majority of adult Americans, often at the expense of social activities outside the home. As a consequence, television privatizes people's leisure time. Putnam suggests that television watchers tend to be loners, not joiners. The more television people watch, the less likely they are to participate in civic and social activities.

Several studies suggest that the Internet may also encourage disengagement from civic and social life. A two-year study of 169 Internet users found that the more time people spent online, the less face-to-face interaction they had with family members and friends. Another survey of more than 4,000 Internet users produced similar results.

Bowling Alone

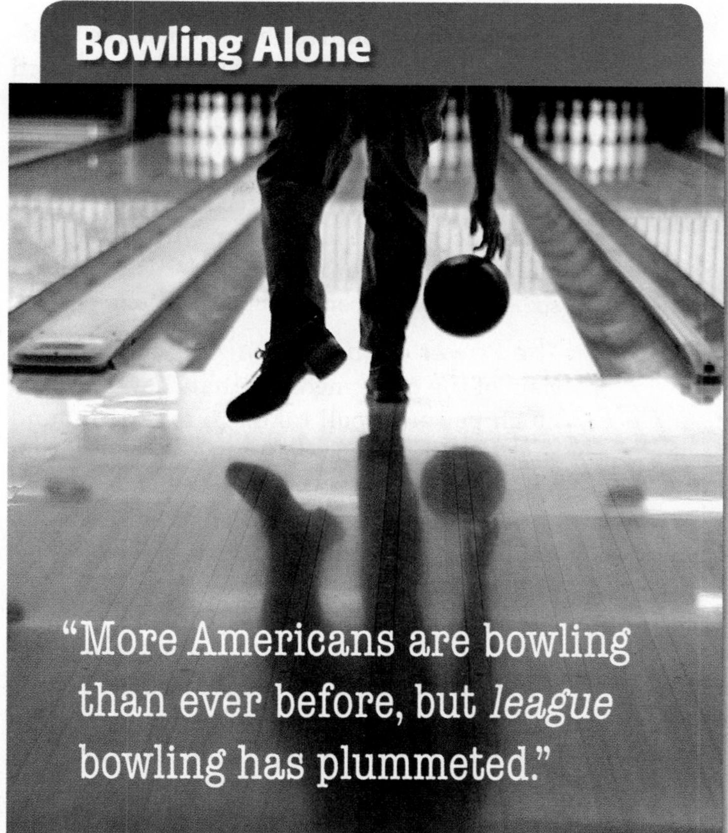

"More Americans are bowling than ever before, but *league* bowling has plummeted."

Robert Putnam uses these words to frame his argument that Americans are increasingly disengaged from social life. Bowling alone, he suggests, is a kind of informal social connectedness that lacks organization and purpose. However, the bowling league, with its rules, regulations, and diverse membership, represents a form of social capital—in other words, a community. ***Do you think the decline of bowling leagues is a good measure of social disengagement? Why or why not?***

Some recent studies, however, have challenged these findings. A 2008 report noted that 45 percent of users said that the Internet was an important way for them to maintain social relationships. The report also found that Internet users spend more time than nonusers in face-to-face interaction with family and friends. The true impact of the Internet on social life, then, remains in question.

The Power of the Media One major criticism of the news media is that they wield too much power. A poll taken in to "2016 found that 66 percent of the American population believes that the news media have too much power and influence in politics. Observers of the media who agree often cite two examples of news-media power—the spiral of silence and agenda setting.

Sociologist Elisabeth Noelle-Neumann suggests that the media are incredibly powerful sources of information that can shape public opinion. She points out that the different forms of news media tend to cover the same stories, often bombarding the public with the same information and the same opinions on these stories. As more and more people accept these opinions, people who disagree are less likely to voice their views. Noelle-Neumann believes that this **spiral of silence** gives the media even more power to influence the way people think.

Other sociologists suggest that the news media do not tell the public what to think but what to think about. They argue that the media set the boundaries of public debate by deciding which issues will receive coverage and which will not, a process known as **agenda setting.** Agenda setting is undertaken by **gatekeepers**—media executives, editors, or reporters who can open or close the "gate" on a particular news story.

However, many people believe that the power of the media is greatly overstated. Some people point out that there are simply too many news outlets for the media to effectively control the flow of information. The public will always be able to find alternative news sources. Others suggest that messages from the media do not directly influence behavior or opinions. Rather, this influence takes place through a multistep flow of communication. The messages are first reviewed and evaluated by **opinion leaders**—respected individuals in the community—who then pass on the information to friends and acquaintances. Still other media watchers note the growth of citizen journalists—people with no ties to the media who share their views of the news, usually on the Internet. Nonetheless, mass media, whatever their real power is, play a large role in American society.

Reading Check **Summarize** What issues have been of concern to media critics in recent years?

SECTION 4 Assessment

Reviewing Main Ideas and Vocabulary

1. **Define** What is the knowledge-gap hypothesis?
2. **Identify** According to Robert Putnam, what are the major components of social capital?
3. **Explain** What role do gatekeepers play in the process of agenda setting?

Thinking Critically

4. **Support a Position** Which perspective is the most useful in analyzing the social impact of mass media? Why?
5. **Make Judgments** What impact do you think the rise of citizen journalists will have on the way that the media report the news? Give reasons for your answer.
6. **Summarize** Using your notes and a graphic organizer like the one here, select one of the mass-media issues and describe how each sociological perspective might view it.

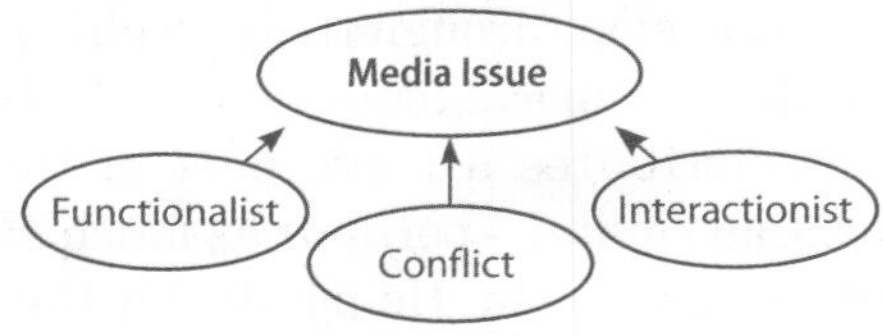

FOCUS ON WRITING

7. **Expository** Write two paragraphs explaining how you think new communication technologies have changed individual and societal behavior. In writing your paragraphs, consider how societal norms and values have changed because of these new technologies.

Video Games and Violence

Since the late 1990s, there has been a spate of school shootings in the United States. The most violent one occurred at Virginia Tech in Blacksburg, Virginia, in 2007. Newspaper reporters discovered that many of the shooters in these incidents had something in common. They all were fanatic players of a violent video game.

Newer video games offer a strong story line, realistic visuals, and believable performances by voice-over actors.

The games played were mostly what are known as first-person shooter games. In such games, players use an assortment of weapons to fight off enemies as they make their way through various levels to their goal. Newspapers quickly linked the violence of these games to the actions of the shooters. With lurid headlines like "Bloodlust Video Games Put Kids in the Crosshairs," they laid the blame for school shootings on the video-game industry.

Over the next few years the premise that violent video games caused young people to carry out violent acts became widely accepted. Sociologist Karen Sternheimer surmised that since video games had become more popular among young people, acts of violence should have increased. However, she discovered that homicide rates among young people had fallen markedly and that school was still one of the safest places for children to be. She wondered why the charge that video games cause violence persisted.

Dozens of studies on the impact of violent media on behavior showed no solid link between on-screen violence and aggression. Studies that focused on video games alone produced contradictory results. One stated that playing video games would "increase aggressive behavior." Another said that it was not possible to determine the impact of these games on aggression.

Sternheimer suggested that the video-game studies had a major weakness—they took violence out of its social context. None of the studies considered the impact of such factors as poverty, neighborhood stability, or family relationships on violent youths. She also noted that the studies might benefit by looking at how the media as a whole influence young people's behavior. She pointed to one study that found that young boys boasted about the horror movies they had seen as a way to underscore their masculinity—they were too tough to be scared. This and similar studies, she proposed, might explain why violent video games attract so many young males.

Linking violent video games to violent behavior, Sternheimer concluded, is too simple. While the impact of the media needs to studied, "if we want to know why young people . . . become homicidal, we need to look beyond the games they play."

The video-game industry, with about $91.5 billion in annual revenues, is an important part of the visual-media market.

Thinking Critically

1. **Identify** What weaknesses did Karen Sternheimer find in the studies of the impact of video games?
2. **Discuss** Do you think there is any connection between violent video games and aggressive behavior? Why or why not?

Lab
Applying What You've Learned

Promoting a Class on Sport and Mass Media

Reading and Activity Workbook

Use the workbook to complete this lab.

What is the best way to encourage students to learn more about social institutions such as sport and mass media?

1. Introduction

In this lab you will create a poster designed to promote a class for high school students on sport and mass media in American society. You will work in two different groups. In the first group you will become experts about one particular aspect of sport and mass media. In the second group you will share your expertise with other group members and construct a poster that promotes a high school class about sport and mass media.

- Following your teacher's instructions, organize the class into five equal-sized groups.
- Your teacher will assign each of these "development" groups one of the following topics: Defining Sport, Issues in American Sport, Influence of Mass Media, Issues in Mass Media, Future of Sport and Mass Media.
- Work with students in your group to become experts on your assigned topic. Write down important terms, concepts, and ideas. All group members should have the same information at the conclusion of this portion of the activity. It is very important that you share information and ideas and write down what you know and learn. You will take this information to a different group, and your classmates in that new group will expect you to be an expert on your topic.
- You may also conduct research online and at the school and public libraries to gather more information about your assigned topic.

2. Sharing Your Expertise

Now that you are an expert, you will be placed in a new group in which every member has a different area of expertise. New groups can easily be formed if each member in a development group is assigned a number. (For example, if there are six students in the development group, each member is assigned a number from 1 to 6.) The "expert" groups will consist of all students with the same number—all 1s form one group, all 2s form another, and so on. As a result, there will be one expert on each topic in the expert group. In your new group, each expert will teach other group members about his or her topic. In teaching other group members, be sure to include the following information:

- Name of your topic
- Important terms and concepts regarding your topic
- How your topic is significant (in what ways it matters for society)
- Specific examples of issues or events from your topic

3. Making the Poster

Once all group members have shared their information, begin to make your poster. The purpose of your poster is to educate high school students about what they should expect in a class on sport and mass media. Your poster must be divided into five sections—one for each topic—and have a title. Each section must include the following:

- Three to five sentences or bulleted points with key information/main ideas
- At least two terms related to the topic (these may be embedded in the sentences)
- An example highlighting how the topic is significant (for example, if your topic is Issues in American Sport, you may provide a specific example of one issue)
- A reason why students should take an interest in this class
- A graphic or illustration that enhances understanding about the topic

4. Exchanging Posters

Once all groups have finished, exchange posters with another group. Review the new poster and make note of information that you did not include in your poster. Also, pay close attention to the examples and illustrations provided by the other group.

5. Discussion

What did you learn from this lab? Hold a group discussion that focuses on the following questions:

- Overall, how successful was the class at creating posters that will encourage students to take a class about sport and the mass media?
- Which topics were easiest to understand and explain?
- Which topics were most difficult to understand and explain?
- What examples were most helpful? Why?
- What illustrations were most helpful? Why?
- How might high school students use this knowledge as they make decisions regarding their education?
- What are the greatest challenges society faces regarding sport? What are the greatest challenges that society faces regarding mass media?
- As technology plays an increasing role in both sport and mass media, how do you think each of these institutions may change during your lifetime?
- Does technology make sport more or less enjoyable? Explain.

PARTICIPATION RATE BY SPORT, 2014

Sport	2014	Percent Change Since 2012
Individual Sports	35.4%	–1.3%
Racquet Sports	13.5%	0.7%
Team Sports	22.4%	0.8%
Outdoor Sports	48.4%	–1%
Water Sports	13.9%	1.4%
Fitness Sports	61%	–0.1%

Source: Physical Activity Council

Participation in sports is a subject covered in most sports courses. How might you incorporate this information in your poster?

CHAPTER 14 Review

Comprehension and Critical Thinking

SECTION 1 *(pp. 338–341)*

1. a. **Define** What three conditions must be present for an activity to be considered a sport?
   b. **Explain** How are rationalization and bureaucratization in sport related?
   c. **Elaborate** How is the development of sport as a social institution an outgrowth of industrial society?

SECTION 2 *(pp. 342–346)*

2. a. **Describe** What functions does sport serve?
   b. **Summarize** What evidence have sociologists found to support the contention that there is race and gender discrimination in sport?
   c. **Develop** How might the three sociological perspectives view the coach–young player relationship?

SECTION 3 *(pp. 347–352)*

3. a. **Identify** What forces combined to encourage the development of the urban newspaper?
   b. **Explain** How do age, education, and income affect media consumption?
   c. **Elaborate** How did cultural and technological advances contribute to the development of the mass media as a social institution?

SECTION 4 *(pp. 353–358)*

4. a. **Recall** According to conflict theorists, how does the knowledge gap help maintain social inequality?
   b. **Explain** What steps do you think should be taken to ensure that advertising aimed at children is ethical and age appropriate?
   c. **Support a Position** Do you think the media wield too much power? Explain your answer.

INTERNET ACTIVITY

5. One form of media convergence involves newspapers offering some of their services via the Internet. Locate a local or regional newspaper's Web site and note the content and services it offers. In a brief illustrated report, compare and contrast the content and services offered in print and on the Web.

Reviewing Vocabulary

Match the terms below with their correct definitions.

6. agenda setting
7. digital divide
8. eligibility
9. gatekeeper
10. information society
11. media convergence
12. secularization
13. sport
14. stacking
15. Title IX

A. competitive games that are won or lost on the basis of physical skills and are played according to specific rules
B. process of moving from the realm of the sacred to that of the profane
C. quality of being qualified or worthy of being chosen
D. practice of assigning people to athletic positions based on their race or ethnicity
E. law that bars discrimination on the basis of gender in any program at educational institutions receiving federal funds
F. community in which the exchange of information is the main social and economic activity
G. merging of the mass media
H. gap between those with access to new technologies and those without
I. deciding which issues will receive media coverage and which will not
J. person who controls the flow of information on a news story

Sociology in Your Life

16. Monitor several newspapers, current-affairs magazines, or television news shows for a week or two to see how many news items feature issues in sport. Categorize the news items according to subject. One category might be major professional sports—baseball, basketball, football, hockey, and so on. Another category might be men's sport, women's sport, and youth sport. Another might be deviance-related issues, such as discrimination, drug abuse, and violence. Also, note the length (number of words or time) of the items. Use your findings to write a brief report on the types of sports stories carried most often in the media.

SKILLS ACTIVITY: INTERPRETING GRAPHS

Study the pie graph on media consumption below. Then use the information to help you answer the questions that follow.

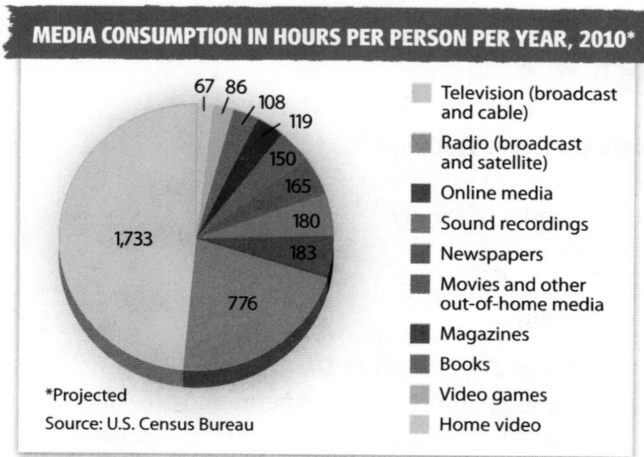

17. Identify About how much time per year does an individual spend using print media?

18. Compare About how much more time is spent on watching television than on listening to the radio and sound recordings?

19. Predict What do you expect this pie graph to look like 10 years from now? Give reasons for your answer.

WRITING FOR SOCIOLOGY

Use your knowledge of the mass media to answer the question below. Do not simply list facts. Present a clear argument based on your critical analysis of the question, using appropriate sociological terminology.

20. Write three paragraphs on what you think will be the impact of citizen journalism on how the news is reported over the next few years. In writing your paragraphs, consider the following issues:

- The methods of gathering and reporting news used by citizen journalists
- Traditional journalistic practices, such as the sourcing of stories
- Balance in reporting controversial stories

Connecting Online

Go online for review and enrichment activities related to this chapter.

KEY TOPICS VIDEOS
View compelling clips on issues in the field.

KEEP IT CURRENT
Link to the Current Events site for regularly updated stories on sociology as well as other social studies topics.

QUICK LAB
Reinforce a key concept with a short lab activity.

CULTURAL DIVERSITY AND SOCIOLOGY

GLOBAL CONNECTIONS

Family Issues Around the World

The family is one topic in sociology that everyone can relate to. While studying families around the world, sociologists learn about the issues families face, such as marriage, divorce, and family size. These issues and the dynamics of family life vary in different regions of the world.

FAMILY SIZE

What's a normal family size?

Family size varies around the world. The average birthrate for the world is 2.36 children per woman. In the United States, the average is 1.9 children. In Europe it is lower, with some countries averaging less than 1.4 children.

Fears about population growth and scarce resources have led some countries to limit family size. In 1979 the Chinese government began limiting most Chinese families to one child. The number of children born per woman has decreased from 2.9 in 1979 to 1.7 today. In 2016, China began allowing couples to have two children. In Rwanda, where the average couple has four children and the population has nearly quadrupled in the past 50 years, government officials are considering limiting each family to three children.

DIVORCE

How common is divorce?

Although most countries permit divorce only under certain circumstances, divorce rates climbed during the 1900s. The United States has one of the highest divorce rates—the number of divorces per 1,000 population—at 3.2. In comparison, the divorce rate in Italy was 0.9 in 2010. Divorce was prohibited in Italy until the 1970s. Also, Italian divorce laws require couples to be separated for at least six months before they can begin divorce proceedings. These factors have helped to keep Italy's divorce rate low. In the Philippines, divorce is still not allowed under most circumstances.

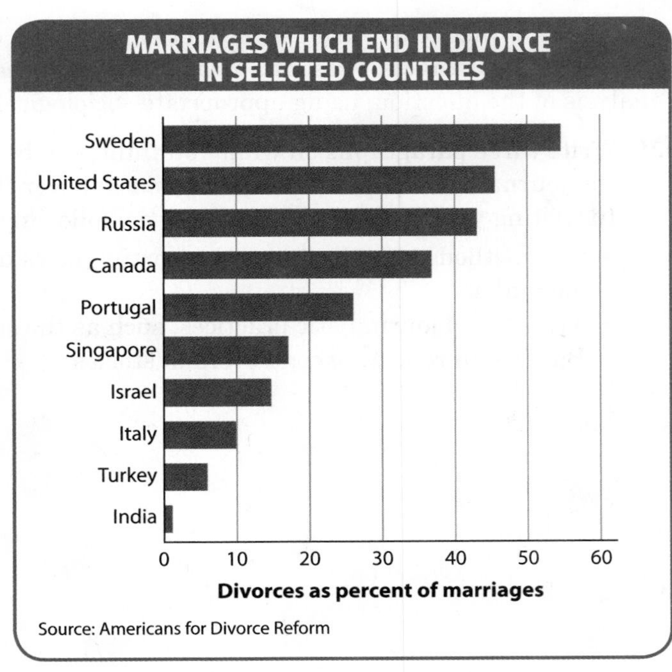

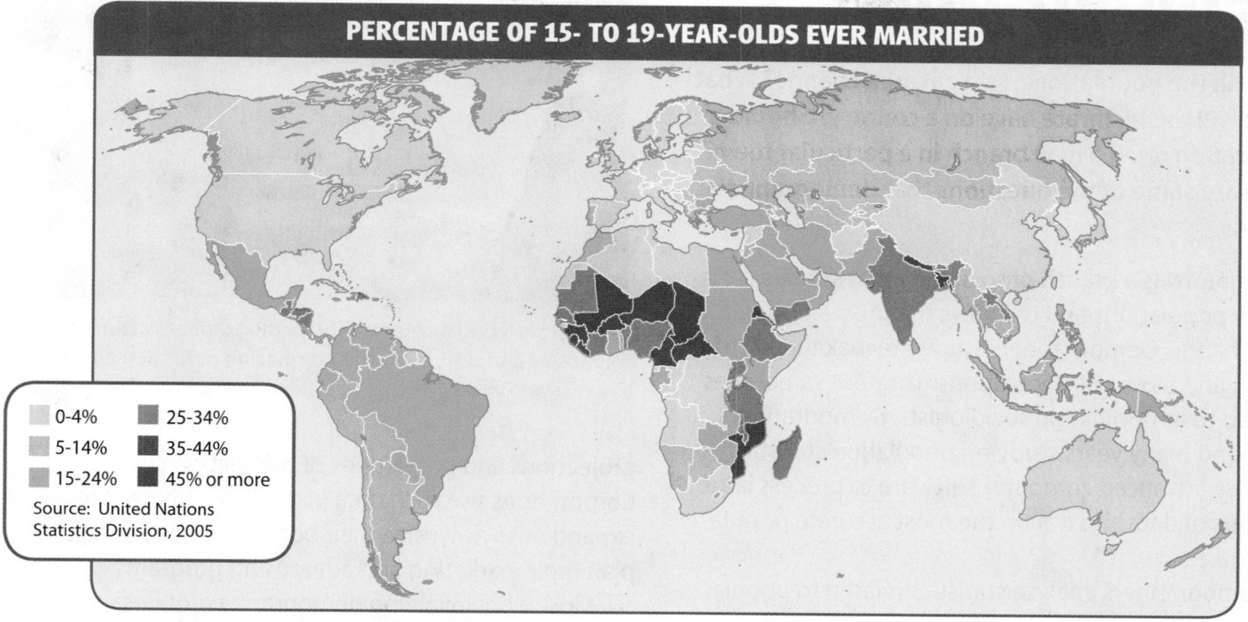

MARRIAGE

What's a normal age to get married?

In many societies, marriage marks a transition to adulthood. As you can see from the map above, the age at which young people first get married varies widely around the world. Countries where the average age at first marriage is later tend to be more urbanized and educated.

Americans have been waiting longer to get married. The median age in the United States at first marriage is 27 for women and 28 for men. As a result, only a small percentage of American teenagers are married.

In recent years, the proportion of teenage women marrying has been declining around the world. However, in some countries over half of girls aged 15 to 19 are married. For example, in Nepal 52 percent of girls aged 15 to 19 are married by age 18; in Niger 77 percent are.

Typically, girls marry young more often than boys because the goal of many early marriages is to begin having children. In some developing nations, especially in rural areas, the family is seen as a source of income, stability, and social status. Children are necessary to maintain the household and preserve its status.

THINKING LIKE A SOCIOLOGIST

What other issues do families around the world face today?

In addition to these issues, families around the world face many other challenges. Using library resources or the Internet, research issues related to families around the world. One good source you can use is the United Nations Programme on the Family Web site. The site contains publications on major trends affecting families around the world under the heading "Resources." Choose at least two of the following issues to research:

1. Caring for elderly family members
2. Role of parents in the family
3. Role of teenagers in the family
4. Divorce rates
5. Age at first marriage
6. Family structure and size

After you have completed your research, write a report on the issues you selected. In your report, address the issues you think families will continue to face in the future.

CAREERS IN SOCIOLOGY

Demographer

How will the population of a local area change? What effect will the birthrate have on a country? Should a corporation open a new branch in a particular town? These are some of the questions that demographers address.

When studying a community, demographers often use maps as a tool to show the population data they gather.

Demography is a branch of sociology that studies human populations and the ways that human populations change. Demographers study the makeup, distribution, and trends of populations. They are sometimes referred to as population sociologists. Demographers can spend many years studying population statistics. They use advanced computer software to process large amounts of data and obtain the most accurate population figures.

Demographers analyze statistics related to population size and population change, such as births, deaths, and marriages. They analyze the data to observe and monitor current trends, as well as to predict future trends. Future population trends are used by government agencies, service agencies, and private businesses for their planning.

Many demographers work for government agencies. The U.S. Census Bureau, for example, employs demographers to analyze census data. Other agencies use demographic information for such issues as planning future immigration policies or analyzing the impact of population growth on the environment.

Some demographers work for corporations by collecting and analyzing data regarding population projections and predictions of population changes. Corporations use such data in deciding whether to expand or to downsize their businesses, and to help plan their marketing and advertising programs.

Most work involving demography requires a master's degree, which generally involves two years of graduate study. Most demographers have a bachelor's degree in sociology or urban planning and have taken courses in statistics, psychology, and economics. Demographers with doctoral degrees often become college professors and teach demography. In addition, some demographers with advanced degrees work as demographic consultants.

Demographers in entry-level positions are often involved in field work, conducting interviews or testing questionnaires. Most demographers work standard hours in offices, where they use computers to analyze the statistics they gather.

Applying ASA Style

Many demographers publish articles in professional journals. The articles often include tables and illustrations, such as graphs, charts, and drawings. In keeping with the guidelines from the **American Sociological Association (ASA)**, these articles follow a similar style for tables and illustrations. The illustrations you include in the papers you write for your sociology class should follow these guidelines, too.

The ASA suggests including tables and illustrations in articles only if they help the reader to better understand the information presented in the article. You should choose the type of table or illustration—bar graph, line graph, circle graph—that best presents your data. Tables and illustrations should contain only essential facts and should be clearly labeled for easy reading and understanding.

Through Think Central you can access the ASA Quick Style Guide for more information. Review the ASA guidelines and then make a list of illustrations you might use to effectively present certain data. An example is provided for you.

Data	Effective Illustration
average annual rainfall in selected countries	bar graph

UNIT 5 The Changing Social World

CHAPTER 15
Population and Urbanization

CHAPTER 16
Collective Behavior and Social Change

CASE STUDY

MEGA CITIES

Travelers flying into São Paulo, Brazil, are immediately struck by the city's endless stretch of skyscrapers that reach as far as the eye can see. Visitors may wonder why there are so many buildings and how so many people can live there. Researchers study enormous cities like São Paulo to answer these questions, among others.

São Paulo is among the 35 cities in the world that have been deemed megacities. A megacity is an urban area with a population of more than 10 million. In 2015 the total population of the world's 35 megacities reached approximately 400 million.

According to the United Nations, a historic milestone was achieved in 2007—more of the world's people now live in cities than in rural areas. By 2050, more than 75 percent of the world's people will live in cities. The world's rural population, in contrast, is expected to decrease by some 28 million, with most of this urban growth occurring in developing countries.

The Megacity Challenges Study In 2007, researchers at GlobeScan published a report on the challenges several megacities around the world face. The study focused on megacities that serve as critical economic centers, such as São Paulo. Because these megacities are major economic centers, people flock to them in search of work. Providing jobs, services, and a workable infrastructure are crucial to a good quality of life in a megacity. With such large populations, megacities face many challenges, including overcrowded public transportation and traffic congestion, increasing electrical consumption, growing demand for health care services, and crime.

Transportation According to the GlobeScan report, maintaining transportation links to, from, and within the city is the biggest challenge megacities face. In order to stay connected to the global economy, cities need to keep their infrastructure of roads, ports, and airports in working order. In a survey of city leaders, the GlobeScan researchers found that leaders are concerned not only about how they will provide transportation to their growing population but also about what the environmental impact of the old public transportation systems will be. As a consequence, cities are looking for greener transportation alternatives. However, new public transportation systems are extremely expensive, and many cities struggle with financing the round-the-clock maintenance on their old transportation systems.

Electricity Sources of energy are crucial to keeping a megacity thriving. Yet in many regions of the world, the demand

With a population of about 21 million, São Paulo is one of the largest megacities in the world.

WORLD'S LARGEST CITIES

1	**Tokyo, Japan**	37,833,000
2	**Delhi, India**	24,953,000
3	**Shanghai, China**	22,991,000
4	**Mexico City, Mexico**	20,843,000
5	**São Paulo, Brazil**	20,831,000

Source: *The Telegraph,* "The World's Biggest Cities," 2016

for electricity is greater than the supply. Researchers at GlobeScan found that city leaders would prefer to use renewable energy sources such as wind energy. However, fossil fuels such as natural gas are much cheaper.

Health Care How the world's megacities will provide health care to their growing populations is also a major concern to city leaders. They wonder how they will afford to take care of their people. For example, although Mumbai is India's richest municipality, it can care for only 20 percent of its population. On the other hand, even with the world's largest concentrations of hospitals, New York struggles with the high cost of health care and an increasing elderly population with diabetes and heart disease.

Crime According to the megacity leaders surveyed, organized crime and terrorist threats are top on the list of challenges their cities face. To fight crime, many cities have installed surveillance cameras on street corners. Researchers found, however, that community involvement reduced crime more effectively than cameras did. For example, the Chicago metropolitan area cut its crime rate 58 percent within a ten-year period by holding monthly community meetings with the law enforcement officers assigned to their neighborhoods.

What do you think?

1. What challenges do megacities face?
2. Which challenge do you think megacities should spend more money on?

CHAPTER 15 POPULATION AND URBANIZATION

Chapter at a Glance

SECTION 1: Population Change

- Three factors affect the growth or decline of a region's population: the birthrate, the death rate, and the rate of migration.
- In the late 1700s, Thomas Malthus predicted that populations around the world would continue to grow rapidly. His theory also stated that a rapidly growing population would outpace food production, which would cause famine.
- Because the demographic transition theory considers a society's level of technological development, most demographers favor that theory to the Malthusian theory.
- Many countries around the world have adopted strategies aimed at controlling their populations, such as family planning and economic improvements.

SECTION 2: Urban Life

- Some sociologists study ways that the movement of populations affects the social world, especially the movement called urbanization. This movement involves the concentration of the population in cities.
- Cities first arose about 6,000 years ago on the fertile banks of major rivers in North Africa and Asia. Many of these early cities were small by modern standards and contained a few thousand people. Most preindustrial cities were very crowded and lacked any kind of sanitation system. As a result, death rates in cities were higher than those in rural areas.
- The industrial city was much larger than the preindustrial city, and commerce was the focal point of urban life. For the first time in history, people worked outside of the home in offices and factories. As industrial cities grew larger, crime, overcrowding, and pollution increased.

SECTION 3: Urban Ecology

- Some sociologists developed urban ecology as an approach to studying cities. This approach examines the relationship between people and the urban environment.
- In addition to studying the structure of cities, sociologists are interested in the nature of life in cities. Several theories try to explain city life—urban anomie, compositional, and subcultural.

SECTION 1

Population Change

Before You Read

Main Idea
The world's population is constantly changing. Demographers study these changes and apply theories to explain them.

Reading Focus
1. How do demographers study world population change?
2. What theories attempt to explain population change?
3. Why do some countries want to control population growth?

Vocabulary
population
demography
birthrate
fertility
fecundity
death rate
life expectancy
migration
growth rate
Malthusian theory
demographic transition theory
family planning

TAKING NOTES Use a graphic organizer like this one to take notes about world population.

World Population	
Population Change	Controlling Growth

A Baby-less Society?

SOCIOLOGY CLOSE UP ***Why are the populations of some countries falling?*** When parents pushing baby strollers are no longer seen on the streets of a country's major cities or hospital maternity wards fall silent, it's a sign that a country is suffering from negative population growth. Countries with a negative, or zero, population growth have more deaths than births or an even number of births.

At 1.6 children per couple, Europe has some of the lowest birthrates in the world. By 2050, demographers predict 30 million Europeans of working age will have vanished. This is shocking news to many Europeans. In a New York Times interview in 2008, Letizia Mencarini, a professor of demography at the University of Turin, Italy explained, "If you would read the documents of demographers 20 years ago, you would see that nobody foresaw that the fertility rate would go so low. In the 1960s, the overall fertility rate in Italy was around two children per couple. Now it is about 1.3, and for some towns in Italy it is less than 1."

To prevent negative population growth, several European nations are giving money to parents who have one or more children. Other countries are providing tax breaks to parents, with the hope that parents pushing strollers will one day fill their city streets again. ■

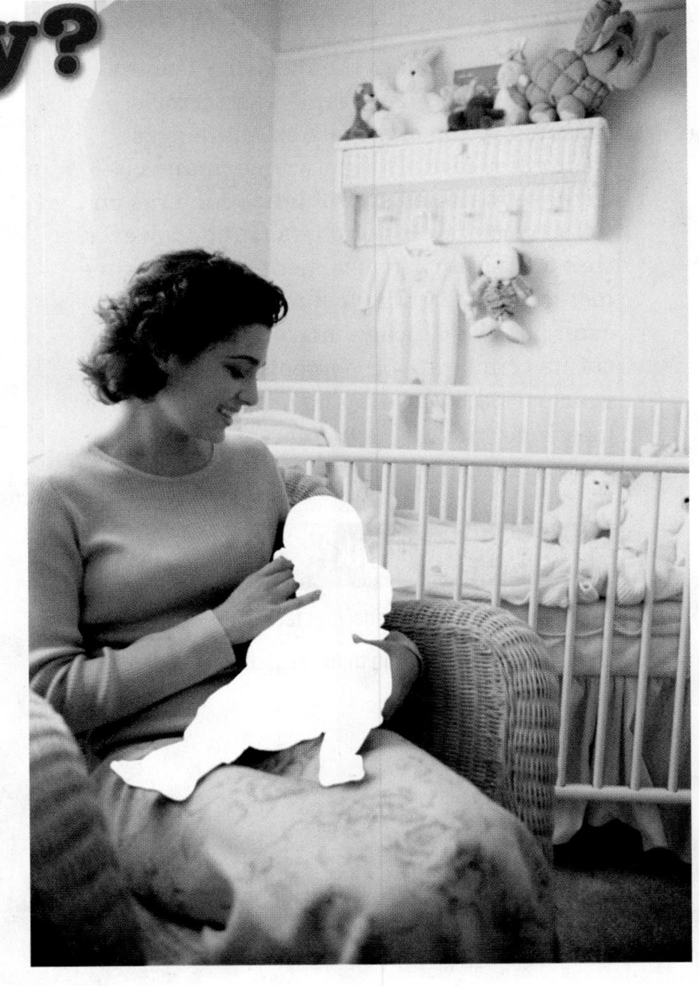

World Population Change

Until relatively recent human history, the world was populated by small bands of people who lived and roamed in primary groups. It took thousands of years for the world population to reach 1 billion. However, in only 150 years it grew to more than 6 billion. Estimates suggest that this figure may exceed 9 billion by 2050.

The rapid population growth of recent years has had a tremendous effect on social life. The study of populations is therefore of great interest to sociologists. A **population** is the number of people living in an area at a particular time. **Demography** is the area of sociology devoted to the study of human populations. One of the major areas of interest to demographers is the measurement of population change.

Three factors affect the growth or decline of a region's population—the birthrate, the death rate, and the rate of migration. These demographic variables determine the size of a population as well as the population's composition and distribution. They also determine how a population changes over time.

World Population About four babies are born in the world every second. As a result, providing food and services to growing populations comes as a challenge to many nations.

7.1 billion World population in 2013

9 billion Projected world population for 2040

#1 China's population ranking in 2016 (with a population of 1.4 billion)

323 million Population of the United States in 2016 (#3 in world rankings)

Skills Focus **INTERPRETING DATA** What is the projected world population for 2040? What do you think the impact of this population increase might be?

Birthrate The measure most often used by demographers to describe the births within a population is the **birthrate.** This term is the annual number of live births per 1,000 members of a population. Demographers calculate the birthrate by dividing the number of live births in a particular year by the total population for that year. This figure is then multiplied by 1,000. Mathematically, the formula is presented as

$$\text{Birthrate} = \frac{\text{Live births}}{\text{Total population}} \times 1{,}000$$

For example, in the United States about 4 million live births occurred in 2013 within a total population of about 317 million people. Dividing the number of live births by the total population and then multiplying that figure by 1,000 produces a birthrate of 12.5. This figure tells us that there were 12.5 live births for every 1,000 members of the U.S. population in 2013. Demographers often refer to the birthrate as the *crude birthrate*. This measure is considered crude because it is based on the total population, including men, children, and women who are past the age of childbearing. Thus, it is somewhat misleading to compare the birthrates of various societies because societies differ a great deal in the numbers of childbearing-age women they contain. Childbearing-age women usually range between the ages of 15 and 44. The crude birthrate also does not take into account the fact that various groups within a society may have different birthrates.

Nevertheless, the birthrate gives a relatively clear picture of the fertility of women in any given society. **Fertility** refers to the actual number of births occurring to women of childbearing age. Demographers distinguish fertility from **fecundity,** the biological capability to bear children. In the approximately 30 years between the onset and end of menstruation, women have the biological capacity to bear between 15 and 30 children. But because of various social, economic, and health factors, most women reproduce far below their biological potential.

Quick Lab

Analyzing Population Statistics

The U.S. Census Bureau is the government agency authorized to collect, tabulate, and publish statistical information about the population of the United States. The Bureau conducts a nationwide survey of the population every 10 years. What can you learn by analyzing these statistics?

PROCEDURE

1. Look at the population figures from the census years, shown in the table below.
2. Using the total population and the Hispanic population, calculate the percentage of Hispanic population for each year.
3. After you calculate the percentages, analyze the differences between the three census years.

ANALYSIS

1. For each census year, draw a pie graph that reflects the percentages you calculated.
2. Use your school library or the Internet to conduct research on the growth of the Hispanic population in the United States since 1980.
3. Write a short report of your findings.

Year	Total Population	Hispanic Population
1980	226,546,000	14,609,000
1990	248,791,000	22,379,000
2000	275,306,000	32,479,000
2010	308,745,538	50,477,594

Death Rate Another factor that affects population is mortality, or the number of deaths within a society. The measure most often used by demographers to describe the deaths in a population is the **death rate.** This term refers to the annual number of deaths per 1,000 members of a population. Demographers calculate the death rate in much the same way as the birthrate. The number of deaths in a particular year is divided by the total population for that year. This figure then is multiplied by 1,000. Mathematically, the formula is presented as

$$\text{Death rate} = \frac{\text{Deaths}}{\text{Total population}} \times 1{,}000$$

In the United States there were approximately 2.6 million deaths in 2013 within a total population of about 317 million people. Dividing the number of deaths by the total population and then multiplying that figure by 1,000 gives a death rate of 8.2. This figure tells us that there were 8.2 deaths for every 1,000 members of the United States population in 2013.

Demographers often refer to the death rate as the crude death rate because it does not take into account the varying death rates among subgroups in the population. Therefore, it is somewhat misleading to compare the death rates of various countries. To get a clearer picture of conditions in different countries, demographers also examine infant mortality rates and life expectancies.

The infant mortality rate is the annual number of deaths among infants under one year of age per 1,000 live births in a population. Demographers calculate the infant mortality rate by dividing the number of deaths of infants under one year of age in a particular year by the number of live births in that same year. This figure then is multiplied by 1,000. The formula can be shown as

$$\text{Infant mortality rate} = \frac{\text{Deaths among infants}}{\text{Total live births}} \times 1{,}000$$

The infant mortality rate provides a general measure of the overall health and quality of life in a society. Infants are particularly open to disease and malnutrition. Thus, the probability of surviving the first year of life is greater in societies that are able to provide their people with adequate medical attention and proper nutrition.

More-developed nations, such as Japan, Singapore, and Sweden, have relatively low rates of infant mortality. More-developed nations have high levels of per capita income, industrialization, and modernization. On the other hand, less-developed nations have low levels of per capita income, industrialization, and modernization. Less-developed nations, such as Ethiopia, Gambia, and Afghanistan, tend to have relatively high rates of infant mortality. For example, in Ethiopia an estimated 41 infants died for every 1,000 children born in 2015.

Examining life expectancies also helps demographers compare the health conditions and quality of life in different countries. **Life expectancy** refers to the average number of years that a person born in a particular year can expect to live. Life expectancy is related to the rate of infant mortality, and life expectancies in more-developed nations are much higher than life expectancies in less-developed nations. For example, in Japan fewer than 3 infants died for every 1,000 born, and life expectancy is 80 years for men and 87 years for women. In Zambia, where 65 infants die for every 1,000 born, life expectancy is only 57 years for men and 60 years for women. Within a single society, life expectancies can differ according to sex, race, ethnicity, and other social factors.

Demographers distinguish between life expectancy and life span—the maximum length of life that is biologically possible. The life span of humans is generally considered to be about 100 years. Although the expectancies in many countries around the world have increased dramatically during the 1900s, life span has not. The increases in life expectancy have been largely due to reductions in infant mortality. It has proved easier to combat the diseases of childhood than it has been to fight the aging process and the diseases common to old age. As a result, life span has remained practically unchanged for centuries.

Migration Rate The third demographic variable is **migration,** or the movement of people from one specified area to another. When measuring migration, demographers examine movement both into and out of an area.

The annual number of people who move into a specified area per 1,000 members of that area's population is called the in-migration rate. The out-migration rate, on the other hand, refers to the annual number of people who move out of a specified area per 1,000 members of a population. Both these processes are often occurring in a specified area at the same time. Because of this, demographers calculate the migration rate as the annual difference between in-migration and out-migration. The effects of the migration rate on population are ordinarily not as significant as the effects of the birthrate and the death rate. One reason for this is that the movement of people does not add to or detract from the global population.

Migration occurs as a result of what demographers call push and pull factors. A push factor is something that encourages people to move out of a certain area. Push factors include religious or political persecution, famine, racial discrimination, overpopulation, and war. A pull factor is something that encourages people to move into a certain area. Religious and political freedom, economic opportunities, and a high standard of living are considered migration pull factors.

Growth Rate Each of the three demographic variables—birthrate, death rate, and migration rate—affects the size of a population. However, demographers tend to focus on birthrates and death rates when considering a population's **growth rate,** or the rate at which a country's population is increasing. Growth rates are calculated by subtracting the death rate from the birthrate and are usually expressed as percentages. As you recall, the United States had a birthrate of 12.5 per 1,000 and a death rate of 8.2 per 1,000 in 2013. Subtracting the death rate from the birthrate leaves 4.3 per 1,000 people. Thus, the United States had a growth rate of 0.4 percent, meaning that about 4 people were added to the population for every 1,000 members.

The growth rates in more-developed countries are typically much lower than the growth rates in less-developed nations because modern industrialized countries generally have low birthrates. Countries with lower levels of technology, on the other hand, usually have birthrates that far exceed their death rates. In Niger, for example, the estimated birthrate for 2015 was 45.5, while the death rate was 12.4. Thus, the growth rate was estimated at 3.3 percent, meaning that 33 people were added to Niger's population for every 1,000 members.

Because growth rates are expressed as percentages, a growth rate of 2.4 appears quite small. In reality, the long-term effect of such a growth rate on population size is enormous because the growth rate is related to a population's doubling time. This period of time is the number of years necessary for a population to double in size, given its current rate of growth.

A population growth rate of only 1 percent will cause that population to double its size in about 70 years. A growth rate of 2 percent doubles the population in about 35 years. The United States has a growth rate of 0.4 percent and will double its population in just over 170 years. In contrast, Niger, at its current growth rate of 3.3 percent, will double its population in just over 20 years.

To illustrate the significance of doubling time, consider the fact that the population of the world doubled from half a billion to 1 billion between 1650 and 1850, a span of 200 years. The population doubled again between 1850 and 1930, reaching 2 billion in only 80 years. Less than 50 years later, in 1975, it doubled to 4 billion. Demographers estimate that at its current rate of growth of 1.1 percent, the world's population will hit the 8 billion mark in 2024.

Population Composition In addition to changes in population size, demographers also study population composition, or the population's structure. Age and sex are the factors most often used to show the composition of a population.

To study population composition, demographers use a population pyramid. A population pyramid is a graphic representation of the age and sex distribution of a population. This two-sided graph shows the percentages of men and women falling into various age groups. The graph is usually shaped like a pyramid because it displays the youngest age group at the bottom and the oldest age group at the top and because the chances of death increase with age.

Demographers gain a great deal of information from population pyramids. For example, the graphs indicate the percentage of older adults within the population who may need care or support. The graphs also show the percentage of childbearing-age women and the percentage of people available for employment. Perhaps most importantly, population pyramids indicate a population's potential for growth. A country with a large percentage of children has an enormous potential for growth. These children will soon grow and have children of their own. A country with a small percentage of children, on the other hand, will have fewer people entering their childbearing years in the future. Therefore, future population growth will be slow.

Look at the population pyramid for the United States on this page. The bulge in the pyramid represents people aged between their late thirties and late forties. This bulge reflects the sharp rise in the birthrate from the late 1940s through the early 1960s as family life resumed following World War II. The pyramid also shows that this baby boom

POPULATION PYRAMIDS

These population pyramids show the percentage of the population of each country at each age group by sex. The birthrate in Sweden has been in a relatively steady decline for a number of years, while Mexico has maintained a high birthrate.

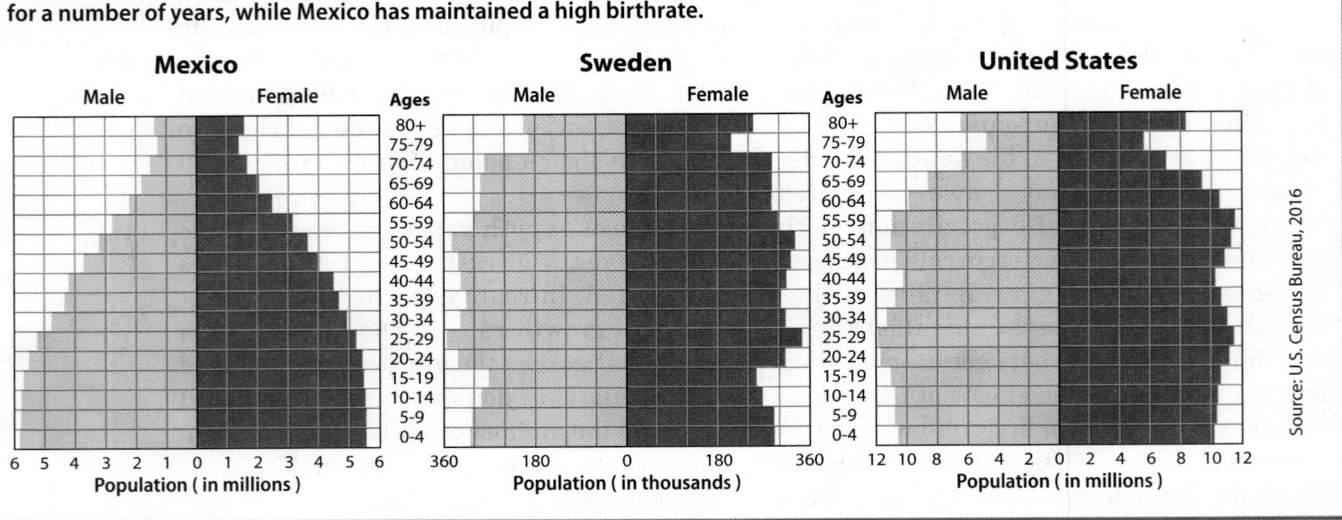

was followed by a "baby bust"—a decline in the birthrate. U.S. birthrates have remained relatively low ever since, making the baby-boom generation the largest percentage of the population. Because the United States has a relatively low birthrate, population growth is likely to be slow.

As you can see in the population pyramid for Sweden, that country's birthrate has been relatively low for a number of years and children make up a small percentage of the population. Sweden is producing fewer young people who will grow up and have children themselves. Therefore, Sweden's future population growth will be slow, slower even than that of the United States. This trend is similar to those in other more-developed nations such as Japan and other countries in northern Europe.

The population pyramid for Mexico stands in sharp contrast to those of the United States and Sweden. Mexico's graph is almost a perfect pyramid shape. This shape indicates that large numbers of children are being born but that few people are living to old age. When today's children reach their childbearing years, the population of Mexico will grow enormously unless the birthrate slows. Mexico's population pyramid is typical of many less-developed nations around the world.

Reading Check **Summarize** What three factors affect a region's growth or decline in population?

Explaining Population Change

A number of theories have been proposed over the years to explain population change. Among the theories most often discussed by demographers are Malthusian theory and demographic transition theory.

Malthusian Theory Thomas Robert Malthus (1766–1834), an English economist, outlined a rather gloomy picture of population growth in his *An Essay on the Principle of Population.* Malthus argued that the already rapidly growing population of the 1700s would continue to grow at ever-faster rates. He based this prediction on the fact that population grows through multiplication. In most instances, this multiplication progresses geometrically. A geometric progression is represented by the series of numbers 2, 4, 8, 16, 32, 64, and so on. Following the progression to its logical conclusion, **Malthusian theory** predicted that world population would soon reach astronomical numbers.

According to Malthusian theory, the geometric progression of population has serious social consequences because food production progresses arithmetically. An arithmetic progression is represented by the series of numbers 2, 3, 4, 5, 6, and so on. Food production is arithmetic because the amount of land available for cultivation is limited. Thus, a rapidly growing population could eventually outpace food production, which would cause famine.

Malthus suggested that two forces could check, or slow, population growth. First, the number of births could be reduced through preventive checks, including birth control, abstinence, and delayed marriage and childbearing. Second, the overall population could be reduced through positive checks, including war, disease, and famine.

Malthus did not think that people would use preventive checks to control what he believed to be a coming disaster. Malthus was also a clergyman, and he rejected the use of artificial birth control. Furthermore, he thought that people would halt their sexual activity only when faced with actual famine conditions. Consequently, Malthus predicted that natural factors, such as disease and famine, would bring the population in line with the available food supply.

Malthus failed to foresee two important developments, however. First, he did not anticipate that advances in agricultural technology would allow farmers to produce more crops on the same amount of land. Second, Malthus foresaw neither the development of effective birth control methods nor their widespread acceptance and use. Modern birth control methods have been particularly effective in reducing the birthrates in more developed nations since the 1960s. In addition, the globalization of the economy has spurred production.

However, some demographers warn that the Malthusian theory is still relevant. They point out that the last documented doubling of the world's population—from 3 billion to 6 billion—took just 39 years. If the population continues to grow at this pace, they argue, there will simply be too many people in need of the world's limited resources.

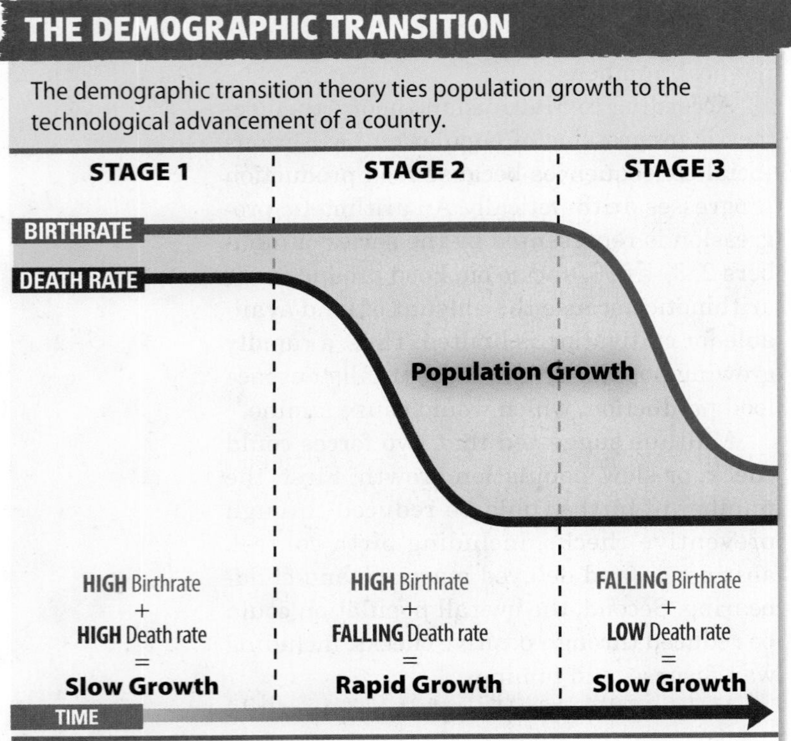

Skills Focus **INTERPRETING GRAPHS** Which growth stage in the demographic transition has a high death rate?

Demographic Transition Theory Malthusian theory has contributed much to our understanding of population change. However, most demographers favor the explanation provided by the **demographic transition theory.** This theory holds that population patterns are tied to a society's level of technological development. Moreover, it tracks three stages of development and is based on the population changes in western Europe over the past 300 years.

In Stage 1, which is typical of preindustrial agricultural societies, both the birthrate and the death rate are high. The birthrate is high in these societies because children are valued as sources of labor and because no effective means of birth control are available. The death rate is high because of the relatively low standard of living and the lack of medical technology to control the spread of disease. The high birthrate and high death rate result in a fairly stable population with little growth and little decline. While all of human society was in Stage 1 until the 18th century, there are no longer any Stage 1 countries in the world.

As societies enter the industrial phase, Stage 2, improved medical techniques, sanitation, and increased food production result in a reduction in the death rate. Children are still highly desired, however, so the birthrate remains high. High birthrates and low death rates combine to produce a rapid growth in population. Developing countries around the world, such as the Democratic Republic of the Congo and Guatemala would fit in Stage 2.

Stage 3 societies have a fully developed industrial economy. During this stage, the birthrate falls because of the increased use of effective birth control methods. Birthrates also decrease because there is a relatively high standard of living and children are no longer needed as workers. The death rate remains low during this stage. The low birthrate and low death rate produce a fairly stable population. Growth occurs very slowly. The world's most technologically advanced countries of the world, such as the United States and Japan, are in Stage 3 of the demographic transition.

Some Stage 3 societies may even approach zero population growth, the point at which nearly equal birthrates and death rates produce a growth rate of zero. In some cases, countries have fallen below zero growth, with birthrates lower than their death rates. In these cases, the populations are shrinking.

Some demographers believe that Stage 2 countries currently experiencing rapid population growth will stabilize as they become more industrially advanced. Critics of the demographic transition theory are less optimistic. These critics believe it is unlikely that all countries will follow the stages of technological development found in Europe and North America. As today's preindustrial countries begin to industrialize, the introduction of modern medicine causes their death rates to drop much more quickly than was the case in western Europe. This difference leads to an increase in population and may hamper modernization in these countries. Any economic gains brought about by industrialization must be used to maintain the same level of subsistence for the rapidly growing population.

Reading Check **Identify Cause and Effect** What happens to a population if the birthrate is lower than the death rate?

Controlling Population Growth

The world now contains over 7.1 billion people. Although the current growth rate is down to 1.1 percent, the population of the world continues to grow. Most of the growth is occurring in the less-developed nations, which are home to 80 percent of the world's population.

Concerns about growth and the desire for economic development have led many countries to adopt strategies aimed at controlling their populations. Two types of basic strategies are being used.

Family Planning One strategy that has been used to lower the birthrate in some countries is **family planning.** This strategy is the conscious decision by couples to have a certain number of children. The goal of family-planning programs is to reduce the number of unplanned pregnancies. Family planning involves the careful use of effective birth-control techniques.

According to demographers, family-planning programs alone have been insufficient to reduce the birthrate in many countries. One reason for the program's lack of success is that these programs are poorly financed. As a result, only a limited number of people are able to use the program services. Moreover, in many less-developed nations children are considered economic assets. In these countries, many people use family-planning programs only after they have several children.

Some countries attempt to reduce population growth by discouraging people from having children. For example, China was involved from the early 1980s until 2016 in a one-child-per-family campaign, which was based on incentives and sanctions. Couples who followed the one-child program received special housing, employment, and financial benefits from the government. Those couples who did not conform to the policy faced large fines and other penalties. China's policy produced a significant reduction in the fertility rate.

Economic Improvements Some critics of family-planning policies believe that economic development must proceed before people in less-developed nations will voluntarily limit their family size. Supporters of economic development believe that better health, higher levels of income, and education will lead to lower birthrates.

However, most less-developed nations do not have the resources to achieve the economic development necessary to raise living standards. Economic assistance packages that are designed to help less-developed nations improve their living conditions often benefit only a very small portion of the population. As a result, the majority of the population of these nations remains in poverty, and birthrates remain high.

Reading Check **Draw Conclusions** How are some nations controlling population growth?

SECTION 1 Assessment

Reviewing Main Ideas and Vocabulary

1. **Define** What is demography?
2. **Recall** What roles do push and pull factors play in the migration of people?
3. **Explain** How did Malthus explain his theory of population change?

Thinking Critically

4. **Compare and Contrast** How is the demographic transition theory similar to and different from the Malthusian theory?
5. **Evaluate** If a country's population pyramid looks like an upside-down pyramid, what does this shape reveal about the age of the country's population?
6. **Categorize** Using your notes and a graphic organizer like this one, identify the three factors that affect the growth or decline of a region's population.

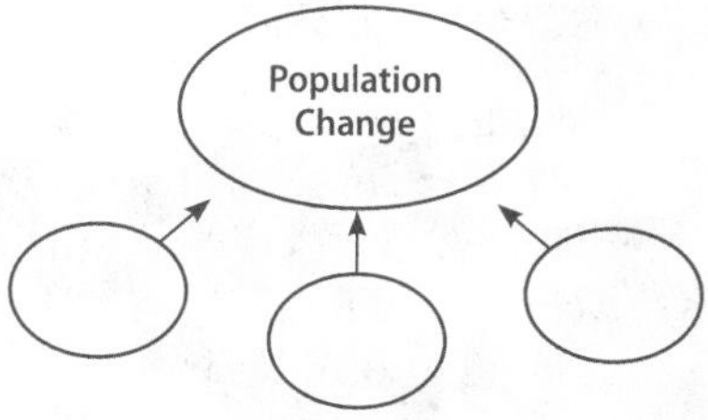

FOCUS ON WRITING

7. **Descriptive** Write two brief paragraphs describing how to calculate the growth rate of a country.

SECTION 2

Urban Life

Before You Read

Main Idea
Cities have evolved through time, and face many challenges today.

Reading Focus
1. How did cities evolve?
2. What are some of the challenges cities face today?

Vocabulary
urbanization
city
overurbanization

TAKING NOTES Use a graphic organizer like this one to take notes on the evolution of the city.

Revisited

SOCIOLOGY CLOSE UP ***Do you think you could live in a city without a car?*** You just might be able to, believe it or not. For the past 25 years, architects and planners have built communities that allow residents to hang up their car keys and walk to the grocery store, entertainment, and even to work. This movement became known as the New Urbanism movement.

In the late 2000s, Market Square in Pittsburgh, Pennsylvania, underwent a series of modernization efforts designed to make the area more friendly to pedestrians. Traffic was diverted around the square, and the availability of outdoor seating was increased. Historic buildings were converted into new apartments and offices. Many new restaurants opened, and pedestrian traffic in the area increased greatly as a result. In a stark contrast to the decline the area had seen in the late 20th century, it now serves as a model for car-free city life. ■

With its pedestrian-friendly streets and open space, Market Square in downtown Pittsburgh, Pennsylvania, provides a sense of community not found in many modern urban areas.

The Evolution of the City

Some sociologists are particularly interested in the ways that the movement of populations affects the social world. In fact, sociology initially developed from the effort to understand the changes accompanying a particular kind of movement—**urbanization.** This movement involves the concentration of the population in cities. A **city** is a permanent concentration of a relatively large number of people who are engaged mainly in nonfarming activities. Urbanization is a relatively recent event in the history of the world. However, it has profoundly changed the way that most people live their lives.

The first recognizable cities appeared between about 5,500 and 7,000 years ago. Yet until very recently, only a small proportion of the population lived in urban areas. As late as 1800 only about 3 percent of the world's population lived in cities of more than 100,000 inhabitants. As of 2014 approximately 54 percent of the world's people live in urban areas, and the world's urban population is growing by over 60 million a year. Demographers estimate that by 2030, urban dwellers will make up about 60 percent of the world's population.

Why did it take so long for urbanization to become commonplace? According to sociologists, the rise of cities appears to be tied to two important developments—the Agricultural Revolution and the Industrial Revolution.

The Agricultural Revolution involved the cultivation of grain, the domestication of animals, and the development of a basic agricultural technology. These developments allowed people to produce a surplus of food for the first time. Food surpluses freed large numbers of people from agricultural activities. In time, these people took up more specialized types of work, such as craftwork and trading. These types of activities are most conveniently pursued where there are large permanent concentrations of people. Thus, cities initially arose when people in specialized roles came together in centralized locations.

The further development and spread of cities did not occur for centuries, until the Industrial Revolution replaced hand tools with machines. The Industrial Revolution also replaced traditional sources of energy such as animal labor with new sources such as coal, water, and steam. These new sources of energy dramatically increased productivity and led to the rise of the factory as a system of production. Factories, which were generally located in or near cities, required large pools of labor. Thus, thousands of people left the countryside in search of employment opportunities in the cities.

The Industrial Revolution also produced more-advanced technologies for the transportation and storage of food. These changes allowed cities to support increasing numbers of people who could fill the labor demands generated by further industrial development.

The Preindustrial City Cities first arose about 6,000 years ago on the fertile banks of rivers such as the Nile in Egypt, the Tigris and Euphrates in what is now Iraq, the Indus in what is now Pakistan, and the Huang in China. Similar urban settlements appeared centuries later in other parts of the world.

Compared with the cities of today, early urban settlements were very small. Most preindustrial cities contained a few thousand people, although some were considerably larger. Population size was limited by the use of inefficient agricultural techniques that could not produce enough food to support more people. In addition, communication and transportation methods were primitive by modern standards. Food had to be carried into the cities from farming areas either by animals or by humans on roads that were typically little more than dirt tracks.

Life in the early cities was quite different from what we know today. Most cities were very crowded and lacked any kind of sanitation system. As a result, death rates in cities were higher than those in rural areas. Ineffective medical techniques and lack of medicines also contributed to the high death rates. Because of these conditions, epidemics could drastically reduce the population of a city in a very short time. For example, the Black Death, or bubonic plague, killed about one third of Europe's population between 1347 and 1350.

ACADEMIC VOCABULARY

epidemic an outbreak of disease affecting large numbers of people

There was no designated downtown area in preindustrial cities. Traders usually worked out of their homes, which they used as shops. People who performed crafts or trades lived and worked in different sectors of the city.

The City Through Time

The Earliest Cities Most early cities contained religious centers such as the temple of Ur in present-day Iraq, which has been partially reconstructed above. Over time, each city and the land it controlled formed a city-state, a political unit with its own government. As the city-states grew, they fought over land and water.

The Preindustrial City The main function of preindustrial cities was to serve as centers of trade. Many preindustrial cities contained a castle, government buildings, and marketplaces. These cities also had defined boundaries marked by defensive walls, as seen in the painting of Genoa, Italy, above.

Generally, each occupational grouping had its own quarter. People were also segregated into classes or castes. Poor people usually lived on the outskirts of the city while those who were wealthy lived in the center.

Finally, day-to-day life in preindustrial cities was built around kinship relations and the extended family. With rare exceptions, city governments were organized as monarchies or oligarchies.

The Industrial City The nature of life in preindustrial cities changed little for almost 5,000 years. Then the Industrial Revolution produced an explosive growth in both the size and number of cities. Mechanization allowed farmers to produce a surplus of food. It also reduced the number of workers needed to work the farms. People no longer needed on the farms moved to the cities, where they filled the need for factory workers. Increased food surpluses as well as improved communication and transportation allowed cities to support ever-increasing numbers of people.

The industrial city differed greatly from the preindustrial city. It covered a greater area and had a much larger population. Commerce became the focal point of life in the industrial city. Central business districts including stores, offices, and banks replaced the segregated trade quarters common in pre-industrial cities.

Social life in the industrial city was also transformed. People began to leave their homes to travel to work in offices or factories. The power of the family over the individual lessened as many single people gained their independence in the city. According to sociologists, urbanization also contributed to the rise of a number of social problems. Crime, overcrowding, and pollution all increased as cities grew larger.

The history of the United States illustrates the rapid urbanization that accompanied the Industrial Revolution. In 1790 only 5 percent of the U.S. population lived in cities. By 1860 about one-fifth of the population lived in urban areas. However, urbanization was largely confined to the Northeast. Today about 81 percent of Americans live in urban areas, and almost every region of the country is heavily urbanized.

Reading Check **Contrast** How did the industrial city differ from the preindustrial city?

Urban Challenges Today

Urbanization in more-developed nations has generally followed an ordered progression. In addition, it has usually resulted in increased rates of literacy, greater economic opportunities, and improved health care. Although problems do exist in the cities of the modern world, urbanization and industrialization

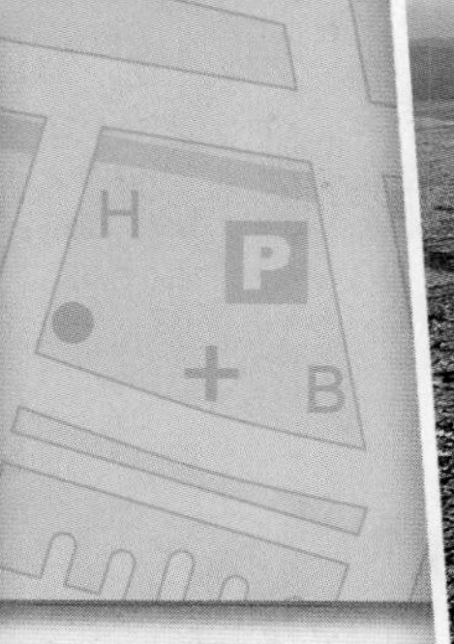

The Industrial City During the Industrial Revolution in the 1800s and early 1900s, cities such as New York evolved into major centers of manufacturing. Factories sprung up to meet the high demand for products such as clothing, processed meats, and steel parts. With factories, cities became a magnet for workers and immigrants looking for jobs.

The City Today Mexico City is a prime example of how cities have spread out, or sprawled, from their centers. This urban sprawl causes excessive pollution and, in some cities, areas of temporary housing called shantytowns. Cities today, such as Mexico City, are more global than the industrial city was and now serve as international economic centers.

have led to a higher standard of living than has ever been known before.

Urbanization in the less-developed nations has been less orderly and more rapid. For example, the population of Mexico City rose from 5 million in 1960 to more than 20 million today. In many of the less-developed nations, the rapid growth of cities has led to **overurbanization**—a situation in which more people live in a city than can be supported in terms of jobs and facilities. As a result, people in overurbanized cities often do not have adequate housing, food, sewage disposal, hospitals, and other key services. The crowded and unsanitary living conditions contribute to high rates of illness and death. Overurbanization and the social problems that accompany it have become a major challenge in parts of Latin America, Asia, and Africa. Despite these challenges, the population of many overcrowded cities continues to grow.

CASE STUDY CONNECTION

Megacities Dealing with overurbanization is another challenge megacities face.

Reading Check **Draw Conclusions** How do you think overurbanization can be prevented?

SECTION 2 Assessment

Reviewing Main Ideas and Vocabulary

1. **Define** What is urbanization?
2. **Describe** How did cities evolve?
3. **Contrast** How has urbanization in less-developed nations differed from urbanization in more-developed nations?

Thinking Critically

4. **Evaluate** How did the Industrial Revolution affect the growth of the industrial cities?
5. **Elaborate** Why do you think less-developed nations have experienced more overurbanization than more-developed nations?
6. **Draw Conclusions** Using your notes and a graphic organizer like the one below, describe the challenges you think cities will face in the next decade.

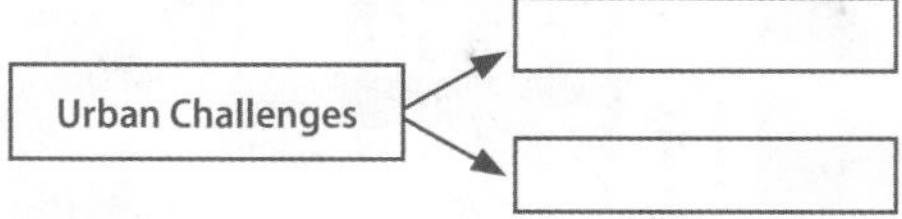

FOCUS ON WRITING

7. **Descriptive** Most cities have evolved over time. Using resources from the library or the Internet describe the evolution of your city, or a city near you.

New York City's Ethnic Neighborhoods

Renovated in 2005, the Apollo Theater in New York's Harlem neighborhood is a landmark for African American culture.

Centuries of migration and immigration have shaped New York City's ethnic makeup. Over time, millions of people from all over the world have settled in various parts of the city. Today New York City contains hundreds of distinct ethnic neighborhoods that have come to reflect the diverse cultures of these immigrants.

Lower East Side Historically, the Lower East Side of New York has been home to a large Jewish population. In 1730, the neighborhood's Jewish residents erected the city's first synagogue. Today New York City metropolitan area's Jewish population is about 2 million. In the Lower East Side, Jewish culture continues to thrive where Yiddish is still heard being spoken and some of the city's best bagel shops and Jewish delis stand.

Chinatown Recognizable by its street signs in both English and Chinese, newsstands selling Chinese-language newspapers and magazines, and smoked ducks hanging in the windows of the neighborhood's restaurants, Chinatown remains a vibrant center of Chinese American culture. New immigrants from mainland China and Taiwan arrive almost daily.

Jackson Heights Some have dubbed one area of Jackson Heights, Queens, "Little India" because of its large population of new immigrants from South Asia. Theaters showing "Bollywood" films from India and some of world's finest Indian restaurants are found in the neighborhood. The rest of Jackson Heights is home to immigrants from Latin America, Eastern Europe, and Russia, making the neighborhood truly diverse.

Little Italy The area of New York labeled "Little Italy" is not as Italian as it used to be. It is more of a tourist destination than a neighborhood, even though the Feast of San Gennaro is still celebrated with a large street fair every year. Much of New York's Italian American population has moved to the borough of Staten Island, where about 45 percent of the population is of Italian descent.

Businesses with signs in Chinese contribute to Chinatown's unique urban landscape.

Harlem Beginning at the turn of the twentieth century, African Americans from other parts of New York and the southern United States began migrating to an area of the city known as Harlem. By the 1920s, Harlem was a center of music and African American culture. Since the 1980s, Harlem has undergone an economic revitalization, which has caused property values to soar into the millions of dollars.

Spanish Harlem Also known as East Harlem, Spanish Harlem is home to much of the city's Hispanic population and has a high concentration of Puerto Ricans. Each year in June, neighborhood leaders hold a Puerto Rican Day parade. This event celebrates Puerto Rican food, music, and dance.

Irish New York In the mid-1800s, about 2 million Irish immigrated to the United States, and many settled in New York. Today New York has more Irish Americans of any city in the country. Irish culture is evident in many different neighborhoods throughout the city—especially on St. Patrick's Day.

Thinking Critically

1. **Contrast** How do New York's ethnic neighborhoods differ?
2. **Discuss** What influence do you think immigrants have on the city's culture?

SECTION 3

Urban Ecology

Before You Read

Main Idea
Researchers have created several models to explain the structure of cities and several theories to explain city life.

Reading Focus
1. What models of city structure are there?
2. How do some theories explain city life?

Vocabulary
urban ecology
concentric zone model
sector model
multiple nuclei model
urban sprawl
urban anomie theory
compositional theory
subcultural theory

TAKING NOTES Use a graphic organizer like this one to take notes on urban ecology.

The City	
Models	Theories

Life in an Eco-city

SOCIOLOGY CLOSE UP ***How are cities helping to protect the environment?*** Look around many big cities today and you might notice gardens on rooftops, zippy Smart cars that park in tiny spaces (bottom left), and skyscrapers powered by solar or wind energy. These are just a few of the ways many cities around the world are becoming more environmentally conscious. For example, developers in Paris are planning a rooftop wind farm that will generate a new building's own heating. A garden that sits atop Chicago's city hall (left) is helping to improve the city's air quality and to lessen the heat the building absorbs from the sun. In Austin, Texas, city leaders promote "green building," which includes the use of sustainable construction materials. Leaders and residents hope these environmentally friendly measures will make the cities of the future greener and healthier places to live. ■

Models of City Structure

During the 1920s and 1930s, sociologists interested in urban life developed an approach to the study of cities called **urban ecology.** This approach examines the relationship between people and the urban environment, such as those relationships mentioned above. Urban ecologists argue that human behavior determines the overall layout of the urban environment. In turn, the urban environment affects human behavior.

ACADEMIC VOCABULARY

model a representation or simulation of an object or a theory

According to sociological studies, urban areas do not develop in random patterns. Rather, different areas of a city tend to be used for different, set purposes. As a result, people, buildings, and activities in a city are distributed in certain patterns. Sociologists have developed three models to describe these patterns: the concentric zone model, the sector model, and the multiple nuclei model. The chart on this page provides a visual representation of each of these models.

Concentric Zone Model In 1925 sociologist Ernest W. Burgess proposed the **concentric zone model** to describe urban structure. According to this model, a typical industrial city spreads outward from the center, resulting in a series of circles, or zones.

Each of these zones differs in terms of land use. The city's central business district, an area used for hotels, banking, commerce, offices, and entertainment, lies at the center. A wholesale-light-manufacturing zone, also called the transition zone, surrounds the city's central business district. Abandoned buildings, poverty, disease, and crime characterize this zone. A series of increasingly expensive residential areas lie beyond the transition zone. The most distant of these areas is the commuters' zone. The city's wealthiest people live in the commuter zone in large, single-family houses away from the noise and bustle of the city. Commuter zone residents travel to their jobs in the city by car or public transportation.

Burgess noted that the city's residential areas are constantly changing. People tend to move to more expensive homes as their socioeconomic status improves. Therefore, the boundaries of the residential zones change over time. He also pointed out that few, if any, cities exactly follow the concentric zone model. Geographic features, such as rivers or lakes and railroad lines, Burgess suggested, might prevent the development of concentric circular zones.

Sector Model Not all sociologists agreed with Burgess's portrayal of city structure. They pointed out that while his model did describe some cities, such as Chicago in the early 1900s, it failed to consider factors such as available forms of urban transportation. Sociologist Homer Hoyt addressed this issue in

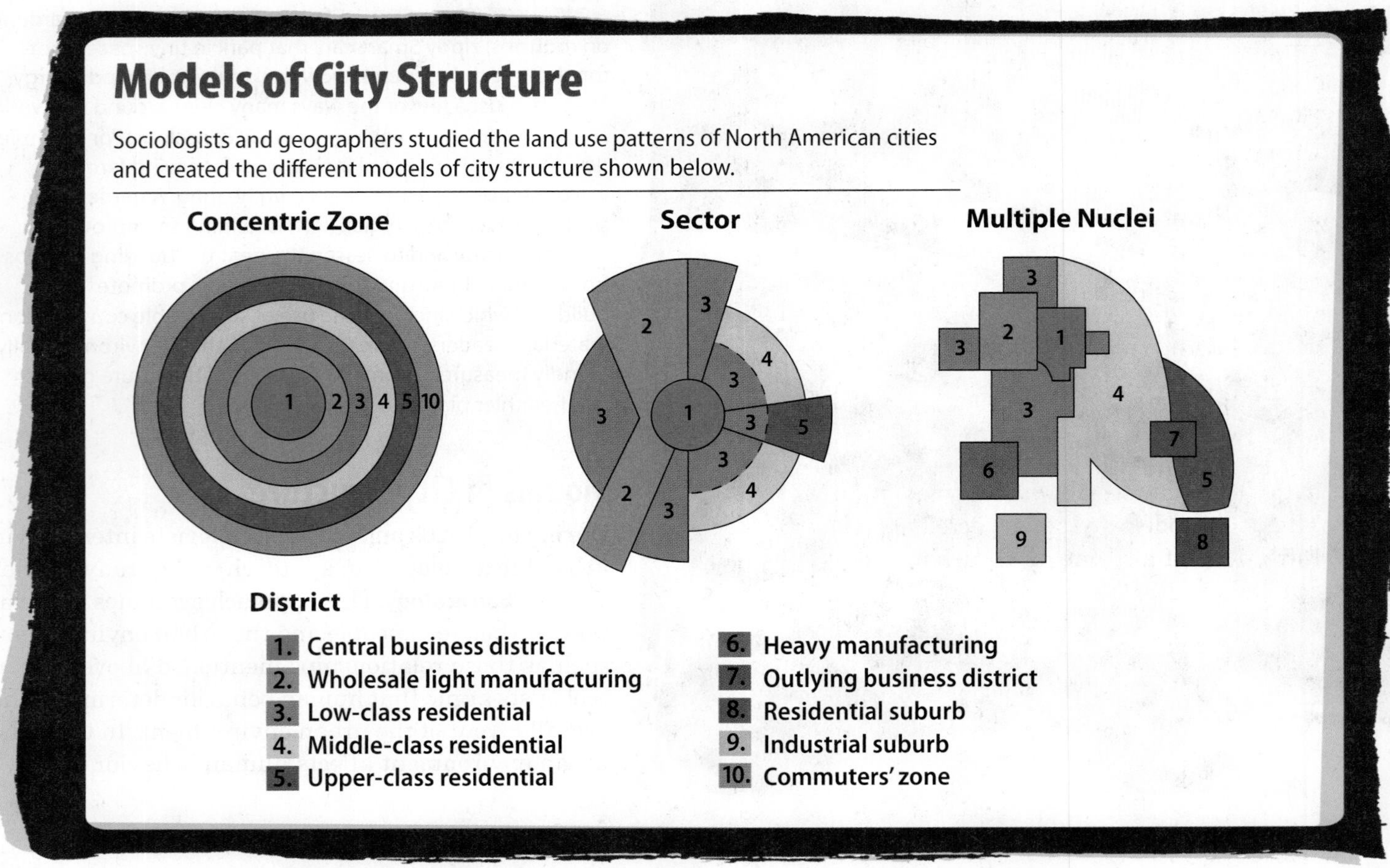

the sector model. Like Burgess, Hoyt proposed that cities grow outward from the center and that the central business district is the core of the city. However, in the **sector model** Hoyt argued that growth occurs in wedge-shaped sectors—not concentric circles—outward from the center to the edge of the city.

According to Hoyt, transportation systems determine land use in the city. For example, warehouses are usually located along railroads that extend from the inner city. Poor people tend to live next to transportation routes that run close to factories. Wealthy people, on the other hand, live near the fastest lines of transportation in attractive areas of the city. Hoyt argued that each sector of land use extends along transportation routes to the edge of the city.

Multiple Nuclei Model Hoyt's sector model painted a fairly accurate picture of the structure of some U.S. cities, such as San Francisco. However, his model focused on transportation systems available before the widespread use of the automobile. Geographers Chauncy Harris and Edward Ullman developed a model that addressed the influence of the automobile on urban ecology.

In their **multiple nuclei model,** Harris and Ullman suggested that a city does not develop around one central core but around several centers of activity, or "nuclei." Each one of these nuclei is devoted to a specialized type of land use. For example, automobile dealerships often cluster together in one or two areas of the city while light-manufacturing industries are often found in industrial parks on the city's edge. For the most part, clustering occurs because it is beneficial. Several stores grouped together will attract more customers than one single store.

Urban Ecology Models—A Critique These three models describe ideal types of cities. Thus, the models are not expected to be exact reflections of any one or all urban areas. In combination, however, they reveal the general pattern of land use in cities. For example, they reflect one of the major trends in urbanization of the 1900s—the movement of populations from the central cities to the suburbs. Still, the models do not reflect several recent developments, such as urban sprawl.

Urban sprawl is characterized by poorly planned development on the edge of cities and towns. Designed with little thought for the surrounding environment, sprawl consumes huge amounts of formerly rural land. These areas have received negative attention from environmentalists in recent years.

This haphazard development does not fit the rather orderly picture of urban ecology that is presented by the models. Further, these models characterize downtown areas as places for mostly business and industry. All residential areas located downtown in the urban ecology models tend to be home to low-income residents. However, in recent years there has been a well-established trend of reverse migration from the suburbs into the central cities.

In addition, these models fail to take full account of how cultural factors affect urban ecology. Walter Firey suggested that culture and sentiment may have an important influence on urban development. Firey cited the Italian American community of Boston's North End neighborhood as an example. Some Italian American families, Firey noted, are wealthy enough to move to more expensive neighborhoods. However, these families tend to stay in the North End because of their cultural attachment to the community.

Reading Check **Summarize** What are the models of city structure?

Theories of City Life

Sociologists are interested not only in the structure of cities but also in the nature of life in cities. Over the years, the following theories have been proposed to explain city life—urban anomie theory, compositional theory, and subcultural theory.

Urban Anomie Theory In a groundbreaking study titled "Urbanism as a Way of Life," sociologist Louis Wirth presented an **urban anomie theory.** According to this theory, the city is an anonymous and unfriendly place, and living there carries serious negative consequences for residents. Wirth argued that the size, density, and diversity of urban life discourage the formation of primary group relationships, especially those relationships based on kinship ties and the neighborhood.

TECHNOLOGY FOCUS

The 22nd Century City

What do you think cities will look like in 100 years? Architects and engineers from across the United States tried to answer this question in a competition held in 2008. Competitors from three cities—Atlanta, San Francisco, and Washington, D.C.—attempted to come up with the most interesting and efficient plan for the city of the future.

The architects representing the San Francisco team created a city plan based on large, white, geothermal "mushrooms" (in the foreground at right) and tall, curvy, algae-harvesting towers (background). Scattered throughout the city, these geo-thermal mushrooms would tap into steam deep in the Earth's crust. The geothermal energy would in turn provide electricity to homes and office buildings.

Hydrogen produced by algae harvested in a "forest" of towers would also generate energy for the city. The hydrogen would be used to power hover cars that would travel through underground tunnels. In addition to algae harvesting, the plans for San Francisco 2108 called for "fog catchers" that would harvest the city's famous fog as a water source.

Architects and city planners created this futuristic view of San Francisco in the year 2108.

Water was also a hot issue for the Atlanta team of architects and planners. They created an enormous system of underground pipes that would filter rainwater throughout the city.

Thinking Critically

Draw Conclusions How do you think society will be different in the 22nd century?

Consequently, life in the city is characterized by relationships only within impersonal secondary groups. According to Wirth, the lack of primary group relationships results in anomie, or normlessness.

Why does city life produce anomie? According to Wirth, city dwellers come into contact with many people on a daily basis. Because most of these people are strangers, interaction tends to be short-lived, formal, and shallow. To keep themselves from having to become personally involved with everyone with whom they come into contact, city dwellers often take on an unfriendly impersonal attitude. This attitude discourages interaction and communication, leading individuals to withdraw further from each other. The result is a lack of involvement with others and thus a feeling of detachment.

In a 1970 study of group behavior, Bibb Latané and John Darley found that the larger the group, the less likely people are to become involved. Latané and Darley proposed that there is a diffusion of responsibility when each group member presumes that someone else will take action. In *Being Urban,* David Karp, Gregory Stone, and William Yoels suggested that this reluctance to get involved is not a result of normlessness. Rather, people are following the norm of noninvolvement. The authors of *Being Urban* argued that the city dwellers' behavior, as described by Wirth, is simply an effective method of handling impersonal city life.

Compositional Theory A number of sociologists have criticized Wirth's theory, saying it portrayed urban life too negatively. In response, they offered several theories that presented a more balanced view of life in the city. These sociologists came up with the **compositional theory,** which examined the ways in which the composition of a city's population influences life in the city. Factors that affect the composition of a city include age, race, ethnicity, education, income, and occupation. Compositional theory argues that the great diversity of people who live in the city leads to a greater variety of lifestyles than is common in most small towns in the United States.

According to sociologist Herbert J. Gans, five identifiable lifestyles can be found among urban dwellers.

- *The cosmopolites* The cosmopolites are the professionals or intellectuals of the city. They are attracted to life in the city because of its culture, entertainment, and excitement.
- *The unmarried or childless* These people work in the city and enjoy the attraction of cultural events and the company of urban friends. Those who marry and decide to have children often move to the suburbs.
- *The ethnic villagers* Ethnic villagers are those people who are attracted to the small ethnic areas typical of big cities, such as "Little Havana" or "Little Italy."
- *The deprived* The deprived are those city dwellers who live in disadvantaged or unfavorable circumstances because of poverty.
- *The trapped* The trapped stay in the city because they cannot afford to leave. Often these are elderly people who are living on fixed incomes.

According to Gans, most people living in cities form communities with others who share the same lifestyle, neighborhood or interests. The city is composed of a number of groups, each providing a community.

Subcultural Theory In *To Dwell Among Friends,* sociologist Claude S. Fischer employed **subcultural theory** to explain the nature of city life. According to Fischer, the characteristics of the city encourage rather than discourage the formation of primary group relationships. Because of the size and diversity of urban populations, it is possible for people to find others who share the same interests and lifestyles.

For example, a person living in a small town who is interested in photography might find only a handful of others with the same interest. In a city, on the other hand, there might be thousands of people who are interested in photography. As a result, clubs, activities, and friendships based on photography could develop from this shared interest.

According to subcultural theory, cities provide a place where people develop close ties with others based on their associations in a number of different groups. These groups may be based on such diverse factors as occupation, hobbies, friendships, ethnicity, or even age. Subcultural theory argues that city dwellers are not separated from others. Rather, they are involved in a rich and diverse social life that includes close relationships with family members, friends, neighbors, and associates.

Reading Check **Explain** How does the subcultural theory describe the formation of relationships?

SECTION 3 Assessment

Reviewing Main Ideas and Vocabulary

1. **Define** What is urban ecology?
2. **Analyze** How do the models of city structure explain city growth?

Thinking Critically

3. **Elaborate** Why is the central business district located in the middle of each model of city structure?
4. **Infer** In what ways does the compositional theory apply or not apply to a city nearest to you?
5. **Explain** How does Louis Wirth's urban anomie theory view city life?
6. **Summarize** Using your notes and a graphic organizer like this one, explain how each theory describes city life.

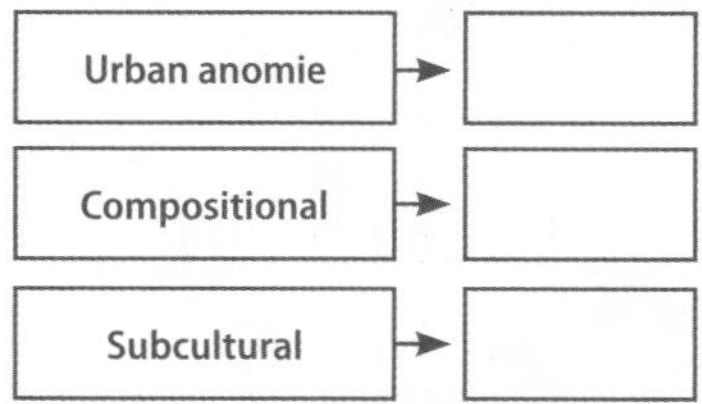

FOCUS ON WRITING

7. **Descriptive** Write two brief paragraphs comparing the models of city structure. Be sure to think about what effects urban sprawl may have on the accuracy of each model.

Lab
Applying What You've Learned

Analyzing World Population Statistics

Use the workbook to complete this lab.

How does the population of the United States differ from the population of other countries?

1. Introduction

This lab will help you analyze population statistics for the United States and one other country. You will work in pairs to gather the population statistics, make a poster, and present your research. To complete this lab, follow the steps below:

- Following your teacher's instructions, organize the class into pairs.
- Your teacher will assign each pair a country to research from the following world regions: Africa, Asia, Europe, North America, or South America.
- Work with your partner to review the chapter material on world population and the demographic variables of birthrate and death rate from Section 1.
- Find the following statistics for the United States and your assigned country: population, percent urban, birthrate, death rate, and growth rate.
- Conduct additional research on the population of the United States and your assigned country by going to the U.S. Census International Data Base (http://www.census.gov/ipc/www/idb). There you will find population pyramids for every country in the world. Print out the population pyramids for the United States and your assigned country.

2. Compiling Statistics and Creating a Poster

Enter your statistics into a table like the Sample Statistics Table below.

- After you and your partner create a statistics table, cut and paste the table onto a large piece of poster board. Also, add a title to your poster by identifying the United States and your assigned country.
- Print out the population pyramids you found and paste them onto your poster. Write at least three sentences under the two pyramids, explaining what the population statistics reveal about each country.
- To make your poster more engaging, you and your partner could also add photographs or illustrations. Try to find images from magazines or newspapers that would best represent your country's population statistics. For example, if the urban percentage is low you could show an image of a rural area with few people.

Sample Statistics Table

	United States	India
Population		
% Urban		
Birthrate		
Death rate		
Growth rate		

From thew classroom of **Connie L. Cooley, The Academy of Irving, Irving, TX**

3. Presenting Your Poster

After you and your partner have completed your poster, choose who will present each part of the poster to the class.

- One person might want to talk about the statistics table, and one person might want to talk about the population pyramids.
- The person who presents the statistics table may want to explain how different or similar the population of their assigned country is to the population of the United States.
- When presenting, remember to look at your audience and speak loud enough for the entire class to hear you clearly.
- Have notes on the population of your assigned country with you so you can present your findings and the conclusions you and your partner agreed on.
- Point to the images you included on the poster and explain the reason you feel they best represent the population of your assigned country.

4. Discussion

What did you learn from this lab? Hold a group discussion that focuses on the following questions:

- What are the differences and similarities of the population of the United States and the countries your class researched?
- Do you think the growth rate of a country affects that country's society? Explain.
- Looking at statistics on the percentage of urban areas in each country your class researched, how does the United States compare? How do these percentages reflect how people live in these countries?
- Which assigned country has the lowest birthrate? Discuss how you think this figure would affect that society.
- According to your population pyramids, which country has the largest percentage of teenagers aged 15 to 19?
- According to your population pyramids, which country has the largest percentage of people over age 65?
- How do a country's birthrate, death rate, and growth rate influence the shape of its population pyramid?

With an urban population of only 33 percent, Vietnam is mostly rural. More than half of the country's population works in agriculture.

The population of Argentina is 92 percent urban. The capital, Buenos Aires, is home to about 13 million people.

CHAPTER 15 Review

Comprehension and Critical Thinking

SECTION 1 *(pp. 370–377)*

1. a. Recall What is the demographic transition theory?

b. Summarize What are the demographic variables that determine the size of a population?

c. Elaborate What are some of the programs that have been used to control population growth?

SECTION 2 *(pp. 378–381)*

2. a. Define What is overurbanization?

b. Analyze In what ways did the Industrial Revolution affect the development of cities? How do you think people living in industrial cities adapted to these changes?

SECTION 3 *(pp. 383–387)*

3. a. Identify What models do sociologists use to explain the structure of cities?

b. Explain What kind of place did Louis Wirth describe the city as being?

c. Develop According to the subcultural theory, what are the benefits of living in a city? Would you want to live in a city for these reasons? Why or why not?

INTERNET ACTIVITY

4. Many cities around the United States are "going green." In what ways has a city near you made efforts to protect the environment? Use the Internet to research environmentally-friendly efforts such as recycling, alternative fuel use, or green building projects that are going on in a community near you. Write a short report that summarizes your findings.

Reviewing Vocabulary

Fill in each blank with the term that correctly completes the sentence.

5. The area of sociology devoted to the study of human populations is called ________.

6. The ________ is the measure most demographers use to describe the deaths in a population.

7. Because population growth follows a geometric progression, ________ predicted that the population would soon reach astronomical numbers.

8. ________ is one strategy that has been used to lower the birthrate in some countries.

9. A permanent concentration of a relatively large number of people who are engaged in nonfarming activities is called a(n) ________.

10. ________ is a situation in which more people live in a city than can be supported in terms of jobs and facilities.

11. Sociologists developed an approach called ________, which examines the relationship between people and the urban environment.

12. A(n) ________, is a representation or simulation of an object or a theory.

13. The ________ states that the city is an anonymous and unfriendly place and that living there carries serious negative consequences.

Sociology in Your Life

14. Go to the U.S. Census Web site and search the "State and Metropolitan Area Data Book 2006" for population statistics for your state. What statistics show a change in population between the last two census years? How did the birthrate change? Write an essay analyzing how the population of your state has changed and how that has led to changes in society.

SKILLS ACTIVITY: INTERPRETING GRAPHS

Study the graph below. Then use the information to help you answer the questions that follow.

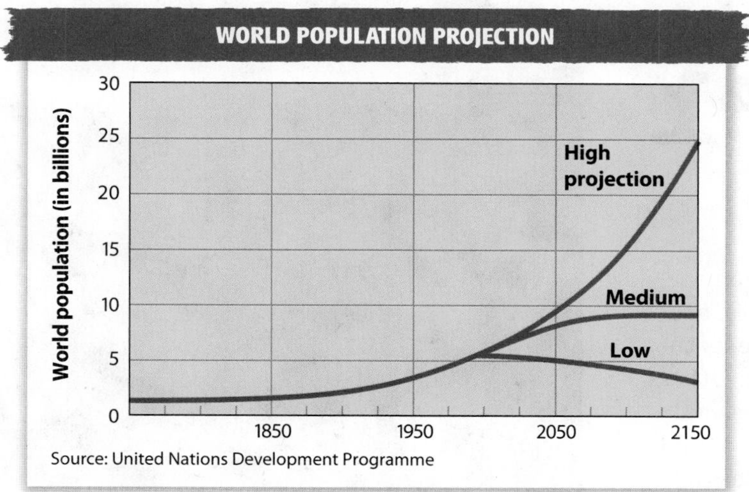

15. Identify What is the approximate medium population projection for the year 2150?

16. Analyze Looking at the high projection, how much is the world population projected to grow between the year 2050 and 2150?

17. Predict Which projection do you think most accurately predicts future population patterns? Why?

WRITING FOR SOCIOLOGY

Use your knowledge of population change, urban life, and urban ecology to answer the question below. Do not simply list facts. Present a clear argument based on your critical analysis of the question using appropriate sociological terminology.

18. Briefly describe each of the terms below from a sociological perspective. For each term, include a general description and a review of major characteristics and trends. Then use real-world examples to help explain the term within the context of American society.

- migration
- urbanization
- compositional theory

Connecting Online

Go online for review and enrichment activities related to this chapter.

KEY TOPICS VIDEOS
View compelling clips on issues in the field.

KEEP IT CURRENT
Link to the Current Events site for regularly updated stories on sociology as well as other social studies topics.

QUICK LAB
Reinforce a key concept with a short lab activity.

CASE STUDY

Why Social Movements Matter

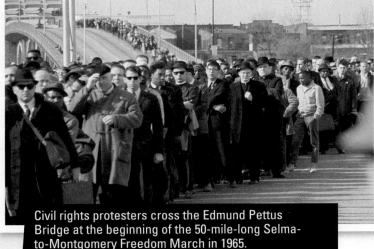

Civil rights protesters cross the Edmund Pettus Bridge at the beginning of the 50-mile-long Selma-to-Montgomery Freedom March in 1965.

Do social movements matter? Some people, especially social activists, are too ready to claim every change as the result of some social movement. Others are rather too quick to dismiss social movements, saying that change would have come with or without protest and activism. Sociological analysis on the subject tends to provide a more balanced picture. As sociologist David S. Meyer notes, social movements "crest and wane, often failing to attain their immediate goals, but they can lastingly change political debates, governmental institutions and the wider culture." The civil rights movement in the United States provides an illustration of this.

In the mid-1900s, African Americans were treated as second-class citizens throughout much of the southern United States. De jure and de facto segregation limited where African Americans could live, go to school, sit on buses, and eat lunch. Furthermore, African Americans were denied the right to vote. A civil rights movement grew in response to this situation. Civil rights lawyers took the fight to the courtroom, challenging the constitutionality of segregation laws. Movement members—both black and white—staged boycotts, marches, and demonstrations to publicize the plight of African Americans. Authorities sometimes reacted violently to these actions, beating and imprisoning the marchers and demonstrators. Television pictures of such police responses helped to create a groundswell of national support for the civil rights movement.

Responding to public pressure, Congress began to chip away at the foundations of segregation by passing a number of civil rights laws. But how successful was the civil rights movement in attaining its goals? In the 1990s, historian Robert Weisbrot reviewed the movement's record.

> *Like other reform movements the crusade for racial justice inevitably fell short of the utopian goals that sustained it. Still, if America's civil rights movement is to be judged by the distance it traveled rather than by the barriers yet to be crossed, a record of substantial achievement unfolds. In communities throughout the South, 'whites only' signs . . . came down from hotels, rest rooms, theaters, and other facilities. Blacks and whites . . . are apt to lunch together at fast-food shops that once drew blacks only for sit-ins. Integration extends equally to Southern workers, whether at diner coun-*

ters or in the high-rise office buildings that now afford every Southern city a skyline.

School desegregation also quickened its pace. . . . Swelling private school enrollments have tarnished but not substantially reversed this achievement. . . .

Protection of voting rights represents the movement's most unalloyed success, more than doubling the black voter registration . . . in the seven states covered by the 1965 [Voting Rights] Act. Winning the vote literally changed the complexion of government service in the South. . . . Mississippi experienced the most radical change, registering 74 percent of its voting-age blacks and leading the nation in the number of elected black officials.

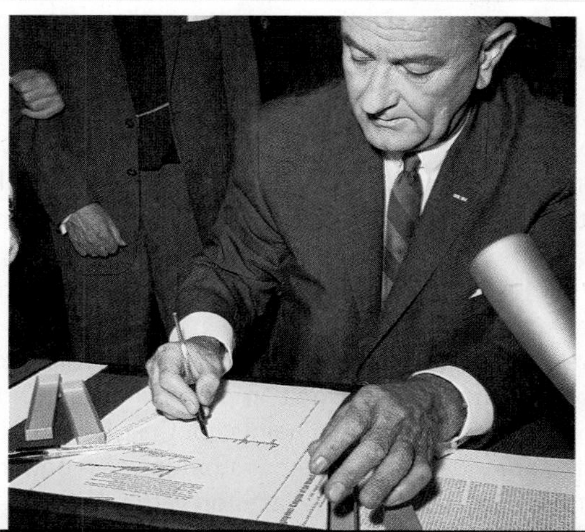

President Lyndon Johnson signs the Voting Rights Act on August 6, 1965.

What do you think?

1. What achievements of the civil rights movement does Weisbrot note?
2. Do you think that David S. Meyer's statement about the power of social movements applies to the civil rights movement ? Why or why not?

CHAPTER 16

COLLECTIVE BEHAVIOR AND SOCIAL CHANGE

Chapter at a Glance

SECTION 1: Collective Behavior

- Collective behavior is the relatively spontaneous social behavior that occurs when people try to develop common solutions to unclear situations. It can be divided into three broad categories: crowds, collective preoccupations, and public opinion.
- Explanations offered for collective behavior include contagion theory, emergent-norm theory, and value-added theory.

SECTION 2: Social Movements

- A social movement is a long-term conscious effort to promote or prevent social change. Sociologists have identified four stages in the life cycle of social movements: agitation, legitimation, bureaucratization, and institutionalization.
- Explanations for the development of social movements include relative deprivation theory and resource-mobilization theory.

SECTION 3: Social Change

- The major factors that stimulate social change are values and beliefs, technology, diffusion, population, the physical environment, and wars and conquests.
- Ethnocentrism, cultural lag, and vested interests all create resistance to social change.

SECTION 4: Theories of Social Change

- The functionalist perspective offers three explanations of social change. Cyclical theory suggests that societies arise, go through various stages of development, then decline. Evolutionary theory holds that societies develop toward increasing complexity. Equilibrium theory holds that change occurs in an effort to maintain social stability.
- From the conflict perspective, change is the result of conflict inherent in society.

SECTION 5: Modernization

- Modernization is the process by which a society's social institutions become more complex.
- Sociologists offer two explanations for this process: modernization theory and world-system theory.

SECTION 1

Collective Behavior

Before You Read

Main Idea
Collective behavior is divided into three broad categories: crowds, collective preoccupations, and public opinion. Sociologists offer three explanations for collective behavior: contagion theory, emergent-norm theory, and value-added theory.

Reading Focus
1. How do sociologists define collective behavior?
2. What kinds of collective behavior do crowds exhibit?
3. What do collective preoccupations involve?
4. How do politicians, businesses, and interest groups try to influence public opinion?
5. What theories have been offered to explain collective behavior?

Vocabulary
collective behavior
crowd
mob
riot
panic
mass hysteria
collective preoccupations
public opinion

TAKING NOTES Use a graphic organizer like this one to take notes about collective behavior.

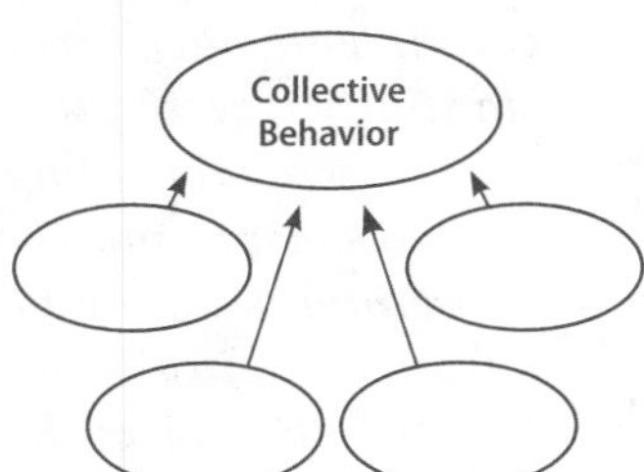

Flash MOB!

SOCIOLOGY CLOSE UP ***What in the world is going on?*** You're downtown waiting to take the bus home. Across the street in front of the art museum you notice a group of people gathering. They are all carrying large plastic bags. Suddenly, they pull pillows from the bags and start a pillow fight. After about five minutes of thrashing and bashing, they stop, put the pillows back in the bags, and disperse. You've just experienced a flash mob—so called because they gather and disperse in a flash.

A flash mob is a group of strangers organized through electronic media to gather at a set place, behave in a set way, and then leave. No one is sure where or when flash mobs began, but in a very short time they were everywhere. On March 22, 2008, for example, flash mob pillow fights took place in more than 25 cities around the world.

What is the purpose of flash mobs? For most people, they are just an excuse to have fun. Because of this, most observers consider flash mobs little more than a fad. However, communications professor Howard Rheingold suggests that they are of great importance. Preferring the term *smart mob,* Rheingold points out that they have been used to organize political demonstrations, to monitor elections, and to organize relief efforts after disasters. ■

A flash mob starts a pillow fight outside St. Paul's Cathedral in London.

Defining Collective Behavior

In general, social behavior is patterned and predictable. People expect others to act in accord with established norms, and usually they do. Sometimes, however, situations occur in which the norms of behavior are unclear. Often in these situations, it appears as though people are making up new norms as they go along. Sociologists refer to this action as **collective behavior**—the relatively spontaneous social behavior that occurs when people try to develop common solutions to unclear situations.

Social scientists have generally found collective behavior to be a difficult topic to study. For one thing, the range of material covered under collective behavior is enormous, including such varied phenomena as lynch mobs, fads, and rumors. Each of these types of collective behavior takes a different form and has different consequences. Collective behavior is also difficult to study because it is relatively short-lived, spontaneous, and emotional. Adding to the problem is the fact that collective behavior usually involves large numbers of people who do not know one another. Because episodes of collective behavior are not enduring aspects of society, it is difficult to subject them to systematic scientific study.

Although collective behavior has always been a fundamental fact of human existence, sociologists in the United States have been systematically studying this type of behavior for little more than a couple of decades. The knowledge they have amassed adds an important dimension to the overall analysis of society. Sociologists call groups that exhibit collective behavior *collectivities*. Generally, three factors distinguish collectivities from social groups. Unlike members of groups, members of collectivities have limited interaction with one another and do not share clearly defined, conventional norms or a sense of group unity.

Collective behavior and the collectivities in which it occurs take many forms. Sociologists identify a wide range of collective behaviors, including crowds, mobs, riots, panics, mass hysteria, crazes, fashions, fads, rumors, urban legends, and public opinion.

Reading Check **Contrast** How do collectivities differ from groups?

GROUPS AND COLLECTIVITIES (QUICK FACTS)

Groups	Collectivities
Members interact directly, often for long periods of time.	Members rarely, if ever, interact directly.
Members share clearly defined and widely understood norms.	Members do not share clearly defined, conventional norms.
Members are united by an awareness of belonging to the group.	Members rarely share a sense of group unity.

Crowds

A **crowd** is a temporary gathering of people who are in close enough proximity to interact. Sociologist Herbert Blumer separated crowds into four classifications: casual, conventional, expressive, and acting.

A *casual crowd* forms spontaneously because some event captures people's attention. It is the least organized and most temporary type of crowd. The people in a casual crowd interact little, if at all. Examples of casual crowds include people waiting in line to buy movie tickets or people watching a street performer.

Behavior in a *conventional crowd* is much more structured than in a casual crowd. People may not interact with one another very much, but they act according to established rules of behavior. Usually they have gathered for a common purpose, such as a religious service, a public lecture, or a baseball game.

An *expressive crowd* has no apparent goal or purpose. This type of crowd forms around emotionally charged activities such as rock concerts, holiday celebrations, or the funeral of a public figure. Laughing, shouting, crying, dancing, cheering, and other behaviors that are common in expressive crowds would be considered inappropriate in many other social situations.

An *acting crowd* is a violent crowd. The emotions that typify an acting crowd are much more intense than those found in an expressive crowd. The emotions are usually hostile and destructive and generally focus on one particular target. An acting crowd is often formed by a dramatic event and results in the violations of established norms.

Some sociologists have added a fifth classification—the protest crowd. While protest crowds sometimes exhibit characteristics of acting crowds, they tend to be better organized and longer lasting. Further, after the protests participants often continue to work together toward a goal.

Mobs and Riots The most violent form of an acting crowd is a **mob.** A mob is an emotionally charged collectivity whose members are united by a specific destructive or violent goal. This type of collectivity usually has leaders who urge the group toward the common action and who enforce conformity among the group's members. Although mobs are generally unstable and limited in duration, their actions represent a threat to social order and a challenge to official authority.

Riots are another violent type of acting crowd. A **riot** is a collection of people who erupt into generalized destructive behavior, the result of which is social disorder. Riots are less unified and less focused than are mobs. People who participate in riots typically lack access to power and so vent their frustrations through destructive actions. A riot often begins when long-standing tensions are triggered by a single event. Unlike mobs, riots end only when the participants exhaust themselves or when officials regain social control.

Panics Some crowd behavior is triggered not by violence but by fear. A **panic** is a spontaneous and uncoordinated group action to escape some perceived threat. Panics generally occur when people believe that their means of escape are limited or are about to be closed off. The fear of being trapped often results in faulty communication about the threat, which fuels the fear and keeps people from forming logical escape plans.

In a panic, mutual cooperation breaks down, and the norms that govern conventional behavior are lost. The panicky reactions of a group sometimes result in more damage than the damage produced by the threat itself. For example, in 1903 a fire broke out in Chicago's Iroquois Theater. Although the fire was quickly put out and actually did little damage to the building, more than 600 people were killed in their panic to reach the exits. Most of these people were smothered or trampled to death in the stampede.

Panics are most likely to occur in situations that are outside the realm of everyday experience, such as fires, floods, and earthquakes. Because few norms of behavior exist for such situations, the response is sometimes irrational and emotional. Occasionally, a panic is avoided when a leader emerges who can channel the behavior of the individuals involved and direct them toward logical action.

A moral panic occurs when people become fearful—often without reason—about behavior that appears to threaten society's core values. Mass media usually identify this behavior and cast it as a major social or moral crisis. Alarmed by the media warnings, the public and various institutions demand action to stamp out the behavior. For example, after several school shootings in the late 1990s, the media in the United States launched a moral panic against violent video games. The media's linking of these games with the shootings resulted in public calls for swift action. Politicians responded by introducing

The Acting Crowd

Herbert Blumer identified four stages in the development of an acting crowd: exciting event, milling behavior, common object, and common impulses. Fanatic supporters of European soccer teams provide a vivid illustration of this process. ***Identify another acting crowd and describe how it follows these four stages of development.***

1 Exciting Event Acting crowds are triggered by an exciting event. For the fanatic soccer crowd, the exciting event is the game. As the day of the game approaches, the event takes on such importance in the minds of supporters that they become completely preoccupied with it.

2 Milling Behavior In the hours before the game, supporters mill around talking about it. As they talk, they develop ideas on how they should think, feel, and act. As more supporters join the crowd, these ideas are reinforced. With the game drawing ever closer, the milling crowd becomes more agitated.

legislation that sought to control the content and sale of video games. Moral panics rarely last long. They are often replaced by another more current public concern.

Mass Hysteria Another form of crowd behavior formed by fear is **mass hysteria.** This is an unfounded anxiety shared by people who can be scattered over a wide geographic area. This anxiety involves irrational beliefs and behaviors that spread among the population. Sometimes this anxiety is unwittingly fueled by the media. Episodes of mass hysteria are usually short-lived, vanishing as people realize that their anxieties have no basis in fact.

One incidence of mass hysteria that had dramatic consequences occurred in 1692 in the Puritan community of Salem, Massachusetts. Tituba, a West Indian slave who lived in Salem, was thought to be skilled in black magic. A group of young girls from the community met regularly with Tituba to listen to her tell exciting and fantastic stories. A few girls in the group began to have strange and unexplainable convulsions, rolling and twisting on the ground as if possessed. Soon, many of the girls in the community were behaving in the same way. Hysteria spread quickly among the villagers, who feared that the girls had been bewitched.

Seeking the source of the bewitchment, Salem's clergy forced the girls to name the people responsible. At first, the girls named only Tituba and two other women as witches. Later, however, few people were safe from the girls' false accusations. The hysteria grew so fevered that friends and neighbors refused to help the accused for fear that they themselves would be branded as witches. Eventually, the girls' accusations were called into question. By that time, the Salem witch trials had resulted in the conviction and execution of 19 innocent people.

Reading Check **Identify Cause and Effect** What types of collective behavior result from violence and fear?

Collective Preoccupations

Collective preoccupations involve people who rarely meet, let alone interact, yet engage in similar behavior and share an understanding of the meaning of that behavior. Typically, they begin with a small group of people and spread to a wider audience through the media or social networks. Fashions, fads, rumors, and urban legends are all examples of collective preoccupations.

Fashions and Fads Fashions refer to enthusiastic attachments among large numbers of people for particular styles of appearance or behavior. Most fashions are related to clothing, but any cultural artifact that gains widespread acceptance can be a fashion. Typically, fashions are short-lived and are subject to continual change.

Fashions are generally identified with modern industrialized societies. In most preindustrial societies, nearly everyone of the same sex and age dresses alike. Styles of clothing in those societies change little, if at all, over the years.

3 Common Object During the game crowd members get caught up in the collective excitement and become fixated on some aspect of the event. Perhaps their team is playing badly, and opposing supporters are taunting them. Conversely, their team is winning, and they taunt opposing supporters.

4 Common Impulses At some point during or after the game, crowd members begin to sense that they agree on what action to take. This common impulse—to attack opposing supporters, perhaps—is stimulated and intensified by a sense of excitement that spreads through the crowd like a contagious disease.

The Acting Crowd This social contagion results in the loss of individual control and the abandonment of accepted social norms. The "infected" individuals act on the common impulse spontaneously. The violent behavior tends to continue until the police regain control.

In industrialized societies, on the other hand, fashions change rapidly. Fashions are prominent in industrialized societies for two reasons. First, change is valued and associated with progress in such societies. For example, in the United States the term *old-fashioned* generally carries a negative meaning. However, the terms *new* and *improved* often bring approval. Second, industrialized societies typically emphasize social mobility. Thus, they give people more opportunities to take on new social statuses and the symbols of these statuses, such as automobiles, clothing, homes, adornments, and points of view.

Fads are somewhat similar to fashions. A fad is an unconventional object, action, or idea that a large number of people are attached to for a very short period of time. Fads differ from fashions in that they are less predictable and less enduring. People who embrace fads are sometimes seen as frivolous by the majority of the population. Sociologist John Lofland divided fads into four groups: objects, activities, ideas, and personalities. Object fads include such items as hula hoops, Pet Rocks, mood rings, Beanie Babies, and Tamagotchi. Activity fads are often bizarre—such as swallowing live goldfish, crowding into telephone booths, and eating lightbulbs. Attempting to see the future through horoscopes is an idea fad whose popularity comes and goes. Justin Timberlake, Beyoncé, and LeBron James have all been the subject of personality fads.

Fads appeal primarily to young people, who participate in them mainly as a way to assert their personal identities. Fads often die out when they become uninteresting to the general public or so widespread that they cease to bring special notice to the participants.

Rumors and Urban Legends All collective preoccupations rely on communication among the participants. Some consist solely of communication. For example, a rumor is an unverified piece of information that is spread rapidly from one person to another. Rumors, which may be true or false, thrive when large numbers of people lack definite information about a subject of interest.

The content of a rumor is likely to change over time as it passes from person to person. Each person evaluates the truth of the rumor and, when transmitting it, may emphasize some aspects of the rumor and eliminate others. The changes that the rumor goes through as it circulates among people reflect each person's hopes, fears, and biases about the information. Rumors are generally difficult to control, and some may persist for years. Once a rumor begins, the number of people who are aware of it increases dramatically as each individual spreads the rumor to several others. Rumors typically end only when substantiated evidence is widely provided. Even then, some people continue to believe the rumor.

One of the stranger rumors involves Paul McCartney of the Beatles. In the late 1960s several college newspapers reported that McCartney had been killed in an automobile accident and that the band had replaced him with a look-alike. As the story spread, supporting evidence was added. Album-cover photographs supposedly provided clues. In one, McCartney is shown wearing a patch with the initials *O.P.D.,* which supposedly stands for "officially pronounced dead." In another, McCartney is shown barefoot—imagined to be the sign of a corpse. Some rumors suggested that a few of the Beatles' songs contained hidden messages when played backwards. Various members of the band can supposedly be heard singing such things as "Turn me on, Dead Man," and "Paul is dead, miss him." Despite strong denials from McCartney and other band members, people continued to repeat the story. Even today, some 50 years after the rumor started, the story that McCartney is actually a talented look-alike named William Campbell is still being spread.

Urban legends are another collective preoccupation based on communication. Urban legends are stories that teach a lesson and seem realistic but are untrue. Like rumors, urban legends arise and spread because of unclear situations. They seem realistic because they are usually attributed to specific times and places and are sometimes said to have happened to someone known to the storyteller. The stories quickly become a sort of urban folklore, the purpose of which is to clarify situations by teaching moral lessons.

One typical urban legend called "The Boyfriend's Death" tells the story of a boy and his date who park their car off a secluded road. After spending some time there, the girl says that she needs to go home. However, the car will not start. After telling the girl to lock herself in the car, the boy starts out for a nearby motel, where he plans to call for help. Much time goes by, but the boy does not return. Eventually, the girl hears a scratching noise on the roof of the car. Too afraid to investigate the sound, she stays in the car all night long. At daylight, some people come by and help the girl out of the car. She looks up to find that her boyfriend is hanging from the tree and that his shoes have been scraping the roof of the car.

This story appears in many versions in many places, but the moral of the tale is always the same—teenagers should not park in secluded places. This story also represents the uneasiness parents feel about the freedom that automobiles give to teenagers. Other unclear situations, such as hitchhiking and teenage sexuality, also provoke the growth and spread of urban legends.

Reading Check **Find the Main Idea** What are collective preoccupations, and how do they spread?

Public Opinion

Another form of collective behavior that depends mainly on communication is public opinion. Although it is common to refer to everyone in a society as the public, social scientists reserve that term for a group of geographically scattered people who are concerned with or engaged in a particular issue. Therefore, societies actually contain many publics because there is a different public for each social issue. The public for each single issue changes as people gain or lose interest in it. The interest that a public has in an issue takes the form of attitudes, or opinions, concerning the issue.

Public opinion, then, refers to the collection of differing attitudes that members of a public have about a particular issue. Public opinion is subject to rapid change because members of a public very often change their views on issues. Nevertheless, democratic capitalist countries such as the United States pay an enormous amount of attention to public opinion. People seeking elected office depend on public-opinion polls to identify important political issues. Businesses use market research and analysis to identify consumer demands.

Types of Collective Behavior

Collective behavior is the relatively spontaneous social behavior that occurs when people try to develop common solutions to unclear situations. There are three broad categories of collective behavior: crowds, collective preoccupations, and public opinion.

Crowds A crowd is a temporary gathering of people who are in close enough proximity to interact. This crowd is responding to the emotionally charged atmosphere of a rock concert.

Collective Preoccupations Collective preoccupations involve people who exhibit similar behavior and share understandings of what that behavior means. Fashions, such as the black clothing of the Goth subculture, are a form of collective preoccupation.

Public Opinion Public opinion refers to the differing attitudes that the public has about an issue. Sometimes the viewing public is asked to express its opinion on participants in television talent contests by casting votes.

Public opinion has such an important place in American society that politicians, interest groups, and businesses spend billions of dollars each year to influence it. Propaganda is the most effective way to influence what people think. Although this term is usually thought of in a negative way, propaganda does not necessarily contain only false information. Like rumors, propaganda may be true, partly true, or false. However, the intent of propaganda is always the same—to shape the opinions of a public toward some specific conclusion.

ACADEMIC VOCABULARY
propaganda organized and deliberate attempt to shape public opinion

A democratic country such as the United States depends on citizens who can make wise, informed decisions both when they cast their votes and when they make their purchases. Thus, it is important for people to be alert to the techniques that propagandists use to sway public opinion. Social scientists have identified seven such techniques: testimonials, transfer, bandwagon, name calling, plain-folks appeal, glittering generalities, and card stacking.

The testimonials technique refers to the use of endorsements by famous people to sell products or secure votes. Advertisers often use sports heroes to promote sports equipment or clothing. Also, famous actors are often enlisted to make speeches on behalf of politicians. The goal is to persuade people to transfer their admiration for a celebrity to the products or candidates endorsed by that celebrity.

The transfer technique is similar to testimonials in that it attempts to associate a product or candidate with something that the public approves of or respects. For example, advertisers might display their product with national symbols, such as the flag and historic monuments, suggesting that buying the product is patriotic. The transfer technique can also be used negatively by linking a competitor's product or an opposing candidate to something the public dislikes.

The bandwagon technique appeals to a public's desire to conform. For example, a politician or product may be promoted as the one already most popular with the public. This technique assumes that people want to be on the winning side of an election or to own what appear to be highly desirable products.

The name-calling technique refers to the use of negative labels or images in order to make competitors appear in an unfavorable light. For example, politicians may accuse their opponents of being reckless spenders or uncaring about the needs of the public. The aim of this technique is to persuade the public to associate the politician or the product with the unfavorable label.

The plain-folks appeal attempts to sway public opinion by appealing to the average American. Thus, a politician may be portrayed as a hard-working American who just wants to do good. Similarly, average Americans with whom everyone can identify may be shown endorsing a product or candidate.

The glittering generalities technique refers to the use of words that sound positive but have little real meaning. For example, to say that a politician believes in freedom, democracy, and the American way sounds positive. However, it says little about the politician's views on important issues.

Quick Lab

Creating an Advertisement

How do advertisers use propaganda to sway public opinion and persuade consumers to buy products?

PROCEDURE

1. Come up with an imaginary product that is being introduced at your school. For example, it could be a new course, a new item on the cafeteria menu, or a candidate for the student council.
2. Use one of the seven propaganda techniques—testimonials, transfer, bandwagon, name calling, plain-folks appeal, glittering generalities, or card stacking—to create an advertisement to sell this product to your classmates.

ANALYSIS

1. Share your advertisement with your classmates.
2. Discuss why you chose to use the technique that you did. Was it the most effective technique for your product? How would your advertisement have been different if you had chosen another technique?
3. As a class, select the most effective advertisements. Discuss what makes them effective. What propaganda techniques do your selected advertisements employ?

Card stacking is the practice of presenting facts in a way that places politicians or products in a favorable light. For example, newspapers may give a great deal of attention to politicians they favor and little attention to those they do not. Similarly, advertisers may present statistics or survey results in a way that favors their products over those of their competitors.

Reading Check **Identify Supporting Details** What techniques are used to sway public opinion?

Explaining Collective Behavior

A number of theories have been proposed over the past century to explain collective behavior. These theories are most useful for explaining types of collective behavior in which people are in close proximity with one another, such as crowds, mobs, riots, and panics. Foremost among the theories of collective behavior are contagion theory, the emergent-norm theory, and the value-added theory.

Contagion Theory The French sociologist Gustave Le Bon developed the first systematic theory of collective behavior. According to his contagion theory, the hypnotic power of a crowd encourages people to give up their individuality to the stronger pull of the group. Individuals become anonymous, with no willpower or sense of responsibility. The crowd, in effect, becomes a single organism operating under one collective mind. In this situation, conventional social norms lose their meaning and, as emotion sweeps through the crowd, behavior becomes unrestrained.

According to Le Bon, three factors give crowds power over individuals. First, because of the sheer numbers of people in a crowd, individuals gain an anonymity that makes them feel unconquerable. Second, the spread of emotion is so rapid that it overtakes the members of a crowd like an epidemic. Third, members of a crowd rapidly enter a state of suggestibility, during which time they are not conscious of their actions. This suggestibility makes them particularly receptive to the manipulations of charismatic leaders.

Contagion theory has its limitations, however. Studies have shown no indication that a collective mind exists in crowds. Any number of motivations for behavior can be found among crowd participants. In addition, behavior in crowds is usually not as uniform as Le Bon suggested. Nonetheless, contagion theory is helpful in explaining how behavior spreads among crowd members, freeing them from the restraints of conventional social norms. This theory also provides insight into how emotions encourage people toward collective action.

Emergent-Norm Theory Sociologists Ralph Turner and Lewis Killian, rather than seeing crowd members as acting with one collective mind, acknowledged that the individuals in a crowd have different attitudes, behaviors, and motivations. They sought an explanation of crowd behavior in the social-control function of social norms.

According to their emergent-norm theory, the people in a crowd are often faced with a situation in which traditional norms of behavior do not apply. In effect, they find themselves with no clear standards for behavior. Through interaction, new norms gradually emerge when one or more leaders initiate new behaviors. These new norms then provide a common motivation for group action where none existed before. For example, when a film being shown in a movie theater breaks, one person may start stamping his or her feet. Even though this behavior does nothing to help fix the film, the action quickly spreads among the people in the theater. Even if individuals inwardly disagree with the action, they often feel obliged to conform to this newly emerged group norm. Crowd behavior therefore appears to be unanimous when, in fact, it may not be.

Value-Added Theory With his value-added theory, sociologist Neil Smelser attempted to predict if collective behavior would occur and the direction it might take. Smelser borrowed the value-added concept from economics. In the production process, which transforms raw materials into finished products, each step adds value. Each step is necessary for the addition of value in the next step. As the process moves forward, the range of possibilities narrows, limiting what the finished product might become.

In applying the value-added concept, Smelser compared the production process to the way collective behavior develops. He identified six preconditions for collective behavior.

These are structural conduciveness, structural strain, growth and spread of a generalized belief, precipitating factors, mobilization for action, and social control. These preconditions build on one another, and each one is necessary for the next to occur. The more preconditions that are present, the greater the likelihood of a particular type of collective behavior. Applying the six preconditions to the Los Angeles riots of 1992 offers a real-life illustration of Smelser's theory.

Structural conduciveness refers to the surrounding social structure that makes it possible for a particular type of collective behavior to occur. For example, in 1991 a bystander videotaped the beating of Rodney King, an African American, by four white Los Angeles police officers. The four officers faced charges in a well-publicized trial. The acquittal of the police officers ignited three days of rioting in South Central Los Angeles, leaving more than 50 people dead and some 2,300 injured. The repeated broadcast of the videotape and the intense media coverage of the trial fueled the conditions for this collective behavior.

Structural strain refers to social conditions that put strain on people and thus encourage them to seek collective means of relief. Structural strain can be produced by poverty, overcrowding, discrimination, and conflict. At the time of the trial, these conditions were present in the predominantly African American area of South Central Los Angeles. The growth of a generalized belief makes the structural strain personally meaningful for people. Individuals begin to identify the problem, form opinions about it, and share ways of dealing with it. For example, in South Central Los Angeles, many residents strongly resented the police and hoped that the four officers would be found guilty. At the same time, many residents doubted that the all-white jury would return a fair verdict.

Precipitating factors, the fourth precondition for collective behavior, refer to triggering mechanisms that set off the behavior. These factors are usually quite dramatic and confirm the generalized belief. The confirming evidence then adds to the structural strain felt by people. In the case of the Los Angeles riots, the news that the jury had found the white officers not guilty provided this triggering mechanism.

The first four preconditions in the sequence of collective behavior set the stage for people to act. When the Los Angeles residents realized that community leaders could do nothing to change the verdict, many mobilized to express their collective anger and frustration through looting and random acts of destruction. By the time community leaders attempted to intervene, the rioting was out of control. At this point in the sequence, collective behavior can be controlled if mechanisms exist to prevent or minimize the situation. In the case of the Los Angeles riots, the governor of California called in the National Guard and the mayor imposed a curfew. In addition, President George H.W. Bush sent in federal troops. These actions helped end the riots.

Reading Check **Contrast** How do the three theories differ in how they explain collective behavior?

SECTION 1 Assessment

Reviewing Main Ideas and Vocabulary

1. **Define** What is collective behavior?
2. **Contrast** How are mobs different from riots?
3. **Identify** What are collective preoccupations? Illustrate your answer with examples.

Thinking Critically

4. **Draw Conclusions** Why do you think sociologists have difficulty studying collective behavior?
5. **Make Judgments** What impact do you think the electronic media will have on the spread of collective preoccupations? Give reasons for your answer.
6. **Elaborate** Using your notes and a graphic organizer like the one here, describe how a riot or mob situation might develop based on Smelser's preconditions for collective behavior.

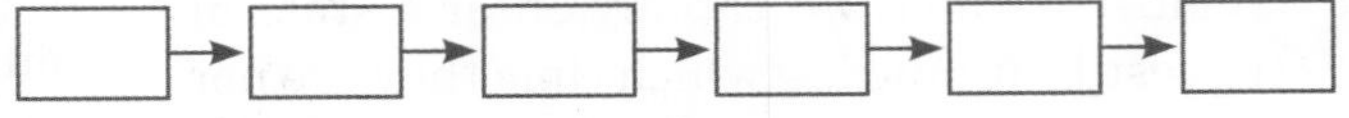

FOCUS ON WRITING

7. **Expository** Identify a specific panic, mass hysteria, fad, fashion, rumor, or urban legend. Write a paragraph noting which theory discussed in the section you think best explains this type of collective behavior. Explain your choice of theory.

Responding to Terrorism

On the morning of September 11, 2001, terrorists launched attacks on New York and Washington, D.C. Although deeply shocked by these horrendous actions, Americans immediately came together in a collective response. For example, there was strong agreement on how the government should respond to the attacks. As time has passed, however, American attitudes toward terrorism and the appropriate reaction to terrorist acts such as 9/11 have shifted somewhat.

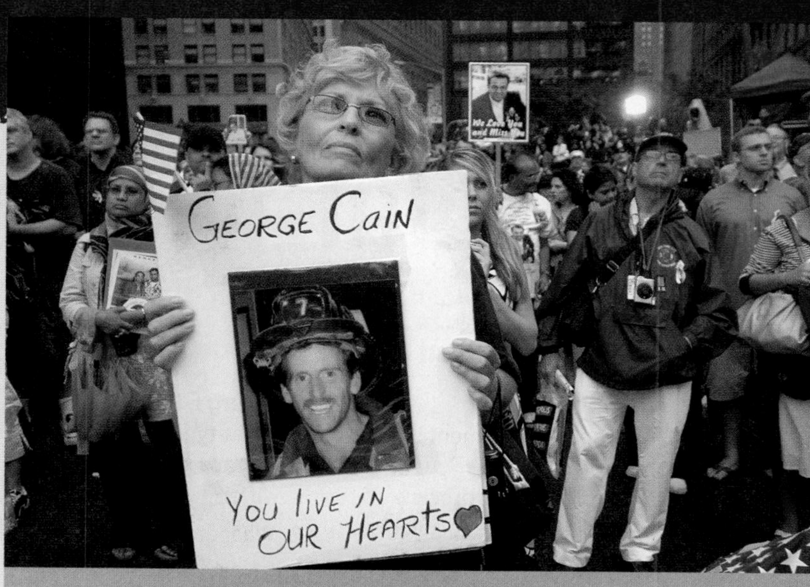

A woman holds a photograph of a victim of the 9/11 terrorist attacks during a 2007 commemoration ceremony held in New York City.

Early Response In the aftermath of the attacks, Americans showed considerable commonality in their attitudes. For most Americans, the initial response was shock and anger. After a short time, many—about 75 percent—began to express anxiety over further attacks. More than half stated that their personal sense of security had been shaken. Furthermore, nearly three-quarters said that they felt depressed, half said that they had trouble concentrating at work, and a third admitted that they had difficulty sleeping. Over time, however, these feelings of anxiety declined.

A vast majority of Americans also felt that 9/11 had changed the country in a lasting way. Many Americans found hope in how the country showed a spirit of unity in its response to the attacks. More than 60 percent said this unity made the country stronger. Moreover, nearly 40 percent said that what they had gone through since the attacks had changed them personally and made them better Americans.

Attitudes on how the country should respond to terrorism also showed considerable unity. A large majority favored giving the police and security services greater powers, even though these powers might adversely affect civil liberties.

Most Americans strongly supported taking military action against the ruling regime of Afghanistan, which had aided al-Qaeda, the terrorist group that carried out the attacks. Most Americans stated a belief that the war on terrorism would be a long one and would take resources away from other important programs. However, about half said that stamping out terrorism was worth this expense. Many Americans also expressed a greater trust in the U.S. government after September 11.

Later Response In 2003, President George W. Bush widened the war on terrorism by invading Iraq, which he charged was a terrorist nation. Initially there was strong support for the president's action. In the months immediately after the invasion of Iraq, some 70 percent of Americans approved of his handling of the war on terror (CBS News, 2007). However, with a growing death toll among American soldiers in Iraq, support plummeted. By late 2007, only about 40 percent approved of the management of the war on terror.

Americans also expressed doubts about the effectiveness of the war on terror. About 53 percent opposed sending ground troops to Iraq and Syria to assist groups that are fighting Islamic militants (Gallup, 2016). Others worried that some actions, particularly the war in Iraq, had made the United States more vulnerable to terrorism (CBS News). And while many said that they felt less concerned about an imminent terrorist attack, 44 percent were not confident the government could protect them from future acts of terrorism (Gallup, 2015). So, while terrorism continues to be a concern, Americans seem to be less certain on how to respond.

Thinking Critically

1. **Contrast** How have American attitudes to the war on terror changed?
2. **Discuss** Do you think changes in the United States since 9/11 have been positive? Why or why not?

SECTION 2

Social Movements

Before You Read

Main Idea

A social movement is a long-term conscious effort to promote or prevent social change. Sociologists have identified four stages in the life cycle of social movements: agitation, legitimation, bureaucratization, and institutionalization.

Reading Focus

1. What types of social movements exist, and how do they differ?
2. What are the stages of the life cycle of social movements?
3. How do sociologists explain the existence of social movements?

Vocabulary

social change
social movement
reactionary movement
conservative movement
revisionary movement
revolutionary movement
resource mobilization

TAKING NOTES Use a graphic organizer like this one to take notes on social movements.

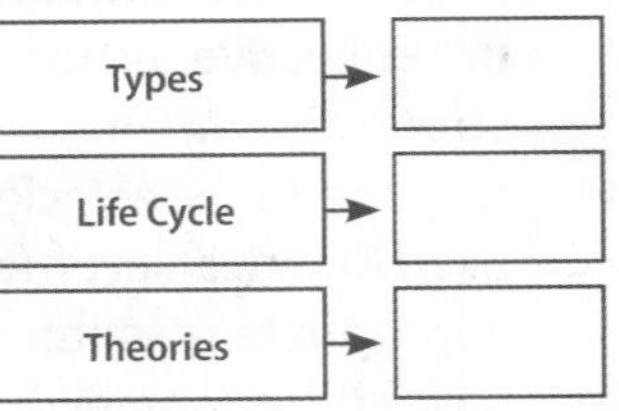

Going Green

Two environmentalists make a point about global warming by dressing as penguins.

SOCIOLOGY CLOSE UP ***How do social movements arise and flourish?*** Environmentalism—the idea that the environment should be protected—has been alive in the United States for a long time. Henry David Thoreau wrote about it extensively in the mid-1800s. However, a well-organized environmental movement did not develop until more than 100 years after Thoreau's death.

From the late 1800s to the mid-1900s, the United States grew into a great industrial power. But the process of industrialization took a huge toll on the environment. By the 1960s, the situation was so bad that some Americans decided to take action. Rachel Carson's book, *Silent Spring* (1962)—which dealt with the dangers of pesticides—forced people to focus on environmental issues. Later, annual Earth Day celebrations heightened environmental awareness. Growing concern among the American public led to government action. During the 1970s, some 35 environmental laws were enacted, covering everything from conserving energy resources to controlling auto emissions.

Other green, or environmental, issues—nuclear safety and global warming, for example—have kept interest in the movement high. Another reason for the continued health of the movement is its approach. While the movement's issues are global, it urges members to "act locally." So, anyone who recycles cans and bottles or walks instead of driving can feel involved. ■

Types of Social Movements

The types of collectivities discussed in the previous section are generally short-lived. Also, while some of these collectivities may bring **social change,** or alterations in various aspects of society over time, they rarely have a serious effect on society as a whole. Social movements, however, are much more deliberate and long-lasting forms of collective behavior. A **social movement** may be defined as a long-term conscious effort to promote or prevent social change. Social movements may develop around any issue of public concern.

Three factors distinguish social movements from other forms of collective behavior. First, social movements are long-lasting. Second, they possess a highly structured organization with formally recognized leaders. Finally, social movements make a deliberate attempt to institute or block societal change. These factors combine to give social movements the potential to attract memberships that number in the millions.

The goal of most social movements is to change society. However, they differ in the amount of change they seek. Sociologist William Bruce Cameron identified four types of social movements based on the level of change sought. These are reactionary movements, conservative movements, revisionary movements, and revolutionary movements.

Reactionary Movements The main goal of a **reactionary movement** is to reverse current social trends—essentially to "turn back the clock." The members of a reactionary movement are suspicious of and hostile toward social change. They want to return society to the way they believe it existed in the past. For example, the Ku Klux Klan is a reactionary movement that wants to reimpose the system of racial segregation that existed before the passage of civil rights laws in the mid-1900s. The Ku Klux Klan, like other reactionary movements, has often used fear and violence in support of its cause.

Conservative Movements The members of a **conservative movement** try to protect what they see as society's prevailing values from change that they consider to be a threat to those values. For example, the religious right seeks to uphold what it views as traditional family and social values. To do that, the religious right has launched political campaigns to elect candidates who support its views and to defeat candidates who oppose them. The religious right has also organized boycotts of television networks that show "antifamily values" programs and of companies that support such programming with advertising.

Revisionary Movements Improving, or revising, some part of society through social change is the goal of a **revisionary movement.** Revisionary movements usually use legal channels to seek change because they generally support the existing social system as a whole. This type of movement typically focuses on a single issue. For example, the women's suffrage movement of the early 1900s attempted to reform laws that prevented women from voting. The members of the women's suffrage movement used political campaigns, political lobbyists, and the courts to seek reform.

CASE STUDY CONNECTION

Why Social Movements Matter The civil rights movement was a revisionary movement because it used mostly legal methods to end discrimination against African Americans.

Revolutionary Movements The main goal of a **revolutionary movement** is a total and radical change of the existing social structure. The ultimate aim of revolutionary movements is to overthrow the existing government and to replace it with their own version of how a government should work. Revolutionary movements involve violent or illegal actions and can sometimes result in drastic and widespread social change. This type of movement usually arises when people see no chance for reform to occur. Examples of revolutionary movements include the American Revolution, the Bolshevik Revolution in Russia, and Fidel Castro's revolution in Cuba.

Reading Check **Contrast** How do the four types of social movements differ in terms of the level of social change they seek?

Life Cycle of Social Movements

Although social movements differ in the goals they hope to attain, successful movements appear to have certain characteristics in common. Many of these movements proceed through a series of stages that eventually lead to their acceptance by society. Sociologists Malcolm Spector and John Kitsuse identified four stages in the life cycle of social movements: agitation, legitimation, bureaucratization, and institutionalization.

Agitation Social movements typically emerge out of the belief that a problem exists and that solutions need to be found. In this early stage of the life cycle, a small group of people with a strong commitment to the cause attempts to stir up public awareness of the problem. This agitation, they hope, will garner widespread support for the social movement. More often than not, potential social movements die out at this point. Either they fail to gain meaningful support for their cause or they lack the resources to continue their agitation efforts.

Legitimation Movements that do find support for their concerns enter the legitimation stage of the life cycle. In this stage, the social movement becomes more respectable as it gains increasing acceptance among the population. The leaders of the movement, who were previously dismissed as cranks, are now seen as legitimate spokespeople of a just cause. Governmental or other authorities also begin to recognize the movement's concerns as legitimate.

At this point, the movement often attracts media attention, which in turn serves to bring the movement's goals to the notice of increasing numbers of people. Demonstrations and rallies add to the visibility of the movement. Commitment to the cause remains high, particularly among new members.

Bureaucratization As the organizational structure of the movement becomes more formal, it enters the third stage of the life cycle—bureaucratization. At this point, the movement has developed a ranked structure of authority, official policies, and efficient strategies for the future. The original goals of the movement are sometimes swept aside during this stage because increasing amounts of time and energy are needed to handle the day-to-day running of the organization.

Institutionalization In the final, or institutional stage, the movement has become an established part of society. Bureaucrats who oversee daily operations replace the idealistic leaders who helped found the movement. Often these bureaucrats care more about their position in the organization than about the goals of the movement. As a result, the movement frequently resists proposals for change. Many members, feeling that the movement has abandoned its original cause, drift away. As membership dwindles, the movement goes into decline.

Reading Check **Sequence** What are the stages in the life cycle of social movements?

Picketers march in support of a strike by the Writers Guild of America. The strike held up television and film production for several months in 2007 and 2008.

Life Cycle of the Labor Movement

The American labor movement, which had its beginnings in the late 1800s, provides an illustration of the life cycle of a social movement.

Agitation Low pay and harsh working conditions led many workers to seek support for unions that would protect employee interests.

Legitimation After many years of often violent confrontations between workers and management and after years of resistance from many segments of the population, labor unions received official governmental recognition.

Bureaucratization Over the years, labor unions grew in size and number. Today they are firmly established and are powerful organizations.

Institutionalization Labor unions are now so well established in society that they resist attempts to change their operating procedures, even though many of these procedures may not benefit the membership. Some members, feeling that labor unions no longer serve their needs, begin to leave.

Explaining Social Movements

Social scientists have proposed a number of theories to explain the existence of social movements. Psychological explanations were popular until about the 1960s. Gustave Le Bon offered one such explanation. He believed that only psychologically disturbed people would question the existing social order. Le Bon therefore viewed social movements as little more than irrational, moblike collectivities. Similar psychological theories hold that social movements are made up of people who have some kind of personality defect. According to these theories, people join movements as a way to hide from their personal problems and to satisfy their psychological needs for purpose and meaning.

Sociologists tend to reject the notion that people join social movements because something is wrong with them as individuals. Rather, sociologists look to problems in the social structure to explain the existence of social movements. The leading sociological explanations of the emergence of social movements are relative deprivation theory and resource-mobilization theory.

Relative Deprivation Theory One school of sociological thought suggests that social movements arise when large numbers of people feel economically or socially deprived of what they think they deserve. This deprivation is not measured in absolute terms but in comparison to the conditions of others or in comparison to what people expect society to provide. From the perspective of relative deprivation theory, people join social movements because they feel deprived relative to other people or groups with whom they identify. Through these social movements, people seek to gain access to things they lack but others have—such as higher incomes, better working and living conditions, and broader political rights.

Relative deprivation theory is often used to explain revolutionary social movements. Interestingly, Karl Marx used a similar argument to explain one of the causes of revolution. In *Wage-Labor and Capital,* Marx noted that capitalism might well give workers higher incomes and better living conditions. However, the workers' dissatisfaction will rise because the wealth of the capitalists will grow at an even greater rate. Marx used the example of houses to illustrate this point. A worker may live in a small house, Marx said. As long as all his neighbors live in small houses, he is content. However, if a palace arises in the neighborhood, the worker will feel "more uncomfortable, more dissatisfied, more cramped within his four walls."

Explaining the Women's Movement

"Two leading explanations of social movements are relative deprivation theory and resource-mobilization theory."

Relative deprivation theorists would explain the development of the women's movement by suggesting that women feel deprived relative to men, particularly in the areas of income and employment opportunities. The resource-mobilization theorist, on the other hand, would point to the movement's ability to garner resources such as money, people with specialized skills, and access to the media. ***What are the weaknesses of these two theories?***

Resource-Mobilization Theory Today most sociologists agree that feelings of deprivation alone are not sufficient to trigger social movements. Some level of deprivation is common among groups in all societies. Yet not all situations of deprivation lead people to organize into social movements.

Most contemporary sociologists believe that social movements can occur only if people are successful in **resource mobilization,** or the organization and effective use of resources. According to resource-mobilization theory, not even the most ill-treated group with the most just cause will be able to bring about change without resources. The resources necessary to generate a social movement include a body of supporters, financial resources, and access to the media.

The body of supporters must include talented people who have the time and skills necessary to work toward change. College students are particularly likely to support efforts for change because they have time and are well educated. College students were very active in the civil rights movement, organizing sit-ins and participating in demonstrations, marches, and voter registration drives in the South.

Leadership and organizational abilities are crucial to the ongoing success of a social movement. Leaders need administrative skills to carry out day-to-day tasks, such as fund-raising and recruitment. Further, leaders need to be strong negotiators in order to reach compromises among members who may differ over policies and goals. In addition, leaders must be charismatic and well-spoken so that others will be encouraged to join the movement.

ACADEMIC VOCABULARY

charismatic having a special charm or appeal that arouses loyalty or enthusiasm

In addition, social movements must be able to mobilize financial resources. Money is needed to print leaflets and posters, travel to demonstrations and rallies, rent meeting places, and hire press agents and lawyers. Legal defense is often needed to protect the legal rights of demonstrators who are arrested. Legal actions are also particularly helpful in bringing the concerns of the movement to the attention of the public. Some social movements spend a great deal of time and energy searching for and raising financial resources to support their causes.

Resource-mobilization theory emphasizes that successful social movements need to gain access to the media. Wide media coverage is the surest way to bring the movement to the attention of the most people possible. Media coverage, which in effect is free publicity, also serves to help movements reserve some of the finances they would normally spend on publicizing the movement.

While resource-mobilization theory helps explain how social movements get started and become successful, it has been criticized for minimizing the importance of deprivation and dissatisfaction. Some sociologists suggest that both deprivation and resource mobilization are necessary for the creation of social movements. People will not mobilize resources unless the perception arises that change is needed. Moreover, the move to make changes will not be successful unless the needed resources can be mobilized.

Reading Check **Summarize** What are the two major sociological theories on the development of social movements?

SECTION 2 Assessment

Reviewing Main Ideas and Vocabulary

1. **Define** What is social change?
2. **Contrast** How do social movements differ from other collectivities, such as crowds and collective preoccupations?
3. **Identify** What do sociologists mean by the term *resource mobilization?*

Thinking Critically

4. **Explain** How do the various types of social movements differ? Illustrate your answer with examples of each social movement.
5. **Elaborate** According to resource-mobilization theory, leadership is essential for the development of social movements. Explain how leadership can be successfully mobilized.
6. **Categorize** Using your notes and a graphic organizer like the one below, describe the life cycle of a social movement.

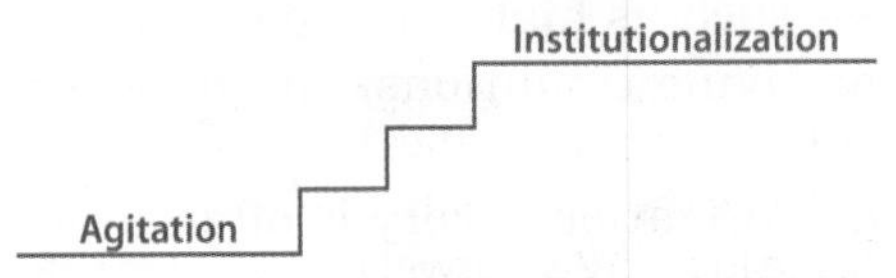

FOCUS ON WRITING

7. **Descriptive** Write two paragraphs describing how relative deprivation theory and resource mobilization theory would explain the rise of the civil rights movement in the United States.

SECTION 3

Social Change

Before You Read

Main Idea
The major factors that stimulate social change are values and beliefs, technology, diffusion, population, the physical environment, and wars and conquests. Ethnocentrism, cultural lag, and vested interests all create resistance to social change.

Reading Focus
1. What are the main sources of social change?
2. Why is there resistance to social change?

Vocabulary
ideology
technology
reformulation

TAKING NOTES Use a graphic organizer like this one to take notes on social change.

Social Change	
Sources of Change	Types of Resistance

Healthy Living

SOCIOLOGY CLOSE UP ***How do changes in values affect day-to-day life?***

In recent years, sociologists have traced the development of self-fulfillment as an important American value. One aspect of self-fulfillment is the desire to follow a healthy lifestyle. Since the early 1990s, the number of health clubs in the United States has more than doubled. So, too, has the number of people with health-club memberships—more than 50 million. Also, since 2000 the number of people who regularly do some type of fitness exercise has grown by nearly 40 percent.

The desire for a healthy lifestyle has begun to change the American diet. Since the late 1990s, the sales of organic food grew between 15 and 20 percent each year until 2007, after which they dropped to about 10 percent growth each year. Organic foods are grown without the use of chemicals, pesticides, or genetically altered seeds and are considered healthier for human consumption. Not only is organic food growing in popularity, so too is fresh, locally grown produce. The number of green, or farmers', markets—markets where farmers sell their products directly to consumers—is growing at the same rate as organic food sales. If, as a French writer suggested, you are what you eat, then Americans are getting healthier. ■

This farmers' market in San Francisco is one of more than 3,400 across the United States that provide city-dwellers access to locally grown fresh fruits and vegetables.

Sources of Social Change

The modern world changes rapidly. Each week brings new material goods, new styles of dress, new ways of doing things, and new ideas. What causes all of these changes? There are many factors that stimulate change, but the most important are values and beliefs, technology, diffusion, population, the physical environment, and wars and conquests.

Values and Beliefs As functionalist sociologists have noted, society is a system of interrelated parts. A change in one aspect of society produces change throughout the system. Changes in values and beliefs, therefore, can have far-reaching consequences for society. These consequences are particularly noticeable when new values and beliefs are part of a larger ideology. An **ideology** is a system of beliefs or ideas that justifies the social, moral, religious, political, or economic interests held by a group or by society.

Ideologies often are spread through social movements. As you recall, a social movement is a long-term conscious effort to promote or prevent social change. The consequences of shifts in ideology can be seen by examining how the social movement for civil rights changed politics in the United States. As recently as the 1950s, African Americans were forced to live as second-class citizens throughout the United States, particularly in the South. Laws limited where they could live, go to school, sit on buses, and eat lunch. Through legal and illegal means, African Americans were denied the right to vote or to hold public office. Civil rights supporters staged boycotts, marches, and demonstrations to publicize this situation. A surge of support for change soon developed. Responding to public pressure, Congress passed a number of civil rights laws, including the Voting Rights Act of 1965. This act outlawed the methods that had been used to deny African Americans the vote.

CASE STUDY CONNECTION

Why Social Movements Matter Sociologists consider the civil rights movement one of the most successful social movements, since it achieved many of its goals.

The changes brought about by the civil rights movement transformed the American political landscape. Today African Americans are a powerful group of voters. The number of African American elected officials has jumped from fewer than 1,500 in 1970 to more than 9,400 in the early 2000s. Nearly two-thirds of these officials hold offices in southern states.

Technology Social change also occurs when people find new ways to manipulate their environment. The knowledge and tools that people use to adjust and adapt their environment are called **technology.** Two ways that new technologies arise are through discovery and invention.

Discovery occurs when people recognize new uses for existing elements in the world or begin to understand them in new ways. Examples of discoveries include atomic fission, chewing gum, and oil shale. Oil shale was discovered by accident. Many stones along the banks of the Colorado River contain rock shale saturated with oil. According to one story, a man used these stones to construct a fireplace. When he lit a fire in the fireplace, the fireplace itself burst into flames! Regardless of how it was discovered, using oil shale as fuel provided new resources for America's growing industrial society.

Invention occurs when people use existing knowledge to create something that did not exist before. Inventions can take the form of material objects, ideas, or patterns of behavior. New tools, such as a gadget to take the pits out of cherries or a computer small enough to hold in your hand, are examples of material inventions. Examples of nonmaterial inventions include political and religious movements, hobbies, and business organizations.

Diffusion People often borrow cultural traits—ideas, beliefs, and material objects—from other societies. As you recall, this process of spreading culture from one society to another is called cultural diffusion. The more contact among societies, the greater the level of diffusion. Today, with mass transportation and instant communication, diffusion takes place constantly.

Generally, societies adopt material culture and technology more freely than ideas and beliefs. For example, most societies readily accept tools and weapons that are superior to their own. Societies often adapt the culture traits they borrow to suit their own particular needs. Many of the societies in Africa, Asia, and South America that adopted Christianity have blended Christian beliefs with elements of their traditional religions. Sociologists refer to this process of adapting borrowed cultural traits as **reformulation.**

Technology and Change

The Impact of the Automobile The invention of the automobile did more than furnish Americans with a new form of transportation. Over time, it also brought huge changes to American social life. To begin with, the automobile changed the country's human geography by making living in the suburbs much easier. Cars changed architecture, too, with houses with attached garages becoming the standard in home construction. In addition, cars affected the way people shopped, making huge suburban shopping malls and drive-through restaurants and banks possible. Finally, the automobile helped to create several new service industries, such as car repair, gas stations, and roadside motels.

Cultural diffusion is a two-way process. As a result of contact with other societies, Americans eat foods such as pasta from Italy, sushi from Japan, Mongolian barbecue, hummus from the Middle East, and baklava from Greece. At the same time, American movies, music, automobiles, farm machinery, soft drinks, and fast foods can be found in countries throughout the world.

Population A change in the size of the population may bring about changes in the culture. For example, the population of the United States has increased rapidly since the early 1900s. The arrival of new groups of people with their own unique cultural traits and values has influenced American culture. For example, foods brought to this country by immigrant groups—such as Mexicans, Chinese, and Italians—have become common in American kitchens.

Population increases and decreases affect the economy, too. By increasing the demand for goods and services, a growing population may increase employment and stimulate the economy. On the other hand, a community with a declining population may need fewer goods and services. As a result, there may be limited employment opportunities for the people who remain.

An increase in the general population also means that there are more people occupying the same amount of space, which creates more crowded conditions. In addition, the larger population brings increased demand for energy, food, housing, schools, stores, and transportation.

People bring about changes simply by moving from one place to another. When a family moves to a new community, change is stimulated both in the community the family leaves and in the new community it enters. Migrations of people within a country can cause social changes, such as the loss of regional distinction within the country.

Social and cultural changes also result from changes in the average age of a population. When fewer families are having babies, for example, there is less need for schools, recreation centers, and other services geared toward children. The need for specialized services geared toward elderly people, on the other hand, increases as more people live into old age.

The Physical Environment The environment provides conditions that may encourage or discourage social change. People in some societies wholly rely on foods that they can grow locally. Other societies must import much of their food or adapt new crops to grow in their area. The introduction of new foods or the scarcity of a familiar food can bring about cultural change.

Natural disasters such as droughts, floods, earthquakes, tornadoes, and tidal waves can also produce social and cultural change. These disasters can destroy whole communities. Afterward, people often take precautions for the future. Dams may be built to lessen the effects of floods and droughts. People may also use new construction materials or adopt new construction methods to enable buildings to better withstand earthquakes or tornadoes.

A change in the supply of natural resources may bring about change. For example, in the 1970s high fuel prices and fuel shortages caused long lines at American gasoline stations. This shortage encouraged Americans to seek alternative sources of energy and to develop smaller, more fuel-efficient cars. The search for alternative forms of energy slowed in the 1980s in part because the fuel shortages eased. In addition, the production of less-fuel-efficient cars, such as high-performance sports cars, increased once again.

Wars and Conquests Wars and conquests are not as common as other sources of social change. However, they probably bring about the greatest change in the least amount of time. War causes the loss of many lives. It brings about the destruction of property and leads to the rise of new cities and towns that must be built to replace those destroyed. In addition, war causes changes in the economy as industry focuses on producing war materials rather than consumer goods. For example, after September 11, 2001, some industries contributed to the wars in Afghanistan and Iraq by providing military supplies and services. War can also promote advances in technology and medicine that can have civilian applications. War may also result in changes in government as new rulers come to power. These changes may contribute to new economic policies and political rights.

Reading Check **Summarize** What are the six major factors that cause social change?

Resistance to Social Change

Social change, regardless of its source, rarely occurs without some opposition. For each change introduced in society, there are usually people who strongly oppose it. Social change often results from a compromise between opposing forces. This is true both on an interpersonal level and on a societal level. Many people, after time, may accept a new idea that they strongly resisted at first. Other people may never accept the new idea but may simply adapt. Changes in the role of women in the workplace first met with some resistance that has waned in recent years. Ethnocentrism, cultural lag, and vested interests are among the reasons that people resist change.

Ethnocentrism Change that comes from outside a society often meets with strong resistance. People tend to believe that their own ideas and ways of doing things are best. This tendency to view one's own culture or group as superior to others is called ethnocentrism. Extreme ethnocentrism can make cultural borrowing difficult or even impossible.

The "Buy American" campaign of the 1970s and 1980s provides an example of how ethnocentrism can affect one culture's acceptance of another culture's material objects and ideas. One target of the campaign was the importation of Japanese automobiles. Allowing these cars into the United States, campaign supporters said, would put Americans out of work. Some Americans agreed with this view and refused to buy Japanese cars, stating that this refusal was the patriotic thing to do. Some American autoworkers went further. They demonstrated their feelings by publicly demolishing Japanese cars. While economic factors certainly were at work, ethnocentrism led to this anti-Japanese-car bias.

In time this bias decreased, and Japanese cars gained wide acceptance in the United States. Indeed, today it can be difficult to differentiate between Japanese and American cars. Some Japanese cars are now made by American workers at factories in the United States. At the same time, some American automobiles are assembled at factories in foreign countries.

Cultural Lag As you recall from Chapter 2, not all cultural traits change at the same rate. Material culture usually changes quickly and nonmaterial culture lags behind. Often, cultural lag results from technological change.

Sociologist James M. Henslin identified the traditional school year as an example of cultural lag. In the 1800s the United States was a largely rural, agricultural country. At that time, farming was a very labor-intensive activity. A long summer break from school was needed so that children could work on the farms. Over time, technological developments transformed the United States into a mostly urban and industrial country. Today, therefore, a long summer break is not needed. Even so, the traditional school year persists. Efforts to introduce year-round schooling have met with significant opposition.

The development of computers and the growth of the Internet in the 1990s also led to cultural lag. Computers and the Internet offer many educational opportunities. However, because of costs and other factors, some school districts have yet to put this new technology to effective use in the classroom. In addition, some elements of Internet technology—notably the "trapping" and storing of information about users—have created questions concerning privacy that the U.S. legal system is struggling to address.

Vested Interests A person who is satisfied with the way things are now is likely to resist change. Some individuals feel that the present, even if somewhat imperfect, is better than an unknown future. They will resist any change that threatens their security or standard of living. In other words, they have a vested interest to protect. For example, workers may oppose the introduction of new technology because they fear the technology may replace them and cost them their jobs.

Entire industries also have vested interests to protect. Consider the American oil industry, for example. During the energy crisis of the 1970s, oil prices rose dramatically. Many people around the country called for a new energy policy. Successive presidents in the 1990s and early 2000s passed legislation that tinkered with but did not really change the country's approach to energy. Indeed, critics charged that these policies did not focus enough on conservation or on the use of renewable fuels.

Resisting Change

Skills Focus INTERPRETING CARTOONS
What type of resistance to change does this cartoon illustrate?

One reason it was difficult to implement an energy policy that would permanently solve the energy problems of the 1970s and 1980s was that many people in the oil industry benefited from the high prices of petroleum products. To protect their vested interests, oil companies and workers in the oil industry lobbied the government to protect their industry and interests in the energy issue.

Reading Check **Find the Main Idea** What forms does resistance to social change take?

SECTION 3 Assessment

Reviewing Main Ideas and Vocabulary

1. **Define** What is an ideology?
2. **Recall** What are two processes through which new technologies arise?
3. **Identify** What term do sociologists use to describe the process of adapting borrowed cultural traits?

Thinking Critically

4. **Explain** How is the women's movement an example of social change?
5. **Elaborate** How have new electronic technologies such as digital music faced resistance to change?
6. **Identify Cause and Effect** Using your notes and a graphic organizer like the one below, explain how changes in values and beliefs can lead to social change.

FOCUS ON WRITING

7. **Descriptive** Write two paragraphs describing how cultural diffusion has changed eating habits in the United States.

Globalization and Social Change

One of the most powerful forces influencing life today is globalization, the process by which societies around the world become increasingly interconnected and interdependent. Globalization increases interaction among societies, which leads to an almost constant exchange of material objects, ideas, and beliefs. This process of cultural exchange, or diffusion, is one of the major sources of social change.

American fast-food restaurants are a common feature of large Chinese cities, such as Shenzhen.

Economic Globalization A prominent feature of economic globalization is the multinational corporation—a company that has factories and offices in several countries. Many of the largest and most powerful multinationals originated in the United States, and foreign markets have become the major focus for most American multinationals. Some companies now receive 50 percent or more of their profits from overseas operations, and their expansion plans are concentrated more on overseas countries than on the United States. American multinationals have spread both products and business ideas to other countries. For example, many foreign companies have adopted the business approach used by the American fast-food industry. Sociologist George Ritzer dubbed this trend the McDonaldization of society.

The exchange of products and ideas is not one way, however. For example, American consumers are able to buy South Korean cars, Japanese audio equipment, Mexican food products, and a variety of other items from a host of countries. Many American corporations have adopted management techniques long practiced by Japanese companies.

Globalization and Transportation Globalization has also helped transform the world's transportation systems. Since multinational corporations have their operations dispersed across the globe, their goods and employees require the ability to move efficiently around the world. Transportation systems have been improved to ensure that raw materials reach their factories and that finished products reach their markets. As a result, the volume of international transportation has grown markedly in recent years.

Air transportation offers a vivid illustration of this growth. Airlines carry tons of cargo and billions of passengers each year. In 2006, the global air carrier industry transported 2.1 billion passengers a total of 3.9 trillion revenue passenger kilometers (RPKs). Observers estimate that worldwide RPKs increased over 6 percent in 2007. Cargo demand increased by more than 4 percent the same year.

Tourism This rise in international transportation is also reflected in the increase in travel and tourism. In 2007, some 56 million tourists from 213 countries visited the United States, a 9 percent increase since the year 2000. Some 64 million Americans traveled abroad, with each averaging 2.7 international trips per year. Increased international tourism tends to promote face-to-face interactions among people of differing cultural backgrounds. This interaction, in turn, increases the chance of cultural diffusion and social change.

Diversity in America One way in which American society has changed in recent years is that it has become much more diverse. Globalization has played a part in this change. Many foreign multinational corporations have established operations in the United States, bringing with them workers from many different cultural backgrounds. These visitors have tried to maintain their own culture while living in the United States. For example, many foreign workers from Asia have established their own houses of worship so that they can more easily practice their religion.

Thinking Critically

1. **Explain** How does globalization contribute to social change?
2. **Discuss** How has globalization affected your community? What changes has globalization brought to your life?

SECTION 4

Theories of Social Change

Before You Read

Main Idea
Sociologists have developed theories to describe how and why social change occurs. Functionalist theories suggest that change takes place to maintain balance in the social order. Conflict theory focuses on conflict among groups as a source of change.

Reading Focus
1. What functionalist theories have been offered to explain social change?
2. How does conflict theory explain social change?

Vocabulary
cyclical theory
principle of immanent change
evolutionary theory
equilibrium theory
class conflict

Use a graphic organizer like this one to take notes on the theories of social change.

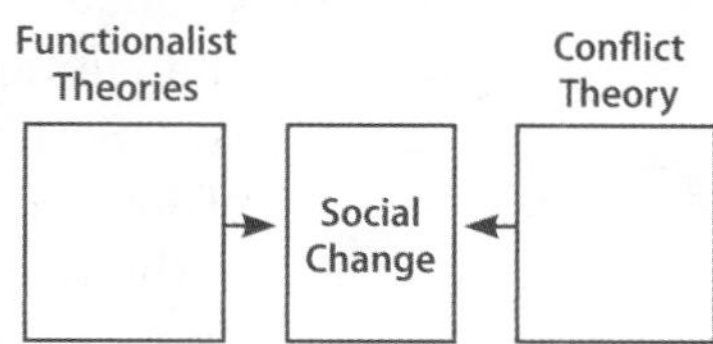

A Lost Civilization

SOCIOLOGY CLOSE UP

Why do societies rise and fall? Some time between 2000 and 1500 B.C., a people known as the Maya established farming villages in present-day Mexico and Central America. The soil was fertile, and farming thrived. With more food, the Maya became healthier and their population grew. In time, the Maya built an advanced civilization based on huge cities. These cities served as trade and religious centers. Each one contained pyramids topped by temples, great palaces, broad plazas, and ball courts.

A king governed each city and the surrounding area. Sometimes kings declared war on neighboring cities. The victorious kings gained control of important trade routes. They also received tribute from vanquished cities—in the form of precious metals and stones, other trade goods, and slaves.

Beginning in the A.D. 800s, the Maya began to abandon their cities. At the same time, their population declined sharply. In time, all that was left of this great civilization were huge stone ruins surrounded by rain forest. Historical explanations for this decline vary. Over-farming may have damaged the environment, and this led to food shortages and famine. Or the Maya may have suffered famine because of a long-lasting drought. Other possible reasons include constant warfare among the cities, foreign invasion, and peasant revolts. As you will read, sociological explanations for great social changes like the fall of civilizations vary, too. ■

The ruins of the great Mayan city of Uxmal push through the rain forest canopy on Mexico's Yucatán Peninsula.

Functionalist Theories

Sociology grew out of the social turmoil of the 1700s and 1800s. Thus, it is not surprising that sociologists devote considerable attention to the study of social change. Through the years, sociologists have provided many descriptions of how social change takes place. They have also suggested numerous theories to explain the process of social change. The most significant functionalist theories can be grouped into three categories: cyclical theory, evolutionary theory, and equilibrium theory.

Cyclical Theory The **cyclical theory** of social change views change from a historical perspective. Societies arise, go through various stages of development, and then decline. Social change is the result of this natural tendency for societies to pass through stages of development. Cyclical theories are likely to gain popularity during periods of extreme social upheaval because people often view events as beyond their control. Cyclical theories are reassuring because they see change as part of a continuing process. German historian Oswald Spengler and Russian American sociologist Pitirim Sorokin are, perhaps, the most notable proponents of the cyclical theory of social change.

Spengler was deeply troubled by the brutality of World War I, which led him to question whether social change always results in progress. In his study *The Decline of the West,* Spengler suggested that all societies pass through four stages—childhood, youth, adulthood, and old age. Western society, Spengler argued, had reached the prime of adulthood during the Enlightenment. By the early 1900s, it was well into the decline associated with old age. This process, he added, was inevitable. Like other great civilizations of the past, Western civilization was bound to decline and disappear.

Sorokin presented a different view, stating that all societies fluctuate between two extreme forms of culture. At one extreme are ideational cultures, in which truth and knowledge are sought through faith or religion. At the other extreme are sensate cultures, in which people seek knowledge through science. Ideational cultures are likely to be devoted to spiritual pursuits, and sensate cultures are likely to be practical and materialistic.

ACADEMIC VOCABULARY

linear relating to or resembling a straight line

According to Sorokin, the tendency toward change is present at a society's birth. So, something in the society's structure causes it to swing back and forth between an ideational and a sensate culture. Sorokin referred to this natural tendency toward social change as the **principle of immanent change.**

Critics of cyclical theories point out that such explanations often describe what is rather than attempt to determine *why* things happen. From a sociological perspective, the interesting point is not that societies have a life cycle. The real point of interest is why some societies decline or disappear while others continue to grow and adapt to changing conditions. Studying the history of past civilizations might help answer this question.

Evolutionary Theory In contrast to cyclical theories, the **evolutionary theory** of social change views change as a process that moves in one direction—toward increasing complexity. As members of society attempt to adapt to social and physical conditions in their environment, they push the society forward in development. Each new adaptation serves as the basis for future adaptations. Thus, change is seen as an additive process.

Evolutionary theorists of the 1800s, such as Auguste Comte, Herbert Spencer, and Émile Durkheim believed that all societies progress through distinct stages of social development. Each stage is supposed to bring with it improved social conditions and increased societal complexity. These early theorists viewed Western civilization as the height of social development.

Critics of early evolutionary theory note that it had ideological bias—it justified the social and political conditions in Europe and the United States. Further, critics note that it did not attempt to explain *why* social change takes place. Instead, evolutionary theorists merely provided scattered data to support their view that all societies were traveling along the path toward industrialization.

Later evolutionary theory abandoned many of the ideas that its critics had challenged. For example, modern evolutionary theorists reject the idea of the linear progression of society toward some Western ideal. Rather, they hold that societies have a *tendency* to become more complex over time.

Change can result from many sources and can take many paths. Modern social evolutionists do not assume that change always produces progress nor that progress means the same thing in all societies.

Also unlike earlier theorists, modern evolutionary theorists attempt to explain *why* societies change. According to social scientists Gerhard and Jean Lenski, social evolution takes place because of changes in a society's economic base and its level of technology. Technological advances enable a society to change its subsistence strategy. As a result, the other social institutions of that society are changed to some degree. Each new level of technological development provides the basis for future changes.

Critics of modern evolutionary theory agree that it has avoided many of the problems that plagued earlier evolutionary theories; modern theories do provide a limited explanation of social change. However, they do not attempt to explain events such as wars or short-term changes within individual societies.

Equilibrium Theory As you know, functionalist theory focuses on the ways in which societies maintain order. Sociologist Talcott Parsons's **equilibrium theory** of social change recognized this. Parsons argued that a change in one part of the social system produces changes in all of the other parts of the system. According to functionalist theory, this phenomenon occurs because a social system, like a living organism, attempts to maintain stability. When stability is disrupted by change in one part of the system, the other parts of the system adjust to the degree needed to bring the system back into balance, or equilibrium. Although order has been restored, the new system is slightly different from the old system. Thus, social change takes place.

Critics of equilibrium theory note that it suffers from the same problems that face all functionalist theories. The emphasis on social order makes it difficult for equilibrium theory to explain widespread, violent social change, such as revolution. In addition, equilibrium theory tends to characterize societies as more stable than they really are.

Reading Check **Summarize** How do cyclical theory, evolutionary theory, and equilibrium theory explain social change?

Marx's Theory of Social Change

Karl Marx saw social change as the result of conflict between the classes.

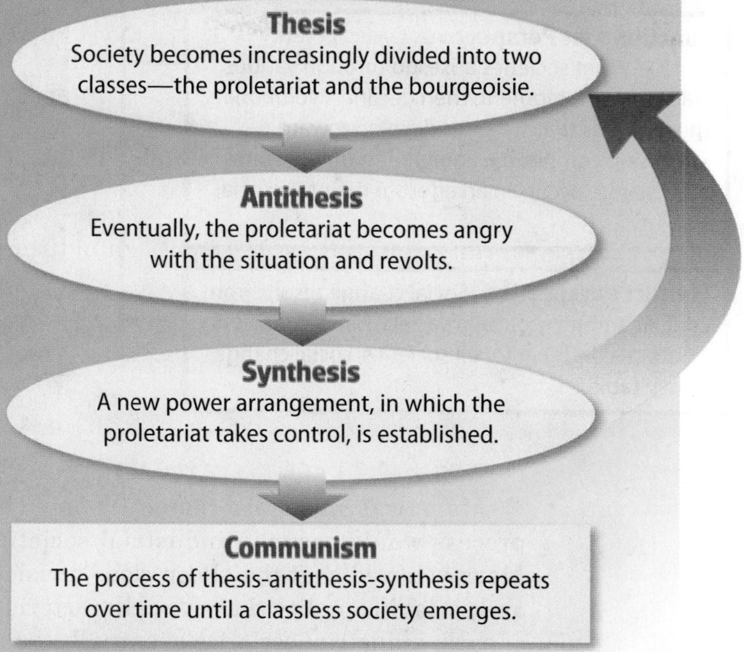

Thesis
Society becomes increasingly divided into two classes—the proletariat and the bourgeoisie.

Antithesis
Eventually, the proletariat becomes angry with the situation and revolts.

Synthesis
A new power arrangement, in which the proletariat takes control, is established.

Communism
The process of thesis-antithesis-synthesis repeats over time until a classless society emerges.

Conflict Theory

According to conflict theorists, change results from conflicts between groups with opposing interests. In most cases, conflicts arise from disputes over access to power and wealth. Because conflict theorists view conflict as a natural condition in all societies, they see social change as inevitable.

Conflict theory is rooted in Karl Marx's ideas on class struggle, which he developed in the mid-1800s. Over the years, most conflict theorists have moved away from the emphasis on class. Rather, they take a much broader view, focusing on social conflict in general.

Marx and Class Conflict Karl Marx held that all of human history is the history of **class conflict.** By that he meant that all societies throughout history have been subject to conflicts between the people who have power and those who lack power. According to Marx, social change results from the efforts of the powerless to gain power. Usually, those efforts involve the violent overthrow of the people in power. Thus, Marx saw violence as a necessary part of social change.

Perspectives on Social Change

Functionalist Perspective Cyclical theory suggests that societies arise, go through various stages of development, then decline. Evolutionary theory holds that societies develop toward increasing complexity. Equilibrium theory states that change occurs in an effort to maintain social stability.

Conflict Perspective Social change results from conflict among groups in society. Since conflict is a natural condition for all societies, social change is inevitable.

Marx was most interested in how this process would occur in industrial societies. Marx believed that the sharp class divisions and social inequality that were characteristic of early industrial societies eventually would lead the proletariat to overthrow the bourgeoisie. After a revolution, a dictatorship of the proletariat would be established to assist in the transformation to communism—the classless society that Marx considered the ultimate goal of all social evolution.

Class conflict has not resulted in revolution in most modern industrial societies. As a result, most conflict theorists have abandoned Marx's emphasis on class conflict. Instead, they focus on a range of social factors that can produce conflict in societies. Ralf Dahrendorf's work is representative of this approach.

Dahrendorf and Social Conflict Ralf Dahrendorf, like all conflict theorists, agrees with Marx's belief that conflict is a central feature of all societies. However, he disagrees with Marx's idea that class conflict is the moving force in human history. Instead, Dahrendorf holds that social conflict can take many forms. Conflict between racial or ethnic groups, religious or political groups, men and women, and the young and the old all can lead to social change. Nor does Dahrendorf believe that revolution is the principal way in which conflicts are resolved. In many instances, interest groups are able to institute social change through compromise and adaptation.

Critics of modern conflict theory note that it suffers from the same problem that troubles equilibrium theory. It has too narrow an emphasis. By concentrating on conflict as the principal cause of social change, conflict theorists ignore changes that occur in the absence of conflict. For example, technological innovations generally do not arise in response to conflict. Nevertheless, they have a profound effect on society. In addition, conflict theory ignores those elements in society that serve to maintain the social order.

No single theory provides a full explanation of all aspects of social change. Given the complex nature of social change, it is very likely that no single theory could ever prove adequate. Therefore, many social scientists combine elements of the various theories in an attempt to gain a better understanding of the nature of social change.

Reading Check **Contrast** How do Dahrendorf's views on social change differ from Marx's views?

SECTION 4 Assessment

Reviewing Main Ideas and Vocabulary

1. **Define** What is the principle of immanent change?
2. **Identify** What did Marx mean by the term *class conflict?*

Thinking Critically

3. **Infer** Cyclical theories of change are popular during times of extreme social turmoil. Why do you think this is so?
4. **Explain** Why do conflict theorists view social change as inevitable?
5. **Elaborate** Using your notes and a graphic organizer like the one to the right, explain how functionalist and conflict theorists would explain the decline of the Maya civilization.

Functionalist Theory

Conflict Theory

FOCUS ON WRITING

6. **Persuasive** Write a paragraph discussing which of the theories covered in this section provides the best explanation of social change.

SECTION 5

Modernization

Before You Read

Main Idea
Modernization is the process by which a society's social institutions become more complex. Sociologists offer two explanations of this process: modernization theory and world-system theory.

Reading Focus
1. How do sociologists explain the process of modernization?
2. What impact has modernization had on social life and the natural environment?

Vocabulary
modernization
modernization theory
world-system theory
infrastructure

TAKING NOTES Use a graphic organizer like this one to take notes on modernization.

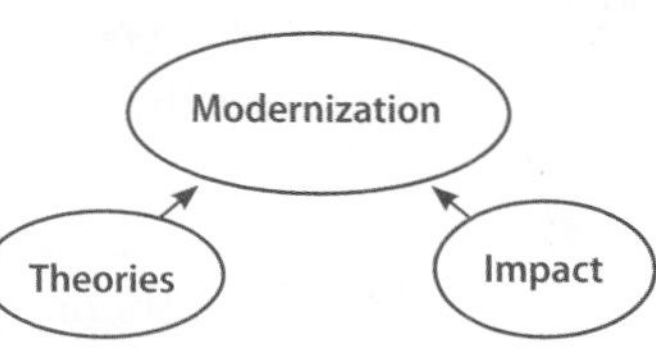

The Olympic National Stadium in Beijing, known as the "Bird's Nest," symbolizes China's push for modernization.

SOCIOLOGY CLOSE UP ***What are the costs of modernization?*** In the late 1970s, the Chinese government set an ambitious goal—China would become a leading industrial power and join the ranks of the world's modernized nations by the early 2000s. Since that time, China has made enormous strides toward that goal. Perhaps the best evidence of this can be found in Beijing, the country's capital. The city's skyline is dotted by towering office and apartment blocks interspersed with futuristic buildings constructed for the 2008 Olympic Games.

This rapid development did not come without costs, however. Statistics show that there has been a dramatic increase in the number of industrial accidents in China. These have killed thousands of workers and injured nearly 2 million more, cost the government dearly in lost economic production, and done irreparable damage to the environment. Modernization has affected social life in China, too. Western-style development has brought a range of Western problems. The number of cars on China's streets has multiplied rapidly over the last few years, for example, creating heavy traffic congestion in the country's big cities. Also, auto emissions add to the already problematic levels of air pollution. Fast-food restaurants are becoming more prevalent and more popular, especially among the young. The high fat content in fast food may be a contributing factor to rising rates of obesity and heart disease in China. Reviewing this situation, many Chinese hope there is a way to reap the benefits of modernization while avoiding such negative consequences. ■

The Process of Modernization

Many sociologists interested in social change focus on **modernization,** the process by which a society's social institutions become increasingly complex as the society moves toward industrialization. Social scientists usually divide the countries of the world into two groups—more developed and less developed. The more-developed nations include the United States, Canada, Japan, Australia, and Western European countries. Most of the less-developed nations are found in Latin America, Africa, and Asia. The more-developed nations have modernized much more rapidly than the less-developed nations. But why is this so? Modernization theory and world-system theory offer two different explanations.

Modernization Theory According to sociologists' view of **modernization theory,** the more-developed nations modernized because they were the first to industrialize. Once less-developed nations begin to industrialize, they too will undergo modernization. Therefore, modernized countries serve as a model and a source for technology and information for those undergoing the modernization process. In addition, modernizing countries will go through the same development stages as those that have undergone modernization. In time, less-developed nations will resemble the more-developed nations in terms of economic and social structure.

The view that less-developed nations follow the same modernizing pattern as more-developed nations forms the basis of modernization theory. According to this view, the extended family will be replaced by the nuclear family as less-developed nations modernize. Similarly, the role of religion in guiding social interaction will decrease, modern systems of medicine and mass education will arise, and most people will move to the cities.

Modernization theory had a large following during the mid-1900s. Sociologists of this era believed that modernization was a cure for social and economic problems that plagued many less-developed nations. These theorists assumed that through modernization less-developed nations would be able to raise their standard of living and become full partners in the world economy. To speed up the process, many industrialized nations established assistance programs. Money, technology, and economic advisers flooded into the less-developed nations. Yet, these assistance programs had little effect. Many less-developed countries still face major economic and social challenges. As a result, support for modernization theory has weakened over the years.

Why have the predictions of modernization theorists not come true? Critics argue that the theory failed to acknowledge that the less-developed nations face conditions that are different from those faced by the more-developed nations. When the more-developed nations began to modernize, they had large amounts of resources and relatively self-sufficient economies. The less-developed nations, however, have a long history of economic dependence on the West. This economic dependence has many causes, but some sociologists point out that many less-developed nations were once colonies of the world's industrial powers. These sociologists note that the colonial powers used their colonies as sources of raw

CHARACTERISTICS OF MODERNIZED AND NONMODERNIZED SOCIETIES

QUICK FACTS

Characteristics	Modernized Societies	Nonmodernized Societies
Family	Nuclear	Extended
Family Size	Smaller	Larger
Population	Urban	Rural
Life Expectancy	Higher	Lower
Infant Mortality	Lower	Higher
Religious Orientation	Less	More
Formal Education	Widespread	Little
Technology	Complex	Simple
Division of Labor	Complex	Simple
Statuses	Mostly Achieved	Mostly Ascribed
Social Stratification	More Open	Rigid
Social Change	Rapid	Gradual

Statistically Speaking...

World-System Theory World-system theorists use several political, social, and economic measures to establish where nations are located on the development continuum. One often-used economic measure is gross domestic product (GDP), the value of finished goods and services produced in a country in a given time period. The bar graph to the right shows the GDP for several core, semiperipheral, and peripheral nations.

Skills Focus **INTERPRETING GRAPHS** How do GDPs among the core, semiperipheral, and peripheral nations compare?

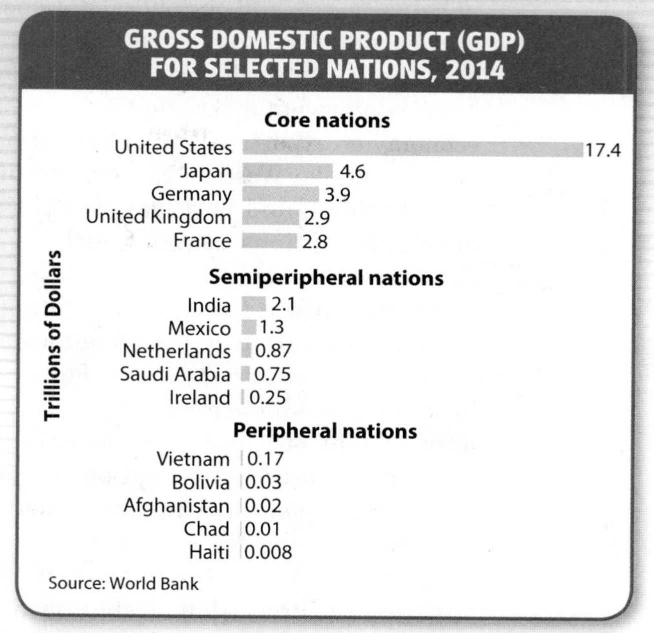

GROSS DOMESTIC PRODUCT (GDP) FOR SELECTED NATIONS, 2014

Trillions of Dollars

Core nations	
United States	17.4
Japan	4.6
Germany	3.9
United Kingdom	2.9
France	2.8
Semiperipheral nations	
India	2.1
Mexico	1.3
Netherlands	0.87
Saudi Arabia	0.75
Ireland	0.25
Peripheral nations	
Vietnam	0.17
Bolivia	0.03
Afghanistan	0.02
Chad	0.01
Haiti	0.008

Source: World Bank

materials and cheap labor. While this helped the colonial powers to industrialize, it slowed economic development in the colonies.

In addition, the population pressures faced by less-developed nations are very different from those faced by more-developed nations. For example, during its modernization period the United States had a relatively small population and a great deal of land. Thus, population growth did not present a serious problem. Less-developed nations, on the other hand, begin the modernization process with large populations. Further, as less-developed nations begin to industrialize, improved medical care causes their death rates to drop markedly. Because birthrates remain high while death rates decline, the population grows at a very fast rate. Most of the economic gains produced by industrialization must be used to maintain the existing standard of living for an expanding population. As a result, the modernization process in such countries slows.

Modernization is also slowed by antimodernization sentiment. For example, in some Islamic countries, modernization is seen as a threat to traditional social and religious values. The revolution that overthrew the shah of Iran in 1979 was, in part, a reaction to the shah's support of modernization based on a Western model.

World-System Theory Sociologist and historian Immanuel Wallerstein offers a different explanation for why societies modernize at different rates. His **world-system theory** views modernization in terms of the world economy. According to Wallerstein, the world system comprises three types of nations—core, peripheral, and semiperipheral. Core nations are the most powerful developed nations—the United States, Canada, Japan, and the countries of Western Europe. They form the center, or core, of the world economy and control most of the world's productive, technological, and financial resources. Core nations have diversified economies with strong manufacturing and service sectors.

Peripheral nations are the poor countries in Latin America, Africa, and Asia. They control few productive resources, and they depend on the core nations for financial aid, technology, and manufactured goods. They also depend on the core nations to buy their main products—mostly raw materials and farm goods, such as coffee, cocoa, and sugar. Many peripheral nations have economies that rely heavily on the exportation of a single product.

Semiperipheral nations are somewhere in between core and peripheral nations. They may be industrialized but may not play a central role in the world economy. Or they may be only somewhat diversified in terms of their economy or exports. Semiperipheral nations include smaller Western European countries, such as Spain and Portugal, and the newly developed nations of Asia, such as South Korea and Taiwan.

On the surface, the economic relationships among these various types of nations appear to be a positive arrangement. For example, by locating production facilities in peripheral nations or by purchasing raw materials from them, businesses in core nations are able to lower production costs. In return, peripheral nations receive technological and economic assistance from the core nations. World-system theorists argue that, despite such apparent benefits, peripheral nations actually gain little. They note that the arrangement creates a lack of economic diversity, dependence on exports and foreign assistance, and increased economic inequality in peripheral nations.

Some sociologists and economists have observed that when core nations are heavily involved in the economy of a peripheral nation, economic activity concentrates in those areas that meet the needs of the core nations. Obviously, such concentration prevents the peripheral nation from diversifying its economy. Export dependency and reliance on foreign financial aid also result from this concentration of economic activity. Because most economic activity in a peripheral nation is tied to meeting the needs of core nations, the peripheral nation seldom produces enough goods and services to have a self-sufficient economy. As a result, the peripheral nation's economic survival is dependent on exporting goods or raw materials to the core nations. If world demand for these goods declines, the peripheral nation's economy suffers greatly, and the peripheral nation often turns to the core nations for loans and other types of financial aid. Because of a lack of economic growth, the peripheral nation may find it difficult to repay its loans. Therefore, it remains forever in debt to the core nations.

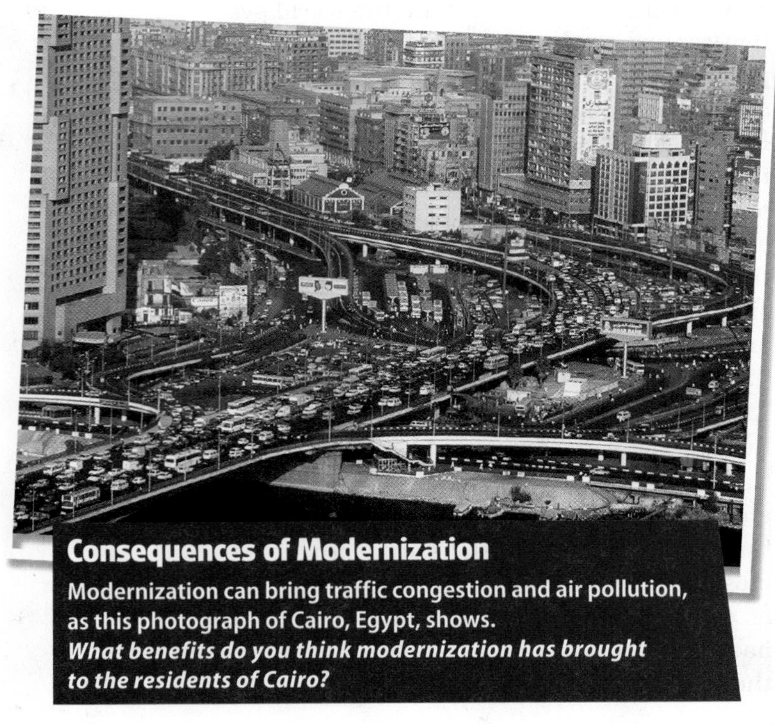

Consequences of Modernization

Modernization can bring traffic congestion and air pollution, as this photograph of Cairo, Egypt, shows.
What benefits do you think modernization has brought to the residents of Cairo?

World-system theorists argue that economic dependence and the lack of economic diversification work together to increase social stratification in peripheral nations. Money likely becomes concentrated in the hands of a few people who have close ties to the core nations. These people, therefore, have a vested interest in maintaining the system. As a result, most peripheral nations remain at a low level of modernization.

Many critics of world-system theory admit that it is useful in explaining why many of the less-developed nations have low levels of economic growth. However, they point out that the theory does not explain why certain core nations emerged as industrial powers. In addition, critics note that the theory does not explain why some semiperipheral nations, such as China, South Korea, and Taiwan, have modernized to the point that they are able to challenge the core nations economically.

Modernization and world-system theories share certain characteristics. They both define modernization in terms of economic development. They also use development in the West as the model for modernization. Some sociologists have suggested that, particularly because of the process of globalization, a new approach to modernization is needed.

Reading Check **Contrast** How do modernization theory and world-system theory differ in the way they look at modernization?

The Impact of Modernization

Modernization has both positive and negative consequences for social life and the natural environment. The most notable positive consequence of modernization is an increase in a country's standard of living. Modernization brings with it longer life expectancies, lower birthrates, higher rates of literacy, a decrease in economic and social inequality, and more personal comforts. Modernization, which brings industrial expansion and technological innovation, can greatly improve a country's infrastructure. An **infrastructure** is a system of roads, ports, and other facilities needed by a modern economy.

Modernization is often accompanied by the arrival of electricity and communication technology such as telephones and computers. These services raise the quality of life for residents. Modernizing countries also benefit from the establishment of colleges and universities. These educational institutions train professionals and improve the quality of life in developing nations.

Modernization also has some costs. The very same changes that bring improvements to social life may also give rise to problems. For example, the family and religion lose some of their traditional authority in a modernizing society. The government, on the other hand, takes on a larger role in directing people's lives. Because people move more frequently in modern societies, social relationships are likely to be weaker than they are in traditional societies. Thus, feelings of social isolation and role conflict are more common.

Modern technology also gives rise to moral and ethical questions. For example, at what point should doctors give up the fight to keep terminally ill patients alive through the use of modern medical technology? Or, now that humans have the ability to destroy the world through nuclear warfare, what steps should be taken to prevent such warfare? These questions and many others like them arise in modern society.

The effects of modernization on the natural environment also cannot be ignored. Modernization has brought with it the problems of soil, water, and air pollution. The use of pesticides in agriculture and chemicals in manufacturing have created serious environmental and health problems—most of them unanticipated. For example, each year modern societies are faced with finding safe ways to dispose of huge amounts of hazardous waste—the by-products of industry. Although many advanced countries have been able to set environmental standards, less-developed nations often face major environmental challenges as they attempt to modernize.

Reading Check **Summarize** What are some of the positive and negative consequences of the modernization process?

SECTION 5 Assessment

Reviewing Main Ideas and Vocabulary

1. **Define** What is modernization?
2. **Identify** What is the name given to Immanuel Wallerstein's explanation of modernization?
3. **Explain** Why would improvement of the infrastructure be considered a benefit of modernization?

Thinking Critically

4. **Infer** Which sociological perspectives do you think modernization theory and world-system theory represent? Give reasons for your answer.
5. **Evaluate** Why do you think some traditional societies are so opposed to the modernization process?
6. **Elaborate** Using your notes and a graphic organizer like the one here, explain how modernization affects different social institutions.

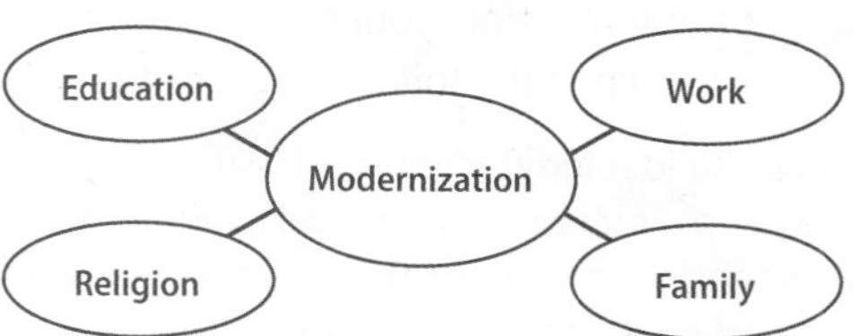

FOCUS ON WRITING

7. **Expository** Write a brief essay exploring why some sociologists feel that the modernization and world-system theories are ethnocentric. In writing your essay, consider the focus of these two theories.

Creating a Social Movement

What methods can be used to attract support for a social movement?

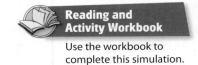

Reading and Activity Workbook
Use the workbook to complete this simulation.

1. Introduction

- This simulation will help you review collective behavior and social movements. You will work in small groups to think of a social change you can imagine happening in the future. Then your group will act as a committee of public opinion responsible for popularizing the social movement using Web sites. Finally, the entire class will evaluate each Web site to determine the type of propaganda being implemented. To complete this simulation, follow the steps below.
- Following your teacher's instructions, organize the class into six groups.
- Your teacher will instruct each group to think of an ideology around which you will organize a social movement.
- Work with students in your group to review the chapter material on social movements. Pay attention to the different types of social movements and how each achieves its goal as well as the different theories that explain why social movements develop.

2. Identifying a Social Movement

Review the types and examples of social movements provided in this chapter. After reviewing this information, your first task as a group is to think of a social movement to promote. Remember, social movements either seek to promote or prevent social change. In order to complete this part of the simulation, your group must have written responses for each of the following prompts.

- What is our ideology? Identify an issue that you think will unite people for either promoting or preventing change. This movement must have the three distinguishing characteristics of a social movement—it is long-lasting, has a highly organized structure, and takes deliberate action to promote or block societal change.
- Which type of social movement are we promoting?
  Reactionary?
  Conservative?
  Revisionary?
  Revolutionary?
- Which theory best explains why our social movement will develop?
  Relative deprivation?
  Resource-mobilization?

3. Simulating a Public Opinion Committee

Your group will now act as the public opinion committee of your social movement. The committee's task is to design and construct a Web site that will help to popularize the movement. If you have access to Web design software, create an actual Web page. If you do not, then draw your Web site design on poster boards. After reviewing the chapter material on public opinion and propaganda, design a Web site that meets the following criteria:

- Implements one of the propaganda techniques identified in this chapter.
- Includes a memorable logo, theme, or motto.
- Has pictures or illustrations that make the social movement and its cause more meaningful.
- Emphasizes the ideology that drives the social movement.

4. Identifying Propaganda Techniques

Before the class tries to determine which propaganda technique has been implemented in each Web site, briefly review the propaganda techniques covered in this chapter. Refer to the chart on this page for a complete list of the techniques. To review the techniques and make your determinations, follow these steps:

- Within your group, think of a way that you could have used each of the described techniques to promote your social movement.
- Your teacher will then ask each group to present its Web site.
- After each Web site is presented, jot down on a piece of paper which propaganda technique you think was being implemented and why.
- Your teacher will then ask the class to vote on which propaganda technique was implemented. After the vote, briefly discuss the Web site, its contents, and the approach used to determine the correct answer.

5. Discussion

What did you learn from this simulation? Hold a group discussion that focuses on the following questions:

- Overall, how successful was the class at determining which propaganda technique was being implemented?
- Overall, how successful was the class at using the various propaganda techniques to promote a social movement?
- Were some techniques particularly difficult to use? If so, which ones and why? Were some techniques particularly easy to use? If so, which ones and why?
- Describe several ongoing social movements. What propaganda techniques do these movements use? How successful do you think their efforts to sway public opinion have been?
- Which propaganda techniques do you think work best in influencing public opinion? Why?
- Is it appropriate for social movements, businesses, or the government to use propaganda to influence your opinions and behavior? Why or why not?

PROPAGANDA TECHNIQUES

Technique	Description
Testimonial	Uses endorsements by famous people to secure support for the social movement. The goal is to persuade people to transfer their admiration for a celebrity to the social movement.
Transfer	Attempts to associate the social movement with something that the public approves of or respects, such as patriotic symbols.
Bandwagon	Appeals to the public's desire to conform by promoting the social movement as already very popular with the public.
Name Calling	Uses negative labels or images in order to make opponents of the social movement appear in an unfavorable light.
Plain-folks Appeal	Attempts to sway public opinion by appealing to the "average American." Average Americans with whom everyone can identify may be shown as supporters of the social movement.
Glittering Generalities	Uses words that sound positive but have little real meaning. This technique paints the social movement in a very positive light but provides little real information.
Card Stacking	Presents facts in a way that puts the social movement in a favorable light. For example, presents statistics or survey results in a way that favors the social movement over its opponents.

CHAPTER 16 Review

Comprehension and Critical Thinking

SECTION 1 *(pp. 394–402)*

1. a. **Identify Main Ideas** How do mobs and riots differ from panics and mass hysteria?
   b. **Draw Conclusions** Some sociologists suggest that protest movements should be classified as a fifth type of crowd. Why do you think this is so?
   c. **Support a Position** Which sociological theory best explains collective behavior? Give reasons for your answer.

SECTION 2 *(pp. 404–408)*

2. a. **Identify** According to resource-mobilization theory, what kinds of resources are needed for a social movement to be successful?
   b. **Explain** Why are the original goals of a social movement sometimes swept aside during the bureaucratization stage of the movement's life cycle?
   c. **Elaborate** Which explanation of the development of social movements would a conflict theorist likely adopt? Give reasons for your answer.

SECTION 3 *(pp. 409–413)*

3. a. **Identify Cause and Effect** Describe some social changes caused by technological innovations in online media.
   b. **Develop** Describe an instance in which vested interests have slowed social change. How has this resistance to change affected everyday life?

SECTION 4 *(pp. 415–418)*

4. a. **Describe** How do modern evolutionary theories of social change attempt to avoid the criticisms leveled against early evolutionary theories?
   b. **Compare and Contrast** How are the functionalist and conflict perspectives of social change similar? How are they different?

SECTION 5 *(pp. 419–423)*

5. a. **Draw Conclusions** Why has modernization theory lost favor over the years?
   b. **Support a Position** Do you think the benefits of modernization outweigh the disadvantages? Give reasons for your answer.

Reviewing Vocabulary

Identify the term from the chapter that best fits each of the following descriptions.

6. the relatively spontaneous social behavior that occurs when people try to develop common solutions to unclear situations
7. a spontaneous and uncoordinated group action to escape some perceived threat
8. an organized and deliberate attempt to shape public opinion
9. alterations in various aspects of society over time
10. a long-term conscious effort to promote or prevent social change
11. a system of beliefs or ideas that justifies the social, moral, religious, political, or economic interests held by a group or society
12. the process of adapting borrowed cultural traits
13. explanation of social change that states that societies arise, go through various stages of development, and then decline
14. conflict between the people who have power and those who lack power
15. the process by which a society's social institutions become increasingly complex as the society moves toward industrialization

INTERNET ACTIVITY

16. Use the Internet to research fads and fashions from an earlier time—the 1920s, perhaps—and fads and fashions today. Note how the fads and fashions started and how long they lasted. Use your findings to create an illustrated pamphlet on fads in the past and today.

Sociology in Your Life

17. For one week, watch television during prime-time hours to record the commercials shown. For each commercial, make note of the product, the propaganda technique used, and how the technique is used. At the end of the week, write a brief report on your findings, noting which technique is used most often and if there is any correlation between types of products and propaganda techniques.

Skills Activity: Interpreting Primary Sources

In the following excerpt, from a review of *We Believe the Children* by Richard Beck, writer Maura Casey describes the hysteria that surrounded day-care centers in the 1980s amid accusations of "Satanic ritual abuse." Study the excerpt and answer the questions that follow.

> "TV news was no friend to those of us who had small children in the 1980s. Allegations of child sexual abuse in day-care centers swept the nation, with high-profile cases in California, North Carolina, New Jersey, Massachusetts, Minnesota and other states, leading to empty playgrounds, hyper-vigilant parents and the implication that behind every tree lurked a pedophile waiting to snatch our children. Sexual abuse is an awful crime, but the perpetrators are usually relatives or family friends, and fewer than 1 percent of cases take place in day-care centers. Nonetheless, 30 years ago America was described as experiencing an "epidemic" of sexual abuse in day care. . . .
>
> "We believe the children" became both the unofficial motto of advocates for the prosecution and a catch-all response to those few who asked whether the accusers had completely lost their minds. The approach was based largely on the work of psychiatrist Roland Summit, who claimed that, of every 1,000 children who say they were sexually abused, only two or three are guilty of inventing or exaggerating. He also said it was normal for children who had been sexually abused to retract their claims and say they made it all up. The upshot: No matter what children said, they were sexually abused, and if you didn't believe them, something was wrong with you. . . .
>
> Some have drawn parallels between the Salem witch trials of 1692 and the false accusations of sexual abuse that swept America in the 1980s. The difference is this: Those falsely accused in Salem got public apologies from their accusers and reparations. No such luck for the dozens of day-care workers and others who were falsely accused and imprisoned in modern-day America. We should be ashamed."
>
> **—Maura Casey, "How the Daycare Child Abuse Hysteria of the 1980s Became a Witch Hunt," *Washington Post*, July 31, 2015, review of *We Believe the Children: A Moral Panic in the 1980s* (Public Affairs, 2015), by Richard Beck**

18. Identify Main Ideas What kind of collective behavior does the excerpt describe?

19. Identify Cause and Effect On what did those making accusations base their belief that children were always to be believed?

20. Evaluate How might this episode help in understanding rumors and "urban legends"?

Writing for Sociology

Use your knowledge of collective behavior to answer the question below. Do not simply list facts. Present a clear argument based on your critical analysis of the question, using appropriate sociological terminology.

21. Write a brief analysis of three urban legends. Your analysis should include information on each of the topics listed below:

- Source of legend
- Summary of legend
- Moral lesson of legend

Connecting Online

Go online for review and enrichment activities related to this chapter.

KEY TOPICS VIDEOS
View compelling clips on issues in the field.

KEEP IT CURRENT
Link to the Current Events site for regularly updated stories on sociology as well as other social studies topics.

QUICK LAB
Reinforce a key concept with a short lab activity.

Global Issues Around the World

As you have read, globalization is the development of economic, political, and social relationships that stretch worldwide. Many sociologists study globalization to learn about its effects on the world's societies.

EFFECTS OF GLOBALIZATION

What do people around the world think about globalization?

In late 2001, researchers conducted the largest-ever public opinion poll on globalization by interviewing 25,000 people in 25 countries. The researchers asked those surveyed whether they thought globalization had made their quality of life "better" or "worse." As seen in the graph below, the effects of globalization on the environment, poverty and homelessness, and the number of available jobs are the greatest concern of those surveyed. However, those surveyed thought that access to foreign markets and cheaper goods were the most positive effects.

EFFECTS OF GLOBALIZATION: SURVEY RESULTS

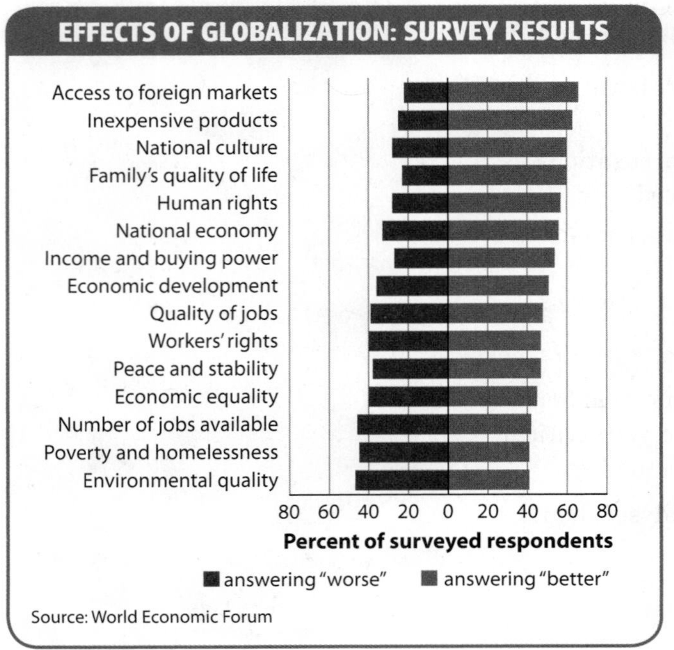

Source: World Economic Forum

GLOBAL CULTURE

How is globalization affecting world cultures?

Globalization contributes to changes in popular culture—specifically culture traits such as food, sports, and music, that are common within a group of people. In addition, globalization causes cultural diffusion, or the spread of culture traits from one region to another. As people travel more and more and are exposed to different cultures, they take back culture traits from the places they visit. The availability of media from different countries is also affecting world cultures. For example, via satellite dishes people can access news, TV shows, and movies from all over the world.

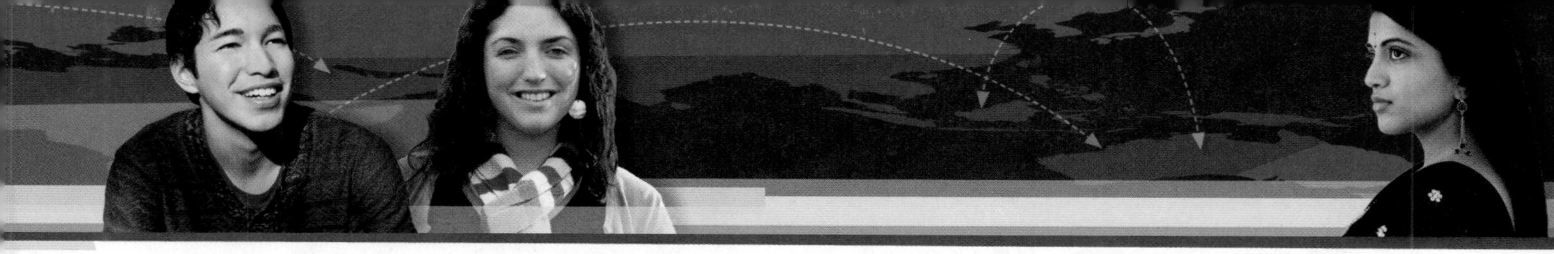

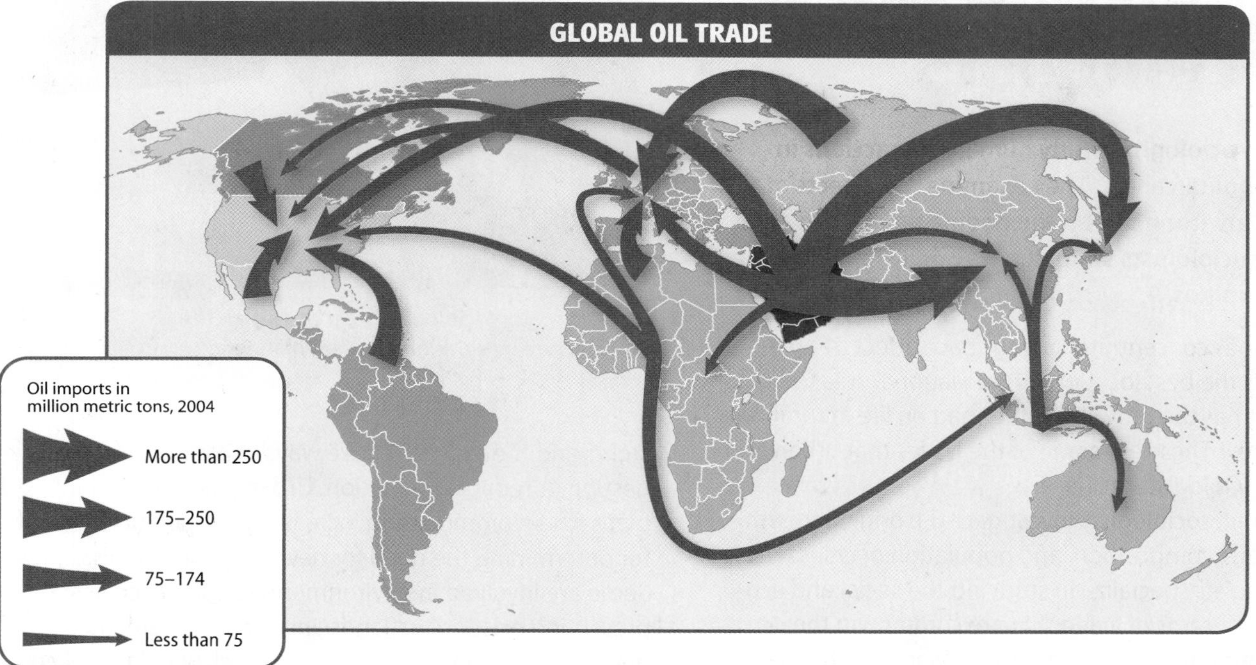

GLOBAL TRADE

What effects does global trade have on the world's societies?

One significant effect of globalization is the rise of global trade. Every day, more and more goods are traded among countries around the world. This growth in world trade increasingly ties countries together economically and politically, and as products flow back and forth, societies are affected.

Consider oil, for example. Oil is a valuable resource that is freely traded on the global market, as you can see on the map. Many developed countries need oil to run their transportation and power systems. They purchase oil from countries all around the globe. Without oil, the technologies, infrastructure, lifestyles, and societies in these countries would be very different. At the same time, oil-rich countries are increasingly tied to the countries that purchase their oil—and to the global economy in general. If changing economic conditions cause many countries to purchase more or less oil, that can have a huge affect on societies in other places.

THINKING LIKE A SOCIOLOGIST

Which countries of the world are the most global?

With the world becoming more connected through economics, politics, and culture, globalization has resulted in a much smaller world. Each year, Foreign Policy journal publishes a "Globalization Index," which measures globalization by using four key components—political engagement (includes participation in international organizations, and peacekeeping), technological connectivity (includes number of Internet users, hosts, and servers), personal contact (includes telephone use and travel), and economic integration (includes international trade and foreign investment).

Go to the journal's Web site and select one country to research. Be sure to study the globalization index data for your selected country in terms of the four key components listed above. How do you think the society of your selected country is affected by globalization? If needed, conduct additional library and Internet research on your selected country. When you are done, write a report that summarizes your findings.

CAREERS IN SOCIOLOGY

Urban and Rural Sociologists

Urban sociologists study human interactions in metropolitan areas. They examine the effects of the urban environment on the people who live in cities. Rural sociologists study the way of life in rural communities.

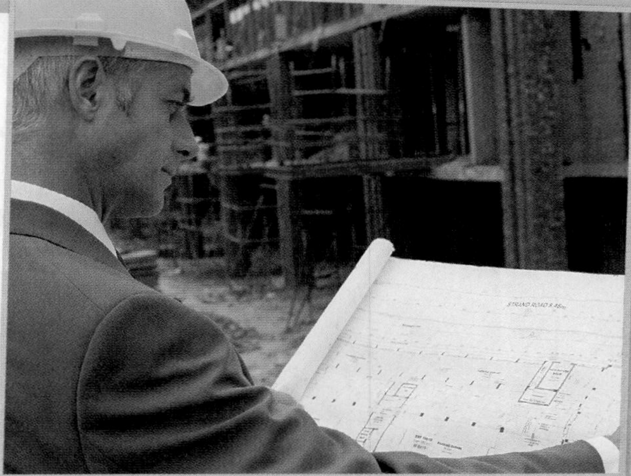

Many urban sociologists help cities plan for the future by working as urban planners.

How does concentrated living space affect people? What is the best location for recreational areas? What impact has the growth of cities had on life in rural communities? These are some of the issues that urban and rural sociologists tackle.

Urban sociologists investigate the origin, growth, structure, composition, and population of cities. These sociologists specialize in studying the social and economic patterns of living that are common in the city environment. They explore the reasons for changes in settlement in urban areas and examine the effect that living in increasingly concentrated areas has on the quality of life.

Some urban sociologists are interested in how people interact in urban spaces. Some study the problems of urban living, such as transportation needs, race relations, and poverty. Others observe population changes and trends. The studies and observations of urban sociologists provide information for planning and policy making by city government leaders.

Many urban sociologists work as urban planners. They help cities plan for the needs of urban populations. Planners determine the best locations for new houses or stores and the most effective ways of easing traffic congestion or reducing pollution. Urban planners design plans for accommodating increases in population and for determining the need for new roads or schools. Some are involved in environmental issues, such as preserving existing wetlands and forests located near developing urban areas. They may work with lawmakers to draft legislation on environmental issues.

Urban sociology is related to rural sociology. Rural sociologists study the way of life in rural communities and the contrasts between rural and urban living. They study the effects that the extension of cities and suburbs into rural areas and the loss of farmland have on people living in rural communities. Some rural sociologists study the social factors that lead to environmental problems and the actions that people in rural communities take to address these problems. Others examine the ways that agricultural technologies affect family farming.

Applying ASA Style

Many urban sociologists publish articles in professional journals in which they refer to people of different races, gender, ethnicity, or religion. In keeping with the guidelines from the **American Sociological Association (ASA)**, the writers try to eliminate language that reflects any bias or stereotyping of groups. The papers you write for your sociology class should follow these guidelines, too.

ASA guidelines call for writers to be as specific as possible in identifying ethnic and racial groups. For example, a sociologist writing about ethnic groups in an urban area would refer to Chinese or Japanese groups rather than using the general term Asian.

Through Think Central you can access the ASA Quick Style Guide for more information on avoiding bias and stereotypes and on using precise racial and ethnic terms. Review the ASA guidelines that you find at the Web site. Then write several imprecise terms, along with corrected terms. An example is provided for you.

Imprecise Term	Preferred Term
Hispanic	Cuban

Reference Section

The ASA Code of Ethics

INTRODUCTION

AMERICAN SOCIOLOGICAL ASSOCIATION'S CODE OF ETHICS

The American Sociological Association's (ASA's) Code of Ethics sets forth the principles and ethical standards that underlie sociologists' professional responsibilities and conduct. These principles and standards should be used as guidelines when examining everyday professional activities. They constitute normative statements for sociologists and provide guidance on issues that sociologists may encounter in their professional work.

ASA's Code of Ethics consists of an Introduction, a Preamble, five General Principles, and specific Ethical Standards. This Code is also accompanied by the Rules and Procedures of the ASA Committee on Professional Ethics which describe the procedures for filing, investigating, and resolving complaints of unethical conduct.

The Preamble and General Principles of the Code are aspirational goals to guide sociologists toward the highest ideals of sociology. Although the Preamble and General Principles are not enforceable rules, they should be considered by sociologists in arriving at an ethical course of action and may be considered by ethics bodies in interpreting the Ethical Standards.

The Ethical Standards set forth enforceable rules for conduct by sociologists. Most of the Ethical Standards are written broadly in order to apply to sociologists in varied roles, and the application of an Ethical Standard may vary depending on the context. The Ethical Standards are not exhaustive. Any conduct that is not specifically addressed by this Code of Ethics is not necessarily ethical or unethical.

Membership in the ASA commits members to adhere to the ASA Code of Ethics and to the Policies and Procedures of the ASA Committee on Professional Ethics. Members are advised of this obligation upon joining the Association and that violations of the Code may lead to the imposition of sanctions, including termination of membership. ASA members subject to the Code of Ethics may be reviewed under these Ethical Standards only if the activity is part of or affects their work-related functions, or if the activity is sociological in nature. Personal activities having no connection to or effect on sociologists' performance of their professional roles are not subject to the Code of Ethics.

PREAMBLE

This Code of Ethics articulates a common set of values upon which sociologists build their professional and scientific work. The Code is intended to provide both the general principles and the rules to cover professional situations encountered by sociologists. It has as its primary goal the welfare and protection of the individuals and groups with whom sociologists work. It is the individual responsibility of each sociologist to aspire to the highest possible standards of conduct in research, teaching, practice, and service.

The development of a dynamic set of ethical standards for a sociologist's work-related conduct requires a personal commitment to a lifelong effort to act ethically; to encourage ethical behavior by students, supervisors, supervisees, employers, employees, and colleagues; and to consult with others as needed concerning ethical problems. Each sociologist supplements, but does not violate, the values and rules specified in the Code of Ethics based on guidance drawn from personal values, culture, and experience.

GENERAL PRINCIPLES

The following General Principles are aspirational and serve as a guide for sociologists in determining ethical courses of action in various contexts. They exemplify the highest ideals of professional conduct.

PRINCIPLE A: PROFESSIONAL COMPETENCE

Sociologists strive to maintain the highest levels of competence in their work; they recognize the limitations of their expertise; and they undertake only those tasks for which they are qualified by education, training, or experience. They recognize the need for ongoing education in order to remain professionally competent; and they utilize the appropriate scientific, professional, technical, and administrative resources needed to ensure competence in their professional activities. They consult with other professionals when necessary for the benefit of their students, research participants, and clients.

PRINCIPLE B: INTEGRITY

Sociologists are honest, fair, and respectful of others in their professional activities—in research, teaching, practice, and service. Sociologists do not knowingly act in ways that jeopardize either their own or others' professional welfare. Sociologists conduct their affairs in ways that inspire trust and confidence; they do not knowingly make statements that are false, misleading, or deceptive.

PRINCIPLE C: PROFESSIONAL AND SCIENTIFIC RESPONSIBILITY

Sociologists adhere to the highest scientific and professional standards and accept responsibility for their work. Sociologists understand that they form a community and show respect for other sociologists even when they disagree on theoretical, methodological, or personal approaches to professional activities. Sociologists value the public trust in sociology and are concerned about their ethical behavior and that of other sociologists that might compromise that trust. While endeavoring always to be collegial, sociologists must never let the desire to be collegial outweigh their shared responsibility for ethical behavior. When appropriate, they consult with colleagues in order to prevent or avoid unethical conduct.

PRINCIPLE D: RESPECT FOR PEOPLE'S RIGHTS, DIGNITY, AND DIVERSITY

Sociologists respect the rights, dignity, and worth of all people. They strive to eliminate bias in their professional activities, and they do not tolerate any forms of discrimination based on age; gender; race; ethnicity; national origin; religion; sexual orientation; disability; health conditions; or marital, domestic, or parental status. They are sensitive to cultural, individual, and role differences in serving, teaching, and studying groups of people with distinctive characteristics. In all of their work-related activities, sociologists acknowledge the rights of others to hold values, attitudes, and opinions that differ from their own.

PRINCIPLE E: SOCIAL RESPONSIBILITY

Sociologists are aware of their professional and scientific responsibility to the communities and societies in which they live and work. They apply and make public their knowledge in order to contribute to the public good. When undertaking research, they strive to advance the science of sociology and to serve the public good.

ETHICAL STANDARDS

1. Professional and Scientific Standards

Sociologists adhere to the highest possible technical standards that are reasonable and responsible in their research, teaching, practice, and service activities. They rely on scientifically and professionally derived knowledge; act with honesty and integrity; and avoid untrue, deceptive, or undocumented statements in undertaking work-related functions or activities.

2. Competence

(a) Sociologists conduct research, teach, practice, and provide service only within the boundaries of their competence, based on their education, training, supervised experience, or appropriate professional experience.

(b) Sociologists conduct research, teach, practice, and provide service in new areas or involving new techniques only after they have taken reasonable steps to ensure the competence of their work in these areas.

(c) Sociologists who engage in research, teaching, practice, or service maintain awareness of current scientific and professional information in their fields of activity, and undertake continuing efforts to maintain competence in the skills they use.

(d) Sociologists refrain from undertaking an activity when their personal circumstances may interfere with their professional work or lead to harm for a student, supervisee, human subject, client, colleague, or other person to whom they have a scientific, teaching, consulting, or other professional obligation.

3. Representation and Misuse of Expertise

(a) In research, teaching, practice, service, or other situations where sociologists render professional judgments or present their expertise, they accurately and fairly represent their areas and degrees of expertise.

(b) Sociologists do not accept grants, contracts, consultation, or work assignments from individual or organizational clients or sponsors that appear likely to require violation of the standards in this Code of Ethics. Sociologists dissociate themselves from such activities when they discover a violation and are unable to achieve its correction.

(c) Because sociologists' scientific and professional judgments and actions may affect the lives of others, they are alert to and guard against personal, financial, social, organizational, or political factors that might lead to misuse of their knowledge, expertise, or influence.

(d) If sociologists learn of misuse or misrepresentation of their work, they take reasonable steps to correct or minimize the misuse or misrepresentation.

4. Delegation and Supervision

(a) Sociologists provide proper training and supervision to their students, supervisees, or employees and take reasonable steps to see that such persons perform services responsibly, competently, and ethically.

(b) Sociologists delegate to their students, supervisees, or employees only those responsibilities that such persons, based on their education, training, or experience, can reasonably be expected to perform either independently or with the level of supervision provided.

5. Nondiscrimination

Sociologists do not engage in discrimination in their work based on age; gender; race; ethnicity; national origin; religion; sexual orientation; disability; health-conditions; marital, domestic, or parental status; or any other applicable basis proscribed by law.

6. Non-exploitation

(a) Whether for personal, economic, or professional advantage, sociologists do not exploit persons over whom they have direct or indirect supervisory, evaluative, or other authority such as students, supervisees, employees, or research participants.

(b) Sociologists do not directly supervise or exercise evaluative authority over any person with whom they have a sexual relationship, including students, supervisees, employees, or research participants.

7. Harassment

Sociologists do not engage in harassment of any person, including students, supervisees, employees, or research participants. Harassment consists of a single intense and severe act or of multiple persistent or pervasive acts which are demeaning, abusive, offensive, or create a hostile professional or workplace environment. Sexual harassment may include sexual solicitation, physical advance, or verbal or non-verbal conduct that is sexual in nature. Racial harassment may include unnecessary, exaggerated, or unwarranted attention or attack, whether verbal or non-verbal, because of a person's race or ethnicity.

8. Employment Decisions

Sociologists have an obligation to adhere to the highest ethical standards when participating in employment related decisions, when seeking employment, or when planning to resign from a position.

8.01 Fair Employment Practices

(a) When participating in employment-related decisions, sociologists make every effort to ensure equal opportunity and fair treatment to all full- and part-time employees. They do not discriminate in hiring, promotion, salary, treatment, or any other conditions of employment or career development on the basis of age; gender; race; ethnicity; national origin; religion; sexual orientation; disability; health conditions; marital, domestic, or parental status; or any other applicable basis proscribed by law.

(b) When participating in employment-related decisions, sociologists specify the requirements for hiring, promotion, tenure, and termination and communicate these requirements thoroughly to full- and part-time employees and prospective employees.

(c) When participating in employment-related decisions, sociologists have the responsibility to be informed of fair employment codes, to communicate this information to employees, and to help create an atmosphere upholding fair employment practices for full- and part-time employees.

(d) When participating in employment-related decisions, sociologists inform prospective full- and part-time employees of any constraints on research and publication and negotiate clear understandings about any conditions that may limit research and scholarly activity.

8.02 Responsibilities of Employees

(a) When seeking employment, sociologists provide prospective employers with accurate and complete information on their professional qualifications and experiences.

(b) When leaving a position, permanently or temporarily, sociologists provide their employers with adequate notice and take reasonable steps to reduce negative effects of leaving.

9. Conflicts of Interest

Sociologists maintain the highest degree of integrity in their professional work and avoid conflicts of interest and the appearance of conflict. Conflicts of interest arise when sociologists' personal or financial interests prevent them from performing their professional work in an unbiased manner. In research, teaching, practice, and service, sociologists are alert to situations that might cause a conflict of interest and take appropriate action to prevent conflict or disclose it to appropriate parties.

9.01 Adherence to Professional Standards

Irrespective of their personal or financial interests or those of their employers or clients, sociologists adhere to professional and scientific standards in (1) the collection, analysis, or interpretation of data; (2) the reporting of research; (3) the teaching, professional presentation, or public dissemination of sociological knowledge; and (4) the identification or implementation of appropriate contractual, consulting, or service activities.

9.02 Disclosure

Sociologists disclose relevant sources of financial support and relevant personal or professional relationships that may have the appearance of or potential for a conflict of interest to an employer or client, to the sponsors of their professional work, or in public speeches and writing.

9.03 Avoidance of Personal Gain

(a) Under all circumstances, sociologists do not use or otherwise seek to gain from information or material received in a confidential context (e.g., knowledge obtained from reviewing a manuscript or serving on a proposal review panel), unless they have authorization to do so or until that information is otherwise made publicly available.

(b) Under all circumstances, sociologists do not seek to gain from information or material in an employment or client relationship without permission of the employer or client.

9.04 Decisionmaking in the Workplace

In their workplace, sociologists take appropriate steps to avoid conflicts of interest or the appearance of conflicts, and carefully scrutinize potentially biasing affiliations or relationships. In research, teaching, practice, or service, such potentially biasing affiliations or relationships include, but are not limited to, situations involving family, business, or close personal friendships or those with whom sociologists have had strong conflict or disagreement.

9.05 Decisionmaking Outside of the Workplace

In professional activities outside of their workplace, sociologists in all circumstances abstain from engaging in deliberations and decisions that allocate or withhold benefits or rewards from individuals or institutions if they have biasing affiliations or relationships. These biasing affiliations or relationships are: 1) current employment or being considered for employment at an organization or institution that could be construed as benefiting from the decision; 2) current officer or board member of an organization or institution that could be construed as benefiting from the decision; 3) current employment or being considered for employment at the same organization or institution where an individual could benefit from the decision; 4) a spouse, domestic partner, or known relative who as an individual could benefit from the decision; or 5) a current business or professional partner, research collaborator, employee, supervisee, or student who as an individual could benefit from the decision.

10. Public Communication

Sociologists adhere to the highest professional standards in public communications about their professional services, credentials and expertise, work products, or publications, whether these communications are from themselves or from others.

10.01 Public Communications

(a) Sociologists take steps to ensure the accuracy of all public communications. Such public communications include, but are not limited to, directory listings; personal resumes or curriculum vitae; advertising; brochures or printed matter; interviews or comments to the media; statements in legal proceedings; lectures and public oral presentations; or other published materials.

(b) Sociologists do not make public statements that are false, deceptive, misleading, or fraudulent, either because of what they state, convey, or suggest or because of what they omit, concerning their research, practice, or other work activities or those of persons or organizations with which they are affiliated. Such activities include, but are not limited to, false or deceptive statements concerning sociologists' (1) training, experience, or competence; (2) academic degrees; (3) credentials; (4) institutional or association affiliations; (5) services; (6) fees; or (7) publications or research findings. Sociologists do not make false or deceptive statements concerning the scientific basis for, results of, or degree of success from their professional services. (c) When sociologists provide professional advice or comment by means of public lectures, demonstrations, radio or television programs, prerecorded tapes, printed articles, mailed material, or other media, they take reasonable precautions to ensure that (1) the statements are based on appropriate research, literature, and practice; and (2) the statements are otherwise consistent with this Code of Ethics.

10.02 Statements by Others

(a) Sociologists who engage or employ others to create or place public statements that promote their work products, professional services, or other activities retain responsibility for such statements.

(b) Sociologists make reasonable efforts to prevent others whom they do not directly engage, employ, or supervise (such as employers, publishers, sponsors, organizational clients, members of the media) from making deceptive statements concerning their professional research, teaching, or practice activities.

(c) In working with the press, radio, television, or other communications media or in advertising in the media, sociologists are cognizant of potential conflicts of interest or appearances of such conflicts (e.g., they do not provide compensation to employees of the media), and they adhere to the highest standards of professional honesty (e.g., they acknowledge paid advertising).

11. Confidentiality

Sociologists have an obligation to ensure that confidential information is protected. They do so to ensure the integrity of research and the open communication with research participants and to protect sensitive information obtained in research, teaching, practice, and service. When gathering confidential information, sociologists should take into account the long-term uses of the information, including its potential placement in public archives or the examination of the information by other researchers or practitioners.

11.01 Maintaining Confidentiality

(a) Sociologists take reasonable precautions to protect the confidentiality rights of research participants, students, employees, clients, or others.

(b) Confidential information provided by research participants, students, employees, clients, or others is treated as such by sociologists even if there is no legal protection or privilege to do so. Sociologists have an obligation to protect confidential information, and not allow information gained in confidence from being used in ways that would unfairly compromise research participants, students, employees, clients, or others.

ETHICAL PRINCIPLES OF SOCIOLOGISTS

(c) Information provided under an understanding of confidentiality is treated as such even after the death of those providing that information.

(d) Sociologists maintain the integrity of confidential deliberations, activities, or roles, including, where applicable, that of professional committees, review panels, or advisory groups (e.g., the ASA Committee on Professional Ethics).

(e) Sociologists, to the extent possible, protect the confidentiality of student records, performance data, and personal information, whether verbal or written, given in the context of academic consultation, supervision, or advising.

(f) The obligation to maintain confidentiality extends to members of research or training teams and collaborating organizations who have access to the information. To ensure that access to confidential information is restricted, it is the responsibility of researchers, administrators, and principal investigators to instruct staff to take the steps necessary to protect confidentiality.

(g) When using private information about individuals collected by other persons or institutions, sociologists protect the confidentiality of individually identifiable information. Information is private when an individual can reasonably expect that the information will not be made public with personal identifiers (e.g., medical or employment records).

11.02 Limits of Confidentiality

(a) Sociologists inform themselves fully about all laws and rules which may limit or alter guarantees of confidentiality. They determine their ability to guarantee absolute confidentiality and, as appropriate, inform research participants, students, employees, clients, or others of any limitations to this guarantee at the outset consistent with ethical standards set forth in 11.02(b).

(b) Sociologists may confront unanticipated circumstances where they become aware of information that is clearly health- or life-threatening to research participants, students, employees, clients, or others. In these cases, sociologists balance the importance of guarantees of confidentiality with other principles in this Code of Ethics, standards of conduct, and applicable law.

(c) Confidentiality is not required with respect to observations in public places, activities conducted in public, or other settings where no rules of privacy are provided by law or custom. Similarly, confidentiality is not required in the case of information available from public records.

11.03 Discussing Confidentiality and Its Limits

(a) When sociologists establish a scientific or professional relationship with persons, they discuss (1) the relevant limitations on confidentiality, and (2) the foreseeable uses of the information generated through their professional work.

(b) Unless it is not feasible or is counter-productive, the discussion of confidentiality occurs at the outset of the relationship and thereafter as new circumstances may warrant.

11.04 Anticipation of Possible Uses of Information

(a) When research requires maintaining personal identifiers in data bases or systems of records, sociologists delete such identifiers before the information is made publicly available.

(b) When confidential information concerning research participants, clients, or other recipients of service is entered into databases or systems of records available to persons without the prior consent of the relevant parties, sociologists protect anonymity by not including personal identifiers or by employing other techniques that mask or control disclosure of individual identities.

(c) When deletion of personal identifiers is not feasible, sociologists take reasonable steps to determine that appropriate consent of personally-identifiable individuals has been obtained before they transfer such data to others or review such data collected by others.

11.05 Electronic Transmission of Confidential Information

Sociologists use extreme care in delivering or transferring any confidential data, information, or communication over public computer networks. Sociologists are attentive to the problems of maintaining confidentiality and control over sensitive material and data when use of technological innovations, such as public computer networks, may open their professional and scientific communication to unauthorized persons.

11.06 Anonymity of Sources

(a) Sociologists do not disclose in their writings, lectures, or other public media confidential, personally identifiable information concerning their research participants, students, individual or organizational clients, or other recipients of their service which is obtained during the course of their work, unless consent from individuals or their legal representatives has been obtained.

(b) When confidential information is used in scientific and professional presentations, sociologists disguise the identity of research participants, students, individual or organizational clients, or other recipients of their-service.

11.07 Minimizing Intrusions on Privacy

(a) To minimize intrusions on privacy, sociologists include in written and oral reports, consultations, and public communications only information germane to the purpose for which the communication is made.

(b) Sociologists discuss confidential information or evaluative data concerning research participants, students, supervisees, employees, and individual or organizational clients only for appropriate scientific or professional purposes and only with persons clearly concerned with such matters.

11.08 Preservation of Confidential Information

(a) Sociologists take reasonable steps to ensure that records, data, or information are preserved in a confidential manner consistent with the requirements of this Code of Ethics, recognizing that ownership of records, data, or information may also be governed by law or institutional principles.

(b) Sociologists plan so that confidentiality of records, data, or information is protected in the event of the sociologist's death, incapacity, or withdrawal from the position or practice.

(c) When sociologists transfer confidential records, data, or information to other persons or organizations, they obtain assurances that the recipients of the records, data, or information will employ measures to protect confidentiality at least equal to those originally pledged.

12. Informed Consent

Informed consent is a basic ethical tenet of scientific research on human populations. Sociologists do not involve a human being as a subject in research without the informed consent of the subject or the subject's legally authorized representative, except as otherwise specified in this Code. Sociologists recognize the possibility of undue influence or subtle pressures on subjects that may derive from researchers' expertise or authority, and they take this into account in designing informed consent procedures.

12.01 Scope of Informed Consent

(a) Sociologists conducting research obtain consent from research participants or their legally authorized representatives (1) when data are collected from research participants through any form of communication, interaction, or intervention; or (2) when behavior of research participants occurs in a private context where an individual can reasonably expect that no observation or reporting is taking place.

(b) Despite the paramount importance of consent, sociologists may seek waivers of this standard when (1) the research involves no more than minimal risk for research participants, and (2) the research could not practicably be carried out were informed consent to be required. Sociologists recognize that waivers of consent require approval from institutional review boards or, in the absence of such boards, from another authoritative body with expertise on the ethics of research. Under such circumstances, the confidentiality of any personally identifiable information must be maintained unless otherwise set forth in 11.02(b).

(c) Sociologists may conduct research in public places or use publicly available information about individuals (e.g., naturalistic observations in public places, analysis of public records, or archival research) without obtaining consent. If, under such circumstances, sociologists have any doubt whatsoever about the need for informed consent, they consult with institutional review boards or, in the absence of such boards, with another authoritative body with expertise on the ethics of research before proceeding with such research.

(d) In undertaking research with vulnerable populations (e.g., youth, recent immigrant populations, the mentally ill), sociologists take special care to ensure that the voluntary nature of the research is understood and that consent is not coerced. In all other respects, sociologists adhere to the principles set forth in 12.01(a)-(c).

(e) Sociologists are familiar with and conform to applicable state and federal regulations and, where applicable, institutional review board requirements for obtaining informed consent for research.

12.02 Informed Consent Process

(a) When informed consent is required, sociologists enter into an agreement with research participants or their legal representatives that clarifies the nature of the research and the responsibilities of the investigator prior to conducting the research.

(b) When informed consent is required, sociologists use language that is understandable to and respectful of research participants or their legal representatives.

(c) When informed consent is required, sociologists provide research participants or their legal representatives with the opportunity to ask questions about any aspect of the research, at any time during or after their participation in the research.

(d) When informed consent is required, sociologists inform research participants or their legal representatives of the nature of the research; they indicate to participants that their participation or continued participation is voluntary; they inform participants of significant factors that may be expected to influence their willingness to participate (e.g., possible risks and benefits of their participation); and they explain other aspects of the research and respond to questions from prospective participants. Also, if relevant, sociologists explain that refusal to participate or withdrawal from participation in the research involves no penalty, and they explain any foreseeable consequences of declining or withdrawing. Sociologists explicitly discuss confidentiality and, if applicable, the extent to which confidentiality may be limited as set forth in 11.02(b).

(e) When informed consent is required, sociologists keep records regarding said consent. They recognize that consent is a process that involves oral and/or written consent.

(f) Sociologists honor all commitments they have made to research participants as part of the informed consent process except where unanticipated circumstances demand otherwise as set forth in 11.02(b).

12.03 Informed Consent of Students and Subordinates

When undertaking research at their own institutions or organizations with research participants who are students or subordinates, sociologists take special care to protect the prospective subjects from adverse consequences of declining or withdrawing from participation.

12.04 Informed Consent with Children

(a) In undertaking research with children, sociologists obtain the consent of children to participate, to the extent that they are capable of providing such consent, except under circumstances where consent may not be required as set forth in 12.01(b).

(b) In undertaking research with children, sociologists obtain the consent of a parent or a legally authorized guardian. Sociologists may seek waivers of parental or guardian consent when (1) the research involves no more than minimal risk for the research participants, and (2) the research could not practicably be carried out were consent to be required, or (3) the consent of a parent or guardian is not a reasonable requirement to protect the child (e.g., neglected or abused children).

(c) Sociologists recognize that waivers of consent from a child and a parent or guardian require approval from institutional review boards or, in the absence of such boards, from another authoritative body with expertise on the ethics of research. Under such circumstances, the confidentiality of any personally identifiable information must be maintained unless otherwise set forth in 11.02(b).

12.05 Use of Deception in Research

(a) Sociologists do not use deceptive techniques (1) unless they have determined that their use will not be harmful to research participants; is justified by the study's prospective scientific, educational, or applied value; and that equally effective alternative procedures that do not use deception are not feasible, and (2) unless they have obtained the approval of institutional review boards or, in the absence of such boards, with another authoritative body with expertise on the ethics of research.

(b) Sociologists never deceive research participants about significant aspects of the research that would affect their willingness to participate, such as physical risks, discomfort, or unpleasant emotional experiences.

(c) When deception is an integral feature of the design and conduct of research, sociologists attempt to correct any misconception that research participants may have no later than at the conclusion of the research.

(d) On rare occasions, sociologists may need to conceal their identity in order to undertake research that could not practicably be carried out were they to be known as researchers. Under such circumstances, sociologists undertake the research if it involves no more than minimal risk for the research participants and if they have obtained approval to proceed in this manner from an institutional review board or, in the absence of such boards, from another authoritative body with expertise on the ethics of research. Under such circumstances, confidentiality must be maintained unless otherwise set forth in 11.02(b).

12.06 Use of Recording Technology

Sociologists obtain informed consent from research participants, students, employees, clients, or others prior to videotaping, filming, or recording them in any form, unless these activities involve simply naturalistic observations in public places and it is not anticipated that the recording will be used in a manner that could cause personal identification or harm.

13. Research Planning, Implementation, and Dissemination

Sociologists have an obligation to promote the integrity of research and to ensure that they comply with the ethical tenets of science in the planning, implementation, and dissemination of research. They do so in order to advance knowledge, to minimize the possibility that results will be misleading, and to protect the rights of research participants.

13.01 Planning and Implementation

(a) In planning and implementing research, sociologists minimize the possibility that results will be misleading.

(b) Sociologists take steps to implement protections for the rights and welfare of research participants and other persons affected by the research.

(c) In their research, sociologists do not encourage activities or themselves behave in ways that are health- or life-threatening to research participants or others.

(d) In planning and implementing research, sociologists consult those with expertise concerning any special population under investigation or likely to be affected.

(e) In planning and implementing research, sociologists consider its ethical acceptability as set forth in the Code of Ethics. If the best ethical practice is unclear, sociologists consult with institutional review boards or, in the absence of such review processes, with another authoritative body with expertise on the ethics of research.

(f) Sociologists are responsible for the ethical conduct of research conducted by them or by others under their supervision or authority.

13.02 Unanticipated Research Opportunities

If during the course of teaching, practice, service, or non-professional activities, sociologists determine that they wish to undertake research that was not previously anticipated, they make known their intentions and take steps to ensure that the research can be undertaken consonant with ethical principles, especially those relating to confidentiality and informed consent. Under such circumstances, sociologists seek the approval of institutional review boards or, in the absence of such review processes, another authoritative body with expertise on the ethics of research.

13.03 Offering Inducements for Research Participants

Sociologists do not offer excessive or inappropriate financial or other inducements to obtain the participation of research participants, particularly when it might coerce participation. Sociologists may provide incentives to the extent that resources are available and appropriate.

13.04 Reporting on Research

(a) Sociologists disseminate their research findings except where unanticipated circumstances (e.g., the health of the researcher) or proprietary agreements with employers, contractors, or clients preclude such dissemination.

(b) Sociologists do not fabricate data or falsify results in their publications or presentations.

(c) In presenting their work, sociologists report their findings fully and do not omit relevant data. They report results whether they support or contradict the expected outcomes.

(d) Sociologists take particular care to state all relevant qualifications on the findings and interpretation of their research. Sociologists also disclose underlying assumptions, theories, methods, measures, and research designs that might bear upon findings and interpretations of their work.

(e) Consistent with the spirit of full disclosure of methods and analyses, once findings are publicly disseminated, sociologists permit their open assessment and verification by other responsible researchers with appropriate safeguards, where applicable, to protect the anonymity of research participants.

(f) If sociologists discover significant errors in their publication or presentation of data, they take reasonable steps to correct such errors in a correction, a retraction, published errata, or other public fora as appropriate.

(g) Sociologists report sources of financial support in their written papers and note any special relations to any sponsor. In special circumstances, sociologists may withhold the names of specific sponsors if they provide an adequate and full description of the nature and interest of the sponsor.

(h) Sociologists take special care to report accurately the results of others' scholarship by using correct information and citations when presenting the work of others in publications, teaching, practice, and service settings.

13.05 Data Sharing

(a) Sociologists share data and pertinent documentation as a regular practice. Sociologists make their data available after completion of the project or its major publications, except where proprietary agreements with employers, contractors, or clients preclude such accessibility or when it is impossible to share data and protect the confidentiality of the data or the anonymity of research participants (e.g., raw field notes or detailed information from ethnographic interviews).

(b) Sociologists anticipate data sharing as an integral part of a research plan whenever data sharing is feasible.

(c) Sociologists share data in a form that is consonant with research participants' interests and protect the confidentiality of the information they have been given. They maintain the confidentiality of data, whether legally required or not; remove personal identifiers before data are shared; and if necessary use other disclosure avoidance techniques.

(d) Sociologists who do not otherwise place data in public archives keep data available and retain documentation relating to the research for a reasonable period of time after publication or dissemination of results.

(e) Sociologists may ask persons who request their data for further analysis to bear the associated incremental costs, if necessary.

(f) Sociologists who use data from others for further analyses explicitly acknowledge the contribution of the initial researchers.

14. Plagiarism

(a) In publications, presentations, teaching, practice, and service, sociologists explicitly identify, credit, and reference the author when they take data or material verbatim from another person's written work, whether it is published, unpublished, or electronically available.

(b) In their publications, presentations, teaching, practice, and service, sociologists provide acknowledgment of and reference to the use of others' work, even if the work is not quoted verbatim or paraphrased, and they do not present others' work as their own whether it is published, unpublished, or electronically available.

15. Authorship Credit

(a) Sociologists take responsibility and credit, including authorship credit, only for work they have actually performed or to which they have contributed.

(b) Sociologists ensure that principal authorship and other publication credits are based on the relative scientific or professional contributions of the individuals involved, regardless of their status. In claiming or determining the ordering of authorship, sociologists seek to reflect accurately the contributions of main participants in the research and writing process.

(c) A student is usually listed as principal author on any multiple authored publication that substantially derives from the student's dissertation or thesis.

ETHICAL PRINCIPLES OF SOCIOLOGISTS

16. Publication Process

Sociologists adhere to the highest ethical standards when participating in publication and review processes when they are authors or editors.

16.01 Submission of Manuscripts for Publication

(a) In cases of multiple authorship, sociologists confer with all other authors prior to submitting work for publication and establish mutually acceptable agreements regarding submission.

(b) In submitting a manuscript to a professional journal, book series, or edited book, sociologists grant that publication first claim to publication except where explicit policies allow multiple submissions. Sociologists do not submit a manuscript to a second publication until after an official decision has been received from the first publication or until the manuscript is withdrawn. Sociologists submitting a manuscript for publication in a journal, book series, or edited book can withdraw a manuscript from consideration up until an official acceptance is made.

(c) Sociologists may submit a book manuscript to multiple publishers. However, once sociologists have signed a contract, they cannot withdraw a manuscript from publication unless there is reasonable cause to do so.

16.02 Duplicate Publication of Data

When sociologists publish data or findings that they have previously published elsewhere, they accompany these publications by proper acknowledgment.

16.03 Responsibilities of Editors

(a) When serving as editors of journals or book series, sociologists are fair in the application of standards and operate without personal or ideological favoritism or malice. As editors, sociologists are cognizant of any potential conflicts of interest.

(b) When serving as editors of journals or book series, sociologists ensure the confidential nature of the review process and supervise editorial office staff, including students, in accordance with practices that maintain confidentiality.

(c) When serving as editors of journals or book series, sociologists are bound to publish all manuscripts accepted for publication unless major errors or ethical violations are discovered after acceptance (e.g., plagiarism or scientific misconduct).

(d) When serving as editors of journals or book series, sociologists ensure the anonymity of reviewers unless they otherwise receive permission from reviewers to reveal their identity. Editors ensure that their staff conform to this practice.

(e) When serving as journal editors, sociologists ensure the anonymity of authors unless and until a manuscript is accepted for publication or unless the established practices of the journal are known to be otherwise.

(f) When serving as journal editors, sociologists take steps to provide for the timely review of all manuscripts and respond promptly to inquiries about the status of the review.

17. Responsibilities of Reviewers

(a) In reviewing material submitted for publication, grant support, or other evaluation purposes, sociologists respect the confidentiality of the process and the proprietary rights in such information of those who submitted it.

(b) Sociologists disclose conflicts of interest or decline requests for reviews of the work of others where conflicts of interest are involved.

(c) Sociologists decline requests for reviews of the work of others when they believe that the review process may be biased or when they have questions about the integrity of the process.

(d) If asked to review a manuscript, book, or proposal they have previously reviewed, sociologists make it known to the person making the request (e.g., editor, program officer) unless it is clear that they are being asked to provide a reappraisal.

18. Education, Teaching, and Training

As teachers, supervisors, and trainers, sociologists follow the highest ethical standards in order to ensure the quality of sociological education and the integrity of the teacher-student relationship.

18.01 Administration of Education Programs

(a) Sociologists who are responsible for education and training programs seek to ensure that the programs are competently designed, provide the proper experiences, and meet all goals for which claims are made by the program.

(b) Sociologists responsible for education and training programs seek to ensure that there is an accurate description of the program content, training goals and objectives, and requirements that must be met for satisfactory completion of the program.

(c) Sociologists responsible for education and training programs take steps to ensure that graduate assistants and temporary instructors have the substantive knowledge required to teach courses and the teaching skills needed to facilitate student learning.

(d) Sociologists responsible for education and training programs have an obligation to ensure that ethics are taught to their graduate students as part of their professional preparation.

18.02 Teaching and Training

(a) Sociologists conscientiously perform their teaching responsibilities. They have appropriate skills and knowledge or are receiving appropriate training.

(b) Sociologists provide accurate information at the outset about their courses, particularly regarding the subject matter to be covered, bases for evaluation, and the nature of course experiences.

(c) Sociologists make decisions concerning textbooks, course content, course requirements, and grading solely on the basis of educational criteria without regard for financial or other incentives.

(d) Sociologists provide proper training and supervision to their teaching assistants and other teaching trainees and take reasonable steps to ensure that such persons perform these teaching responsibilities responsibly, competently, and ethically.

(e) Sociologists do not permit personal animosities or intellectual differences with colleagues to foreclose students' or supervisees' access to these colleagues or to interfere with student or supervisee learning, academic progress, or professional development.

19. Contractual and Consulting Services

(a) Sociologists undertake grants, contracts, or consultation only when they are knowledgeable about the substance, methods, and techniques they plan to use or have a plan for incorporating appropriate expertise.

(b) In undertaking grants, contracts, or consultation, sociologists base the results of their professional work on appropriate information and techniques.

(c) When financial support for a project has been accepted under a grant, contract, or consultation, sociologists make reasonable efforts to complete the proposed work on schedule.

(d) In undertaking grants, contracts, or consultation, sociologists accurately document and appropriately retain their professional and scientific work.

(e) In establishing a contractual arrangement for research, consultation, or other services, sociologists clarify, to the extent feasible at the outset, the nature of the relationship with the individual, organizational, or institutional client. This clarification includes, as appropriate, the nature of the services to be performed, the probable uses of the services provided, possibilities for the sociologist's future use of the work for scholarly or publication purposes, the timetable for delivery of those services, and compensation and billing arrangements.

20. Adherence to the Code of Ethics

Sociologists have an obligation to confront, address, and attempt to resolve ethical issues according to this Code of Ethics.

20.01 Familiarity with the Code of Ethics

Sociologists have an obligation to be familiar with this Code of Ethics, other applicable ethics codes, and their application to sociologists' work. Lack of awareness or misunderstanding of an ethical standard is not, in itself, a defense to a charge of unethical conduct.

20.02 Confronting Ethical Issues

(a) When sociologists are uncertain whether a particular situation or course of action would violate the Code of Ethics, they consult with other sociologists knowledgeable about ethical issues, with ASA's Committee on Professional Ethics, or with other organizational entities such as institutional review boards.

(b) When sociologists take actions or are confronted with choices where there is a conflict between ethical standards enunciated in the Code of Ethics and laws or legal requirements, they make known their commitment to the Code and take steps to resolve the conflict in a responsible manner by consulting with colleagues, professional organizations, or the ASA's Committee on Professional Ethics.

20.03 Fair Treatment of Parties in Ethical Disputes

(a) Sociologists do not discriminate against a person on the basis of his or her having made an ethical complaint.

(b) Sociologists do not discriminate against a person based on his or her having been the subject of an ethical complaint. This does not preclude taking action based upon the outcome of an ethical complaint.

20.04 Reporting Ethical Violations of Others

When sociologists have substantial reason to believe that there may have been an ethical violation by another sociologist, they attempt to resolve the issue by bringing it to the attention of that individual if an informal resolution appears appropriate or possible, or they seek advice about whether or how to proceed based on this belief, assuming that such activity does not violate any confidentiality rights. Such action might include referral to ASA's Committee on Professional Ethics.

20.05 Cooperating with Ethics Committees

Sociologists cooperate in ethics investigations, proceedings, and resulting requirements of the American Sociological Association. In doing so, they make reasonable efforts to resolve any issues of confidentiality. Failure to cooperate may be an ethics violation.

20.06 Improper Complaints

Sociologists do not file or encourage the filing of ethics complaints that are frivolous and are intended to harm the alleged violator rather than to protect the integrity of the discipline and the public.

Note: This revised edition of the ASA Code of Ethics builds on the 1989 edition of the Code and the 1992 version of the American Psychological Association's Ethical Principles of Psychologists and Code of Conduct.

English and Spanish Glossary

MARK	AS IN	RESPELLING	EXAMPLE
a	alphabet	a	*AL-fuh-bet
ā	Asia	ay	AY-zhuh
ä	cart, top	ah	KAHRT, TAHP
e	let, ten	e	LET, TEN
ē	even, leaf	ee	EE-vuhn, LEEF
i	it, tip, British	i	IL, TIP, BRIT-ish
ī	site, buy, Ohio	y	SYT, BY, oh-HY-oh
	iris	eye	EYE-ris
k	card	k	KAHRD
ō	over, rainbow	oh	OH-vuhr, RAYN-boh
u̇	book, wood	ooh	BOOHK, WOOHD
ȯ	all, orchid	aw	AWL, AWR-kid
ȯi	foil, coin	oy	FOYL, KOYN
au̇	out	ow	OWT
ə	cup, butter	uh	KUHP, BUHT-uhr
ü	rule, food	oo	ROOL, FOOD
yü	few	yoo	FYOO
zh	vision	zh	VIZH-uhn

*A syllable printed in capital letters receives heavier emphasis than the other syllable(s) in a word.

Phonetic Respelling and Pronunciation Guide

Some of the vocabulary terms in this textbook have been respelled to help you pronounce them. The letter combinations used in the respelling throughout the narrative are explained in the following phonetic respelling and pronunciation guide. The guide is adapted from *Merriam-Webster's Collegiate Dictionary, 11th Edition; Merriam-Webster's Geographical Dictionary;* and *Merriam-Webster's Biographical Dictionary.*

A

absolute monarchy an authoritarian type of government in which the hereditary ruler holds absolute power (p. 296)
monarquía absoluta tipo de gobierno autoritario en el que el gobernante hereditario tiene poder absoluto (pág. 296)

abstinence voluntarily not engaging in sexual behavior (p. 122)
abstinencia privación voluntaria de la actividad sexual (pág. 122)

accommodation a state of balance between cooperation and conflict (p. 60)
acomodación estado de equilibrio entre la cooperación y el conflicto (pág. 60)

achieved status a status acquired by an individual on the basis of some special skill, knowledge, or ability (p. 55)
estatus adquirido estatus alcanzado por un individuo por medio de destrezas, conocimientos o habilidades especiales (pág. 55)

acquired immune deficiency syndrome (AIDS) a fatal disease that attacks an individual's immune system, leaving the person vulnerable to a host of deadly infections (p. 248)
síndrome de inmunodeficiencia adquirida (SIDA) enfermedad mortal que ataca el sistema inmunológico del individuo y provoca que la persona sea vulnerable a una gran cantidad de infecciones fatales (pág. 248)

adolescence the period between the normal onset of puberty and the beginning of adulthood (p. 111)
adolescencia período comprendido entre el comienzo normal de la pubertad y el inicio de la adultez (pág. 111)

ageism the belief that one age category is by nature superior to another age category (p. 239)
discriminación por edad creencia de que una categoría de edad es naturalmente superior a otra (pág. 239)

agenda setting an argument that the media sets the boundaries of public debate by deciding which issues will receive coverage and which will not (p. 358)
teoría de la *agenda-setting* argumento que establece que los medios de comunicación definen la opinión pública al determinar qué temas deben tratarse y cuáles no (pág. 358)

agents of socialization specific individuals, groups, and institutions that enable socialization to take place (p. 100)
agentes de socialización individuos, grupos e instituciones que hacen posible la socialización (pág. 100)

alienation the feeling of powerlessness in, and disassociation from, social situations (p. 78)
alienación sentimiento de impotencia en situaciones sociales y disociación de ellas (pág. 78)

alternative medicine treating illnesses with unconventional methods such as acupuncture, acupressure, biofeedback, massage, meditation, yoga, herbal remedies, and relaxation techniques (p. 248)
medicina alternativa tratamiento de enfermedades con métodos no convencionales, como la acupuntura, la digitopuntura, la biorretroalimentación, los masajes, la meditación, el yoga, las hierbas medicinales y las técnicas de relajación (pág. 248)

Alzheimer's disease an organic condition that results in the progressive destruction of brain cells (p. 148)
enfermedad de Alzheimer enfermedad orgánica que produce la destrucción progresiva de las células cerebrales (pág. 148)

animism a belief system in which natural objects such as plants and animals are embodied spirits, which are active in influencing human life (p. 325)
animismo conjunto de creencias según las cuales los objetos naturales, como las plantas y los animales, están habitados por espíritus, que influyen activamente en la vida humana (pág. 325)

anomie (A-NUH-MEE) the situation that arises when the norms of society are unclear or are no longer applicable (p. 164)
anomia situación que se produce cuando las normas de la sociedad no son claras o ya no se aplican (pág. 164)

anthropology the comparative study of various aspects of past and present cultures (p. 5)
antropología estudio comparativo de varios aspectos de las culturas del pasado y del presente (pág. 5)

anticipatory socialization learning the rights, obligations, and expectations of a role to prepare for assuming that role in the future (p. 113)
socialización anticipada aprendizaje de los derechos, las obligaciones y las expectativas de un rol con el fin de prepararse para asumir ese rol en el futuro (pág. 113)

anti-Semitism discrimination and prejudice that targets Jews (p. 224)
antisemitismo discriminación y prejuicios contra los judíos (pág. 224)

aptitude a capacity to learn a particular skill or acquire a specific body of knowledge (p. 91)
aptitud capacidad de aprender una destreza particular o adquirir un conjunto específico de conocimientos (pág. 91)

ascribed status a status assigned according to standards that are beyond a person's control. Age, sex, family heritage, and race are examples of ascribed statuses (p. 55)
estatus adscrito estatus asignado según valores que no se pueden controlar; la edad, el sexo, la herencia familiar y la raza son ejemplos de estatus adscritos (pág. 55)

assimilation the blending of culturally distinct groups into a single group with a common culture and identity (p. 215)
asimilación combinación de grupos culturalmente distintos en un único grupo que comparte una cultura y una identidad (pág. 215)

authoritarianism a type of government in which power rests firmly with the state (p. 296)
autoritarismo tipo de gobierno en el que el estado ejerce fuertemente el poder político (pág. 296)

B

baby-boom generation collective term for the approximately 76 million children born in the United States from 1946 through 1964 (p. 239)
generación del *baby boom* término colectivo que designa a los 76 millones de niños que nacieron en Estados Unidos entre 1946 y 1964 (pág. 239)

barter the practice of exchanging one good for another (p. 64)
trueque práctica que consiste en el intercambio de bienes (pág. 64)

bilingual education a system in which non-English-speaking students are taught academic subjects in their native languages until they are prepared to attend classes taught in English (p. 320)
educación bilingüe sistema en el que los estudiantes que no hablan inglés aprenden materias académicas en su lengua materna hasta estar preparados para tomar clases en inglés (pág. 320)

birthrate the annual number of live births per 1,000 members of a population (p. 371)
tasa de natalidad cantidad anual de nacidos vivos en una población cada 1,000 personas (pág. 371)

bourgeoisie (BOORZH-wah-zee) owners of the means of production in a capitalist society (p. 188)
burguesía propietarios de los medios de producción en una sociedad capitalista (pág. 188)

bureaucracy a ranked authority structure that operates according to specific rules and procedures (p. 75)
burocracia estructura jerárquica de autoridad que opera según reglas y procedimientos específicos (pág. 75)

C

capitalism an economic model in which the factors of production are owned by individuals and that is regulated by the forces of profit and competition (p. 284)
capitalismo modelo económico regulado por las fuerzas de las ganancias y la competencia en el que los propietarios de los factores de producción son individuos (pág. 284)

case study an intensive analysis of a person, group, event, or problem (p. 25)
estudio de caso análisis intensivo de una persona, un grupo, un suceso o un problema (pág. 25)

caste system a system of social stratification in which resources and rewards are distributed on the basis of ascribed statuses (p. 187)
sistema de castas sistema de estratificación social en el que los recursos y las recompensas se distribuyen en base al estatus adscrito (pág. 187)

charismatic authority power that is legitimated on the basis of the personal characteristics of the individual exercising the power (p. 294)
autoridad carismática poder legitimizado en base a las características personales del individuo que ejerce el poder (pág. 294)

charter schools alternative schools that are funded by public money but are privately operated (p. 318)
escuelas *charter* escuelas alternativas financiadas con fondos públicos, pero administradas de manera privada (pág. 318)

city a permanent concentration of relatively large numbers of people who are engaged mainly in non-agricultural pursuits (p. 379)
ciudad concentración permanente de una cantidad relativamente grande de personas que se dedican principalmente a actividades no agrícolas (pág. 379)

class conflict the conflict between people who have power and those who lack power (p. 417)
conflicto de clases conflicto entre los que tienen poder y los que no tienen poder (pág. 417)

class system a system of social stratification in which distribution of scarce resources and rewards is determined on the basis of achieved statuses (p. 188)
sistema de clases sistema de estratificación social en el que los recursos escasos y las recompensas se distribuyen en base al estatus adquirido (pág. 188)

collective behavior the relatively spontaneous social behavior that occurs when people try to develop common solutions to unclear situations (p. 395)
comportamiento colectivo conducta social relativamente espontánea que surge cuando un grupo de personas busca soluciones comunes a situaciones poco claras (pág. 395)

collective preoccupation an action involving people who rarely meet yet engage in similar behavior and share an understanding of the meaning of that behavior (p. 397)
pensamientos colectivos acción de personas que no suelen encontrarse pero que tienen una conducta similar y comprenden el significado de esa conducta (pág. 397)

communism a political and economic system in which property is communally owned (p. 286)
comunismo sistema político y económico en el que la propiedad pertenece a la comunidad (pág. 286)

competition interaction that occurs when two or more people or groups oppose each other to achieve a goal that only one can attain (p. 59)
competencia interacción que se produce cuando dos o más personas o grupos se enfrentan para lograr un objetivo que solo uno puede alcanzar (pág. 59)

compositional theory a theory of city life that examines the ways in which the composition of a city's population influences life in the city. According to this theory, individuals are able to protect themselves from the anonymity of the city by forming primary groups with others who are like themselves (p. 386)
teoría composicional teoría acerca de la vida urbana que analiza los efectos de la composición poblacional de las ciudades en la vida urbana; según esta teoría, los individuos pueden protegerse del anonimato que provoca la ciudad formando grupos primarios junto con otras personas similares (pág. 386)

concentric zone model a model of urban structure proposed by Ernest W. Burgess in which the typical industrial city is said to spread outward from the center in a series of circles within circles (p. 384)
modelo de círculos concéntricos modelo de estructura urbana propuesto por Ernest W. Burgess, que establece que la típica ciudad industrial se expande hacia afuera desde el centro en una serie de círculos concéntricos (pág. 384)

conflict the deliberate attempt to oppose, harm, control by force, or resist the will of another person or persons (p. 59)
conflicto intento deliberado por oponerse a la voluntad de otra u otras personas, dañarla, controlarla por la fuerza o resistirla (pág. 59)

conflict perspective a theoretical perspective that focuses on those forces in society that promote competition and change (p. 16)
perspectiva de conflicto perspectiva teórica que se centra en las fuerzas de la sociedad que promueven la competencia y el cambio (pág. 16)

conservative movement a social movement that tries to protect from change what they see as society's prevailing values (p. 405)
movimiento conservador movimiento social cuyo objetivo es evitar que cambien los valores sociales que se consideran preponderantes (pág. 405)

constitutional monarchy a type of government in which the ruler, or monarch, is nothing more than the symbolic head of state. Constitutional monarchies are considered democratic because the ultimate power rests with elected officials (p. 295)
monarquía constitucional tipo de gobierno en el que el gobernante, o monarca, es tan solo el jefe de estado simbólico; se considera que las monarquías constitucionales son democráticas porque el poder máximo está en manos de autoridades electas (pág. 295)

content analysis the research method used to analyze existing sources that involves counting the number of times a particular word, phrase, idea, event, symbol, or other element appears in a given context (p. 25)
análisis de contenido método de investigación usado para analizar fuentes que consiste en contar la cantidad de veces que aparece una palabra, una frase, una idea, un suceso, un símbolo o cualquier otro elemento particular en un contexto dado (pág. 25)

control theory a theory of deviant behavior in which deviance is seen as a natural occurrence and conformity is seen as the result of social ties among individuals (p. 166)
teoría del control teoría de la desviación en la que la conducta desviada se considera natural y la conformidad a las normas se percibe como el resultado de los vínculos sociales entre individuos (pág. 166)

cooperation interaction that occurs when two or more persons or groups work together to achieve a goal that will benefit many people (p. 60)
cooperación interacción que se produce cuando dos o más personas o grupos trabajan en conjunto para alcanzar un objetivo que beneficiará a muchas personas (pág. 60)

corporation a business organization that is owned by stockholders and is treated by law as if it were an individual person (p. 288)
sociedad anónima organización comercial que pertenece a un grupo de accionistas y que responde ante la ley como si fuera una persona individual (pág. 288)

corrections sanctions such as imprisonment, parole, probation, and community service used to punish criminals (p. 173)
penas sanciones usadas para castigar a los delincuentes, como la prisión, la libertad condicional, la libertad provisional y el servicio comunitario (pág. 173)

correlation a situation that exists when a change in one variable is regularly associated with a change in another variable (p. 23)
correlación situación que se presenta cuando un cambio en una variable se suele asociar con un cambio en otra variable (pág. 23)

counterculture a group that rejects the values, norms, and practices of the larger society and replaces them with a new set of cultural patterns (p. 40)
contracultura grupo que rechaza los valores, las normas y las prácticas de la mayor parte de la sociedad y los reemplaza con un nuevo conjunto de modelos culturales (pág. 40)

courtship a social interaction similar to dating but with the sole purpose of eventual marriage (p. 116)
cortejo interacción social similar al noviazgo pero cuyo único propósito es, en última instancia, el matrimonio (pág. 116)

crime any act that is labeled as such by those in authority and is prohibited by law (p. 169)
delito todo acto que las autoridades clasifican como tal y que está prohibido por la ley (pág. 169)

crime syndicate a large-scale organization of professional criminals that controls some vice or legitimate business through violence or the threat of violence (p. 170)
organización mafiosa gran organización de delincuentes profesionales que controlan actividades relacionadas con el vicio o los negocios legítimos por medio de la violencia o amenazas de violencia (pág. 170)

criminal-justice system the system of police, courts, and corrections that has jurisdiction once a crime has been committed (p. 172)
sistema de justicia penal sistema compuesto por la policía, los tribunales y las penas que tiene jurisdicción cuando se ha cometido un delito (pág. 172)

crowd a temporary gathering of people who are in close enough proximity to interact (p. 395)
multitud reunión temporaria de personas que están a una distancia bastante cercana para interactuar (pág. 395)

cult a small, unorthodox religious group (p. 326)
culto pequeño grupo religioso no ortodoxo (pág. 326)

cultural diffusion the process of spreading cultural traits from one society to another (p. 42)
difusión cultural proceso por el cual las características culturales se transmiten de una sociedad a otra (pág. 42)

cultural lag a situation in which some aspects of the culture change less rapidly, or lag behind, other aspects of the same culture (p. 42)
retraso cultural situación en la que algunos aspectos de la cultura cambian con menor rapidez, o se retrasan, con respecto a otros aspectos de la misma cultura (pág. 42)

cultural leveling the process through which cultures become more and more alike (p. 42)
nivelación cultural proceso por el cual las culturas se asemejan cada vez más (pág. 42)

cultural pluralism a policy that allows each group within society to keep its unique cultural identity (p. 215)
pluralismo cultural política mediante la cual se permite que cada grupo de una sociedad mantenga su propia identidad cultural (pág. 215)

cultural relativism a belief that cultures should be judged by their own standards (p. 41)
relativismo cultural creencia de que las culturas se deben juzgar según sus propios valores (pág. 41)

cultural transmission theory a theory of deviant behavior that views deviance as a learned behavior transmitted through interaction with others (p. 166)
teoría de la transmisión cultural teoría de la desviación según la cual ese tipo de conducta es aprendida y se transmite mediante la interacción con otras personas (pág. 166)

cultural universals common features that are found in all human cultures (p. 39)
universales culturales características comunes a todas las culturas humanas (pág. 39)

culture shared products of human groups, which include both physical objects and the beliefs, values, and behaviors shared by the group (p. 34)
cultura productos compartidos por un grupo humano; entre ellos, los objetos físicos, las creencias, los valores y las conductas que comparte el grupo (pág. 34)

cyclical theory a historical view of social change in which societies are seen as rising and then falling or as continuously moving back and forth between stages of development (p. 416)
teoría cíclica visión histórica del cambio social según la cual las sociedades crecen y luego decaen, o avanzan y retroceden continuamente a lo largo de las etapas de desarrollo (pág. 416)

D

dating a social behavior that allows individuals to choose their own marriage partners (p. 116)
noviazgo conducta social en la que los individuos pueden elegir a sus propios cónyuges (pág. 116)

death rate the annual number of deaths per 1,000 members of a population (p. 372)
tasa de mortalidad cantidad anual de muertes en una población cada 1,000 personas (pág. 372)

demographic transition theory a theory of population in which population patterns are said to be tied to a society's level of technological development. Theoretically, a society's population progresses through three distinct stages (p. 376)
teoría de la transición demográfica teoría poblacional según la cual los patrones de población de una sociedad dependerían de su nivel de desarrollo tecnológico; en teoría, la población de una sociedad atraviesa tres etapas distintas (pág. 376)

demography the scientific study of human populations (p. 371)
demografía estudio científico de las poblaciones humanas (pág. 371)

denomination a well-established religious organization in which a substantial portion of the population are members (p. 326)
denominación organización religiosa establecida cuyos miembros representan una parte importante de la población (pág. 326)

dependency the shift from being an independent adult to being dependent on others for physical or financial assistance (p. 149)
dependencia proceso por el cual se deja de ser un adulto independiente y se comienza a depender de otras personas para obtener asistencia física o financiera (pág. 149)

dependency ratio the number of workers for each person receiving Social Security benefits (p. 240)
índice de dependencia cantidad de trabajadores por cada persona que recibe beneficios de la seguridad social (pág. 240)

deviance a behavior that violates significant social norms (p. 162)
desviación conducta que desobedece normas sociales importantes (pág. 162)

dictatorship an authoritarian type of government in which power is in the hands of a single individual (p. 296)
dictadura tipo de gobierno autoritario en el que el poder está en manos de un solo individuo (pág. 296)

differential association a concept that refers to the frequency and closeness of associations a person has with deviant and nondeviant individuals (p. 166)
asociación diferencial concepto que hace referencia a la frecuencia y a la intensidad con que una persona interactúa con individuos desviados y con individuos no desviados (pág. 166)

digital divide the gap between those with access to new technologies and those without (p. 355)
brecha digital distancia que separa a las personas que tienen acceso a las nuevas tecnologías de las que no lo tienen (pág. 355)

discrimination a denial of equal treatment to individuals based on their group membership (p. 213)
discriminación trato diferenciado de individuos en base a su grupo de pertenencia (pág. 213)

division of labor the specialization by individuals or groups in the performance of specific economic activities (p. 63)
división del trabajo especialización de individuos o grupos para realizar determinadas actividades económicas (pág. 63)

dominant group a group that possesses the ability to discriminate by virtue of their greater power, privilege, and social status in a society (p. 211)
grupo dominante grupo que tiene la habilidad de discriminar en virtud de su mayoría de poder, privilegios y estatus social en una sociedad (pág. 211)

dramaturgy a theory that proposes that social interaction is like a drama being performed on a stage (p. 98)
dramaturgia teoría que postula que la interacción social es como una obra de teatro que se representa en un escenario (pág. 98)

drug a substance that changes mood, behavior, or consciousness (p. 124)
droga sustancia que altera el estado de ánimo, la conducta o la conciencia (pág. 124)

dual-earner families families in which both husband and wife have jobs (p. 267)
familias de doble ingreso familias en las que trabajan tanto el esposo como la esposa (pág. 267)

dyad (DY-ad) a group with two members (p. 69)
díada grupo de dos miembros (pág. 69)

dysfunction a negative consequence an element has for the stability of the social system (p. 16)
disfunción efecto negativo que produce un elemento sobre la estabilidad del sistema social (pág. 16)

E

early adulthood the first era of adulthood, spanning ages 17 through 39 (p. 137)
adultez temprana primera parte de la etapa adulta que se extiende de los 17 a los 39 años (pág. 137)

ecclesia (i-KLEE-zee-uh) a type of religious organization in which all people in the society are members by virtue of their birth (p. 326)
ecclesia tipo de organización religiosa que considera que todos los integrantes de la sociedad son miembros de esa organización por el hecho de haber nacido (pág. 326)

e-commerce economic transactions that occur over the Internet or other electronic communication systems (p. 290)
comercio electrónico transacciones económicas realizadas por Internet u otros sistemas de comunicación electrónicos (pág. 290)

economic institution a system of roles and norms that governs the production, distribution, and consumption of goods and services (p. 283)
institución económica sistema de roles y normas que rige la producción, la distribución y el consumo de bienes y servicios (pág. 283)

economics the study of the choices people make in an effort to satisfy their wants and needs (p. 5)
economía estudio de las elecciones que hacen las personas para satisfacer sus deseos y necesidades (pág. 5)

education a system of roles and norms that ensures the transmission of knowledge, values, and patterns of behavior from one generation to the next (p. 309)
educación sistema de roles y normas que asegura la transmisión de conocimientos, valores y patrones de conducta de una generación a otra (pág. 309)

electronic community a group made up of people who interact with one another regularly through the Internet or other forms of electronic communication (p. 72)
comunidad electrónica grupo de personas que interactúan regularmente a través de Internet u otras formas de comunicación electrónica (pág. 72)

endogamy marriage within one's own social category (p. 187)
endogamia matrimonio dentro de la propia categoría social (pág. 187)

environmental racism racial bias in environmental policies and practices (p. 220)
racismo ambiental sesgo racial en las políticas y prácticas ambientales (pág. 220)

ENGLISH AND SPANISH GLOSSARY

equilibrium theory Talcott Parsons's view of social change in which society is likened to a living organism. Change in one part of the social system produces change in all other parts as the system attempts to regain balance, or equilibrium (p. 417)
teoría del equilibrio visión del cambio social de Talcott Parsons en la que la sociedad se compara con un organismo vivo; los cambios que ocurren en una parte del sistema social suscitan cambios en todas las partes a medida que el sistema trata de recuperar el equilibrio (pág. 417)

ethicalism a belief system in which moral principles have a sacred quality (p. 325)
doctrina ética sistema de creencias en el que los principios morales tienen calidad de sagrados (pág. 325)

ethnic cleansing the process of removing a group from a particular area through terror, expulsion, and mass murder (p. 217)
limpieza étnica proceso de eliminar a un grupo de un área determinada por medio del terror, la expulsión y los asesinatos en masa (pág. 217)

ethnic group individuals who share a common cultural background and a common sense of identity (p. 210)
grupo étnico individuos que comparten un mismo origen cultural y sentido de la identidad (pág. 210)

ethnicity a set of cultural characteristics that distinguishes one group from another group (p. 210)
etnia conjunto de características culturales que distinguen a un grupo de otro (pág. 210)

ethnocentrism the tendency to view one's own culture and group as superior to all other cultures and groups (p. 41)
etnocentrismo tendencia a considerar que la cultura y el grupo propios son superiores a todas las otras culturas y los otros grupos (pág. 41)

evolutionary theory a view of social change in which change is seen as a process that moves toward increasing complexity (p. 416)
teoría de la evolución visión del cambio social en la que el cambio es un proceso que avanza hacia una complejidad cada vez mayor (pág. 416)

exchange an individual, group, or societal interaction undertaken in an effort to receive a reward in return for actions (p. 59)
intercambio interacción individual, grupal o social que se realiza con el fin de recibir una recompensa a cambio de acciones (pág. 59)

exchange theory a theory that holds that people are motivated by self-interests in their interactions with others (p. 59)
teoría del intercambio teoría que postula que las personas interactúan con otros individuos motivadas por intereses propios (pág. 59)

exogamy marriage outside of one's own social category (p. 187)
exogamia matrimonio con personas de distinta categoría social (pág. 187)

experiment a research method in which data is gathered under controlled conditions set by the researcher (p. 26)
experimento método de investigación en el que los datos se reúnen en condiciones controladas que determina el investigador (pág. 26)

extended family a family form that consists of three or more generations of a family sharing the same residence (p. 261)
familia extensa tipo de familia en la que tres o más generaciones de una familia conviven en el mismo hogar (pág. 261)

F

factors of production the resources that can be used to produce and distribute goods and services (p. 283)
factores de producción recursos que pueden usarse para producir y distribuir bienes y servicios (pág. 283)

family a group of people who are related by marriage, blood, or adoption and who live together and share economic resources (p. 261)
familia grupo de personas vinculadas por matrimonio, sangre o adopción, que viven juntas y comparten los recursos económicos (pág. 261)

family of orientation a nuclear family into which a person is born or adopted (p. 261)
familia de orientación núcleo familiar en el que nace una persona o al cual se la adopta (pág. 261)

family of procreation a nuclear family consisting of an individual, his or her spouse, and their children (p. 261)
familia de procreación familia nuclear compuesta por un individuo, su cónyuge y sus hijos (pág. 261)

family planning a conscious decision by married couples to have only a certain number of children (p. 377)
planificación familiar decisión que toman a conciencia los matrimonios de tener solo cierta cantidad de hijos (pág. 377)

fecundity the biological potential for reproduction (p. 371)
fecundidad potencial biológico de reproducción (pág. 371)

feminist perspective a theoretical perspective that involves viewing society as a system of gender inequality in which men dominate women (p. 16)
perspectiva feminista perspectiva teórica según la cual la sociedad es un sistema de desigualdad de género, en el que los hombres dominan a las mujeres (pág. 16)

fertility the actual number of births per 1,000 women of childbearing age in a population (p. 371)
fertilidad cantidad de nacimientos en una población cada 1,000 mujeres en edad fértil (pág. 371)

folkways norms that do not have great moral significance attached to them—the common customs of everyday life (p. 36)
cultura popular normas que no poseen gran significado moral; las costumbres comunes de todos los días (pág. 36)

formal group a group in which the structure, goals, and activities of the group are clearly defined (p. 70)
grupo formal grupo en el que la estructura, los objetivos y las actividades están definidos claramente (pág. 70)

formal organization a large, complex secondary group that has been established to achieve specific goals (p. 75)
organización formal grupo secundario, grande y complejo creado para lograr objetivos específicos (pág. 75)

formal sanction a reward or punishment that is given by some formal organization or regulatory body, such as a school, business, or government (p. 160)
sanción formal recompensa o castigo otorgados por una organización formal o un ente regulador, como una escuela, una empresa o el gobierno (pág. 160)

free enterprise system an economic system with limited government control of business operations (p. 285)
sistema de libre empresa sistema económico en el que el gobierno ejerce un control limitado de las operaciones comerciales (pág. 285)

free trade trade between nations that is unrestricted by trade barriers (p. 288)
libre comercio intercambio comercial entre naciones libre de barreras comerciales (pág. 288)

function a positive consequence that an element of society produces for the maintenance of the social system (p. 12)
función efecto positivo que produce un elemento de la sociedad para mantener el sistema social (pág. 12)

functionalist perspective a theoretical perspective that views society as a set of interrelated parts that work together to produce a stable social system (p. 16)
perspectiva funcionalista perspectiva teórica según la cual la sociedad es un conjunto de partes interrelacionadas que funcionan en conjunto con el fin de alcanzar un sistema social estable (pág. 16)

fundamentalism a type of religion involving rigid adherence to rules and practices and the belief that religion should be the primary force in one's life. (p. 329)
fundamentalismo tipo de religión en la que las reglas y prácticas deben cumplirse rigurosamente y en la que se cree que la religión debe ser la fuerza principal en la vida de una persona (pág. 329)

G

gatekeepers media executives, editors, or reporters who can open or close the "gate" on a particular news story (p. 358)
***gatekeepers* o porteros** ejecutivos de los medios de comunicación, editores o periodistas que pueden abrir o cerrar las "puertas de acceso" a una noticia particular (pág. 358)

Gemeinshaft (guh-MYN-shahft) societies in which most members know one another, relationships are close, and activities center on the family and the community (p. 66)
Gemeinshaft sociedades en las que la mayoría de los miembros se conocen, los vínculos son estrechos y las actividades se centran en la familia y la comunidad (pág. 66)

gender the behavioral and psychological traits considered appropriate for men and women (p. 233)
género características conductuales y psicológicas que se consideran adecuadas para el hombre y la mujer (pág. 233)

gender identity the awareness of being masculine or feminine as those traits are defined by culture (p. 233)
identidad de género la conciencia de ser masculino o femenino según la definición que da la cultura de esas características (pág. 233)

gender roles the specific behaviors and attitudes that a society establishes for men and women (p. 233)
roles de género conductas y actitudes específicas que la sociedad determina para el hombre y la mujer (pág. 233)

generalized other the internalized attitudes, expectations, and viewpoints of society that guide our behavior and reinforce our sense of self (p. 97)
otro generalizado actitudes, expectativas y visiones de la sociedad que están internalizadas, guían nuestra conducta y refuerzan nuestra percepción del yo (pág. 97)

genocide extermination aimed at intentionally destroying an entire targeted population (p. 217)
genocidio exterminio cuyo fin es destruir intencionalmente y por completo a una población determinada (pág. 217)

gerontology the scientific study of the processes and phenomena of aging (p. 147)
gerontología estudio científico de los procesos y los fenómenos relacionados con el envejecimiento (pág. 147)

Gesellshaft (guh-ZEL-shahft) societies in which social relationships are based on need rather than on emotion, relationships are impersonal and temporary, and individual goals are more important than group goals (p. 66)
Gesellshaft sociedades en las que las relaciones sociales están basadas en la necesidad antes que en las emociones, las relaciones son impersonales y temporarias y los objetivos individuales son más importantes que los grupales (pág. 66)

glass ceiling the invisible barrier that prevents women from gaining upper-level positions in business (p. 237)
techo de cristal barrera invisible que no permite que las mujeres accedan a altos puestos de trabajo profesionales (pág. 237)

globalization the development of economic, political, and social relationships that stretch worldwide (p. 18)
globalización desarrollo de relaciones económicas, políticas y sociales en todo el mundo (pág. 18)

graying of America a phenomenon of the growing percentage of elderly Americans as part of the total U.S. population (p. 239)
envejecimiento de la población estadounidense fenómeno que se produce por el aumento de la población de estadounidenses ancianos respecto de la población total de ese país (pág. 239)

group a set of two or more people who interact on the basis of shared expectations and who possess some degree of common identity (p. 63)
grupo conjunto de dos o más personas que interactúan a partir de expectativas comunes y que comparten cierto grado de identidad común (pág. 63)

growth rate the birthrate minus the death rate, or the rate at which a country's population is increasing (p. 373)
tasa de crecimiento la tasa de natalidad menos la tasa de mortalidad, o el ritmo al que aumenta la población de un país (pág. 373)

H

heredity the transmission of genetic characteristics from parents to children (p. 91)
herencia transmisión de rasgos genéticos de padres a hijos (pág. 91)

heterogamy (he-tuh-RAH-guh-mee) the tendency for individuals to marry people who have social characteristics different from their own (p. 267)
heterogamia tendencia a casarse con personas que tienen características distintas de las propias (pág. 267)

hidden curriculum transmission by schools of cultural goals that are not openly acknowledged (p. 312)
currículo oculto transmisión por parte de la escuela de metas culturales que no se reconocen abiertamente (pág. 312)

historical method a research method that involves the examination of any materials from the past that contain information of sociological interest (p. 25)
método histórico método de investigación que consiste en analizar materiales del pasado que contienen información de interés sociológico (pág. 25)

history the study of the people and events of the past (p. 6)
historia estudio de las personas y los sucesos del pasado (pág. 6)

homeschooling a system in which a child's main education is undertaken by parents at home (p. 318)
educación doméstica sistema en el que los padres imparten la educación principal de los niños en el hogar (pág. 318)

homogamy (hoh-MAH-guh-mee) the tendency of individuals to marry people with social characteristics similar to their own (p. 118)
homogamia tendencia a casarse con personas con características sociales similares a las propias (pág. 118)

horizontal mobility a type of social mobility in which an individual moves within a social class (p. 195)
movilidad horizontal tipo de movilidad social en la que un individuo se mueve dentro de una clase social (pág. 195)

hypothesis a statement that predicts the relationship between two or more variables (p. 21)
hipótesis enunciado que predice la relación entre dos o más variables (pág. 21)

I the unsocialized, spontaneous, self-interested component of the personality and self-identity (p. 97)
yo componente de la personalidad y de la propia identidad que no está socializado, es espontáneo y se guía por los propios intereses (pág. 97)

ideal type a description comprised of the essential characteristics of some aspect of society (p. 12)
tipo ideal descripción que incluye las características esenciales de algún aspecto de la sociedad (pág. 12)

ideology a system of beliefs or ideas that justifies some social, moral, religious, political, or economic interests held by a social group or by society (p. 410)
ideología sistema de creencias o ideas que justifica los intereses sociales, morales, religiosos, políticos o económicos que tiene un grupo social o una sociedad (pág. 410)

impression management an effort to present the self well and manage the impressions that the audience receives (p. 98)
manejo de impresiones intento por dar una buena impresión de uno mismo y controlar las impresiones que se forma la audiencia (pág. 98)

industrial society a type of society in which the mechanized production of goods is the main economic activity (p. 65)
sociedad industrial tipo de sociedad en la que la principal actividad económica es la producción mecanizada de bienes (pág. 65)

informal group a group in which there is no official structure or established rules of conduct (p. 70)
grupo informal grupo que no tiene una estructura oficial ni reglas de conducta establecidas (pág. 70)

informal sanction a spontaneous expression of approval or disapproval given by an individual or a group (p. 160)
sanción informal expresión espontánea de aprobación o desaprobación por parte de un individuo o grupo (pág. 160)

information society a society in which the exchange of information is the main social and economic activity (p. 350)
sociedad de la información sociedad cuya principal actividad económica y social es el intercambio de información (pág. 350)

infrastructure a system of roads, ports, and other facilities needed by a modern economy (p. 423)
infraestructura sistema de caminos, puertos y otros servicios que necesita una economía moderna (pág. 423)

in-group a group that an individual belongs to and identifies with (p. 71)
endogrupo grupo al que pertenece un individuo y con el que se identifica (pág. 71)

instinct an unchanging, biologically inherited behavior pattern (p. 91)
instinto patrón de conducta invariable y heredado biológicamente (pág. 91)

institutionalized discrimination discrimination that is an outgrowth of the structure of society (p. 213)
discriminación institucionalizada discriminación que es producto de la estructura de la sociedad (pág. 213)

interactionist perspective a theoretical perspective that focuses on how individuals interact with one another in society (p. 17)
perspectiva interaccionista perspectiva teórica que se centra en la manera en que los individuos interactúan en la sociedad (pág. 17)

interest group an organization that attempts to influence the political decision-making process (p. 299)
grupo de interés organización que intenta influir en el proceso político de toma de decisiones (pág. 299)

intergenerational mobility a form of vertical mobility in which social status differs between generations in the same family (p. 195)
movilidad intergeneracional forma de movilidad vertical en la que el estatus social varía en cada generación dentro de la misma familia (pág. 195)

internalization the process by which a norm becomes a part of an individual's personality, thus conditioning that individual to conform to society's expectations (p. 159)
internalización proceso de incorporación de una norma a la personalidad de un individuo; de ese modo, el individuo queda condicionado a cumplir con las expectativas de la sociedad (pág. 159)

intragenerational mobility a form of vertical mobility in which social status changes during one individual's life (p. 195)
movilidad intrageneracional forma de movilidad vertical en la que un individuo cambia de estatus social durante su vida (pág. 195)

iron law of oligarchy a tendency of organizations to become increasingly dominated by small groups of people (p. 78)
ley de hierro de la oligarquía tendencia de las organizaciones a estar cada vez más controladas por pequeños grupos de personas (pág. 78)

junta (HOOHN-tuh) an authoritarian type of government in which political power has been seized from the previous government by force (p. 296)
junta tipo de gobierno autoritario en el que el poder político ha sido arrebatado del gobierno anterior por la fuerza (pág. 296)

kinship a network of people who are related by marriage, birth, or adoption (p. 261)
parentesco red de personas vinculadas por matrimonio, nacimiento o adopción (pág. 261)

knowledge-gap hypothesis a theory that states as new information enters society, wealthy and better-educated members acquire it at a faster rate than poor and less-educated people (p. 355)
hipótesis de la brecha del conocimiento teoría que postula que, a medida que ingresa información nueva en la sociedad, los miembros más ricos y educados incorporan esa información a un ritmo mayor que las personas pobres y menos educadas (pág. 355)

labeling theory a theory of deviant behavior that focuses on how individuals come to be labeled as deviant (p. 167)
teoría del etiquetado teoría de la desviación que se centra en la manera en que se caracteriza a los individuos como desviados (pág. 167)

labor force all individuals 16 and older who are employed in paid positions or who are seeking paid employment (p. 142)
mano de obra todos los individuos mayores de 16 años que tienen un empleo pago o que buscan un puesto de trabajo pago (pág. 142)

laissez-faire capitalism a pure form of capitalism in which the government does not interfere in the economy (p. 285)
capitalismo del *laissez-faire* forma pura del capitalismo en la que el gobierno no interfiere en la economía (pág. 285)

late adulthood the third and last era of adulthood, spanning ages 60 and over (p. 137)
adultez tardía tercera y última etapa de la vida adulta, que comienza a partir de los 60 años (pág. 137)

latent function an unintended and unrecognized consequence of some element of society (p. 16)
función latente efecto involuntario y no reconocido de determinado elemento de la sociedad (pág. 16)

law of demand a principle that states that the demand for a product increases as the price of the product decreases and demand decreases as price increases (p. 285)
ley de la demanda principio que establece que la demanda de un producto aumenta a medida que el precio baja y disminuye a medida que el precio aumenta (pág. 285)

law of supply a principle that states that producers will supply more products when they can charge higher prices and fewer products when they must charge lower prices (p. 285)
ley de la oferta principio que establece que los productores ofrecen más productos cuando pueden aumentar los precios y menos productos cuando deben bajar los precios (pág. 285)

laws written rules of conduct that are enacted and enforced by the government (p. 37)
leyes reglas de comportamiento escritas que promulga y hace cumplir el gobierno (pág. 37)

leaders people who influence the attitudes and opinions of others (p. 73)
líderes personas que influyen en las actitudes y opiniones de otras personas (pág. 73)

legal discrimination discrimination that is upheld by law (p. 213)
discriminación legal discriminación avalada por la ley (pág. 213)

legitimacy the right of those people in power to control, or govern, others (p. 293)
legitimidad derecho que poseen las personas que están en el poder de controlar o gobernar a otras personas (pág. 293)

life chances the likelihood that individuals have of sharing in the opportunities and benefits of society (p. 200)
oportunidades de vida probabilidad que tienen los individuos de participar de las oportunidades y los beneficios de la sociedad (pág. 200)

life expectancy the average number of years a person born in a particular year can be expected to live (pp. 200, 373)
esperanza de vida promedio de la cantidad de años que se espera que viva una persona que nació en un año determinado (pág. 200, 373)

life structure the combination of statuses, roles, activities, goals, values, beliefs, and life circumstances that characterize an individual (p. 137)
estructura de vida combinación de las condiciones, los roles, las actividades, los objetivos, los valores, las creencias y las circunstancias de vida que caracterizan a un individuo (pág. 137)

looking-glass self the interactive process by which we develop an image of ourselves based on how we imagine we appear to others (p. 96)
yo espejo proceso interactivo mediante el cual formamos una imagen de nosotros mismos a partir de la imagen que creemos tener frente a otras personas (pág. 96)

M

macrosociology a level of analysis that involves the study of large-scale systems or society as a whole; employed by the functionalist and conflict perspectives (p. 18)
macrosociología nivel de análisis empleado por la perspectiva funcionalista y la perspectiva del conflicto según el cual se estudian los sistemas en gran escala y la sociedad como un todo (pág. 18)

Malthusian theory (mal-THOO-zhuhn) a theory of population proposed by Thomas Malthus, in which population increases geometrically and the food supply increases arithmetically. Because the food supply cannot keep up with the expanding population, Malthus predicted widespread starvation would result (p. 375)
teoría malthusiana teoría poblacional propuesta por Thomas Malthus, que postula que la población crece en progresión geométrica y la producción de alimentos crece en progresión aritmética; como la producción de alimentos no puede mantenerse a la par del crecimiento de la población, Malthus predijo que esa situación produciría hambrunas generalizadas (pág. 375)

managed care alternative health-insurance plans used to help control health care costs (p. 245)
administración de servicios médicos planes alternativos de seguros médicos usados para controlar los costos de los servicios médicos (pág. 245)

manifest function an intended and recognized consequence of some element of society (p. 16)
función manifiesta efecto voluntario y reconocido de un elemento de la sociedad (pág. 16)

mass hysteria an unfounded anxiety shared by people who are scattered over a wide geographic area (p. 397)
histeria colectiva estado de ansiedad infundado que comparten un grupo de personas situadas en un área geográfica extensa (pág. 397)

mass media the instruments of communication that reach large audiences with no personal contact between the individuals sending the information and those receiving it, such as newspapers, magazines, books, television, radio, films, and the Internet (p. 101)
medios masivos de comunicación instrumentos de comunicación que llegan a una gran audiencia sin que haya contacto personal entre los individuos que envían la información y los que la reciben; algunos ejemplos son los periódicos, las revistas, los libros, la televisión, la radio, las películas e Internet (pág. 101)

master status the status that plays the greatest role in shaping a person's life and determining his or her social identity (p. 55)
estatus principal el estatus que más influye en la conformación de la vida de una persona y la determinación de su identidad social (pág. 55)

material culture physical objects created by human groups (p. 35)
cultura material objetos físicos creados por grupos humanos (pág. 35)

me the part of the identity that is aware of the expectations and attitudes of society, or the socialized self (p. 97)
mí parte de la identidad que conoce las expectativas y actitudes de la sociedad, o el yo socializado (pág. 97)

mechanical solidarity the close-knit social relationships common in preindustrial societies that result when a small group of people share the same values and perform the same tasks (p. 66)
solidaridad mecánica relación social estrecha, común en las sociedades preindustriales, que aparece cuando un pequeño grupo de personas comparten los mismos valores y realizan las mismas actividades (pág. 66)

media convergence the idea that mass media are merging and are no longer separate entities (p. 351)
convergencia de medios la idea de que los medios de comunicación masivos ya no son entidades separadas, sino que se unen (pág. 351)

Medicaid the state and federally funded health-insurance program for low-income individuals (p. 241)
Medicaid programa de asistencia médica financiado con recursos estatales y federales que está dirigido a personas de bajos ingresos (pág. 241)

Medicare the government-sponsored health insurance plan for elderly Americans and Americans with disabilities (p. 241)
Medicare plan de seguros financiado por el gobierno y dirigido a la población estadounidense anciana y discapacitada (pág. 241)

mentor someone who fosters an individual's development by believing in the person, sharing the person's dreams, and helping the person achieve those dreams (p. 138)
mentor persona que fomenta el desarrollo de un individuo creyendo en él, compartiendo los sueños de ese individuo y ayudándolo a alcanzarlos (pág. 138)

microsociology the level of analysis that involves looking at small-scale settings and everyday interaction among group members; employed by the interactionist perspective (p. 18)
microsociología nivel de análisis empleado por la perspectiva interaccionista según el cual se estudian los entornos pequeños y la interacción cotidiana entre los miembros de un grupo (pág. 18)

middle adulthood the second era of adulthood, spanning the ages 40 through 59 (p. 137)
adultez intermedia segunda etapa de la vida adulta que se extiende de los 40 a los 59 años (pág. 137)

middle-old a term used to refer to people aged 75 to 84 (p. 147)
mayores-adultos término usado para referirse a las personas que tienen entre 75 y 84 años de edad (pág. 147)

migration the movement of people from one specified area to another (p. 373)
migración el movimiento de personas de un área específica a otra (pág. 373)

minority group a group of people who are singled out and unequally treated because of their physical characteristics or cultural practices (p. 211)
grupo minoritario grupo de personas disgregadas que reciben un trato desigual a causa de sus rasgos físicos o prácticas culturales (pág. 211)

mob an emotionally charged collectivity whose members are united by a specific, and often destructive or violent, goal (p. 396)
banda grupo unido emocionalmente cuyos miembros se reúnen con un objetivo específico y por lo general violento y destructivo (pág. 396)

modernization the process by which a society's social institutions become increasingly complex as the society moves toward industrialization (p. 420)
modernización proceso por el cual las instituciones sociales de una sociedad se vuelven cada vez más complejas a medida que la sociedad avanza hacia la industrialización (pág. 420)

modernization theory a theory of modernization that argues that the more-developed nations of the world were the first to modernize because they were the first to industrialize (p. 420)
teoría de la modernización teoría que postula que las naciones más desarrolladas del mundo fueron las primeras en modernizarse porque se industrializaron antes que el resto (pág. 420)

monogamy the practice of being married to only one spouse at a time (p. 262)
monogamia el régimen de casarse con sólo una persona a la vez (pág. 262)

monotheism the belief that there is only one god (p. 325)
monoteísmo la creencia de que existe un solo dios (pág. 325)

mores (MAWR-ayz) norms that have great moral significance attached to them (p. 37)
normas morales normas que poseen gran significado moral (pág. 37)

multinational a corporation that has factories and offices in several countries (p. 288)
multinacional sociedad comercial que posee fábricas y oficinas en varios países (pág. 288)

multiple-nuclei model a model of urban structure proposed by Chauncey Harris and Edward Ullman in which the city is said to have a number of specialized centers devoted to different types of land use (p. 385)
modelo de los núcleos múltiples modelo de estructura urbana propuesto por Chauncey Harris y Edward Ullman según el cual la ciudad cuenta con un número de centros especializados a los que se les asignan distintos usos de la tierra (pág. 385)

N

narcissism (NAHR-suh-si-zuhm) the feeling of extreme self-centeredness (p. 47)
narcisismo sentimiento de egocentrismo excesivo (pág. 47)

negative sanction a punishment or the threat of punishment used to enforce conformity (p. 159)
sanción negativa castigo o amenaza de castigo usada para hacer cumplir las normas (pág. 159)

nonmaterial culture abstract human creations, such as language, ideas, beliefs, rules, skills, family patterns, work practices, and political and economic systems (p. 35)
cultura no material creaciones humanas abstractas, como el lenguaje, las ideas, las creencias, las normas, las destrezas, los modelos familiares, las prácticas laborales y los sistemas políticos y económicos (pág. 35)

norms shared rules of conduct that tell people how to act in specific situations (p. 36)
normas reglas de comportamiento compartidas que indican cómo actuar en determinadas situaciones (pág. 36)

novice phase a term proposed by Daniel Levinson and his colleagues for the first three stages of the early adulthood era, during which a person prepares for entry into the adult world (p. 138)
etapa de "noviciado" término propuesto por Daniel Levinson y sus colegas para designar las tres primeras etapas de la adultez temprana, durante las cuales una persona se prepara para entrar en el mundo adulto (pág. 138)

nuclear family a family form that consists of one or both parents and their children (p. 261)
familia nuclear forma familiar compuesta por uno o los dos padres y sus hijos (pág. 261)

O

objective method a technique used to rank individuals according to social class in which sociologists define social class in terms of factors such as income, occupation, and education (p. 193)
método objetivo técnica usada para clasificar a los individuos según su clase social; en esta técnica, los sociólogos definen una clase social teniendo en cuenta factores como los ingresos, la ocupación y la educación (pág. 193)

old-old a term used to refer to people aged 85 and older (p. 147)
mayores-mayores término usado para referirse a las personas que tienen 85 años o más (pág. 147)

oligopoly (ah-luh-GAH-puh-lee) a situation that exists when a few people control an industry (p. 288)
oligopolio situación que se presenta cuando una industria en manos de unas pocas personas (pág. 288)

opinion leaders respected individuals in the community (p. 358)
líderes de opinión individuos respetados dentro de la comunidad (pág. 358)

organic solidarity impersonal social relationships, common in industrial societies, that arise with increased job specialization (p. 66)
solidaridad orgánica relaciones sociales impersonales que suelen darse en sociedades industriales y que surgen como resultado de la creciente especialización laboral (pág. 66)

out-group any group that an individual does not belong to or identify with (p. 71)
exogrupo todo grupo al que un individuo no pertenece o con el que no se identifica (pág. 71)

outsourcing a practice that involves moving business units and jobs across national boundaries, where operating and labor costs are less expensive (p. 144)
tercerización práctica que consiste en trasladar unidades de negocios y puestos de trabajo a países extranjeros, donde los costos operativos y los costos de mano de obra son más bajos (pág. 144)

overurbanization a situation in which more people live in the city than the city can support in terms of jobs and facilities (p. 381)
urbanización excesiva situación que se presenta cuando en una ciudad viven más personas de las que se puede albergar en términos de puestos de trabajo y servicios (pág. 381)

P

pan-Indianism a social and political movement that unites culturally distinct tribes to work together on issues that affect all Native Americans (p. 223)
panindianismo movimiento político y social que une a tribus de distintas culturas para trabajar en conjunto sobre temas que afectan a todos los indígenas norteamericanos (pág. 223)

panic a spontaneous and uncoordinated group action to escape some perceived threat (p. 396)
pánico acción grupal espontánea y no coordinada que busca escapar de algo que se percibe como una amenaza (pág. 396)

participant observation a research method in which researchers become directly involved in the situation under investigation (p. 25)
observación participante método de investigación mediante el cual los investigadores se relacionan directamente con la situación investigada (pág. 25)

patriarchy a system in which men are dominant over women (p. 234)
patriarcado sistema en el que los hombres dominan a las mujeres (pág. 234)

peer group a primary group composed of individuals of roughly equal age and similar social characteristics (p. 100)
grupo de pares grupo primario compuesto por individuos de aproximadamente la misma edad y características sociales similares (pág. 100)

personality the sum total of behaviors, attitudes, beliefs, and values that are characteristic of an individual (p. 90)
personalidad conjunto de conductas, actitudes, creencias y valores que caracterizan a un individuo (pág. 90)

plea bargaining the process of legal negotiation that allows an accused person to plead guilty to a lesser charge in return for a lighter sentence (p. 173)
negociación de la sentencia proceso de negociación legal por el cual el acusado puede declararse culpable de un cargo menor a cambio de una sentencia más leve (pág. 173)

pluralist model a model in which the political process in the United States is said to be controlled by interest groups that compete with one another for power (p. 300)
modelo pluralista modelo que establece que los procesos políticos en Estados Unidos están controlados por grupos de interés que compiten entre sí por el poder (pág. 300)

police discretion the power held by police officers to decide who is actually arrested (p. 172)
discreción policial poder que tienen los agentes de policía para decidir a quién arrestar (pág. 172)

political institution a system of roles and norms that governs the distribution and exercise of power in society (p. 293)
institución política sistema de roles y normas que rige la distribución y el ejercicio del poder en la sociedad (pág. 293)

political party an organization that seeks to gain power in the government through legitimate means (p. 298)
partido político organización que busca acceder al poder en el gobierno por medios legítimos (pág. 298)

political science the study of the principles, organization, and operation of government (p. 5)
ciencias políticas estudio de los principios, la organización y el funcionamiento del gobierno (pág. 5)

polygamy a marriage with multiple partners (p. 262)
poligamia matrimonio entre varias personas (pág. 262)

polytheism the belief in more than one god (p. 325)
politeísmo la creencia de que existe más de un dios (pág. 325)

population the number of people living in an area at a particular time (p. 371)
población cantidad de personas que habitan un área en un momento determinado (pág. 371)

positive sanction an action that rewards a particular kind of behavior (p. 159)
sanción positiva acción que premia determinado tipo de conducta (pág. 159)

postindustrial society a type of society in which economic activity centers on the production of information and the provision of services (p. 65)
sociedad postindustrial tipo de sociedad en la que la actividad económica gira en torno a la creación de información y la provisión de servicios (pág. 65)

poverty a standard of living that is below the minimum level considered adequate by society (p. 198)
pobreza estándar de vida inferior al nivel mínimo que la sociedad considera adecuado (pág. 198)

poverty level the minimum annual income needed by a family to survive as defined by the U.S. Census Bureau (p. 198)
nivel de pobreza ingreso mínimo anual que necesita una familia para vivir definido por la Oficina del Censo de EE.UU. (pág. 198)

power the ability to control the behavior of others, with or without their consent (p. 188)
poder habilidad para controlar la conducta de otras personas con su consentimiento o sin él (pág. 188)

power-elite model a model in which political power in the United States is said to be exercised by and for the privileged few in society (p. 300)
modelo de la élite del poder modelo que establece que el poder político de Estados Unidos estaría en manos de un grupo de privilegiados dentro de la sociedad y serviría a sus intereses (pág. 300)

preindustrial society a type of society in which food production—carried out through the use of human and animal labor—is the main economic activity (p. 63)
sociedad preindustrial tipo de sociedad en el que la principal actividad económica es la producción de alimentos (realizada por mano de obra humana y animal) (pág. 63)

prejudice an unsupported generalization about a category of people (p. 213)
prejuicio generalización infundada acerca de una categoría de personas (pág. 213)

prestige the respect, honor, recognition, or courtesy an individual receives from other members of society (p. 189)
prestigio respeto, honor, reconocimiento o cortesía que recibe un individuo de parte de otros miembros de la sociedad (pág. 189)

primary deviance the occasional violation of norms; the individuals who commit it do not see themselves as deviant and neither does society (p. 167)
desviación primaria conducta que se opone a las normas y que no es detectada por las autoridades; tanto los individuos que tienen esa conducta como la sociedad no se consideran desviados (pág. 167)

primary group a small group of people who interact over a relatively long period of time on a direct and personal basis (p. 70)
grupo primario pequeño grupo de personas que interactúan directa y personalmente durante un período de tiempo relativamente largo (pág. 70)

primary sector a sector of the economy that deals with the extraction of raw materials from the environment (p. 283)
sector primario sector de la economía que se ocupa de la extracción de materias primas del medio ambiente (pág. 283)

principle of immanent change according to Pitirim Sorokin's cyclical theory of social change, the natural tendency of a society's structure to swing back and forth between and ideational and sensate culture (p. 416)
principio del cambio inmanente según la teoría cíclica del cambio social que postula Pitirim Sorokin, tendencia natural de la estructura de una sociedad a oscilar entre una cultura sensata y una cultura ideacional (pág. 416)

profane anything considered to be part of the ordinary world and thus commonplace and familiar; not sacred (p. 323)
profano todo lo que se considera parte del mundo común y, por lo tanto, es frecuente y familiar; no sagrado (pág. 323)

profession a high-status occupation that requires specialized skills obtained through formal education (p. 142)
profesión ocupación de estatus alto que requiere destrezas especializadas adquiridas por medio de la educación formal (pág. 142)

proletariat workers who sell their labor in exchange for wages in a capitalist society (p. 188)
proletariado en una sociedad capitalista, trabajadores que venden su mano de obra a cambio de salarios (pág. 188)

proportional representation a system in which a party receives a number of seats in government related to the popular votes they receive (p. 298)
representación proporcional sistema en el que la cantidad de puestos políticos que ocupa un partido depende de los votos populares que recibe (pág. 298)

protectionism the use of trade barriers to protect domestic manufacturers from foreign competition (p. 288)
proteccionismo el uso de barreras comerciales para proteger la producción local de la competencia extranjera (pág. 288)

psychology the social science that studies the behavior and mental processes of individuals (p. 5)
psicología ciencia social que estudia la conducta y los procesos mentales de los individuos (pág. 5)

puberty the physical maturing that makes an individual capable of sexual reproduction (p. 111)
pubertad etapa de maduración física que prepara a un individuo para la reproducción sexual (pág. 111)

public opinion a collection of differing attitudes that members of a public have about a particular issue (p. 399)
opinión pública conjunto de actitudes distintas que tienen los miembros de un público respecto de un tema específico (pág. 399)

R

race the category of people who share inherited physical characteristics and who are perceived by others as being a distinct group (p. 209)
raza categoría de personas que comparten características físicas heredadas y se los reconoce como un grupo diferenciado (pág. 209)

racial profiling a practice of assuming that nonwhite Americans are more likely to commit crimes than white Americans (p. 173)
uso de perfiles raciales práctica que consiste en suponer que es más probable que los estadounidenses que no son blancos cometan delitos que los estadounidenses blancos (pág. 173)

racism the belief that one's own race or ethnic group is naturally superior to other races or ethnic groups (p. 214)
racismo creencia de que la raza o el grupo étnico propio es naturalmente superior a otras razas o grupos étnicos (pág. 214)

rationality the process of subjecting every feature of human behavior to calculation, measurement, and control (p. 75)
racionalidad proceso de someter todos los aspectos de la conducta humana a cálculos, mediciones y controles (pág. 75)

rationalization the processes by which every feature of human behavior becomes subject to calculation, measurement, and control (p. 340)
racionalización procesos por los cuales todos los aspectos de la conducta humana se someten a cálculos, mediciones y controles (pág. 340)

rational-legal authority power that is legitimated by formal rules and regulations (p. 293)
autoridad legal racional poder legitimado por reglas y reglamentos formales (pág. 293)

reactionary movement a social movement with a goal to reverse current social trends (p. 405)
movimiento reaccionario movimiento social cuyo objetivo es revertir las tendencias sociales actuales (pág. 405)

recidivism (ri-SI-duh-vi-zuhm) repeated criminal behavior (p. 174)
reincidencia conducta delictiva recurrente (pág. 174)

reciprocity the idea that if you do something for someone, that person owes you something in return (p. 59)
reciprocidad idea de que si uno hace algo por alguien, esa persona debe darle algo a cambio (pág. 59)

reference group any group with whom individuals identify and whose attitudes and values they often adopt (p. 71)
grupo de referencia grupo con el que se identifican los individuos y cuyas actitudes y valores suelen adoptar (pág. 71)

reformulation the process of adapting borrowed cultural traits (p. 410)
reformulación el proceso de adaptar características culturales no propias (pág. 410)

religion a system of roles and norms organized around the sacred realm that binds people together in social groups (p. 323)
religión sistema de roles y normas organizados en torno a lo sagrado que une a las personas en grupos sociales (pág. 323)

religiosity the importance of religion in a person's life (p. 329)
religiosidad importancia que una persona da a la religión (pág. 329)

reputational method a technique used to rank individuals according to social class in which individuals in the community rank other community members based on what they know of their characters and lifestyles (p. 193)
método de clasificación por reputación técnica usada para clasificar a los individuos según su clase social; mediante esta técnica, los individuos de la comunidad clasifican a otros miembros de la comunidad basándose en el conocimiento que tienen acerca de su personalidad y estilo de vida (pág. 193)

resocialization a break with past experiences and the learning of new values and norms (p. 102)
resocialización abandono de las experiencias pasadas y aprendizaje de normas y valores nuevos (pág. 102)

resource mobilization the organization and effective use of resources essential to social movements (p. 408)
movilización de recursos organización y uso efectivo de recursos como parte esencial de los movimientos sociales (pág. 408)

revisionary movement a social movement that tries to improve or revise some part of society through social change (p. 405)
movimiento revisionista movimiento social cuyo objetivo es mejorar o revisar algún aspecto de la sociedad mediante el cambio social (pág. 405)

revolutionary movement a type of social movement, the goal of which is a total and radical change of the existing social structure (p. 405)
movimiento revolucionario tipo de movimiento social cuyo objetivo es lograr un cambio total y radical de la estructura social existente (pág. 405)

riot a crowd that erupts in generalized destructive behavior, the purpose of which is social disorder (p. 396)
motín multitud que se levanta con una conducta generalizada destructiva, cuyo propósito es provocar desorden social (pág. 396)

ritual an established pattern of behavior through which a group of believers experiences the sacred (p. 324)
ritual patrón de conducta establecido mediante el cual un grupo de creyentes experimentan lo sagrado (pág. 324)

role the behavior expected of someone occupying a particular status (p. 55)
rol conducta que se espera de alguien que ocupa determinado estatus (pág. 55)

role conflict a situation that occurs when fulfilling the expectations of one status makes it difficult to fulfill the expectations of another status (p. 57)
conflicto de roles situación que se presenta cuando el cumplimiento de las expectativas de un estatus dificulta el cumplimiento de las expectativas de otro estatus (pág. 57)

role exit the process that people go through to detach from a role that has been central to their self-identity (p. 57)
separación del rol proceso que atraviesan las personas para separarse de un rol que ha sido fundamental en su propia identidad (pág. 57)

role set different roles attached to a single status (p. 56)
conjunto de roles distintos roles relacionados con un único estatus (pág. 56)

role strain a situation that occurs when a person has difficulty meeting the expectations of a single status (p. 57)
sobrecarga de rol situación que se presenta cuando una persona tiene dificultades para cumplir con las expectativas de un único estatus (pág. 57)

role-taking taking on or pretending to take on the role of others (p. 96)
adoptar el rol del otro tomar el rol de otra persona o fingir que se lo toma (pág. 96)

S

sacred anything that is considered to be part of the supernatural world and that inspires awe, respect, and reverence (p. 323)
sagrado todo aquello que se considera parte del mundo sobrenatural y que inspira admiración, respeto y reverencia (pág. 323)

sample a small but representative selection of people studied in a survey or other research project (p. 24)
muestra selección de personas pequeña pero representativa que se estudia en una encuesta u otros proyectos de investigación (pág. 24)

sanctions the rewards or punishments used to enforce conformity to norms (p. 159)
sanciones recompensas o castigos usados para hacer cumplir las normas (pág. 159)

sandwich generation a group of Americans caught between the needs of their children and their aging parents (p. 273)
generación sándwich grupo de estadounidenses atrapados entre las necesidades de sus hijos y las de sus padres envejecidos (pág. 273)

scapegoating the practice of placing blame for one's troubles on an innocent individual or group (p. 214)
búsqueda del chivo expiatorio la práctica de echar la culpa de los problemas propios a un individuo o grupo inocente (pág. 214)

school choice a system of schooling offering alternatives to local public schools, to which parents can choose to send their children (p. 318)
libre elección de escuelas sistema educativo que ofrece alternativas a las escuelas públicas locales, adonde los padres pueden enviar a sus hijos si así lo desean (pág. 318)

schooling instruction by specially trained teachers who follow officially recognized policies (p. 309)
escolarización instrucción que imparten maestros capacitados especialmente para ello, que cumplen con políticas reconocidas oficialmente (pág. 309)

scientific method an objective, logical, and systematic way of collecting empirical data and arriving at reasoned conclusions (p. 21)
método científico forma objetiva, lógica y sistemática de reunir datos empíricos y llegar a conclusiones razonadas (pág. 21)

secondary deviance a lifestyle of deviance; results in the individuals who commit it being labeled as deviant and accepting that label as true (p. 167)
desviación secundaria conducta que se opone a las normas y provoca que los individuos que muestran esa conducta sean categorizados como desviados y que acepten esa clasificación como verdadera (pág. 167)

secondary group a group in which interaction is impersonal and temporary in nature (p. 70)
grupo secundario grupo en el que la interacción es de naturaleza impersonal y temporaria (pág. 70)

secondary sector the sector of the economy that concentrates on the use of raw materials to manufacture goods (p. 283)
sector secundario sector de la economía que se ocupa del uso de las materias primas para producir bienes (pág. 283)

second shift a phenomenon of individuals having to complete household duties after working away from home (p. 237)
doble turno fenómeno por el cual los individuos deben hacer tareas domésticas en el hogar cuando salen de su trabajo (pág. 237)

sect a relatively small religious organization that typically has split off from a denomination because of doctrinal differences (p. 326)
secta organización religiosa relativamente pequeña que suele separarse de una denominación por diferencias doctrinales (pág. 326)

sector model a model of urban structure proposed by Homer Hoyt in which the growth of a city is said to occur in wedge-shaped sectors that extend outward from the center to the edge of the city (p. 385)
modelo sectorial modelo de estructura urbana propuesto por Homer Hoyt según el cual el crecimiento de una ciudad se daría en sectores con forma de cuña que se extienden hacia afuera, desde el centro de la ciudad hacia la periferia (pág. 385)

secular non-religious (p. 329)
secular no religioso (pág. 329)

secularization the process of moving from the realm of the sacred to that of the profane (p. 340)
secularización proceso por el cual se va del dominio de lo sagrado al dominio de lo profano (pág. 340)

segregation the physical separation of a minority group from the dominant group (p. 216)
segregación separación física de un grupo minoritario del grupo dominante (pág. 216)

ENGLISH AND SPANISH GLOSSARY

self the conscious awareness of possessing a distinct identity that separates one from other members of society (p. 96)
el yo la percepción consciente de que uno tiene una identidad única que lo distingue de otros miembros de la sociedad (pág. 96)

self-fulfilling prophecy a prediction that results in behavior that makes the prediction come true (p. 214)
profecía autocumplida predicción que provoca una conducta que hace que se cumpla la predicción (pág. 214)

self-fulfillment a commitment to the full development of one's personality, talents, and potential (p. 47)
autorrealización compromiso a desarrollar plenamente la personalidad, los talentos y el potencial propios (pág. 47)

sexism the belief that one sex is by nature superior to the other (p. 235)
sexismo la creencia de que un sexo es naturalmente superior al otro (pág. 235)

sexually transmitted diseases (STDs) diseases acquired through sexual activity (p. 123)
enfermedades de transmisión sexual (ETS) enfermedades contraídas por medio de la actividad sexual (pág. 123)

significant others specific people, such as parents, siblings, relatives, and others, who directly influence our socialization (p. 96)
otros significativos determinadas personas, como los padres, los hermanos, los parientes y otros, que tienen una influencia directa sobre nuestra socialización (pág. 96)

social capital the social networks and the reciprocal norms associated with these networks that encourage people to do things for each other (p. 357)
capital social redes sociales y normas de reciprocidad asociadas a esas redes que fomentan la colaboración entre las personas (pág. 357)

social change alterations in various aspects of a society over time (p. 405)
cambio social alteraciones en varios aspectos de la sociedad que ocurren en el tiempo (pág. 405)

social class a grouping of people with similar levels of wealth, power, and prestige (p. 188)
clase social agrupación de personas con niveles similares de riqueza, poder y prestigio (pág. 188)

social control enforcing of norms through either internal or external means (p. 160)
control social proceso de hacer cumplir las normas por medios internos o externos (pág. 160)

social Darwinism the perspective that holds that societies evolve toward stability and perfection and only the fittest societies survive over time (p. 10)
darwinismo social perspectiva que sostiene que las sociedades evolucionan hacia la estabilidad y la perfección y solo sobreviven los más aptos (pág. 10)

social gerontology a subfield of gerontology that studies the nonphysical aspects of aging (p. 147)
gerontología social rama derivada de la gerontología que estudia los aspectos no físicos del envejecimiento (pág. 147)

social inequality the unequal sharing of scarce resources and social rewards (p. 187)
desigualdad social distribución desigual de recompensas sociales y recursos escasos (pág. 187)

social institution a system of statuses, roles, values, and norms that is organized to satisfy one or more of the basic needs of society (p. 57)
institución social sistema de estatus, roles, valores y normas que está organizado para satisfacer una o más necesidades básicas de la sociedad (pág. 57)

social integration the degree of attachment people have to social groups or to society as a whole (p. 126)
integración social grado de integración de las personas a los grupos sociales o a la sociedad en su totalidad (pág. 126)

social interaction how people relate to one another and influence each other's behavior (p. 5)
interacción social formas que tienen las personas de relacionarse e influir en la conducta propia y ajena (pág. 5)

socialism an economic model in which the factors of production are owned by the government, which regulates all economic activity (p. 284)
socialismo modelo económico en el que los factores de producción están en manos del gobierno, que regula todas las actividades económicas (pág. 284)

socialization the interactive process through which people learn the basic skills, values, beliefs, and behavior patterns of a society (p. 95)
socialización proceso de interacción mediante el cual los individuos aprenden las destrezas, los valores, las creencias y los patrones de conducta básicos de una sociedad (pág. 95)

social mobility the movement between or within social classes (p. 195)
movilidad social movimiento entre clases sociales o dentro de ellas (pág. 195)

social movement a long-term conscious effort to promote or prevent social change (p. 405)
movimiento social intento consciente a largo plazo de promover o evitar el cambio social (pág. 405)

social network the web of relationships that is formed by the sum total of an individual's interactions with other people (p. 72)
red social trama de relaciones compuesta por el total de las interacciones de un individuo con otras personas (pág. 72)

social phenomena (fi-NAH-muh-nuh) observable facts or events that involve human society (p. 5)
fenómenos sociales hechos o sucesos observables relacionados con la sociedad humana (pág. 5)

social psychology the study of how the social environment affects an individual's behavior and personality (p. 5)
psicología social estudio de los efectos que tiene el ambiente social sobre la conducta y la personalidad de un individuo (pág. 5)

social sciences related disciplines that study various aspects of human social behavior (p. 5)
ciencias sociales disciplinas relacionadas que estudian varios aspectos de la conducta social humana (pág. 5)

social stratification the process of dividing societies into categories, ranks, or classes based on certain characteristics (p. 187)
estratificación social el proceso de dividir a las sociedades en categorías, rangos o clases según ciertas características (pág. 187)

social structure a network of interrelated statuses and roles that guides human interaction (p. 55)
estructura social red de estatus y roles interrelacionados que guían la interacción humana (pág. 55)

society a group of interdependent people who have organized in such a way as to share a common culture and have a feeling of unity (p. 35)
sociedad grupo de personas interdependientes organizadas de manera que pueden compartir una cultura común y tener un sentido de unidad (pág. 35)

sociobiology the systematic study of the biological basis of all social behavior (p. 91)
sociobiología estudio sistemático de las bases biológicas de todas las conductas sociales (pág. 91)

socioeconomic status a rating that combines social factors such as level of education, occupational prestige, and place of residence with the economic factor of income in order to determine an individual's relative position in a stratification system (p. 189)
estatus socioeconómico clasificación que combina factores sociales, como el nivel de educación, el prestigio ocupacional y el lugar de residencia, con el factor económico de los ingresos con el fin de determinar la posición relativa de un individuo dentro de un sistema de estratificación (pág. 189)

sociological imagination the ability to see the connection between the larger world and our personal lives (p. 7)
imaginación sociológica habilidad de ver la conexión que existe entre el mundo y nuestra vida personal (pág. 7)

sociological perspective a viewing of the behavior of groups in a systematic way (p. 7)
perspectiva sociológica visión sistemática de las conductas de los grupos (pág. 7)

sociology the social science that studies human society and social behavior (p. 5)
sociología ciencia social que estudia la sociedad humana y la conducta social (pág. 5)

spiral of silence a belief that as more people accept common opinions the people who disagree are less likely to voice their views (p. 358)
espiral del silencio creencia de que, a medida que se generalizan las opiniones compartidas, es menos probable que aquellos que no están de acuerdo expresen su punto de vista (pág. 358)

sport competitive games that are won or lost on the basis of physical skills and played according to specific rules (p. 339)
deporte juegos competitivos en los que se pierde o se gana según la destreza física y se juega con reglas específicas (pág. 339)

stacking the practice of assigning people to central or noncentral athletic positions on the basis of race or ethnicity (p. 344)
discriminación por raza en el deporte la práctica de asignar posiciones centrales o no centrales en disciplinas deportivas por cuestiones de raza o etnia (pág. 344)

statistical analysis a research method that entails analyzing data that have already been collected to determine the strength of the relationship that may exist between two or more variables (p. 26)
análisis estadístico método de investigación que consiste en analizar datos recolectados para determinar la intensidad de la relación que puede existir entre dos o más variables (pág. 26)

status a socially defined position in a group or in a society (p. 55)
estatus posición dentro de un grupo o sociedad, definida socialmente (pág. 55)

stereotype an oversimplified, exaggerated, or unfavorable generalization about a category of people (p. 213)
estereotipo generalización exagerada, desfavorable o excesivamente simplificada de una categoría de personas (pág. 213)

stigma a mark of social disgrace that sets a deviant individual apart from the rest of society (p. 163)
estigma marca de desacreditación social que separa a un individuo desviado del resto de la sociedad (pág. 163)

strain theory a theory of deviant behavior that views deviance as the natural outgrowth of the values, norms, and structure of society (p. 164)
teoría de la tensión teoría de la desviación que considera que ese tipo de conducta es la consecuencia natural de los valores, las normas y las estructuras de la sociedad (pág. 164)

subcultural theory a theory of city life in which the characteristics of the city are said to encourage rather than discourage the formation of primary group relationships (p. 387)
teoría de las subculturas teoría acerca de la vida urbana que postula que las características de la ciudad fomentarían la formación de relaciones entre grupos primarios en lugar de desalentarla (pág. 387)

subculture a group with its own unique values, norms, and behaviors that exists within a larger culture (p. 40)
subcultura grupo que posee sus propios valores, normas y comportamiento únicos, y que existe dentro de una cultura mayor (pág. 40)

subjective method a technique used to rank individuals according to social class in which the individuals themselves are asked to determine their own social rank (p. 193)
método subjetivo técnica usada para clasificar a los individuos según su clase social; mediante esta técnica, los individuos mismos deben determinar su propio rango social (pág. 193)

subjugation the maintaining of control over a group through force (p. 216)
subyugación el acto de mantener el control sobre un grupo mediante la fuerza (pág. 216)

subsistence strategies ways in which a society uses technology to provide for the needs of its members (p. 63)
estrategias de subsistencia maneras en que la sociedad usa la tecnología para satisfacer las necesidades de sus miembros (pág. 63)

suffrage the right to vote (p. 235)
sufragio derecho al voto (pág. 235)

survey a research method that allows data on attitudes and opinions to be collected from large numbers of people (p. 24)
encuesta método de investigación con el que se pueden recolectar datos sobre las actitudes y opiniones de muchas personas (pág. 24)

symbol anything that stands for something else and has a shared meaning attached to it, such as language, gestures, images, sounds, physical objects, events, and elements of the natural world that convey a particular meaning (p. 17)
símbolo todo aquello que representa otra cosa y posee un significado compartido, como el lenguaje, los gestos, las imágenes, los sonidos, los objetos físicos, los sucesos y los elementos del mundo natural que tienen un significado particular (pág. 17)

symbolic interaction interaction among people that takes place through the use of symbols (p. 18)
interacción simbólica interacción entre personas mediante el uso de símbolos (pág. 18)

T

technology the knowledge and tools that people use to manipulate their environment (p. 410)
tecnología conocimientos y herramientas que usan las personas para manipular su ambiente (pág. 410)

tertiary sector (TUHR-shee-er-ee) a sector of the economy that concentrates on the provision of services (p. 283)
sector terciario sector de la economía que se ocupa de la oferta de servicios (pág. 283)

theism (THEE-i-zuhm) the belief in a god or gods (p. 325)
teísmo la creencia en uno o varios dioses (pág. 325)

theoretical perspective a general set of assumptions about the nature of phenomena; in sociology, a theoretical perspective outlines certain assumptions about the nature of social life (p. 16)
perspectiva teórica conjunto general de suposiciones acerca de la naturaleza de los fenómenos; en la sociología, una perspectiva teórica define ciertas suposiciones acerca de la naturaleza de la vida social (pág. 16)

theory a systematic explanation of the relationship among phenomena (p. 16)
teoría explicación sistemática de las relaciones entre los fenómenos (pág. 16)

total institution a setting in which people are isolated from the rest of society for a specific period of time and subjected to tight control (p. 102)
institución total lugar donde las personas están aisladas del resto de la sociedad durante un tiempo determinado y están bajo un control estricto (pág. 102)

Title IX a section of the Education Amendment Act of 1972 that bars discrimination on the basis of gender in any program—including athletics—at any educational institution receiving federal funds (p. 345)
Título IX sección de la Enmienda Educativa de 1972 que prohíbe la discriminación de género en todos los programas, incluso en el atletismo, de todas las instituciones educativas que reciben fondos federales (pág. 345)

totalitarianism the most extreme form of authoritarian government. Under totalitarianism, government leaders accept few limits on their authority (p. 296)
totalitarismo la forma más extrema de gobierno autoritario; bajo el totalitarismo, los líderes políticos aceptan pocos límites a su autoridad (pág. 296)

tracking the assignment of students to different types of educational programs (p. 312)
agrupar según las habilidades o *tracking* la asignación de diferentes programas educativos a los estudiantes (pág. 312)

traditional authority the power that is legitimated by long-standing customs (p. 293)
autoridad tradicional poder legitimado por antiguas costumbres (pág. 293)

transfer payments a method used by the government to attempt to reduce social inequality by redistributing money among various segments of society (p. 200)
pagos de transferencias método usado por el gobierno para reducir la desigualdad social por medio de la redistribución de dinero entre varios segmentos de la sociedad (pág. 200)

triad three-person group (p. 69)
tríada grupo de tres personas (pág. 69)

U

unemployment a situation that occurs when people do not have jobs but are actively seeking employment (p. 143)
desempleo situación que se presenta cuando las personas no tienen trabajo pero lo buscan activamente (pág. 143)

unemployment rate a percentage of the civilian labor force that is unemployed but actively seeking employment (p. 143)
tasa de desempleo porcentaje de la mano de obra civil que no tiene trabajo pero lo busca activamente (pág. 143)

urban anomie theory a theory of city life in which the city is seen to be an anonymous and unfriendly place that carries serious negative consequences for those who live there (p. 385)
teoría de la anomia urbana teoría de la vida urbana que percibe la ciudad como un lugar anónimo y hostil que produce graves efectos negativos sobre sus habitantes (pág. 385)

urban ecology an approach that examines the relationship between people and the urban environment (p. 383)
ecología urbana enfoque que analiza la relación que existe entre las personas y el medio ambiente urbano (pág. 383)

urban sprawl a phenomenon characterized by poorly planned development on the edge of cities and towns (p. 385)
expansión urbana fenómeno caracterizado por el desarrollo urbano no planificado en la periferia de ciudades y pueblos (pág. 385)

urbanization the concentration of the population in cities (p. 379)
urbanización concentración de la población en la ciudad (pág. 379)

V

values shared beliefs about what is good or bad, right or wrong, desirable or undesirable (p. 35)
valores creencias compartidas acerca de lo que está bien y lo que está mal, lo correcto y lo incorrecto, lo deseable y lo no deseable (pág. 35)

variable a characteristic that can differ from one individual, group, or situation to another in a measurable way (p. 22)
variable característica que puede cambiar de un individuo, un grupo o una situación a otro y que se puede medir (pág. 22)

vertical mobility a type of social mobility in which an individual moves from one social class to another (p. 195)
movilidad vertical tipo de movilidad social en la que un individuo cambia de clase social (pág. 195)

Verstehen (fer-SHTAY-en) an empathetic understanding of the meanings others attach to their actions (p. 12)
Verstehen comprensión empática de los significados que otros otorgan a sus acciones (pág. 12)

voluntary association a nonprofit association formed to pursue some common interest (p. 75)
asociación voluntaria asociación sin fines de lucro creada en pos de un interés común (pág. 75)

voluntary childlessness the conscious choice to remain childless (p. 273)
decisión voluntaria de no tener hijos elección hecha a conciencia de no tener hijos (pág. 273)

wage gap the level of women's income relative to that of men (p. 236)
brecha salarial el nivel de ingresos de las mujeres en comparación con el de los hombres (pág. 236)

wealth a combination of an individual's assets—the value of everything the person owns—and income—money earned through salaries and investments (p. 188)
riqueza combinación de los activos de un individuo (el valor de todo lo que posee una persona) y sus ingresos (dinero que se gana con salarios y jornales) (pág. 188)

white-collar crime a crime that is committed by people of high social status in the course of their professional lives (p. 170)
delito de cuello blanco delito cometido por un individuo o individuos de estatus social alto durante su desempeño profesional (pág. 170)

white ethnics the collective reference to immigrants from the predominantly Catholic countries of Ireland, Italy, France, Poland, and Greece (p. 224)
etnias blancas referencia colectiva a los inmigrantes provenientes de los países donde predomina el catolicismo: Irlanda, Italia, Francia, Polonia y Grecia (pág. 224)

work all of the tasks necessary for producing goods and providing services that meet human needs (p. 142)
trabajo todas las actividades necesarias para producir bienes y ofrecer servicios que satisfacen las necesidades humanas (pág. 142)

world-system theory a theory of modernization, proposed by Immanuel Wallerstein, in which the spread of capitalism is seen as producing an international division of labor between more-developed and less-developed nations. According to this view, the more-developed nations control the factors of production and the less-developed nations serve as sources of cheap labor and raw materials (p. 421)
teoría del sistema mundial teoría de la modernización propuesta por Immanuel Wallerstein según la cual la expansión del capitalismo produce una división internacional del trabajo entre naciones más desarrolladas y naciones menos desarrolladas; según esta visión, las naciones más desarrolladas controlan los factores de producción y las naciones menos desarrolladas son fuente de mano de obra barata y materias primas (pág. 421)

young-old a term used to refer to people aged 65 to 74 (p. 147)
mayores jóvenes término usado para referirse a las personas que tienen entre 65 y 74 años (pág. 147)

zero tolerance a set of strict policies to prevent school violence (p. 319)
tolerancia cero conjunto de políticas estrictas cuyo fin es prevenir la violencia escolar (pág. 319)

Index

KEY TO INDEX

c = chart g = graph m = map
q = quotation p = picture

A

B

C

D

INDEX

E

F

INDEX

N

O

P

R

INDEX

W

Credits and Acknowledgments

Cover: © Janet Woolley/Illustration Works/Corbis

FRONT MATTER: Table of Contents iv © Phillip Jarrell/Digital Vision/Alamy Ltd; v (bl) © Banana Stock/PunchStock; (br) © Banana Stock/age fotostock; (t) © Banana Stock/age fotostock; vi (t) © Sylvia Plachy/Redux; (b) AP/ Wide World Photos; vii © Charles Gatewood/The Image Works; viii (t) © David Coleman/Alamy Ltd; (b) *We Can Do It!,* about 1942, J. Howard Miller. Photo © Corbis; ix (t) © Scott J. Ferrell/Congressional Quarterly/Getty Images; (b) © Reggie Casagrande/Getty Images; x (t) © Masterfile; (b) © Mike Blake/Reuters/Corbis; xi (t) Courtesy IwamotoScott Architecture; (b) © Saipul Siagiancheers/epa/Corbis; **Features** xii (t) © Jim Mahoney/Dallas Morning News/Corbis; (b) © Corbis; xiii © Fly Fernandez/zefa/Corbis; xiv *all* © Jerzyworks/Masterfile; xvii (l) © Gianni Dagli Orti/Corbis; (r) © Per-Andre Hoffmann/LOOK Die Bildagentur der Fotografen GmbH/Alamy Ltd; **Time Line of Sociology** xx (tl) Engraving after Harriet Martineau (1873), Alonzo Chappel. Photo © Bettmann/Corbis; (br) Courtesy UIC Photographic Services; (bc) © Michael Nicholson/Corbis: (tc) © Hulton-Deutsch Collection/Corbis; (tr) © Bettmann/Corbis; xxi (c) The Granger Collection, New York; (tr) © Pasieka/Science Photo Library/Photo Researchers, Inc.; (tl) © Bettmann/ Corbis; (br) © Tom Stoddart Archive/ Hulton Archive/Getty Images; (bc) AP/Wide World Photos; **Skills Handbook** S11 © Edward Beardwell/ www.CartoonStock.com; S14 © American Sociological Association, www.asanet.org.

UNIT 1: Page 1 *masai warriors herding cattle* © Vera Bogaerts/ShutterStock; *waitress holding tray* © Kuznetsov Dmitriy/ShutterStock; *african brother and sister* © Lucian Coman/ ShutterStock; *township in south africa* © Socrates/ShutterStock; *smiling businesswoman* © Jose AS Reyes/ ShutterStock; *contractors in suits* © Stephen Coburn/ShutterStock.

CHAPTER 1: Page 2 (t) © Melanie Dunea/Creative Photographers Inc.; (b) AP/Wide World Photos; 4 © David Lees/ Taxi/Getty Images;

6 © Michael Gottschalk/DDP/AFP/ Getty Images; (inset) AP/Wide World Images; 8 *Houndsditch from London: A Pilgrimage,* 1872, after Gustave Doré. Wood engraving. The Granger Collection, New York; 10 (l) © Hulton Archive/Getty Images; (r) Engraving after Harriet Martineau (1873), Alonzo Chappel. Photo © Bettmann/Corbis; 11 (l) © Hulton-Deutsch Collection/Corbis; (r) © Michael Nicholson/Corbis; 12 (l) © Bettmann/ Corbis; (r) The Granger Collection, New York; 13 (t) © Bettmann/Corbis; 14 © Corbis; 15 AP/Wide World Images; 17 (l) © Chris Hondros/Getty Images; (c) © Dynamic Graphics/Jupiterimages/Alamy Ltd; (r) © Ian Shaw/Alamy Ltd; 19 (t) © Phillip Jarrell/Digital Vision/Alamy Ltd; 20 © Ovie Carter; 23 © Dennis MacDonald/Alamy Ltd; 24 © CMCD, Inc.; 26 © Dennis Hallinan/Alamy Ltd; (inset and bkgd) D.M. Kirke, 1996; 29 (bkgd) AP/Wide World Photos; (t) © Jim Mahoney/Dallas Morning News/Corbis; (b) © Corbis. **CHAPTER 2:** Page 31 © Jim Sizemore/www.CartoonStock.com; 32 © image100/Corbis; 33 © image100/ Corbis; 34 © Car Culture/Collection Mix: Subjects/Getty Images; (inset) © Lake County Museum/Corbis; 36 (l) © Jeff Sherman/Taxi/Getty Images; (r) © Alan Thornton/Stone/Getty Images; 37 (l) © Christopher Morris/Corbis; (r) © Alan Schein/zefa/Corbis; (c) Photo © Steven E. Aufrect/Northern Development Foundation, Thailand, www.whatdoino-steve.blogspot.com; 38 © Charles Gupton/ Stone/Getty Images; 43 © Rudi Von Briel/PhotoEdit; 44 © The New Yorker Collection 1996 Tom Cheney from cartoonbank.com. All Rights Reserved.

CHAPTER 3: Page 52 (tl) © PhotoAlto Agency RF/PunchStock; (tr) © Banana Stock/age fotostock; (bl) © BananaStock/ PunchStock; (br) © Banana Stock/ age fotostock; 53 (t) © Banana Stock/ age fotostock; (b) © Banana Stock/age fotostock; 60 (l) © Eileen Bach/Digital Vision/Alamy Ltd; (r) © Paulo Fridman/ Corbis; 61 (l) AP/Wide World Photos; (c) © Coby Burns/ZUMA/Corbis; (r) © Ramin Talaie/Corbis; 62 © Christophe Boisvieux/Corbis; 64 (r) Ploughing scene from 21st dynasty, Egypt. Museo Egizio, Turin, Italy. Photo © Nimatallah/ Art Resource, New York; (l) Prehistoric Rock art from Wadi Anshal, Jebel Acacus, Southern Lybia. Photo © age fotostock/SuperStock; (l) © Marie-france Bélanger/iStockphoto; (l bkgd) © Jon Larson/iStockphoto; (r bkgd) © Christopher Bazeley/iStockphoto; 65 (l inset) The Granger Collection, New York; (r) © Stewart Cohen/Pam Ostrow/Blend Images/Alamy Ltd; 67 (l) © Walter Hodges/Stone/Getty Images; (r) © Pictor International/ ImageState/Alamy Ltd; 68 © Betsy Streeter/www.CartoonStock.com; 71 © Fly Fernandez/zefa/Corbis; 74 *Civil Service Exam Under Emperor Jen-Tsung* from *The Lives of the Emperors of China,* 17th–18th century AD, Qing Dynasty. Watercolor on silk. Bibliotheque Nationale, Paris. Photo © Bridgeman-Giraudon/Art Resource, New York; 77 © Jim Craigmyle/Corbis; 79 © Aly Song/Reuters/Corbis; (inset) © Steven Puetzer/Masterfile; **Global Connections** 84 (t) © Peeter Viisimaa/ iStockphoto.com; (b) © Layne Kennedy/ Corbis; 85 (tl) © A J James/Digital Vision/Getty Images; (tc) © Frank Herholdt/Digital Vision/Getty Images; (tr) © Image Source Black/ Jupiterimages Corporation; **Careers in Sociology** 86 © Ted Foxx/Alamy Images.

UNIT 2 CHAPTER 4: Page 88 (tl) Courtesy Paula Bernstein; (tr) Courtesy Elyse Schein; (b) © Elena Seibert; 90 (t) © MedicalRF.com/Corbis; (c) © Erik Isakson/Blend Images/Getty Images; (b) © Mitchell Funk/Photographer's Choice/ Getty Images; 97 (t) © SW Productions/ Digital Vision/Alamy Ltd; (c) © Getty Images; (b) © RPM Pictures/Riser/Getty Images; 99 (inset) © Historical Picture Archive/Corbis; © Getty Images; 101 © Peter Cade/Iconica/Getty Images; 102 © Peter Turnley/Corbis; 103 (t) © Brooks Kraft/Sygma/Corbis; (b) AP/ Wide World Photos.

CHAPTER 5: Page 108 (tl) AP/Wide World Photos; (tr) © Ingrid Young/The New York Times/Redux Pictures; 112 © Brad Wilson/Photonica/Getty Images;

114 (t) © P. Deliss/Godong/Corbis; (b) © 2004 Sylvia Plachy/Redux; 115 Book illustration of *Romeo and Juliet,* John Henry Frederick Bacon. From *Children's Stories from Shakespeare,* Edith Nesbit. Published by Raphael Tuck and Sons Ltd., London. Private Collection. Photo © Bridgeman Art Library; 116 Letter from Walter Reed to Emilie B. Lawrence (September 28, 1874). From the Philip S. Hench Walter Reed Yellow Fever Collection. Image Courtesy Historical Collections and Services of the Health Sciences Library, University of Virginia; 117 (l) © Alfred Eisenstaedt/Time and Life Pictures/Getty Images; (l inset) © H. Armstrong Roberts/Retrofile/Getty Images; (r inset) © SuperStock/Alamy Ltd.; (r) © Rolf Bruderer/Corbis; 119 Image courtesy of Dr. Victor Johnson/ New Mexico State University; 129 © LuckyPix/Veer; 131 © Meth Project Foundation, Inc., 2005-2008. All rights reserved. **CHAPTER 6:** Page 134 © Jacky Chapman/Photofusion Picture Library/ Alamy Ltd; 135 © Flying Colours Ltd/ Digital Vision/Alamy Ltd; 136 © Peter Augustin/Stone/Getty Images; 137 (t) © Creatas/Jupiterimages Corporation; (c) © Construction Photography/Corbis; (b) © Digital Vision/Alamy Ltd; 139 © Lisa F. Young/Shutterstock; 141 (r) AP/Wide World Photos; (l) © Mark Evans/iStockphoto; 143 (t) © Bob Riha/ Childrens Hospital Los Angeles/Getty Images; (tc) © dotshock/Shutterstock; (c) © Chuck Savage/Corbis; (bc) © Jean Louis Batt/Stone/Getty Images; (b) AP/Wide World Photos; 144 © Jan Tadeusz/Alamy Ltd; 146 © AFP; (inset) © Narendra Shrestha/epa/ Corbis; 151 AP/Wide World Photos; 153 © Highwaystarz-Photography/Getty Images.

CHAPTER 7: Page 156 © Charles Gatewood/The Image Works; 158 © image100/Corbis; 162 © MCT/Tribune News Service/Getty Images; 165 (t) © Andy Aitchison/Corbis; (b) © Dennis M. Sabangan/epa/Corbis; 172 © Flying Colours Ltd/Digital Vision/ Getty Images; 175 © Kin Cheung/ Reuters/Corbis; **Global Connections** 180 (t) © Peeter Viisimaa/iStockphoto.com; (b) © Diego Goldberg; 181 (tl) © A J James/Digital Vision/Getty Images; (tc) © Frank Herholdt/Digital Vision/Getty Images; (tr) © Image Source Black/ Jupiterimages Corporation; **Careers in Sociology** 182 © Benjamin Sklar/The New York Times/Redux.

UNIT 3 CHAPTER 8: Page 184 AP/ Wide World Photos; 185 AP/Wide World Photos; 186 *boy holding briefcase* © Image Source/Getty Images; *young woman in prom dress* © Image Source/ Getty Images; *two girls in dance dresses* © moodboard/Corbis; *football player* © Mark Stout Photography/ShutterStock; (tr) © @erics/ShutterStock; 191 (t) © Adrian Arbib/Corbis; (b) © Bruce Bi/ age fotostock/Alamy; 194 (l) © Hans Neleman/Zefa RF/Alamy Ltd; (c) © Rob Melnychuk/Photodisc/Getty Images; (r) © Sean Justice/image100/Alamy Ltd; 195 (l) © Rob Bartee/Alamy Ltd; (c) © Benjamin Lowy/Corbis; (r) © 2008 Ingram Publishing/Jupiterimages Corporation; 197 AP/Wide World Photos; (inset) © Joe Raedle/Getty Images; 205 © Ed Fischer/www.cartoonstock. com. **CHAPTER 9:** Page 206 (t) © Layne Kennedy/Corbis; (b) Photo by Charlotte Buttons for the ABC News documentary program *The Eye of the Storm.* Courtesy of ABC News; 208 *head* © Kristy-Anne Glubish/Design Pics/Corbis; 209 © Ted Thai/Time and Life Pictures/Getty Images; 212 (t) © Bettmann/Corbis; (c) © Bettmann/Corbis; (b) © Bettmann/ Corbis; 216 (t) AP/Wide World Photos; (c) The Granger Collection, New York; (b) © Bettmann/Corbis; 218 *saguaro cactus* © tbkmedia.de/Alamy Ltd; *city skyline* © Uta Nueman/fStop/Alamy Ltd; *fireworks* © Tetra Images/Corbis; *jumping woman* © Corbis; *smiling woman* © Randy Faris/Corbis; *children in parade* © Ariel Skelley/Corbis; *business man* © PunchStock; *teenage girl* © PunchStock; *bagpipers* AP/Wide World Images; *woman wearing glasses* © Jupiterimages Corporation; *stir-fry noodles* © D. Hurst/Alamy Ltd; 220 AP/Wide World Photos; 221 © Gilles Mingasson/Getty Images; 222 © David Coleman/Alamy Ltd; 223 © Tim Sloan/ AFP/Getty Images; 225 (t) © Paul Conklin/PhotoEdit; (b) © Bill Pugliano/ Getty Images. **CHAPTER 10:** Page 230 *all* © Jerzyworks/Masterfile; 232 © SuperStock, Inc./SuperStock; 234 AP/ Wide World Photos; 235 (t) © Bettmann/ Corbis; (c) We Can Do It!, about 1942, J. Howard Miller. Photo © Corbis; (b) © Charles Gatewood/The Image Works; 238 AP/Wide World Photos; 242 © Belushi/Shutterstock; 243 AP/Wide World Photos; 245 © Science Source/ Photo Researchers, Inc.; 253 © Harley Schwadron/www.CartoonStock. com;

Global Connections 254 (t) © Peeter Viisimaa/iStockphoto.com; (b) © Jon Hrusa/epa/Corbis; 255 (tl) © A J James/ Digital Vision/Getty Images; (tc) © Frank Herholdt/Digital Vision/Getty Images; (tr) © Image Source Black/ Jupiterimages Corporation; (b) © STRDEL/AFP/Getty Images; **Careers in Sociology** 256 © Dana White/ PhotoEdit.

UNIT 4 CHAPTER 11: Page 258 © Corbis; 259 © Ariel Skelley/Taxi/Getty Images; 260 © Preeti Moberg/Getty Images; 264 © Jason Smalley/Wildscape/Alamy Ltd; 266 AP/Wide World Images; 269 © Mike Kemp/Rubberball/Jupiterimages Corporation; 271 © Reggie Casagrande/ Getty Images; 274 © Bubbles Photolibrary/Alamy Ltd.
CHAPTER 12: Page 280 *cottage-style home* © iolo72/iStockphoto. com; *foreclosure sign* © Andy Dean/ iStockphoto.com; *lender owned sign* © Tim McCaig/iStockphoto.com; *for sale by owner* sign © Milan Lusacek/ iStockphoto.com; *homes on curving street* © Tim McCaig/iStockphoto.com; *bank owned sign* © Tim McCaig/iStockphoto. com; 281 (l) © Courtney Weittenhiller/ iStockphoto.com; (r inset) © Tim McCaig/iStockphoto.com; 282 (t) AP/ Wide World Photos; (b) © Don Emmert/ AFP/Getty Images; 284 (l) The Granger Collection, New York; (r) Karl Marx, about 1915–1935, Emil Dreyer. Photo © The Art Archive/Corbis; 285 (l) © Walter Stoneman/Hulton Archive/ Getty Images; (r) © Hulton Archive/ Getty Images; 287 Photo by Robb D. Cohen; (inset) © Cesar Ivan Salazar; (inset border) © Marie-france Bélanger/ iStockphoto; 290 © Bloomberg/Getty Images; 292 (t) © Mark Ralston/AFP/ Getty Images; (b) © PCL/Alamy Ltd; 297 © Edward Beardwell/www.CartoonStock. com; 300 © Scott J. Ferrell/Congressional Quarterly/Getty Images.
CHAPTER 13: Page 306 © Landon Nordeman/National Geographic/ Getty Images; 308 © Michael Ventura/ PhotoEdit; 310 © Jetta Productions/ Lifesize/Getty Images; 316 © Masterfile; 317 © Aaron Bacall/www.CartoonStock. com; 318 © Maria Stenzel/National Geographic/Getty Images; 321 AP/Wide World Photos; 323 (t) © Ali Mubarak/age fotostock; (c) © Khin Maung Win/AFP/ Getty Images; (b) © Masterfile; 327 © 2005 Nina Berman/Redux Pictures; 331 (t) AP/Wide World Photos; (c) AP/ Wide World Photos; (b) © Marc Asnin/ Corbis SABA; 333 Copyright © Pittsburgh Bost-Gazette, 2008, all rights reserved. Reprinted with permission.

CHAPTER 14: Page 336 © David Sherman/National Basketball Association/Getty Images; 338 © Lou Dematteis/Reuters; 339 (t) © Mike Blake/Reuters/Corbis; (c) © Peter Kneffel/epa/Corbis; (b) © Michael Weber/imagebroker/Alamy Ltd; 341 © Photodisc/Stockbyte/Alamy Ltd; 342 (t) © Dave King/Dorling Kindersley; (b) AP/Wide World Photos; 348 (l) © Gianni Dagli Orti/Corbis; (r) © Per-Andre Hoffmann/LOOK Die Bildagentur der Fotografen GmbH/Alamy Ltd; 349 (tl) © Bettmann/Corbis (bl) © Mansell/Time and Life Pictures/Getty Images; 351 (tl) © Alex Segre/Alamy Ltd; (cl) © Brendan McDermid/Reuters; (cr) AP/Wide World Photos; (b) © Ablestock.com/Jupiterimages Corporation; 352 © The New Yorker Collection 2002 Barbara Smaller from cartoonbank.com. All Rights Reserved; 353 © Paul Kane/Getty Images; 354 Photo by Vivan Zink/Everett Collection. © ABC; 356 © OJO Images Ltd/Alamy Ltd; 357 © Steve Boyle/NewSport/Corbis; 359 (t) © Cate Gillon/Getty Images; (b) AP/Wide World Photos; **Global Connections** 364 (t) © Peeter Viisimaa/iStockphoto.com; (tr) © Image Source Black/Jupiterimages Corporation; 365 (tl) © A J James/Digital Vision/Getty Images; (tc) © Frank Herholdt/Digital Vision/Getty Images; (b) © Patrick Field/Eye Ubiquitous/Corbis; **Careers in Sociology** 366 © RosaIreneBetancourt 7/Alamy.

UNIT 5 CHAPTER 15: Page 368–369 © Masterfile; 370 © Purestock/Getty Images; 371 © Vladimir Wrangel\Fotolia; 378 (t) © Zlatko Guzmic/ShutterStock; (b) © Richard Cummins/Getty Images; 380 (l) The Granger Collection, New York; (r) The Granger Collection, New York; 380–381 (bkgd) © Robert Adrian Hillman/ShutterStock; 381 (l) © Corbis; (r) © areialarchives.com/Alamy Ltd; 382 (t) © Alan Schein Photography/Corbis; (b) © Spencer Platt/Getty Images; 383 Courtesy of DOE/NREL/Katrin Barth-Scholz; (inset) © E.J. Baumeister Jr./Alamy Ltd; 386 Courtesy IwamotoScott Architecture; 389 (l) © Tony Duy/Shutterstock; (r) © Jon Hicks/Corbis.

CHAPTER 16: Page 392 © Flip Schulke/Corbis; 393 © Bettmann/Corbis; 394 © David Hoffman Photo Library/Alamy Ltd; 396–397 (b) © Sergei Supinsky/AFP/Getty Images; 399 (t) AP/Wide World Photos; (c) © Waltraud Grubitzsch/dpa/Corbis; (b) © Chris Ryan/Corbis; 403 © David Handschuh-Pool/Getty Images; 404 © Saipul Siagiancheers/epa/Corbis; 406 AP/Wide World Photos; 407 AP/Wide World Photos; 409 AP/Wide World Photos; 411 © Masterfile; 413 Speed Bump ©2005 Dave Coverly. Used with the permission of Dave Coverly and the Cartoonist Group. All rights reserved; 414 © Bloomberg/Getty Images; 415 (b) © Ian Dagnall/Alamy Ltd; 415 (t) © Ian Dagnall/Alamy Ltd; 419 © Marcel Lam/Arcaid/Corbis; 422 © The Photolibrary Wales/Alamy Ltd; **Global Connections** 428 (t) © Peeter Viisimaa/Stockphoto.com; (b) © SambaPhoto/Paulo Fridman/Getty Images; 430 (t) © Jupiterimages Corporation.

For permission to reprint copyrighted material, grateful acknowledgment is made to the following sources:

American Sociological Association: "The American Sociological Association Code of Ethics." Copyright © 1999 by the American Sociological Association.

Basic Books, a member of Perseus Books LLC: Excerpt from *Corporate Cultures: The Rites and Rituals of Corporate Life* by Terrence Deal and Allen Kennedy. Copyright © 1982 by Addison-Wesley Publishing Company, LLC.

Business Week: Excerpt from "Hispanic Nation" by Brian Grow, Ronald Grover, Arlene Weintraub, Christopher Palmeri, Mara Der Hovanesian, and Michael Eidam, from *Business Week,* March 15, 2004. Copyright © 2004 by The McGraw–Hill Companies.

Henry Holt and Company, LLC: Excerpt from "The Authoritarian Character," from *Escape from Freedom* by Erich Fromm. Copyright © 1941 and renewed © 1969 by Erich Fromm.

W.W. Norton & Company, Inc.: Excerpt from *Freedom Bound: A History of America's Civil Rights Movement* by Robert Weisbrot. Copyright © 1990 by Robert Weisbrot.

Springer Science and Business Media: Excerpts from "The Saints and the Roughnecks" by William J. Chambliss, from *Society,* Vol. 11, No 1. Copyright © 1973 by Society.

The Washington Post: Excerpt from "How the Daycare Child Abuse Hysteria of the 1980s became a Witch Hunt" from *The Washington Post,* July 31, 2015. Text copyright © 2015 by The Washington Post. Reprinted by permission of PARS International on behalf of the The Washington Post.